Introduction to Management Accounting: A User Perspective

Third Edition

Michael L. Werner
University of Miami

Kumen H. Jones
Arizona State University, Retired

Kendall Hunt
publishing company

Kendall Hunt
publishing company

www.kendallhunt.com
Send all inquiries to:
4050 Westmark Drive
Dubuque, IA 52004-1840

This book was previously published by Pearson Education, Inc.

ISBN 978-0-7575-7054-4

Printed in the United States of America
10 9 8 7 6 5 4 3

Contents

Preface

Business people must be prepared to perform tasks that only people can perform; in particular, they must be able to communicate, to think, and to make solid, well-informed decisions. Decision making is the critical skill in today's business world, and *Introduction to Management Accounting—A User Perspective 3rd Edition* helps students to better use accounting information to improve their decision making skills.

This text provides a solid management accounting foundation within the context of business and business decisions. Readers will explore accounting information's role in the decision making process and learn how to use the accounting information typically provided to company managers. Seeing how accounting information can be used to make better business decisions will benefit all students, regardless of their major course of study or chosen career.

This text is purposely written so students will find it easy to read and understand. The conversational tone of the text and the logical presentation of topics all contribute to the ability of this text to meet that goal. In addition, we have included the exhibits necessary to get important points across, but we intentionally have not included an array of glitz and graphics that can break up the flow and distract student attention. Generally, we have not segregated material into special presentation boxes that might be skipped by students attempting to focus on the most relevant points. All the points of interest and examples we present are woven into the body of the text.

Support for the Interactive Classroom

We believe this text provides tools to actively involve students in their learning processes. Several features are particularly important in developing a classroom atmosphere in which students share ideas, ask questions, and relate their learning to the world around them. For example, throughout each chapter of the text, you will find Discussion Questions (DQs) that challenge students to reach beyond the surface of the written text to determine answers. Far from typical review questions, for which the students can scan a few pages of the text to locate an answer, many of the DQs provide relevant learning by relating students' personal experiences to the knowledge they gain through the text. The DQs provide a variety of classroom experiences:

- Many DQs provide the basis for classroom discussions, requiring students to think about issues and formulate or defend their opinions.

- Some DQs are springboards for group assignments (in or out of the classroom) to put cooperative learning into practice.
- DQs may be assigned as individual writing assignments to allow students to practice and develop their writing skills.
- Combining individually written DQ responses with follow-up group discussions can spark lively debate!
- Having students keep a journal of their responses to all DQs (regardless of whether they are used in another way) encourages contemplation of accounting concepts.

The DQs are designed to emphasize important points that students may skim across in their initial reading. Even if they are not formally part of the required work for your course, students will gain a greater understanding of the concepts discussed when they take time to consider each question as part of the text.

Flexibility Regarding Recording Procedures (Debit and Credit Entries)

Aside from its support for the interactive classroom, another distinction of this text is its separation of the use of accounting information and its preparation. Coverage of recording procedures (debit and credit entries) differs from school to school. Some schools choose to have all students learn basic accounting procedures; others require only accounting majors to acquire these skills. Our text offers institutions the flexibility to cover accounting procedures to a significant degree, to cover just the basics, or to omit the coverage of accounting procedures entirely. We do not use debits and credits or journal entries to demonstrate or explain characteristics and uses of accounting information. However, the recording process is covered in detail where appropriate. For those institutions that would like to include accounting procedures in their introductory accounting curriculum, these chapters demonstrate most of the basic management accounting journal entries including the journal entries for standard costing. Institutions that desire to omit recording procedures from the introductory curriculum entirely would simply skip the recording process portion of these chapters from their course coverage.

Assignment Material

The text includes an array of assignment material including the following:

- *Discussion Questions.* As we have already mentioned, throughout each chapter of the text, you will find Discussion Questions (DQs) that challenge students to reach beyond the text material to determine answers.
- *Review the Facts.* Students can use these basic, definitional questions to review the key points of each chapter. The questions are in a sequence reflecting the coverage of topics in the chapter.
- *Apply What You Have Learned.* Many of these end-of-chapter assignments can be used as the basis for classroom discussions; they will also work well as group assignments. There are three versions of most problems—one to use as an example in class, one for homework, and one extra.

Topics and Sequence of Coverage

We have carefully considered the inclusion or exclusion of topics and feel that our coverage has resulted in a balanced text consistent with our pedagogical goal of building a foundation that supports effective student learning. We will continue to gather information regarding topical coverage to make future editions even better. We feel that this text covers those topics that every accounting student should leave the course understanding well. For example, in the cost behavior chapter (Chapter 5), instead of demonstrating the calculations for regression analysis, we demonstrate how to use *Microsoft* Excel to prepare cost behavior charts and insert trend lines. This allows us to focus on the usefulness of cost behavior rather than on tedious number crunching, which, in practice, is generally done by a computer.

We have carefully chosen the sequence of coverage so the material flows from one topic to the next. Not only does this make accounting easier to teach, but it is more understandable for the students as well. We have developed a logical flow of topics so that each chapter builds on what the student has already learned. Students can easily understand how the topics fit together logically and how they are used together to make good decisions. Moreover, students can see that accounting and the information it provides is not merely something that exists unto itself, but rather it is something developed in response to the needs of economic decision makers.

If you could read the entire text before using it in your classroom, you would have a very clear picture of the experience awaiting your students. However, even a short tour through the material covered in each chapter will show you how we have structured our presentation of the topics to maximize student learning.

Chapter Highlights

Chapter 1 explores management accounting, its environment and future. The chapter introduces management accounting and contrasts it with financial accounting. The chapter explores ethical considerations and discusses where management accounting fits in a company as well as the origin and evolution of management accounting and the challenges and trends that lie ahead.

Chapter 2 explores various cost classifications and concepts; it covers product costs and period costs for merchandisers and manufacturers as well as cost of services and period costs for service firms. The chapter discusses direct material, direct labor, and manufacturing overhead as well as the various manufacturing inventories (raw materials, work-in-process, finished goods). Chapter 2 also provides a comparison of merchandising, manufacturing, and service costs. The chapter covers the accounting procedures (journal entries) for simple manufacturing environments where manufacturing overhead is recorded directly in work-in-process inventory. (Overhead allocation techniques and the associated journal entries are covered in Chapter 3.)

Chapter 3 describes how companies determine the cost of their products. The chapter covers job order costing and introduces overhead allocation. The chapter also covers process costing in a simplified presentation that makes process costing basics very understandable. Only the average cost flow method is presented, but the presentation includes both the situation where the percentage complete for direct materials, direct labor, and manufacturing overhead is the same, and the situation where completion percentages differ between direct materials and conversion cost. Also covered in the chapter are accounting procedures including journal entries for manufacturing overhead allocation.

Chapter 4 covers cost allocation and the use of activity-based costing (ABC). The chapter takes a closer look at overhead allocation by further examining traditional overhead allocation and introduces ABC. Basic concepts of ABC are explored including its implementation, ABC calculations, and benefits and drawbacks of using ABC.

Chapter 5 covers cost behavior including fixed costs, variable costs, and the relevant range. The chapter also introduces the concept of mixed cost and includes an easy-to-understand presentation of techniques to separate mixed costs into fixed and variable components. Step-by-step calculations are presented for the scatter graph and high-low methods. Regression analysis is discussed and the chapter includes a step-by-step presentation of scatter graphing using *Microsoft* Excel.

Chapter 6 explores business decisions using cost behavior. The contribution income statement and cost–volume–profit (CVP) analysis for single-product and multiple-product situations are introduced and explored. The chapter includes step-by-step presentations of breakeven and the calculations to determine sales needed to meet target profit. The chapter also introduces a CVP graph and sensitivity analysis. Income statements under variable costing and absorption costing are also explored.

Chapter 7 explores the use of relevant information for decision making. The chapter describes relevant information, costs and benefits and their characteristics. Qualitative and quantitative considerations are discussed. The chapter demonstrates the importance of relevant information with a series of examples including equipment replacement, special orders, outsourcing—the make or buy decision, and discontinuance of business segments.

Chapter 8 introduces various aspects of business planning and explores capital budgeting and evaluating capital expenditures. The chapter introduces the business planning process and setting company goals, the strategic plan, the capital budget, and the operating budget. Then, it explores the capital budget, the cost of capital and the evaluation of potential capital projects. The chapter demonstrates discounted cash flow capital budgeting decision methods such as net present value and internal rate of return using both financial tables and a financial calculator. Thus, the chapter supports instructors demonstrating concepts using financial tables, or a financial calculator, or both. The chapter also demonstrates non-discounted cash flow capital budgeting decision methods, including payback period and accounting rate of return. Appendix A to this chapter demonstrates detailed future value and present value calculations using financial tables. Appendix B demonstrates using a financial calculator for future and present value calculations.

Chapter 9 explores the operating budget. The chapter is presented in two parts. Part One presents an overview of the operating budget including the benefits of budgeting, the contents of the operating budget (it also introduces various operating budgets), and approaches to budgeting. Part Two covers preparing and using the operating budget. It includes step-by-step presentations of the preparation of various budgets from the sales budget to budgeted financial statements. Flexible budgeting is covered near the end of the chapter.

Chapter 10 explores standard costing. The chapter explains why standard costing is used, discusses ideal versus practical standards, and describes some of the problems with standard costing. The chapter demonstrates basic standard costing for a manufacturer using an easy-to-understand example based on a small student-owned company manufacturing wooden mailboxes in a rented garage. Calculations are shown for the direct material variances, direct labor variances, variable manufacturing overhead variances, and fixed manufacturing overhead variances. The chapter concludes with a look at variance analysis and using variances to manage by exception and a demonstration of the journal entries used in standard costing.

Chapter 11 covers various aspects of evaluating performance. Business segments and the segmented income statement are presented and the pitfalls of allocating common fixed costs are discussed. The chapter discusses the basics of service department cost allocation and activity-based service department cost allocation. The chapter discusses revenue centers, cost centers, profit centers, and investment centers. Return on investment, residual income and economic value added (EVA™) are discussed and demonstrated. The chapter also briefly introduces a number of cutting-edge management and management accounting developments including:

- The Balanced Scorecard
- E-commerce
- Process Management
- Enterprise Information Systems
- Six-Sigma
- Theory of Constraints
- Lean Manufacturing

Other Important Features of This Text

In addition to the Discussion Questions, our text offers these features to enhance the learning process:

- *Learning Objectives.* Previewing each chapter with these objectives allows students to see what direction the chapter is taking, which makes the journey through the material a bit easier.
- *Marginal Glossary.* Students often find the process of learning accounting terminology to be a challenge. As each new key word is introduced in the text, it is shown in bold and also defined in the margin. This feature offers students an easy way to review the key terms and locate their introduction in the text.
- *Summary.* This concise summary of each chapter provides an overview of the main points, but is in no way a substitute for reading the chapter.
- *Key Terms.* At the end of each chapter, a list of the new key words directs students to the page on which the key word or phrase was introduced.
- *Review the Facts.* Students can use these basic, definitional questions to review the key points of each chapter. The questions are in a sequence reflecting the coverage of topics in the chapter.
- *Apply What You Have Learned.* Our end-of-chapter assignment materials include a mix of traditional types of homework problems and innovative assignments requiring critical thinking and writing. Many of the requirements can be used as the basis for classroom discussions. You will find matching problems, short essay questions, and calculations. Assignments dealing directly with the use of financial statements are also included. Many of these applications also work well as group assignments. There are three versions of most problems—one to use as an example in class, one for homework, and one extra.

- *Glossary of Accounting Terms.* An alphabetical listing of important accounting terms, including all of the key terms.
- *Company Index.* A listing of the companies used in the text as examples or in assignment material.

Supplements for Use by the Instructor

Additional support for your efforts in the classroom is provided by our group of supplements.

- *Solutions Manual:* Solutions for all end-of-chapter material.
- *Test Item File:* A ready-to-use bank of testing material. Each chapter includes a variety of types of questions, including true/false, multiple choice, problems, and essay questions. Intended for ease of use, each question is linked to chapter objectives, and also provides a suggested difficulty level.
- *PowerPoint Presentations:* Complete PowerPoint presentations for each chapter. Instructors may download and use each presentation as is or customize the slides to create a tailor-made slide show. Each presentation allows instructors to offer a more interactive experience with outlines of chapter material and graphical explanations of each topic.
- *Course Web site at http://www.khwebcom.com/mgmtaccounting:* A complete online resource that offers a variety of Internet-based teaching and learning support. Our website provides a wealth of resources for students and faculty adopters. These resources include:
    - Downloadable Supplements
    - PowerPoint Presentations
    - Teaching/Lecture Outlines for Faculty
    - Solutions Manual

Acknowledgments

This project would not have been possible without support and encouragement from a number of people, and the faith in the concept's value from Kendall Hunt Publishing Company.

In particular, we thank Stefani DeMoss, Senior Regional Project Coordinator, and Marla W. Swartz, Senior Acquisitions Editor for their patience, determination, and faith in the project. We also thank Stacy L. (Beyer) Raap, Instructional Technology Consultant, and Rebecca Wagner, Web Project Editor, for their valuable contributions and assistance with the various computer and web-based supplements associated with this project.

We also express our gratitude to Clay Johnson, Senior Acquisitions Editor, for his persistence and his faith in the project.

We express our thanks to Stephen Speace for his contributions, editorial help and guidance and to Nancy Flores for her help with the Test Item File.

We are grateful for the inspiration and encouragement of Sherry Shu Zhang, Tom and Cathy Norris, and Geng Yue Bin. We also thank Thomas Greco, Manta Racing; Bruce Perlmuter, The Perlmuter Printing Company; and Stacy Sexton, who contributed editorial help and assignment material.

We thank Linda H. Tarrago, Hillsborough Community College for her most valuable input regarding the topics, coverage, and the presentation of material. We would also like to thank Olga Quintana, University of Miami for her help with the PowerPoint presentations for each chapter and Jacklyn Collins, University of Miami for her contributions to the Test Item File.

We thank our friends Professor Zhang Ai Min, East China University of Science and Technology and Professor Chai Quing Fu, Shanghai Li Xin University of Commerce for their valuable guidance, assistance and suggestions throughout the course of this project. We also thank Hou Yong, University of North Dakota for his help, encouragement and support for this project.

We thank our colleagues for their intellectual contributions and friendship that have helped to enrich this book including Thomas R. Robinson, Oscar J. Holzmann, Paul Munter, Frank Collins, Jacklyn Collins, Olga Quintana, Mark Friedman, Kay Tatum, University of Miami. We thank Kathy Terrell and Robert Terrell, University of Central Oklahoma for their contributions, support and friendship.

We would also like to thank the following reviewers for their recommendations on prior editions or our work: Mark E. Bettini, University of California–Berkeley; Joseph H. Bylinski, University of North Carolina at Chapel Hill; Cherie Francisco, Simpson College; Cheryl Mitchem, Virginia State University; Sally J. Nelson, Northeast Iowa Community College; Michael R. Palma, Gwinnett Technical Institute; S. E. C. Purvis, California State University–San Bernadino; Olga Quintana, University of Miami; Nanette Sanders-Cobb, Craven Community College; and Ann E. Selk, University of Wisconsin–Green Bay. Other colleagues who have provided suggestions as adopters, as focus group members, or as reviewers of previous editions of our material: Jeffrey J. Archambault, Clarkson University; Lorren H. Beavers, University of Central Oklahoma; Roger K. Doost, Clemson University; Suzanne Elsea, Anheuser–Busch Corporation; Jessica J. Frazier, Eastern Kentucky University; Edward S. Goodhart, Shippensburg University; Bambi A. Hora, University of Central Oklahoma; Steven D. Hunter, Western Baptist College; Thomas A. Jones; Raymond L. Larson, Appalachian State University; Mary D. Maury, St. John's University; Alfonso R. Oddo, Niagara University; Charles J. Pineno, Clarion University; Joanne Sheridan, Montana State University–Billings; Sheldon R. Smith, Brigham Young University–Hawaii; Patricia M. Sommerville, Saint Mary's University; Carolyn Streuly; Marilyn T. Zarzeski, University of Central Florida.

Kumen Jones expresses a very special thanks to Dane Kay, Jim Salisbury, Scott Petersen, and Steve "Cub" Petersen, whose generosity and support made his involvement in this project possible.

Michael Werner would like to thank Vice President Xu Fu Yuan and Dean Wang Heng Shan, University of Shanghai for Science and Technology, for their help, guidance, and research collaboration which aided in the development of this text. I would also like to thank Professor Chen Xiao, Chairman of the Department of Accounting at Tsinghua University for his help encouragement, guidance, and friendship. I thank Professor Cui Guo Wen, Professor Song Yan Heng, Professor Wang Kun, Mr Lin Zhao Guang, John McVay and my many other friends and colleagues at Tsinghua University for their friendship, suggestions and support. I thank Vice President Tu Shang Zong and Professor Xi Gui Ping, East China University of Science and Technology for their contributions to this project and their support and friendship over the years.

We believe the approach we have taken will help students see how accounting fits into the "big picture of business". We hope students will find that what they learn from this text and in their accounting class relates directly to them, regardless of their career path. Please feel free to contact us at *mwerner@miami.edu* with your comments or suggestions.

Michael L. Werner
University of Miami

Kumen H. Jones
Arizona State University, Retired

1

Management Accounting: Its Environment and Future

People make decisions every day. Obviously, making good decisions is easier when we have relevant information regarding the pros and cons of the various alternatives under consideration. Without meaningful information, selecting one alternative over another can not only be frustrating, but more importantly, very often results in making the wrong choice.

When business professionals make decisions, they need relevant and reliable information upon which to base their decisions. In almost all instances, accounting information is a significant and critical part of what is needed. The purpose of accounting, in fact, is to provide useful information to economic decision makers. The area of accounting that specializes in providing managers and employees with the information they need to make decisions on behalf of their companies is called management accounting.

Accounting is essentially a response function. As decision makers determine the nature of the accounting information they need, accountants provide it. If those decision makers do not make that determination, there is only a remote chance that accounting will provide the right information.

In today's global marketplace, American businesses must compete not only with firms from down the street but also with the firms from around the world. Managers in the United States have come to realize that they must implement more effective and efficient business and production techniques to effectively compete with foreign companies. Accordingly, successful companies have worked hard to improve business prospects through developing and using more advanced management techniques. As new management techniques are adopted, companies often find that the accounting information they have been using no longer suits their needs. Because the nature of business operations is changing, the nature of the accounting information required by management is also changing. Managers and accountants must work closely together to develop and use more sophisticated and modern management accounting techniques to provide the information managers need.

In the current global business environment it is not enough for business men and women to simply be familiar with the management accounting techniques their companies currently use. Instead, they must be aware of the various management accounting techniques they can employ to improve their management and decision making capabilities as needs arise.

Although business management and management accounting are inescapably connected, our focus in this text will not be on specific management techniques themselves. Those subjects are better suited to management courses. Our focus will be on the management accounting techniques, decision models, and other accounting information managers need to help them effectively run their businesses.

Learning Objectives

After completing your work on this chapter, you should be able to do the following:

1. Describe management accounting and contrast it with financial accounting.
2. Explain major historical developments that have affected management accounting.
3. Describe the relationship between business management and management accounting.
4. Describe how changes in management accounting affect today's businesses.
5. Explain how businesspeople use management accounting information and skills.

What Is Management Accounting?

It is almost impossible to make any decision unless you have the information you need to select the best alternative. In business, decision makers depend on accounting to provide much of the information they need to make sound decisions. The purpose of accounting is to provide information. The branch of accounting that provides information to managers within an organization is management accounting.

management accounting The branch of accounting designed to provide information to the firm's internal economic decision makers.

Management accounting is the branch of accounting designed to provide information to the firm's internal economic decision makers. It is also sometimes called managerial accounting or cost accounting. Because accounting literature often uses these three terms interchangeably, confusion can result. Management accounting is

> *. . . the process of identification, measurement, accumulation, analysis, preparation, interpretation, and communication of financial information used by management to plan, evaluate, and control . . . an organization . . .*
>
> —Statement on Management Accounting
> (No. lA. IMA, 1981)

managerial accounting Another name for management accounting.

cost accounting A narrow application of management accounting dealing specifically with procedures designed to determine how much a particular item (usually a unit of manufactured product) costs.

Management accounting and **managerial accounting** mean exactly the same thing. We will use the term management accounting throughout our discussions of the subject. However, in references to other writings you may see the term managerial accounting.

The third term, cost accounting, is a narrow application of management accounting. **Cost accounting** deals specifically with procedures designed to determine how much a particular item (usually a unit of manufactured product) costs. Technically then, cost accounting is a part of management accounting. In other words, the two terms are not really interchangeable, but it is quite common for some managers to use the term cost accounting when they are describing management accounting.

Institute of Management Accounting (IMA)

In 1919, the **Institute of Management Accountants (IMA)** was formed in the United States. The formation of this professional organization signified that management accounting was a recognized branch of the accounting profession separate and distinct from financial accounting. Among other purposes, the IMA provided the same sort of professional status for management accountants as the **American Institute of Certified Public Accountants (AICPA)** did for financial accountants. On its official website (www.imanet.org) the IMA states its purpose as follows:

> *"IMA is dedicated to rebalancing the accountancy profession by educating society regarding the business building role of management accountants and finance professionals working inside organizations."*

Further, the websites states that the IMA's expressed mission is:

> *"To provide a dynamic forum for management accounting and finance professionals to develop and advance their careers through certification, research and practice development, education, networking, and the advocacy of the highest ethical and professional practices."*

Certified Management Accountant (CMA®)—The Gold Standard

As part of its effort in fulfilling its purpose and mission, the IMA developed and offers its prestigious global certification, the **Certified Management Accountant (CMA®)**. CMA certification is awarded by the IMA to highly qualified accountants and it is intended for accountants and other finance professionals that provide accounting services to a particular company or organization in industry. To become a CMA, a candidate must pass a rigorous three day exam, complete a two year experience requirement, and comply with the IMA's Ethical Standards.

Certified Management Accountant (CMA®) Certification awarded to highly qualified accountants intended for those providing accounting services to a particular company or organization in industry.

Although both certifications are intended to enhance the professional standard of the individuals that possess them, there are some differences between the CMA designation and the **Certified Public Accountant (CPA)** certification. In contrast to the CMA designation, CPA certification is actually a license awarded by a state government to highly qualified accountants and is intended for accountants that work for accounting firms that provide accounting services to the public. In almost all states, an accountant must be a CPA to provide assurance services (sometimes called audit services) where the CPA attests to the reasonableness of disclosures, the freedom from material misstatement, and the adherence to the applicable generally accepted accounting principles (GAAP) in financial statements.

Certified Public Accountant (CPA) A license awarded by state government to highly qualified accountants and is intended for accountants that work for accounting firms that provide accounting services to the public.

Ethical Standards for Management Accountants

The early years of this century were not good ones for the overall reputation of the accounting profession. Seemingly every day brought a new report of another scandal, a part of which at least involved unethical behavior by accountants. The fraudulent financial reports of **Enron**, **WorldCom**, **Global Crossing**, **Tyco International** and many others were shown to involve the willing participation by accountants and finance personnel both within the companies themselves, and in some cases by accounting professionals working for the independent auditors whose job it was to attest to the results reported in the financial reports. The result was disgrace and even prison terms for some financial executives of these companies. Another casualty was the accounting firm of **Arthur Andersen**, the largest CPA firm in the world. As a result of the complicity of some its senior executives, Arthur Andersen actually went out of business causing literally thousands of honest, hard working accountants to lose their jobs.

As a result of these and other financial scandals, both the financial accounting and the management accounting branches of the accounting profession have placed a renewed emphasis on the critical need for ethical behavior on the part of accountants in performing their jobs. The IMA's *Statement of Ethical Professional Practice* is reproduced as Exhibit 1-1. This statement provides sound advice for management accountants and other financial professionals. It not only outlines the principles and standards required of management accountants, but also provides guidance on how to resolve ethical conflicts. We hope you will take the time to read the entire exhibit, because the items discussed therein are good recommendations for all of us.

International Federation of Accountants (IFAC)

The **International Federation of Accountants (IFAC)** is a global organization of accountants and other financial professionals. It works with its members and associates in more than 120 countries and jurisdictions to encourage high quality practices by the world's accountants. IFAC members and associates are primarily national professional accountancy bodies, representing more than 2.5 million accountants employed in public practice, industry and commerce, government, and education.

The IFAC develops international standards on ethics, auditing and assurance, education, and public sector accounting. It also provides guidance to professional accountants in business, small and medium practices, and developing nations.

On its official website (www.ifac.org) the IFAC describes its mission as follows:

> *"To serve the public interest, IFAC will continue to strengthen the worldwide accountancy profession and contribute to the development of strong international economies by establishing and promoting adherence to high-quality professional standards, furthering the international convergence of such standards and speaking out on public interest issues where the profession's expertise is most relevant."*

Sarbanes-Oxley

Sarbanes-Oxley Act A United States federal law enacted in 2002 that establishes new or strengthened standards for all U.S. publicly traded companies boards of directors, management, and the public accounting firms that deal with them.

The **Sarbanes-Oxley Act** of 2002 is a United States federal law enacted on July 30, 2002 in response to the major corporate and accounting scandals we discussed briefly in the preceding section of this chapter under ethical standards for management accountants. These scandals, which cost investors billions of dollars when the share prices of the affected companies collapsed, severely undermined public confidence in the nation's securities markets.

This law established new or strengthened standards for all U.S. publicly traded companies boards of directors, management, and the public accounting firms that deal with them. The law contains provisions ranging from additional corporate board

Exhibit 1-1 Ethical Standards for Management Accountants

Members of IMA shall behave ethically. A commitment to ethical professional practice includes overarching principles that express our values, and standards that guide our conduct.

PRINCIPLES

IMA's overarching ethical principles include: Honesty, Fairness, Objectivity, and Responsibility. Members shall act in accordance with these principles and shall encourage others within their organizations to adhere to them.

STANDARDS

A member's failure to comply with the following standards may result in disciplinary action.

I. COMPETENCE

Each member has a responsibility to:

1. Maintain an appropriate level of professional expertise by continually developing knowledge and skills.
2. Perform professional duties in accordance with relevant laws, regulations, and technical standards.
3. Provide decision support information and recommendations that are accurate, clear, concise, and timely.
4. Recognize and communicate professional limitations or other constraints that would preclude responsible judgment or successful performance of an activity.

II. CONFIDENTIALITY

Each member has a responsibility to:

1. Keep information confidential except when disclosure is authorized or legally required.
2. Inform all relevant parties regarding appropriate use of confidential information. Monitor subordinates' activities to ensure compliance.
3. Refrain from using confidential information for unethical or illegal advantage.

III. INTEGRITY

Each member has a responsibility to:

1. Mitigate actual conflicts of interest, regularly communicate with business associates to avoid apparent conflicts of interest. Advise all parties of any potential conflicts.
2. Refrain from engaging in any conduct that would prejudice carrying out duties ethically.
3. Abstain from engaging in or supporting any activity that might discredit the profession.

IV. CREDIBILITY

Each member has a responsibility to:

1. Communicate information fairly and objectively.
2. Disclose all relevant information that could reasonably be expected to influence an intended user's understanding of the reports, analyses, or recommendations.
3. Disclose delays or deficiencies in information, timeliness, processing, or internal controls in conformance with organization policy and/or applicable law.

RESOLUTION OF ETHICAL CONFLICT

In applying the Standards of Ethical Professional Practice, you may encounter problems identifying unethical behavior or resolving an ethical conflict. When faced with ethical issues, you should follow your organization's established policies on the resolution of such conflict. If these policies do not resolve the ethical conflict, you should consider the following courses of action:

1. Discuss the issue with your immediate supervisor except when it appears that the supervisor is involved. In that case, present the issue to the next level. If you cannot achieve a satisfactory resolution, submit the issue to the next management level. If your immediate superior is the chief executive officer or equivalent, the acceptable reviewing authority may be a group such as the audit committee, executive committee, board of directors, board of trustees, or owners. Contact with levels above the immediate superior should be initiated only with your superior's knowledge, assuming he or she is not involved. Communication of such problems to authorities or individuals not employed or engaged by the organization is not considered appropriate, unless you believe there is a clear violation of the law.
2. Clarify relevant ethical issues by initiating a confidential discussion with an IMA Ethics Counselor or other impartial advisor to obtain a better understanding of possible courses of action.
3. Consult your own attorney as to legal obligations and rights concerning the ethical conflict.

responsibilities to criminal penalties for corporate executives who knowingly certify fraudulent corporate financial reports.

Sarbanes-Oxley also severely limits the kinds of services CPA firms are allowed to perform for their clients. Prior to the enactment of this law, large CPA firms routinely performed management advisory services to their clients in addition to performing an annual audit. The result was that these CPA firms wound up auditing the very accounting and internal control systems they, themselves, had installed. At a very minimum this situation created the appearance of a lack of independence. With the passage of Sarbanes-Oxley, a CPA firm that performs an annual audit for a company is no longer allowed to perform management advisory services for that company.

There is a continuing debate over the perceived benefits and costs of Sarbanes-Oxley. Supporters contend that the legislation was necessary and has played a useful role in restoring public confidence in the nation's capital markets by, among other things, strengthening corporate accounting controls. Opponents claim that its cost far outweighs any real benefit and that compliance reduces the ability of U.S. companies to compete globally against foreign companies which are not bound by the provisions of the law.

More detailed information about Sarbanes-Oxley can be obtained from the **American Institute of Public Accountants (AICPA)** at http://thecaq.aicpa.org/Resources/Sarbanes+Oxley/

Next we will look at the differences between financial accounting and management accounting.

Contrasting Financial and Management Accounting

financial accounting The branch of accounting designed to provide information to external decision makers such as stockholders and creditors.

Financial accounting provides information to external decision makers—people outside the company. Management accounting, in contrast, provides information to internal decision makers. Internal decision makers are those that work *for* the company. You might think that anyone who owns a part of a company is an internal decision maker. However, this is not the case. To be considered an internal decision maker, one must work for the company. Exhibit 1-2 lists only some of the many external and internal users of a company's accounting information.

Exhibit 1-2 External and Internal Decision Makers

External—Those that do not work for the company	Internal—Those that work for the company (Employees)
• Stockholders (present and potential)	• Marketing managers
• Banks and other lending institutions	• Salespersons
• Bondholders (present and potential)	• Production managers
• Suppliers	• Production supervisors
• Customers	• Strategic planners
• Competitors	• Company president
• Governments	• Company engineers

This text is an extract from www.ifac.org, published by the International Federation of Accountants (IFAC) in July 2009 and is used with permission of IFAC.

Discussion Questions

1-1. For each of the external parties listed in Exhibit 1-2, suggest one economic decision they might make regarding a company.

1-2. Name an external party in addition to those listed in Exhibit 1-2, and provide an example of an economic decision that party might make regarding a company.

1-3. For each of the internal parties listed in Exhibit 1-2, describe one economic decision they might make regarding their company.

1-4. Name two more internal parties in addition to those listed in Exhibit 1-2, and give an example of an economic decision each might make regarding the company.

Discussion Questions 1-1 through 1-4 highlight the different nature of the decisions made by external and internal parties. If you review your answers to these questions, you will discover that the decisions external parties make focus on the company as a whole, whereas the decisions internal parties make usually center on some part of the company. Because people use financial accounting information and management accounting information differently, the nature of the two differs.

Traditionally, financial accounting has focused primarily on a company's overall profitability, solvency, and liquidity. Management accounting, on the other hand, focuses on the efficiency, productivity, and product or service quality of a company's various operating functions. Logically, increasing efficiency, productivity, and product or service quality should ultimately lead to increased profitability, solvency, and liquidity. The emphasis of management accounting, however, is on the means to those ends, not the ends themselves.

Accounting Rules

Financial accounting information must be prepared in accordance with rules, such as **Generally Accepted Accounting Principles (GAAP)** or **International Financial Reporting Standards (IFRS)**. These rules are necessary to provide assurance to external parties that the information they receive from a company has been prepared in conformance with a consistently applied set of standards. Because management accounting information is prepared for use by those working within the company, its users can question the content, meaning, level of detail, and validity of the accounting information they receive. Therefore, management accounting is not required to conform to GAAP. Internal users can also determine the format of the information. As discussed later, in addition to accountants, managers may also gather and prepare management accounting information. In conclusion, accounting standards are not necessary to protect internal decision makers because they can generally demand that the information they receive from their accountants is exactly what they want. Financial accounting standards are in place to protect the interests of external decision makers because they must accept the financial accounting information they receive, like it or not.

Generally Accepted Accounting Principles (GAAP) Financial accounting rules establishing how financial accounting information is to be prepared and presented.

International Financial Reporting Standards (IFRS) International financial accounting rules establishing how financial accounting information is to be prepared and presented.

Level of Detail

The financial statements prepared for use by external parties under financial accounting are known as general-purpose financial statements. There are four of them (the income statement, balance sheet, statement of shareholders' equity, and statement of cash flows) and the format of the statements is remarkably similar for all companies. This means that financial statements prepared by companies such as **General Motors**, **Intel**, **McDonalds**, and **Campbell Soup** follow the same general format, even though they are in vastly different industries. These financial statements contain very little detail, but they are accompanied by explanatory notes and supporting schedules that provide an added measure of information beyond that provided by the financial statements themselves.

In contrast to the general-purpose nature of financial accounting information, firms prepare management accounting information to address specific company issues. Therefore, it is often much more detailed than financial accounting information. For example, it may be fine for a potential investor to know that **Dell's** sales were $61.1 billion in 2008, but this information would be nearly useless to the national sales manager for **Dell** laptop computers. Rather than total sales for the company, the manager needs to know details about **Dell's** laptop sales. For a given internal decision, a user may need specific information for a division, product line, product, or department. The company's accountants should be able to customize management accounting information so that it includes sufficient detail to meet the user's needs.

Honeywell International, Inc., for example, has a production facility on 53rd Avenue and Bell Road in Phoenix, Arizona. This facility requires various types of maintenance, including mowing the lawn and weeding the flower beds outside the buildings. This maintenance costs money. The amount spent for grounds maintenance at this **Honeywell** facility is totally irrelevant to external parties. The maintenance supervisor at that facility, however, would find that amount quite relevant. **Honeywell's** accountants should be able to customize a report providing the supervisor with pertinent cost information.

Discussion Question

1-5. In addition to sales information, what other accounting information would you want if you were the national sales manager for **Dell** laptops?

Timeliness

Timeliness is important to both financial and management accounting information users. Regardless of whether the user is external or internal accounting information is useful only if it is available in time to help the decision maker.

Because it has become customary, users of financial accounting information expect that financial results will be available quarterly. However, managers making frequent decisions need information much more often. They need information monthly, weekly, or even daily, so they can make informed decisions. Because of the fast pace of business decision-making, sometimes it is better to sacrifice precision in favor of speed. Management accountants must strike a balance between information accuracy and timeliness to provide managers with information that is accurate enough to make good decisions, and yet timely enough to make a difference.

Future Orientation

Although financial accounting information must have either predictive value or feedback value if it is to be useful, it primarily presents historical results. In contrast, management accounting has a forward-looking orientation. Management accounting focuses on estimating future revenues, costs, and other measures to forecast future activities and their results. Firms use these forecasts to plan their course of action toward future goals.

As you can see, because of the fundamental differences between the information needs of external and internal parties, financial and management accounting differ. Exhibit 1-3 summarizes the differences we have discussed.

Exhibit 1-3 Contrast of Financial and Management Accounting

	Financial Accounting	Management Accounting
Principal users	External parties	Internal parities
Rules and regulations	Governed by GAAP	No rules
Level of detail	Deals with the company as a whole	Deals with various parts of the company
Timeliness	Quarterly and annually provided in a reasonable amount of time	As users need provided very quickly
Orientation	The past	The future

Where Accounting Fits in a Company

Exhibit 1-4 presents a typical corporate organizational structure. Note where financial and management accounting fit within a company.

Exhibit 1-4 Corporate Organization

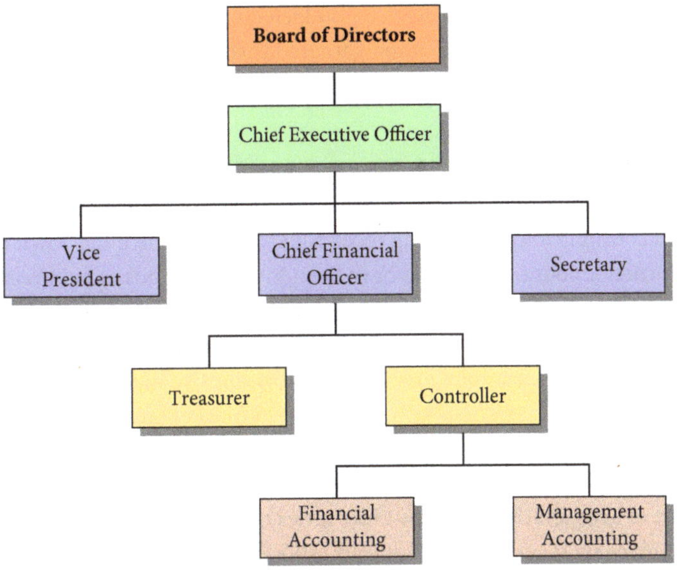

The accounting function centers on the treasurer and the controller. The **treasurer** is a corporate officer and is generally responsible for cash and credit management, obtaining external financing, and making investments for the company. The **controller** is a company's chief accountant, and is responsible for preparing accounting reports for both external and internal decision makers. Whereas the controller likely has a degree in accounting, the treasurer may have a degree in finance.

treasurer The corporate officer that is generally responsible for cash and credit management, obtaining external financing, and making investments for the company.

controller A company's chief accountant responsible for preparing accounting reports for both external and internal decision makers.

In a large company, such as **Intel** or **Coca-Cola** the treasurer and controller are both likely to have large staffs reporting to them. At a midsized company one or two people may perform all the duties of the treasurer and controller. In small firms, one person may perform all the functions.

Discussion Question

1-6. What possible problems may arise when the same accountants prepare reports for both external parties and internal parties?

Accounting's Role in Planning, Directing, Motivating, and Controlling

Things go better if you have a plan. In business, managers spend a considerable amount of time planning for the future. Company accountants can assist managers by helping them formalize business plans in a meaningful way. The business plans that accountants prepare based on the input of managers and other employees are often called budgets. In addition to budgets, company accountants can help managers with the planning process by providing information about past business activity and by providing various decision models to help managers select the best decision alternatives.

Once managers have developed their business plans, they direct employees and motivate them to fulfill the plans. To help direct employees, managers must communicate with the employees about the plans. Managers often use the budgets and other information accounting provides to communicate their plans to employees. Often the budgets and plans are detailed enough to also help motivate employees to fulfill specific objectives of the plan such as meeting sales targets or reducing costs.

As plans are put into action, accounting may also provide tools to help managers evaluate employee performance and control the progress toward fulfillment of company goals. Accounting does this by preparing reports for managers and employees that compare the plans (budgeted amounts) to actual results. These accounting reports usually show differences (variances) between budgeted and actual results. These differences are then investigated. The information gathered through this investigation is used to make needed correction to the operation of the firm and also to help refine the process of planning.

The Origin and Evolution of Management Accounting

Accounting and accounting records have existed since the dawn of civilization. Indeed, formal accounting systems have been in use for thousands of years. The need for accounting information for management decision-making purposes, however, did not exist until the early 19th century in the United States. Before that time almost all businesses were proprietorships or small partnerships. Businesses had no permanent employees to speak of and no management as we know it today. Management usually consisted of the proprietor or partners and immediate family members. Because businesses had no management, they had little need for management accounting information. Virtually all transactions were between the company and parties outside the company. Transactions with external parties such as suppliers, contract labor, and customers were easy to measure and evaluate: A company was successful if it collected more cash from its customers than it paid to suppliers and contract laborers.

Beginning in the 1820s and continuing for roughly 100 years, however, four significant changes took place in American business operation and organization: the emergence of permanent employees, the Industrial Revolution, the rise of scientific management, and diversification. Combined, these changes radically altered the way businesses operated, and in the process altered the nature of the accounting information managers needed in order to operate successfully. The changed nature of needed accounting information led to the development of what we now know as modern management accounting.

Emergence of Permanent Employees

For the most part, U.S. businesses had few employees before the 1880s. Companies purchased labor with a piece rate contract and hired independent contractors to complete most of their production functions. A chair manufacturer, for example, purchased wood at a certain price per board foot. Then the company contracted someone to turn the wood into legs, arms, seats, and backs at some specified rate per item. When the pieces were produced and paid for, the company contracted someone else to assemble the chairs, and paid that person some specified amount per chair assembled. Determining the cost of a chair produced was very simple—the sum of the wood cost, the amount paid per component piece (arm, leg, and so on), and the cost of assembling it. The company was not terribly interested in how long it took any of these contractors to complete their tasks, so long as they met the needs of the company. In other words, the purchasing company was not really concerned with the contractors' efficiency, so long as the component parts arrived on time, at an acceptable cost.

Gradually, however, companies began hiring permanent employees to fill the role of the independent contractors. Why the switch to permanent employees took place is not completely certain, but from the company's standpoint, moving from a contract system to a wage system gave the firm greater control of the production process and, in fact, created what we now know as the factory. From the laborer's standpoint, the change was likely an exchange of personal freedom for the security of a regular paycheck.

Discussion Questions

1-7. In what ways do you think hiring permanent employees gives a company greater control of the production process?

1-8. What kinds of personal freedom do you think permanent employees exchange for the security of a regular paycheck?

When we see the word factory, we tend to think of the huge factories of today. Actually, early factories in the United States were still small businesses. Management accounting did not develop because of the size or complexity of organizations. Rather, it developed because the accounting systems then in existence did not provide business people with enough information to determine the cost of a manufactured product. Nor did these systems provide information about a company's efficiency, productivity and product or service quality.

Discussion Question

1-9. Why do you think the emergence of factories (even small ones) made it more difficult to determine the cost of a manufactured product?

The Industrial Revolution

The **Industrial Revolution** was the 19th-century transition of the United States and other western countries from agricultural-based economies to manufacturing-based economies. In the years following the first third of the 19th century, businesses began to greatly increase their investment in property, plant, and equipment and began to rely more on machines instead of human labor to produce products. As companies grew in size and complexity, owners found it impossible to be in all places at all times. They were forced to create hierarchical levels of management for their organizations. These managers sought needed information to control costs and production processes. Over time, businesses developed methods to measure the conversion of raw materials into units of finished product. These methods were the foundation for present-day management accounting. Their focus was on the effectiveness and efficiency of various internal processes, rather than on the overall profitability of the company.

Industrial Revolution A term used to describe the transition in the United States from an agricultural-based economy to a manufacturing-based economy.

Scientific Management

scientific management A management philosophy based on the notion that management should maximize the prosperity of the employer and employees by improving worker efficiency through the use of standard amounts of time it should take workers to produce whatever the company manufactures.

The scientific management movement began near the end of the 19th century and had a tremendous influence on business management and management accounting. The most influential person in this movement was Frederick Winslow Taylor. His work continues to influence management practices even today. The basic philosophy of **scientific management** as stated in Taylor's writings is that the principal object of management should be to maximize the prosperity of the employer, but also to maximize the prosperity of each employee. To illustrate the application of this philosophy, he used the simple example of a shoemaker who employs one employee. Said he:

> *"If you and your workman have become so skilful that you and he together are making two pairs of shoes in a day, while your competitor and his workman are making only one pair, it is clear that after selling your two pairs of shoes you can pay your workman much higher wages than your competitor who produces only one pair of shoes is able to pay his man, and that there will still be enough money left over for you to have a larger profit than your competitor."*
>
> —Fundamentals of Scientific Management, P2

In order to produce that extra pair of shoes in a day, it follows that your operation must be more efficient than that of your competitor. Obviously, attaining that increased efficiency is the key to scientific management. And while an in-depth discussion of the many facets of scientific management theory and practice is beyond the scope of this text, we should note that an essential feature is determining a standard amount of time it should take a worker to produce whatever the company manufactures.

One of the techniques employed by Frederick Taylor to determine a standard amount of labor required in production was stop-watch timing as the basis of observation. It was he who coined the term "time study", later expanded to the term "time-and-motion study" employed today. In a tool-manufacturing company, for instance, managers can conduct time-and-motion studies to set a standard for the time workers should take to convert a given amount of resources into a finished product, such as a hammer.

These standards of performance were quickly adapted to accounting for the purpose of determining how much it should cost to manufacture a product. Experts, often engineers, determined how much material, labor, and other resources a business needed to manufacture a single unit of product. This information served as a yardstick to measure whether resources were used efficiently or squandered during the production process. Such standards were the beginning of what is referred to today as standard costing, one of the most important developments in management accounting. We will discuss standard costing in greater detail in Chapter 10.

Discussion Questions

Assume a company manufactures tables. Scientific management studies show that each tabletop requires 4 square feet of wood, and it takes a worker 45 minutes to convert the wood into a tabletop.

1-10. If the wood costs the company $2 per square foot and the company's workers are paid $10 per hour, how much does each tabletop cost to produce?

1-11. What other costs should the company consider in calculating of the cost to produce the tabletop? Explain.

Diversification

During the first two decades of the 20th century, companies in the U.S. and other western countries began to diversify. Before this time, virtually all companies undertook only one activity. For example, railroad companies were strictly in the railroad business and steel companies were strictly in the steel business. The emergence of diversified, multi-activity companies changed the nature of decision making.

Discussion Question

1-12. Why do you think companies began to diversify in the early years of the 20th century?

Owners of diversified companies could not directly manage all the various business operations. Instead, they relied on others to manage operations that they could not personally oversee; and they obtained additional management accounting information from the various parts of the business so they could plan, control, and evaluate performance. Company accountants tailored reports to meet the needs of managers at each level of the organization. Lower-level managers, such as production supervisors, received reports that focused on production efficiencies. Higher level managers received reports that focused on product profits.

Challenges and Trends in Management Accounting

It is generally acknowledged that as we approached the end of the 20th Century, United States industries had lost much of their dominance relative to those from other countries, and that by the 1980s the U.S. had experienced serious erosion in its position as the world's business leader. Industry after industry suffered from the effects of significant foreign competition. At the time, experts offered many reasons to explain what was happening. But whatever else contributed to the decline, American industries had clearly become complacent. They had been dominant for so long, they seemed to feel that they did not need to make any significant changes in the way they operated.

Until the 1970s, the lack of competition from outside the country allowed U.S. companies to flourish. Because many industries lacked serious competition, many decisions—even those made without adequate management accounting information—led to favorable financial results. If satisfactory decisions could be made without more sophisticated accounting information, why would management even recognize that improvements were needed? Even business executives who were convinced of the weaknesses in their management accounting systems did not believe changes were worth making because they felt they were no worse off than their competition.

By the early 1980s, however, competition from foreign companies with more sophisticated management accounting techniques forced U.S. companies to pay more attention to the relevance of the accounting information they were using to make short-term and long-term business decisions.

By the mid-1980s, U.S. companies in many different industries had realized the need to change business operations to remain competitive. Beginning in the 1980s and continuing into the 21st Century, many U.S. businesses began to take significant steps to increase their competitiveness.

American businesses began using production and management techniques that were initiated in the Far East and Europe. As they examined and reorganized their operations to become more competitive, they also examined the way they use accounting information to make decisions. As a result, managers and accountants in the U.S. are implementing or at least considering various new operating methods, which has led to adoption of new techniques in management accounting. Just-in-time inventory (JIT), activity-based costing (ABC), and the balanced scorecard, are just a few of the management accounting techniques that many American industries have adopted over the past two decades in an effort to restore their ability to compete in today's global marketplace.

At present, management accountants all over the world are facing critical problems concerning intense competition, increased risk and social responsibility. Although they have recently devised various novel methods and models, they are not yet likely to resolve the problems even if these novelties lead to increased efficiency and effectiveness. Management accountants and operating managers of all types must continue to look for improved performance and measurement techniques. We anticipate that the coming decades will see vastly more sophisticated and innovative ways to achieve those improvements.

Consumers of Management Accounting Information

To make effective decisions, business managers must understand the firm's management accounting system, know whether the information is reliable, and recognize that no system will provide perfect information. Decision-making by its very nature is forward-looking, and the future always contains elements of uncertainty. Managers should look for ways to reduce the number of these elements.

Regardless of your career, at some point you will probably use accounting information to make a decision. If you are studying marketing, you may start as an assistant who helps prepare and implement marketing programs. As you advance in your career, you may manage a staff of people who handle marketing programs, so you will need the accounting tools to make well-informed decisions. When you are responsible for the well-being of a company, department, division, or management team, you will face decisions that depend on your using management accounting information. The following chapters will teach you to be a careful consumer of accounting information.

Summary

The function of accounting is to provide economic decision makers with the financial information they need to make informed decisions.

Management accounting is the branch of accounting designed to provide information to the firm's internal economic decision makers. Financial accounting provides information to external decision makers—people outside the company. In contrast to financial accounting, management accounting provides information to internal decision makers, does not have to conform to GAAP, provides information about various parts of a company, is provided as quickly as users need information, and has more of a future orientation.

The Institute of Management Accountants provides the same sort of professional status for management accountants as the American Institute of Certified Public Accountants (AICPA) does for financial accountants. The International Federation of Accountants (IFAC) is a global organization of accountants and other financial professionals. The Sarbanes-Oxley Act is a United States federal law that established new standards for all U.S. publicly traded companies, company management, public accounting firms, and financial analysts.

As companies grew in size and complexity in the 19th and 20th centuries, owners developed methods to measure the conversion of raw materials into units of finished product. These methods were the foundation for present-day management accounting. The scientific management movement had a tremendous influence on business management and management accounting.

As companies diversified, their owners could not directly manage all the various business operations and because they relied on others to manage operations, they obtained additional management accounting information from the various parts of the business so they could plan, control, and evaluate performance.

Currently managers and accountants in the U.S. are implementing or at least considering various new operating methods, which has led to adoption of new techniques in management accounting. Just-in-time inventory (JIT), activity-based costing (ABC), and the balanced scorecard are just a few of the management accounting techniques that many American industries have adopted over the past two decades in an effort to restore their ability to compete in today's global marketplace.

To make effective decisions, business managers must understand the firm's management accounting system, Decision making by its very nature is forward-looking, and the future always contains an element of uncertainty. Management accounting provides useful information that helps managers to reduce the amount of that uncertainty.

Key Terms

Review the Facts

A. What are the differences among management accounting, managerial accounting, and cost accounting?

B. What is the purpose of management accounting?

C. What are the primary differences between financial accounting and management accounting?

D. Financial accounting information must be prepared in conformity with GAAP. Why are there no such rules for management accounting?

E. List four significant changes in business that led to the development of management accounting.

F. What is the IMA and what is its purpose?

G. Why is an understanding of management accounting an important ingredient of success in your career?

Apply What You Have Learned

LO 1: Contrast Management Accounting and Financial Accounting

1-13. Following are certain characteristics of either financial accounting information or management accounting information.

1. _____ Must conform to GAAP.
2. _____ Tends to be quite detailed.
3. _____ Generally limited to presenting historical information.
4. _____ Need not conform to a formal set of rules and standards.
5. _____ Information prepared primarily for external users.
6. _____ Tends to include only a limited amount of detail.
7. _____ Information prepared on a quarterly or yearly basis.
8. _____ Information prepared on a monthly, weekly, or daily basis.
9. _____ Information often includes future projections.
10. _____ Information prepared for use by internal parties.

Required

Designate each of the characteristics as pertaining to (a) financial accounting information or (b) management accounting information.

LO 1: Describe Management Accounting

1-14. Is management accounting important for not-for-profit organizations as well as for-profit organizations? Explain.

LO 1: Describe Management Accounting

1-15. If you were the manager of **a Blockbuster Entertainment** Store, what accounting information would you desire to help you do your job better?

LO 4: Changes in Management Accounting

1-16. Explain why there has been a renewed emphasis on the development of management accounting in the United States in the last few decades.

LO 1: Contrast Management Accounting and Financial Accounting

1-17. Following are examples of users of financial accounting information and users of management accounting information.

1. _____ Sales supervisor
2. _____ Salespersons
3. _____ Wall Street analyst
4. _____ Suppliers
5. _____ Current shareholders
6. _____ Potential shareholders
7. _____ Personnel manager
8. _____ Maintenance supervisor
9. _____ Maintenance worker
10. _____ Loan officer at a company's bank

Required

Designate each of the users of accounting information as either (a) external party or (b) internal party.

2

Classifying Costs

Suppose for a moment that you work for a large clothing store chain that sells online. Your boss has asked you to organize the company website of all the clothes the company sells. You need to categorize the products so users of your website will be able to find information easily. After thinking about your task for a while, you make a list of product classifications—design, price, gender of user and age of user. It looks like this:

Classification	Type of Clothes
Age of User	Clothes for babies
	Clothes for young children
	Clothes for teenagers
	Clothes for adults
Gender of User	Clothes for females
	Clothes for males
	Clothes for both males and females
Price	Clothes that cost less than $10
	Clothes that cost $10 to $50
	Clothes that cost $51 to $99
	Clothes that cost more than $100
Design	Casual clothing
	Sportswear
	Formalwear

Your boss wants you to pick only one or two categories by which to organize the catalog. You scan your list to see which classifications will be most useful, but you realize that the catalog must include all of them to be as useful as possible, because purchasers may need different information for different decisions. For instance, let's say someone is choosing clothes to donate to the annual clothing drive for needy children. They may want to focus on price so they can donate several articles of clothing, and may want to use the gender classification to find clothes for all children because they would not know in advance whether the child receiving the clothes is a girl or a boy.

Another shopper may be looking for a birthday present intended for a two-year-old relative, so he would need to use the age classification to find the appropriate clothing. And because he has a budget, this shopper will also want to use the price category to help decide on the gift. As these examples show, even in making just one decision, more than one classification may provide useful information.

Like our hypothetical clothing buyers, managers must have information to make effective planning and controlling decisions. Cost information is one of the key components of financial decision making, but what exactly is a cost? In accounting, a cost is how much we have to give up to get something. Put more formally, a **cost** is the dollar amount of resources forfeited to receive some goods or services. Note that cost is different from price. Price is what we charge; cost is what we pay.

cost The resources forfeited to receive some goods or services.

Business managers classify costs in many different ways because, just like the vast array of clothes, there are many types of costs. Each classification can provide managers with useful information. In this chapter, we explore several different cost classifications that managers use to make decisions.

Learning Objectives

After completing your work on this chapter, you should be able to do the following:

1. Classify costs by cost objects, and distinguish between direct and indirect costs.
2. Distinguish between product costs and period costs, and contrast their accounting treatment.
3. Explain the differences between product cost for a merchandiser and for a manufacturer.
4. Describe the components of the costs included in each of the three types of inventory in a manufacturing operation.
5. Calculate cost of goods manufactured and cost of goods sold.
6. Describe the components of the cost of services provided by a service firm.
7. Prepare basic journal entries for a manufacturer.

Major Cost Classifications

Businesses incur many different costs as they operate and there are many useful ways to classify these costs. As managers make each internal business decision, they must determine what cost classifications will help them most. We will first identify important cost terms and investigate several cost classifications.

Assigning Costs to Cost Objects

One of the most useful classifications of cost is by cost object. A **cost object** is any activity or item for which we desire a separate cost measurement. Think of any noun associated with business and you have a potential cost object. Exhibit 2-1 lists some cost objects commonly used by companies.

cost object Any activity or item for which a separate cost measurement is desired.

Exhibit 2-1 Common Cost Object Designations

Cost Object	Examples
• Activity	• Repairing equipment, testing manufactured products for quality
• Product	• Paper towels, personal computers, automobiles (These can be either purchased or manufactured products.)
• Service	• Performing surgery, accounting work, legal work
• Project	• Constructing a bridge, designing a house
• Geographic region	• A state, a city, a county
• Department	• Marketing department, accounting department

We identify a cost object to determine the cost of that particular object. Such classification can provide useful information. For example, **Harley-Davidson** may need information about the cost to manufacture one of its motorcycles. In this case, the individual products are the cost objects. All costs associated with a particular product are grouped to determine the full cost of that product. Managers may also want to determine the cost associated with a group of products, such as a fleet of delivery trucks.

When we assign costs to cost objects, we classify costs as direct or indirect. A cost that is easily traced to individual cost objects is a **direct cost**. Many times, however, a cost may benefit more than one cost object, so tracing that cost to individual cost objects becomes difficult or even impossible. A cost that supports more than one cost object is an **indirect cost**. An indirect cost may also be called a **common cost**, because it is common to more than one cost object.

direct cost A cost that can be easily traced to an individual cost object.

indirect cost A cost that supports more than one cost object.

common cost Another name for indirect cost.

To illustrate the difference between direct and indirect costs, consider 12 **Wal-Mart** stores in New York. Each store has a manager who is responsible for the day-to-day operation of that store. **Wal-Mart** also has a general manager who is responsible for the operation of all the stores in the state. If we define each of the 12 stores as cost objects, the salary of each store manager is a direct cost to his or her store. The salary of the *general manager* however is not incurred to support any one of the 12 stores—rather, it supports all 12 stores. Therefore, the general manager's salary is an indirect cost to each cost object (the individual stores).

Discussion Questions

Assume that instead of defining each individual Wal-Mart store as a cost object, we define the entire Wal-Mart operation in New York as a cost object.

2-1. In this case, would the salaries of the 12 store managers be considered direct or indirect costs? Explain your reasoning.

2-2. Would the salary of the general manager be considered a direct or an indirect cost? Explain your reasoning.

2-3. Why do you think managers at various levels in a company would find it useful to classify costs as direct or indirect?

Product Cost

product cost The cost of the various products a company sells.

When you see inventory on store shelves, you know the store did not get the inventory for free. Rather, each unit of product had some cost. The cost of the various products a company sells is called **product cost**. More specifically, product costs are the costs associated with making the products available and ready to sell. For a bookstore, such as **B. Dalton Booksellers** or **Barnes & Noble**, product cost is the cost of the books it purchases for resale, the freight to get the books to the store (also known as freight-in), and other costs involved in getting the books ready to sell.

inventoriable cost Another name for product cost.

Product costs are also known as **inventoriable costs** because they become part of a company's inventory until the goods associated with those costs are sold. Because a product held for sale is considered an asset, its cost is shown on the balance sheet (inventory) until the product is actually sold. When the goods are sold, the product cost is converted from an asset on the balance sheet to an expense (cost of goods sold) on the income statement.

For example, when **Payless Shoe Source** buys shoes to sell, the cost of the shoes is a product cost and is added to inventory on the balance sheet. The cost remains in inventory on the balance sheet until the shoes are sold. When the shoes are sold, the reality of the reduced inventory caused by the sale is reflected in the company's accounting records by reducing inventory on the balance sheet and increasing cost of goods sold on the income statement.

Period Cost

period cost All costs incurred by a company that are not considered product cost. Includes selling and administrative cost.

Period costs are all the costs a company incurs that are not considered product costs. They include selling and administrative expenses, but not any costs associated with acquiring product or getting it ready to sell. For **Payless Shoe Source** this would include costs of employees in accounting, finance, marketing, advertising, and certain executives such as the company president.

Selling Cost

selling cost The cost of locating customers, attracting customers, convincing customers to buy, and the cost of necessary paperwork to document and record sales.

Selling cost includes the cost of locating customers, attracting them, convincing them to buy, and the cost of necessary paperwork to document and record sales. Examples of selling cost include salaries paid to members of the sales force, sales commissions, and advertising.

Two selling costs are less obvious: the cost of delivering product to customers (also known as freight-out) and the cost of storing merchandise inventory. The reason delivery cost is considered a selling cost is that companies probably would not provide delivery unless it helped sell more product. If customers would buy with or without free delivery, the seller would likely not offer it.

Do not confuse freight-out (period cost) with freight-in (product cost). The key to keeping the two straight is to think about when they are incurred. Freight-in is a cost incurred before the product is ready to sell and is therefore a product cost. Freight-out is incurred after the product is ready for sale and is therefore classified as a period cost. For companies like **Dell Computers**, freight-in is part of the cost to get the raw material to assemble its computers and freight-out is the cost to ship the finished computers to its customers.

The cost of storing merchandise inventory is also classified as a selling cost, because merchandise in stock enhances its sales potential. Businesses cannot easily sell what they do not have. For example, if you go to your local music shop to buy a compact disc and the salesperson tells you, "We don't keep that CD in stock, but we'll be glad to order it for you," you may decide to go to another store that carries a better-stocked inventory of CDs rather than wait. Because both delivery and merchandise inventory enhance sales, these items are considered selling costs.

Administrative Cost

Administrative cost includes all costs that are not product or selling costs. These costs are typically associated with support functions—areas that offer support to the product and selling areas, such as accounting, finance, human resources, and executive functions.

administrative cost All costs incurred by a company that are not product costs or selling costs. Includes the cost of accounting, finance, employee relations, and executive functions.

Generally, period costs are shown as operating expenses (selling and administrative expenses) on the income statement. Most period costs—administrators' salaries, for example—are presented as expenses when the expenditure is made. When long-lived assets that will be used for selling or administrative functions are purchased, a slightly different treatment is necessary. At the time they are purchased, the cost of long-lived assets is shown on the balance sheet. As time passes, the depreciation expense associated with these assets becomes part of selling and administrative expense.

Discussion Questions

Assume that you are using a felt-tip highlighter to mark this book as you read it. Assume further that you purchased the marker at the college bookstore.

2-4. What costs associated with the marker do you think the bookstore would consider to be product costs? Explain your reasoning for each cost you included.

2-5. What costs associated with operating the bookstore do you think would be considered period costs (selling and administrative)? Explain your reasoning for each cost you included.

Comparing Product and Period Costs

The distinction between product cost and period cost is based on whether the cost in question benefits the process of getting products ready for sale (product cost), or the selling and administrative functions (period cost). Let's look at some examples to make sure you understand the distinction. The cost of a factory security guard is a product cost because it benefits the plant. Conversely, the cost of a security guard in the sales office is a selling expense, which is a period cost. The classification depends on the company function that benefits from the cost.

What about the salary of the vice president of manufacturing? Even though vice president of manufacturing may sound like an administrative position, the cost benefits the manufacturing function, so it is a product cost. Further, all costs associated with that position, including, for example, the depreciation on the vice president's desk, the cost of his or her support personnel, and travel costs, are classified as product costs. Likewise, the salary of the vice president of marketing and the costs of that position are period costs, as they benefit the sales area of the company.

Next, we examine how manufacturing, merchandising, and service firms identify their product costs.

Product Cost Identification for Merchandising Firms

Merchandising firms such as **Macy's** and **Nordstrom** purchase products ready to sell, add a markup, and resell the goods. Regardless of whether they are wholesale or retail merchandising firms they generate profits by selling merchandise for a price that is higher than its cost.

Wholesalers generally buy products from manufacturers (or other wholesalers) and then sell them to retailers. Retailers buy from manufacturers or wholesalers and sell their products to the final consumers. In this section we explore how a merchandising company identifies product costs and how those product costs flow through the balance sheet and income statement.

For a merchandising firm, product cost includes the cost of the merchandise itself, freight costs to obtain the merchandise, and any other costs incurred to get the product ready to sell. Because merchandisers buy goods for resale, often the cost of getting products ready to sell is minor or nonexistent. Product cost does not include any cost incurred after the product is in place and ready to sell.

Product cost is often the most significant of all costs for a merchandiser. It is not uncommon for merchandising companies to have cost of goods sold as high as 80 percent of the selling price of the product sold, meaning that they have a gross profit as low as 20 percent. Besides increasing sales, managers are always interested in reducing expenses, which is impossible without an understanding of what items are included in product cost. Efforts to reduce total cost of goods sold may focus on any component of that expense, that is, any component of product cost.

The Flow of Product Cost—Merchandising Company

If you were responsible for the profitability of a product or group of products, not only would you want to know total product cost, but you would also want to know and understand the various components of each product's cost. With this understanding, you could analyze reports detailing these products' cost components and work to isolate costs that could be reduced or eliminated. The diagram in Exhibit 2-2 illustrates the flow of costs in a merchandising operation.

Exhibit 2-2 Flow of Product Costs—Merchandising Company

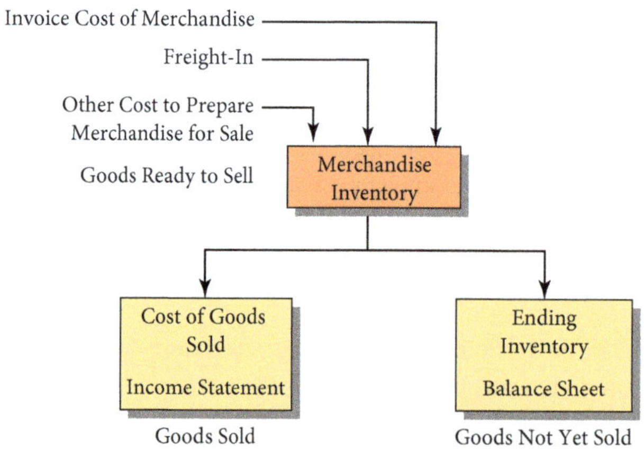

Exhibit 2-2 indicates that as goods are purchased, their cost is classified as merchandise inventory. In fact, all product costs are originally shown like those in Exhibit 2-2, as an asset on the balance sheet. Typically, a merchandising firm has only one inventory classification, which is usually referred to as *merchandise inventory* or, simply, *inventory*. As the units of product are sold, their cost is converted to an expense and shown on the income statement as the cost of goods sold.

Cost of Goods Sold

Exhibit 2-3 is a cost of goods sold schedule for Jason's Supply Company. As the exhibit shows, Jason adds purchases to the inventory on hand at the beginning of the period to arrive at the goods available for sale. Generally, one of two things can happen to the goods available for sale: They are either sold (cost of goods sold) or remain on hand at the end of the period (ending inventory). Thus, when ending inventory is subtracted from the goods available for sale, Jason can determine the cost associated with the products that have been sold—that is, the company can determine the cost of goods sold.

Exhibit 2-3 Cost of Goods Sold Schedule

Jason's Supply Company
Cost of Goods Sold Schedule
For the Year Ending December 31, 2008

	Beginning Inventory (1/1/08)	$ 23,000
+	Purchases during 2008	300,000
=	Goods Available for Sale in 2008	$323,000
–	Ending Inventory (12/31/08)	(30,000)
=	Cost of Goods Sold for 2008	$293,000

The beginning inventory amount shown in Exhibit 2-3 is actually the ending inventory from Jason's balance sheet at December 31, 2007, and the ending inventory amount shown is from Jason's balance sheet at December 31, 2008. The cost of goods sold amount is included as an expense item on the company's income statement for the year ending December 31, 2008.

Discussion Question

2-6. Accounting for the flow of product cost for a merchandiser seems to be a lot of bother. If all merchandise inventory will eventually be sold anyway, why not just record it as an expense (cost of goods sold) on the income statement when it is purchased?

Any company that sells tangible, physical product must sell its product for more than the product cost or it will eventually go bankrupt. This may seem very obvious, and in fact, good business managers are well aware of this necessity. Understanding the need is one thing; making sure it happens is another. Competitive pressures in most industries cause companies to sell their products for less than they would like to. Managers of these businesses must have a solid understanding of the relationship between the selling price of their products and the cost of those products, or they may actually sell a product for less than it costs.

It's like the two guys—Harry and George—who bought watermelons for $1 each and were selling them for $0.90 each. Business was certainly brisk because they were underselling all their competition. Still, they were not making a profit. Finally, George turned to his friend and said, "Harry, we need to get a bigger truck." What George and Harry didn't understand is that they could never sell enough watermelons at $.90 each to be profitable because they were selling each melon for less than it cost. Without a thorough understanding of the relationship between the cost of a product and the selling price of that product, managers cannot hope to make prudent business decisions.

Product Cost Identification for Manufacturing Firms

Virtually all the products that consumers purchase have undergone some manufacturing process. In this section we explore how a manufacturing company identifies product costs and how those product costs flow through the balance sheet and income statement. As in merchandising firms, product cost for a manufacturer includes all costs associated with acquiring the product and getting it ready to sell. For manufacturers, however, getting the product ready to sell is usually an extensive process requiring the use of factory facilities such as production machinery and factory workers.

For a manufacturer, units of product are normally considered cost objects and their cost encompasses three distinct elements. We will introduce them briefly here and then discuss each of them in more detail a bit later. As we present each of the elements, think back to our discussion earlier in the chapter about cost objects and direct versus indirect costs.

direct materials cost The cost of all raw materials that can be traced directly to a unit of manufactured product.

Direct materials cost. Direct materials cost is the cost of all raw materials that can be traced directly to a unit of manufactured product. For **Ford Motor Company's** Mustang this would include the cost of metal, tires, engines, belts, seats, etc. Direct materials cost is not the cost of all materials used in the manufacture of the product. In most manufacturing operations some materials costs are incurred for multiple cost objects. These costs are indirect materials cost and accountants generally consider them a part of manufacturing overhead.

direct labor cost The cost of all production labor that can be traced directly to a unit of manufactured product.

Direct labor cost. Direct labor cost is the cost of all production labor that can be traced directly to a unit of manufactured product. Direct labor is also sometimes called **touch labor** because it is the cost of the workers who actually touch the product being manufactured. For **Ford's** Mustang, this would include the cost of assembly line workers. Direct labor cost is not the cost of all labor incurred in the manufacture of product. In most manufacturing operations some labor costs benefit multiple cost objects. Accountants generally consider that indirect labor cost a part of manufacturing overhead, discussed next.

manufacturing overhead cost All costs associated with the operation of the manufacturing facility besides direct materials cost and direct labor cost. It is composed entirely of indirect manufacturing cost incurred to support multiple cost objects.

Manufacturing overhead cost. Manufacturing overhead is all the costs associated with the operation of the manufacturing facility other than direct materials cost and direct labor cost. It is composed entirely of indirect manufacturing cost—that is, manufacturing cost incurred to support multiple cost objects. Among others, manufacturing overhead includes indirect materials and indirect labor as discussed previously. For **Ford's** Mustang, manufacturing overhead cost would include a portion of costs for the factory's security, telephone, electricity, insurance, property taxes, and factory depreciation.

Prime Cost and Conversion Cost

prime cost The combined total of direct material cost and direct labor cost.

conversion cost The combined total of direct labor cost and manufacturing overhead cost.

Sometimes managers use the terms *prime cost* and *conversion* cost to describe the cost of manufacturing their products. The combined total of direct material cost and direct labor cost is called **prime cost**. The cost of manufacturing overhead is not considered a part of prime cost. **Conversion cost** is the combined total of direct labor cost and manufacturing overhead cost. Conversion cost does not include the cost of the direct material itself, rather it is the cost of the direct labor and manufacturing overhead the company uses to convert the direct material into a finished product.

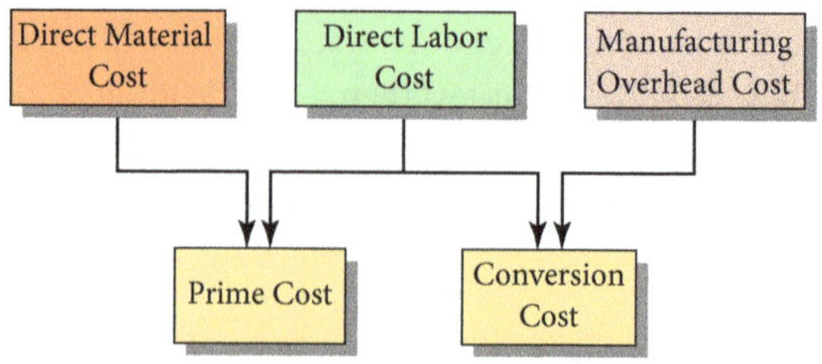

Inventory Classifications

As with merchandising firms, product costs for a manufacturer are inventoriable costs. However, manufacturing companies have not just one, but three types of inventory: raw materials, work in process, and finished goods. Note that these three types of inventory are not the same as the three elements of manufactured product we just introduced. Rather, these inventory classifications specify where manufactured product is at any given time in the production process.

As we discuss the three inventory classifications used by manufacturers, consider the following thoughts. First, our discussion in this chapter is intended to serve only as a broad introduction to the flow of product cost through a manufacturing company. The next two chapters deal with specific methods used to accumulate product cost for a manufacturer. Second, there is a difference between reality and the measurement of reality. Reality is the physical units of product moving through the production process, separate from our attempt to measure that reality.

Raw Materials Inventory

Raw materials inventory, sometimes called **material stores**, consists of materials that have been purchased but have not yet entered the production process. Raw materials inventory includes all the materials that will eventually be accounted for as either direct or indirect materials. For example, **Steelcase, Inc.** manufactures metal desks, filing cabinets, and other metal office furniture. Raw materials inventory consists of the sheet metal, screws, paint, and glue **Steelcase** has on hand with which to make metal office furniture. It would not include any of the material in the office furniture the company has begun to manufacture but has not yet finished, nor would it include the material in the office furniture that has been completed and ready for sale. Until raw materials actually enter the production process, the cost associated with those materials is classified as raw materials inventory on the balance sheet.

raw materials inventory Materials that have been purchased but have not yet entered the production process.

material stores Another name for raw materials inventory

Work-in-Process Inventory

Work-in-process inventory consists of products that have entered the production process but have not yet been completed—those units currently on the production line or in the production process. In our **Steelcase** example, work-in-process inventory consists of the desks, filing cabinets, and other metal office furniture that have been started but are not yet finished. The reality is partially completed desks, filing cabinets, and other metal office furniture. The measurement of reality counts the costs associated with these partially completed units of product and classifies them as work-in-process inventory on the balance sheet. These costs include the cost of the materials associated with these units, the labor cost incurred so far in the production process, and some amount of manufacturing overhead applied to each of the partially completed units of product.

work-in-process inventory Products that have entered the production process but have not yet been completed.

Work-in-process inventory does not include the cost of raw materials that have not yet entered the production process, nor does it include the cost associated with products that have been completed and ready for sale.

Finished Goods Inventory

Finished goods inventory, as you might imagine, consists of products that have been completed and are ready to sell. With respect to **Steelcase**, finished goods inventory consists of the pieces of metal office furniture completed but not yet sold. Remember, these are real units of finished product: They are reality. They have completed the production process and are sitting in a warehouse somewhere waiting to be sold. The measurement of that reality is a classification of inventory on the balance sheet called finished goods inventory. Included in that amount are all the materials, labor, and manufacturing overhead costs accumulated for those units completed, but not yet sold.

finished goods inventory Products that have been completed and are ready to sell.

Discussion Question

2-7. Why do you think managers of a manufacturing firm would find it beneficial to separate the amount and cost of inventory items into raw materials, work in process, and finished goods?

If managers in manufacturing businesses are to make prudent production decisions, they must have relevant information. The decisions they must make include how much and what type of materials they need to purchase, how many production workers are needed, what skill level these workers must possess, and whether production capacity is sufficient to produce the product required. The information managers need to help them make these and many other production decisions includes the amount and cost of raw materials on hand, the composition of the labor force, the capacity and cost of production facilities, and the amount and cost of both work-in-process and finished goods inventory.

Although much of the relevant information managers need to make these decisions is provided by non-accountants such as marketing and sales personnel, accountants provide vital information concerning the cost of raw materials, work in process, and finished goods. All three classifications of inventory have one or more of the product cost elements introduced earlier: direct material, direct labor, and manufacturing overhead. We will now discuss each of those elements in more detail.

Direct Material

direct material The raw material that becomes a part of the final product and can be easily traced to the units produced.

Direct material is the raw material that becomes part of the final product and can be easily traced to the individual units produced. Obviously, direct materials cost is the cost of these raw materials. Examples of direct materials used in the manufacture of automobiles are sheet metal, plastic, and window glass. In the manufacture of computers, direct materials include circuit boards, memory chips, and other items. At **Steelcase**, direct materials include the sheet metal used to manufacture the desks, filing cabinets, and other metal office furniture.

Often, the final product of one company is purchased by another to be used as part of its raw material in the manufacturing process. For example, direct materials used in the manufacture of **Cessna** aircraft include aluminum, wheels, tires, cables, and engines. The tires that **Cessna** uses as raw materials in the manufacture of its aircraft are the finished product of one of the company's suppliers, **Goodyear Tire and Rubber Company**.

Discussion Questions

2-8. In addition to the tires supplied by **Goodyear**, what other finished products do you think **Cessna** uses in its production of small aircraft? What companies might produce these products?

2-9. Name three additional pairs of manufacturing companies that have a supplier-buyer relationship—that is, the finished product of one company becomes the raw material of another company.

When materials are purchased for use in the manufacture of products, their cost at first is added to raw materials inventory. Once the material has entered the production process (reality), its cost is removed from raw materials inventory and added to work-in-process inventory (measurement of reality). Thus, in our **Steelcase** example, as sheet metal is purchased, its cost is added to raw materials. Once the metal has been used to make a desk or other piece of office furniture, its cost is removed from raw materials inventory and becomes part of work-in-process inventory.

Direct Labor

Direct labor hours are defined as the time spent by production workers as they transform raw materials into units of finished products. Direct labor costs are the salaries and wages paid to these workers, which can be easily traced to the products they produce.

direct labor hours The time spent by production workers as they transform raw materials into units of finished products.

Think about some article of clothing, say a pair of pants, you are wearing right now. Certainly there is material in the pants. But how did the pants become pants? Well, you may not know all the steps, but you do know that somewhere, someone sat at a sewing machine and stitched the cut material into a pair of pants. The money paid to that person, whether in China, Korea, or the United States, is considered direct labor, because her or his efforts (and therefore cost) can easily be traced to that single cost object (the pair of pants).

The accounting treatment of direct labor cost may surprise you. Direct labor needed to get products ready to sell is a product cost that enhances the value of direct material. Because product costs are inventoriable costs, direct labor cost is added to the value of work-in-process inventory, along with the cost of direct material. Why? Because the work of production-line personnel increases the value of material as it is fabricated, assembled, painted, or processed. As a result, the cost of production-line labor should increase the value of inventory, shown as an asset on the balance sheet and ultimately as cost of goods sold on the income statement. In our **Steelcase** example, then, wages paid to workers who actually make the desks, filing cabinets, and other metal office furniture is considered direct labor and added to work-in-process inventory.

Thus far we have explored two elements of product costs for a manufacturing firm: direct material and direct labor. Next, we consider the third and last element of manufacturers' product costs—manufacturing overhead.

Manufacturing Overhead

Manufacturing overhead is defined as all activities involved in the manufacture of products besides direct materials or direct labor. Manufacturing overhead cost, then, is the cost of these indirect manufacturing activities. It is also referred to as **factory overhead**, **factory burden**, or simply **overhead**. In recent years, manufacturing companies have begun to call the cost of manufacturing overhead **indirect manufacturing cost**, which is certainly more descriptive than any of its other names. Old habits die hard, however, so we will call it manufacturing overhead because this term has been and remains universally understood in business.

manufacturing overhead All activities involved in the manufacture of products besides direct materials or direct labor.

factory overhead Another name for manufacturing overhead cost.

factory burden Another name for manufacturing overhead cost.

overhead In a manufacturing company, another name for manufacturing overhead cost; in a service type business, the indirect service cost.

To be considered part of manufacturing overhead, a cost must be associated with the manufacturing facility, not some other aspect of the company such as selling or administrative functions. Manufacturing overhead includes three groups of costs—indirect materials, indirect labor, and other indirect manufacturing costs.

Indirect Material

Indirect materials are those consumed in a manufacturing facility in support of multiple cost objects. There are two types of indirect material costs in manufacturing. The first is the cost of raw materials so insignificant that the added benefit of physically tracing these materials to individual products is not worth the effort. Examples include glue, rivets, solder, small nails, and caulking. In fact, businesses could physically trace all material cost to their products.

indirect materials Materials consumed in support of multiple cost objects.

In the case of indirect materials, however, the effort required to trace the cost outweighs the benefit of the additional information. The second type of indirect material is factory supplies. These are materials used in the manufacturing facility but not incorporated into the product. Examples include paper towels, janitorial supplies, and lubricants for production machinery. The cost of all indirect materials, whether the materials actually become part of manufactured product, is added to the cost of the product as part of manufacturing overhead.

Indirect Labor

indirect labor The labor incurred in support of multiple cost objects

Indirect labor is labor incurred in a manufacturing facility in support of multiple cost objects. As was the case with indirect material costs, there are two types of indirect labor in manufacturing. The first is the cost associated with factory workers who are neither on the production line nor directly involved in the manufacturing process. Examples include the cost of materials handlers, production supervisors, plant security personnel, plant janitorial personnel, factory secretarial and clerical personnel, and the vice president of manufacturing. Although the effort of these workers is important to the production process, their labor costs are not easily traceable to products. They are therefore classified as indirect labor.

The second type of indirect labor is the cost of wages paid to direct labor employees when they are doing something other than working on the product they produce. These activities might include setting up equipment for production runs or sweeping up at the end of a shift. The idea is that direct labor should include only the cost of direct labor personnel when they are actually working on the product. The cost of all indirect labor is added to the cost of the product as part of manufacturing overhead.

Some manufacturers in the United States now consider *all* labor as indirect labor. In some types of operations, the direct labor element of a manufactured product is as low as four percent of the total manufacturing cost. If managers believe labor cost is insignificant, they may choose not to separate it into direct and indirect labor cost and may instead classify all labor costs as indirect.

Other Manufacturing Overhead Costs

In addition to indirect material and indirect labor, manufacturing overhead includes other costs associated with the production facility. Examples include depreciation on the factory building, rent paid for production equipment, factory insurance, property taxes for the factory, and telephone service for the factory. All the costs in this category are associated with the operation of the production facility.

We have seen that manufacturing overhead is the sum of all indirect material, indirect labor, and other manufacturing overhead costs. Manufacturing overhead costs are necessary costs to produce products and enhance the value of the goods being manufactured. Accordingly, as products are being manufactured, manufacturing overhead costs are added to work-in-process inventory.

Discussion Question

2-10. The textbook you are reading was printed (manufactured) by the publisher. What costs of manufacturing this book do you think the publisher would include as

a. direct materials?

b. direct labor?

c. manufacturing overhead?

The Flow of Product Cost—Manufacturing Company

In a manufacturing environment, just as in merchandising operations, managers must understand the flow of product costs to successfully control and plan for them. Product cost information is also an essential element of the information needed when making pricing and sales decisions. How could a business price a product if none of its managers knew how much the product cost to produce? Having the information is not enough, though. Managers must also understand the components of product cost and the way these costs will affect the company's assets as reported on the balance sheet and the profits as reported on the income statement. Exhibit 2-4 shows the flow of product costs through a manufacturing operation.

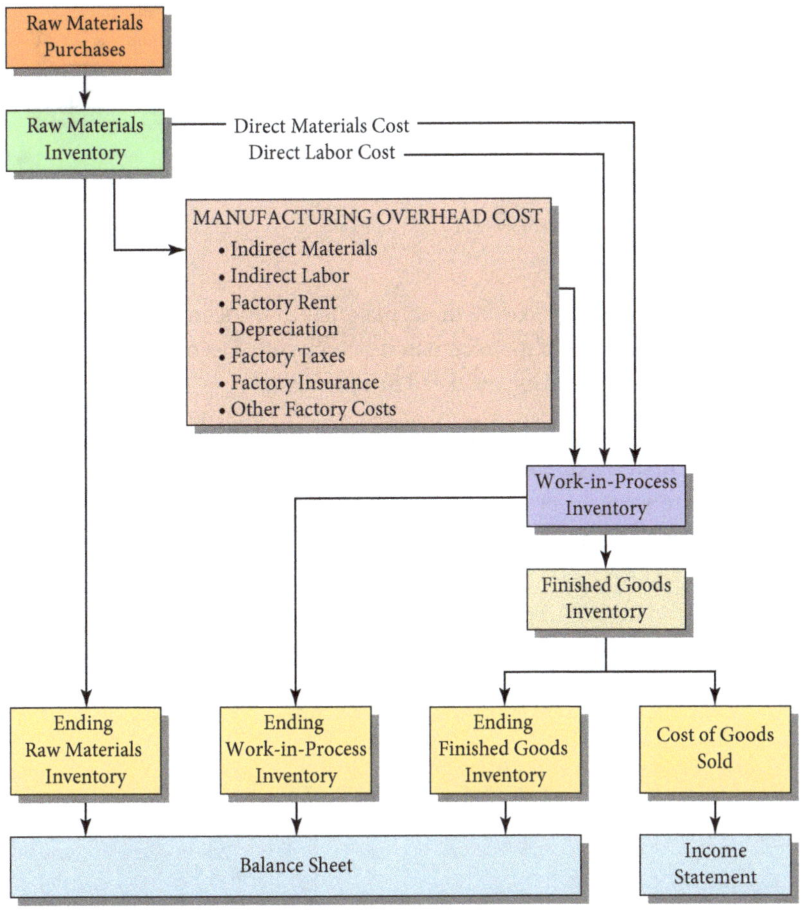

Exhibit 2-4 The Flow of Product Costs—Manufacturing Company

Exhibit 2-4 looks more complicated than it really is. In fact, this exhibit summarizes our entire discussion of product cost identification for a manufacturer. Let's take some time to walk through the diagram.

As raw materials are purchased, they become part of raw materials inventory (a).

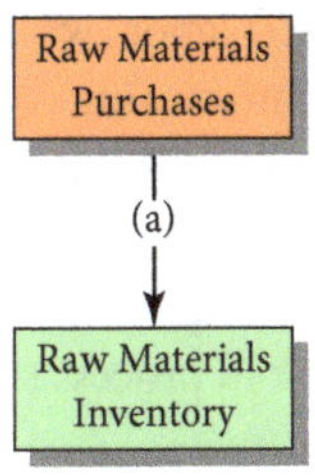

When materials actually enter the production process, we classify their cost as either direct materials (b) or indirect materials (c) depending on the type of material. We classify the cost of any raw materials still on hand at the end of the production period as ending raw materials inventory on the balance sheet at the end of the period (d).

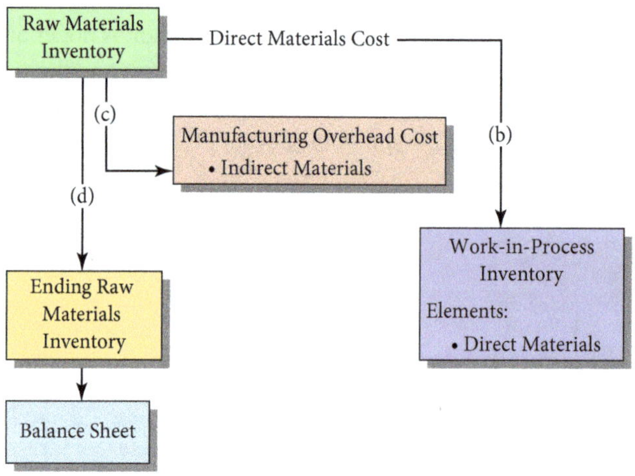

Note that we add the cost of direct materials to work-in-process inventory at this point, whereas the cost of indirect materials is classified as manufacturing overhead. We will return to manufacturing overhead in a moment.

We now have one of the three elements of product cost in work-in-process inventory (direct materials). The next element added is labor. Note that we add direct labor (e) directly to work-in-process inventory, whereas indirect labor (f) is classified as manufacturing overhead.

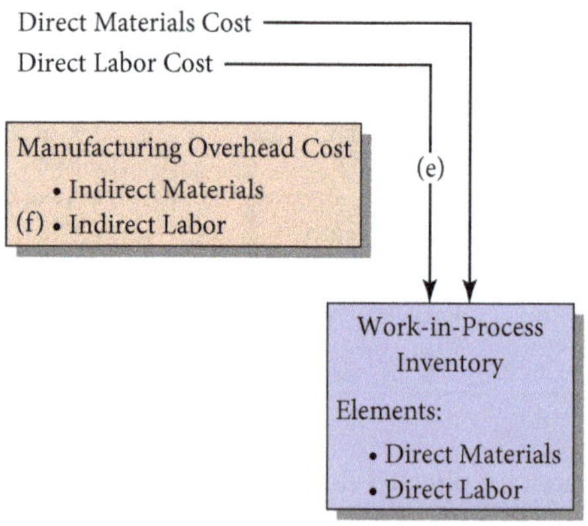

We now have two of the three elements of product cost in work-in-process inventory (direct materials and direct labor). The last element added is manufacturing overhead. In addition to indirect materials and indirect labor (which we classified as manufacturing overhead earlier), all other indirect manufacturing costs are classified as manufacturing overhead (g). The ones we have provided in Exhibit 2-4 are representative only. In reality, the list is almost endless.

Once we accumulate the manufacturing overhead items and amounts, we add the cost of manufacturing overhead to work in process (h).

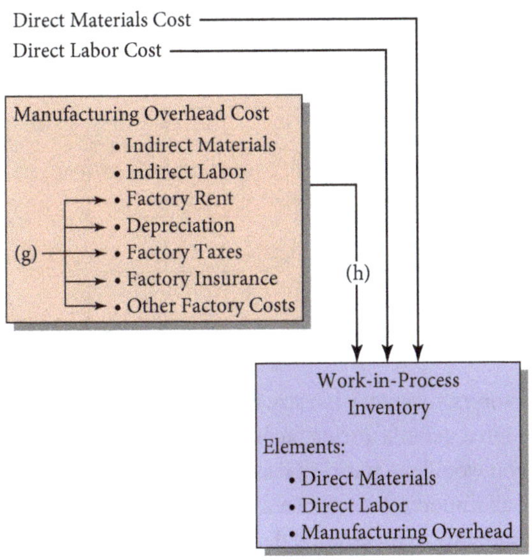

Work-in-process inventory, then, consists of the direct material, direct labor, and manufacturing overhead cost associated with goods that are currently in production. As units are completed, we transfer the cost associated with these units from work-in-process inventory to finished goods inventory (i). We classify the cost of product still in production at the end of the production period as ending work-in-process inventory on the balance sheet at the end of the period (j).

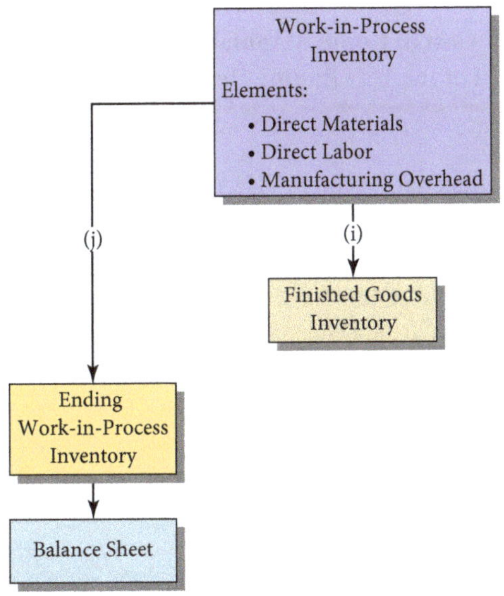

Once finished units of product (and their cost) have been transferred to finished goods inventory, usually only one of two things will happen to the actual units—either they will be sold by the end of the accounting period or they will not be sold. If they are sold, we transfer the cost associated with them to cost of goods sold (k). We classify the cost of the finished product still on hand at the end of the accounting period as ending finished goods inventory on the balance sheet at the end of the period (1).

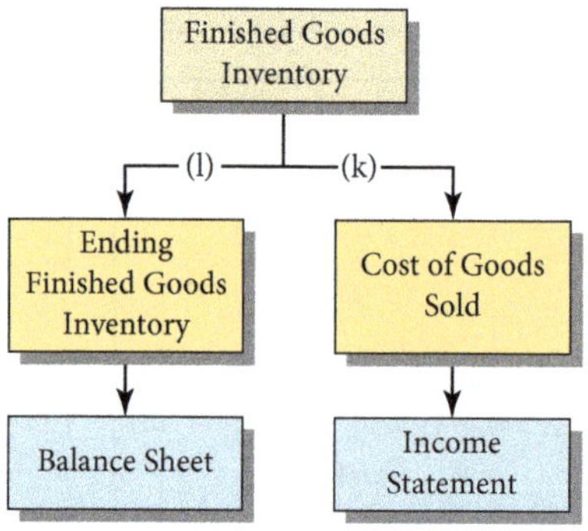

For most manufacturers, inventory is a sizeable asset requiring considerable financial resources. A walk through a manufacturing facility would make you aware of the significance of inventory, because you would see stacks of it sitting there. Raw materials, work in process, and finished goods are all important assets of a manufacturer. Proper measurement of these assets is crucial if managers are to make good decisions about inventory management. For this reason, business people should understand the component costs of each type of inventory.

Cost of Goods Manufactured

We have seen that a manufacturer's product cost consists of direct material, direct labor, and manufacturing overhead. These three product classifications are summarized on the cost of goods manufactured schedule. You will find a typical presentation of this schedule for Zhang Manufacturing, Inc. in Exhibit 2-5.

Exhibit 2-5 Cost of Goods Manufactured Schedule

Zhang Manufacturing, Inc.
Cost of Goods Manufactured Schedule
For the Year Ending December 31, 2008

	Direct Materials:		
	Beginning Direct Material Inventory (1/1/08)	$ 13,000	
+	Purchases during 2008	400,000	
=	Materials Available during 2008	$413,000	
−	Ending Direct Material Inventory (12/31/08)	(20,000)	
=	Direct Materials Used during 2008		$ 393,000
	Direct Labor during 2008		220,000
	Manufacturing Overhead Cost:		
	Indirect Materials	$ 5,000	
	Indirect Labor	20,000	
	Factory Rent	144,000	
	Depreciation of Equipment	250,000	
	Repairs and Maintenance on Equipment	40,000	
	Utilities	39,000	
	Property Taxes	15,000	
	Total Manufacturing Overhead Cost during 2008		513,000
	Manufacturing Cost for Current Period		$1,126,000
+	Beginning Work-in-Process Inventory (1/1/08)		41,000
=	Cost of Goods Available to be Finished in 2008		$1,167,000
−	Ending Work-in-Process Inventory (12/31/08)		(65,000)
=	Cost of Goods Manufactured during 2008		$1,102,000

Although this schedule looks quite involved, it consists of four relatively simple parts.

1. Direct Materials Section. This section is similar in format to the cost of goods sold section of the income statement. In both cases, we deal with costs stored in inventory to determine the cost of the inventory that has been used.

Zhang Manufacturing, Inc.
Cost of Goods Manufactured Schedule
Direct Materials Section
For the Year Ending December 31, 2008

	Direct Materials:		
	Beginning Direct Material Inventory (1/1/08)	$ 13,000	
+	Purchases during 2008	400,000	
=	Materials Available during 2008	$413,000	
−	Ending Direct Material Inventory (12/31/08)	(20,000)	
=	Direct Materials Used during 2008		$ 393,000

2. Direct Labor Section. We see that the direct labor section of Zhang Manufacturing's cost of goods manufactured schedule consists of only one line, which is a common way to present this information. Remember, direct labor represents the cost of employees directly involved in the production process.

Zhang Manufacturing, Inc.
Cost of Goods Manufactured Schedule
Direct Labor Section
For the Year Ending December 31, 2008

Direct Labor during 2008	220,000

3. The Manufacturing Overhead Section. This section lists manufacturing overhead costs by functional description. Depending on the level of detail desired, this section can be as short as one line, which depicts total manufacturing overhead. Zhang's cost of goods manufactured schedule provides several lines detailing the various components of manufacturing overhead.

Zhang Manufacturing, Inc.
Cost of Goods Manufactured Schedule
Manufacturing Overhead Section
For the Year Ending December 31, 2008

Manufacturing Overhead Cost:		
Indirect Materials	$ 5,000	
Indirect Labor	20,000	
Factory Rent	144,000	
Depreciation of Equipment	250,000	
Repairs and Maintenance on Equipment	40,000	
Utilities	39,000	
Property Taxes	15,000	
Total Manufacturing Overhead Cost during 2008		513,000

4. Cost Summary and Work-in-Process Section. The last section of the cost of goods manufactured schedule summarizes the current period's product cost and incorporates the beginning and ending work-in-process inventory balances. Note that as in a cost of goods sold schedule, beginning inventory is added and ending inventory is subtracted to arrive at inventory completed.

Zhang Manufacturing, Inc.
Cost of Goods Manufactured Schedule
Cost Summary and Work-in-Process Section
For the Year Ending December 31, 2008

	Manufacturing Cost for Current Period	$1,126,000
+	Beginning Work-in-Process Inventory (1/1/08)	41,000
=	Cost of Goods Available to be Finished in 2008	$1,167,000
−	Ending Work-in-Process Inventory (12/31/08)	(65,000)
=	Cost of Goods Manufactured During 2008	$1,102,000

Using the information from the cost of goods manufactured schedule, we can prepare a cost of goods sold schedule, such as the one for Zhang Manufacturing, Inc. shown in Exhibit 2-6.

Exhibit 2-6 Cost of Goods Sold Schedule

Zhang Manufacturing, Inc.
Cost of Goods Sold Schedule
For the Year Ending December 31, 2008

	Beginning Finished Goods Inventory (1/1/08)	$ 70,000
+	Cost of Goods Manufactured during 2008	1,102,000
=	Goods Available for Sale in 2008	$1,172,000
−	Finished Goods Inventory (12/31/08)	(28,000)
=	Cost of Goods Sold for 2008	$1,144,000

Product Cost Identification for Service Firms

In contrast to both merchandisers and manufacturers, service type businesses such as law firms, health care providers, airlines, and accounting firms do not sell tangible, physical products. Many service firms are huge. For example, **Hilton Hotels Corporation** is a diversified service company in the hospitality industry. The company reported revenues from hotel and casino services of over $8 billion for 2007.

Service companies offer their customers a product just as real as those sold by merchandisers and manufacturers, but service products lack physical substance. Determining the cost of its product is just as important for a service company as it is for merchandisers and manufacturers, but the procedures differ because service type businesses have no inventory.

Costs can be accumulated for almost any facet of a service company's operation. To illustrate, let us consider the Marston Medical Clinic. The three doctors at the clinic (Dr. Helen Marston and two of her medical school classmates) perform routine physical exams, examinations in response to specific patient symptoms, immunizations, and minor surgery (they perform major surgery at a local hospital). Any one of these services can be designated as a cost object, and cost can be accumulated for a particular service provided to an individual patient. Likewise, costs can be accumulated for a particular category of procedure, for a department or a particular area of the medical practice, or for each of the three doctors or the five nurses.

The three broad cost classifications included in the cost of services provided are materials, labor, and indirect service cost (sometimes called overhead). The cost classifications for a service firm are very similar to the classifications used in costing manufactured products, but there are some important differences.

Materials

The materials used in performing services are normally incidental supplies, and the cost of these materials is relatively insignificant compared to the direct materials used in the production of manufactured products. In the case of Marston Medical Clinic, materials include items such as tongue depressors, the needles and serum used for immunizations, and bandages.

Some service companies separate material that is significant enough to trace to individual cost objects from insignificant material that they simply treat as indirect overhead cost. In many cases, however, the materials used in performing a service are actually more like the indirect materials used by a manufacturer. Whereas a manufacturer such as **Steelcase** might consider glue and screws to be indirect materials, a legal firm would probably consider legal pads, computer discs, and pens as indirect materials, and all costs of materials are treated as indirect (overhead) cost.

Labor

Generally, service businesses are labor intensive, meaning that the largest component of product cost for service organizations is often labor cost. It includes costs of those people who perform part or all the service. In the case of Marston Medical Clinic, labor cost certainly includes the salaries of the three doctors and the five nurses. It does not, however, include the amount paid to the receptionist or bookkeeper. Even though their work is important, these employees do not perform the health care services provided by the clinic. The labor cost of the receptionist and bookkeeper, then, is a period cost.

Overhead or Indirect Service Costs

The overhead costs in a service business are similar to those for a manufacturer. They are costs that are associated specifically with performing the services provided but that cannot easily be traced to one specific cost object. In the case of the Marston Clinic, rent on the clinic building is an indirect cost of providing health care—the building is necessary to provide patient services. However, its cost is difficult to trace to one cost object, so it is considered an overhead cost.

Discussion Question

2-11. Airline companies such as **Delta Airlines**, often define the routes they fly as cost objects. Given that definition, consider a specific route from New York to Los Angeles and describe the costs you believe **Delta** would include as

a. materials

b. labor

c. overhead

The Flow of Service Cost—Service Company

Just as managers in manufacturing and merchandising operations must understand the flow of costs associated with products they sell, managers of service type businesses must understand the flow of service costs if they are to control and plan for them. Also, service cost information is an essential element of the information needed when making pricing and sales decisions. Simply having the information, however, is not enough. Managers must also understand how these costs will affect the company's assets as reported on the balance sheet and profits as reported on the income statement. The flow of costs through a typical service firm is shown in Exhibit 2-7.

Exhibit 2-7 The Flow of Service Costs—Service Company

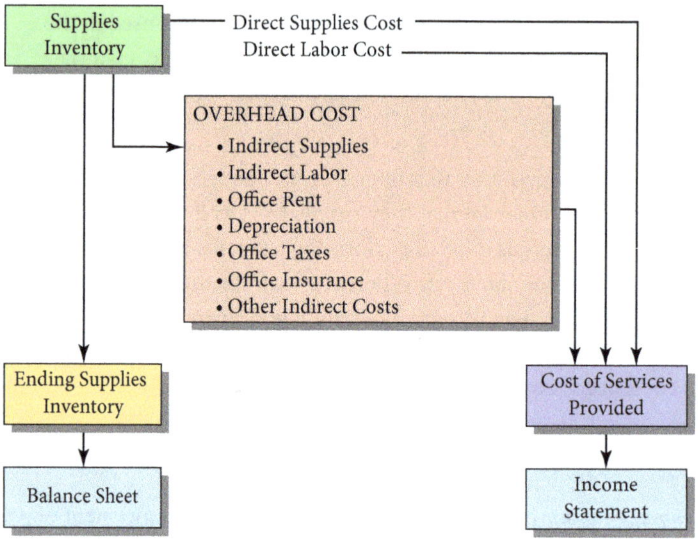

Cost of Services

As Exhibit 2-7 indicates, cost of services has three parts: direct labor, direct supplies, and overhead. With this in mind, we can easily create a schedule computing the cost of services produced. As an example, the schedule in Exhibit 2-8 computes the cost of medical services for Marston Medical Clinic.

Exhibit 2-8 Cost of Services Schedule

Marston Medical Clinic
Cost of Services Schedule
For the Year Ending December 31, 2008

Direct Labor Cost		$ 940,000
Direct Supplies Cost		20,000
Overhead Cost:		
Indirect Supplies	$12,000	
Office Rent	24,000	
Depreciation	18,000	
Office Taxes	2,000	
Office Insurance	8,000	
Other Indirect Costs	6,000	
Total Overhead Cost		70,000
Cost of Services Provided		$1,030,000

Exhibit 2-8 shows that the cost of services for Marston Medical Clinic was $1,030 for the year ended December 31, 2008. The total cost included the three components service product cost: direct labor, direct supplies, and overhead.

We have examined how service firms identify product costs and how those costs flow through the firm. We now turn briefly to hybrid firms, which produce both goods and ser

Hybrid Firms

Some companies, called **hybrid firms**, generate revenue from both providing servic selling products. For example, although the majority of **Blockbuster Entertainmen** enue comes from its DVD rental service, the company also generates significant rev from DVD product sales. In accounting for an operation that combines service and products, companies such as **Blockbuster** must incorporate techniques used by both service and merchandising firms. A single company, such as **General Motors**, might actually be a manufacturer (making cars and trucks), a merchandiser (selling floor mats and other accessories to **GM** dealers), and a service type business (offering **GMAC Financing**).

Merchandising, Manufacturing, and Service—A Comparison

Now that we have explored how merchandising, manufacturing, and service businesses identify their product costs and how those costs flow through each type of operation, we can see how these businesses present product costs and period costs on their income statements. We begin with a merchandising operation, and then we look at a manufacturer and a service business.

Exhibit 2-9 illustrates how a merchandiser reports its product costs and period costs on an income statement. This exhibit shows the 2008 income statement for Jason's Supply Company and includes the cost of goods sold schedule we developed for Jason earlier in the chapter (presented as Exhibit 2-3).

Exhibit 2-9 Product Costs and Period Costs on the Income Statement—Merchandiser

Jason's Supply Company
Cost of Goods Sold Schedule
For the Year Ending December 31, 2008

Beginning Inventory (1/1/08)	$ 23,000
+ Purchases during 2008	300,000
= Goods Available for Sale in 2008	$323,000
− Ending Inventory at (12/31/08)	(30,000)
= Cost of Goods Sold for 2008	$293,000

Jason's Supply Company
Income Statement
For the Year Ending December 31, 2008

Sales		$673,000
Cost of Goods Sold		293,000
Gross Profit		$380,000
Operating Expenses:		
Selling Expense	$120,000	
Administrative Expense	80,000	
Total Operating Expenses		200,000
Operating Income		$180,000

As Exhibit 2-9 indicates, the amount of product cost Jason recognized as expense (cost of goods sold) on its 2008 income statement ($293,000) is calculated in the cost of goods sold schedule. The period cost recognized is the total of the operating expenses ($200,000).

Exhibit 2-10 illustrates how a manufacturer reports its product costs and period costs on an income statement. This exhibit shows the 2008 income statement for Zhang Manufacturing, Inc. and includes the cost of goods manufactured schedule and cost of goods sold schedule we developed for Zhang and presented as Exhibit 2-5 and Exhibit 2-6 earlier in the chapter.

...ibit 2-10 Product Cost ...nd Period Cost on the Income Statement—Manufacturer

Zhang Manufacturing, Inc.
Cost of Goods Manufactured Schedule
For the Year Ending December 31, 2008

Direct Materials:		
Beginning Direct Material Inventory (1/1/08)	$ 13,000	
+ Purchases during 2008	400,000	
= Materials Available during 2008	$413,000	
− Ending Direct Material Inventory (12/31/08)	(20,000)	
= Direct Materials Used during 2008		$ 393,000
Direct Labor during 2008		220,000
Manufacturing Overhead Cost:		
Indirect Materials	$ 5,000	
Indirect Labor	20,000	
Factory Rent	144,000	
Depreciation of Equipment	250,000	
Repairs and Maintenance on Equipment	40,000	
Utilities	39,000	
Property Taxes	15,000	
Total Manufacturing Overhead Cost during 2008		513,000
Manufacturing Cost for Current Period		$1,126,000
+ Beginning Work-in-Process Inventory (1/1/08)		41,000
= Cost of Goods Available to be Finished in 2008		$1,167,000
− Ending Work-in-Process Inventory (12/31/08)		(65,000)
= Cost of Goods Manufactured during 2008		$1,102,000

Cost of Goods Sold Schedule
For the Year Ending December 31, 2008

Beginning Finished Goods Inventory (1/1/08)	$ 70,000
+ Cost of Goods Manufactured during 2008	1,102,000
= Goods Available for Sale in 2008	$1,172,000
− Finished Goods Inventory (12/31/08)	(28,000)
= Cost of Goods Sold for 2008	$1,144,000

Income Statement
For the Year Ending December 31, 2008

Sales		$1,884,000
Cost of Goods Sold		1,144,000
Gross Profit		$ 740,000
Operating Expenses:		
Selling Expense	$250,000	
Administrative Expense	180,000	
Total Operating Expenses		430,000
Operating Income		$ 310,000

As Exhibit 2-10 indicates, the amount of product cost Zhang recognized as expense (cost of goods sold) on its 2008 income statement ($1,144,000) is calculated in the cost of goods manufactured schedule and the cost of goods sold schedule. The period cost recognized is the total of the operating expenses ($430,000).

Exhibit 2-11 illustrates how a service type company reports its cost of services and period costs on an income statement. This exhibit shows the 2008 income statement for Marston Medical Clinic and includes the cost of services schedule we developed for Marston earlier in the chapter (presented as Exhibit 2-8).

Exhibit 2-11 Cost of Services and Period Costs on the Income Statement—Service Type Company

Marston Medical Clinic
Cost of Services Schedule
For the Year Ending December 31, 2008

Direct Labor Cost		$ 940,000
Direct Supplies Cost		20,000
Overhead Cost:		
Indirect Supplies	$ 12,000	
Office Rent	24,000	
Depreciation	18,000	
Office Taxes	2,000	
Office Insurance	8,000	
Other Indirect Costs	6,000	
Total Overhead Cost		70,000
Cost of Services Provided		$1,030,000

Income Statement
For the Year Ending December 31, 2008

Service Revenue		$1,260,000
Cost of Services		1,030,000
Gross Margin on Services		$ 230,000
Operating Expenses:		
Selling Expense	$ 45,000	
Administrative Expense	130,000	
Total Operating Expenses		175,000
Operating Income		$ 55,000

As Exhibit 2-11 indicates, the amount of services cost Marston recognized as expense (cost of services) on its 2008 income statement ($1,030,000) is calculated in the cost of services schedule. The period cost recognized is the total of the operating expenses ($175,000).

Whether the costs are related to products purchased for sale, products manufactured for sale, or services provided, cost information is an important input in the decision making process. Remember that management accounting information helps internal decision makers plan and control the firm's future. In the chapters that follow, you will see how the cost classifications and cost flows you learned about in this chapter will help you understand and apply management accounting decision making techniques.

Recording Manufacturing Costs

To fully understand the material in this section, it is best if you have a basic understanding of debit and credit accounting procedures including general journal entries and the use of t-accounts. If this is not the case, we suggest that you review the accounting procedures section of any introductory financial accounting text. After completing your work on this section of the chapter, you should be able to prepare basic manufacturing journal entries.

The recording process for manufacturing involves six basic types of transactions:

Transaction 1—Purchasing raw material

Transaction 2—Using direct material in the manufacturing process

Transaction 3—Using direct labor in the manufacturing process

Transaction 4—Using manufacturing overhead in the manufacturing process

Transaction 5—Transferring the cost of completed units from work in process to finished goods

Transaction 6—Selling finished goods

To record these transactions accountants generally use the following general ledger accounts:

1. *Cash*
2. *Accounts receivable*
3. *Raw materials inventory*
4. *Work-in-process inventory*
5. *Finished goods inventory*
6. *Accounts payable*
7. *Sales*
8. *Cost of goods sold*

Remember that debits increase and credits decrease assets, expenses, and losses. Further recall that credits increase and debits decrease liabilities, equity, revenues, and gains. Lastly, recall that debits and credits must equal for each journal entry.

We will now examine a series of journal entries that a manufacturer would make. When it is appropriate and non-repetitive, we will analyze each transaction using the following four steps.

1. Determine if and when a transaction occurred, what accounts were affected, which account balances should increase, which should decrease, and by how much.
2. Determine which accounts we should debit and which we should credit.
3. Make the journal entry.
4. Review the entry to ensure it is in proper form and that the debits equal the credits.

Transaction 1: Purchased $95,000 of raw material on account on January 2, 2008.

1. This transaction took place on January 2, 2008. The transaction affects the raw materials inventory account and the accounts payable account. We should increase the balances of both accounts by $95,000.
2. Because raw materials inventory is an asset account we increase it with a debit. Accounts payable is a liability account so we increase it with a credit.
3. The general journal entry:

2008				
Jan.	2	Raw Materials Inventory	95,000	
		Accounts Payable		95,000
		To record the purchase of raw material.		

4. A final check of the entry reveals that we dated it correctly, made the debit part of the entry first, indented the credit account title, and the dollar amount of the debits equals that of the credits. The entry is fine.

Transaction 2: Transferred $70,000 of direct material to production on January 3, 2008.

1. This transaction took place on January 3, 2008. The transaction affects the work-in-process inventory and raw materials inventory accounts. We should increase the balance of the work-in-process inventory account by $70,000 and decrease the balance of the raw materials inventory account by the same amount.
2. Because work-in-process materials inventory is an asset account we increase it with a debit. Raw materials inventory is also an asset account so we decrease it with a credit.
3. The general journal entry:

2008				
Jan.	3	Work-In-Process Inventory	70,000	
		Raw Material Inventory		70,000
		To record the transfer of direct		
		material to production.		

4. A final check of the entry reveals the entry is fine.

Transaction 3: On January 31, paid $80,000 for direct labor cost incurred during January 2008.

1. For this entry, we will use January 31, the date we paid the wages as the transaction date. Recall that direct labor cost becomes part of work-in-process inventory so the transaction affects the work-in-process inventory account and the cash account. We should increase the work-in-process inventory account by $80,000 and decrease the cash account by the same amount.
2. Because work-in-process materials inventory is an asset account we increase it with a debit. Cash is also an asset account so we decrease it with a credit.

3. The general journal entry:

2008				
Jan.	31	Work-In-Process Inventory	80,000	
		Cash		80,000
		To record wages paid for direct labor		
		in January.		

4. A final check of the entry reveals the entry is fine.

Transaction 4: Incurred various factory overhead costs totaling $110,000 during January 2008. Assume that $10,000 of the overhead costs was paid in cash and the balance of $100,000 was on account.

To keep the example simple, we will record the manufacturing overhead directly in work-in-process inventory. As you will see in the next chapter, manufacturing overhead is generally allocated to production which necessitates using more complicated accounting procedures.

1. So that our example remains straightforward, we will make a single journal entry on January 31 for all of the manufacturing overhead cost incurred during the period. In practice, a manufacturing company would make an entry each time an overhead cost is incurred. Recall that manufacturing overhead costs becomes part of work-in-process inventory so the transaction affects the work-in-process inventory account. The transaction also affects the cash and accounts payable accounts. We should increase the balance in the work-in-process inventory account by $110,000, we should decrease the balance in the cash account for the $10,000 of manufacturing overhead costs paid for, and we should increase the balance of the accounts payable account by $100,000 for the manufacturing overhead purchased on account.
2. Because work-in-process materials inventory is an asset account we increase it with a debit. Cash is also an asset account so we decrease it with a credit. Accounts payable is a liability so we increase it with a credit.
3. The general journal entry:

2008				
Jan.	31	Work-In-Process Inventory	110,000	
		Cash		10,000
		Accounts Payable		100,000
		To record manufacturing overhead		
		for January.		

4. A final check of the entry reveals the entry is fine.

Transaction 5: On January 31, transferred goods costing $230,000 from work in process to finished goods.

1. On January 31, goods costing $230,000 to manufacture were completed and transferred to finished goods inventory so the transaction took place on January 31, 2008.

The transaction affects the finished goods inventory and work-in-process inventory accounts. We should increase the balance of the finished goods inventory account by $230,000 and decrease the balance of the work-in-process inventory account by the same amount.

2. Because finished goods inventory is an asset account we increase it with a debit. Work-in-process inventory is also an asset account so we decrease it with a credit.

3. The general journal entry:

2008				
Jan.	31	Finished Goods Inventory	230,000	
		Work-In-Process Inventory		230,000
		To transfer completed goods from		
		production to finished goods.		

4. A final check of the entry reveals the entry is fine.

Transaction 6: On January 31, the company sold finished goods costing $210,000 to manufacture for a selling price of $300,000. The goods were sold on account.

1. This transaction took place on January 31. Generally, transactions for the sale of goods have two distinct parts. First, the transaction affects the accounts receivable and sales accounts, and we should increase the balances of both these accounts by $300,000. Second, the transaction also affects the cost of goods sold and finished goods inventory accounts because the company has delivered merchandise to the customer from its inventory. We should increase the balance of the cost of goods sold account by $210,000 and decrease the balance of the finished goods inventory account by the same amount.

2. Accounts receivable is an asset account so we increase it with a debit. Sales is a revenue account so we increase it with a credit. Cost of goods sold is an expense account so we increase it with a debit. Finished goods inventory is an asset account so we decrease it with a credit.

3. This transaction can be recorded either by making two separate entries or one compound entry. The two separate entries are:

2008				
Jan.	31	Accounts Receivable	300,000	
		Sales		300,000
		To record sales on account.		
2008				
Jan.	31	Cost of Goods Sold	210,000	
		Finished Goods Inventory		210,000
		To record the cost of goods sold		

Or, to accomplish the same changes to the account balances, we can make the following compound entry:

2008				
Jan.	31	Accounts Receivable	300,000	
		Cost of Goods Sold	210,000	
		Sales		300,000
		Finished Goods Inventory		210,000
		To record sales on account and cost of goods sold.		

4. A final check of both sets of entries (two separate or one compound) reveals that the dollar amount of the debits equals that of the credits.

The following t-accounts depict balances after recording all of the entries including the $300,000 sale and the $210,000 cost of goods sold. We will assume no beginning balances in raw materials inventory, work-in-process inventory and finished goods inventory.

Raw Materials Inventory

	Debit	Credit	
1-2-08	95,000	70,000	*1-3-08*
Balance	25,000		

Cash

	Debit	Credit	
		80,000	*1-31-08*
		10,000	*1-31-08*

Work-in Process Inventory

	Debit	Credit	
1-3-08	70,000	230,000	*1-31-08*
1-31-08	80,000		
1-31-08	110,000		
Balance	30,000		

Accounts Receivable

	Debit	Credit	
1-31-08	300,000		

Finished Goods Inventory

	Debit	Credit	
1-31-08	230,000	210,000	*1-31-08*
Balance	20,000		

Sales

	Debit	Credit	
		300,000	*1-31-08*

Cost of Goods Sold

	Debit	Credit	
1-31-08	210,000		

Accounts Payable

	Debit	Credit	
		95,000	*1-2-08*
		100,000	*1-31-08*

Recording basic manufacturing entries involves eight accounts: cash, accounts receivable, accounts payable, raw material inventory, work-in-process inventory, finished goods inventory, cost of goods sold, and sales. The basic flow through the accounts is depicted in Exhibit 2-12.

Exhibit 2-12 Basic Flow of Costs through Manufacturing Accounts

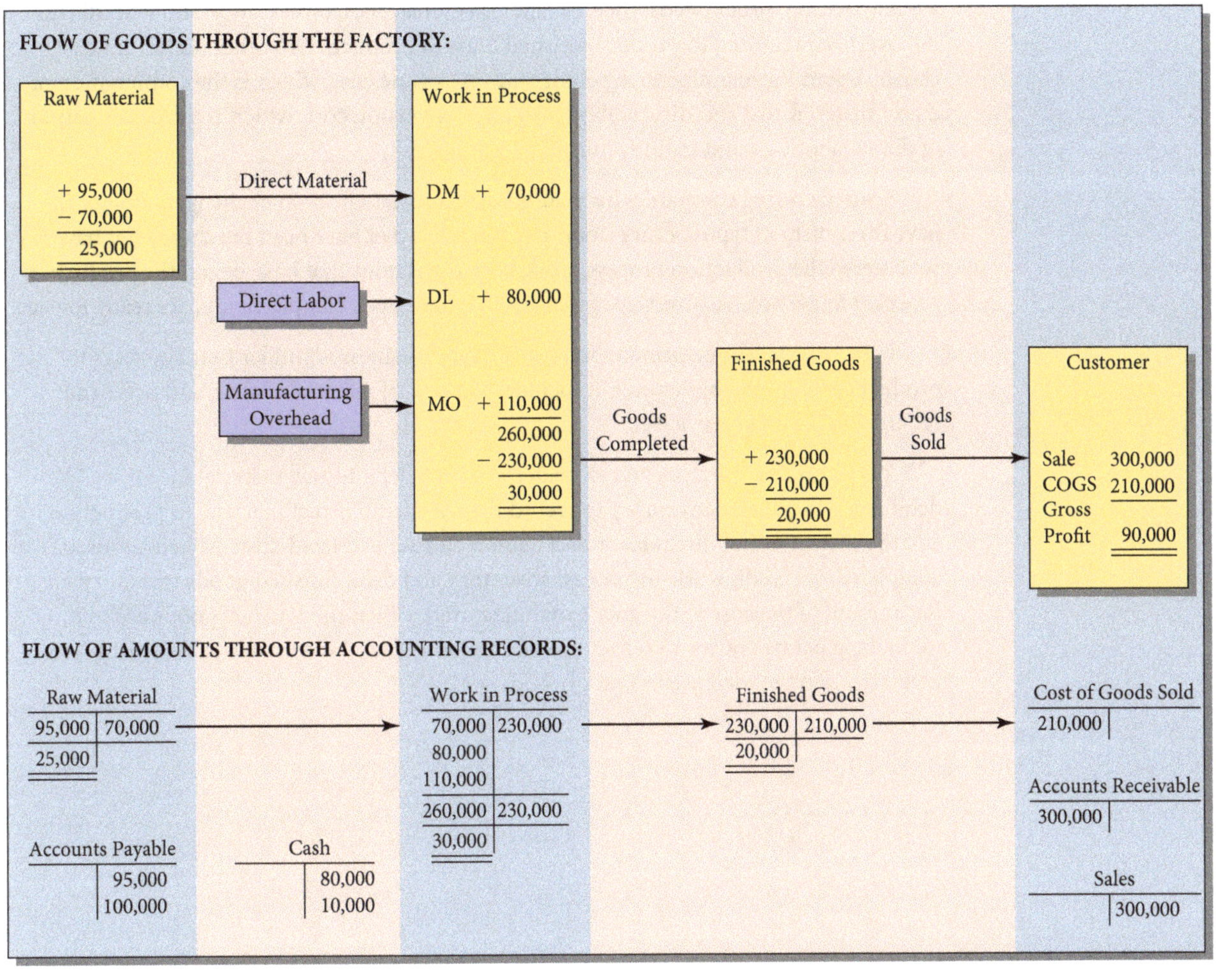

Summary

Businesses incur many different costs as they operate in the modern business world. These costs can be classified in a variety of ways and managers must determine what cost classifications will be most helpful if they are to make effective planning and control decisions.

Costs can be accumulated by cost object, which is any activity or item for which we desire a separate cost measurement. Some of the costs associated with a cost object can be traced directly to that cost object. These are called direct costs. Other costs incurred to support multiple cost objects are known as indirect costs.

The classification of costs as either product cost or period cost is very important because it determines how costs are reported on a company's financial statements. Product cost is the sum of all costs required to make the products available and ready to sell. Product cost is reported as an asset (Inventory) on the balance sheet until the product is sold. When the product is sold, product cost is reported as an expense (cost of goods sold) on the income statement. Period costs are all costs a company incurs that are not classified as product cost. Period costs are divided into selling and administrative costs and are reported on the income statement as expenses.

There are significant differences in the way product cost is determined for merchandising companies and for manufacturing companies. For a merchandiser, product cost includes the cost of the merchandise itself and freight costs to obtain the merchandise. For a manufacturer, product cost includes the direct materials, direct labor, and manufacturing overhead required to produce finished units of product. Two other important cost classifications for manufacturing companies are prime cost, which is the combination of direct material cost and direct labor cost, and conversion cost, which is the combination of direct labor cost and manufacturing overhead cost.

Manufacturing companies have additional cost classification challenges because they have three distinct types of inventory: raw materials that have been purchased but have not yet entered the production process, work-in-process units that have begun the production process but are not yet complete, and units that have been completed and are ready for sale.

Cost of services performed for a service type business is similar in many ways to product cost for a manufacturer. It includes the cost of materials, labor, and overhead required to perform services.

We record the purchase of raw material with a debit to raw material inventory. We debit work-in-process inventory to record the transfer of direct material to production and the incurrence of direct labor and manufacturing overhead costs. When goods are completed, we credit work-in-process inventory and debit finished goods inventory for the amount of the cost of the goods manufactured. When the finished goods are sold, we make separate entries to reflect the sale and to reflect the decrease in finished goods inventory and the increase in cost of goods sold.

Key Terms

Term	Page
administrative cost	23
common cost	21
conversion cost	26
cost	20
cost object	21
direct cost	21
direct labor cost	26
direct labor hours	29
direct material	28
direct materials cost	26
factory burden	29
factory overhead	29
finished goods inventory	27
hybrid firms	39
indirect cost	21
indirect labor	30
indirect materials	29
inventoriable costs	22
manufacturing overhead	29
manufacturing overhead cost	26
material stores	27
overhead	29
period costs	22
prime cost	26
product cost	22
raw materials inventory	27
selling cost	22
work-in-process inventory	27

Review the Facts

A. What is a cost object?

B. What is the difference between a direct cost and an indirect cost?

C. What is product cost?

D. What is period cost?

E. Why is the cost of delivering merchandise to customers included in selling expense?

F. Why is the cost of storing inventory that is ready to sell included in selling expense?

G. What classification includes costs that are neither product costs nor costs directly associated with selling activities?

H. Why are product costs called inventoriable costs?

I. Describe the difference between the accounting treatment for product costs and period costs.

J. Describe the flow of inventory costs for a merchandising operation as goods are bought and then sold.

K. What are the inventory classifications for a manufacturing type firm?

L. What are the three main cost components included in product cost for a manufacturing type firm?

M. What is the difference between direct material and indirect material?

N. What is the difference between direct labor and indirect labor?

O. In which product cost classification would you most likely find indirect material and indirect labor?

P. What is included in prime cost?

Q. What is included in conversion cost?

R. With respect to the cost of goods sold section of an income statement, what is the similarity between purchases for a merchandising type company and cost of goods manufactured for a manufacturing type company?

S. What is included in the cost of services provided for a service type firm?

Apply What You Have Learned

LO 1: Distinguish between Direct and Indirect Costs

2-12. Brittany operates a small chain of five children's shoe stores called Baby Feet. She employs a store manager and two sales clerks for each store. In addition, she rents office space which houses her office, the personnel department, and the bookkeeping department for the chain.

Brittany has collected the following information regarding the stores and has asked you to determine which costs are direct and which are indirect costs.

Required:

For each of the following items, indicate which would describe a direct cost (D) for the store at the corner of Elm Street and Main and which would describe an indirect cost (I) for an individual store.

1. _____ Rent for the office space
2. _____ Rent for the store
3. _____ Brittany's salary
4. _____ The store manager's salary
5. _____ The company personnel manager's salary
6. _____ Bookkeeper's salary
7. _____ Maintenance cost for the store
8. _____ Depreciation on sales equipment
9. _____ Depreciation on bookkeeping computer
10. _____ Sales clerks' salaries
11. _____ Cost of shoes
12. _____ Advertising cost for the chain

LO 1: Distinguish between Direct and Indirect Costs

2-13. Sue Lee is the president of Baby Care. The company operates a chain of four child care centers in southern Florida. In addition to the four Baby Care locations, the company rents office space which is used by the company's bookkeeper and Sue Lee.

Required:

a. List four costs that would be considered direct costs of one of the four child care centers.

b. List four costs that would be considered indirect costs of one of the four child care centers.

LO 1: Distinguish between Direct and Indirect Costs

2-14. Blue Water Travel operates a chain of travel agent offices in the eastern United States. Blue Water Travel's home office is in New York. There are six sales offices and a district office located in Florida.

Required:

If the cost object is one of the sales offices in Florida, indicate which of the following would describe a direct cost (D) and which would describe an indirect cost (I).

1. _____ Rent for the Florida district office building
2. _____ Rent for the home office building in New York
3. _____ Rent for the sales office
4. _____ The company president's salary
5. _____ The salary of the vice president in charge of the Florida division
6. _____ The salary of a sales office manager
7. _____ The salary of a sales associate

LO 2: Types of Cost for a Manufacturer

2-15. Following are several representative costs incurred in a typical manufacturing company. For each of the costs, indicate in the space provided whether the cost is a direct material (DM), direct labor (DL), manufacturing overhead (MO), selling (S), or administrative (A) cost.

1. _____ Material incorporated into products
2. _____ Sales supplies
3. _____ Supplies used in the factory
4. _____ Wages of plant security guard
5. _____ Wages of security guard for the sales office
6. _____ Depreciation on a file cabinet used in the factory
7. _____ Depreciation on a file cabinet used in the general accounting office
8. _____ President's salary
9. _____ President's secretary's salary
10. _____ Manufacturing vice president's salary
11. _____ Salary of the manufacturing vice president's secretary

12. _____ Wages paid to production-line workers

13. _____ Factory rent

14. _____ Accounting office rent

15. _____ Depreciation on a copy machine used in the sales department

16. _____ Depreciation on a copy machine used to copy work orders in the factory

17. _____ Salary of plant supervisor

LO 2: Types of Cost for a Manufacturer

2-16. Following are several representative costs incurred in a typical manufacturing company. For each of the costs, indicate in the space provided whether the cost is a product cost (PR) or a period cost (PE).

1. _____ Material incorporated into products

2. _____ Sales supplies

3. _____ Supplies used in the factory

4. _____ Wages of plant security guard

5. _____ Wages of security guard for the sales office

6. _____ Depreciation on a file cabinet used in the factory

7. _____ Depreciation on a file cabinet used in the general accounting office

8. _____ President's salary

9. _____ President's secretary's salary

10. _____ Manufacturing vice president's salary

11. _____ Salary of the manufacturing vice president's secretary

12. _____ Wages paid to production-line workers

13. _____ Factory rent

14. _____ Accounting office rent

15. _____ Depreciation on a copy machine used in the sales department

16. _____ Depreciation on a copy machine used to copy work orders in the factory

17. _____ Salary of plant supervisor

LO 5: Calculate Costs for a Manufacturer, No Inventories

2-17. The following data pertain to the Anderson Table Manufacturing Company for January 2007. The company made 1,000 tables during January, and there are no beginning or ending inventories.

Wood used in production	$25,000
Cleaning supplies used in the factory	300
Machine lubricants used in the factory	100
Factory rent	2,000
Rent on the sales office	3,000
Sales salaries	20,000
Production-line labor cost	50,000
Plant security guard cost	1,200
Plant supervision	2,500
Sales office supervision	3,000
Depreciation on production equipment	4,000
Depreciation on sales office equipment	1,000

Required:

a. What is the cost of direct material used in production during January 2007?

b. What is the cost of direct labor for January 2007?

c. What is the cost of manufacturing overhead for January 2007?

d. What is the total cost of tables manufactured in January 2007?

e. What is the cost of each table manufactured in January 2007?

f. Do you think the cost per table is valuable information for Carole Anderson, the company's owner? How might she use this information?

LO 5: Calculate Ending Inventory

2-18. Steinmann Window Company makes aluminum window units. At the beginning of November, the company's direct material inventory included 900 square feet of window glass. During November Steinmann purchased another 12,000 square feet of glass. Each completed window unit requires 9 square feet of glass. During November, 9,900 square feet of glass was transferred to the production line.

Required:

How many square feet of glass remain in the ending direct material inventory?

LO 4: Analyzing Inventory

2-19. Van Kirk Manufacturing Company has been in business for many years. Dottie Van Kirk, the company president, is concerned that the cost of raw material is skyrocketing. The production foreman assured Van Kirk that the use of direct material actually dropped in 2009.

Van Kirk has engaged your services to provide insight into what she thinks may be a sizable problem. Not only does it seem that the cost of direct material is increasing, but it also seems that her production foreman is being less than honest with her.

The following information is available:

Van Kirk Manufacturing Company Direct Materials Schedule For the Year Ending December 31, 2008	
Beginning Direct Material Inventory	$ 25,000
Purchases during 2008	435,000
Materials Available during 2008	$460,000
Ending Direct Material Inventory	(30,000)
Direct Materials Used during 2008	$430,000

Van Kirk Manufacturing Company Direct Materials Schedule For the Year Ending December 31, 2009	
Beginning Direct Material Inventory	$ 30,000
Purchases during 2009	501,000
Materials Available during 2009	$531,000
Ending Direct Material Inventory	(103,000)
Direct Materials Used during 2009	$428,000

Required:

Examine the information presented and write a brief report to Dottie Van Kirk detailing your findings relative to her concerns.

LO 3: Analyze Costs of a Merchandiser

2-20. Ralph Brito opened Brito Auto Sales several years ago. Since then, the company has grown and sales have steadily increased. In the last year, however, income has declined despite successful efforts to increase sales. In addition, the company is forced to borrow more and more money from the bank to finance the operation.

The following information is available:

Brito Auto Sales Income Statement For the Year Ending December 31, 2009		
Sales		$758,000
Cost of Goods Sold		
Beginning Inventory	$ 66,000	
+ Cost of Goods Purchased	639,000	
= Goods Available for Sale	$705,000	
− Ending Inventory	85,000	
= Cost of Goods Sold		620,000
Gross Profit		$138,000
Operating Expense:		
Selling Expense	$ 55,000	
Administrative Expense	60,000	(115,000)
Operating Income		$ 23,000

(Continued)

Brito Auto Sales
Income Statement
For the Year Ending December 31, 2010

Sales			$890,000
Cost of Goods Sold			
	Beginning Inventory	$ 85,000	
+	Cost of Goods Purchased	799,000	
=	Goods Available for Sale	$884,000	
−	Ending Inventory	123,000	
=	Cost of Goods Sold		761,000
Gross Profit			$129,000
Operating Expense:			
	Selling Expense	$ 66,000	
	Administrative Expense	60,000	(126,000)
Operating Income			$ 3,000

Required:

Assume that you are hired by Mr. Brito as a consultant. Review the Brito income statement and write a report to Mr. Brito that addresses his concerns.

LO 4: Calculate Ending Direct Material Inventory for a Manufacturer

2-21. Matheis Designs, Inc. manufactures swimming suits. At the beginning of October 2007, the company had $1,450 worth of cloth on hand which was included in its direct material inventory. During October, Matheis purchased cloth costing $12,360 and used material costing $12,750 in production.

Required:

What is the cost of the ending direct material inventory of cloth for Matheis Designs, Inc.?

LO 4 & 7: Calculate Direct Material Used and Prepare Basic Journal Entries for a Manufacturer

2-22. The following information relates to the Penny Manufacturing Company.

Beginning direct material inventory	$ 540,000
Ending direct material inventory	$ 480,000
Direct material purchased	$4,680,000

Required:

a. Compute the cost of direct material used in production.

b. Prepare the journal entry dated January 3, 2008 to record the purchase of the direct material on account.

c. Prepare a journal entry dated January 31, 2008 to record the use of direct material in production.

LO 4 & 7: Calculate Direct Material Used and Prepare Basic Journal Entries for a Manufacturer

2-23. The following information relates to the Montoya Manufacturing Company.

Beginning direct material inventory	$ 40,000
Ending direct material inventory	$ 48,000
Direct material purchased	$437,000

Required:

a. Compute the cost of direct material used in production.

b. Prepare the journal entry dated January 3, 2008 to record the purchase of the direct material on account.

c. Prepare a journal entry dated June 30, 2008 to record the use of direct material used in production.

LO 4: Calculate the Cost of Supplies Used

2-24. The following information relates to Pons Maintenance Service.

Maintenance supplies at January 1, 2008	$ 4,210
Maintenance supplies at December 31, 2008	$ 3,840
Maintenance supplies purchased during 2008	$27,530

Required:

What was the cost of maintenance supplies consumed by Pons Maintenance Service during 2008?

LO 6: Calculate Cost of Materials Used by a Service Company

2-25. On January 1, 2007, Bowden Auto Repair had $3,560 worth of auto parts on hand. During the year, Bowden purchased auto parts costing $286,000. At the end of 2007, the company had parts on hand amounting to $4,260.

Required:

What was the cost of the auto parts used by Bowden Auto Repair during 2007?

LO 3: Calculate the Cost of Goods Sold for a Merchandiser

2-26. On January 1, 2008, the cost of merchandise on hand at Margaret's Fashions was $56,530. Purchases during the month amounted to $488,668 and the cost of merchandise on hand at the end of January was $52,849.

Required:

Determine January's cost of goods sold for Margaret's Fashions.

LO 5: Inventory and Production Costs for a Manufacturer

2-27. The following data pertain to the Hudik Manufacturing Company for the year ended December 31, 2008. The company made 115,000 light fixtures during 2008. There are no beginning or ending inventories.

Metal used in production	$750,000
Wire used in production	40,000
Factory supplies	5,200
Depreciation on the factory	48,000
Depreciation on the sales office	3,000
Sales salaries	90,000
Assembly-line labor cost	960,000
Factory security guard cost	8,200
Factory supervision	62,500
General accounting cost	43,000
Depreciation on production equipment	454,850
Depreciation on sales office equipment	9,200

Required:

a. What is the cost of direct material used during 2008?

b. What is the cost of direct labor during 2008?

c. What is the cost of manufacturing overhead during 2008?

d. What is the total product cost for 2008 production?

e. What is the cost per light fixture for 2008?

LO 5: Inventory and Production Costs Including Cost of Goods Manufactured and Cost of Goods Sold.

2-28. The following data pertain to the Elsea Manufacturing Company for the year ended December 31, 2008. The company made 60,000 SW20 switching units during 2008.

Beginning direct material inventory	$ 42,000
Ending direct material inventory	48,000
Beginning work-in-process inventory	84,000
Ending work-in-process inventory	93,000
Beginning finished goods inventory	124,000
Ending finished goods inventory	133,000
Direct material purchased	850,000
Indirect material used in production	4,000
Factory supplies	6,200
Depreciation on the factory	60,000
Depreciation on the sales office	4,000
Depreciation on the administrative office	3,000
Sales salaries	120,000
Assembly-line labor cost	820,000
Factory security guard cost	12,000
Factory supervision	82,600
Depreciation on production equipment	560,000
Depreciation on sales office equipment	22,200

Required:

a. What is the cost of direct material used during 2008?

b. What is the cost of direct labor during 2008?

c. What is the cost of manufacturing overhead for 2008?

d. What is total manufacturing cost incurred during 2008?

e. What is the cost of goods manufactured for 2008?

f. What is the cost of goods sold for 2008?

LO 5: Inventory and Production Costs Including Cost of Goods Manufactured and Cost of Goods Sold

2-29. The following data pertain to the Miami Manufacturing Company for the year ended December 31, 2008.

Beginning finished goods inventory	$ 255,000
Ending finished goods inventory	270,000
Beginning direct material inventory	82,000
Ending direct material inventory	98,000
Beginning work-in-process inventory	164,000
Ending work-in-process inventory	184,000
Direct material purchased	1,740,000
Indirect material used in production	3,000
Factory supplies	12,500
Depreciation on the factory	134,000
Depreciation on the sales office	14,000
Depreciation on the administrative office	9,000
Sales salaries	350,000
Assembly-line labor cost	2,120,000
Factory security guard cost	22,000
Factory supervision	183,500
Depreciation on production equipment	1,340,000
Depreciation on administrative office equipment	52,200

Required:

a. What is the cost of direct material used during 2008?

b. What is the cost of direct labor during 2008?

c. What is the cost of manufacturing overhead for 2008?

d. What is total manufacturing cost incurred during 2008?

e. What is the cost of goods manufactured for 2008?

f. What is the cost of goods sold for 2008?

LO 5: Inventory and Production Costs Including Cost of Goods Manufactured and Cost of Goods Sold

2-30. The following data pertain to the Seth Levine Manufacturing Company for the year ended December 31, 2008.

Beginning direct material inventory	$ 2,000
Ending direct material inventory	3,000
Beginning work-in-process inventory	4,000
Ending work-in-process inventory	5,000
Beginning finished goods inventory	9,500
Ending finished goods inventory	8,000
Direct material purchased	22,000
Factory supplies	12,500
Depreciation on the factory	34,000
Assembly-line labor cost	120,000
Depreciation on production equipment	42,000
Other indirect factory costs	12,000

Required:

a. What is the cost of direct material used during 2008?

b. What is the cost of direct labor during 2008?

c. What is the cost of manufacturing overhead for 2008?

d. What is total manufacturing cost incurred during 2008?

e. What is the cost of goods manufactured for 2008?

f. What is the cost of goods sold for 2008?

LO 5: Inventory and Production Costs Including Cost of Goods Manufactured and Cost of Goods Sold

2-31. The following data pertain to the Sexton Manufacturing Company for the year ended December 31, 2009.

Beginning direct material inventory	$ 22,000
Ending direct material inventory	28,000
Beginning finished goods inventory	30,000
Ending finished goods inventory	28,000
Beginning work-in-process inventory	16,000
Ending work-in-process inventory	15,000
Direct material purchased	280,000
Production worker labor cost	290,000
Depreciation on production equipment	80,000
Factory rent	24,000
Other indirect factory costs	36,000

Required:

a. What is the cost of direct material used during 2009?

b. What is the cost of direct labor during 2009?

c. What is the cost of manufacturing overhead for 2009?

d. What is total manufacturing cost incurred during 2009?

e. What is the cost of goods manufactured for 2009?

f. What is the cost of goods sold for 2009?

LO 5: Preparation of Cost of Goods Manufactured and Cost of Goods Sold Schedules

2-32. The following data pertain to the Adler Manufacturing Company for the year ended December 31, 2008.

Beginning direct material inventory	$ 12,000
Ending direct material inventory	13,000
Beginning work-in-process inventory	24,000
Ending work-in-process inventory	25,000
Beginning finished goods inventory	29,500
Ending finished goods inventory	28,000
Direct material purchased	122,000
Factory utilities	2,500
Rent on the factory	64,000
Assembly worker labor cost	86,000
Depreciation on production equipment	92,000
Other indirect factory costs	22,000

Required:

a. Prepare a cost of goods manufactured schedule for 2008.

b. Prepare a cost of goods sold schedule for 2008.

LO 5: Preparation of Cost of Goods Manufactured and Cost of Goods Sold Schedules

2-33. The following data pertain to the Clifford Manufacturing Company for the year ended December 31, 2009.

Beginning direct material inventory	$ 2,300
Ending direct material inventory	3,400
Beginning work-in-process inventory	5,500
Ending work-in-process inventory	4,100
Beginning finished goods inventory	6,500
Ending finished goods inventory	5,100
Direct material purchased	12,300
Factory supplies used	500
Depreciation on the factory	22,000
Assembly-line labor cost	48,600
Depreciation on production equipment	12,000
Other indirect factory costs	4,700

Required:

a. Prepare a cost of goods manufactured schedule for 2009.

b. Prepare a cost of goods sold schedule for 2009.

LO 5: Preparation of Cost of Goods Manufactured Schedule, Cost of Goods Sold Schedule, and Multiple-step Income Statement

2-34. The following data pertain to the Zhang Manufacturing Company for the year ended December 31, 2009.

Sales	$1,267,000
Beginning direct material inventory	40,000
Ending direct material inventory	50,000
Beginning work-in-process inventory	70,000
Ending work-in-process inventory	60,000
Beginning finished goods inventory	90,000
Ending finished goods inventory	80,000
Direct material purchased	350,000
Indirect material used in production	24,000
Factory supplies used	6,000
Depreciation on the factory	90,000
Depreciation on the sales office	24,000
Depreciation on the administrative office	36,000
Sales salaries	110,000
Assembly-line labor cost	220,000
Factory security guard cost	22,000
Factory supervision	42,000
Depreciation on production equipment	160,000
Depreciation on general accounting office equipment	16,000

Required:

a. Prepare a cost of goods manufactured schedule for 2009.

b. Prepare a cost of goods sold schedule for 2009.

c. Prepare a multiple-step income statement for 2009.

LO 5: Preparation of Cost of Goods Manufactured Schedule, Cost of Goods Sold Schedule, and Multiple-step Income Statement

2-35. The following data pertain to the Quintana Manufacturing Company for the year ended December 31, 2009.

Sales	$1,302,000
Beginning finished goods inventory	93,000
Ending finished goods inventory	86,000
Beginning direct material inventory	45,000
Ending direct material inventory	56,000
Beginning work-in-process inventory	72,000
Ending work-in-process inventory	77,000
Direct material purchased	370,000
Indirect material used in production	34,000
Depreciation on production equipment	145,000
Depreciation on sales office equipment	19,000
Factory supplies used	8,000
Depreciation on the factory	96,000

(Continued)

Depreciation on the sales office	$ 34,000
Depreciation on the administrative office	30,000
Sales salaries	122,000
Assembly-line labor cost	240,000
Factory security guard cost	32,000
Factory supervision	48,000

Required:

a. Prepare a cost of goods manufactured schedule for 2009.

b. Prepare a cost of goods sold schedule for 2009.

c. Prepare a multiple-step income statement for 2009.

LO 5: Preparation of Cost of Goods Manufactured Schedule, Cost of Goods Sold Schedule, and Multiple-step Income Statement

2-36. The following data pertain to the Rodriguez Manufacturing Company for the year ended December 31, 2008.

Sales	$1,124,000
Beginning direct material inventory	55,000
Ending direct material inventory	56,000
Beginning finished goods inventory	83,000
Ending finished goods inventory	96,000
Beginning work-in-process inventory	62,000
Ending work-in-process inventory	67,000
Direct material purchased	290,000
Direct labor cost	220,000
Manufacturing overhead	286,000
Selling expense	122,000
Administrative expense	140,000

Required:

a. Prepare a cost of goods manufactured schedule for 2008.

b. Prepare a cost of goods sold schedule for 2008.

c. Prepare a multiple-step income statement for 2008.

LO 5: Preparation of Cost of Goods Manufactured Schedule, Cost of Goods Sold Schedule, and Multiple-step Income Statement

2-37. The following data pertain to the Avener Manufacturing Company for the year ended December 31, 2008.

Sales	$333,000
Beginning direct material inventory	5,000
Ending direct material inventory	4,000
Beginning work-in-process inventory	6,000
Ending work-in-process inventory	7,000
Beginning finished goods inventory	8,000

(Continued)

Ending finished goods inventory	$10,000
Direct material purchased	56,000
Direct labor cost	96,000
Manufacturing overhead	86,000
Selling expense	46,000
Administrative expense	34,000

Required:

a. Prepare a cost of goods manufactured schedule for 2008.

b. Prepare a cost of goods sold schedule for 2008.

c. Prepare a multiple-step income statement for 2008.

LO 5 & 7: Prepare the Cost of Goods Manufactured Schedule and Prepare Basic Journal Entries for a Manufacturer

2-38. The following information is for Megan Hat Manufacturing Company.

Inventory information:		
	January 1, 2009	December 31, 2009
Raw materials inventory	$ 9,000	$11,000
Work-in-process inventory	22,000	18,000
Finished goods inventory	42,000	38,000
Other information:		
Direct materials purchases	$120,000	
Direct labor cost	250,000	
Manufacturing overhead	140,000	

Required:

a. What is the cost of direct material used in production?

b. Prepare a cost of goods manufactured schedule in good form.

c. Prepare a cost of goods sold schedule.

d. Prepare journal entries to record the following (Note: Instead of dating the entries, number them 1 through 6.):

1. The purchase of direct material assuming it was purchased on account
2. The use of direct material in production
3. Direct labor cost
4. Manufacturing overhead cost (Use "various accounts" for the credit side of the entry.)
5. The cost of goods manufactured
6. The sale of finished goods assuming the sale price was $600,000 and the sale was on account.

LO 5 & 7: Prepare the Cost of Goods Manufactured Schedule and Prepare Basic Journal Entries for a Manufacturer

2-39. The following information is for Friedman Shelving Manufacturing Company.

Inventory information:	January 1, 2009	December 31, 2009
Raw materials inventory	$22,000	$24,000
Work-in-process inventory	42,000	43,000
Finished goods inventory	82,000	78,000

Other information:	
Direct materials purchases	$280,000
Direct labor cost	540,000
Manufacturing overhead	240,000

Required:

a. What is the cost of direct material used in production?

b. Prepare a cost of goods manufactured schedule in good form.

c. Prepare a cost of goods sold schedule.

d. Prepare journal entries to record the following (Note: Instead of dating the entries, number them 1 through 6.):

1. The purchase of direct material assuming it was purchased on account
2. The use of direct material in production
3. Direct labor cost
4. Manufacturing overhead cost (Use "various accounts" for the credit side of the entry.)
5. The cost of goods manufactured
6. The sale of finished goods assuming the sale price was $1,400,000 on account

LO 5 & 7: Preparation of Cost of Goods Manufactured Schedule and Prepare Basic Journal Entries for a Manufacturer

2-40. The following information is for Tatum Manufacturing Company.

Inventory information:	January 1, 2009	December 31, 2009
Raw materials inventory	$2,000	$4,000
Work-in-process inventory	4,000	3,000
Finished goods inventory	8,000	6,000

Other information:	
Direct materials purchases	$ 8,000
Direct labor cost	12,000
Manufacturing overhead	9,000

Required:

a. Prepare a cost of goods manufactured schedule in good form.

b. Prepare journal entries to record the following (Note: Instead of dating the entries, number them 1 through 6.):

1. The purchase of direct material on account
2. The use of direct material in production
3. Direct labor cost
4. Manufacturing overhead cost (Use "various accounts" for the credit side of the entry.)
5. The cost of goods manufactured
6. The sale of finished goods assuming the sale price was $40,000 and it was a cash sale

LO 5 & 7: Preparation of Cost of Goods Manufactured Schedule and Prepare Basic Journal Entries for a Manufacturer

2-41. The following information is for Munter Manufacturing Company.

Inventory information:			
	January 1, 2009		December 31, 2009
Raw materials inventory	$6,000		$5,000
Work-in-process inventory	3,000		4,000
Finished goods inventory	7,000		9,000
Other information:			
Direct materials purchases		$ 9,000	
Direct labor cost		10,000	
Manufacturing overhead		11,000	

Required:

a. Prepare a cost of goods manufactured schedule in good form.

b. Prepare journal entries to record the following (Note: Instead of dating the entries, number them 1 through 6.):

1. The purchase of direct material on account
2. The use of direct material in production
3. Direct labor cost
4. Manufacturing overhead cost (Use "various accounts" for the credit side of the entry.)
5. The cost of goods manufactured
6. The sale of finished goods assuming the sale price was $39,000 on account

LO 5: Preparation of Cost of Goods Manufactured Schedule and Multiple-step Income Statement

2-42. The following information is for Collins Manufacturing Company.

Inventory information:	January 1, 2009	December 31, 2009
Raw materials inventory	$16,000	$14,000
Work-in-process inventory	23,000	25,000
Finished goods inventory	33,000	36,000

Other information:	
Sales	$760,000
Direct materials purchases	159,000
Direct labor cost	110,000
Manufacturing overhead	221,000
Selling expense	62,000
Administrative expense	47,000

Required:

a. Prepare a cost of goods manufactured schedule in good form.

b. Prepare a multiple-step income statement in good form.

LO 5: Preparation of Cost of Goods Manufactured Schedule and Multiple-step Income Statement

2-43. The following information is for Richard Manufacturing Company.

Inventory information:	January 1, 2009	December 31, 2009
Raw materials inventory	$14,000	$16,000
Work-in-process inventory	25,000	28,000
Finished goods inventory	32,000	36,000

Other information:	
Sales	$790,000
Direct materials purchases	162,000
Direct labor cost	140,000
Manufacturing overhead	234,000
Selling expense	72,000
Administrative expense	57,000

Required:

a. Prepare a cost of goods manufactured schedule in good form.

b. Prepare a multiple-step income statement in good form.

LO 3: Preparation of a Multiple-step Income Statement for a Merchandiser

2-44. Bonnie's Pet Cage Company has the following information for 2008:

Sales	$300,000
Cost of goods manufactured	200,000
Selling expense	30,000
Administrative expense	25,000
Beginning finished goods inventory	21,000
Ending finished goods inventory	28,000

Required:

Prepare a multiple-step income statement for Bonnie's Pet Cage Company for 2008.

LO 3: Preparation of a Multiple-step Income Statement for a Manufacturer

2-45. Albert's Manufacturing Company has the following information for 2008:

Beginning finished goods inventory	$ 41,000
Ending finished goods inventory	58,000
Sales	600,000
Cost of goods manufactured	400,000
Selling expense	90,000
Administrative expense	60,000

Required:

Prepare a multiple-step income statement for Albert's Manufacturing Company for 2008.

LO 5: Preparation of a Multiple-step Income Statement for a Merchandiser

2-46. Phillips Merchandising Company has the following information for 2008:

Sales	$400,000
Cost of merchandise purchased	300,000
Selling expense	30,000
Administrative expense	20,000
Beginning finished goods inventory	40,000
Ending finished goods inventory	50,000

Required:

Prepare a multiple-step income statement for Phillips Merchandising Company for 2008.

LO 5: Preparation of a Multiple-step Income Statement for a Merchandiser

2-47. Robinson Merchandising Company has the following information for 2009:

Beginning finished goods inventory	$ 60,000
Ending finished goods inventory	50,000
Sales	840,000
Cost of merchandise purchased	630,000
Selling expense	90,000
Administrative expense	40,000

Required:

Prepare a multiple-step income statement for Robinson Merchandising Company for 2009.

LO 6: Determine the Cost of Services Provided and Preparation of a Single-Step Income Statement for a Service Company

2-48. Butterfield's Bookkeeping Service began operations on January 1, 2009. The following information is taken from its accounting records as of December 31, 2009.

Bookkeeping service revenue	$80,000
Bookkeeping salaries	42,000
Bookkeeping office rent	12,000
Depreciation on bookkeeping equipment	2,000
Bookkeeping supplies used	700
Advertising	800

Required:

a. What is the cost of services provided?

b. Prepare a single-step income statement for Butterfield's Bookkeeping Service for 2009.

LO 6: Determine the Cost of Services Provided and Preparation of a Single-Step Income Statement for a Service Company

2-49. Tony's Film Delivery Service began operations on January 1, 2009. The following information is taken from its accounting records as of December 31, 2009.

Delivery revenue	$40,000
Driver wages	22,000
Depreciation on truck	4,000
Fuel cost	2,700
Advertising	800
Bookkeeping cost	240

Required:

a. What is the cost of services provided?

b. Prepare a single-step income statement for Tony's Film Delivery Service.

LO 3: Preparation of a Multiple-step Income Statement for a Merchandiser

2-50. Cam's Swimsuit Shop provided the following information for 2009.

Merchandise inventory, January 1. 2009	$ 16,000
Merchandise inventory, December 31, 2009	19,000
Sales	190,000
Advertising	1,200
Store rent	2,400
Purchases of merchandise	82,000
Sales salaries	22,000
Store utilities	3,600
Sales supplies used during 2009	1,000
Sales supplies on hand, December 31, 2009	500
Administrative office rent	800
Administrative salaries	18,000

Required:

Prepare a multiple-step income statement for Cam's Swimsuit Shop for 2009.

LO 3: Preparation of a Multiple-step Income Statement for a Merchandiser
2-51. Leroy's Auto Parts provided the following information for 2009.

Merchandise inventory, January 1, 2009	$ 19,000
Merchandise inventory, December 31, 2009	21,000
Sales	280,000
Advertising	2,200
Depreciation on the store	18,000
Purchases of merchandise	182,000
Sales salaries	21,000
Store utilities	1,200
Depreciation on administrative office building	4,000
Administrative salaries	15,000
Administrative office utilities	600

Required:

Prepare a multiple-step income statement for Leroy's Auto Parts for 2009.

LO 6: Preparation of a Single-Step Income Statement for a Service Company
2-52. Dan's Security Service provided the following information for 2009.

Security revenue	$480,000
Advertising	12,000
Depreciation on the home office building	12,000
Security guard wages	362,000
Administrative salaries	21,000
Sales salaries	24,000
Utilities	1,200

Required:

Prepare a single-step income statement for Dan's Security Service for 2009.

LO 3: Preparation of a Multiple-step Income Statement for a Merchandiser
2-53. Margaret's Flower Shop provided the following information for 2009.

Merchandise inventory, January 1, 2009	$ 1,000
Merchandise inventory, December 31, 2009	1,200
Sales	42,400
Advertising	3,200
Store rent	1,200
Purchases of merchandise	18,000
Sales salaries	21,000
Utilities	1,300
Sales supplies used during 2009	9,000
Sales supplies on hand, December 31, 2009	300

Required:

Prepare a multiple-step income statement for Margaret's Flower Shop for 2009.

LO 2, 3, & 4: Understanding Cost of Goods Sold

2-54. The management of Diversified Incorporated is concerned that few of its employees understand cost of goods sold. The company president has decided that a series of presentations will be made focusing on cost of goods sold.

Assume that the company has formed two teams, Team A and Team B. You and several of your classmates have been assigned to Team B.

Team A is given the responsibility of preparing a presentation detailing the cost of goods sold pertaining to a subsidiary that operates a chain of hardware stores. Team B, your team, has been given the responsibility of preparing a presentation detailing the cost of goods sold of a subsidiary that manufactures electronic calculators.

In short order, Team A has completed its assignment and is ready to make its presentation. Your team, however, is still working. Company executives question why Team A is so far ahead of your team's progress.

Required:

Working as a group, develop a response to the concerns relating to your teams slow progress. Explain why Team A could complete their assignment so quickly and why your team will have to work longer.

LO 6: Understanding Service Company Costs

2-55. Assume that you are the manager of an accounting practice. You are concerned about billing your clients so that the company covers all costs and makes a reasonable profit.

Required:

a. What information might you desire to help develop a method of billing clients?

b. How would you use the information to ensure that costs are covered and profits result?

LO 1, 2, & 4: Understanding Inventory Cost Classifications

2-56. The inventory of a manufacturer is typically grouped into one of three classifications-raw material inventory, work-in-process inventory, and finished goods inventory.

Required:

Discuss why it provides more useful information to use three classifications of inventory rather than one for a manufacturer.

LO 1, 2, & 4: Understanding Inventory Costs

2-57. Assume that you work for the Acme Wire Manufacturing Company. Some employees in the company are unsure of which costs should be included in inventories and which costs should not. There is also some confusion regarding the logic of including some items while excluding others.

You have been assigned to a group that is responsible for making a presentation on which of Acme's costs would properly be classified as inventory costs and which would not.

Required:

Prepare a presentation describing the type of items that would be included in inventories and those that would not. Comment on the logic of including some cost items in inventory while excluding others.

LO 1, 2, & 3: General Inventory and Cost Analysis

2-58. One year ago, Herb Smith quit his job at Adcox Medical where he earned $28,000 a year as a health care technician to start the Super CD Store. He invested almost his entire life's savings in the venture and is now concerned. He notes that, when his money was in the bank, he earned about 4% interest. Now, when he compares his company profits to the amount invested in the store, the profits seem lower than what he could have earned if he had simply left the money in the bank. The following information is available for the company's first year of business:

Annual sales	$600,000
Cost of goods sold	450,000
Selling expense	90,000
Administrative expense	50,000
Inventory	300,000
Other assets	30,000
Total liabilities	50,000

The administrative expense includes $30,000 received by Herb in the form of salary. Herb's friend Bill has suggested that a simple $5,000 computer might help with company record keeping and ordering inventory.

Herb has indicated that he does not mind the added work or ordering the merchandise without a computer. In fact, when it comes to ordering product, he seems quite proud of the job he is doing as he almost always has the CDs his customers want. Herb has engaged your services as a consultant to determine whether his feelings are correct about the low earnings of the company and to suggest some possibilities to improve the situation. Also, Herb would like some input regarding the computer.

Required:

Prepare a report for Herb addressing each of his concerns.

LO 1, 2, & 3: General Inventory and Cost Analysis

2-59. Alberto Manufacturing Company has been in business for many years. Toward the end of 2008, management began to notice that the company had to rely more and more on borrowing to support the cash flow needs of the operation. Although sales increased in 2009, profits declined and the cash flow problem worsened. The company president is very concerned that the cash shortfall is caused by mismanagement of the daily operation of the factory. Managers argue that the company's operations are quite satisfactory. They cite that expenses have increased only slightly as sales have risen, and that production levels have been dictated by customer demand.

The president has hired your team of consultants to review the situation and comment on the possible problems that exist. The following information is available for 2008 and 2009.

Alberto Manufacturing Company
Schedule of Cost of Goods Manufactured
For the Year Ending December 31, 2008

Direct Materials:		
Beginning Direct Material Inventory	$ 15,000	
Purchases during 2008	420,000	
Materials Available during 2008	$ 435,000	
Ending Direct Material Inventory	(45,000)	
Direct Materials Used during 2008		$ 390,000
Direct Labor during 2008		225,000
Total Manufacturing Overhead Cost during 2008		415,000
Manufacturing Cost for Current Period		$1,030,000
Beginning Work-in-Process Inventory 12/31/07		40,000
Cost of Goods Available to be Finished		$1,070,000
Ending Work-in-Process Inventory 12/31/08		(82,000)
Cost of Goods Manufactured during 2008		$ 988,000

Alberto Manufacturing Company
Income Statement
For the Year Ending December 31, 2008

Sales		$1,758,000
Cost of Goods Sold		
Beginning Finished Goods Inventory	$ 65,000	
+ Cost of Goods Manufactured	988,000	
= Goods Available for Sale in 2008	$1,053,000	
− Ending Finished Goods Inventory	(75,000)	
= Cost of Goods Sold for 2008		978,000
Gross Profit		$ 780,000
Operating Expense:		
Selling Expense	$ 355,000	
Administrative Expense	190,000	(545,000)
Operating Income		$ 235,000

Alberto Manufacturing Company
Schedule of Cost of Goods Manufactured
For the Year Ending December 31, 2009

Direct Materials:		
Beginning Direct Material Inventory	$ 45,000	
Purchases during 2009	457,000	
Materials Available during 2009	$ 502,000	
Ending Direct Material Inventory	(73,000)	
Direct Materials Used during 2009		$ 429,000
Direct Labor during 2009		263,000
Total Manufacturing Overhead Cost during 2009		450,000
Manufacturing Cost for Current Period		$1,142,000
Beginning Work-in-Process Inventory 1/1/09		82,000
Cost of Goods Available to be Finished		$1,224,000
Ending Work-in-Process Inventory 12/31/09		(154,000)
Cost of Goods Manufactured during 2009		$1,070,000

Alberto Manufacturing Company
Income Statement
For the Year Ending December 31, 2009

Sales		$1,772,000
Cost of Goods Sold		
Beginning Finished Goods Inventory	$ 75,000	
+ Cost of Goods Manufactured during 2009	1,070,000	
= Goods Available for Sale in 2009	$1,143,000	
− Ending Finished Goods Inventory	(93,000)	
= Cost of Goods Sold for 2009		$1,052,000
Gross Profit		720,000
Operating Expense:		
Selling Expense	$ 365,000	
Administrative Expense	228,000	(593,000)
Operating Income		$ 127,000

Required:

Your team should review the provided information and comment on problems that exist. It may help to segment the statements into sections and assign group members to a particular area. For example, a group member might be assigned to review the purchase and use of direct material, another member might be assigned the direct labor and manufacturing overhead areas, and so forth. Each group member should comment on his or her assigned area as it pertains to cash flow and income.

3

Determining Costs of Products

Every year **Fortune** magazine compiles a list of the top 500 publicly traded companies in the United States. This prestigious list is called the *Fortune 500*. Of the top 25 Fortune 500 companies, there are more manufacturing companies than any other classification, demonstrating that manufacturing plays a pivotal role in the United States.

In recent years, however, manufacturing companies from outside the United States have begun to exert significant competitive pressure on U.S. manufacturers. The new global marketplace has forced U.S. manufacturers to take a hard look at both the way they operate and the way the results of their operations are measured and evaluated.

One area of vital importance to manufacturing companies is determining the cost of the products they manufacture. If you are the sales manager for **Dell's** laptop computer division for example, you must be sure that the selling price you establish is high enough to earn a profit. To ensure that the selling price of each computer exceeds its cost, you need accurate product cost information.

Besides the product pricing decision, there are several other uses of information about product cost. First, a company must determine the cost of products to compute cost of goods sold on its income statement for a particular period. Second, a company must have product cost information to determine the value of inventories shown on its balance sheet. Third, product cost information helps managers evaluate the efficiency and productivity of a company's manufacturing facility.

In Chapter 2 we stated that the three elements of product cost for a manufacturer are direct material, direct labor, and manufacturing overhead. We also presented an overview of the product costing process. In this chapter we will delve more deeply into the methods that manufacturers use to determine the cost of the individual units of product they produce.

Learning Objectives

After completing your work on this chapter, you should be able to do the following:

1. Compare and contrast process costing with job order costing.
2. Describe how process costing and job order costing work.

3. Describe the documents used to help control the costs of manufacturing products.
4. Describe how overhead costs are allocated to products.
5. Determine the cost of products using job order costing.
6. Determine the cost of products using process costing.
7. Prepare basic manufacturing journal entries.

Accumulating Product Cost—Cost Accounting

The process of assigning manufacturing costs to manufactured products is called *cost accounting*. When we first introduced this term in Chapter 1, we said that it is often used interchangeably with the terms *management accounting* and *managerial accounting*, but that cost accounting is actually a narrow application of management accounting dealing with costing products. Cost accounting information can help managers plan and control their operations, make decisions about investments in property, plant, and equipment, establish selling prices, and determine the value of inventories on the balance sheet. Cost accounting information also affects reported net income on the income statement, because the cost of the products sold during the income statement period is reported as cost of goods sold.

Units of Product as Cost Objects

Recall from Chapter 2 that a cost object is any activity or item for which a separate cost measurement is desired. For our purposes in this chapter, we will consider a unit of manufactured product as the cost object. As we said earlier, the cost of a unit of manufactured product includes the cost of the direct material, direct labor, and manufacturing overhead required to produce that unit of product. The amount of direct material included in each unit of production can actually be traced to finished products. Assigning the cost of direct material to production is relatively simple, then, as long as the company keeps track of the amount of material used to produce each unit of product. Similarly, if a company keeps track of the amount of direct labor used to produce each unit of product, it can readily assess the cost of direct labor used to produce each unit. Unlike direct material and direct labor, however, the amount of manufacturing overhead cost associated with particular units of production is quite abstract.

Manufacturing overhead cost includes all manufacturing cost except direct material and direct labor costs. Accordingly, it includes a wide assortment of factory related items. Some examples are production design setup, plant security, supervisory salaries, raw materials storage, building maintenance, and factory supplies.

Product Costing Methods

Manufacturers generally use one of two methods for determining the cost of products—the job order cost method and the process cost method. Although both methods are used, they are not interchangeable. A company must select the method best suited to the type of products it makes and to the manufacturing process itself. The key consideration for choosing between process costing and job order costing is whether the goods produced consume similar enough amounts of factory resources (direct material, direct labor, and manufacturing overhead) that an average cost per unit would be an accurate reflection of the product's cost. This is process costing. If the units consume very different amounts of factory resources, an average cost per unit is meaningless, and job order costing should be used.

Job Order Costing Basics

Job order costing accumulates the cost of production for each job, each individual unit of production, each order, or each product. This method is used to accumulate the cost of one-of-a-kind and custom-made goods such as custom furniture or custom cabinets, ships, airplanes, bridges, buildings, and advertising posters. For instance, when **Boeing** manufactured the five **Boeing** 777-200 passenger jets ordered by **Air China**, the airplane manufacturer used job order costing to determine how much each aircraft costs.

job order costing A costing method that accumulates cost by a single unit or production or batch of units.

Under job order costing, managers keep close track of the material and labor associated with each job. The "job" may consist of a single unit or a batch of units. For example, a job for **Boeing** would consist of a single airplane. For **Perlmuter Printing**, however, a job would consist of a batch of 20,000 advertising posters. In either case, the cost of direct material, direct labor, and manufacturing overhead are accumulated and totaled for each job. (See Exhibit 3-1)

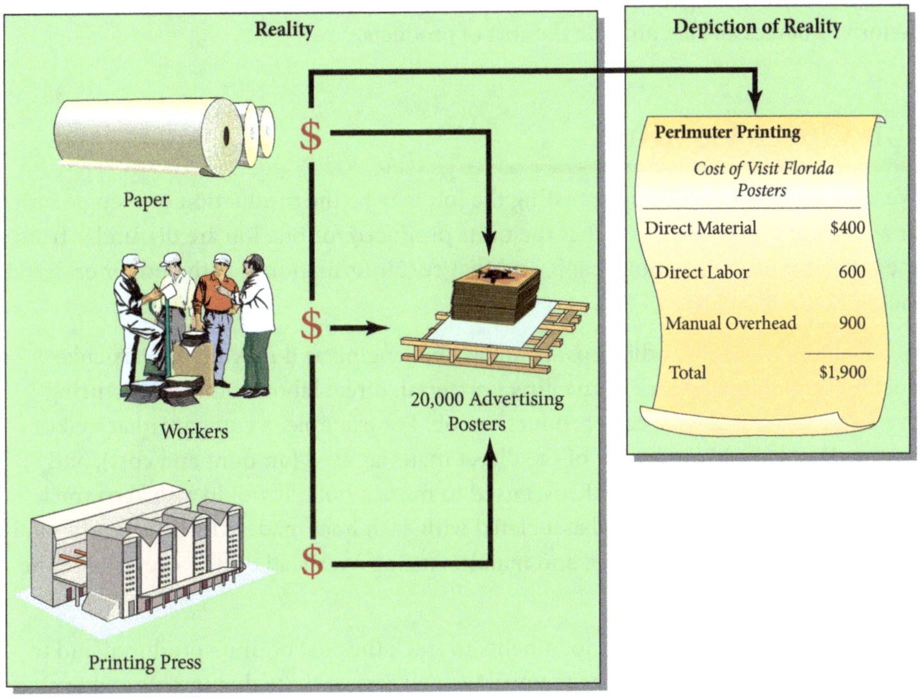

Exhibit 3-1 Cost of Advertising Posters

Process Costing Basics

Process costing is a method of allocating manufacturing cost to products to determine an average cost per unit. Companies use process costing when units of production are identical, or almost identical, and each unit of production receives the same manufacturing input as the next. Examples of such products are milk, soda, canned goods, breakfast cereal, household cleaners, motor oil, and gasoline. For example, **Eastman Kodak** uses process costing to determine the cost of the color paper it produces.

process costing A method of allocating manufacturing cost to products to determine an average cost per unit.

Under process costing, total manufacturing cost is divided by the number of units produced to arrive at a per unit cost. For example, if a toothbrush factorywakes 2 million toothbrushes and the total production cost is $400,000, then the cost per tooth brush is $0.20, computed as follows:

$$\frac{\text{Total productiqn cost}}{\text{Number of units produced}} = \text{Cost per unit}$$

$$\frac{\$400{,}000}{2{,}000{,}000 \text{ units produced}} = \$0.20 \text{ per unit}$$

The reason this simple method is adequate for a product such as toothbrushes is that each toothbrush is identical to, and consumes the same amount of resources as the next. Accordingly, an average cost per toothbrush provides an accurate unit's cost.

Discussion Questions

3-1. Name four products (other than those mentioned in the text) for which process costing would be appropriate.

3-2. Name four products (other than those mentioned in the text) for which job order costing would be appropriate.

3-3. Are any products difficult to classify? If so, list some and explain the difficulty.

The first product costing method we will explore in detail is job order costing. As we cover job order costing, we will also look at the documents manufacturers use to control factory resources and accumulate the cost of products.

Job Order Costing

We have seen that in job order costing the job may be the production of a single unit, or a batch of units. The key is that the units produced for one job are dissimilar from the units produced for another job, and that cost information is gathered for each individual production job.

Keeping track of product cost is not as challenging as it may seem. Particular documents help keep track of the direct material, direct labor, and manufacturing overhead associated with each production job. For example, a company that makes custom boats would keep a list of the direct material used (amount and cost), and direct labor hours (amount and cost) used to make a boat. It would also keep track of the manufacturing overhead associated with each boat made. The firm would total the direct material, direct labor, and manufacturing overhead costs to determine the boat's cost.

Managers use a system of documents to track the cost of units produced and to control the costs incurred in the factory. We will review these documents and explore job order costing procedures in the following sections, using **Manta Power Boats** for our example. **Manta** is a top-quality, custom boat manufacturer located in Hollywood, Florida. In contrast to production-line boats—boats made in large quantities that are nearly identical—**Manta's** boats are manufactured to each customer's specifications. Customers select the boat style, interior, engines, construction material, and paint scheme they want. No two boats are alike.

Documentation Relating to Job Order Costing

job cost sheet A document that tracks the cost of products and organizes and summarizes the cost information for each job.

When a company uses job order costing, a document called a **job cost sheet** simplifies tracking the costs of products because it organizes and summarizes the cost information for each job. An example of a job cost sheet is shown in Exhibit 3-2.

The job cost sheet in Exhibit 3-2 will eventually list the manufacturing costs for Job Number 97384, a 28-foot Open Fisherman. An entry will be made on the job cost sheet each time direct material, direct labor, and manufacturing overhead costs are incurred in connection with this job. **Manta's** managers can refer to a job cost sheet any time they need information about the cost of producing a particular boat.

Manta Power Boats
Job Cost Sheet

Job Number: 97384 **Date Promised:** 7-11-08
Customer: Bill Hudik **Date Started:** 6-2-08
Product Description: 28 Open Fisherman

Direct Material			Direct Labor		Manufacturing Overhead			Total
Date	Req.#	Amount	Date	Amount	Base	Rate	Amount	
		$		$				
Total		$						$

Date Completed: ______

Exhibit 3-2. Job Cost Sheet for **Manta Power Boats**

Job cost sheets not only help keep track of the costs of current production, but they also provide historical information that can help managers estimate the cost of future production. For example, if an order is received for a boat similar to one that **Manta** has made in the past, the company's owner, Tom Greco, can look at the first boat's job cost sheet to help estimate how much the next boat will cost.

Now let's look at how these costs are monitored and measured. We begin with an analysis of direct material.

Cost Information for Raw Materials

Manufacturers such as **Manta** generally keep close track of raw material cost because it is such a large percentage of manufacturing cost. The raw materials **Manta** needs to build power boats include fiberglass cloth, polyester resin, wood, plastic, aluminum, engines, and much more. Because these materials are so costly, **Manta**, like other manufacturers, does not allow just any employee to buy raw material on behalf of the company. An unqualified employee might buy too much or too little, or they may buy the wrong raw material altogether. In most manufacturing companies, the employee in charge of monitoring the raw materials inventory levels makes a request for material. This person may be in charge of the materials store room or perhaps is the production supervisor. At **Manta**, Karl Bevins is that person. Karl monitors the amount of material on hand, and when polyester resin is needed, Karl requests that more be purchased. This purchase request comes in the form of a purchase requisition.

A **purchase requisition** is a request form that lists the quantity and description of the materials needed. This form helps to control and monitor all materials requested to ensure that the company secures the right amount and quality. Copies of the completed purchase requisition are forwarded to **Manta's** purchasing department and to the accounts payable clerk in charge of paying the company's bills. Exhibit 3-3 shows the completed materials requisition for **Manta Power Boats**.

purchase requisition A request form that lists the quantity and description of the materials needed.

Exhibit 3-3 Purchase Requisition for **Manta Power Boats**

Manta Power Boats
Purchase Requisition

Name: Karl Bevins **Number:** 1001

Department: Production Material Stores **Date:** 6-4-08

Quantity	Description
110 Gal.	Polyester Resin

Signature: Karl Bevins

purchasing department A department that specializes in purchasing all the goods required by a company or organization.

The **purchasing department** is a specialized department that purchases all the goods the company requires. In the purchasing department, trained individuals called purchasing agents contact several competing vendors (suppliers) to obtain the highest-quality material at the lowest cost.

purchase order A document a company or organization uses to order materials from a vendor.

Once the purchasing agent has selected a vendor, the agent issues a **purchase order**, a formal document created to order material from a vendor. The purchase order specifies the quantity, type and cost of the material, payment terms, and method of delivery. Copies of the purchase order are distributed to the receiving department, the accounts payable department, and the vendor. A sample purchase order for **Manta Power Boats** is shown in Exhibit 3-4.

Exhibit 3-4 Purchase Order for **Manta Power Boats**

Manta Power Boats
Purchase Order

Vendor: Pitman Sales Company **PO No.:** 06059702
Address: 8650 S W 132 Street **Order Date:** 6-5-08
Miami, FL 33156 **Delivery Date:** 6-7-08
Phone: 305-256-9558

Purchase Requisition No.: 1001 **Department:** Prod. Mat. Stores

Quantity	Description	Unit Cost	Total Cost
110 Gal.	Polyester Resin	$6.00	$660.00

Purchasing Agent Signature: Bob Pass

When **Manta's** receiving department receives the material from the supplier, the receiving clerk compares the material received to the purchase order and completes a receiving report. The **receiving report** is a document that indicates the quantity of each item the company receives. It is used to note any differences between the goods ordered and the goods received. Lauren Elsea, **Manta's** receiving clerk, completes a receiving report for each delivery received as shown in Exhibit 3-5.

receiving report A document that indicates the quantity and condition of each item received.

Manta Power Boats
Receiving Report

Vendor: Pitman Sales Company **Number:** 1234

Purchase Order No.: 06059702 **Date Received:** 6-7-08

Quantity	Description
110 Gal.	Polyester Resin

Receiving Clerk Signature: Lauren Elsea

Exhibit 3-5 Receiving Report for **Manta Power Boats**

A copy of the receiving report is sent to the accounts payable department. Manta's accounts payable clerk now has three documents related to the purchase: (1) the purchase requisition, (2) the purchase order, and (3) the receiving report. When the accounts payable clerk receives the vendor's invoice for the material, information on the invoice is matched to these three documents. If everything is correct, the clerk pays the invoice according to the payment terms.

Discussion Question

3-4. The accounts payable department verifies that the information on the vendor's invoice matches the purchase requisition, the purchase order, and the receiving report. In each of the following situations, what would the discrepancy indicate?

a. The receiving report conflicts with the vendor's invoice.

b. The purchase order conflicts with the receiving report.

c. The purchase requisition conflicts with the purchase order.

Once the materials have been checked in, they are stored in the materials stores warehouse until they are needed for production. Generally, such storage space is quite secure to protect the raw materials from damage and theft.

When material is needed for production, **Manta's** production manager, Kevin Dunn, completes a materials requisition. The **materials requisition** is a formal request to transfer materials from the raw materials storage area to production. This document lists the type of material and the quantity needed. To begin work on the 28-foot Open Fisherman boat for Job Number 97384, Kevin needs fiberglass and polyester resin, so he prepares the materials requisition shown in Exhibit 3-6 to transfer this material into production.

materials requisition A formal request for material to be transferred from the raw materials storage area to production.

Keep in mind that a *materials requisition* is different from a *purchase requisition*. The purchase requisition is a request to purchase materials, whereas the materials requisition is a request by manufacturing personnel to transfer previously purchased materials from the materials stores warehouse to production.

The materials requisition is a useful tool for accumulating the cost of products. Materials requisitions show how much material is being used, for what purpose, and at what cost. The information from the materials requisitions is transferred to the job cost sheets to show the quantity and cost of materials used for each job. Exhibit 3-7 shows how the

Exhibit 3-6 Materials Requisition for **Manta Power Boats**

Manta Power Boats
Materials Requisition

Job Number: 97384

Number: 98765
Date: 6-16-08

Quantity	Description	Unit Cost	Total Cost
55 Gal.	Polyester Resin	$6.00	$330.00

Issued By: Karl Bevins
Received By: Kevin Dunn

Exhibit 3-7 Transfer of Information from a Materials Requisition Form to a Job Cost Sheet

MATERIALS REQUISITION REQ# 1998

JOB #: 97384
DATE: 6/2/08

Quantity	Item #	Description	Unit Cost	Total Cost
9700	FG12	Fiberglass	.50	4,850

Issued By: Carl Bevans
Received By: Bill Smith

MATERIALS REQUISITION REQ# 2002

JOB #: 97384
DATE: 6/16/08

Quantity	Item #	Description	Unit Cost	Total Cost
55Gal	PR55X	Polyester Resin	6.00	330.00

Issued By: Carl Bevans
Received By: Kevin Dunn

JOB COST SHEET

JOB #: 97384 DATE PROMISED: 7/11/08
CUSTOMER: Bill Hudik DATE STARTED: 6/2/08
PRODUCT DESCRIPTION:

DIRECT MATERIALS			DIRECT LABOR		NAME OVERHEAD			
DATE	REQ #	AMT.	DATE	AMT.	BASE	RATE	AMT.	TOTAL
6/2/08	1998	$4,850						
6/11/08	2002	330						
6/19/08	2124	4,510						
6/23/08	2216	5,310						
TOTAL		$15,000						

Date Completed

MATERIALS REQUISITION REQ# 2124

JOB #: 97384
DATE: 6/19/08

Quantity	Item #	Description	Unit Cost	Total Cost
60 ft	RR4	Rubrail	1.40	84
1	W520	WindShield		210
1	1248	Steering Wheel		156
1	564	Alm. Top		4,060
				4,510

Issued By: Carl Bevans
Received By: Bill Smith

MATERIALS REQUISITION REQ# 2216

JOB #: 97384
DATE: 6/23/08

Quantity	Item #	Description	Unit Cost	Total Cost
1	MC520	Engine Package	5,310	5,310

Issued By: Carl Bevans
Received By: Kevin Dunn

accounting department at **Manta Power Boats** transfers information from the materials requisition to the job cost sheet for Job Number 97384.

Materials requisitions are also valuable tools for controlling the movement of materials in the factory. Because the movement is documented, it is easier to monitor employees' use of materials. This record helps prevent theft, waste, or other inappropriate use of materials.

Cost Information for Direct Labor

Once raw materials enter the production process, factory workers begin working with it, converting the materials into finished product. Remember from Chapter 2 that the cost of the raw materials incorporated into the product *and* the labor of production workers increase the value of the goods in work-in-process inventory. Therefore, in accounting records, work-in-process inventory is increased not only by the cost of direct material, but also by the cost of direct labor. The combination of the cost of direct material and the cost of direct labor is also referred to as the prime cost in manufacturing.

labor time ticket A document that tracks the amount of time each employee works on a particular job or a particular task in a factory or organization.

Manufacturers use **labor time tickets** to track the amount of time each employee works on a particular production job or a particular task in the factory. Exhibit 3-8 shows a sample labor time ticket for **Manta Power Boats**.

Exhibit 3-8 Labor Time Ticket for **Manta Power Boats**

Manta Power Boats
Labor Time Ticket

Employee: Edward Clark
Employee Number: 127 **Week Ending:** 6-8-08

Job No.	M	T	W	T	F	S	S	Total
97384	8	8	4		8			28
97383			4	8				12

Supervisor: Seth Levine **Employee:** Edward Clark

Labor time tickets include information regarding the amount of direct labor associated with each production job. As was the case with the materials requisitions, company accountants transfer cost information from the labor time tickets to the job cost sheet for each job. Exhibit 3-9 shows the transfer of information from the labor time tickets to the job cost sheet for Job Number 97384 at **Manta Power Boats**.

Most companies now use computer technology to make entries on labor time tickets. They issue identification cards to employees that are scanned by a card reader. The employees then enter codes to indicate the duties they are performing and the job or jobs to which these duties relate. Information from the electronic labor time tickets is stored in a computer file and transferred electronically to electronic job cost sheets.

The information from the materials requisitions and labor time tickets makes it easy to trace direct material cost and direct labor cost to individual jobs. Tracing manufacturing overhead is not quite as straightforward. What follows is a general treatment of the

Exhibit 3-9 Transfer of Information from Labor Time Tickets to a Job Cost Sheet at **Manta Power Boats**

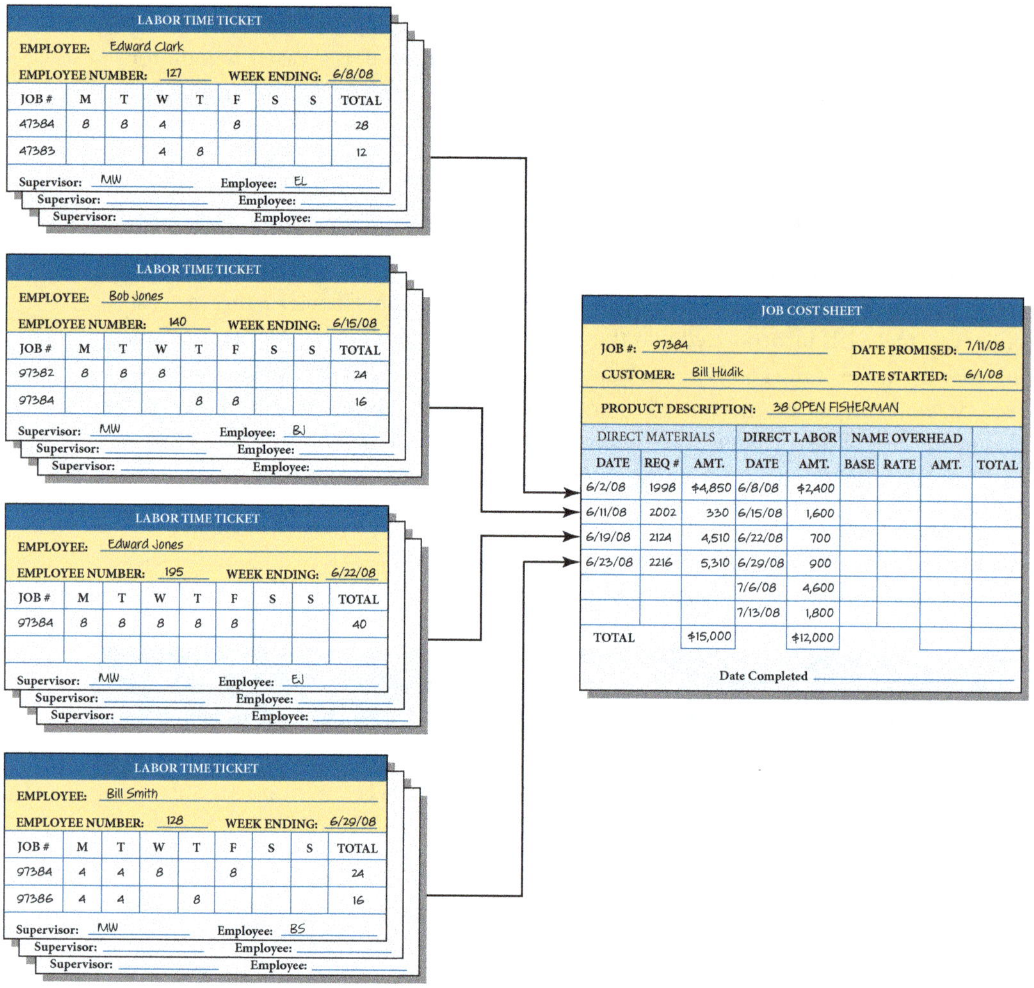

topic of manufacturing overhead allocation. The subject is presented in greater detail in the next chapter.

Manufacturing Overhead

Manufacturing overhead generally benefits the factory as a whole and therefore all units produced. It is very difficult to accurately assign manufacturing overhead costs to units produced because the benefit of these expenditures cannot be traced to individual jobs or units of production. Because it can't be traced to individual units, manufacturing overhead must be allocated to the units produced based on some reasonable basis of distribution. This allocation has traditionally been a two-stage process.

cost pool An accumulation of the costs associated with a specific cost object.

allocation base An item or activity associated with cost objects that can be used to proportionately distribute manufacturing overhead costs to each cost object.

The first stage is to gather manufacturing overhead into a cost pool. A **cost pool** is an accumulation of the costs associated with a specific cost object—in this instance all manufacturing overhead costs. The second stage is to allocate the manufacturing overhead to the units of product produced by way of an application rate. Determining this rate requires the selection of some allocation base. An **allocation base** is some item or activity used to proportionately distribute manufacturing overhead cost to the product being produced. Companies attempt to identify an allocation base that indicates the relative amounts of indirect factory resources consumed in the manufacture of individual units of product.

As seen in Exhibit 3-10, generally the cost to be allocated is divided by the total allocation base to determine the amount to allocate per occurrence of the allocation base.

$$\frac{\text{Cost to be allocated}}{\text{Total occurrences of the allocation base}} = \text{Cost per occurrence of the allocation base}$$

Exhibit 3-10 General Formula to Allocate a Cost

Choosing an appropriate allocation base is critical if a company is to establish a reasonable application rate. One alternative is to use the number of units produced as the allocation base.

If we use the number of units produced as an allocation base, we divide the manufacturing overhead by the number of units to arrive at an amount of manufacturing overhead per unit. This method of allocation provides an equal amount of manufacturing overhead cost for each unit of production. When the products a company produces are different from one another, however, a uniform cost per unit is generally inadequate. If the manufacturing overhead for **Manta Power Boats**, for instance, is $75,000 and the company makes five boats, the manufacturing overhead per boat would be $15,000 for each boat produced, as calculated in Exhibit 3-11.

$$\frac{\text{Total manufacturing overhead}}{\text{Total number of units produced}} = \text{Manufacturing overhead per unit}$$

$$\frac{\$75{,}000}{\text{5 Boats}} = \$15{,}000 \text{ per boat}$$

Manufacturing Overhead Cost

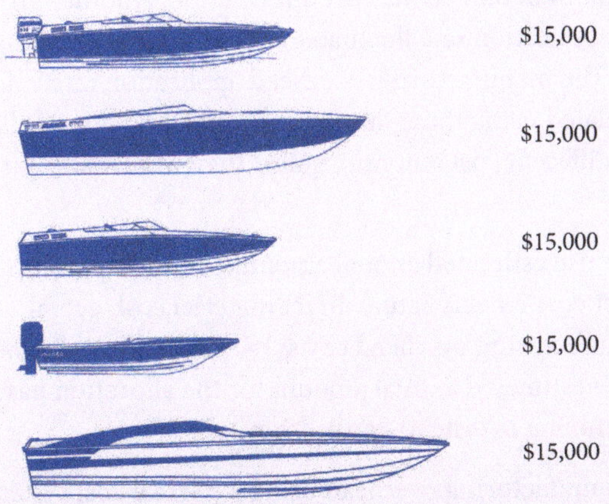

Exhibit 3-11 Allocating Manufacturing Overhead Based on the Number of Units Produced

However, this allocation of $15,000 per boat is not appropriate because the boats are so different from one another. It stands to reason that building a large boat would consume more factory resources and should receive a higher manufacturing overhead cost allocation than a small boat. It would be more accurate to allocate the manufacturing overhead cost according to the resources consumed instead of allocating the exact same amount to each boat produced.

When we select an allocation base, we should strive to find one that will distribute manufacturing overhead cost reasonably. The best allocation base would be one that *causes* the cost which is to be allocated; but, when a single cost pool is used for manufacturing overhead, it is impossible to find a single allocation base that causes all the cost in the pool. Instead, we attempt to find an allocation base that has the second-best attribute for cost allocation, an allocation base that is correlated to the incurrence of cost. Thus, we should try to find an allocation base that is correlated to the amount of manufacturing overhead resources consumed by each unit produced. Historically, manufacturers have most often used some measure of direct labor as the allocation base in applying manufacturing overhead to production. For this reason, the combination of direct labor cost and manufacturing overhead cost is referred to as the conversion cost in manufacturing. More recently, machine hours has also been used as the allocation base.

Taking a closer look at our boat company example, we note that no two boats are identical and manufacturing a larger or more complicated boat would, in all likelihood, consume more manufacturing overhead than a smaller or less complicated boat. As a start, we should find an allocation base that would apportion more manufacturing overhead to a boat that uses up more manufacturing overhead resources and less to a boat that likely uses less. It seems reasonable that a correlation exists between the amount of direct labor cost and the amount of manufacturing overhead resources consumed to make each boat. Therefore, for our example, we will use **Manta Power Boats**' direct labor cost as the allocation base for manufacturing overhead.

actual cost system A system in which product cost reflects actual direct material cost, actual direct labor cost and actual manufacturing overhead cost.

When we calculate product cost using actual amounts for direct material, direct labor, and manufacturing overhead, the system is called an **actual cost system**. Manufacturing overhead is allocated to production based on actual manufacturing overhead cost and the actual amount of the allocation base. For example, we use actual direct labor to allocate actual manufacturing overhead.

Unfortunately, when we do this, several problems emerge. First, managers must wait until the end of the production period to obtain actual cost information. Another problem is that the manufacturing overhead application rate fluctuates as actual manufacturing overhead and direct labor fluctuate. The manufacturing overhead application rate will be different for each period if it is calculated using these fluctuating actual amounts. This results in identical products having different cost amounts unless they were made during the same production period.

normal cost system A system in which product cost reflects actual direct material cost, actual direct labor cost and estimated manufacturing overhead cost.

predetermined manufacturing overhead application rate A manufacturing overhead allocation rate calculated using estimated annual manufacturing overhead cost and the estimated annual amount for the allocation base.

To eliminate these problems, we use estimated annual amounts. In this approach, called a **normal cost system**, product cost reflects actual direct material cost, actual direct labor cost, and estimated manufacturing overhead costs. We use estimated annual manufacturing overhead cost and the estimated annual amount for the allocation base to calculate a **predetermined manufacturing overhead application rate.**

Manta Power Boats allocates manufacturing overhead using a normal cost system and has selected direct labor cost as its allocation base. Suppose that **Manta's** estimated annual manufacturing overhead is $1 million and estimated annual direct labor cost is $1,250,000. In this case, the predetermined manufacturing overhead application rate is 80 percent ($1,000,000 ÷ $1,250,000) of direct labor cost. To determine the manufacturing overhead cost for the 28-foot Open Fisherman boat for Job Number 97384, we must know the direct labor cost. According to the job cost sheet in Exhibit 3-9, the direct labor cost for this job was $12,000. Using the manufacturing overhead application rate of 80 percent of direct labor cost, we calculate the manufacturing overhead associated with this job as follows: $12,000 × 80% = $9,600.

The total cost for Job Number 97384 is $15,000 for direct material, $12,000 for direct labor, and $9,600 for manufacturing overhead. These costs are summarized in the job cost sheet in Exhibit 3-12.

Manta Power Boats Job Cost Sheet									
Job Number: 97384						Date Promised: 7-11-08			
Customer: Bill Hudik						Date Started: 6-2-08			
Product Description: 28 Open Fisherman									
Direct Material			Direct Labor		Manufacturing Overhead				
Date	Req.#	Amount	Date	Amount	Base	Rate	Amount	Total	
6-2-08	1998	$ 4,850	6-8-08	$ 2,400	DL$	80%	$ 1,920		
6-16-08	2002	330	6-15-08	1,600	DL$	80%	1,280		
6-19-08	2124	4,510	6-22-08	700	DL$	80%	560		
6-23-08	2216	5,310	6-29-08	900	DL$	80%	720		
			7-6-08	4,600	DL$	80%	3,680		
			7-13-08	1,800	DL$	80%	1,440		
Total		$15,000		$12,000			$9,600	$36,600	
					Date Completed: 7-11-08				

Exhibit 3-12 Completed Job Cost Sheet for Job 97384

A normal cost system generally is superior to an actual cost system because it smoothes out the fluctuations in product cost due to monthly differences in manufacturing overhead cost and the allocation base. In addition, because the manufacturing overhead application rate is calculated at the very beginning of the year, there is no need to wait until actual manufacturing overhead cost information is available to determine product cost.

Over or Under Applied Manufacturing Overhead

As you might imagine, the actual amount of manufacturing overhead cost a company incurs will be different than the amount applied to production. In a given month, the actual amount of manufacturing overhead may be more than the amount allocated and in another month it may be less. The hope is that the differences will just about balance out during the year. If the amount allocated to production exceeds the actual manufacturing overhead amount, manufacturing overhead is **over applied**. If the amount applied to production is less than the actual manufacturing overhead amount, manufacturing overhead is **under applied**. The under or over application of manufacturing overhead is monitored during the year but generally no accounting entries are made to dispense with the amount until the end of the year. In most cases, an accounting entry is made at year end to close the manufacturing overhead incurred, and manufacturing overhead applied to cost of goods sold. Because the amount of under or over applied manufacturing overhead is generally relatively small, and most product cost ends up in cost of goods sold by year end, closing the manufacturing overhead accounts to cost of goods sold is adequate for most companies.

over applied manufacturing overhead When more manufacturing overhead cost is applied to production than the actual manufacturing overhead costs incurred.

under applied manufacturing overhead When less manufacturing overhead cost is applied to production than the actual manufacturing overhead costs incurred.

Introduction to Process Costing

Process costing is a method of allocating manufacturing cost to products to determine an average cost per unit. Companies use process costing when units of production are identical, or almost identical, and each unit of production receives the same manufacturing input as the next. Examples of such products are milk, soda, canned goods, breakfast cereal, household cleaners, motor oil, and gasoline.

Under process costing, total manufacturing cost is divided by the number of units produced to arrive at a per-unit cost. For example, if a toothbrush factory makes 2 million toothbrushes and the total production cost is $400,000, then the cost per tooth brush is $0.20, computed as follows:

$$\frac{\text{Total production cost}}{\text{Number of units produced}} = \text{Cost per unit}$$

$$\frac{\$400{,}000}{2{,}000{,}000 \text{ Units produced}} = \$0.20 \text{ per unit}$$

Because each toothbrush is identical to the next, the 20 cents per unit would be an accurate measure of the cost of each unit. This method only works well if all the units produced are the same. That is, if each unit of production is identical to the next, with the exception of minor variations such as color. When units of production differ significantly from one another, job order costing would work better than process costing to determine the cost of individual products.

Companies use per unit costs to determine the cost of ending work-in-process inventories and to determine the cost of units completed and transferred out of the production department. In addition, among other things, per unit costs can help companies set selling prices and to determine the profitability of their products.

Process costing presents some challenges, however, because there are usually some units of product that are only partially completed at the end of the production period. These partially completed units remain in work-in-process inventory. To reflect reasonably accurate cost amounts, process costing calculations must accommodate situations where some units are only partially completed.

Process costing helps managers determine the cost of products. It provides several key items of information:

1. The number of equivalent units of production
2. The cost per equivalent unit of production
3. The cost of the units that remain in ending work-in-process inventory
4. The cost of the completed units

Let's take a closer look at process costing and the complexities related to beginning and ending work-in-process inventories. As an example, assume Ross Atkinson Company manufactures decorative pink flamingos. The process to make the decoration is simple. A worker coats the inside of a mold with liquid plastic, and then, when the plastic has cured and hardened, another worker pulls the mold apart and removes the bird figure. The bird is finished by employees who trim off the excess plastic, paint the eyes and beaks, and add the legs.

Generally acceptable accounting principles allow companies to use the first in first out (FIFO), last in first out (LIFO), or the average cost flow method for inventories. In process costing, the FIFO and average cost flow methods are popular. The method chosen has a significant impact on various process costing calculations. For example, the FIFO cost flow method assumes that the cost of the first units added to inventory is the first cost removed from inventory. Thus, the cost of units must be tracked through the inventory records so the first cost in is the first cost out. As you might expect, this complicates process costing calculations. To keep our example simple, we will assume that Ross Atkinson Company uses the average inventory cost flow method to calculate its inventory amounts.

Equivalent Units

Atkinson must calculate the number of units produced before it can determine a cost per unit. For our example, assume that 10,000 flamingos were completed during the production period and another 1,000 were only partially completed at the end of the period. The 1,000 units still in production comprise the work-in-process inventory. Obviously the 10,000 units completed should be included in the number of units produced, but what about the 1,000 units that were not yet finished? By definition, units in ending work-in-process inventory are incomplete. Thus, it would be inaccurate to assign the same cost per unit to these units as to the completed units. They did, however, require expenditures for direct material, direct labor, and manufacturing overhead to bring them to their present state of completion. So, some cost should be assigned to these units.

The 1,000 flamingos in work-in-process inventory are at various stages of completion. It would be impractical to determine the percentage of completeness for each individual unit of production, so Atkinson calculates an average. In this example, on average, the flamingos in work-in-process inventory are approximately 40 percent complete. Exhibit 3-13 presents a summary of units and completion percentages.

Exhibit 3-13 Decorative Flamingos Example—Units and Completion Percentages

Units to be accounted for:	Units	Percent Complete
Beginning work-in-process	1,070	30%
Units started into production	9,930	
Units to be accounted for	11,000	
Units accounted for:		
Units completed	10,000	100%
Ending work-in-process	1,000	40%
Units accounted for	11,000	

The *units to be accounted for* come from the beginning work-in-process inventory and additional units started into production during the period. Of course, the beginning inventory for the current period is made up of units from the ending inventory of the prior period. Although they provide interesting background information, for our process costing calculations we will not need to use the amounts for beginning work-in-process inventory or units started into production.

Because the flamingos in the ending work-in-process inventory are only 40 percent complete, Atkinson should not include the entire 1,000 units in the number of units produced. The company is interested in the portion of units complete, which we can calculate by multiplying the number of units in ending work-in-process inventory by their average completion percentage. Because the 1,000 flamingos are on average 40 percent complete, they are the equivalent of 400 completed flamingos (1,000 × 40% = 400 equivalent units).

equivalent units The theoretical number of units that would have been completed if all production efforts resulted in only completed units.

In process costing, **equivalent units** are the number of units that would have been completed if all production efforts resulted in only completed units. When the average cost flow method is used, we can calculate the total number of equivalent units by adding the number of completed units to the number of equivalent units in ending work-in-process. That is, we add the number of completed units to the number of raw units in ending work-in-process times their completion percentage. Exhibit 3-14 presents the calculations for the number of equivalent units of production, which totals 10,400 units.

Exhibit 3-14 Decorative Flamingos Example—Equivalent Units of Production

	Number of Raw Units		Percent Complete		Equivalent Units
Units completed	10,000	×	100%	=	10,000
Ending work-in-process	1,000	×	40%	=	400
Total equivalent units					10,400

In actual practice, the percentage of completion for direct material is likely different from that of direct labor or manufacturing overhead. Product costs would be more accurate if we used separate completion percentages for direct material, direct labor, and manufacturing overhead. Manufacturers do, in fact, calculate separate completion percentages to determine equivalent units of production. Such precise calculations complicate process costing, so to keep our first example simple and more understandable, we will use a single percentage to represent the degree of completion for direct material, direct labor, and manufacturing overhead. Then, we will present a second example that demonstrates the calculations when the percentage of completion varies among cost classifications.

Cost Per Equivalent Unit

Now let's examine the cost associated with producing the 10,400 equivalent units in Atkinson's flamingo factory. Assume the production costs are $5,408 as summarized in Exhibit 3-15.

Exhibit 3-15 Decorative Flamingos Example—Summary of Production Cost

Cost of beginning work-in-process	$ 500
Current month's production cost	4,908
Total production cost	$5,408

To compute process costing cost per unit when the average cost flow method is used, we divide the total production cost by the number of equivalent units as Exhibit 3-16 presents.

Exhibit 3-16 Decorative Flamingos Example—Cost per Equivalent Unit

$$\frac{\text{Total production cost}}{\text{Equivalent units}} = \text{Cost per equivalent unit}$$

$$\frac{\$5{,}408}{10{,}400 \text{ equivalent units}} = \$0.52 \text{ per equivalent unit}$$

In our example we see that Atkinson's cost per flamingo is $0.52. Now that we know the cost of each unit produced, we can determine the cost of the ending work-in-process inventory and the cost of the units completed. Barring theft or other losses, units of production are either completed and transferred to finished goods inventory, or they remain in ending work-in-process inventory. Therefore, it stands to reason that production costs are associated either with completed units or with units in ending work-in-process inventory.

Cost of Ending Work-in-Process Inventory

The cost of ending work-in-process inventory is shown as an asset on the balance sheet. To determine this cost, we multiply the number of equivalent units in ending work-in-process inventory by the cost per unit. For Atkinson, 400 equivalent units are in ending work-in-process inventory and the cost per unit is $0.52. Therefore, the cost of the ending work-in-process inventory is $208 as shown in Exhibit 3-17.

Number of Equivalent Units	×	Cost per Unit	=	Cost of Ending Work-in-Process Inventory
400	×	$0.52	=	$208

Exhibit 3-17 Decorative Flamingos Example—Cost of Ending Work-in-Process Inventory

Cost of Completed Units

To determine the cost of completed units, we multiply the number of completed units by the cost per unit. For Atkinson, the 10,000 completed units are multiplied by the $0.52 cost per unit. The cost of the completed units then is $5,200, calculated as shown in Exhibit 3-18.

Number of Units	×	Cost Per Unit	=	Cost of Units Completed and Transferred to Finished Goods Inventory
10,000	×	$0.52	=	$5,200

Exhibit 3-18 Decorative Flamingos Example—Cost of Units Completed

The cost of completed units is important because initially it becomes part of finished goods inventory. Then, as products are sold, the cost of sold units becomes part of cost of goods sold on the income statement.

Assuming no units are spoiled, stolen, or otherwise lost, the cost of production is either transferred to finished goods inventory or remains as the cost of ending work-in-process inventory. Therefore, the total cost of the ending work in process inventory and the cost of the completed units should equal the total manufacturing cost as shown in Exhibit 3-19.

Cost to account for:	Manufacturing Cost
Beginning work-in process	$ 500
Cost added during the period	4,908
Total cost to account for	$5,408
Cost accounted for:	Manufacturing Cost
Ending work-in process	$ 208
Completed units	5,200
Total cost accounted for	$5,408

Exhibit 3-19 Decorative Flamingos Example—Accounting for Manufacturing Cost

As you might imagine, companies must account for all manufacturing costs so the *costs to be accounted for* must equal the *cost accounted for*.

In our decorative flamingo example the total manufacturing cost was $5,408. Part of the total manufacturing cost is transferred to finished goods inventory and the remainder reflects the cost of the units that remain in ending work-in-process inventory as shown in Exhibit 3-20.

Exhibit 3-20 Decorative Flamingos Example—Flow of Manufacturing Cost

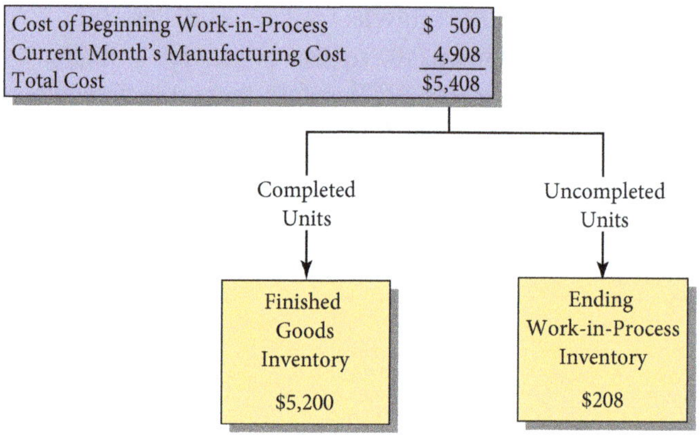

If the company sells 9,000 of the units produced for $1.25 each, its gross profit on the sale would be $6,570 (9,000 units × ($1.25 − $0.52)).

Next we will explore process costing when the completion percentage varies among cost classifications.

Process Costing When the Percentage of Completion Varies

In the example we presented for the decorative flamingos, we assumed the units in ending work-in-process inventory were 40% complete as to direct material, 40% complete as to as to direct labor, and 40% complete as to as to manufacturing overhead. Situations where units in work-in-process inventory are the same percentage complete with respect to all three cost classifications almost never exist. In the prior example we made this assumption so we could present the process costing calculations in a very simple, easy-to-follow manner.

In reality, the completion percentages will differ for the various cost categories in ending work-in-process inventory. For example, in situations where all the direct material is added at the very beginning of the production process, direct material would be 100 percent complete while direct labor and manufacturing overhead might be only be 20 percent complete.

In our next example, we assume that the completion percentage differs for the various cost classifications. As you will see, the basic calculations stay exactly the same as before, but we must repeat each of them for each cost classification.

For this example we will examine another product from the Ross Atkinson Company—the garden gnome.

The Garden Gnome

Background Information and Assumptions

Atkinson manufactures its garden gnomes by pouring liquid plastic into a mold. Once the plastic hardens, the gnomes are removed from the molds and are ready for the direct labor force to begin the work to finish them. The direct labor force grinds off any excess plastic and smoothes the edges and contours of the figures and then they apply paint as the final step in the manufacturing process. To simplify our example, we will assume that the paint is considered indirect material, and therefore, part of manufacturing overhead.

Direct Material

Generally, direct material can be added at any time during the production process. Therefore, the direct material completion percentage for units in ending work-in-process inventory could be any amount. For our example, we will assume that all of the direct material for our garden gnomes is added at the very beginning of the production process. That is, the gnomes are put into production when all the direct material, which consists of liquid plastic, is poured into the mold. In situations when all of the direct material is added at the very beginning of the production process, all units are 100% complete with respect to direct material.

Direct Labor, Manufacturing Overhead, and Conversion Cost

The completion percentage for direct labor may differ from that of manufacturing overhead. However, in many process costing situations companies assume the completion percentage for manufacturing overhead follows hand in hand with the completion percentage for direct labor. This is especially true when companies allocate manufacturing overhead to production based on direct labor. When this happens, we can treat the combined total of direct labor and manufacturing overhead as a single cost category.

The total of direct labor cost and manufacturing overhead cost is called **conversion cost**.

Direct labor + Manufacturing overhead = Conversion cost.

For our garden gnome example, we will assume that the completion percentage for direct labor is equal to that of manufacturing overhead. With this in mind, we are able to simplify the calculations by doing the process costing calculations for conversion cost instead of doing calculations for direct labor and manufacturing overhead individually.

Exhibit 3-21 presents information regarding the number of garden gnomes produced by Atkinson.

Units to be accounted for:	Units	Direct Material Percent Complete	Conversion Cost Percent Complete
Beginning work-in-process	9,000	100%	70%
Units started into production	112,000		
Units to be accounted for	121,000		
Units accounted for:			
Units completed	110,000	100%	100%
Ending work-in-process	11,000	100%	40%
Units accounted for	121,000		

Exhibit 3-21 Garden Gnome Example—Units in Production

Exhibit 3-22 shows Atkinson's direct material, direct labor, and manufacturing overhead cost for their garden gnomes. The exhibit also shows how we combined the direct labor and manufacturing overhead costs to form conversion cost.

Exhibit 3-22 Garden Gnome Example—Cost Information

	Direct Material	Direct Labor	Manufacturing Overhead	Total
Beginning work-in-process	$ 21,440	$ 9,307	$ 6,980	$ 37,727
Cost added during the period	327,040	193,345	145,008	665,393
Total cost to account for	$348,480	$202,652	$151,988	$703,120

	Direct Material	Conversion Cost	Total
Beginning work-in-process	$ 21,440	$ 16,287	$ 37,727
Cost added during the period	327,040	338,353	665,393
Total cost to account for	$348,480	$354,640	$703,120

Equivalent Units of Production

As we said in the flamingo example, we calculate the number of equivalent units by adding the number of completed units to the number of equivalent units in ending work-in-process inventory, which is the number of units in ending work-in-process inventory times their completion percentage. Since the completion percentage differs between direct material and conversion cost, two calculations are necessary. The method for calculating the amount for each classification is the same as the one we presented in the earlier example, but here we are repeating the calculation for each of the two cost classifications. Exhibit 3-23 presents the calculations for the number of equivalent units of production for the garden gnomes.

Exhibit 3-23 Garden Gnome Example—Equivalent Units of Production

	Direct Material					Conversion				
	Number of Raw Units		Percent Complete		Equivalent Units	Number of Raw Units		Percent Complete		Equivalent Units
Units completed	110,000	×	100%	=	110,000	110,000	×	100%	=	110,000
Ending work-in-process	11,000	×	100%	=	11,000	11,000	×	40%	=	4,400
Total equivalent units					121,000					114,400

As Exhibit 3-23 shows, the equivalent units of production are 121,000 for direct material and 114,400 for conversion cost.

Cost Per Equivalent Unit

As mentioned earlier, to compute cost per unit when the average cost flow method is used, we divide the total production cost by the number of equivalent units.

$$\frac{\text{Total production cost}}{\text{Equivalent units}} = \text{Cost per equivalent unit}$$

Since we need the cost per equivalent unit for direct material and for conversion cost, we must do the calculation for each of the cost classifications. Exhibit 3-24 presents the cost per unit calculations for the garden gnomes.

Exhibit 3-24 Garden Gnome Example—Costs per Equivalent Unit

	Direct Material		Conversion		Total
Total cost	$\frac{\$348,480}{121,000}$ = $2.88 Cost per unit		$\frac{\$354,640}{114,400}$ = $3.10 Cost per unit		
Equivalent Units	$2.88 Cost per unit	+	$3.10 Cost per unit	=	$5.98 Total Cost per unit

In our garden gnome example, we see that the cost per unit is $2.88 for direct material and $3.10 for conversion cost. The total cost per gnome is $5.98 ($2.88 + $3.10). With these per unit amounts, we can determine the cost of the ending work-in-process inventory and the cost of the units completed.

Cost of Ending Work-in-Process Inventory

The cost of ending work-in-process inventory is shown as an asset on the balance sheet. As we mentioned earlier, to determine this cost, we multiply the number of equivalent units in ending work-in-process inventory by the cost per unit. By examining the equivalent units calculations in Exhibit 3-23, we see that there are 11,000 equivalent units for direct material and 4,400 equivalent units for conversion cost remaining in work-in-process inventory.

Now that we know the number of equivalent units and the costs per unit ($2.88 for direct material and $3.10 for conversion cost as calculated in Exhibit 3-24), we can calculate the cost of the ending work-in-process inventory as shown in Exhibit 3-25.

Exhibit 3-25 Garden Gnome Example—Cost of Ending Work-in-Process Inventory

Direct Material				Conversion				Total Cost of Ending W.I.P. Inventory
Number of Equivalent Units	Cost per Unit	Cost in Ending W.I.P. Inventory		Number of Equivalent Units	Cost per Unit	Cost in Ending W.I.P Inventory		
11,000	× $2.88 =	$31,680		4,400	× $3.10 =	$13,640		
		$31,680	+			$13,640	=	$45,320

Note that the calculation to determine the cost of the ending work-in-process is the same as the one we presented earlier for the flamingo example, except that we are doing the calculation for each of the two cost classifications and then adding the amounts together to get the total cost of the ending work-in-process inventory.

Cost of Completed Units

To determine the cost of completed units when the weighted average method is used, we multiply the number of completed units by the cost per unit. For Atkinson's garden gnomes, the 110,000 units completed is multiplied by the total cost per unit of $5.98. The cost of the completed units is $657,800 as shown in Exhibit 3-26.

Exhibit 3-26 Garden Gnome Example—Cost of Completed Units

Number of Units	×	Cost per Unit	=	Cost of Units Completed and Transferred to Finished Goods Inventory
110,000	×	$5.98	=	$657,800

The above calculation could be expanded to show the calculations for direct material and conversion cost independently as shown in Exhibit 3-27.

Exhibit 3-27 Garden Gnome Example—Detailed Cost of Completed Units

Direct Material						Conversion						Total Cost of Completed Units
Number Completed Units		Cost per Unit		Cost of Completed Units		Number Completed Units		Cost per Unit		Cost of Completed Units		
110,000	×	$2.88	=	$316,800		110,000	×	$3.10	=	$341,000		
				$316,800	+					$341,000	=	$657,800

Accounting for Total Manufacturing Cost

In our garden gnome example the total manufacturing cost is $703,120. Assuming no units are spoiled, stolen, or otherwise lost, the total cost of the ending work in process inventory and the cost of the completed units should equal the total manufacturing cost. This can be calculated for total cost and also for each of the product cost classifications as shown in Exhibit 3-28.

Exhibit 3-28 Garden Gnome Example—Accounting for Total Manufacturing Cost

Cost to account for:	**Direct Material Cost**	+	**Conversion Cost**	=	**Total Cost**
Beginning work-in process	$ 21,440	+	$ 16,287	=	$ 37,727
Cost added during the period	327,040	+	338,353	=	665,393
Total Cost to account for	$348,480	+	$354,640	=	$703,120
Cost accounted for:	**Direct Material Cost**	+	**Conversion Cost**	=	**Total Cost**
Ending work-in process	$ 31,680	+	$ 13,640	=	$ 45,320
Completed Units	316,800	+	341,000	=	657,800
Total cost accounted for	$348,480	+	$354,640	=	$703,120

As you might imagine, companies must account for all manufacturing costs so the *cost to be accounted for* must equal the *cost accounted for*.

Assuming no units are spoiled, stolen, or otherwise lost, the cost of production is either transferred to finished goods inventory or remains as the cost of ending work-in-process inventory. If no units are lost or spoiled during production, the actual units are completed and physically transferred to finished goods or they remain in ending work-in-process inventory. Part of the total manufacturing cost is transferred to finished goods inventory and the remainder reflects the cost of the units that remain in ending work-in-process inventory as shown in Exhibit 3-29.

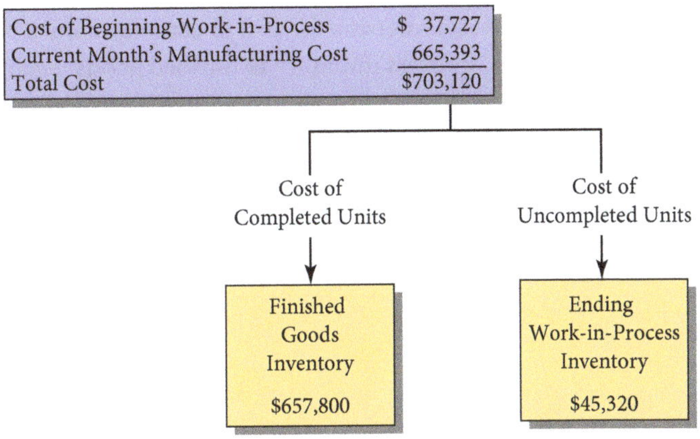

Exhibit 3-29 Garden Gnome Example—Flow of Manufacturing Cost

If the company sells 95,000 of the units produced for $7.00 each, its gross profit on the sale would be $96,900 (95,000 units × ($7.00 − $5.98)).

It is important for managers, to know how much products cost. Otherwise, how could managers determine which products are profitable and which are not? Process costing can help determine the costs of products when units are identical or nearly identical to one another. Whether it is being used to determine the company's cost of goods sold, the cost of inventories shown on the balance sheet, or to help set selling prices and determine the profitability of individual products, accurate product cost information is essential.

Recording Manufacturing Costs

To fully understand the material in this section, it is best if you have a basic understanding of debit and credit accounting procedures including general journal entries and the use of t-accounts. If this is not the case, we suggest that you review the accounting procedures section of any introductory financial accounting text.

This chapter reviews some of the entries included in Chapter 2. The main difference lies in the treatment of manufacturing overhead. In Chapter 2, manufacturing overhead was recorded directly in work-in-process inventory. This chapter demonstrates the entries manufacturers use when actual manufacturing overhead costs are recorded in a *manufacturing overhead* account and then allocated to work in process using the allocation procedures described in this chapter.

After completing your work on this section of the chapter, you should be able to prepare basic manufacturing journal entries including those to record manufacturing overhead allocation.

The recording process for manufacturing costs including overhead allocation involves eight basic types of transactions:

Transaction 1—Purchasing raw materials

Transaction 2—Using direct material to manufacture goods

Transaction 3—Using direct labor to manufacture goods

Transaction 4—Incurring manufacturing overhead costs

Transaction 5—Allocating manufacturing overhead cost to production

Transaction 6—Transferring the cost of completed units or jobs from work-in-process inventory to finished goods inventory

Transaction 7—Selling finished goods

Transaction 8—Closing manufacturing overhead accounts

To record these transactions we will use the following general ledger accounts:

1. *Cash*
2. *Raw materials inventory*
3. *Work-in-process inventory*
4. *Manufacturing overhead incurred*
5. *Manufacturing overhead applied*
6. *Finished goods inventory*
7. *Accumulated depreciation*
8. *Accounts payable*
9. *Sales*
10. *Cost of goods sold*

Remember that debits increase and credits decrease assets, expenses, and losses. Further recall that credits increase and debits decrease liabilities, equity, revenues, and gains. Lastly, recall that debits and credits must equal for each journal entry.

We will now examine a series of journal entries that a manufacturer would make. When it is appropriate and non-repetitive, we will analyze each transaction using the following four steps.

1. Determine if and when a transaction occurred, what accounts were affected, which account balances should increase, which should decrease, and by how much.
2. Determine which accounts we should debit and which we should credit.
3. Make the journal entry.
4. Review the entry to ensure it is in proper form and that the debits equal the credits.

The following transactions are based on information from the **Manta Power Boats** example presented in this chapter. For example, the first entry records the June 7 purchase of raw materials, The remaining entries are based on other transactions that occurred in connection with **Manta's** 28 Open Fisherman, Job Number 97384.

Transaction 1: $660 of raw materials was purchased on account on June 7, 2008. (See Exhibits 3-4 and 3-5.)

1. This transaction took place on June 7, 2008. The transaction affects the raw materials inventory account and the accounts payable account. We should increase the balances of both these accounts by $660.

2. Because raw materials inventory is an asset account we increase it with a debit. Accounts payable is a liability account so we increase it with a credit.

3. The general journal entry:

2008				
Jun.	7	Raw Materials Inventory	660	
		Accounts Payable		660
		To record the purchase of raw materials.		

4. A final check of the entry reveals that we dated it correctly, made the debit part of the entry first, indented the credit account title, and the dollar amount of the debits equals that of the credits. The entry is fine.

Transaction 2: Based on the information from Materials Requisition in Exhibit 3-6, Direct material costing $330 was transferred to production on June 16, 2008.

1. This transaction took place on June 16, 2008. The transaction affects the work-in-process inventory and raw materials inventory accounts. We should increase the balance of the work-in-process inventory account by $330 and decrease the balance of the raw materials inventory account by the same amount.

2. Because work-in-process inventory is an asset account, we increase it with a debit. Raw materials inventory is also an asset account so we decrease it with a credit.

3. The general journal entry:

2008				
Jun.	16	Work-In-Process Inventory	330	
		Raw Materials Inventory		330
		To record the transfer of direct		
		material to production for Job 97384.		

4. A final check of the entry reveals the entry is fine.

Transaction 3: Based on information from the Job Cost Sheet in Exhibit 3-12, we determine that Manta paid $1,600 on June 15 for direct labor for Job Number 97384.

1. This transaction took place on June 15, 2008. Recall that direct labor cost becomes part of work-in process inventory so the transaction affects the work-in-process inventory account. It also affects the cash account. We should increase the balance of the work-in-process inventory account by $1,600 and decrease the balance of the cash account by the same amount.

2. Because work-in-process inventory is an asset account we increase it with a debit. Cash is also an asset account so we decrease it with a credit.

3. The general journal entry:

2008				
Jun.	15	Work-In-Process Inventory	1,600	
		Cash		1,600
		To record wages paid for direct labor		

4. A final check of the entry reveals the entry is fine.

Transaction 4: Let's assume that Manta's actual manufacturing overhead cost for June was $75,000 made up of the following items:

Factory rent paid on June 30	$33,000
Factory utilities paid on June 30	11,000
Indirect labor costs such as factory supervision paid on June 30	23,000
Depreciation on production equipment for June	8,000
Total actual manufacturing overhead cost	$75,000

1. We will assume that these transactions occurred on June 30, 2008. They affect the manufacturing overhead incurred account, the cash account, and the accumulated depreciation account. As you learned in Chapter 2 and in this chapter, manufacturing overhead eventually becomes part of the cost of goods in work-in-process inventory. But when a manufacturer *allocates* cost to production using a manufacturing overhead application rate, the company initially records actual manufacturing overhead costs in an account called *manufacturing overhead cost incurred* or another similar title. In practice, a manufacturer would make separate entries for each of the manufacturing overhead costs incurred, so recording actual manufacturing overhead costs consists of a series of many entries. For each of **Manta's** manufacturing overhead costs we should increase the balance of the manufacturing overhead incurred account. We should decrease the balance of the cash account by $33,000, $11,000, and $23,000 for the paid items. We should increase the balance of the accumulated depreciation account by $8,000 for the depreciation on production equipment.

2. We increase the manufacturing overhead cost incurred account with debits. We decrease the cash account with credits and we increase the accumulated depreciation account with a credit.

3. The general journal entries:

2008				
Jun.	30	Manufacturing Overhead Cost Incurred	33,000	
		Cash		33,000
		To record factory rent for June.		
	30	Manufacturing Overhead Cost Incurred	11,000	
		Cash		11,000
		To record factory utilities for June.		
	30	Manufacturing Overhead Cost Incurred	23,000	
		Cash		23,000
		To record indirect labor for June.		
	30	Manufacturing Overhead Cost Incurred	8,000	
		Accumulated Depreciation		8,000
		To record depreciation on production		
		equipment for June.		

4. A final check of the entries reveals that they are fine.

Transaction 5: According to the Job Cost Sheet in Exhibit 3-12, Manta applied manufacturing overhead cost of $9,600 to Job 97384. To keep our example simple, we will allocate the entire amount in a single entry dated July 11, 2008.

1. The manufacturing overhead cost applied to production becomes part of work-in-process inventory so this transaction affects the work-in-process inventory account. Because **Manta** uses a normal cost system, the transaction also affects an account called *manufacturing overhead applied.* When we allocate manufacturing overhead to production in a normal cost system, we use a different account than the one we used when we recorded the actual manufacturing overhead costs. By using two separate accounts, managers can keep track of both the actual manufacturing overhead costs incurred and the amount applied to production. We should increase the balances of both the work-in-process inventory and the manufacturing overhead applied accounts by $9,600.

2. We increase the work-in-process inventory with a debit and the manufacturing overhead applied account with a credit.

3. The general journal entry:

2008				
Jul.	11	Work-In-Process Inventory	9,600	
		Manufacturing Overhead		
		Applied		9,600
		To record the allocation of		
		manufacturing overhead to production.		

4. A final check of the entry reveals the entry is fine.

Transaction 6: On July 11, 2008, Job Number 97384 was completed and transferred from work-in-process inventory to finished goods. According to the job cost sheet in Exhibit 3-12 the total cost of the job was $36,600.

1. This transaction took place on July 11, 2008. The transaction affects the finished goods inventory account and the work-in-process inventory account. We should increase the balance of the finished goods inventory account by $36,600 and decrease the balance of the work-in-process inventory account by the same amount.
2. We increase the finished goods inventory account with a debit and decrease the work-in-process inventory account with a credit.
3. The general journal entry:

2008				
Jul.	11	Finished Goods Inventory	36,600	
		Work-In-Process Inventory		36,600
		To transfer Job 97384 from work-in-process inventory to finished goods.		

4. A final check of the entry reveals the entry is fine.

Transaction 7: Assume that on July 12, 2008, Manta sold the 28 Open Fisherman boat for cash of $50,000. In other words, Job Number 97384 which cost $36,600 to manufacture was sold for $50,000.

1. This transaction took place on July 12. As we mentioned in Chapter 2, transactions for the sale of goods have two distinct parts. First, this transaction affects the cash and sales accounts, and we should increase the balances of both these accounts by $50,000. Second, the transaction also affects the cost of goods sold and finished goods inventory accounts because the company has delivered merchandise to the customer from its inventory. We should increase the balance of the cost of goods sold account by $36,600, and decrease the balance of the finished goods inventory account by the same amount.
2. We increase the cash account with a debit and the sales account with a credit. We increase the cost of goods sold account with a debit and decrease the finished goods inventory account with a credit.
3. This transaction can be recorded either by making two separate entries or one compound entry. The two separate entries are:

2008				
Jul.	12	Cash	50,000	
		Sales		50,000
		To record the sale of Job 97384 for cash.		
	12	Cost of Goods Sold	36,600	
		Finished Goods Inventory		36,600
		To record the cost of goods sold for Job 97384.		

Or, to accomplish the same changes to the account balances, we can make the following compound entry:

2008				
Jul.	12	Cash	50,000	
		Cost of Goods Sold	36,600	
		Sales		50,000
		Finished Goods Inventory		36,600
		To record the cash sale of Job 97384		
		and cost of goods sold.		

4. A final check of both sets of entries reveals that the dollar amount of the debits equals that of the credits.

Transaction 8: On December 31, Manta closed its under applied manufacturing overhead. Assume that the year end balance in the manufacturing overhead incurred account is $1,091,000 debit and the balance in the manufacturing overhead applied accounts is a credit of $1,072,000. In this case, manufacturing overhead is under applied by $19,000.

1. This transaction took place on December 31, 2008. Recall from our discussion of this topic in the chapter that the two manufacturing overhead accounts are usually closed to cost of goods sold, so the closing process affects the manufacturing overhead incurred account, the manufacturing overhead applied account, and the cost of goods sold account. We should decrease the balance of the manufacturing overhead incurred account by $1,091,000 (making the balance zero) and decrease the balance of the manufacturing overhead applied account by $1,072,000 (making the balance zero). We should increase the balance of the cost of goods sold account by $19,000 (the amount of the under applied manufacturing overhead).

2. The manufacturing overhead incurred account has a debit balance so we decrease it with a credit. The manufacturing overhead applied account has a credit balance so we decrease it with a debit. We increase the cost of goods sold account with a debit.

3. This transaction can recorded in a single entry, or two separate entries. The entries are:

2008				
Dec.	31	Manufacturing Overhead Applied	1,072,000	
		Cost of Goods Sold	19,000	
		Manufacturing Overhead Incurred		1,091,000
		To close manufactured overhead		
		incurred to cost of goods sold.		

Or, to accomplish the same thing, the following two entries can be made:

2008				
Dec.	31	Cost of Goods Sold	1,091,000	
		Manufacturing Overhead Incurred		1,091,000
		To close manufactured overhead		
		incurred to cost of goods sold.		
	31	Manufacturing Overhead Applied	1,072,000	
		Cost of Goods Sold		1,072,000
		To close manufactured overhead		
		applied to cost of goods sold.		

4. A final check reveals that the entries are fine.

Summary

As American manufacturing companies experience increasing competition—both domestic and foreign—accurate costing of the products they produce becomes ever more important. Information about the cost of manufactured product is useful in establishing a selling price for the products, determining cost of goods sold on the income statement, and valuing inventories on the balance sheet.

The cost of a manufactured product is composed of the cost of direct material, direct labor, and manufacturing overhead associated with the units of product produced. Although accounting for the cost of direct material and direct labor is relatively straightforward, determining the amount of manufacturing overhead to include in a unit of manufactured product is more difficult because these costs must be allocated to the units of product produced.

The traditional method of allocating manufacturing overhead to product uses a two stage process. First, we accumulate overhead cost in a single cost pool. Second, we develop a manufacturing overhead application rate based on some allocation base. Using that application rate, we then apply manufacturing overhead to production.

Job order costing is one of two main methods used to accumulate product costs and is most appropriate when units or batches of production are unique. Under this method, cost information is gathered for each production job. The second of the two main product costing methods is called process costing and is most appropriate when units of production are identical and each unit of production receives the same manufacturing input as the next.

Regardless of whether the job order costing method or the process costing method is used, the overall purpose of accumulating product costs is to provide managers with the information they need to make many of the decisions necessary to plan and control their operations.

Work-in-process inventory is debited to record the transfer of direct material to production and to record direct labor cost. Manufacturing overhead incurred is debited to record the actual amount of manufacturing overhead cost incurred. To apply manufacturing overhead to production, work-in-process is debited and manufacturing overhead applied is credited. If the amount applied to production exceeds the actual manufacturing overhead amount, manufacturing overhead is over applied. If the amount applied to production is less than the actual manufacturing overhead amount, manufacturing overhead is under applied. Manufacturers generally make an accounting entry at year end to close the manufacturing overhead incurred and manufacturing overhead applied accounts to cost of goods sold. When products are completed, finished goods is debited and work-in-process is credited for the cost of those products.

Key Terms

actual cost system 86

allocation base 84

conversion cost, ... 34

cost pool 84

equivalent units 90

job cost sheet 78

job order costing 77

labor time ticket 83

materials requisition 81

normal cost system 86

over applied manufacturing overhead 87

predetermined manufacturing overhead application rate 86

process costing 77

purchase order 80

purchase requisition 79

purchasing department 80

receiving report 80

under applied manufacturing overhead 87

Review the Facts

A. What are the general characteristics of products for which process costing would be used?

B. What are the general characteristics of products for which job order costing would be used?

C. What is the purpose of a job cost sheet?

D. Which form is sent to a vendor to order materials and supplies?

E. What is the purpose of a receiving report?

F. What is the difference between a purchase requisition and a materials requisition?

G. What is the difference between an actual cost system and an normal cost system?

H. Which type of form is used to track the amount of labor associated with various jobs?

I. List the four key items of information provided by process costing.

J. Define the term equivalent units as used in process costing.

Apply What You Have Learned

LO 1: Compare Process Costing with Job Order Costing

3-5. Following is a list of several products.

1. _____ Commercial jetliners
2. _____ Hair spray
3. _____ Oil tankers
4. _____ Breakfast cereal
5. _____ Office buildings
6. _____ Aspirin
7. _____ Dog food
8. _____ Advertising posters
9. _____ Custom kitchen cabinets
10. _____ Gasoline

Required:

For each item, indicate whether job order costing (J) or process costing (P) would be the preferred costing method.

LO 4: Calculate and Describe How Overhead Costs Are Allocated to Products

3-6. The Jessie Lynne Company manufactures playground equipment. For 2008, budgeted manufacturing overhead is $240,000. Budgeted direct labor is 30,000 hours at a cost of $384,000. Budgeted machine hours are 12,500.

Required:

a. When production begins on January 1, 2008, would it be a good idea for the managers to determine the cost of the manufacturing overhead associated with each swing set produced, or should managers wait for this information until actual overhead cost amounts are available at the end of the year?

b. If we assume that managers need to know the manufacturing overhead cost associated with the playground equipment as soon as the equipment is manufactured, would actual overhead cost information be available when the first few swing sets are made in January?

c. If we assume managers need to know the overhead cost associated with the playground equipment as soon as the equipment is made, and it is too early in the year to have actual overhead cost information, what overhead cost information must be used to allocate overhead cost to playground equipment produced by the company?

d. Determine the overhead application rates based on the following:

   1. Direct labor hours

   2. Direct labor cost

   3. Machine hours

e. If you were asked to help select an allocation base for the Jessie Lynne Company, which of the three used in (d) would you recommend? Which would you not recommend? Why?

LO 4: Calculate Traditional Overhead Allocation

3-7. The Griswald Company allocates manufacturing overhead to production based on direct labor hours. The following information is available for Griswald:

Estimated manufacturing overhead	$403,200
Actual manufacturing overhead	$378,000
Estimated direct labor hours	21,000
Actual direct labor hours	20,000

Required:

a. Compute Griswald's overhead application rate.

b. Assuming that Griswald's overhead application rate is $19, calculate the amount of overhead that should be allocated to production.

LO 7: Prepare Manufacturing Overhead Journal Entries

3-8. This problem is a continuation of problem 3-7. Prepare journal entries based on the overhead calculations for the Griswald Company.

Required:

Prepare the following journal entries:

1. Record the actual manufacturing overhead. (Use "various accounts" for the credit side of the entry.)
2. Assuming that Griswald's overhead application rate is $19, record the overhead applied to production.
3. Close the over or under application of overhead.

LO 4: Calculate Overhead Allocation

3-9. The Anderson Company allocates manufacturing overhead to production based on machine hours. The following information is available for Anderson:

Estimated manufacturing overhead	$2,000,000
Actual manufacturing overhead	$2,100,000
Estimated machine hours	125,000
Actual machine hours	140,000

Required:

a. Compute Anderson's overhead application rate.

b. Assume that Anderson's overhead application rate is $18. Calculate the amount of overhead that should be applied to production.

LO 7: Prepare Manufacturing Overhead Journal Entries

3-10. This problem is a continuation of problem 3-9. Prepare journal entries based on the overhead calculations for the Anderson Company.

Required:

Prepare the following journal entries:

1. Record the actual manufacturing overhead. (Use "various accounts" for the credit side of the entry.)
2. Assuming that Anderson's overhead application rate is $18, record the overhead applied to production.
3. Close the over or under application of overhead.

LO 4: Calculate Traditional Overhead Allocation

3-11. The Nunez Company allocates manufacturing overhead to production based on cost of direct labor. The following information is available for Nunez:

Estimated manufacturing overhead	$3,500,000
Actual manufacturing overhead	3,485,000
Estimated cost of direct labor	1,750,000
Actual cost of direct labor	1,700,000

Required:

a. Compute the overhead application rate for the Nunez Company.

b. Assume that the overhead application rate for Nunez is 190%. Calculate the amount of overhead that should be applied to production.

LO 4 & 5: Calculate Traditional Overhead Allocation and Determine the Cost of Products Using Job Order Costing

3-12. Slater Industries makes custom optical glass equipment. The company began two jobs during January 2008. There was no beginning inventory. The following information is available:

	Job 7	Job 8
Direct material	$7,250	$3,640
Direct labor	$4,251	$5,125
Direct labor hours	212	234

Slater's estimated manufacturing overhead for 2008 is $110,400, and the company estimates that labor force will work 9,200 direct labor hours. Slater applies overhead to production based on direct labor hours.

Required:

a. Calculate the cost of Job 7.

b. Calculate the cost of Job 8.

LO 4 & 5: Calculate Traditional Overhead Allocation and Determine the Cost of Products Using Job Order Costing

3-13. Willig-Davis Cleaning Equipment began two jobs during March 2008. There was no beginning inventory. The following information is available:

	Job 10	Job 15
Direct material	$14,350	$23,530
Direct labor	$ 7,231	$15,125
Machine hours	124	236

The company estimated manufacturing overhead for 2008 is $307,200, and the company estimates that 4,800 machine hours will be used during the year. Willig-Davis applies overhead to production based on machine hours.

Required:

a. Calculate the cost of Job 10.

b. Calculate the cost of Job 15.

LO 4 & 5: Calculate Overhead Allocation and Determine the Cost of Products Using Job Order Costing—No Beginning Work-In-Process Inventory

3-14. Williams Company began operations in June 2008. During that month, two jobs were started. The following costs were incurred:

	Job 101	Job 202
Direct material	$3,000	$4,000
Direct labor	6,000	7,000

Factory overhead is applied at 60% of direct labor cost. During the month, Job 101 was completed but not sold. Job 202 is yet to be completed.

Required:

a. Calculate the cost of the ending work-in-process inventory as of June 30, 2008.

b. Calculate the cost of the finished goods inventory as of June 30, 2008.

LO 4 & 5: Calculate Overhead Allocation and Determine Product Costs and Inventory Values Using Job Order Costing—No Beginning Work-In-Process Inventory

3-15. Seth Levine Manufacturing began operations in August 2008. During that month, two jobs were started. The following costs were incurred:

	Job 1	Job 2
Direct material	$5,400	$8,900
Direct labor	6,500	9,000

Factory overhead is applied at 50% of direct labor cost. During the month, Job 1 was completed but not sold. Job 2 has not been completed.

Required:

a. Calculate the cost of the ending work-in-process inventory as of August 31, 2008.

b. Calculate the cost of the finished goods inventory as of August 31, 2008.

LO 4 & 5: Calculate Overhead Allocation and Determine Product Costs and Inventory Values Using Job Order Costing—No Beginning Work-In-Process Inventory

3-16. Stacy Sexton Manufacturing began operations in September 2008. During that month, two jobs were started. The following costs were incurred:

	Job A	Job B
Direct material	$2,500	$5,000
Direct labor	7,000	9,500

Factory overhead is applied at 120% of direct labor cost. During the month, Job A was completed but not sold. Job B has not been completed.

Required:

a. Calculate the cost of the ending work-in-process inventory as of September 30, 2008.

b. Calculate the cost of the finished goods inventory as of September 30, 2008.

LO 7: Prepare Manufacturing Journal Entries

3-17. This problem is a continuation of problem 3-16. Prepare journal entries based on the calculations in problem 3-16 for Stacy Sexton Manufacturing.

Required:

Prepare the following journal entries:

1. Record direct material for each job.
2. Record direct labor for each job.
3. Record the application of manufacturing overhead for each job.
4. Record the transfer to finished goods of Job A.

LO 4 & 5: Calculate Overhead Allocation and Determine Product Costs and Inventory Values Using Job Order Costing—No Beginning Work-In-Process Inventory

3-18. Mendelsohn Manufacturing began two jobs during the month of January 2008. There was no beginning inventory. The following costs were incurred:

	Job A	Job B
Direct material	$2,000	$3,000
Direct labor	4,000	5,000

Mendelsohn's estimated manufacturing overhead for 2008 is $117,000, and the estimated direct labor cost is $90,000. Mendelsohn applies overhead to production based on direct labor cost. During the month, Job A was completed but not sold. Job B has not been completed.

Required:

a. Calculate the cost of the ending work-in-process inventory as of January 31, 2008.

b. Calculate the cost of the finished goods inventory as of January 31, 2008.

LO 7: Prepare Manufacturing Journal Entries

3-19. This problem is a continuation of problem 3-18. Prepare journal entries based on the calculations in problem 3-18 for Mendelsohn Manufacturing.

Required:

Prepare the following journal entries:

1. Record direct material for each job.
2. Record direct labor for each job.
3. Record the application of manufacturing overhead for each job.
4. Record the transfer to finished goods of Job A.

LO 4 & 5: Determine Product Costs and Inventory Values Using Job Order Costing—Includes Beginning Work-In-Process Inventory

3-20. Speace Automotive Security converts regular automobiles to armored cars. Each car is custom made to conform to the needs of each individual customer. Modifications may be as minor as the addition of bullet-resistant windows or as extravagant as full armor. The following information is presented for March 2008.

Beginning work-in-process inventory:		
Job 2727	Direct material	$24,000
	Direct labor	9,000
	Manufacturing overhead	5,400

Cost for current month:

	Direct Material	Direct Labor	Manufacturing Overhead
Job 2727	$ 8,000	$4,000	$2,400
Job 2728	11,000	6,000	3,600

Job 2727 was completed and sold in March, and Job 2728 was not complete as of March 31.

Required:

a. What is the cost of the beginning work-in-process inventory for March 2008?

b. What is the cost of the ending work-in-process inventory for March 2008?

c. 1. What is the cost of Job 2727?

2. How would Job 2727 appear on the financial statements?

LO 4 & 5: Challenging—Calculate Overhead Allocation and Determine Product Costs and Inventory Values Using Job Order Costing—Includes Beginning Work-In-Process Inventory

3-21. Crespin Brothers Equipment Company began two jobs during March 2008. At the beginning of March, Job 303 was the only job in work-in-process inventory. There was no finished goods inventory. The cost in beginning work-in-process inventory for Job 303 consisted of $5,450 in direct material cost, $8,825 in direct labor cost, and manufacturing overhead cost of $7,354. The following information is available for costs added during March:

	Job 303	Job 304	Job 305
Direct material	$4,350	$12,650	$11,300
Direct labor	$8,400	$ 8,125	$ 6,750
Direct labor hours	560	520	480

Job 303 was completed and sold during March. Job 304 was completed but has yet to be sold, and Job 305 remains in production.

Crespin's estimated manufacturing overhead for 2008 is $225,000, and the company estimates that the labor force will work 18,000 hours during the year. Crespin applies overhead to production based on direct labor hours.

Required:

a. Calculate the cost of the ending work-in-process inventory as of March 31, 2008.

b. Calculate the cost of the finished goods inventory as of March 31, 2008.

c. Calculate the cost of goods sold for March.

LO 4 & 5: Challenging—Calculate Overhead Allocation and Determine Product Costs and Inventory Values Using Job Order Costing—Includes Beginning Work-In-Process Inventory

3-22. Greenberg and Son Manufacturing began two jobs during July 2008. At the beginning of July, Job 227 was the only job in work-in-process inventory. There was no finished goods inventory. The cost in beginning work-in-process inventory for Job 227 consisted of $1,500 in direct material cost, $2,000 in direct labor cost, and manufacturing overhead cost of $4,500. Total manufacturing overhead for the month was $16,054. The following information is available for costs added during July:

	Job 227	Job 228	Job 229
Direct material	$ 935	$2,850	$1,300
Direct labor	$1,840	$3,225	$1,975
Direct labor hours	184	310	204

Job 227 was completed and sold during July. Job 228 was completed but has yet to be sold, and Job 229 remains in production.

Greenberg's estimated manufacturing overhead for 2008 is $180,000, and the company estimates that the labor force will work 8,000 hours during the year. Greenberg applies overhead to production based on direct labor hours.

Required:

a. Calculate the cost of the ending work-in-process inventory as of July 31, 2008.

b. Calculate the cost of the finished goods inventory as of July 31, 2008.

c. Calculate the cost of goods sold for July.

LO 4 & 5: Challenging—Calculate Overhead Allocation and Determine Product Costs and Inventory Values Using Job Order Costing—Includes Beginning Work-In-Process Inventory

3-23. Baillie Manufacturing began two jobs during May 2008. At the beginning of May, Job 411 was the only job in work-in-process inventory. There was no finished goods inventory. The cost in beginning work-in-process inventory for Job 411 consisted of $4,000 in direct material cost, $6,000 in direct labor cost, and manufacturing overhead cost of $8,000. Total manufacturing overhead for the month was $22,050. The following information is available for costs added during May:

	Job 411	Job 412	Job 413
Direct material	$2,000	$4,000	$6,000
Direct labor	$2,500	$6,500	$8,500
Direct labor hours	225	570	780

Job 411 was completed and sold during May. Job 412 was completed but has yet to be sold, and Job 413 remains in production.

Baillie's estimated manufacturing overhead for 2008 is $277,875, and the company estimates that the labor force will work 19,500 hours during the year. Baillie applies overhead to production based on direct labor hours.

Required:

a. Calculate the cost of the ending work-in-process inventory as of May 31, 2008.

b. Calculate the cost of the finished goods inventory as of May 31, 2008.

c. Calculate the cost of goods sold for May.

LO 4 & 5: Challenging—Calculate Overhead Allocation and Determine Product Costs and Inventory Values Using Job Order Costing—Includes Beginning Work-In-Process Inventory

3-24. LHE Custom Truck Containers makes aluminum truck containers for medium and large trucks. The estimated manufacturing overhead for 2008 is $40,000, and the estimated direct labor cost is $60,000. Manufacturing overhead is applied to production based on direct labor cost.

The following information pertains to truck containers manufactured during February 2008.

Beginning work-in-process inventory:		
Job 101	Direct material	$1,000
	Direct labor	2,000
Job 102	Direct material	750
	Direct labor	1,200
Cost for current month:		
Direct material	Job 101	$ 500
	Job 102	1,100
	Job 103	2,300
Direct labor	Job 101	$ 800
	Job 102	1,300
	Job 103	3,200

Job 101 was completed and sold in February and Job 102 was completed, but has not been sold. Job 103 remains in production.

Required:

a. What is the cost of LHE's beginning work-in-process inventory for February 2008?

b. What is the cost of LHE's ending work-in-process inventory for February 2008?

c. 1. What is the cost of Job 101?

 2. How would Job 101 appear on LHE's financial statements?

d. 1. What is the cost of Job 102?

 2. How would Job 102 appear on LHE's financial statements?

LO 6: Determine the Cost of Products Using Process Costing—No Beginning or Ending Inventory

3-25. Daysi's Specialty Food Company makes canned chili. The following cost information is available for March 2008:

Units produced	25,000 units
Direct material cost	$ 8,000
Direct labor cost	$ 3,000
Manufacturing overhead costs	$ 2,000

There were no beginning or ending inventories.

Required:

a. What is the total production cost for Daysi's Specialty Food Company?

b. What is the cost per unit?

c. If the chili sold for $0.82 per can, what is the gross profit for the company?

LO 6: Determine the Number of Equivalent Units

3-26. The following information relates to the Collins Company for 2009:

	Units	Percent Complete
Units completed	138,000	
Work-in-process at December 31	17,000	50%

Required:

Calculate the number of equivalent units of production.

LO 6: Determine the Number of Equivalent Units

3-27. The following information relates to the Munter Company for June 2008:

	Percent Units	Complete
Units completed	1,850,000	
Work-in-process at June 30	65,000	30%

Required:

Calculate the number of equivalent units of production.

LO 6: Determine the Number of Equivalent Units

3-28. The following information relates to the Holder Company for July 2008:

	Percent Units	Complete
Units completed	72,000	
Work-in-process at July 3 1	3,000	20%

Required:

Calculate the number of equivalent units of production.

LO 6: Determine the Number of Equivalent Units

3-29. The following information relates to the Mayber Company for May 2008:

	Percent Units	Complete
Work-in-process at May 1	5,000	45%
Units started into production	77,000	
Units completed	70,000	
Work-in-process at May 31	12,000	35%

Required:

Calculate the number of equivalent units of production.

LO 6: Determine the Number of Equivalent Units

3-30. The following information relates to the Strayform Company for August 2008:

	Percent Units	Complete
Work-in-process at August 1	7,000	95%
Units started into production	87,000	
Units completed	87,500	
Work-in-process at August 31	6,500	25%

Required:

Calculate the number of equivalent units of production.

LO 6: Determine the Number of Equivalent Units

3-31. The following information relates to the Golden Company for February 2009:

	Percent Units	Complete
Work-in-process at February 1	22,500	80%
Units started into production	185,000	
Units completed	193,000	
Work-in-process at February 28	14,500	25%

Required:

Calculate the number of equivalent units of production.

LO 6: Determine the Cost of Products Using Process Costing With Beginning Inventory

3-32. The following information relates to the Smithfield Company for July 2008:

	Units	Percent Complete
Units completed in July	231,000	
Work-in-process at July 31	8,500	40%
Cost information:		
Cost of the beginning work-in-process		$ 7,020
Current month's production cost		$166,436

Required:

a. Calculate the number of equivalent units of production.

b. Calculate the cost per equivalent unit of production.

c. Calculate the cost of the ending work-in-process inventory.

d. Calculate the cost of the completed units.

LO 6: Determine the Cost of Products Using Process Costing With Beginning Inventory

3-33. The following information relates to the Richard Renick Company for 2009:

	Units	Percent Complete
Units completed in 2009	390,000	
Work-in-process at December 31	72,000	20%
Cost information:		
Cost of the beginning work-in-process		$ 14,280
Current year's production cost		$248,580

Required:

a. Calculate the number of equivalent units of production.

b. Calculate the cost per equivalent unit of production.

c. Calculate the cost of the ending work-in-process inventory.

d. Calculate the cost of the completed units.

LO 6: Determine the Cost of Products Using Process Costing With Beginning Inventory

3-34. The following information relates to the Robert Lewis Manufacturing Company for 2008:

	Units	Percent Complete
Units completed in 2008	1,290,000	
Work-in-process at December 31	130,000	70%
Cost information:		
Cost of the beginning work-in-process		$ 40,200
Current year's production cost		$1,768,910

Required:

a. Calculate the number of equivalent units of production.

b. Calculate the cost per equivalent unit of production.

c. Calculate the cost of the ending work-in-process inventory.

d. Calculate the cost of the completed units.

LO 6: Determine the Cost of Products Using Process Costing With Beginning Inventory

3-35. The cost of the work-in-process inventory at January 1 for Ralph Robinson Manufacturing was $7,420. An additional 130,000 units were started into production during the year. The cost of direct material, direct labor, and manufacturing overhead added during the year amounted to $280,680. The units completed and transferred to finished goods totaled 125,000. The ending work-in-process inventory consisted of 15,000 units which were 60% complete.

Required:

a. Calculate the number of equivalent units of production.

b. Calculate the cost per equivalent unit of production.

c. Calculate the cost of the ending work-in-process inventory.

d. Calculate the cost of the completed units.

LO 6: Determine the Cost of Products Using Process Costing with Beginning Inventory

3-36. The cost of the work-in-process inventory at January 1 for Jim Mays Manufacturing was $61,875. An additional 150,000 units were started into production during the year. The cost of direct material, direct labor, and manufacturing overhead added during the year amounted to $1,872,855. The units completed and transferred to finished goods totaled 145,000. The ending work-in-process inventory consisted of 16,000 units which were 65% complete.

Required:

a. Calculate the number of equivalent units of production.

b. Calculate the cost per equivalent unit of production.

c. Calculate the cost of the ending work-in-process inventory.

d. Calculate the cost of the completed units.

LO 6 & 7: Determine the Cost of Products Using Process Costing with Beginning Inventory and Prepare Manufacturing Journal Entries

3-37. The cost of the work-in-process inventory at January 1 for Hanamura Manufacturing was $119,805. An additional 750,000 units were started into production during the year. The cost of direct material, direct labor, and manufacturing overhead added during the year amounted to $2,627,820. The units completed and transferred to finished goods totaled 790,000. The ending work-in-process inventory consisted of 72,500 units which were 25% complete.

Required:

a. Calculate the number of equivalent units of production.

b. Calculate the cost per equivalent unit of production.

c. Calculate the cost of the ending work-in-process inventory.

d. Calculate the cost of the completed units.

e. Prepare a journal entry to transfer the cost of completed goods from work-in-process.

LO 6 & 7: Determine the Cost of Products Using Process Costing and Prepare Manufacturing Journal Entries

3-38. The following information relates to the Zhang Manufacturing Company for 2008:

	Units	Cost
Work-in-process at January 1	18,500	$ 35,668
Units started into production	190,000	
Units completed in 2008	187,000	
Work-in-process at December 31	21,500	
Current production cost		$1,873,052

The beginning work-in-process inventory is 20% complete and the ending work-in-process inventory is 55% complete.

Required:

a. Calculate the number of equivalent units of production.

b. Calculate the cost per equivalent unit of production.

c. Calculate the cost of the ending work-in-process inventory.

d. Calculate the cost of the completed units.

e. Prepare a journal entry to transfer the cost of completed goods from work-in-process.

LO 6 & 7: Determine the Cost of Products Using Process Costing and Prepare Manufacturing Journal Entries

3-39. The following information relates to the Mathias Manufacturing Company for 2008:

	Units	Cost
Work-in-process at January 1	77,000	$ 107,415
Units started into production	602,500	
Units completed in 2008	587,500	
Work-in-process at December 31	92,000	
Current production cost		$2,979,922

The beginning work-in-process inventory is 30% complete and the ending work-in-process inventory is 80% complete.

Required:

a. Calculate the number of equivalent units of production.

b. Calculate the cost per equivalent unit of production.

c. Calculate the cost of the ending work-in-process inventory.

d. Calculate the cost of the completed units.

e. Prepare a journal entry to transfer the cost of completed goods from work-in-process.

LO 6 & 7: Determine the Cost of Products Using Process Costing and Prepare Manufacturing Journal Entries

3-40. The following information relates to the Heromi Manufacturing Company for 2008:

	Units	Cost
Work-in-process at January 1	13,000	$ 4,368
Units started into production	83,500	
Work-in-process at December 31	7,500	
Units completed in 2008	89,000	
Current production cost		$37,262

The beginning work-in-process inventory is 70% complete and the ending work-in-process inventory is 20% complete.

Required:

a. Calculate the number of equivalent units of production.

b. Calculate the cost per equivalent unit of production.

c. Calculate the cost of the ending work-in-process inventory.

d. Calculate the cost of the completed units.

e. Prepare a journal entry to transfer the cost of completed goods from work-in-process.

LO 6: Determine the Cost of Products Using Process Costing With Beginning Inventory

3-41. Dunn Electronic Manufacturing Company makes low-cost calculators. The following information is available for January 2008:

	Units	Percent Complete	Cost
Beginning work-in-process inventory	700	40%	$224
Ending work-in-process inventory	900	60%	?
Units completed	12,000 calculators		
Manufacturing cost for January 2008 is $10,659.			

Required:

a. What is the number of equivalent units of production for January 2008?

b. What is the cost per equivalent unit?

c. What is the cost of the 900 calculators in the ending work-in-process?

d. What is the cost of the calculators that were completed during January?

e. If 11,000 of the completed calculators were sold for $1.12 each, what is the gross profit for the Dunn Electronic Manufacturing Company?

f. 1. Do you think there is a benefit for Dunn's managers to know the cost of the calculators that are in ending work-in-process inventory? Explain.

2. Where would the cost of the ending inventory appear on the financial statements?

3. Do you think there is a benefit for Dunn's managers to know the cost of the calculators completed during January? Explain.

4. Where would the cost of the 11,000 sold calculators be found on the financial statements?

5. Where would the cost of the calculators that were completed, but not yet sold be found on the financial statements?

LO 6: Determine the Cost of Products Using Process Costing With Beginning Inventory

3-42. The following information is for Suzanne's Volleyball Manufacturing Company for February 2008:

	Units	Percent Complete	Cost
Beginning work-in-process inventory	2,400	80%	$2,304
Ending work-in-process inventory	3,200	50%	

64,000 Volleyballs were completed in February. Manufacturing cost for February is $86,256.

Required:

a. What is the number of equivalent units of production for February?

b. What is the cost per equivalent unit for February?

c. What is the cost of the 3,200 volleyballs in the ending work-in-process inventory for February?

d. What is the cost of the volleyballs that were completed during February?

e. If 50,000 of the completed volleyballs were sold for $1.80 each, what is the gross profit for Suzanne's Volleyball Manufacturing Company?

LO 6: Determine the Cost of Products Using Process Costing No Beginning Inventory

3-43. Valentine's Manufacturing makes candy. During 2009, the company's first year of operations, the company completed 200,000 boxes of candy and incurred direct material cost of $160,800, direct labor cost of $40,200, and manufacturing overhead cost of $60,300. There were 2,000 boxes of candy that were 50% complete in the production process at the end of the year.

Required:

a. What is the number of equivalent units of production for 2009?

b. What is the cost per equivalent unit of production for 2009?

c. What is the cost of the 2009 ending work-in-process inventory?

d. What is the cost of the boxes of candy that were completed in 2009?

LO 6: Determine the Number of Equivalent Units

3-44. The following information relates to the Olympic Manufacturing Company for 2007:

	Units	Direct Material Percent Complete	Conversion Cost Percent Complete
Units completed	150,000		
Work-in-process at December 31	20,000	100%	20%

Required:

Calculate the number of equivalent units of production for direct material and for conversion cost.

LO 6: Determine the Number of Equivalent Units

3-45. The following information relates to the Richmond Company for 2007:

	Units	Direct Material Percent Complete	Conversion Cost Percent Complete
Units completed	140,000		
Work-in-process at December 31	30,000	90%	30%

Required:

Calculate the number of equivalent units of production for direct material and for conversion cost.

LO 6: Determine the Number of Equivalent Units

3-46. The following information relates to the Florence Company for May 2008:

	Units	Direct Material Percent Complete	Conversion Cost Percent Complete
Work-in-process at May 1	6,000	100%	45%
Units started into production	70,000		
Units completed	60,000		
Work-in-process at May 31	16,000	100%	35%

Required:

Calculate the number of equivalent units of production for direct material and for conversion cost.

LO 6: Determine the Number of Equivalent Units

3-47. The following information relates to the Gem Company for June 2008:

	Units	Direct Material Percent Complete	Conversion Cost Percent Complete
Work-in-process at June 1	16,000	90%	45%
Units started into production	170,000		
Units completed	160,000		
Work-in-process at June 30	26,000	80%	35%

Required:

Calculate the number of equivalent units of production for direct material and for conversion cost.

LO 6: Determine the Cost of Products Using Process Costing With Beginning Inventory
3-48. The following information relates to the Smith Company for July 2008:

	Units	Direct Material Percent Complete	Conversion Cost Percent Complete
Units completed in July	227,000		
Work-in-process at July 31	26,000	100%	30%
Cost information:			
		Direct Material	**Conversion Cost**
Cost of the beginning work-in-process		$ 29,040	$ 10,627
Current month's production cost		$358,050	$451,929

Required:

a. Calculate the number of equivalent units of production.

b. Calculate the cost per equivalent unit of production.

c. Calculate the cost of the ending work-in-process inventory.

d. Calculate the cost of the completed units.

LO 6: Determine the Cost of Products Using Process Costing With Beginning Inventory
3-49. The following information relates to the Field Company for August 2008:

	Units	Direct Material Percent Complete	Conversion Cost Percent Complete
Units completed in August	128,500		
Work-in-process at August 31	10,500	100%	60%
Cost information:			
		Direct Material	**Conversion Cost**
Cost of the beginning work-in-process		$ 78,340	$ 46,622
Current month's production cost		$786,240	$1,057,390

Required:

a. Calculate the number of equivalent units of production.

b. Calculate the cost per equivalent unit of production.

c. Calculate the cost of the ending work-in-process inventory.

d. Calculate the cost of the completed units.

LO 6: Determine the Cost of Products Using Process Costing With Beginning Inventory

3-50. The cost of the work-in-process inventory at January 1 for Ralph Manufacturing was $17,220 for direct material and $35,800 for conversion cost. An additional 130,000 units were started into production during the year. Direct material cost of $232,700, direct labor cost of $280,042 and manufacturing overhead cost of $206,030 was added during the year. The units completed and transferred to finished goods totaled 125,000. All direct material is added at the beginning of production. The ending work-in-process inventory consisted of 17,000 units which were 60% complete as to conversion cost.

Required:

a. Calculate the number of equivalent units of production.

b. Calculate the cost per equivalent unit of production.

c. Calculate the cost of the ending work-in-process inventory.

d. Calculate the cost of the completed units.

LO 6: Determine the Cost of Products Using Process Costing With Beginning Inventory

3-51. The cost of the work-in-process inventory at January 1 for Robinson Manufacturing was $29,280 for direct material and $7,923 for conversion cost. An additional 192,000 units were started into production during the year. Direct material cost of $268,800, direct labor cost of $120,400, and manufacturing overhead cost of $101,192 was added during the year. The units completed and transferred to finished goods totaled 195,000. All direct material is added at the beginning of the manufacturing process. The ending work-in-process inventory consisted of 21,000 units which were 65% complete as to conversion cost.

Required:

a. Calculate the number of equivalent units of production.

b. Calculate the cost per equivalent unit of production.

c. Calculate the cost of the ending work-in-process inventory.

d. Calculate the cost of the completed units.

LO 6: Determine the Cost of Products Using Process Costing

3-52. The following information relates to the Zhang Manufacturing Company for 2007:

	Units	Direct Material Cost	Conversion Cost
Work-in-process at January 1	18,500	$3,090	$ 6,387
Units started into production	190,500		
Units completed in 2007	187,000		
Work-in-process at December 31	22,000		
Current production cost		$53,340	$127,010

All direct material is added at the beginning of the production process. With respect to conversion cost, the beginning work-in-process inventory was 20% complete and the ending work-in-process inventory is 55% complete.

Required:

a. Calculate the number of equivalent units of production.

b. Calculate the cost per equivalent unit of production.

c. Calculate the cost of the ending work-in-process inventory.

d. Calculate the cost of the completed units.

LO 6: Determine the Cost of Products Using Process Costing

3-53. The following information relates to the Jessie Lynne Manufacturing Company for 2007:

	Units	Direct Material Cost	Conversion Cost
Work-in-process at January 1	1,200	$ 1,059.00	$ 647.60
Units started into production	13,500		
Units completed in 2007	12,200		
Work-in-process at December 31	2,500		
Current production cost		$10,260.00	$12,558.40

All direct material is added at the beginning of the production process. With respect to conversion cost, the beginning work-in-process inventory is 70% complete and the ending work-in-process inventory is 80% complete.

Required:

a. Calculate the number of equivalent units of production.

b. Calculate the cost per equivalent unit of production.

c. Calculate the cost of the ending work-in-process inventory.

d. Calculate the cost of the completed units.

LO 6: Determine the Cost of Products Using Process Costing With Beginning Inventory

3-54. Canton Electronic Manufacturing Company makes low-cost calculators. All direct material is added at the very beginning of the production process. The following information is available for January 2008:

	Units	Conversion Cost Percent Complete	Total Cost
Beginning work-in-process	7,000	45%	$977.50
Ending work-in-process	9,000	60%	?
Units completed	120,000 calculators		

The beginning inventory cost included $718.00 for direct material, $155.70 for direct labor, and $103.80 for manufacturing overhead. Manufacturing cost for January 2008 is $14,762.00 for direct material, $11,882.70 for direct labor and $7,921.80 for manufacturing overhead.

Required:

a. What is the number of equivalent units of production for January 2008?

b. What is the cost per equivalent unit?

c. What is the cost of the 9,000 calculators in the ending work-in-process?

d. What is the cost of the calculators that were completed during January?

e. If 110,000 of the completed calculators were sold for $1.12 each, what is the gross profit for the Canton Electronic Manufacturing Company?

f. 1. Do you think there is a benefit for Canton's managers to know the cost of the calculators that are in ending work-in-process inventory? Explain.

2. Where would the cost of the ending inventory appear on the financial statements?

3. Do you think there is a benefit for Canton's managers to know the cost of the calculators completed during January? Explain.

4. Where would the cost of the 110,000 sold calculators be found on the financial statements?

5. Where would the cost of the calculators that were completed, but not yet sold be found on the financial statements?

LO 6: Determine the Cost of Products Using Process Costing With Beginning Inventory

3-55. The following information is for Suzanne's Basketball Manufacturing Company for February 2008:

	Units	Direct Material Percent Complete	Conversion Cost Percent Complete
Beginning work-in-process	2,400	90%	70%
Ending work-in-process	3,200	80%	30%

The cost of the beginning inventory was $864.80 for direct material and $1,098.72 for conversion cost. 64,000 Basketballs were completed in February. Manufacturing cost for February is $29,752.80 for direct material and $56,066.08 for conversion cost.

Required:

a. What is the number of equivalent units of production for February?

b. What is the cost per equivalent unit for February?

c. What is the cost of the 3,200 basketballs in the ending work-in-process inventory for February?

d. What is the cost of the basketballs that were completed during February?

e. If 50,000 of the completed basketballs were sold for $1.80 each, what is the gross profit for Suzanne's Basketball Manufacturing Company?

LO 6: Determine the Cost of Products Using Process Costing With Beginning Inventory

3-56. The following information is for Sherry's Manufacturing Company for February 2008:

	Units	Direct Material Percent Complete	Conversion Cost Percent Complete
Beginning work-in-process	6,800	80%	65%
Ending work-in-process	3,800	90%	70%

The cost of the beginning inventory was $2,261.44 for direct material and $3,777.88 for conversion cost. 76,500 units were completed in February. Manufacturing cost for February is $44,092.16 for direct material and $74,590.52 for conversion cost.

Required:

a. What is the number of equivalent units of production for February?

b. What is the cost per equivalent unit for February?

c. What is the cost of the 3,800 units in the ending work-in-process inventory for February?

d. What is the cost of the units that were completed during February?

e. If 50,000 of the completed units were sold for $2.80 each, what is the gross profit for Sherry's Manufacturing Company?

LO 6: Determine the Cost of Products Using Process Costing With Beginning Inventory

3-57. The following information is for Steve's Manufacturing Company for February 2008:

	Units	Direct Material Percent Complete	Conversion Cost Percent Complete
Beginning work-in-process	10,000	95%	70%
Ending work-in-process	15,000	90%	60%

The cost of the beginning inventory was $8,914 for direct material and $11,156 for conversion cost. 95,000 units were completed in February. Manufacturing cost for February is $97,416 for direct material and $171,884 for conversion cost.

Required:

a. What is the number of equivalent units of production for February?

b. What is the cost per equivalent unit for February?

c. What is the cost of the 15,000 units in the ending work-in-process inventory for February?

d. What is the cost of the units that were completed during February?

e. If 80,000 of the completed units were sold for $4.24 each, what is the gross profit for Steve's Manufacturing Company?

4

Cost Allocation and Activity Based Costing

Jim Smith is a product manager for the Buck Slade Company, a manufacturer of cutting blades used in knives, scissors and industrial machinery. In recent years, profits at Slade have begun to decline and Jim is trying to improve the situation. Jim's plan is to determine which of the company's products are the most profitable, and then focus the company's sales efforts on these profitable products. He may also discontinue some of the less profitable products to preserve company resources for those that are more lucrative. But how can Jim determine which products to promote and which to discontinue? This is where the company's management accounting system comes into play. Jim calls upon the company's cost accounting department to provide revenue and cost information for the various products the company manufactures. He is hoping that he will be able to use the information to make the decisions that will curb the declining profit trend.

After reviewing the revenue and cost information, Jim notices that the reports generally indicate that complex, low volume products are much more profitable than the simple, high volume ones. Jim thinks this is because Slade charges a premium price for its complex products such as their complex cutters. Other manufacturers are not as competitive with these products, so customers seldom complain about the higher prices Slade charges. In fact, the company recently raised its selling price on complex cutters by 10 percent and, although some customers voiced their displeasure about the price hike, not one switched to another supplier. On the other hand, simple, high volume products, such as Slade's simple trimming blades, are very price competitive. It seems that there are many other manufacturers making this type of product and price competition is fierce. In fact, Slade must sell many of its simple, high volume products at cost or even below cost just to be competitive in the marketplace. Exhibit 4-1 shows revenue and cost information for a typical complex, low volume products and a simple, high volume product.

Slade uses job-order costing, which we demonstrated in Chapter 3, to cost its products. The company's cost accounting department traces direct material and direct labor costs directly to individual products while manufacturing overhead is allocated to various products based on direct labor hours.

Exhibit 4-1 Revenue and Cost Report for Representative Complex, Low Volume and Simple, High Volume Products

	Complex Cutters		Simple Trimming Blades	
Sales		$19,500		$53,000
Cost:				
Direct material cost	$4,500		$10,000	
Direct labor cost	1,200		6,000	
Manufacturing overhead cost	8,000		40,000	
Total cost		(13,700)		(56,000)
Gross profit		$ 5,800		$ (3,000)

Assuming that Exhibit 4-1 is representative of the profitability of the company's simple and complex products, what does the information suggest? Based on the information Jim received from his cost accounting department, what should Jim do to improve company profits? Well, the information clearly indicates that Jim should focus the company's efforts on shifting production and sales toward complex, low volume products and that he should probably discontinue producing and selling simple, high volume products. Management accounting information seems to make Jim's decisions easier because it is, in effect, telling Jim what to do. But, is it telling him the right thing to do?

As we learned in Chapter 3, direct material and direct labor cost can be traced directly to individual products or batches of products. Manufacturing overhead, however, is another matter. Because manufacturing overhead is an indirect cost and benefits more than one product, it is difficult if not impossible to determine the true overhead cost associated with individual products produced. For example, it is easy for ***Wilson Sporting Goods*** to trace the direct material and direct labor costs to a batch of its basketballs, but it is nearly impossible for the company to trace manufacturing overhead costs such as the cost of factory insurance, electricity, and depreciation of production machinery to individual batches of production.

The resources included in manufacturing overhead are an important component of manufacturing product. Even though their cost cannot easily be traced to individual units of production, manufacturing overhead resources are all necessary to produce products, and therefore, their cost should be included in the cost of products produced. The problem is, however, that because the cost of manufacturing overhead resources and activities cannot be traced directly to the units of product produced, their cost must be allocated to production.

Consider the cost of factory lighting, for example. As units of product make their way through the production process, the factory lights are illuminated and lighting cost is incurred. Without light, it would be impossible for workers to manufacture the products, so it follows that a certain amount of the cost for lighting should be included in the cost of each unit of product manufactured. However, when the power company sends the bill at the end of the month, there is no breakdown as to how much lighting cost is to be included in each unit of product produced. The bill only shows the total cost of electricity used, say $10,000. The manufacturer has to determine how to allocate some portion of the lighting cost to each unit produced. **Manufacturing overhead allocation** is a process of assigning or allotting an amount of manufacturing overhead cost to each unit of product produced based on some reasonable basis of distribution.

manufacturing overhead allocation The process of assigning or allotting an amount of manufacturing overhead cost to each unit of product produced based on some reasonable basis of distribution.

Learning Objectives

After completing your work on this chapter, you should be able to do the following:

1. Describe how manufacturing overhead costs are traditionally allocated to products and how they are allocated using activity based costing.
2. Define the term cost driver.
3. Calculate product costs using activity based costing and traditional manufacturing overhead allocation.
4. Compare and contrast activity based costing with traditional manufacturing overhead allocation with respect to product cost accuracy, cost control, and the cost and complexity of the cost systems.

As we discussed in the previous chapter, when we allocate manufacturing overhead using actual amounts for direct material, direct labor, and manufacturing overhead, the system is called an **actual cost system**. Unfortunately, using the actual amount of manufacturing overhead and the actual amount of the allocation base to allocate manufacturing overhead has several problems. First, managers must wait until the end of the accounting period to receive actual cost information. Another problem with using actual amounts to allocate manufacturing overhead is that the manufacturing overhead application rate would fluctuate as actual manufacturing overhead and the actual activity base fluctuated. The manufacturing overhead application rate will be different for each period if it is calculated using these fluctuating actual amounts. This will result in identical products having different cost amounts unless they were made during the same accounting periods.

actual cost system A system in which product cost reflects actual direct material cost, actual direct labor cost and actual manufacturing overhead cost.

As we mentioned in Chapter 3, to eliminate these problems we use estimated annual amounts. In this approach, called a **normal cost system**, product cost reflects actual direct material cost, actual direct labor cost, and estimated manufacturing overhead costs. Estimated annual manufacturing overhead cost and the annual estimated amount for the allocation base are used to calculate a **predetermined manufacturing overhead application rate**.

normal cost system A system in which product cost reflects actual direct material cost, actual direct labor cost and estimated manufacturing overhead cost.

predetermined manufacturing overhead application rate An overhead allocation rate calculated using estimated annual manufacturing overhead cost and an annual estimated amount for the allocation base.

Traditional Manufacturing Overhead Allocation

Manufacturing overhead allocation has traditionally been a two-stage process. The first stage is to gather manufacturing overhead cost into a **cost pool**. A cost pool is an accumulation of the costs associated with a specific cost object. Traditionally, the cost of manufacturing overhead has been gathered into one or very few large cost pools, including all manufacturing costs except for direct material and direct labor.

cost pool An accumulation of the costs associated with a specific cost object.

The second stage is to assign the manufacturing overhead cost gathered in the pool to units of product manufactured. Manufacturers attempt to allocate the amount of manufacturing overhead cost that corresponds to the overhead resources consumed to make the product. For example, if $1,000 of manufacturing overhead resources were consumed to manufacture a pool table, then, ideally $1,000 should be allocated to that pool table and included on the pool table's cost reports as shown in Exhibit 4-2.

Because it is impractical if not impossible for managers to know the exact cost of the manufacturing overhead resources used to make each unit of product, an equitable basis for cost allocation must be determined.

Exhibit 4-2 Ideal Allocation of Manufacturing Overhead Cost

Manufacturing Overhead
Resources Used
To Make a Pool Table:

- Factory Supplies
- Factory Supervision
- Factory Lighting
- Production Equipment
- Materials Handling
- Setting-up Production Equipment
- Product Quality Testing

- Total $1,000

→

Manufacturing Overhead
Allocated to the Pool Table

- Cost of Factory Supplies Used
- Cost of Factory Supervision Used
- Cost of Factory Lighting Used
- Cost of Production Equipment Used
- Cost of Materials Handling Used
- Cost of Setting-up Production Equipment
- Cost of Product Quality Testing Done

- Total $1,000

cost allocation base An item, activity, or cost associated with cost objects that is used to proportionately distribute cost to each cost object.

A **cost allocation base** is an item, activity, or cost associated with cost objects that is used to proportionately distribute costs to those cost objects. The traditional approach to allocating manufacturing overhead costs to units produced is to identify something that can be used as an indicator of the relative amounts of indirect factory resources used to make each unit of product. That is, to find some other item, activity, or cost that is correlated to the consumption of manufacturing overhead, and then use it as the allocation base. Direct labor hours, direct labor cost, and machine hours are common traditional manufacturing overhead allocation bases. Traditionally, companies have used one or very few overhead allocation bases to allocate overhead.

It seems logical that a larger unit of production would require the use of more factory resources than a smaller unit of production, which may mean more direct labor, direct materials, machine time, or some combination of these. The idea behind using an allocation base such as direct labor hours is that if a unit of product requires a large amount of direct labor hours, it follows that its manufacture would probably use a large amount of overhead resources. So the relative amount of direct labor hours may be a good indication of the relative amount of manufacturing overhead resources used to make the product. If it took a lot of direct labor hours to make a particular product, it probably took a lot of manufacturing overhead resources too.

As an example, we will take a closer look at the Buck Slade Company and examine how the company's cost accounting department determined the manufacturing overhead costs presented in Exhibit 4-1. Slade uses direct labor hours as the allocation base for manufacturing overhead. Assume Slade estimates that its annual manufacturing overhead will be $1million and direct labor hours are expected to total 10,000 hours for the year. Slade can express the relationship between these two items by dividing the $1 million estimated annual manufacturing overhead by the 10,000 estimated direct labor hours. Notice that we are dividing the cost we wish to allocate (the $1 million manufacturing overhead) by the allocation base (the 10,000 direct labor hours). The result is the company's manufacturing overhead application rate. Slade will allocate manufacturing overhead cost to the units of manufactured product at a rate of $100 per direct labor dollar as follows:

$$\frac{\text{Estimated annual manufacturing overhead cost}}{\text{Estimated annual allocation base}} = \text{Manufacturing overhead application rate}$$

$$\frac{\$1{,}000{,}000}{10{,}000 \text{ direct labor hours}} = \$100 \text{ per direct labor hour}$$

What this means is that for every direct labor hour it takes to manufacture a product, $100 of manufacturing overhead cost will be added to the product's cost. A product that requires little direct labor will receive a small allocation of manufacturing overhead. The total direct material cost, direct labor cost, and the total allocated manufacturing overhead cost are then added together to determine the cost of the manufactured product.

As an example, let's calculate the cost of the two Buck Slade products mentioned earlier in the chapter. Assume that it takes 80 direct labor hours to make the 15,000 complex cutters and 400 direct labor hours to make the 100,000 simple trimming blades. Based on the fact that the complex cutters required a total of 80 direct labor hours, the manufacturing overhead allocation would be $8,000, calculated as follows:

Direct labor hours	×	Manufacturing overhead application rate	=	Total manufacturing overhead allocation
80	×	$100	=	$8,000

The 100,000 simple trimming blades required 400 direct labor hours so the manufacturing overhead allocation for them would be $40,000, calculated as follows:

Direct labor hours	×	Manufacturing overhead application rate	=	Total manufacturing overhead allocation
400	×	$100	=	$40,000

Using the total sales, the direct material cost, and the direct labor cost included in Exhibit 4-1 along with the manufacturing overhead allocations we have calculated, we can calculate the gross profit for each of the two Slade products as shown in Exhibit 4-3.

Exhibit 4-3 Summary of Gross Profit Calculations for Buck Slade Products Using Traditional Manufacturing Overhead Allocation

	Complex Cutters		**Simple Trimming Blades**	
Sales		$19,500		$53,000
Cost:				
Direct material cost	$4,500		$10,000	
Direct labor cost	1,200		6,000	
Manufacturing overhead cost	8,000		40,000	
Total cost		(13,700)		(56,000)
Gross profit		$ 5,800		$(3,000)

Exhibit 4-3 presents the exact same information that we presented in the opening to this chapter. Only this time we know how the company calculated the manufacturing overhead cost for each of the products. Note that the complex cutter, a complex, low volume product, earned a gross profit of $5,800 while the simple trimming blade, a simple, high volume product, has a negative gross profit of $3,000.

The manufacturing overhead allocation technique we just examined uses a single manufacturing overhead cost pool and a single, plant-wide manufacturing overhead application rate. Virtually all manufacturers in the United States used this method until the 1980s, and many still do today.

During the mid-1980s, some companies realized that a plant-wide manufacturing overhead application rate has significant weaknesses. The difficulty is that manufacturing overhead costs are typically caused by (or related to) many different activities—the activity that drives one cost may be totally different from the activity that drives another cost. To use one activity (such as direct labor hours) as the allocation base for applying *all* manufacturing overhead cost will likely cause some products to be overcosted and others to be undercosted. For example, assume that a company uses direct labor hours to allocate all manufacturing overhead cost, and its factory has five machines, two of which use significant amounts of water for cooling. The manufacturing overhead cost per direct labor hour will include an amount for cooling water. The amount will be allocated to products whether they are produced on a machine that requires cooling water or not. Therefore, products that are produced on machines that do not require cooling water will be overcosted and, because some of the cost of cooling water is allocated to products produced on machines that do not require cooling water, products produced on the machines that do require cooling water will be undercosted.

In an attempt to improve the accuracy of their manufacturing overhead allocation, many companies have begun to study their business activities and the costs these activities cause. The result was the development of a new costing method that provides more realistic and reasonable cost for units of manufactured product. This method is called activity-based costing.

Activity-Based Costing

activity based costing A technique to allocate indirect cost to cost objects based on activities that cause the cost to occur. It is more accurate than traditional cost allocation.

Activity-based costing (ABC) is a more accurate technique for allocating indirect cost to cost objects based on activities that cause the cost to occur.

ABC improves on traditional manufacturing overhead allocation in two ways. First, an analysis of activities, costs, and the causes of cost may result in the reclassification of certain costs from manufacturing overhead to direct material, direct labor, or some other direct cost classification. That is, some costs traditionally viewed as indirect can actually be traced directly to units of product and need not be allocated. This contributes to a more accurate unit cost because less cost remains to be allocated. Second, ABC allocates manufacturing overhead more accurately. ABC achieves a more accurate allocation by breaking total manufacturing overhead down into small cost pools and then allocating them based on activities that cause the costs to occur. Rather than allocating all manufacturing overhead to products using one plant-wide allocation base, ABC allocates various manufacturing overhead costs using cost drivers. A **cost driver** is an activity used as an allocation base for a particular cost pool that actually *causes* the cost to occur. Therefore, unlike traditional manufacturing overhead allocation that allocates cost using allocation bases that are believed to correlate to the incurrence of cost, ABC allocates costs using activities that cause cost. This results in more accurate cost allocation.

cost driver An activity used as an allocation base for a particular cost that causes the cost to occur.

Determining Product Cost Using ABC

As an example of how companies determine product costs when they use ABC, let's revisit the Buck Slade Company. Recall that Buck Slade estimated total manufacturing overhead cost of $1 million and 10,000 direct labor hours. To allocate manufacturing overhead costs using ABC we will employ the five step process shown in Exhibit 4-4.

Exhibit 4-4 Steps to Employ ABC

Step 1 *Review manufacturing overhead cost and remove any direct costs from manufacturing overhead.*
Step 2 *Identify major activities.*
Step 3 *Pool the costs of major activities.*
Step 4 *Determine multiple cost application rates.*
Step 5 *Determine the cost of manufacturing overhead allcated to individual products.*

Step 1. *Review manufacturing overhead costs and remove any direct costs from manufacturing overhead.* The reason companies allocate manufacturing overhead cost to products is because these costs cannot be traced directly to those products. When manufacturing overhead includes costs that can actually be traced to individual products, removing these costs from manufacturing overhead and treating them as direct product costs is a good first step in improving product cost accuracy. For example, if we determine that some indirect material and indirect labor costs included in manufacturing overhead can actually be traced to individual products, we should remove them from manufacturing overhead and treat them as direct material or direct labor. By the same token, if we can trace the benefit of a particular manufacturing overhead cost to individual products, we should remove that cost from manufacturing overhead and treat it as a direct cost of the products benefited. For example, let's say **Honeywell** uses a particular machine solely to manufacture a circuit board for one of its government contracts. The company should probably not include the cost associated with the machine in manufacturing overhead, but rather treat it as a direct cost of manufacturing the circuit boards.

With respect to our Buck Slade example, assume that the company has analyzed its manufacturing overhead and has reclassified \$220,000 of the \$1 million in manufacturing overhead to direct cost because the company found that, using modern technology, it could readily trace those costs directly to units of product as they are produced.

Step 2. *Identify major activities.* Once direct costs have been removed from manufacturing overhead, the next step is to determine major business activities. For example, depending on the company, manufacturing activities may include designing how products will be manufactured, setting up production machinery, moving raw material into production, manufacturing product, testing for product quality, and moving the goods in production from one manufacturing station to the next and then to finished goods. Manufacturing activities will vary from one company to the next. The major manufacturing activities for the Buck Slade Company, along with the estimated annual quantity measures for those activities are shown in Exhibit 4-5.

Number of parts	750,000
Number of production runs	25
Number of machine hours	2,000
Number of components tested	25,000
Number of direct labor hours	10,000

Exhibit 4-5 Major Manufacturing Activities for the Buck Slade Company

Step 3. *Pool the costs of major activities.* In this step the cost of the resources consumed by each activity should be determined. Once determined, cost pools are formed for each activity.

Slade determines the cost of the resources consumed by each activity and groups the costs into a cost pool for each. Recall that Slade reclassified \$220,000 from manufacturing overhead to direct cost. The remaining \$780,000 manufacturing overhead cost consists of the items listed in Exhibit 4-6.

Step 4. *Determine multiple cost application rates.* Instead of using one plant-wide application rate and a single allocation base, ABC uses several application rates. Basically, this is done by dividing the amount of each cost pool determined in Step 3 by its corresponding activity from Step 2. When an activity actually causes factory resources to be consumed it is called a cost driver. If we can determine the activities that drive the costs, it makes sense to use those activities to allocate the costs they cause.

It is impossible or impractical to determine cost drivers for every manufacturing overhead cost. This is because it may be difficult to determine the activity that causes a particular cost, or perhaps the activity that causes a cost is not really related to products or is not otherwise suitable to be used as a cost driver. For example, consider the cost of maintenance on

Exhibit 4-6 Remaining Manufacturing Overhead for Buck Slade Company

Costs associated with activities listed in Step 2:	
Materials purchasing and handling cost	$ 75,000
Production engineering and design	60,000
Production machine set-up	40,000
Production machine depreciation	300,000
Production machine maintenance	50,000
Quality testing	100,000
Costs not associated with the activities listed in Step 2:	
Plant security	25,000
Plant supervision	70,000
Building maintenance	10,000
Factory supplies	20,000
Factory insurance	30,000
Total manufacturing overhead	$780,000

the factory building. A fresh coat of paint on the cafeteria walls is not related to any product that the factory produces. For such situations, the company will probably continue using a traditional allocation base such as direct labor hours, direct labor cost or machine hours.

Costs should be paired with activities that cause the cost to occur. In other words, companies should pair costs with cost drivers. In the Buck Slade example, one of the logical pairs would be production machine set-up cost and the number of production runs. This is because production runs cause set-up cost to occur. Think about it. If the company had no production runs, there would be no need to set up production equipment and therefore, no set-up cost would occur. On the other hand, if the company has many production runs, the production machines must be set up for each run so set-up cost would be substantial.

As we have already mentioned, sometimes it is impossible or impractical to find cost drivers for each and every manufacturing overhead cost. For Slade, we will use direct labor hours to allocate these costs. Our pairing of cost pools with their respective cost drivers is shown in Exhibit 4-7.

Exhibit 4-7 Pairing of Cost Pools and Cost Drivers for Buck Slade Company

Manufacturing Overhead Cost Pool		Cost Driver
Pool 1	Materials Purchasing and Handling Cost	Number of Parts
Pool 2	Production Engineering and Design Cost and Production Machine Set-up Cost	Number of Production Runs
Pool 3	Production Machine Depreciation and Production Machine Maintenance	Number of Machine Hours
Pool 4	Quality Testing	Number of components tested
Pool 5	Remaining Manufacturing Overhead Costs	Because it is impossible or impractical to determine cost drivers for these remaining costs, a traditional allocation base, direct labor hours, will be used.

As we have already mentioned, the basic calculation to allocate manufacturing overhead is do divide the total estimated manufacturing overhead by the total estimated allocation base. This basic calculation is also used for ABC. Therefore, to calculate the application rate for an individual cost pool for Slade, we divide the estimated annual cost of the pool by the estimated number of occurrences of its cost driver.

$$\frac{\text{Estimated annual cost of the pool}}{\text{Estimated annual occurrences of the cost driver}} = \text{Manufacturing overhead application rate}$$

The manufacturing overhead application rate calculations for Slade are presented in Exhibit 4-8.

Exhibit 4-8 Manufacturing Overhead Application Rate Calculations for the Buck Slade Company

Manufacturing Overhead Pool	Cost Driver (Allocation Base)	Application Rate Based on Occurrence of the Cost Driver
POOL 1 Materials purchasing and handling cost	Number of Parts	\$75,000 ÷ 750,000 = \$0.10 per part
POOL 2 Production engineering and design and Production machine set-up	Number of production runs	\$100,000 ÷ 25 = \$4,000 per production run
POOL 3 Production machine depreciation and Production machine maintenance	Number of machine hours	\$350,000 ÷ 2,000 = \$175 per machine hour
POOL 4 Quality testing	Number of components tested	\$100,000 ÷ 25,000 = \$4 per component tested
POOL 5 Plant security Plant supervision Building maintenance Factory supplies Factory insurance	Number of direct labor hours	\$155,000 ÷ 10,000 = \$15.50 per direct labor hour

Based on the calculations in Exhibit 4-8, for every part added to a unit of product, \$0.10 of manufacturing overhead cost is added to the product as well (Pool 1). Every time a production run is made, \$4,000 of manufacturing is added to the cost of the products in that production run (Pool 2). For every machine hour devoted to the unit of product, \$175 of manufacturing overhead is added (Pool 3). For every component tested, \$4 of manufacturing overhead is added (Pool 4). And for every hour of direct labor, \$15.50 of manufacturing overhead is added to the cost of the product (Pool 5). The total direct material cost, direct labor cost, and total allocated manufacturing overhead cost are then added together to determine the cost of the product.

Step 5. *Determine the cost of manufacturing overhead allocated to individual products.* In this step we determine the amount of manufacturing overhead applied to each product by multiplying the application rate determined in Step 4 by the number of occurrences of the cost driver for each product. To allocate Slade's manufacturing overhead cost, we need to know more about the activities required to manufacture each of the example products. Exhibit 4-9 shows information for the two Buck Slade products mentioned earlier in this chapter.

Exhibit 4-9 Information for Buck Slade's Complex Cutters and Simple Trimming Blades

	Complex Cutters	Simple Trimming Blades
Number of units produced	15,000	100,000
Number of parts per unit	3	1
Number of production runs	1	1
Number of machine hours	16	48
Number of components tested	1,000	100
Number of direct labor hours	80	400

As Exhibit 4-9 shows, each complex cutter is made of three parts. In addition, it takes 16 machine hours and 80 direct labor hours to produce the 15,000 cutters. Also, during production a sample consisting of 1,000 cutters is tested for sharpness. To calculate the manufacturing overhead cost allocation for the cutters, we will multiply each activity by the corresponding application rate. Exhibit 4-10 shows the manufacturing overhead cost allocated to the cutters under ABC.

Exhibit 4-10 ABC Manufacturing Overhead Cost Allocation for Complex Cutters

Manufacturing Overhead Pool	Cost Allocation
POOL 1 Materials purchasing and handling cost	15,000 × 3 × \$0.10 = \$4,500
POOL 2 Production engineering and design and Production machine set-up	1 × \$4,000 = \$4,000
POOL 3 Production machine depreciation and Production machine maintenance	16 × \$175 = \$2,800
POOL 4 Quality testing	1,000 × \$4 = \$4,000
POOL 5 Plant security Plant supervision Building maintenance Factory supplies Factory insurance	80 × \$15.50 = \$1,240
Total manufacturing overhead for 15,000 cutters	\$16,540
Manufacturing overhead per cutter (\$16,540 ÷ 15,000)	\$ 1.103 (rounded)

Notice that the \$16,540 of overhead allocated for the complex cutters under ABC is more than double the \$8,000 allocated when a traditional allocation method is used (See Exhibit 4-3). The cutters are not more expensive to make when ABC is used; rather, the amount of manufacturing overhead allocated to the cutters under ABC more accurately represents the true cost of producing the cutters.

Now let's turn our attention to Slade's 100,000 simple trimming blades. As Exhibit 4-9 shows, each blade is made of one part. In addition, it takes 48 machine hours and 400 direct labor hours to produce the 100,000 blades. Finally, a sample of 100 blades is tested for sharpness. Exhibit 4-11 shows the manufacturing overhead cost allocated to the blades under ABC.

Manufacturing Overhead Pool	Cost Allocation
POOL 1 Materials purchasing and handling cost	100,000 × 1 × \$0.10 = \$10,000
POOL 2 Production engineering and design and Production machine set-up	1 × \$4,000 = \$4,000
POOL 3 Production machine depreciation and Production machine maintenance	48 × \$175 = \$8,400
POOL 4 Quality testing	100 × \$4 = \$400
POOL 5 Plant security Plant supervision Building maintenance Factory supplies Factory insurance	400 × \$15.50 = \$6,200
Total manufacturing overhead for the 100,000 blades	\$29,000
Manufacturing overhead per blade (\$29,000 ÷ 100,000)	\$ 0.29

Exhibit 4-11 ABC Manufacturing Overhead Cost Allocation for Simple Trimming Blades

The manufacturing overhead allocated to the simple trimming blades assuming traditional manufacturing overhead allocation was used is $40,000 (See Exhibit 4-3) while the manufacturing overhead allocated under ABC is only $29,000.

Discussion Questions

4-1. Why is the amount of manufacturing overhead allocated to the simple trimming blades under ABC different from what it was under traditional manufacturing overhead allocation?

4-2. Which manufacturing overhead allocation do you think more accurately reflects the cost of the manufacturing overhead resources consumed to make the simple trimming blades? Why?

With the manufacturing overhead allocations we have calculated, we can calculate the gross profit for each of the two Slade products under ABC. Exhibit 4-12 shows a comparison of the gross profit calculations for Buck Slade using traditional manufacturing overhead allocation and ABC.

Exhibit 4-12 Summary of Gross Profit Calculations for Buck Slade Products Using Traditional Manufacturing Overhead Allocation and ABC

Costs Using Traditional Manufacturing Overhead Allocation:

	Complex Cutters		Simple Trimming Blades	
Sales		$19,500		$53,000
Cost:				
Direct material cost	$4,500		$10,000	
Direct labor cost	1,200		6,000	
Manufacturing overhead cost	8,000		40,000	
Total cost		(13,700)		(56,000)
Gross profit		$ 5,800		$ (3,000)

Costs Using ABC for Manufacturing Overhead Allocation:

	Complex Cutters		Simple Trimming Blades	
Sales		$19,500		$53,000
Cost:				
Direct material cost	$ 4,500		$10,000	
Direct labor cost	1,200		6,000	
Manufacturing overhead cost	16,540		29,000	
Total cost		(22,240)		(45,000)
Gross profit		$ (2,740)		$ 8,000

In Exhibit 4-12 the cost information for Slade using traditional overhead allocation shows that the complex cutters are quite profitable, while the simple trimming blades are not. But there is a catch. Although the information is prepared using accepted and popular management accounting techniques, it is terribly flawed. This is because when a single plant-wide manufacturing overhead application rate is used, costs are allocated to products whether they consume a particular overhead resource or not. On the other hand, our ABC calculations show that in reality, the simple, high volume products are more profitable than the complex, low volume ones. This is because ABC results in more accurate product costs because it allocates cost to products based on factory resources used to make the product.

If Jim bases his decisions on the flawed costs achieved using traditional manufacturing overhead allocation, Slade's profits will disappear and losses will skyrocket. The trouble with the cost information under traditional manufacturing overhead allocation lies in the fact that allocating manufacturing overhead cost to production using a single allocation base does not do a good job of accurately assigning manufacturing overhead cost to the products that consume the factory's manufacturing overhead resources.

When ABC is used, products are more realistically charged for the manufacturing overhead resources they use. For example, if one product requires more inspections than another, as is the case with Slade's complex cutters, because the allocation is based on the use of the resource (the number of inspections), the product is charged more. Because products are allocated cost based on the manufacturing overhead resources they use, product costs are more accurate.

Comparison of Traditional and ABC Overhead Allocation

Exhibit 4-13 presents a comparison of traditional manufacturing overhead allocation method with the ABC manufacturing overhead allocation method.

	Traditional Manufacturing Overhead Allocation	ABC Manufacturing Overhead Allocation
Number of cost pools	One or few	Several
Number of allocation bases	One or few	Several
Relationship of allocation base with cost	Correlative	Causal
Product cost accuracy	Could be accurate enough for the company as a whole, but the cost of individual products is not very accurate.	More accurate because costs are allocated to products based on the factory resources they use.
Cost control	Does not aid in cost reduction	Aids in cost reduction
Cost system complexity and cost	Simpler, less costly allocation system	More complex, more expensive cost allocation system

Exhibit 4-13 Comparison of Traditional Manufacturing Overhead Allocation Method and ABC Manufacturing Overhead Allocation Method

Product Cost Accuracy

Is traditional manufacturing overhead allocation good enough? Well, for financial reporting and general purpose financial statements, it is accurate enough. This may be why using a single plant-wide allocation base is so popular. Unfortunately however, the costs of products that result when a single allocation base is used are generally not accurate enough for many management decisions. For example, if Jim, Buck Slade's product manager, had shifted the company's focus based on information presented in Exhibit 4-1, it is likely that the company's profits would have disappeared.

When Does ABC Result in More Accurate Product Costs?

When a company manufactures products that differ or when manufacturing processes differ from one product to the next, that is, when diversity exists, ABC will probably result in more accurate product cost. On the other hand, when a company manufactures only one product or when products and processes to manufacture those products are nearly identical, activity based costing will probably not result in more accurate product costs. For example, if the tires that ***Goodyear Tire and Rubber Company*** makes in one of its factories are identical to one another, ABC would not render more accurate product costs. However, since the models of tires **Goodyear** makes differ from one another with respect to the production machinery used, production processes, and production volumes, ABC would render more accurate product costs.

Diversity in manufacturing can take many forms. A company has diversity due to product complexity when it manufactures some simple products and some complex ones. Differences in complexity can be as subtle as manufacturing some products that require many component parts and manufacturing other products that require only a few. Alternatively, products could require varying amounts of engineering, materials handling, or quality testing. Diversity also exists when some products require the use of more costly factory resources than others. For example, some products must be produced on a machine that costs $1 million while others can be made on a machine that costs only $100,000. Diversity may also be in the form of volume, as in a company that produces both low volume and high volume products.

When diversity exists, using ABC will usually result in more accurate product costs. This is because each product is costed based on the activities required to make that product. For example, if diversity exists because some products require more quality inspections than others, ABC will allocate cost based on the number of inspections required to make each product. Products requiring more inspections will receive a high inspection cost allocation, while products requiring fewer inspections will receive one that is lower.

Reducing Cost by Using ABC

ABC can actually help firms reduce costs in at least three ways. First, costs are more closely scrutinized when ABC is used. Second, the smaller ABC cost pools make it more difficult to hide questionable costs. And third, to reduce costs allocated to their products, managers will attempt to reduce the allocation base, which for ABC are cost causes. Reducing the activities that cause cost will lead to actual cost reduction. Let's look at each of these more closely.

Closer Cost Scrutiny

Under ABC, costs are more closely scrutinized, especially during the process of establishing an ABC system. As you recall, when an ABC system is established, managers attempt to determine which costs can be removed from manufacturing overhead and treated as direct costs. In addition, managers work to separate manufacturing overhead into several smaller cost pools and to match these cost pools with cost drivers. With all this cost examination, managers are bound to find unnecessary costs. For example, a cost that has been the norm for years, such as the cost of maintaining and changing decorative plants in factory offices, may become a candidate for elimination when it fails to fit into a cost pool that is associated with an activity that benefits the company's products or services.

Smaller Cost Pools Make It Difficult to Hide Cost

Costs that may be hidden in a single huge cost pool are more difficult to hide in smaller ABC cost pools. Under traditional manufacturing overhead allocation, a single huge cost pool is often used for all manufacturing overhead costs. Even sizable expenditures can be hidden in such a massive cost pool. For example, $20,000 in expenditures for traveling to trade shows may never be noticed in a $1 million cost pool, but may be detected if it is part of one of ten $100,000 cost pools. The fact that costs are more likely to be detected in smaller ABC cost pools may cause managers to think twice before they allow questionable expenditures to occur.

Cost Control by Controlling the Allocation Base

If a company uses a predetermined manufacturing overhead application rate, managers cannot really reduce the manufacturing overhead cost allocated to their products by reducing manufacturing overhead costs directly. For example, assume that a particular ***Dow Chemical*** plant uses direct labor hours to allocate manufacturing overhead. If a **Dow** production manager changes the way his products are made so that it takes less electricity, manufacturing overhead cost to the company will be reduced, but the cost *allocated* to the manager's product will not change. This is because **Dow's** manufacturing overhead application rate would have been established before the year even began. The rate for the next year might be a little lower, but the current year's rate will remain unchanged by the reduced cost of electricity.

Because of the way manufacturing overhead allocation works, managers who desire to reduce the amount of manufacturing overhead cost allocated to their products must reduce the incurrence of the allocation base. In our **Dow Chemical** example, the manager could reduce the manufacturing overhead cost allocated to her products by reducing the number of direct labor hours.

Under traditional manufacturing overhead allocation, reducing the incurrence of the allocation base, however, will not reduce the amount the company actually pays for manufacturing overhead. Unfortunately, in our **Dow Chemical** example, reducing direct labor hours may reduce labor cost, but it is unlikely that it will reduce the amount **Dow** spends for manufacturing overhead. In fact, as the manager calls upon her factory engineers to find ways to reduce direct labor hours, the amount **Dow** pays for manufacturing overhead may actually increase instead of decrease. Manufacturing overhead cost will likely increase due to the added cost of the engineers (a manufacturing overhead cost), and perhaps the added cost of updating or replacing equipment with new labor saving devices. So, while the manufacturing overhead cost allocated to the manager's product may decrease, manufacturing overhead spending for the company as a whole may actually increase.

Under ABC, reducing the incurrence of the allocation base, the cost driver, *will* likely reduce the amount the company actually pays for manufacturing overhead cost. Now let's assume that our **Dow Chemical** plant uses ABC to allocate its manufacturing overhead cost and that the cost driver for inspection cost is the number of inspections. If the production manager would like to reduce the inspection cost allocated to her product, she would attempt to reduce the incurrence of the cost driver, the number of inspections. And, most importantly, since the cost driver (the number of inspections) causes the inspection cost, when the cost driver is reduced the amount the company pays for inspection cost is reduced. By reducing the cost driver, which is a cause of the cost, the company actually saves money. But how can a manager reduce the number of inspections without hindering product quality? Let's assume that in the **Dow Chemical** example, the production manager determined that the blemishes to the product were caused by an uneven cooling process. Assume further, that the manager corrected the problem so that blemishes would no longer occur and therefore the inspections from that time forward found no blemished product. Without the potential for product blemishes, inspections are no longer necessary. Reducing the cost driver (the number of inspections) actually reduced the company's manufacturing overhead cost.

Added Complexity and Cost of ABC

As you have seen with the Buck Slade example, an ABC system is much more complex than a traditional manufacturing overhead allocation system. The added complexity begins with establishing the ABC system itself. Costs must be examined, direct costs must be removed from the manufacturing overhead cost, and cost pools and cost drivers must be established. Then, once the cost pools and cost drivers are established, the company must design and establish systems to properly classify costs, to capture data regarding the occurrences of the various cost drivers, and to allocate the costs. This makes ABC considerably more complex than traditional manufacturing overhead allocation.

The added complexity of an ABC system makes it considerably more costly than traditional manufacturing overhead allocation. It is expensive to design and establish an ABC system, and the time and effort required to examine manufacturing overhead cost and to establish cost pools and cost drivers can be substantial.

ABC and Job Order Costing—Another Look at Manta Power Boats

Let's explore how activity based costing works using job order costing by revisiting our **Manta Power Boats** example introduced in Chapter 3. **Manta's** boats are made of fiberglass and plastic resin formed in molds. A series of molds is used to make the necessary components of each boat. Before a mold can be used, it must be cleaned and waxed to keep the fiberglass and plastic resin from sticking. The process of preparing molds used to make a boat is part of **Manta's** set-up.

When a manufacturer uses ABC, the cost of each manufacturing activity is accumulated in a dedicated cost pool. In the case of **Manta Power Boats**, manufacturing overhead costs are examined and all costs associated with set-up are separated out and grouped in a cost pool. Now set-up cost can be allocated to products separately from other manufacturing overhead costs. Assume the annual set-up cost at **Manta** is $117,000.

Next, a cost driver must be selected to allocate set-up cost. Assume that **Manta** has decided that the number of molds used is that cost driver. The number of molds required to make a single boat varies depending on each boat design. Exhibit 4-14 shows one boat requires the use of 12 molds, while another requires the use of only five molds.

Exhibit 4-14 Number of Molds Used for Each Basic Boat Design

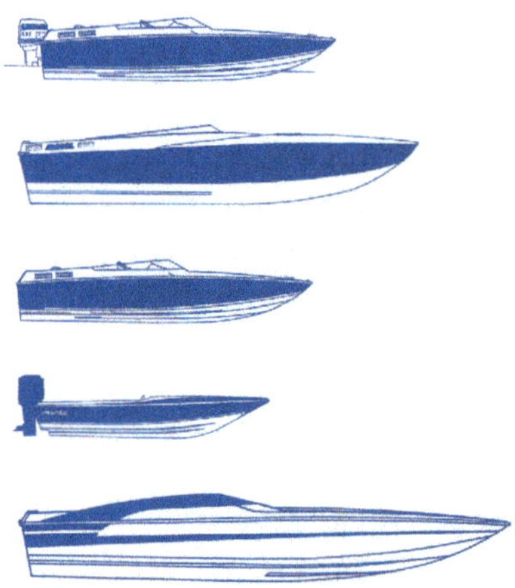

Number of Molds Used

5

10

6

5

12

The effort and cost of set-up varies from boat to boat depending on the number of molds required. By using the number of molds as the cost driver, we can reflect the differing amounts of set-up effort in the costs of each boat produced. For example, the set-up cost for a boat that requires 12 molds will be twice as much as the set-up cost for a boat that requires six molds. The calculations for allocating a manufacturing overhead cost pool using a cost driver are similar to the calculations using a traditional allocation base. The total estimated annual cost for the cost pool is divided by the estimated annual activity of the cost driver to arrive at an application rate per occurrence of the cost driver. The general formula is as follows:

$$\frac{\text{Estimated annual manufacturing overhead cost}}{\text{Estimated annual occurrences of the cost driver}} = \text{Application rate per occurrence of the cost driver}$$

Based on past experience, **Manta** estimates that it will need 360 mold preparations this year to produce 45 boats. Recall that **Manta's** estimated total annual set-up cost is \$117,000. With these numbers, we can find **Manta's** application rate for set-up. **Manta** divides the estimated total estimated set-up cost by the estimated number of mold preparations for the year to determine the application rate for set-up cost.

$$\frac{\text{Estimated annual set-up cost}}{\text{Estimated annual number of mold preparations}} = \text{Cost per mold preparation}$$

$$\frac{\$117{,}000}{\text{360 Mold preparations}} = \$325 \text{ Per mold preparation}$$

We find that with an estimated annual set-up cost of \$117,000 and a total estimated number of mold preparations of 360, the allocation rate is \$325 per mold used.

Discussion Questions

4-3. If you owned a factory, would you prefer that employees spend time setting up production equipment or producing product?

4-4. If the production manager is able to use one fewer mold when making a boat, would the cost allocated to that boat be less? Is it likely that the company's actual set-up cost would also be less?

Using the ABC application rate, we can now allocate set-up cost to each boat based on the number of molds required. For example, boat 1 requires the use of five molds, so its set-up cost would be \$1,625 (5 × \$325 = \$1,625). The set-up cost allocated to boat 2 would be \$3,250 based on the use of 10 molds (10 × \$325 = \$3,250). The more molds required to make a boat, the higher the allocation for set-up cost.

Using traditional manufacturing overhead application cost, a manager can reduce manufacturing overhead cost allocated to a given product by reducing the allocation base used to allocate the cost. For example, if manufacturing overhead is allocated using machine hours, a manager could reduce the manufacturing overhead allocated to his or her product by reducing the amount of machine time it takes to make the product. This process would reduce the manufacturing overhead cost allocated to the given product, but it would generally not affect the various manufacturing overhead costs actually incurred by the company. As we mentioned earlier in this chapter, reducing machine hours has no significant effect on the amount the company spends for manufacturing overhead items such as property taxes, plant insurance, plant security, indirect material, indirect labor, and so forth. Even though accounting records would indicate a lower cost for that product's manufacturing overhead, the reduced machine hours would have little effect on the dollars the company actually spends for manufacturing overhead.

Let's say that Manta Power Boats wants to use ABC to reduce the set-up cost of a particular boat. The manager, then, would try to decrease the number of molds used. For instance, if the number of molds used to make boat 2 were reduced by one mold, the cost allocated to that boat would be reduced by $325. With this cost-reduction technique, the decrease in the allocation base (the cost driver) actually reduces the amount of cost incurred by the company. That is, reducing the number of molds used actually reduces the amount of work that must be done to make a boat. In general, this reduction in work contributes to true cost savings for the company.

Summary

Direct material and direct labor cost can be traced directly to individual products or batches of products. Because manufacturing overhead is an indirect cost and benefits more than one product, it is difficult, if not impossible to determine the true manufacturing overhead cost associated with individual products produced.

The costs included in manufacturing overhead are an important component of manufacturing product. Even though their cost cannot easily be traced to individual units of production, manufacturing overhead resources are all necessary to produce products, and therefore, their cost should be included in the cost of products produced. The problem is, however, that the cost of manufacturing overhead resources and activities cannot be traced directly to the units of product produced. Their cost, therefore, must be allocated to production.

When allocating manufacturing overhead using actual amounts for direct material, direct labor and manufacturing overhead, the system is called an actual cost system. Using a normal cost system, product cost reflects actual direct material cost, actual direct labor cost, and estimated manufacturing overhead costs. Estimated annual manufacturing overhead cost and the estimated annual amount for the allocation base are used to calculate a predetermined manufacturing overhead application rate.

Manufacturing overhead allocation has traditionally been a two-stage process. The first stage is to gather manufacturing overhead cost into a cost pool. The second stage is to assign the manufacturing overhead cost gathered in the pool to units of product manufactured. Manufacturers attempt to allocate the amount of manufacturing overhead cost that corresponds to the overhead resources consumed to make the product.

Because it is impractical if not impossible for managers to know the exact cost of the manufacturing overhead resources used to make each unit of product, an equitable basis for cost allocation must be determined. An allocation base is an amount associated with cost objects that is used to proportionately distribute costs to each cost object. Direct labor hours, direct labor cost, and machine hours are common traditional manufacturing overhead allocation bases.

Traditional overhead allocation uses one or very few manufacturing overhead cost pools and one or very few, plant-wide application rates. Virtually all manufacturers in the United States used this method until the mid-1980s, and many still do today.

During the 1980s, some companies realized that a plant-wide application rate has significant weaknesses. To use one activity (such as direct labor hours) as the allocation base for applying *all* manufacturing overhead cost will likely cause some products to be overcosted and others to be undercosted. In an attempt to improve the accuracy of their manufacturing overhead allocation, many companies have begun to study their business activities and the costs these activities cause. This new method is activity-based costing

(ABC). When ABC is used, products are more realistically charged for the manufacturing overhead resources they use. Because products are allocated cost based on the manufacturing overhead resources they use, product costs are more accurate.

Traditional manufacturing overhead allocation may be accurate enough for financial reporting and general purpose financial statements but, unfortunately, the costs of products that result when a single allocation base is used are generally not accurate enough for many management decisions.

When diversity exists, that is, when products differ or manufacturing processes differ from one product to the next, ABC will usually result in more accurate product cost because each product is costed based on the activities required to make that product.

Key Terms

activity-based costing (ABC) 132
actual cost system 129
cost allocation base 130
cost driver 132
cost pool 129
manufacturing overhead allocation 128
normal cost system 129
predetermined manufacturing overhead application rate 129

Review the Facts

A. Describe two problems associated with using actual amounts instead of estimated annual amounts for allocating manufacturing overhead.

B. What is a cost pool?

C. What is a manufacturing overhead allocation base?

D. List the allocation bases typically used in traditional manufacturing overhead allocation.

E. What is the significant weakness of a plant-wide allocation base?

F. What is activity-based costing?

G. In what two ways does activity-based costing improve upon the traditional approach to manufacturing overhead allocation?

H. Describe a cost driver.

I. What is the difference between a plant-wide cost pool and multiple cost pools?

J. Under what circumstances would ABC probably result in more accurate product costs?

K. List the three ways ABC can actually help firms reduce cost.

L. Which overhead allocation system, traditional or ABC, is more costly to establish and operate?

Apply What You Have Learned

LO 1, 3 & 4: Calculate Traditional and ABC Overhead Allocation and Determine the Cost of Products Using Job Order Costing and Compare the Outcomes of Each Method

4-5. The president of Simple Products, Inc. is attending a management seminar and has just heard about activity-based costing. He wonders whether it would help his company.

Simple Products, Inc. uses common machinery to manufacture two simple products. Each year, there are two production runs for each product requiring similar set-up effort. Manufacturing overhead includes set-up cost of $50,400 per year. Total overhead for the company including the set-up cost is $198,000 annually and direct labor hours are expected to total 18,000 for the year.

The following information is available for products A and B.

	Product A	Product B
Units produced	1,000	8,000
Direct material cost per unit	$ 14	$ 14
Direct labor cost per unit	$ 24	$ 24
Machine hours per unit	1	1
Direct labor hours per unit	2	2

Required:

a. Calculate the cost per unit for each product using traditional overhead allocation.

b. Calculate the cost per unit for each product using activity-based costing.

c. Do you believe activity-based costing would benefit Simple Products, Inc.? Explain your answer.

LO 1, 3 & 4: Calculate Traditional and ABC Overhead Allocation and Determine the Cost of Products Using Job Order Costing and Compare the Outcomes of Each Method

4-6. The president of Complex Products, Inc. is attending a management seminar and has just heard about activity-based costing. She wonders whether it would help her company.

Complex Products, Inc. uses common machinery to manufacture two complex products. Each year, there are two production runs for each product requiring similar set-up effort. Manufacturing overhead includes set-up cost totaling $52,000. To maintain a competitive edge, these products are updated periodically to conform to the latest technological advancements. These engineering changes are considered part of manufacturing overhead and cost $26,000 per year. Total overhead for the company including the cost of set-up and engineering changes is $175,000 per year. Direct labor hours total 7,000 for the year.

The following information is available for products C and D.

	Product C	Product D
Units produced	1,000	1,000
Direct material cost per unit	$ 24	$ 24
Direct labor cost per unit	$ 36	$ 48
Machine hours per unit	6	8
Direct labor hours	3	4
Engineering changes per year	6	2

Required:

a. Calculate the cost per unit for each product using traditional overhead allocation.

b. Calculate the cost per unit for each product using activity-based costing.

c. Do you believe activity-based costing would benefit Complex Products, Inc.? Explain your answer.

LO 3: Calculate Traditional and ABC Overhead Allocation

4-7. The following estimates are available for Violette Manufacturing for 2008.

Violette Manufacturing Estimated Manufacturing Overhead For the Year Ended December 31, 2008	
Materials handling cost	$ 50,000
Product engineering	110,000
Production machine set-up	200,000
Production machine depreciation	450,000
Quality testing	100,000
Other overhead cost	250,000
Total manufacturing overhead	$1,160,000

(Continued)

Estimated Overhead Activities For the Year Ended December 31, 2008	
Number of material movements	200,000
Number of product engineering hours	4,400
Number of machine set-ups	100
Number of machine hours	18,000
Number of tests performed	125,000
Number of direct labor hours	25,000

The following information is available for production runs of two products, the FP111 and the FP222:

	FP111	FP222
Selling price	$ 23	$ 26
Number of units produced	5000	500
Direct material cost	$60,000	$6,000
Direct labor cost	$14,400	$1,440
Number of material movements	10,000	1,000
Number of product engineering hours	100	100
Number of machine set-ups	1	1
Number of machine hours	200	20
Number of tests performed	1,250	125
Number of direct labor hours	800	80

Violette Manufacturing uses a traditional overhead allocation system. Manufacturing overhead is allocated based on direct labor hours.

Violette Manufacturing's sales manager has submitted a proposal that would shift the marketing focus to low-volume products such as the FP222. The proposal is prompted by the higher markups that can be charged for these products without customer complaint. The company president is concerned that the company's cost per unit may be sending the wrong message. He recently learned of activity-based costing and wonders if it might help.

Assume that you are part of a group that has been assigned to review the situation.

Required:

a. Determine the per unit cost for FP111 and FP222 using direct labor hours as the allocation base for all manufacturing overhead cost.

b. Determine the per unit cost for FP111 and FP222 using activity-based costing to allocate manufacturing overhead cost. (Note: Allocate other overhead cost based on direct labor hours.)

c. Discuss the marketing manager's proposal in light of your findings. Discuss what would happen if the marketing manager's sales strategy was adopted.

LO 1, 3 & 4: Calculate Traditional and ABC Overhead Allocation and Determine the Cost of Products Using Job Order Costing and Compare the Outcomes of Each Method

4-8. The following estimates are available for George Manufacturing for 2008.

George Manufacturing Estimated Manufacturing Overhead For the Year Ended December 31, 2008	
Production machine set-up	$ 75,000
Production machine depreciation	240,000
Quality testing	25,000
Other overhead cost	150,000
Total manufacturing overhead	$490,000

Estimated Overhead Activities For the Year Ended December 31, 2008	
Number of machine set-ups	100
Number of machine hours	3,200
Number of tests performed	50,000
Number of direct labor hours	16,000

The following information is available for production of two products, the AA1 and the BB2:

	AA1	BB2
Selling price	$ 2.40	$3.25
Number of units produced	10,000	500
Direct material cost	$ 5,000	$ 250
Direct labor cost	$ 6,400	$ 320
Number of machine set-ups	1	1
Number of machine hours	100	5
Number of tests performed	100	50
Number of direct labor hours	400	20

George Manufacturing uses a traditional overhead allocation system. Manufacturing overhead is allocated based on direct labor hours. George Manufacturing's marketing manager has submitted a proposal that would shift the marketing focus to low-volume products such as the BB2. The proposal is prompted by the higher markups and lack of competition, even at high selling prices.

The company president is concerned that the company's cost per unit may be sending the wrong message. He recently learned of activity based costing and wonders if it might help.

Assume that you are a member of a work team that has been assigned to review the situation.

Required:

a. Determine the per unit cost for AAI and BB2 using direct labor hours as the allocation base for all manufacturing overhead cost.

b. Determine the per unit cost for AAI and BB2 using activity-based costing to allocate manufacturing overhead cost. (Note: Allocate other overhead cost based on direct labor hours.)

c. Discuss the marketing manager's proposal in light of your findings. Discuss what would happen if the marketing manager's sales strategy was adopted.

LO 1, 3 & 4: Calculate Traditional and ABC Overhead Allocation and Determine the Cost of Products Using Job Order Costing and Compare the Outcomes of Each Method

4-9. Salter Equipment Company began the following jobs during March 2008:

	Job 303	Job 304
Direct material	$2,000	$2,000
Direct labor	$3,120	$6,240
Direct labor hours	260	520
Machine hours machine A	5	30
Machine hours machine B	20	0
Machine set-ups	2	1
Engineering changes	22	9

Estimated overhead cost for 2008:	
Depreciation machine A	$ 100,000
Depreciation machine B	500,000
Machine set-up cost	50,000
Engineering cost	200,000
Other overhead cost	150,000
Total	$1,000,000

Estimated activities for 2008:	
Machine hours machine A	1,000
Machine hours machine B	1,000
Number of set-ups	80
Number of engineering changes	800
Number of direct labor hours	20,000

Required:

a. Calculate the cost of each job using direct labor hours as the allocation base for all overhead.

b. Calculate the cost of each job using activity-based costing. Use direct labor hours as the allocation base for "other overhead cost."

LO 3: Calculate Traditional and ABC Overhead Allocation and Determine the Cost of Products Using Job Order Costing

4-10. Jack Klett Equipment Company began the following jobs during August 2008:

	Job 500	Job 600
Direct material	$1,000	$1,000
Direct labor	$1,800	$3,000
Direct labor hours	120	200
Machine hours machine A	10	50
Machine hours machine B	50	0
Machine set-ups	2	1
Material movements	200	75

(Continued)

Estimated overhead cost for 2008:	
Depreciation machine A	$ 50,000
Depreciation machine B	300,000
Machine set-up cost	75,000
Material handling cost	100,000
Other overhead cost	80,000
Total	$605,000

Estimated activities for 2008:	
Machine hours machine A	500
Machine hours machine B	500
Number of set-ups	75
Number of material movements	5,000
Number of direct labor hours	10,000

Required:

a. Calculate the cost of each job using direct labor hours as the allocation base for all overhead.

b. Calculate the cost of each job using activity-based costing. Use direct labor hours as the allocation base for "other overhead cost"

LO 3: Calculate Traditional and ABC Overhead Allocation and Determine the Cost of Products Using Job Order Costing

4-11. Vazquez Manufacturing Company began the following jobs during July 2008:

	Job 901	**Job 922**
Direct material	$3,000	$3,000
Direct labor	$1,800	$3,000
Direct labor hours	250	100
Machine hours machine A	20	12
Machine hours machine B	0	8
Machine set-ups	1	2
Material movements	90	300

Estimated overhead cost for 2008:	
Depreciation machine A	$ 150,000
Depreciation machine B	600,000
Machine set-up cost	175,000
Material handling cost	150,000
Other overhead cost	180,000
Total	$1,255,000

Estimated activities for 2008:	
Machine hours machine A	700
Machine hours machine B	700
Number of set-ups	100
Number of material movements	5,000
Number of direct labor hours	10,000

Required:

a. Calculate the cost of each job using direct labor hours as the allocation base for all overhead.

b. Calculate the cost of each job using activity-based costing. Use direct labor hours as the allocation base for "other overhead cost."

LO 1, 3 & 4: Calculate Traditional and ABC Overhead Allocation and Determine the Cost of Products Using Job Order Costing and Compare the Outcomes of Each Method

4-12. The following estimates are available for Tarrago Manufacturing for 2008.

Estimated Manufacturing Overhead Costs For the Year Ended December 31, 2008	
Production machine set-up	$ 35,000
Production machine depreciation	240,000
Quality testing	75,000
Other overhead cost	150,000
Total manufacturing overhead	$500,000

Estimated Overhead Activities For the Year Ended December 31, 2008	
Number of machine set-ups	100
Number of machine hours	3,000
Number of tests performed	25,000
Number of direct labor hours	12,500

The company makes many products and the following information is available for two sample products, the HV100 and the LV50:

	HV100	LV50
Selling price	$ 3.40	$5.25
Number of units produced	10,000	500
Direct material cost	$ 5,000	$ 250
Direct labor cost	$ 6,400	$ 320
Number of machine set-ups	2	1
Number of machine hours	75	10
Number of tests performed	700	500
Number of direct labor hours	400	20

Tarrago Manufacturing uses a traditional overhead allocation system. Manufacturing overhead is allocated based on direct labor hours. Tarrago Manufacturing's marketing manager has submitted a proposal that would shift the marketing focus to low-volume products such as the LV50. The proposal is prompted by the higher markups and lack of competition, even at high selling prices.

The company president is concerned that the company's cost per unit may be sending the wrong message. She recently learned of activity based costing and wonders if it might help.

Assume that you are a member of a work team that has been assigned to review the situation.

Required:

a. Determine the gross profit per unit for HV100 and LV50 using direct labor hours as the allocation base for all manufacturing overhead cost.

b. Based on the gross profit figures you determined in part a, does the marketing managers plan seem reasonable? Briefly explain.

c. Determine the gross profit per unit for HV100 and LV50 using activity-based costing to allocate manufacturing overhead cost. (Note: Allocate other overhead cost based on direct labor hours.)

d. Discuss the sales manager's proposal in light of your findings. Discuss what would happen if the marketing manager's sales strategy was adopted.

e. Discuss which cost system provides more accurate product costs and why.

f. Discuss which cost system would be more costly to operate and why.

LO 2: Determine Cost Drivers for Various Costs

4-13. Consider the following list of manufacturing overhead items:

1. Setting up a printing press for a large print job
2. Quality testing of complicated electronic components
3. Production engineering
4. Moving direct materials into production
5. Production supervision
6. Production area clean-up
7. Packaging completed products
8. Moving completed products from production to the finished goods warehouse

Required:

Provide at least two possible cost drivers that could be used to allocate the cost of each of the items listed above.

5

Cost Behavior

Laura Jorgensen is the newly-elected social chairperson of her mountain climbing club. Her first duty is to plan the club's big kickoff party for the upcoming year. Funds are limited, so she must plan well and estimate costs carefully. Laura's first step in estimating the total cost of the party is to identify the individual costs involved. As she begins the planning process, she identifies two major costs:

1. Entertainment—A live band is a must.
2. Food and drinks—Plenty for everyone is essential.

When Laura checks the records of last year's social chairperson, she discovers he spent $3,650 on these two items for last year's party ($525 for entertainment and $3,125 for food and drinks). Assuming the prices for entertainment and food and drinks have remained the same, the club should be able to have this year's party for $3,650. In fact, Laura has money to spare because the spending limit for this year's event is $5,500.

But wait. . . . The mountain climbing club has grown, so about 175 guests are expected to attend this year's party, compared to the 125 guests who attended last year. Laura must estimate the party's cost for 175 guests, not 125. How should she begin? To determine the total expected cost of the party, Laura needs to know which costs are affected by the number of guests attending and which costs are not. Let's examine Laura's two major costs for the party:

1. Entertainment: Will the band charge more if more guests attend? No.
2. Food and drinks: Will the caterer charge more if the number of guests increases? Yes.

How should Laura determine the cost of this year's party? She knows her cost for the item that is unaffected by the attendance level (the band), but what about the cost that *is* affected by a change in attendance level (food and drinks)? This chapter will demonstrate how to determine these amounts.

As managers plan for business success, they must know which costs will vary with changes in business activity and which will remain constant. In this context, we are using the term *business activity* in a very broad sense. "Business activity" can refer to almost anything happening in a business. In the mountain climbing club example, the activity is the number of guests attending the party. For a manufacturer, the activity could be the number of products produced; for a shipping department, it could be the number of packages shipped; and for a sales office, it could be the number of sales orders processed. Increases and decreases in any business activity will impact some costs and not others. That is, some costs will increase as business activity increases and others will not. To help them predict and control costs, managers must be able to determine how costs will behave as business activity changes. **Cost behavior** is the reaction of costs to changes in levels of business activity.

cost behavior The reaction of costs to changes in levels of activity.

Learning Objectives

After completing your work on this chapter, you should be able to do the following:

1. Describe the differences between fixed costs and variable costs.
2. Classify costs by cost behavior.
3. Explain the concept of relevant range and its effect on cost behavior information.
4. Describe the characteristics of a mixed cost and the four basic approaches to separating a mixed cost into its fixed and variable components.
5. Determine the fixed and variable components of a mixed cost using scatter graphs and the high-low method.
6. Use **Microsoft** Excel to prepare a cost behavior scatter graph.

Common Cost Behavior Patterns

Costs may react in various ways to changes in activity levels, creating many different cost behavior patterns. In this chapter we describe and compare the two most common patterns: fixed and variable.

Fixed Costs

Fixed costs are costs that remain constant *in total* regardless of the level of activity. In our chapter-opening example, the entertainment cost is a fixed cost. As the number of guests increases, this cost does not change. The band will cost $525 for the night, regardless of how many guests attend the club's party.

fixed cost A cost that remains constant in total regardless of the level of activity.

Suppose Laura is interested in determining the fixed cost *per guest*. Would the fixed cost amount change per guest as the number of guests changes? Let's take a look.

	125 Guests	175 Guests
Total fixed cost	$525	$525
Cost per guest	$525 ÷ 125 = $4.20	$525 ÷ 175 = $3.00

As you can see, the fixed cost *per unit* (in this case, the entertainment cost per guest) changes as the activity level changes. A fixed cost, then, is a cost that remains constant in total, but changes per unit as the activity level changes. Fixed cost per unit decreases as activity increases.

Discussion Question

5-1. Consider the costs involved in operating a fast-food restaurant such as **McDonald's**. What are three examples of fixed costs?

Variable Costs

Variable costs are costs that change *in total* proportionately with changes in the level of activity. As activity increases, total variable cost also increases. In our party example, the variable cost is the catering cost of $25 per guest. We know this because the total cost for food and drinks last year was $3,125 for 125 guests, and $3,125 ÷ 125 = $25. For each additional guest added to the party, the total cost for food and drinks will increase by $25.

variable cost A Cost that change in total proportionately with changes in the level of activity.

If 175 guests attend, the total catering cost is as follows:

$$175 \text{ Guests} \times \$25 = \$4{,}375$$

Variable cost per unit stays the same as activity changes. In our example, the catering cost per guest remains constant regardless of how many guests attend. A variable cost, then, is a cost that increases in total, but remains constant per unit as activity increases.

Discussion Question

5-2. Consider the costs involved in operating a fast-food restaurant such as **McDonald's**. What are three examples of variable costs and the activity or activities that cause them to change?

Comparison of Cost Behaviors

Cost and activity can be plotted on a graph to yield a visual representation of cost behavior. When doing so, we plot the activity on the horizontal axis (the x-axis) and the type of cost on the vertical axis (the y-axis). You may recall from past math classes that *x* is the independent variable, and *y* is the dependent variable, which means that the item depicted on the x-axis (activity) affects the item shown on the y-axis (cost).

A graphical representation of a fixed cost is as follows:

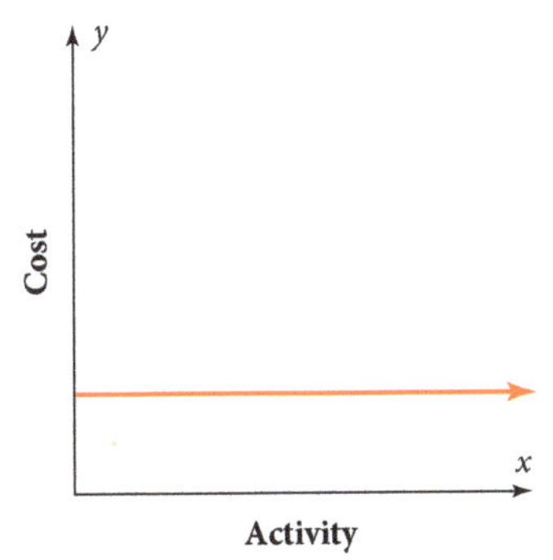

Examples of activities and fixed costs are shown in Exhibit 5-1. Notice that each example in Exhibit 5-1 suggests a cost that remains constant even if the level of the activity changes.

Exhibit 5-1 Examples of Fixed Costs

Activity	Fixed Cost
Production	Rent on the factory building
Production	Depreciation on production equipment
Sales	Salary of vice president of sales
Delivery	Vehicle insurance

From our party example, we can graph the cost of the band as an example of a fixed cost, as shown in Exhibit 5-2.

Exhibit 5-2 Graph of Fixed Cost Behavior Pattern of Entertainment at the Climbing Club Party

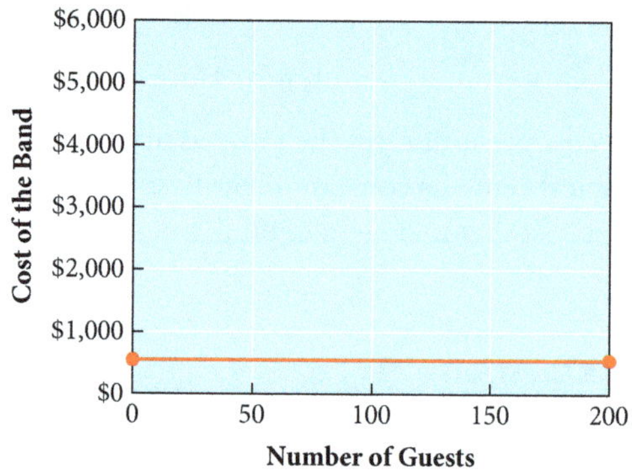

The horizontal line on the graph in Exhibit 5-2 shows that the fixed cost of entertainment stays constant no matter how the number of guests changes.

A graphical representation of variable cost is as follows:

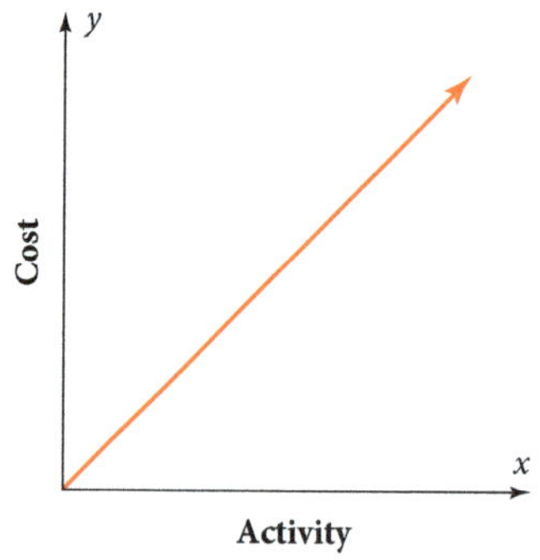

Examples of activities and variable costs are shown in Exhibit 5-3. Notice that for each example in Exhibit 5-3, a change in the level of the activity results in a change in the total cost.

Exhibit 5-3 Examples of Variable Costs

Activity	Variable Cost
Production	Direct material cost
Production	Direct labor cost
Sales	Cost of sales commissions
Delivery	Cost of gasoline used in delivery trucks

From our party example, we can graph the cost of catering as an example of a variable cost, as shown in Exhibit 5-4. The upward sloping line shows us that as the number of guests increases from 125 to 175, the catering cost increases proportionately.

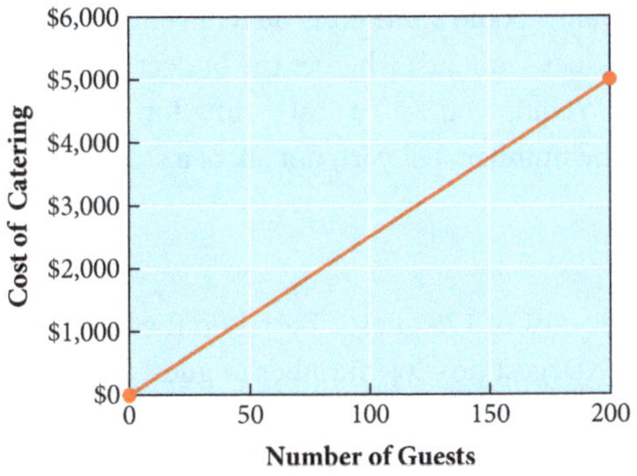

Exhibit 5-4 Graph of Variable Cost Behavior Pattern for Catering Cost at the Climbing Club Party

Discussion Question

5-3. Identify four additional costs of hosting the mountain climbing club party and describe the cost behavior of each if the number of guests changes.

In this section, we defined and compared the two most common types of cost behavior. Next, we see how to estimate the total cost of an activity.

Determining Total Cost

Once managers classify costs according to cost behavior, they can determine the total cost of an activity. The formula for finding total cost is as follows:

$$\text{TOTAL COST} = \text{FIXED COST} + \text{VARIABLE COST}$$

Recall from our example that we have $525 of fixed cost for the band, and $4,375 of variable cost for the food and drinks (based on 175 guests). Using this information, Laura can calculate the total cost of the party as $4,900, as follows:

$$\$4{,}900 = \$525 + \$4{,}375$$

The total cost of the party is shown on the graph in Exhibit 5-5.

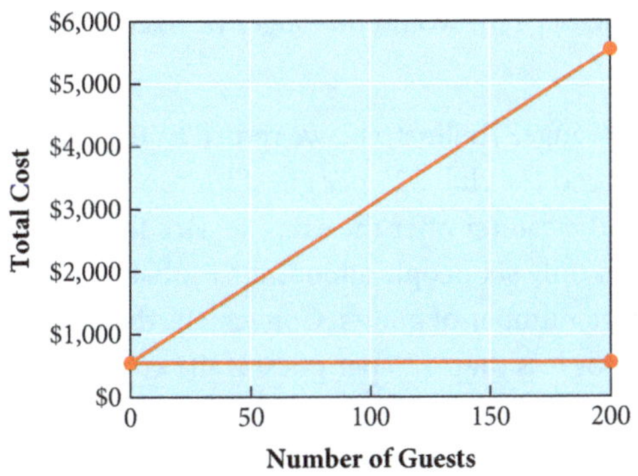

Exhibit 5-5 Graph of Total Climbing Party Cost

The graph in Exhibit 5-5 shows both the horizontal line depicting the fixed cost of the band and the upward sloping line representing the variable cost of the food and drinks. Exhibit 5-5, then, is actually a combination of the graphs in Exhibits 5-2 and 5-4. These graphs are consistent with the statement that total cost equals fixed cost plus variable cost.

Since the budget for the event was $5,500, and Laura plans to spend only $4,900, she must have planned well, right? Not necessarily. Keep in mind that the numbers tell only part of the story. As a decision maker, Laura must not be lulled into thinking that she has made the most effective spending choices just because she failed to spend every budgeted dollar. Is it wise to spend nearly $5,000 on one event? Could some costs be reduced? To make sound decisions, managers must consider all issues—not just whether the budget has been met. In this chapter, we examine cost behavior to equip you with a cost estimation tool. Remember, however, that when making decisions the numbers tell part, not all, of a story.

Discussion Question

5-4. The total cost of $4,900 covers the cost of 175 guests. Based on the cost behavior information available, what is the largest possible number of guests that could attend the party within the $5,500 budget?

Relevant Range

Are there any situations when a cost behavior might change? Well, let's reexamine the cost of entertainment in the party example to answer this question. We assumed the cost of the band would remain fixed if the number of guests attending the party increased; however, if the number of guests increased well outside normal expectations to 500 or 1,000, the guests could not be entertained with a single band. At least two bands would be needed. Once the number of guests exceeds a certain range, the entertainment cost does not remain fixed at $525.

relevant range The range of activity within which cost behavior assumptions are valid.

The range of activity within which cost behavior assumptions are valid is called the **relevant range**. In the party example, the relevant range might be up to 250 guests. If more than 250 guests attend, Laura will need more than one band. For a business, we usually consider the relevant range to be the normal range of activity for the company.

Activity that is outside the relevant range can affect costs in a business setting. For example, in Exhibit 5-1, we described rent for a factory building as a fixed cost relative to production. This fixed cost behavior holds true only within the relevant range. On the one hand, if production dropped to two units there would be no point in having a factory. Work could be contracted to an outside party. Conversely, if the factory building provided just enough space to produce 1,000 units per month, and production requirements increased to 1,500 units per month, a second factory would be needed. If the activity level were higher than the relevant range, factory rent would no longer be fixed at the original cost level.

Variable costs also have a relevant range. To illustrate, we return to the catering costs for the party example. The caterer charged the club $25 per guest for food and drinks for a party with 125 to 175 guests. Would the caterer offer the same service for $25 per guest if the event were a private evening with only six people attending? Probably not. The caterer's fee is based on a relatively large number of guests. Conversely, the caterer might be willing to provide food and drinks for less than $25 per guest if the crowd were significantly larger. For example, the caterer might offer a $25 per guest charge for groups of 50 to 200, and a $20 per guest charge for groups of more than 200. In such a case, the relevant range of the variable cost of $25 per guest would be from 50 to 200 guests.

In business settings, similar types of quantity discounts exist. For example, if **IBM** were to purchase just enough electrical wire to manufacture one computer, it would likely pay a higher price for the wire than if it were buying enough to make 1,000 computers.

Buying enough electrical wire to make 1,000 computers allows **IBM** to obtain quantity discounts that would be unavailable otherwise. At the other extreme, if **IBM** were to make such a large number of computers that it outstripped its normal source for wire and had to resort to secondary, more expensive suppliers, the cost for electrical wire per computer could actually increase as production increased.

With these examples in mind, how can fixed cost be described as a cost that remains constant in total, and variable cost be described as cost that remains constant per unit regardless of activity? For most decision situations, the fixed and variable cost information provided to managers assumes activity will be within the relevant range, that is, the normal operating range for the company. The relevant range can be depicted graphically as shown in Exhibit 5-6.

Exhibit 5-6 Relevant Ranges of Fixed and Variable Costs

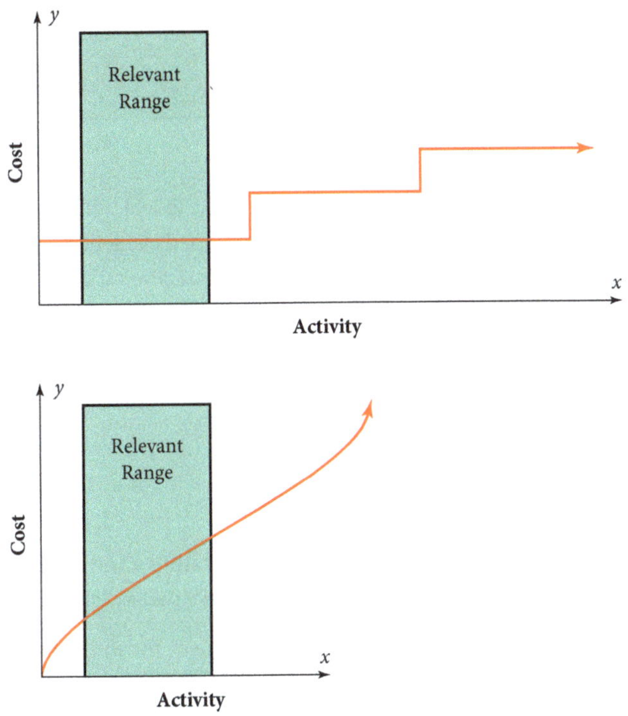

As shown in Exhibit 5-6, the fixed cost remains constant in total and the variable cost is constant per unit within the relevant range.

Decision makers usually assume activity levels will be within a company's relevant range. Activity levels may exceed or fall below the relevant range, such as when growth in production activity is significant. However, unless some evidence suggests the contrary, you should assume in our text discussion and assignment material that the activity levels will be within the relevant range.

Mixed Costs

The costs we have looked at thus far have been either completely fixed or completely variable. Some costs, however, are actually a combination of fixed and variable cost, and are known as mixed costs. A **mixed cost** is a cost that has elements of both fixed and variable costs.

mixed cost A cost that has both a fixed cost and a variable cost component.

For decision making purposes, it is useful to identify the fixed and variable components of a mixed cost. For example, consider the cost of electricity consumed in a manufacturing facility. When production lines are completely shut down on weekends, production is zero. Even without any production, however, the facility still requires minimal electricity to operate water heaters, refrigerators, and security lighting. This minimum cost of keeping the factory ready for use is the fixed portion of electricity cost. When production begins and production machinery cranks up, much more electric power is used. This incremental cost, which is driven by the actual use of the manufacturing facility, is the variable portion of electricity cost. Exhibit 5-7 shows a graph of a mixed cost.

Exhibit 5-7 Graph of a Mixed Cost

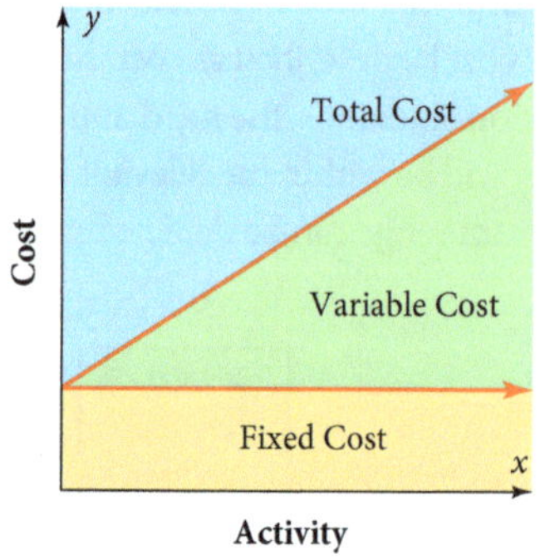

Exhibit 5-7 shows that even when the activity level is at zero (the intercept of the x-axis and the y-axis), cost is incurred. This cost is the fixed element of the mixed cost. As activity increases, the cost rises from that initial point. This cost is the variable component of the mixed cost.

You may have observed that the graph in Exhibit 5-7 is quite similar to that in Exhibit 5-5 depicting the total cost of the climbing club party. This similarity occurs because total cost (which is composed of its fixed costs and its variable costs) could be described as one giant mixed cost.

Discussion Questions

5-5. Consider the costs involved in operating a fast-food restaurant such as **McDonald's**. What are three examples of activities that would have mixed costs?

Assume you are the sales manager for the Hinds Wholesale Supply Company, and you are trying to estimate the cost of operating the fleet of delivery vehicles for the coming year. The only information you have is that $110,000 was spent last year to operate the fleet.

5-6. Would it help you to know which delivery vehicle costs are fixed and which are variable? Why?

5-7. What other information would you need to gather before being able to estimate next year's costs?

5-8. Why would the sales manager at Hinds Wholesale Supply Company be concerned about the cost of delivery vehicles?

Identifying the Fixed and Variable Elements of a Mixed Cost

Even when we know that a cost is a combination of both fixed and variable costs, we have no information to tell us how much of the cost is unaffected by the level of activity (fixed) and how much of it will increase as activity increases (variable). Cost information is much more useful for cost control, planning, and decision making purposes if the manager can determine which part of a mixed cost is fixed and which is variable. In this section we will discuss four methods commonly used to identify the fixed and variable elements of a mixed cost: the engineering approach, scatter graphing, the high-low method, and regression analysis.

The Engineering Approach

The **engineering approach** relies on engineers or other professionals who are familiar with the technical aspect of the activity and the associated cost to analyze the situation and determine which costs are fixed and which are variable. This approach may employ time-and-motion studies or other aspects of scientific management.

engineering approach A method of separating mixed cost into its fixed and variable components using experts that are familiar with the technical aspects of the activity and associated cost.

For example, experts in the field of aviation and aircraft operations could analyze the cost of operating a corporate aircraft to determine which portion of the operating cost increases as aircraft usage increases and which portion of the cost remains constant. Based on the experts' industry experience and evaluations, they would then separate the fixed and variable components of this mixed cost.

Analysts would be likely to use flying time as the activity level base because hours of use will affect costs. They would then classify the cost of insurance and of renting hangar space in which to store the plane as fixed costs. Why? The insurance and rental costs are unaffected by the number of hours the plane may be flown. The cost of the airplane's battery will likely be classified as a fixed cost because the deterioration of this item and the need for replacement are affected more by the passing of time and very little by the number of flight hours.

Aviation experts would probably classify fuel costs and certain expected maintenance and repair costs as variable costs, because both depend on usage. For example, experts may estimate that a plane's engines require an overhaul every 2,000 hours of flight time.

Discussion Questions

Again assume you are a sales manager for the Hinds Wholesale Supply Company trying to estimate the cost of operating the fleet of delivery vehicles for the coming year.

5-9. Would you engage the services of an automotive expert to help separate costs into fixed and variable? Why or why not?

5-10. List four costs you (or the automotive expert) would identify as part of the cost of operating the fleet of delivery trucks. Classify each by its cost behavior and the activity to which it relates.

5-11. If an expert determined that the fixed cost of operating each vehicle is $3,000 per year and the variable cost is $0.10 per mile, what would be the expected cost of operating the fleet next year? (Assume there are eight trucks, and they are each driven an average of 25,000 miles per year.)

The engineering approach to separating mixed cost relies on an expert's experience and judgment to classify costs as fixed or variable. It is often used when the company has no past experience concerning a cost's reaction to activity. In contrast, the other three methods we examine use historical data and mathematical computations to approximate the fixed and variable components of mixed cost.

Scatter Graphing

The **scatter graph approach** plots historical activity and cost data on a graph to see how a cost relates to various levels of activity. An analyst places a straight line through the visual center of

scatter graph approach A method of separating a mixed cost into its fixed and variable components by plotting historical activity and cost data to determine how the cost relates to various levels of activity.

the points plotted on the graph as shown in Exhibit 5-8. Then using some simple calculations, the analyst can approximate the fixed and variable elements of the cost being analyzed.

Exhibit 5-8 Sample Scatter Graph

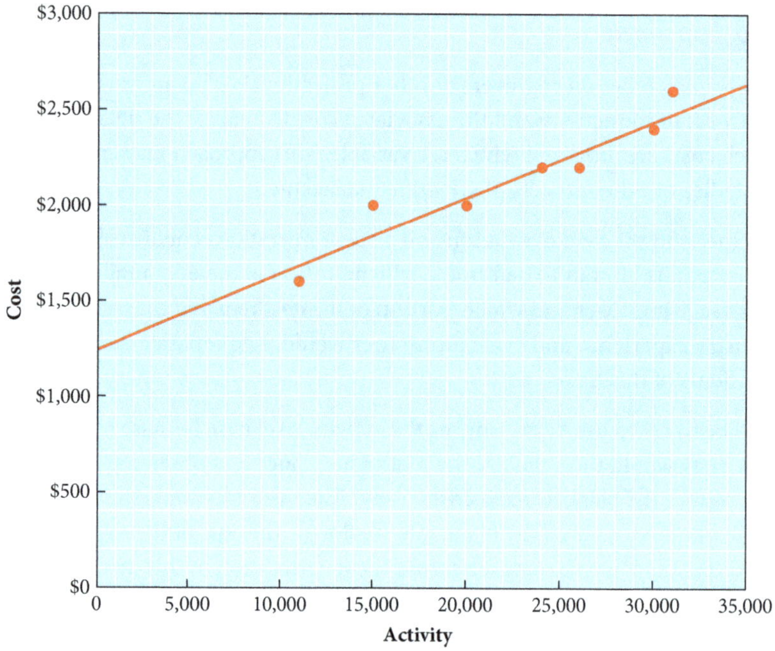

To demonstrate how scatter graphing is used, imagine you are again the sales manager for the Hinds Wholesale Supply Company with the task of estimating the expected delivery vehicle operating cost for 2009. One of the operating costs is vehicle maintenance, which you think is a mixed cost, so you need to determine how much of that cost is fixed, and how much is variable. Your first step is to obtain relevant historical cost data. At your request, the accounting department provides you with the following maintenance cost information about the company's delivery vehicles for 2008:

Truck Number	Maintenance Cost
202	$2,000
204	1,600
205	2,200
301	2,400
422	2,600
460	2,200
520	2,000

You now ask yourself a couple of questions. First, is vehicle maintenance cost a fixed cost? Clearly it is not a fixed cost, because the cost is not the same for all trucks. Second, is this cost a variable cost? Well, if it is a variable cost, it varies based on some activity. After careful consideration, you determine that activity might be either (1) the number of miles driven or (2) the number of packages delivered. On request, the accounting department provides you with the following expanded data for 2008:

Truck Number	Miles Driven	Packages Delivered	Maintenance Cost
202	15,000	1,200	$2,000
204	11,000	1,000	1,600
205	24,000	1,500	2,200
301	30,000	1,500	2,400
422	31,000	500	2,600
460	26,000	1,000	2,200
520	20,000	2,000	2,000

Remember, if a cost is truly variable, it changes proportionately as activity changes. Let's consider miles driven first and see whether there is a proportional change in total vehicle maintenance cost as activity changes. Compare trucks 202 and 301. The miles driven for truck 301 are exactly twice as many as for truck 202. If vehicle maintenance cost is variable based on miles driven, then the cost for truck 301 should be twice the cost for truck 202, but it is not.

Now we look at packages delivered as the activity. Compare truck 204 with truck 422. Truck 204 delivered twice as many packages as truck 422. If vehicle maintenance cost is variable based on the number of packages delivered, the cost for truck 204 should be exactly twice the cost for truck 422. Again, it is not.

If a cost is neither fixed nor variable, then it is mixed, meaning it has both a fixed element and a variable element. This is the case with Hinds' delivery vehicle maintenance cost. Therefore, you must find a way to estimate the amount of fixed and variable costs associated with the maintenance cost if you are to reasonably predict the vehicle maintenance cost for 2009.

To use the scatter graph method to determine the fixed and variable elements of the vehicle maintenance cost, the first step is to plot the information for each observation (in this case, each delivery vehicle) on a graph. Remember, the vertical axis on a graph is the y-axis (total cost), and the horizontal axis is the x-axis (activity). Recall also that the independent variable, shown as the x-axis, is not affected by a change in y. However, the dependent variable value, shown on the y-axis, depends on the numerical value of the x variable. The assumption is that a change in x will lead to a change in y.

If a truck driver travels 1,000 miles, for example, Hinds must spend money on gasoline. In our case, driving is the independent (x) variable and the company's gasoline cost is the dependent (y) variable. Driving affects the company's gasoline cost; however, the reverse does not hold true. The mere purchase of gasoline, which increases the dependent (y) variable, will not cause a change in the number of miles driven.

For mixed cost calculations, the y variable is the cost affected by the activity and it is the cost you are trying to estimate. The x variable represents the activity you believe will affect the cost behavior. Do not fall into the trap of thinking that the dependent variable (y) will be measured in dollars and the independent variable (x) will not. It is possible to predict a cost such as sales commissions, expressed in dollars, based on an activity such as sales, also expressed in dollars.

For the Hinds Wholesale Supply Company example, the data have two possible activity-cost pairs. The first pair is the number of miles driven and vehicle maintenance cost. The second pair is the number of packages delivered and vehicle maintenance cost.

We begin by graphing maintenance cost and miles driven. When we plot the data on a graph, we plot each observation as a pair of values. The maintenance cost for a particular vehicle—the dependent variable—is plotted using the scale on the y-axis. The miles driven for the same vehicle—the independent variable—are plotted using the scale on the x-axis. The position on the graph occupied by the plotted pair of numbers is called a *coordinate*. As the graph in Exhibit 5-9 indicates, each observation is represented by a dot.

Exhibit 5-9 Scatter Graph for Hinds Company Vehicle Maintenance Cost and Miles Driven

DATA:

Truck Number	Miles Driven	Maintenance Cost
202	15,000	$2,000
204	11,000	1,600
205	24,000	2,200
301	30,000	2,400
422	31,000	2,600
460	26,000	2,200
520	20,000	2,000

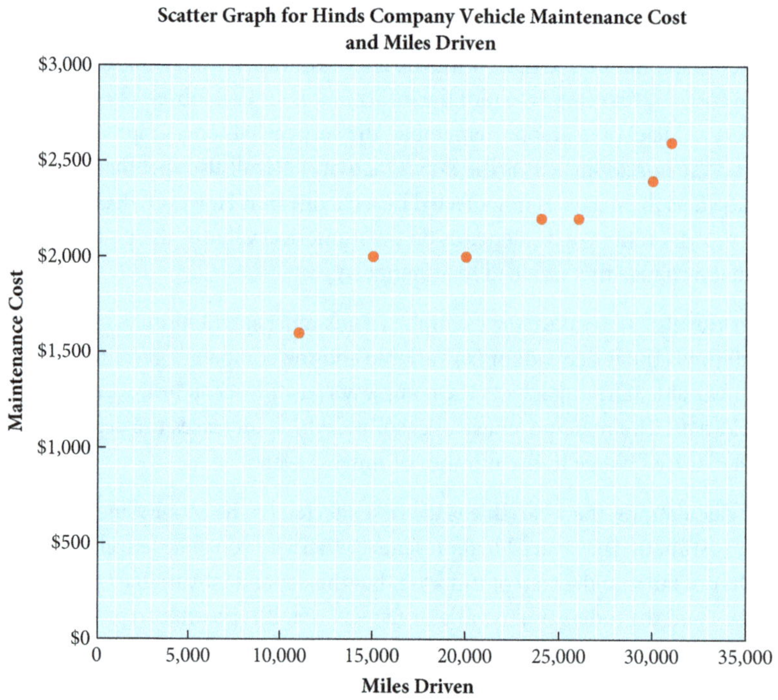

The next step is to place a straight line through the visual center of the plotted coordinates, which we have done in Exhibit 5-10.

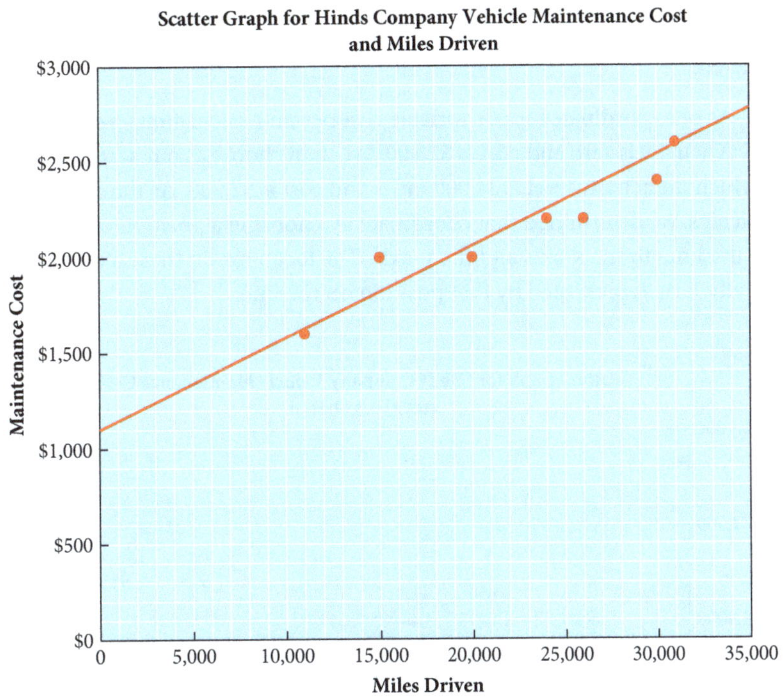

Exhibit 5-10 Scatter Graph for Vehicle Maintenance Cost and Miles Driven

In Exhibit 5-10 it is easy to place the straight line through the points on the graph because they seem to line up in a nearly straight line on their own. This straight line effect occurs when the relationship of the two variables is quite correlated, or linear. The graph in Exhibit 5-10 suggests a relatively constant relationship between the miles driven (x) and maintenance cost (y). The straight line represents the behavior of maintenance cost as it relates to the number of miles driven.

Now that we have a completed scatter graph for Hinds' vehicle maintenance cost, we can employ some simple calculations to approximate the fixed and variable portion of that cost. As you recall from earlier in the chapter:

Total Cost = Fixed Cost + Variable Cost

For total mixed costs we can modify the equation slightly as follows:

Total Mixed Cost = Fixed Cost Element + Variable Cost Element

When using the scatter graph method, we identify the fixed element of the maintenance cost first. Note that in Exhibit 5-10 the straight line that indicates the relationship of miles driven and maintenance cost intercepts the y-axis at $1,100. At this point, the x variable (miles) is zero, which suggests that when activity is zero, maintenance cost will still be $1,100. That $1,100 represents fixed cost. In the scatter graph method, we determine fixed cost simply by noting where the straight line intercepts the y-axis. Thus, in our example we now know the following information:

Total Mixed Cost = $1,100 + Variable Cost Element

Next, we find the variable cost per mile using simple mathematics. First we choose two points from anywhere along the *scatter graph line* to determine the effect of the x

variable on the y variable. *Note:* Because the points must be directly on the line, we can't use any of the points from our original data (unless one happens to be directly on the scatter graph line). Any two positions on the line are fine, but it is better to select points that are somewhat separated. That way, the error caused by our visual estimation in reading the graph will be small relative to the numerical difference between the two points selected.

As one coordinate for our variable cost per unit calculations, we select the point at which activity is zero and cost is $1,100. We then choose as our second point the coordinate at which the activity level is 34,000 miles and cost is $2,700. As the graph in Exhibit 5-11 indicates, we determined that coordinate by choosing a position on the line and following the lines to the x-axis and the y-axis. The locations on these axes indicate the cost and activity level represented by that position on the line.

Exhibit 5-11 Scatter Graph with Activity Points Selected

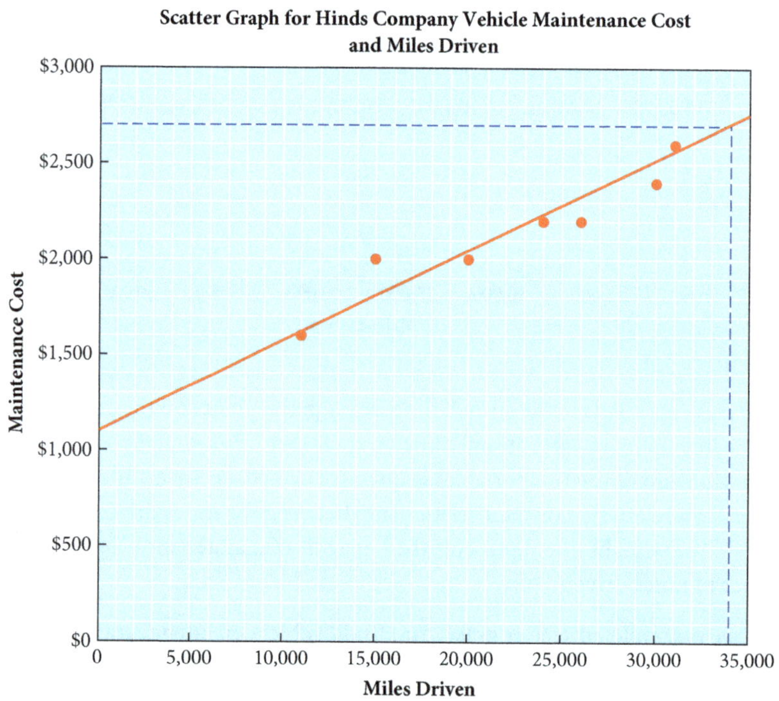

The next step is to determine the mathematical difference between the two coordinates.

Miles	Cost
34,000	$2,700
(0)	(1,100)
34,000	$1,600

We can see from our calculations that the maintenance cost at 34,000 miles is $1,600 higher than it is for zero miles. What do you think caused the $1,600 difference? We assume that the increase was caused exclusively by driving the 34,000 miles.

Now we can calculate the average amount of maintenance cost per mile caused by the additional activity. We do this by dividing the 34,000 mileage difference into the $1,600 increased maintenance cost:

$$\$1{,}600 \div 34{,}000 = \$0.047059, \text{ or about 4.7 cents per mile}$$

The calculations show that each additional mile of driving causes maintenance cost to rise by $0.047. If we combine this information with the fixed cost information determined earlier, we can create a cost formula for vehicle maintenance cost:

$$\text{Vehicle Maintenance Cost} = \$1{,}100 + (\$0.047 \text{ per mile driven})$$

We have now used scatter graphing to separate maintenance cost into its fixed and variable components. With this information, we can project maintenance cost at any level of activity. To do this, we add the fixed cost to the activity multiplied by the cost per unit of activity. For example, the estimated maintenance cost for a single delivery truck that will be driven 28,000 miles is $2,416, calculated as follows:

$$\$2{,}416 = \$1{,}100 + (\$0.047 \times 28{,}000)$$

Discussion Questions

5-12. Based on the information obtained from the scatter graph, what would be the maintenance cost of operating one delivery truck if we expected the truck to be driven 25,000 miles next year?

5-13. Based on the information obtained from the scatter graph, what would be the maintenance cost of operating a fleet of delivery trucks? (Assume there are eight trucks, and they are driven an average of 25,000 miles each.)

Now we turn to the information the accounting department provided about the number of packages delivered. Then we use the scatter graphing method to plot maintenance cost as the dependent (y) variable and packages delivered as the independent (x) variable. Exhibit 5-12 shows a scatter graph of the maintenance cost and packages delivered.

Exhibit 5-12 Scatter Graph for Vehicle Maintenance Cost and Packages Delivered

DATA:

Truck Number	Packages Delivered	Maintenance Cost
202	1,200	$2,000
204	1,000	1,600
205	1,500	2,200
301	1,500	2,400
422	500	2,600
460	1,000	2,200
520	2,000	2,000

Exhibit 5-12 *(Continued)*

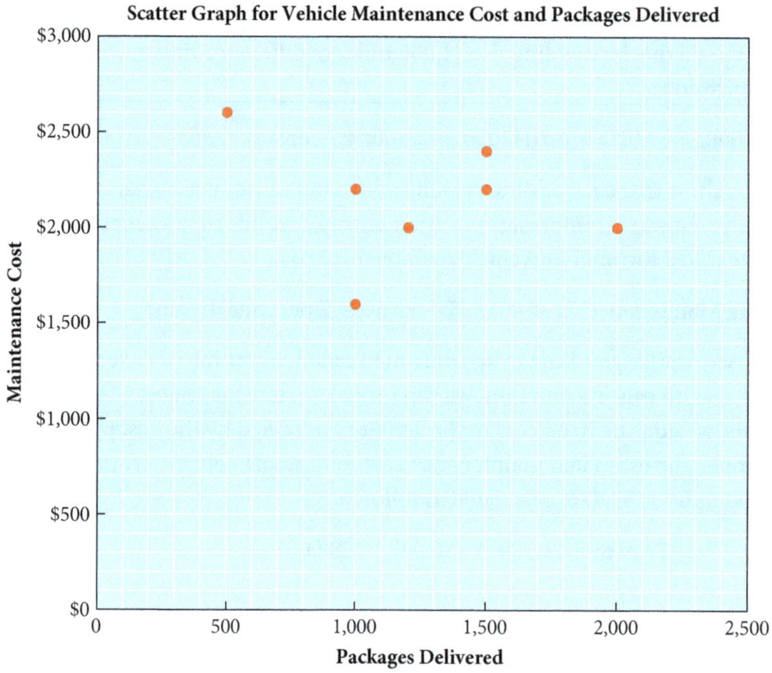

We attempt to draw a meaningful straight line through the points depicted by the observations, as in Exhibit 5-13.

Exhibit 5-13 Scatter Graph for Vehicle Maintenance Cost and Packages Delivered

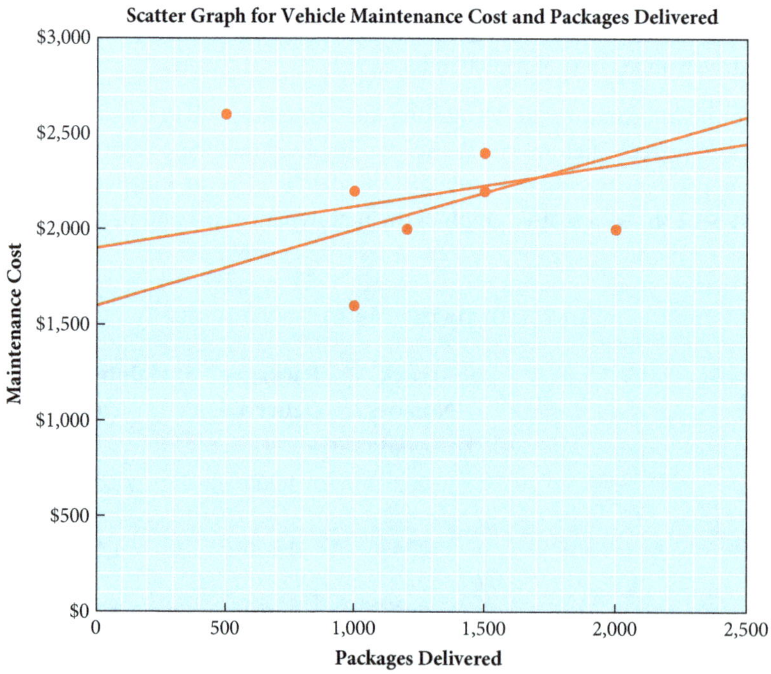

Note in Exhibit 5-13 that placing a straight line through the points on this graph is considerably more challenging than in the previous scatter graph. This is because a straight line could take any one of several paths through the points on the graph. Each of the lines seems to depict the relationship between maintenance cost and packages delivered, but none does a very good job. The reason for the difficulty is that the relationship between the variables is not linear. How do we use this method if the data do not have a clear linear relationship? Well, we don't. Before we employ the scatter graph method, we must be sure the activity we have chosen has a relatively linear relationship with the cost in question. That is, the data should be correlated. If we plot points on a graph and the coordinates resemble a random pattern with little linearity, the data do not indicate a constant relationship between the activity and the cost. In the case of a random pattern, any conclusions drawn from the data will be useless for predicting future cost, and may cause trouble if used. Once we see that random pattern then, we should not use the packages delivered data to estimate the fixed and variable elements of vehicle maintenance cost.

Even if a scatter graph appears to represent a linear relationship between an activity and a cost, we must be cautious to not imply relationships that do not exist. For instance, if we tried to determine cost behavior of vehicle maintenance cost by relating it to an activity such as the number of direct labor hours worked, we might possibly get mathematically reasonable results. However, common sense tells us that no relationship exists between direct labor hours and vehicle maintenance cost, so the results would be meaningless. A random guess would provide as good or better information. The activity and cost should have a clear, common sense relationship.

The High-Low Method

high-low method A method of separating a mixed cost into its fixed and variable components using the mathematical differences between the highest and lowest levels of activity and cost.

Like the scatter graph approach, the **high-low method** uses historical data and mathematical computations to approximate the fixed and variable components of mixed cost. To illustrate the steps required by the high-low method, we review the following vehicle maintenance cost and activity data gathered for the Hinds Wholesale Supply Company:

Truck Number	Miles Driven	Maintenance Cost
202	1,200	$2,000
204	1,000	1,600
205	1,500	2,200
301	1,500	2,400
422	500	2,600
460	1,000	2,200
520	2,000	2,000

The high-low method focuses on the mathematical differences between the highest and lowest observations unless one or both of them is clearly too high or too low to be representative of the rest of the data. In such a case, we would select the next highest or lowest observation. If we examine the data list, we see that the highest observation is 31,000 miles with maintenance cost of $2,600. The lowest observation is 11,000 miles with maintenance cost of $1,600.

Remember, our purpose is to find the amount of the fixed and variable elements of a mixed cost. With the high-low method, we focus on determining the variable component of the cost first. The calculations to determine variable cost per unit are similar to those used in scatter graphing. By comparing the differences in activity and cost between the highest observation and the lowest observation, we can calculate a per unit cost that describes the relationship shown by these differences as follows:

	Miles	Cost
High	31,000	$2,600
Low	(11,000)	(1,600)
Difference	20,000	$1,000

Notice the mileage difference of 20,000 miles is accompanied by a cost difference of $1,000. So, to drive the extra 20,000 miles, the company spent $1,000 more in maintenance cost. We assume that the $1,000 increase in maintenance cost was caused exclusively by the increase in the number of miles from 11,000 to 31,000 miles. The cost per mile, then, is simply the $1,000 increased cost divided by the 20,000 additional miles as shown here:

$$\$1{,}000 \div 20{,}000 = \$0.05, \text{ or 5 cents per mile}$$

Before we calculate the fixed cost element, recall that total mixed cost is total fixed cost plus total variable cost (Total Mixed Cost = Fixed Cost Element + Variable Cost Element). The variable cost element can be calculated by multiplying the variable cost per unit by the activity. In this case we multiply the variable cost per mile by the number of miles. With what we have determined thus far, we can begin to construct a cost formula for vehicle maintenance cost as follows:

$$\text{Total Mixed Cost} = \text{Fixed Cost Element} + (\$0.05 \text{ per mile driven})$$

For each of our observations (high and low), we know the total mixed cost and variable cost element. Therefore, we can easily determine the fixed cost element with simple calculations. Let's determine the fixed cost element associated with the high observation used in our example.

$$\text{Total Mixed Cost} = \text{Fixed Cost Element} + (\$0.05 \text{ per mile driven})$$

$$\$2{,}600 = ? + (\$0.05 \times 31{,}000)$$

$$\$2{,}600 = ? + \$1{,}550$$

To solve the equation, the fixed cost element must be $2,600-$1,550, or $1,050, shown as follows:

$$\text{Total Mixed Cost} = \text{Fixed Cost Element} + (\$0.05 \text{ per mile driven})$$

$$\$2{,}600 = \$1{,}050 + \$1{,}550$$

We now know both the variable cost per mile and the total fixed cost of operating one of the delivery vehicles. To check our math, we can do the same calculation for the low observation, as follows:

$$\text{Total Mixed Cost} = \text{Fixed Cost Element} + (\$0.05 \text{ per mile driven})$$

$$\$1{,}600 = ? + (\$0.05 \times 11{,}000)$$

$$\$1{,}600 = ? + \$550$$

For the low observation, to solve the equation, fixed cost must be $1,600 − $550, or $1,050, as we see next.

Total Mixed Cost	=	Fixed Cost Element	+	($0.05 per mile driven)
$1,600	=	$1,050	+	$550

Note that you must use either the high or the low to determine the fixed cost. Using an observation other than the ones you used for the variable cost calculation will provide an erroneous fixed cost amount.

The high-low method yields a fixed cost for maintenance of $1,050, and a variable cost of 5 cents per mile. As with scatter graphing, to estimate the mixed cost at a particular level of activity we add the fixed cost to the activity multiplied by the cost per unit of activity. For example, the estimated maintenance cost for a single delivery truck that will be driven 28,000 miles is $2,450, calculated as follows:

$$\$2{,}450 = \$1{,}050 + (\$0.05 \times 28{,}000)$$

Discussion Questions

5-14. Using the high-low method and the data from our example, what would be the maintenance cost for operating one of the delivery trucks if we expected the truck to be driven 25,000 miles next year?

5-15. Using the high-low method and the information from our Hinds Company example, what would be the maintenance cost for operating the fleet of eight trucks, if each is to be driven 25,000 miles on average?

When we compare the scatter graph method with the high-low method, we find that the fixed and variable cost results are somewhat different. If you were going to present your cost estimates to the vice president of marketing, which method would you use? Which provides the most dependable information? The scatter graph method is based on visual estimation whereas the high-low method is based on hard mathematics with no visual estimation. Does that make the high-low method better? No, because the high-low method considers only two observations. What if these two observations are not representative of the data in general? Then the cost behavior conclusions will be flawed and possibly misleading.

Another drawback to the high-low method is that users cannot assess whether the data items have a linear relationship, which is necessary to find meaningful results. Because the scatter graph method considers all observations and indicates whether the data items have a linear relationship, practitioners regard it as superior to the high-low method, despite the fact that it is more time consuming to use and it is based on visual estimation.

Regression Analysis

Regression analysis, also called the **least-squares method** or **linear regression analysis**, is a mathematical approach to determining fixed and variable cost with statistical accuracy. The mathematical computations are complex and beyond the scope of this text; however, it is important to note that regression analysis is a more reliable estimation technique than either the scatter graph method or the high-low method. Regression analysis uses the information contained in all the observations in a data set. That thoroughness makes it superior to the high-low method. Because it considers all these points of observation mathematically, rather than visually, regression analysis is also superior to the scatter graph method. The basic mathematical equation for regression analysis follows:

regression analysis A method of separating a mixed cost into its fixed and variable components using fairly complex mathematical formulas.

least-squares method Another name for regression analysis.

linear regression analysis Another name for regression analysis.

$$y = a + bx$$

Where:

y = The dependent variable, or the variable that changes in response to a change in x.

a = The y intercept, or the amount for y when x is zero.

b = The slope coefficient, or the amount by which y changes when x is increased by one.

x = The independent variable

When applying regression analysis to find the fixed and variable elements of a mixed cost, the variables in the regression equation are defined as follows:

y = total cost

a = fixed cost

b = unit variable cost

x = activity level

Results of regression analysis would provide answers to the same questions that we posed for the scatter graph and the high-low methods. In fact, the results of regression analysis allow us to determine total cost, y, for any given level of activity, x. Reexamine the basic regression analysis formula and compare it with the total cost equation. When we rewrite the equation, we see that it translates directly to our earlier total cost equation, as follows:

$$y = a + bx$$

$$\text{Total Cost} = \text{Fixed Cost} + (\text{Unit Variable Cost} \times \text{Activity Level})$$

Although regression analysis is difficult to compute manually, almost all business calculators, such as the ***Hewlett-Packard** 12c*, are programmed to compute linear regression problems. By reading your calculator's instruction manual and practicing a little, you can easily determine fixed and variable cost components of a mixed cost using linear regression. In addition, most spreadsheet software packages provide easy-to-use regression functions. In the following sections we will briefly demonstrate how you can use **Microsoft** Excel, a very popular spreadsheet program, to prepare cost behavior scatter graphs.

Microsoft Excel—Preparing an Excel Scatter Graph

Basically, what we will do here is to use **Microsoft** Excel to prepare the charts we prepared by hand when we covered the scatter-graph approach. As we did with the manual scatter graph approach, we will use historical data and let Excel do the graphing and mathematical computations to approximate costs at various levels of activity.

To illustrate the use of Excel, we will again use the vehicle maintenance cost and activity data gathered for the Hinds Wholesale Supply Company.

Whether you are using Excel 2003 or Excel 2007, to begin, open a new spreadsheet. Use row 1 to put headings in columns A, B, and C. Enter *Truck No.* in cell A1, enter *Miles* in cell B1, and enter *Cost* in cell C1. Now use the truck numbers, the miles each truck was driven, and the maintenance cost for each truck to populate the spreadsheet. We should note here that the information you enter into row 1 and column A will not be used in our calculations. The information in row 1 and column A is solely to identify the data that will be used in the calculations. Now enter the first truck's number (202) in cell A2, the number of miles for the first truck (15,000) in cell B2 and its maintenance cost ($2,000) in cell C2. Do the same thing for the second truck by placing its truck number in cell A3, the miles for the second truck in cell B3 and its maintenance cost in cell C3. Now do this for all of the remaining trucks. It is critical that the amounts for the independent variable (the activity) be entered in the column just before the column for the amounts for the dependant variable (the mixed cost). This is why we used column B for the activity (the miles) and the next column, column C, for the mixed cost (the maintenance cost). When you are done, your spreadsheet should look like the one in Exhibit 5-14.

	A	B	C
1	Truck Number	Miles	Cost
2	202	15,000	$2,000
3	204	11,000	$1,600
4	205	24,000	$2,200
5	301	30,000	$2,400
6	422	31,000	$2,600
7	460	26,000	$2,200
8	520	20,000	$2,000

Exhibit 5-14 **Microsoft** Excel Spreadsheet with Data for Hinds Wholesale Supply Company

Next, highlight all the cells that include the activity and cost data. For our example, highlight only the cells that contain amounts for the number of miles and maintenance costs. Your highlighted spreadsheet should look like the one in Exhibit 5-15.

	A	B	C
1	Truck Number	Miles	Cost
2	202	15,000	$2,000
3	204	11,000	$1,600
4	205	24,000	$2,200
5	301	30,000	$2,400
6	422	31,000	$2,600
7	460	26,000	$2,200
8	520	20,000	$2,000

Exhibit 5-15 **Microsoft** Excel Spreadsheet with Highlighted Data for Hinds Wholesale Supply Company

If you are using Excel 2003, select the **Insert** pull-down menu and click on **chart**. The Chart Wizard box will appear. From the list of **Chart Types**, click **XY (Scatter)** and use the Wizard's default scatter graph. Once you have clicked **XY (Scatter)**, click **Next**. You are now at **Chart Wizard—Step 2 of 4**. For **Step 2**, simply click **Next**. You are now at **Chart Wizard—Step 3 of 4**. In this step, you can customize the labels on your chart so it looks professional. For **Chart title**, enter something like *Hinds Company Vehicle Maintenance Cost and Miles Driven*. For **Value (X) axis** enter *Miles Driven*, and for **Value (Y) axis** enter *Maintenance Cost*. To remove the legend, on the **Legend** tab, click the **Show legend** box to remove the check mark. Then click **Next**. You are now at **Chart Wizard—Step 4 of 4**. Unless you would like the chart to appear on another sheet of your workbook, simply click **Finish**. Your chart should look like the one in Exhibit 5-16.

Exhibit 5-16 **Microsoft** Excel Scatter Graph for the Hinds Company

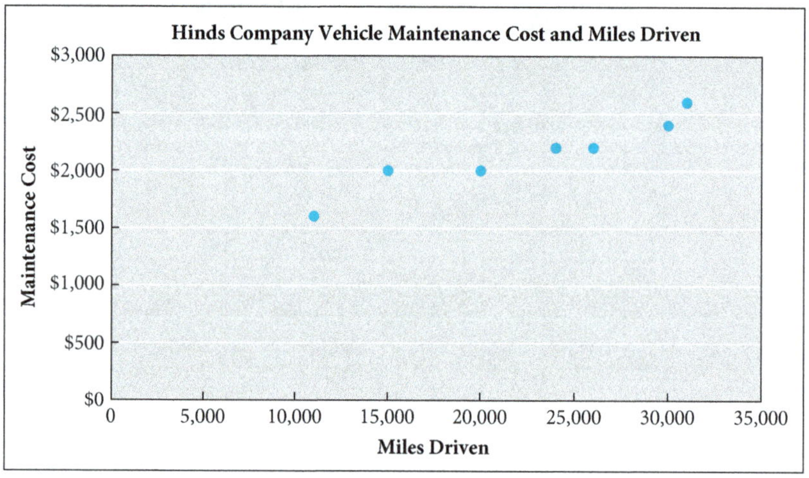

If you are using Excel 2007, select the **Insert** tab. Then from the **Scatter** pull-down menu select the chart that has no lines connecting the plotted points. A basic scatter chart will appear. Next, select the **Layout** tab and use the **Chart Title**, **Axis Titles**, and **Legend** pull-down menus to customize your chart. Once you have added appropriate titles and removed the legend, your chart should look like the one in Exhibit 5-16.

So that the chart can be used to predict costs, we now add a regression line, or what Excel calls a trendline. To do this in Excel 2003, select the **Chart** pull-down menu and click on **Add Trendline**. The **Add Trendline** box will appear. Go with the default trend line (the straight one) and then click on the **Options** tab where you can extend the line forward and backward. If you are using Excel 2007, under the **Layout** tab, use the **Trendline** pull-down menu and select **More Trendline Options** at the bottom. This option will add a linear trend line and allow you to extend or "Forecast" the line forward and backward. It's a good idea to extend the trend line backward to the axis and forward beyond its highest point so the line does not end at the chart's lowest and highest plotted points. Once you are in the Trendline options box, whether you are using Excel 2003 or 2007, to extend the trend line backward enter the lowest *x* value from your data set in **Forecast Backward**. Using the Hinds example, enter 11,000, which is the *x* value for the truck with the fewest miles. In **Forecast Forward**, we will enter 2,000 for this example, which represents the number of miles to extend the trend line forward. Once you have entered the values for **Forecast Backward** and **Forecast Forward**, click **OK** if you are using Excel 2003 or **Close** if you are using Excel 2007. At this point, your chart should look like the one in Exhibit 5-17.

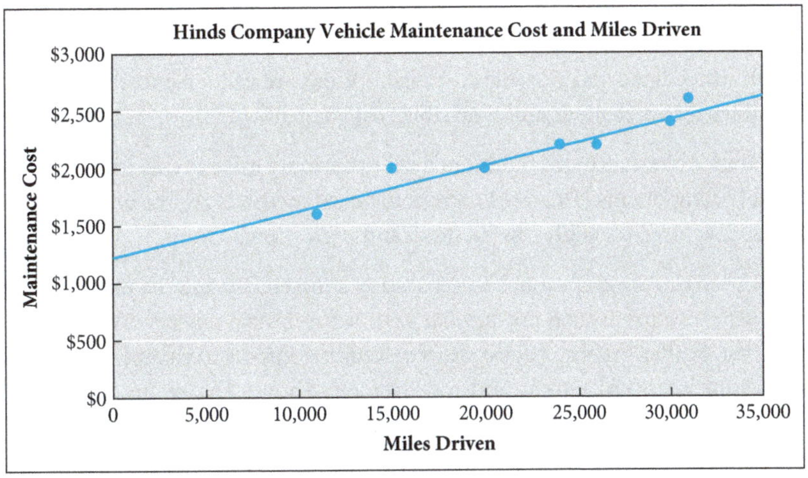

Exhibit 5-17 **Microsoft** Excel Scatter Graph with Trend Line for the Hinds Company

The Excel chart you have just prepared is very similar to the manually prepared ones we demonstrated earlier in this chapter. The most significant difference is that Excel uses regression analysis to precisely plot the chart's trend line, whereas we used visual estimation to plot it manually.

Once you have prepared a chart similar to the one in Exhibit 5-17, you can predict costs for any level of activity shown on the chart. For example, we can readily see that the fixed cost of vehicle maintenance for Hinds is about $1,200. And for a truck driven 25,000 miles, the maintenance cost should be about $2,250.

You can customize the chart, making it easier to use, by adding additional tick marks and making other modifications.

No matter which of the methods a company uses to separate mixed costs into fixed and variable elements, the outcome of the mixed cost analysis is useful information for controlling costs, setting prices, and assessing profitability. Indeed, a variety of internal users of accounting information, from marketing managers to production managers, will want access to such cost behavior information.

Whether large or small, simple or complex, managers of all companies must understand cost behavior. Production managers at companies as diverse as **Caterpillar Tractor** and **Campbell Soup Company** need this information to plan and control their operations. Marketing managers at companies as different as **General Motors** and **Gerber Baby Foods** must know how costs react to activity if they are to do their jobs properly.

Once a determination has been made as to a cost's behavior, an appropriate notation can be made in the accounting records to designate it as fixed, variable, or mixed. Then, the accounting system can produce reports sorted by cost behavior. Internal reports providing cost behavior information are valuable in a variety of decision making settings. We will explore several of these settings in more detail in the next chapter.

Summary

If managers are to plan and control their operations effectively, they must understand cost behavior. Cost behavior is the reaction of costs to changes in levels of business activity.

Common cost behavior patterns are fixed cost, variable cost, and mixed cost. A fixed cost is a cost that remains constant in total regardless of the level of activity within the relevant range. A variable cost is a cost that changes in total proportionately with changes in the level of activity within the relevant range. The relevant range is the range of activity within which fixed and variable cost assumptions are valid. A mixed cost is a cost that has both a fixed cost element and a variable cost element.

Several alternative methods are used to separate mixed costs into their fixed and variable components. The most commonly used methods are the engineering approach, scatter graphing, the high-low method, and regression analysis.

The engineering approach to separating a mixed cost into its fixed and variable components uses experts who are familiar with the technical aspects of the activity and associated cost. Scatter graphing separates a mixed cost into its fixed and variable components by plotting historical activity and cost data to see how a cost relates to various levels of activity. The high-low method uses the mathematical differences between the highest and lowest levels of activity and cost. Regression analysis uses complex mathematical formulas, but the results are more mathematically precise than those of the scatter graph or high-low method. Microsoft Excel uses regression analysis and an easy-to-use chart menus to prepare precise, high quality scatter graphs for mixed costs.

Regardless of the method that managers choose to separate mixed costs into fixed and variable elements, the analysis provides useful information for a myriad of business decisions.

Key Terms

Review the Facts

A. What is cost behavior?

B. For fixed costs, what happens to total cost as activity increases?

C. For fixed costs, what happens to the cost per unit as activity increases?

D. For variable cost, what happens to total cost as activity increases?

E. For variable cost, what happens to the cost per unit as activity increases?

F. With respect to cost behavior, what is the relevant range?

G. Does the relevant range pertain to fixed costs, variable costs, or both fixed and variable costs?

H. What are the two elements of a mixed cost?

I. What are the four methods of separating a mixed cost into its two cost components?

J. Compare the high-low method to the scatter graph method. Which provides the more dependable information?

K. What is the major limitation of the high-low method?

L. What is another name for regression analysis?

M. If you desired the reliability of the regression analysis method but did not want to suffer through the difficulty of doing the mathematics manually, what would you do?

Apply What You Have Learned

LO 2: Classifying Cost by Cost Behavior

5-16. Indicate whether the following costs are more likely to be fixed (F), variable (V), or mixed (M) with respect to the number of units manufactured.

1. _____ Direct material
2. _____ Direct labor
3. _____ Cost of the plant security guard
4. _____ Straight line depreciation on production equipment
5. _____ Maintenance on production equipment
6. _____ Maintenance on factory building
7. _____ Cost of cleaning supplies used in the factory
8. _____ Rent on the factory building
9. _____ Salary for the two factory supervisors
10. _____ Vice president of manufacturing's salary
11. _____ Cost of electricity used in the factory
12. _____ Cost of production machine lubricants

LO 2: Classifying Cost by Cost Behavior

5-17. Assume that you are trying to analyze the costs associated with driving your car. Indicate whether the following costs are more likely to be fixed (F), variable (V), or mixed (M) with respect to the number of miles driven.

1. _____ Cost of the car
2. _____ Insurance cost
3. _____ Maintenance cost
4. _____ Cost of gasoline
5. _____ The cost of a college parking permit
6. _____ AAA membership

LO 2: Classifying Cost by Cost Behavior

5-18. Assume that you are planning a large party. As you are trying to figure out how much the party will cost, you decide to separate the costs according to cost behavior. Indicate whether the following costs are more likely to be fixed (F), variable (V), or mixed (M) with respect to the number of guests attending the party.

1. _____ Rent for the party hall
2. _____ Cost of the band
3. _____ Cost of cold drinks
4. _____ Cost of food
5. _____ Cost of party decorations
6. _____ Cost of renting tables and chairs

LO 2: Classifying Cost by Cost Behavior

5-19. Assume that you have been assigned to analyze the costs associated with operating the law firm of Moore & Moore and Company. The law firm just moved into a new, large office building that it purchased last year. Indicate whether the following costs are more likely to be fixed (F), variable (V), or mixed (M) with respect to the number of attorneys working for the firm.

1. _____ Cost of the new office building
2. _____ Basic telephone service
3. _____ Cost of attorney salaries
4. _____ Cost of the receptionist's wages

LO 2: Classifying Cost by Cost Behavior

5-20. Assume that you have been assigned to analyze the costs of a retail merchandiser, Auto Parts City. Indicate whether the following costs are more likely fixed (F), variable (V), or mixed (M) with respect to the dollar amount of sales.

1. _____ Cost of store rent
2. _____ Basic telephone service
3. _____ Cost of salaries for the two salespeople
4. _____ Cost of advertising

5. _____ Cost of store displays

6. _____ Cost of electricity

7. _____ Cost of merchandise sold

LO 4: Evaluating a Mixed Cost Situation

5-21. Assume that you work for Wilma Manufacturing Company and have been asked to review the cost of delivery truck maintenance. The company president, Wilma Hudik, is dissatisfied with the accounting department's reluctance to calculate the fixed and variable cost of truck maintenance as it pertains to the number of units produced in the factory. The accounting department prepared the following scatter graph:

The accounting department personnel seem unable to use the graph to determine fixed and variable cost. The company president knows that regression analysis will provide mathematically accurate amounts for the fixed and variable truck maintenance cost, but no one in the accounting department seems to know how to do it.

Required:

Prepare a short memo to the president that details the feasibility of using the scatter graph and regression analysis to determine the fixed and variable components of delivery truck maintenance relative to the amount of factory production. In addition, your memo should recommend an alternative approach that could be used to evaluate the cost and cost behavior of truck maintenance.

LO 5: Use of a Scatter Graph for Separating Mixed Cost

5-22. Consider the following scatter graphs:

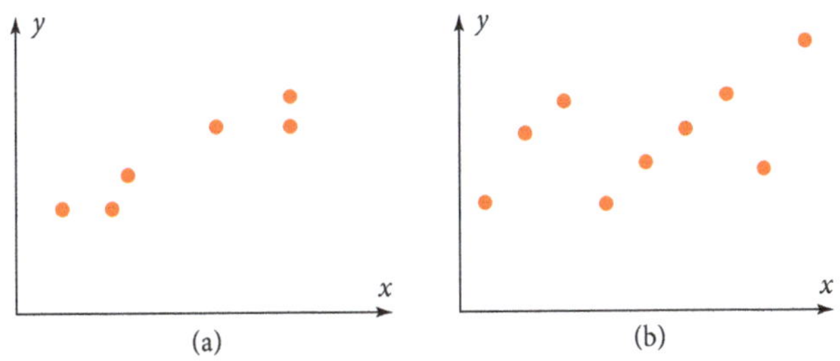

Required:

Which of the scatter graphs (a or b) do you think would be more appropriate for determining the fixed and variable portions of a mixed cost? Explain your reasoning.

LO 5: Separating Mixed Cost Using the High-Low Method

5-23. The following information pertains to Jacobs Incorporated:

2008 Information:	
Sales	$2,300,000
Selling expense	347,000
2009 Information:	
Sales	$2,860,000
Selling expense	369,400

Required:

Using the high-low method, determine the following:

a. The variable cost element for selling expense

b. The fixed selling expense

c. The selling expense that can be expected if sales are $2,500,000

LO 5: Separating Mixed Cost Using the High-Low Method

5-24. The following information pertains to the Robin Rappaport Company:

2008 Information:	
Units packaged	14,500
Packaging cost	$32,567
2009 Information:	
Units packaged	15,300
Packaging cost	$33,191

Required:

Using the high-low method, determine the following:

a. The variable cost element for packaging cost

b. The fixed packaging cost

c. The packaging cost that can be expected if 15,000 units are packaged

LO 5: Separating Mixed Cost Using the High-Low Method

5-25. The inspection department at the Rose Spiegel Company inspects every third unit produced. The following information is available for the inspection department:

2008 Information:	
Number of inspections	41,950
Inspection cost	$77,273
2009 Information:	
Number of inspections	48,600
Inspection cost	$83,790

Required:

Using the high-low method, determine the following:

a. The variable cost element for inspection cost

b. The fixed inspection cost

c. The inspection cost that can be expected if 45,000 units are inspected

LO 5: Separating Mixed Cost Using the High-Low Method

5-26. The plant manager has asked you to analyze the cost of electricity used in the manufacturing facility. Information for 2008 and 2009 follows:

	2008	2009
Machine hours	100,000	120,000
Cost of electricity	$188,000	$221,600

Required:

a. Determine the variable rate for electricity per machine hour.

b. Determine the total fixed cost of electricity.

c. Determine the estimated cost of electricity for next year if machine hours are expected to be 122,500.

LO 5: Separating Mixed Cost Using the High-Low Method

5-27. The office manager has asked you to analyze the cost of service and supplies for the office copy machines. Information for 2008 and 2009 follows:

	2008	2009
Number of copies produced	52,550	77,800
Cost of service and supplies	$1,961.57	$2,592.82

Required:

a. Determine the variable cost per copy.

b. Determine the total fixed cost for service and supplies for the copy machines.

c. Determine the estimated cost of service and supplies for next year if 75,000 copies are made.

LO 5: Separating Mixed Cost Using the High-Low Method

5-28. The production manager has asked you to analyze the cost of materials handling. Information for 2008 and 2009 follows:

	2008	2009
Number of parts handled	154,300	185,400
Materials handling cost	$9,244.77	$10,675.37

Required:

a. Determine the variable cost per part handled.

b. Determine the total fixed cost for materials handling.

c. Determine the estimated cost of materials handling if 160,000 parts are handled next year.

LO 5: Separating Mixed Cost Using the High-Low Method

5-29. The sales manager has asked you to estimate the shipping cost that can be expected for 2010. Following is information for 2008 and 2009:

	2008	2009
Sales in units	15,000	18,000
Shipping cost	$30,000	$35,400

Required:

Estimate 2010 shipping cost assuming sales of 16,500 units.

LO 5: Separating Mixed Cost Using the High-Low Method

5-30. The transportation manager has asked you to estimate the operating cost that can be expected for the company jet for 2010. Following is information for 2008 and 2009:

	2008	2009
Flight time in hours	1,250	1,875
Aircraft operating cost	$1,563,750	$2,148,125

Required:

Estimate the cost of operating the company jet for 2010 assuming that flight time will be 1,500 hours.

LO 5: Separating Mixed Cost Using the High-Low Method

5-31. Tom Robinson is the owner of Robinson Fishing Guide Service. He is trying to estimate the cost of operating his fishing service next year. He expects to have 185 charters during 2010. The following information is available:

	2008	2009
Number of charters	150	190
Operating cost	$7,741	$8,601

Required:

Determine the estimated operating cost for 2010.

LO 5: Separating Mixed Cost Using the High-Low Method

5-32. The following information pertains to Picon Manufacturing for 2008:

	Number of Purchase Orders Issued	Cost of Operating the Purchasing Department
Fourth quarter of 2007	2,500	$130,000
First quarter of 2008	1,000	80,000
Second quarter of 2008	1,500	110,000
Third quarter of 2008	2,000	115,000
Fourth quarter of 2008	3,000	140,000

Required:

Using the high-low method, determine the following:

a. The variable cost per purchase order

b. The fixed cost of operating the purchasing department for one quarter

c. The estimated cost of operating the purchasing department in 2009 assuming that 7,000 purchase orders will be issued. (Hint: Remember that the fixed cost for one year is four times the amount of fixed cost for one quarter.)

LO 5: Separating Mixed Cost Using the Scatter Graph Method

5-33. Refer to the information from problem 5-32.

Required:

Using the scatter graph method, determine the following:

a. The variable cost per purchase order

b. The fixed cost of operating the purchasing department for one quarter

c. The estimated cost of operating the purchasing department in 2009 assuming that 7,000 purchase orders will be issued. (Hint: Remember that the fixed cost for one year is four times the amount of fixed cost for one quarter.)

LO 6: Scatter Graph Using Microsoft Excel

5-34. Refer to the information from problem 5-32.

Required:

a. Use Microsoft Excel to prepare a scatter graph for the data presented.

b. Estimate the fixed cost of operating the purchasing department for one quarter.

c. Estimate the cost of operating the purchasing department for a quarter assuming that 1,500 purchase orders will be issued.

LO 5: Separating Mixed Cost Using the High-Low Method

5-35. The following information pertains to Mendelsohn Bottled Spring Water:

	Number of Sales Invoices Processed	Cost of Operating the Invoicing Department
Fourth quarter of 2007	10,500	$49,310.65
First quarter of 2008	11,000	50,332.12
Second quarter of 2008	15,000	58,120.19
Third quarter of 2008	12,000	51,939.73
Fourth quarter of 2008	9,000	46,240.19

Required:

Using the high-low method, determine the following:

a. The variable cost per invoice processed

b. The fixed cost of operating the invoicing department for one quarter

c. The estimated cost of operating the invoicing department in 2009 assuming that 45,000 invoices will be processed. (Hint: Remember that the fixed cost for one year is four times the amount of fixed cost for one quarter.)

LO 5: Separating Mixed Cost Using the High-Low Method

5-36. The following information pertains to Jillian Munter & Associates:

	Number of Computers Repaired	Cost of Operating the Repair Department
Fourth quarter of 2007	125	$26,100.91
First quarter of 2008	130	26,529.16
Second quarter of 2008	110	25,400.65
Third quarter of 2008	105	25,212.91
Fourth quarter of 2008	115	25,799.88

Required:

Using the high-low method, determine the following:

a. The variable cost per computer repair

b. The fixed cost of operating the repair department for one quarter

c. The estimated cost of operating the repair department in 2009 assuming that 450 invoices will be processed. (Hint: Remember that the fixed cost for one year is four times the amount of fixed cost for one quarter.)

LO 5: Separating Mixed Cost Using the High-Low Method

5-37. The following information is taken from Sweepy Broom Manufacturing Company:

	Number of Brooms Produced	Total Production Cost
January	9,800	$17,100
February	7,000	15,000
March	8,000	16,000
April	7,500	15,500
May	10,100	17,200
June	9,000	17,000
July	10,500	19,000
August	11,600	20,000
September	10,600	18,200
October	8,500	16,800
November	12,100	20,500
December	11,000	18,000

Required:

Using the high-low method, determine the following:

a. The variable production cost per unit
b. The total fixed production cost
c. The expected production cost to produce 12,000 brooms

LO 5: Separating Mixed Cost Using the Scatter Graph Method
5-38. Refer to the information in problem 5-37.

Required:

Using the scatter graph method, determine the following:

a. The variable production cost per unit
b. The total fixed production cost
c. The expected production cost to produce 12,000 brooms

LO 6: Scatter Graph Using Microsoft Excel
5-39. Refer to the information in problem 5-37.

Required:

a. Use Microsoft Excel to prepare a scatter graph for the data presented.
b. Estimate the total fixed production cost.
c. Estimate the expected production cost to produce 12,000 brooms.

LO 5: Separating Mixed Cost Using the High-Low Method
5-40. Ace Computer Training offers short computer courses. The number of course sessions offered depends on student demand. The following information pertains to 2009:

	Number of Sessions	Cost
First quarter	30	$ 75,000
Second quarter	35	78,000
Third quarter	15	42,000
Fourth quarter	20	48,000
Total	100	$243,000

Required:

Using the high-low method, determine the following:

a. The variable cost per session
b. The total fixed cost of operating the company
c. The expected cost for a quarter if 25 sessions are offered

LO 5: Separating Mixed Cost Using the Scatter Graph Method
5-41. Refer to the information in problem 5-40.

Required:

Using the scatter graph method, determine the following:

a. The variable cost per session
b. The total fixed cost of operating the company
c. The expected cost for a quarter if 25 sessions are offered

LO 6: Scatter Graph Using Microsoft Excel

5-42. Refer to the information in problem 5-40.

Required:

a. Use Microsoft Excel to prepare a scatter graph for the data presented.

b. Estimate the total fixed cost of operating the company.

c. Estimate the expected cost for a quarter if 25 sessions are offered.

LO 5: Separating Mixed Cost Using the High-Low Method

5-43. The following information is taken from Miami Avionics Testing Service:

	Number of Tests Performed	Total Cost of Testing
January	61,000	$1,420,000
February	55,000	1,340,000
March	50,000	1,290,000
April	72,000	1,430,000
May	78,000	1,440,000
June	81,000	1,540,000
July	90,000	1,590,000
August	108,000	1,610,000
September	111,000	1,700,000
October	128,000	1,720,000
November	140,000	1,860,000
December	132,000	1,810,000

Required:

Using the high-low method, determine the following:

a. The variable cost per test

b. The total fixed cost of operating the testing facility

c. The expected cost for a month if 125,000 tests are performed

LO 5: Separating Mixed Cost Using the Scatter Graph Method

5-44. Refer to the information in problem 5-43.

Required:

Using the scatter graph method, determine the following:

a. The variable cost per test
b. The total fixed cost of operating the testing facility
c. The expected cost for a month if 125,000 tests are performed

LO 6: Scatter Graph Using Microsoft Excel
5-45. Refer to the information in problem 5-43.

Required:

a. Use Microsoft Excel to prepare a scatter graph for the data presented.
b. Estimate the total fixed cost of operating the testing facility.
c. Estimate the expected cost for a month if 125,000 tests are performed.

LO 5: Separating Mixed Cost Using the High-Low Method
5-46. The following information is for the Valdez Supply Company:

	2009	2010
Sales	$1,000,000	$1,150,000
Costs:		
Cost of goods sold	$ 800,000	$ 920,000
Sales commissions	15,000	17,250
Store rent	3,000	3,000
Depreciation	20,000	20,000
Maintenance cost	3,800	4,100
Office salaries	34,000	35,500

Required:

Assuming sales is the activity base, use the high-low method to determine the variable cost element and the fixed cost component of each of the costs just listed.

LO 5: Separating Mixed Cost Using the High-Low Method
5-47. The following information is for the General Production Company:

	2009	2010
Units produced	257,000	326,000
Costs:		
Direct material	$ 611,660	$ 775,880
Direct labor	1,662,790	2,109,220
Manufacturing overhead	1,781,820	1,868,760

Required:

Assuming units produced is the activity base, use the high-low method to determine the variable cost element and fixed cost component of each of the costs just listed.

LO 5: Separating Mixed Cost Using the High-Low Method

5-48. The following information is for the Maupin Gift Shop:

	2009	2010
Sales	$100,000	$150,000
Costs:		
Cost of goods sold	$ 75,000	$112,500
Sales commissions	5,000	7,500
Store rent	1,000	1,000
Depreciation	500	500
Maintenance cost	200	250
Office salaries	5,000	6,000

Required:

a. Assuming sales is the activity base, use the high-low method to determine the variable cost element and the fixed cost component of each of the costs just listed.

b. Why is it useful to know the information requested in requirement a?

LO 4: Components of Mixed Cost

5-49. Consider the following mathematical formula:

$$y = a + bx$$

Required:

Match the variables to the correct descriptions. Some variables have two correct matches.

1. _____ y
2. _____ a
3. _____ b
4. _____ x

a. Independent variable
b. Variable cost per unit
c. Dependent variable
d. Total fixed cost
e. Activity
f. Total cost

LO 4: Describing the Methods of Separating Mixed Cost

5-50. Mr. Robinson, the director of Medical Diagnostics Clinic, is preparing a presentation to the clinic's board of directors about the fee charged for thallium stress tests. Part of the presentation will include information about the variable cost element and fixed costs associated with the tests. The accounting department has provided the director with a report which details the monthly costs associated with the thallium stress tests and the number of tests performed each month. Mr. Robinson is contemplating whether to use the scatter graph method, the high-low method, or regression analysis to separate the cost into its variable cost element and fixed cost. The director has asked your help in choosing an appropriate method.

Required:

Prepare a short report to Mr. Robinson providing insight into the strengths and weaknesses of the scatter graph method, the high-low method, and regression analysis. Your report should conclude with support for a final recommendation of one of the methods of separating mixed cost.

LO 1, 2, 4, & 5: Analyzing a Situation Using Cost Behavior

5-51. Accents Furniture Company has been in business for two years. When the business began, Accents established a delivery department with a small fleet of trucks. The delivery department was designed to be able to handle the substantial future growth of the company. As expected, sales for the first two years of business were low and activity in the delivery department was minimal.

In an effort to control costs, Accents Furniture Company's store manager is considering a proposal from a delivery company to deliver the furniture sold by Accents for a flat fee of $30 per delivery.

The following information is available regarding the cost of operating Accents's delivery department during its first two years of business.

	2008	**2009**
Number of deliveries	600	700
Cost of operating the delivery department	$25,480	$26,480

Sales and the number of deliveries are expected to increase greatly in the coming years. For example, sales in 2010 will require an estimated 1,250 deliveries, while in 2011, it is expected that 1,775 deliveries will be required.

Due to the high growth rate, the store manager is concerned that the delivery cost will grow out of hand unless the proposal is accepted. He states that the cost per delivery was about $42.47 ($25,480/600) in 2008 and $37.83 ($26,480/700) in 2009. Even at the lower cost of $37.83, it seems the company can save about $7.83 ($30.00 − $37.83) per delivery. For 2011, the store manager believes the proposal can save the company about $13,898.25 (1,775 × $7.83).

Required:

Assume that you have been assigned to a group which has been formed to analyze the delivery cost of Accents Furniture Company. Your group should prepare a report and presentation that indicates the advantage or disadvantage of accepting the proposed delivery contract. Your report and presentation should not only include calculations to support your recommended course of action, but should also address the non-monetary considerations of contracting with an outside source for delivery services.

LO 1, 2, 3, & 4: Addressing a Situation Using Cost Behavior Concepts

5-52. Mr. Reed is considering starting his own business. He has worked for a large corporation all his life and desires a change of pace. He is most interested in retail merchandising, but does not know what products his new business should sell. Mr. Reed is unsure about how to proceed with this major change in his life and has hired a consulting firm to help.

Assume that you have been assigned to the consulting group that will advise Mr. Reed.

Required:

Your group is to prepare a report that recommends a particular product line for Mr. Reed's new retail merchandising business. In addition, your report should recommend ways for Mr. Reed to gather information about the various costs associated with the merchandising business you have recommended. Finally, your report should explain how costs are classified as variable, fixed, and mixed costs, and why such classification by cost behavior is important.

LO 1, 2, & 4: Analyzing a Situation Using Cost Behavior

5-53. The Bowl-O-Mat operates a small chain of bowling alleys in southern Florida. Bowl-O-Mat's president, Al Palmer, is considering adding a supervised playground facility to each of the bowling alley properties. The playgrounds would require that a small addition be built onto each of the bowling alley buildings. Each playground would include a swing, a slide, climbing bars, and some other small-scale playground equipment. Each child would be charged an admission fee to use the facility. It is expected that parents will stay at the bowling alleys longer while their children are occupied in the playground area.

Mr. Palmer is interested in obtaining cost information relative to the proposed playground project. He understands that the more hours each playground area is open for business, the higher the cost of operating the playground will be. Beyond that, he knows nothing of cost behavior patterns.

Required:

Prepare a memorandum to Mr. Palmer that describes the following:

a. The various variable, fixed, and mixed costs that are likely to be associated with the new playground facilities

b. The concept of fixed costs, variable costs, and mixed costs

c. Why an understanding of the methods available for estimating cost behavior patterns will help him to better plan and control his operations

6

Business Decisions Using Cost Behavior

Claudia June owns the Beachside T-Shirt Shop, one of many souvenir shops along Highway A1A in Daytona Beach, Florida. Beachside sold 3,000 T-shirts during 2007 (the company's first year of operation), and Claudia's accountant prepared the following multiple-step income statement for the year.

Beachside T-Shirt Shop
Income Statement
For the Year Ended December 31, 2007

Sales		$36,000
Cost of Goods Sold		21,600
Gross Profit		$14,400
Operating Expense:		
Selling Expense	$9,500	
Administrative Expense	7,900	(17,400)
Operating Loss		$ (3,000)

Claudia was satisfied with the results for 2007 because she didn't expect the store to be profitable in its first year. As she planned for 2008, Claudia figured she needed to increase sales by only 625 T-shirts to break even for the year. Her reasoning? Each T-shirt cost $7.20 and sold for $12, resulting in $4.80 gross profit per T-shirt ($12.00 − $7.20 = $4.80). If the shop sold 3,625 T-shirts, it would earn a gross profit of $17,400 (3,625 × $4.80), which would be exactly enough to cover the selling and administrative expenses of $17,400. If Claudia met her sales goal, the store would break even in its second year of operation. As luck would have it, Beachside T-Shirt Shop sold exactly 3,625 T-shirts during 2008. Each T-shirt sold for exactly $12 and cost the company exactly $7.20. Confident that the shop had broken even for the year, Claudia excitedly opened the envelope from her accountant and found the following multiple-step income statement for 2008.

Beachside T-Shirt Shop Income Statement For the Year Ended December 31, 2008		
Sales		$43,500
Cost of Goods Sold		26,100
Gross Profit		$17,400
Operating Expense:		
Selling Expense	$10,438	
Administrative Expense	8,897	(19,335)
Operating Loss		$ (1,935)

Claudia was disappointed and discouraged when she saw an operating loss of $1,935 for the year. She rechecked the arithmetic and her assumptions about what it would take to break even for 2008 and could not understand why the store had an operating loss. Claudia wasn't aware of cost behavior. She failed to consider that some costs are affected by changes in activity level and others are not. In this chapter, we explore cost-volume-profit analysis and how business people use this analytical technique to predict financial performance effectively.

Learning Objectives

After completing your work on this chapter, you should be able to do the following:

1. Describe the differences between a traditional income statement and a contribution income statement.
2. Determine per unit amounts for sales, variable cost, and the contribution margin.
3. Determine the contribution margin ratio and explain its importance as a management tool.
4. Prepare and analyze a contribution income statement for a merchandising firm.
5. Describe cost-volume-profit (CVP) analysis and explain its importance as a management tool.
6. Use CVP analysis to determine the amount of sales required to break even or to earn a targeted profit.
7. Use CVP to perform sensitivity analysis.
8. Prepare income statements using absorption and variable costing and be able to explain the resulting differences in income and ending inventory and income.

The Contribution Income Statement

As discussed in Chapter 5, classifying costs by cost behavior provides managers insight about forecasting cost at different levels of business activity. You can't find this valuable cost behavior information readily, however, in either the multiple-step or the single-step income statement. The traditional income statement, whether the multiple-step or single-step format is used, classifies costs functionally. Costs are classified on the statement based on their nature or function. For example, all product costs are combined and appear as part of cost of goods sold. Likewise all operating expenses are grouped and listed in the appropriate section of the statement. The **traditional income statement** is sometimes called the **functional income statement**. The traditional multiple-step and the traditional single-step income statement formats conform to Generally Accepted Accounting Principles (GAAP) and companies use them for external financial reporting. For example, the income statement in the annual report for **Barnes & Noble** classifies expenses by the nature of the cost or its function.

traditional income statement An income statement prepared in the multiple-step or single-step income statement format which conforms to Generally Accepted Accounting Principles (GAAP) and can be used for external financial reporting.

functional income statement Another name for the traditional income statement.

Some companies prepare a special income statement format for use internally that categorizes costs by behavior (fixed cost and variable cost) rather than by the cost's nature or function. It is called a **contribution income statement**. This new format is no more complicated than the income statements you studied in earlier chapters. The main difference between the two is that the contribution income statement lists variable costs first, followed by fixed costs. Keep in mind that GAAP and IFRS does not permit businesses to use the contribution income statement for financial accounting—it is used only for internal decision making purposes.

contribution income statement An income statement that classifies cost by behavior (fixed cost and variable cost).

Absorption and Variable Costing

When companies determine the costs of their products they can use either absorption or variable costing. When companies prepare traditional income statements, they use absorption costing. Under **absorption costing**, product cost includes all the costs to acquire products and get them ready to sell regardless of whether the costs are variable or fixed. Generally Accepted Accounting Principles require businesses to use absorption costing for financial accounting.

absorption costing A costing method where product cost includes all the costs to acquire products and get them ready to sell regardless of whether the costs are variable or fixed. Generally Accepted Accounting Principles require businesses to use absorption costing for financial accounting.

When companies prepare contribution income statements, they use variable costing. Under **variable costing**, only the costs to acquire products or to get them ready to sell that vary with output are treated as product costs. In other words, only variable product costs are treated as product costs. All fixed costs associated with acquiring products or getting the products ready to sell are treated as period costs.

variable costing A method of costing where only the costs to acquire products or to get them ready to sell that vary with output are treated as product costs. In other words, only variable product costs are treated as product costs.

For manufacturers, the difference between absorption costing and variable costing is significant. For example, when **Caterpillar** uses absorption costing to determine the cost of manufacturing one of its bulldozers, its product cost includes the direct material, direct labor, variable manufacturing overhead, and fixed manufacturing overhead cost incurred to make the bulldozer. These costs are added to inventory and they are not expensed as cost of goods sold until the bulldozer is sold. However, when **Caterpillar** uses variable costing, product cost includes only direct material, direct labor, and variable manufacturing overhead costs. Under variable costing, all of **Caterpillar's** fixed manufacturing overhead cost is treated as a period cost. When **Caterpillar** uses variable costing only the variable costs are added to inventory (direct material, direct labor, and variable manufacturing overhead). Under variable costing, **Caterpillar** expenses fixed manufacturing overhead as it is incurred just like it does other period costs such as selling and administrative expense.

When companies prepare income statements under absorption costing, they use the traditional income statement format. On the other hand, when companies prepare income statements under variable costing, they generally use the contribution income statement format. Since variable costing and the contribution income statement format do not conform to GAAP or IFRS, the financial statements companies prepare for outsiders always use absorption costing.

Near the end of this chapter we take a closer look at absorption and variable costing along with an example that demonstrates how income will differ between the two methods when inventories are increasing or decreasing.

Purpose of the Contribution Income Statement

Let's return to the Beachside T-Shirt Shop example to see how a contribution income statement could have helped Claudia better predict the future profitability of her merchandising company. The two income statements presented for Beachside (2007 and 2008) were traditional income statements. Beachside's 2007 traditional income statement is reproduced as Exhibit 6-1.

Exhibit 6-1 Beachside's 2007 Traditional Income Statement

Beachside T-Shirt Shop
Traditional Income Statement
For the Year Ended December 31, 2007

	Sales		$36,000
Product Cost ⟶	Cost of Goods Sold		21,600
	Gross Profit		$14,400
	Operating Expense:		
Period Cost ⟶	Selling Expense	$9,500	
	Administrative Expense	7,900	(17,400)
	Operating Loss		$ (3,000)

We see that the cost information in Exhibit 6-1 is separated into product cost (cost of goods sold) and period cost (selling expenses and administrative expenses). Next we will examine how Claudia can convert her traditional income statement into a contribution income statement.

First, Claudia needs additional information about the cost behavior of the expenses in Beachside's 2007 traditional income statement. On request, Claudia's accountant provides the following information:

Cost of goods sold	All variable
Selling expense	40% variable, so 60% must be fixed
Administrative expense	$6,300 Fixed, so $1,600 must be variable

Discussion Question

6-1. With the cost behavior information just presented, discuss how you could determine the change in profit if the company sells 5,000 shirts in 2009. (Remember to look at the 2008 income statement shown at the beginning of the chapter.)

contribution margin The amount remaining after all variable costs have been deducted from sales.

Now that she has Beachside's cost behavior information, Claudia can prepare a contribution income statement for 2007. The contribution income statement lists sales first, with variable costs listed next. These costs are subtracted from sales to arrive at the contribution margin. **Contribution margin** is the amount remaining after all variable costs have been deducted from sales revenue. The contribution margin is an important piece of information for managers, because it tells them how much of their company's original sales dollars remain after deducting variable costs. This remaining portion of the sales dollars contributes to fixed costs and, once fixed costs have been covered, to profit. The contribution margin, then, is the amount available to contribute to covering fixed costs and ultimately toward profits.

Finally, fixed costs are listed and subtracted from the contribution margin to arrive at operating income, as shown in Exhibit 6-2.

Exhibit 6-2 Beachside's 2007 Contribution Income Statement

Beachside T-Shirt Shop
Contribution Income Statement
For the Year Ended December 31, 2007

Sales		$36,000
Variable Cost:		
Cost of Goods Sold	$21,600	
Variable Selling Expense ($9,500 × 40%)	3,800	
Variable Administrative Expense ($7,900 − $6,300)	1,600	
Total Variable Cost		(27,000)
Contribution Margin (Sales Less Total Variable Cost)		$ 9,000
Fixed Cost:		
Fixed Selling Expense ($9,500 × 60%)	$ 5,700	
Fixed Administrative Expense	6,300	
Total Fixed Cost		(12,000)
Operating Loss		$(3,000)

Like a traditional income statement, the contribution income statement can be detailed or condensed depending on the needs of the information users. We can also prepare it showing the per unit costs and percentage of sales calculations. A condensed version of Beachside's 2007 contribution income statement, including per unit and percentage of sales figures, is presented as Exhibit 6-3.

Exhibit 6-3 Beachside's Condensed 2007 Contribution Income Statement

Beachside T-Shirt Shop
Contribution Income Statement
For the Year Ended December 31, 2007

	Total	Per Unit	Percent of Sales
Sales in Units	3,000	1	
Sales	$ 36,000	$12.00	100
Variable Cost	(27,000)	(9.00)	(75)
Contribution Margin	$9,000	$ 3.00	25
Fixed Cost	(12,000)		
Operating Loss	$ (3,000)		

Throughout the rest of the chapter we will use a condensed version of the contribution income statement.

Discussion Question

6-2. How does the gross profit found on the traditional income statement differ from the contribution margin found on the contribution income statement?

Looking at the per unit column in Exhibit 6-3, we note that the contribution margin per unit is $3. We calculate this by dividing the total contribution margin of $9,000 by the number of units sold—in this case 3,000 ($9,000 ÷ 3,000 = $3). The $3 per unit contribution margin means that for every T-shirt sold, the sale generates $3 to contribute toward fixed costs. Then, once fixed costs have been covered, $3 per T-shirt sold contributes to profit. The contribution margin contributes toward fixed cost first, then to profits.

contribution margin ratio The contribution margin expressed as a percentage of sales.

Note in the percentage column of Exhibit 6-3 that the contribution margin is 25 percent of sales. When the contribution margin is expressed as a percentage of sales, it is called the **contribution margin ratio**.

We can calculate the contribution margin ratio by dividing the total contribution margin by total sales, or by dividing the per unit contribution margin by per unit selling price, as follows:

$$\frac{\text{Total contribution margin}}{\text{Total sales}} = \text{Contribution margin ratio}$$

or

$$\frac{\text{Per unit contribution margin}}{\text{Per unit selling price}} = \text{Contribution margin ratio}$$

In the case of Beachside T-shirt Shop, the calculations are as follows:

$$\frac{\$9{,}000}{\$36{,}000} = 25\%$$

or

$$\frac{\$3}{\$12} = 25\%$$

The contribution margin ratio is the same whether we compute it using total figures or per unit figures. This is because we base the contribution margin on sales minus only variable costs and variable costs and the contribution margin change in direct proportion to sales. This proportional relationship holds true whether we are using per unit amounts or amounts in total.

In our example, the 25 percent contribution margin ratio means that, of each sales dollar, 25 percent (or 25 cents) is available to contribute toward fixed cost and then toward profit.

Discussion Question

6-3. If Beachside's sales increase by $20,000 and the contribution margin ratio is 25%, by how much will profits increase?

Predicting Profits Using the Contribution Income Statement

Let's assume that Beachside expects to sell 7,500 shirts in 2009. Claudia can quickly predict the expected profit at that sales level by preparing a contribution income statement, such as that in Exhibit 6-4. To do this, the sales figure equals the number of T-shirts multiplied by the selling price per unit (7,500 × $12 = $90,000). Variable cost is the number of T-shirts sold multiplied by the variable cost per unit (7,500 × $9 = $67,500). The fixed cost of $12,000 remains the same in total. With these three figures in place, simple arithmetic gave us the expected profit of $10,500 if 7,500 T-shirts are sold.

Exhibit 6-4 Beachside's Condensed 2009 Projected Contribution Income Statement

Beachside T-Shirt Shop
Projected Contribution Income Statement
For the Year Ended December 31, 2009

	Total	Per Unit	Percent of Sales
Sales in Units	7,500	1	
Sales	$ 90,000	$12.00	100
Variable Cost	(67,500)	(9.00)	(75)
Contribution Margin	$ 22,500	$ 3.00	25
Fixed Cost	(12,000)		
Operating Income	$ 10,500		

If we did not want to take the time to prepare an actual contribution income statement, we could calculate the company's operating income using the following basic equation.

Sales	−	Variable Costs	−	Fixed Costs	=	Profit
(7,500 × $12)	−	(7,500 × $9)	−	$12,000	=	Profit
$90,000	−	$67,500	−	$12,000	=	$10,500

The sales figure in this calculation is the number of T-shirts multiplied by the selling price per unit (7,500 × $12 = $90,000). Variable cost is the number of T-shirts sold multiplied by the variable cost per unit (7,500 × $9 = $67,500). The fixed cost of $12,000 remains the same in total. With these three figures in place, simple arithmetic gave us the expected profit of $10,500 if 7,500 T-shirts are sold.

The contribution income statement is a wonderful management tool because it allows managers to clearly see the amounts of fixed and variable costs incurred by the company. For example, using the contribution income statement, a manager at **DuPont** could assess the amount of costs that remain constant regardless of activity and the amount of costs that will change as business activity changes, allowing her to make more well-informed management decisions. Understanding which costs are variable and which are fixed is essential if managers are to reasonably predict future costs. More importantly, a solid understanding of the contribution income statement approach and the concept of the contribution margin and contribution margin ratio is the backbone of another important decision-making tool: cost-volume-profit analysis.

Cost-Volume-Profit Analysis

As its name implies, **cost-volume-profit (CVP) analysis** is the analysis of the relationships between cost and volume (the level of sales), and the effect of those relationships on profit. In this section, we examine how managers can use CVP concepts to predict sales levels at which a firm will break even or attain target profits. CVP analysis is a useful tool for managers, business owners, and potential business owners for determining the profit potential of a new company or the profit impact of changes in selling price, cost, or volume on existing businesses.

cost-volume-profit (CVP) analysis The analysis of the relationships between cost and volume and the effect of these relationships on profit.

Thousands of businesses are started every day. Unfortunately, most of them fail a short time later, and the people who start these businesses suffer significant financial and emotional hardship. Such hardships might be avoided if new business owners used CVP analysis to evaluate the potential profit of their business ventures. With CVP analysis, a potential business owner can discover impending disaster before starting the business, thereby preserving funds that could be used more productively elsewhere.

Throughout the remainder of this chapter we will use three basic CVP formulas as shown in Exhibit 6-5. We will use these formulas to determine the sales required to earn a target profit amount. Two of the formulas provide the dollar amount of sales while the other provides sales in units.

Exhibit 6-5 Cost-Volume-Profit Formulas

Formula	Calculation	Purpose
CVP Formula 1	$\frac{\text{Total fixed cost} + \text{target profit}}{\text{Contribution margin ratio}}$	To determine the required sales *in dollars* to achieve a target profit
CVP Formula 2	$\frac{\text{Total fixed cost} + \text{target profit}}{\text{Contribution margin per unit}}$	To determine the required sales *in units* to achieve a target profit
CVP Formula 3	$\frac{\text{Total fixed cost}}{\text{Contribution margin ratio} - \text{target profit percentage}}$	To determine the required sales *in dollars* to achieve a target profit expressed as a percentage of sales

Notice that the first and third formula, the ones that determine required sales in dollars, use the *contribution margin ratio*, while the second formula, the one that determines sales in units, uses the *contribution margin per unit*.

Next, we will use the first and second formula to determine sales required to break even.

Break-Even

break-even The point at which sales and costs are equal so the enterprise generates neither a profit nor a loss.

break-even point The level of sales required to achieve break-even. This can be expressed either in sales dollars or in the number of units sold.

Break-even occurs when a company generates neither a profit nor a loss. The sales volume required to achieve break-even is called the **break-even point**. Because most businesses exist to earn a profit, why would managers be interested in calculating a break-even point? In at least two situations this kind of information is valuable. First, the break-even point tells managers how far sales can decline before the company will incur a loss. This information could provide the encouragement to continue in business, or may provide an early warning of impending business failure. Second, owners and managers may use break-even analysis when starting a business. For example, Claudia could have calculated Beachside's break-even point when she started the company. Even when Claudia tried to calculate the company's break-even point for its second year, she overlooked some important cost behavior considerations. Now, with our understanding of cost behavior and the contribution income statement, we can predict the correct sales level Beachside needs to break even for the year.

Let's look again at the 2007 contribution income statement for Beachside T-Shirt Shop, reproduced in Exhibit 6-6.

Exhibit 6-6 Beachside's Condensed 2007 Contribution Income Statement

Beachside T-Shirt Shop
Contribution Income Statement
For the Year Ended December 31, 2007

	Total	Per Unit	Percent of Sales
Sales in Units	3,000	1	
Sales	$ 36,000	$12.00	100
Variable Cost	(27,000)	(9.00)	(75)
Contribution Margin	$9,000	$ 3.00	25
Fixed Cost	(12,000)		
Operating Loss	$ (3,000)		

We can use either CVP Formula 1 or CVP Formula 2 to calculate break-even for Beachside. We will begin our presentation using CVP Formula 1. Remember that break-even means that profit will be exactly zero. Therefore, we will use a target profit of zero in our break-even calculations for the Beachside T-shirt Shop. To demonstrate the break-even calculation, we use the information provided by Beachside T-Shirt Shop's contribution income statement in Exhibit 6-6. Beachside's contribution margin ratio is 25 percent and the company's fixed costs total \$12,000 per year. With this information, we can use CVP Formula 1 to determine the sales in dollars that Beachside must attain to break even by dividing the contribution margin ratio into the total fixed cost as follows:

CVP Formula 1—To Determine Required Sales in Dollars:

$$\frac{\text{Total fixed cost} + \text{target profit}}{\text{Contribution margin ratio}} = \text{Required sales in dollars}$$

$$\frac{\$12{,}000 + \$0}{25\%} = \$48{,}000$$

Using CVP Formula 1, we determined the sales must total \$48,000 for Beachside to break-even, but what if we wanted to know the number of units the company must sell? Once we know sales in dollars, and we know the selling price per unit, we can simply divide the total sales in dollars by the per unit selling price to determine the number of units the company must sell. Therefore, Beachside must sell 4,000 units (\$48,000 ÷ \$12) in order to break-even.

For situations where it is more convenient to use the per unit contribution margin rather than the contribution margin ratio, we can use CVP Formula 2. This might occur when the contribution margin ratio does not round to an even percentage and per unit amounts are available.

To illustrate how to find the break-even point in units using CVP Formula 2, we will once again use the information in Exhibit 6-6 for the Beachside T-Shirt Shop. Beachside's contribution margin is \$3 per T-shirt, and the company's fixed costs total \$12,000 per year. With this information, we can determine the number of T-shirts Beachside must sell to achieve a break-even point by dividing the contribution margin per unit into the total fixed cost, as follows:

CVP Formula 2—To Calculate Required Sales in Units:

$$\frac{\text{Total fixed cost} + \text{target profit}}{\text{Contribution margin per unit}} = \text{Required sales in units}$$

$$\frac{\$12{,}000 + \$0}{\$3.00} = 4{,}000 \text{ T-shirts}$$

As the calculation shows, Beachside must sell 4,000 T-shirts to break-even. To determine sales in dollars, we simply multiply the number of units by the per unit selling price. For Beachside to break even, the company's sales in dollars must be \$48,000 (4,000 units × \$12).

Notice that we can determine sales in dollars and sales in units by using either one of the first two CVP formulas. But how do we know that our calculations are correct? We can prepare a condensed contribution income statement to check our answers. We have already determined the sales figures for this contribution income statement (4,000 T-shirts, totaling sales of \$48,000). Variable cost is the number of T-shirts sold multiplied by the variable cost per unit (4,000 × \$9 = \$36,000). The fixed cost of \$12,000 remains the same in total. As the contribution income statement in Exhibit 6-7 shows, with these figures in place, profit will be zero if 4,000 T-shirts are sold.

Exhibit 6-7 Beachside's Projected Condensed 2009 Contribution Income Statement

Beachside T-Shirt Shop
Projected Contribution Income Statement
For the Year Ended December 31, 2009

	Total	Per Unit	Percent of Sales
Sales in Units	4,000	1	
Sales (4,000 × \$12)	\$ 48,000	\$12.00	100
Variable Cost (4,000 × \$9)	(36,000)	(9.00)	(75)
Contribution Margin	\$ 12,000	\$ 3.00	25
Fixed Cost	(12,000)		
Operating Income	\$ 0		

We have examined the calculations for break-even point, but as we said earlier, companies are usually not in business to break even. Rather, they are usually interested in earning profits. In the next section, we will discuss how to use the CVP formulas to determine the sales needed to meet a specific profit objective. We will call this profit objective *target profit*. As with the break-even point, we can apply CVP analysis to determine the sales needed to meet target profits in either units or sales dollars.

Determining Sales Required to Meet a Profit Objective

When we determined the break-even point, we calculated the sales required to generate a large enough contribution margin to cover fixed cost. In our present discussion, we are looking for the sales required not only to cover the fixed cost, but also to achieve a specific target profit. To use CVP Formula 1, we simply add the target profit to the total fixed cost and then divide the sum by the contribution margin ratio. This calculation will tell us the sales in dollars Beachside must achieve to cover all its fixed cost and to attain the target profit. If we assume that Claudia targets \$27,000 as Beachside's profit for 2009, the calculation is as follows:

CVP Formula 1—To Determine Required Sales in Dollars:

$$\frac{\text{Total fixed cost} + \text{target profit}}{\text{Contribution margin ratio}} = \text{Required sales in dollars}$$

$$\frac{\$12{,}000 + \$27{,}000}{25\%} = \$156{,}000 \text{ in sales dollars}$$

Discussion Question

6-4. Prove that Claudia' sales must total \$156,000 to earn a \$27,000 profit.

Using CVP Formula 1, we determined the sales dollars required to earn a profit of \$27,000. If we want to know the number of units the company must sell, we simply divide the total sales in dollars by the per unit selling price to determine the number of units the company must sell. In our example, Beachside must sell 13,000 units (\$156,000 ÷ \$12) in order to earn the \$27,000 target profit.

Now let's use CVP Formula 2 to determine the number of T-shirts Beachside must sell to earn a target profit of $27,000. Using CVP Formula 2 to calculate the number of units the company must sell, we simply add the target profit to the total fixed cost and then divide the sum by the contribution margin per unit. This calculation will tell us how many units Beachside must sell to cover all the fixed cost and to attain the target profit. Beachside's calculation is as follows:

CVP Formula 2—To Calculate Required Sales in Units:

$$\frac{\text{Total fixed cost} + \text{target profit}}{\text{Contribution margin per unit}} = \text{Required sales in units}$$

$$\frac{\$12{,}000 + \$27{,}000}{\$3.00} = 13{,}000 \text{ T-shirts}$$

Our calculations confirm that with a fixed cost of $12,000 and a contribution margin per unit of $3, Beachside must sell 13,000 T-shirts to earn $27,000 profit. To determine sales in dollars, we simply multiply the number of units by the per unit selling price. For Beachside to earn a target profit of $27,000, the company's sales in dollars must be $156,000 (13,000 units × $12).

Once again, we see that we can determine sales in dollars and sales in units using either one of the first two CVP formulas. To test the accuracy of our calculations, we can prepare a condensed contribution income statement. We already know that the sales figures for this contribution income statement are $156,000 or 13,000 units. Variable cost is the number of T-shirts sold multiplied by the variable cost per unit (13,000 × $9 = $117,000). The fixed cost of $12,000 remains unchanged. As the contribution income statement in Exhibit 6-8 shows, with these figures in place, profit will be $27,000 if 13,000 T-shirts are sold.

Exhibit 6-8 Beachside's Projected Condensed 2009 Contribution Income Statement

Beachside T-Shirt Shop
Projected Contribution Income Statement
For the Year Ended December 31, 2009

	Total	Per Unit	Percent of Sales
Sales in Units	13,000	1	
Sales (13,000 × $12)	$ 156,000	$12.00	100
Variable Cost (13,000 × $9)	(117,000)	(9.00)	(75)
Contribution Margin	$ 39,000	$ 3.00	25
Fixed Cost	(12,000)		
Operating Income	$ 27,000		

If we did not want to take the time to prepare an actual contribution income statement, we could calculate the same operating income using the following basic equation.

Sales	−	Variable Costs	−	Fixed Costs	=	Profit
(13,000 × $12)	−	(13,000 × $9)	−	$12,000	=	Profit
$156,000	−	$117,000	−	$12,000	=	$27,000

Using the first and second CVP formulas we determined required sales when the target profit is expressed as a dollar amount. We use CVP Formula 3 to determine the sales dollars required to earn a target profit which is expressed as a percentage of sales. In other words, instead desiring a profit of $27,000, let's assume the company desires a target profit of 10 percent of sales in 2009. The calculation in Formula 3 will determine the sales in dollars that Beachside must achieve to cover all its fixed cost and to attain a target profit equal to 10 percent of its sales. The calculation is as follows:

CVP Formula 3—To Determine Required Sales in Dollars to Earn a Percent of Sales Target Profit:

$$\frac{\text{Total fixed cost}}{\text{Contribution margin ratio} - \text{Target profit percentage}} = \text{Required sales in dollars}$$

$$\frac{\$12{,}000}{25\% - 10\%} = \$80{,}000 \text{ in sales dollars}$$

Using CVP Formula 3, we determined that sales of $80,000 are required to earn a profit of 10 percent of sales. If we want to know the number of units the company must sell, we simply divide the total sales in dollars by the per unit selling price to determine the number of units the company must sell. In our example, Beachside must sell 6,667 units ($80,000 ÷ $12, rounded to the nearest full unit) in order to earn the 10 percent of sales profit target. As the contribution income statement in Exhibit 6-9 shows, if sales are $80,000 then profit will be $8,000, which is 10 percent of sales ($80,000 × 10% = $8,000).

Exhibit 6-9 Beachside's Projected Condensed 2009 Contribution Income Statement

Beachside T-Shirt Shop
Projected Contribution Income Statement
For the Year Ended December 31, 2009

	Total	Per Unit	Percent of Sales
Sales in Units ($80,000/$12.00)	6,667*	1	
Sales (from Formula 3)	$ 80,000	$12.00	100
Variable Cost (80,000 × 75%)	(60,000)	(9.00)	(75)
Contribution Margin	$ 20,000	$ 3.00	25
Fixed Cost	(12,000)		
Operating Income	$ 8,000**		

*Rounded to the nearest unit.
** Operating income equals 10 percent of sales.

Cost-Volume-Profit Graph

In addition to the calculations we have been studying, CVP analysis can also be depicted graphically. Exhibit 6-10 shows A CVP graph for Beachside T-Shirt Shop.

The main difference between the CVP graph in Exhibit 6-10 and the cost behavior graphs in Chapter 5 is that the CVP graph shows sales in addition to variable and fixed costs. The cost line (a) on the graph is similar to those in Chapter 5. Note that this line intercepts the *y*-axis at $12,000, the total fixed cost for Beachside T-Shirt Shop. Thus, Beachside incurs $12,000 fixed cost even if the company sells no T-shirts. The cost line slopes upward at $9 for each T-shirt sold (variable cost).

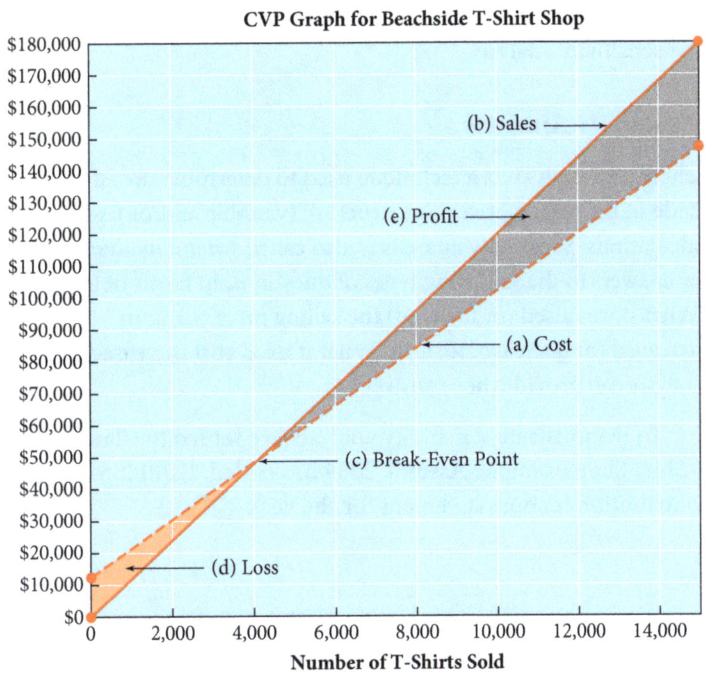

Exhibit 6-10 CVP Graph-Beachside T-Shirt Shop

Now consider the sales line (b) on the graph. If Beachside sells no T-shirts, there would obviously be no sales dollars, which explains why the sales line intercepts the *y*-axis at zero. The line slopes upward at $12 for every T-shirt sold. The point at which the cost line and the sales line cross (c) is Beachside's break-even point, which we know from our calculations in this chapter to be 4,000 T-shirts, or $48,000 in sales revenue. The loss area (d) on the graph and the profit area (e) represent a loss and profit, respectively, for Beachside. Thus, if Beachside sells fewer than 4,000 T-shirts, the company will experience a loss. If it sells more than 4,000 T-shirts, the company will earn a profit.

Discussion Question

6-5. Using the CVP graph in Exhibit 6-10, determine sales level (in units and dollars) where Beachside would earn a profit of

- **a.** $10,500
- **b.** $27,000

The CVP graph is a useful management tool. Although it should not take the place of the calculations we have demonstrated thus far in this chapter, it has a distinct advantage over the calculations in that it allows managers to view the entire cost-volume-profit picture. Claudia June can, for example, assess Beachside's profit potential at any level of business within the relevant range of activity.

Discussion Question

6-6. If Claudia is forced to lower her selling price to $11 per T-shirt, how much profit should she expect in 2009 assuming the company expects to sell 13,000 shirts and its cost structure stays the same?

To demonstrate the basics of CVP analysis, we have assumed that the selling price per unit, variable costs per unit, and total fixed cost all remained unchanged. Businesses, however, experience daily pressures that can cause each of these items to change. CVP analysis can adapt to any such change.

Now that we have covered the basics, we are ready to put CVP to perhaps its greatest use: sensitivity analysis.

Sensitivity Analysis

sensitivity analysis A technique used to determine the effect on cost-volume-profit when changes are made in the selling price, cost structure (variable and/or fixed) and/or volume used in the CVP calculations. Also called *what-if analysis.*

Sensitivity analysis is a technique used to determine the effect on CVP when changes are made in the selling price, cost structure (variable and/or fixed), and volume used in the calculations. Sensitivity analysis is also called *what if analysis.* Managers are often looking for answers to the following types of questions, in terms of the effect on projected profits: "What if we raised (or lowered) the selling price per unit?" "What if variable cost per unit increased (or decreased)?" and "What if fixed cost increased (or decreased)?" Sensitivity analysis can provide those answers.

To demonstrate sensitivity analysis, we return to Claudia June and the Beachside T-Shirt Shop example. Assume 2009 has ended. Exhibit 6-11 presents Beachside's contribution income statement for the year.

Exhibit 6-11 Beachside T-Shirt Shop's 2009 Contribution Income Statement

Beachside T-Shirt Shop
Contribution Income Statement
For the Year Ended December 31, 2009

	Total	Per Unit	Percent of Sales
Sales in Units	11,286	1	
Sales	$ 135,432	$12.00	100
Variable Cost	(101,574)	(9.00)	(75)
Contribution Margin	$ 33,858	$ 3.00	25
Fixed Cost	(12,000)		
Operating Income	$ 21,858		

Although it is less than she had hoped for, Claudia is satisfied with the $21,858 profit Beachside earned in 2009 and is aiming for a target profit of $27,000 in 2010 (the same target profit as 2009). However, a new T-shirt shop just opened three doors from Beachside. Claudia feels she must lower her selling price to $11 due to competitive pressure and wants to know how many T-shirts her shop must now sell to attain the $27,000 target profit. Claudia can use CVP analysis to determine the required sales level to achieve a targeted profit even if she changes her selling price.

Change in Selling Price

If the selling price changes but variable cost does not, sales required to attain a target profit can be determined using CVP Formula 1 and a recalculated contribution margin ratio based on the new selling price. In the case of Beachside T-Shirt Shop, the new per unit contribution margin is $2 (new selling price of $11 − variable cost of $9) and the new contribution margin ratio is 18.1818 percent (rounded), which we calculate by dividing the new $11 selling price into the new $2 contribution margin ($2 ÷ $11 = 18.1818%) We now apply this new information to CVP Formula 1. Remember the target profit is still $27,000 and that fixed cost remains unchanged at $12,000.

CVP Formula 1—To Determine Required Sales in Dollars:

$$\frac{\text{Total fixed cost} + \text{target profit}}{\text{Contribution margin ratio}} = \text{Required sales in dollars}$$

$$\frac{\$12{,}000 + \$27{,}000}{18.1818\%} = \$214{,}500 \text{ sales dollars (rounded)}$$

By applying the revised contribution margin ratio to CVP Formula 1, we see that Beachside will need $214,500 in sales to achieve the target profit of $27,000. By dividing the $214,500 in sales by the new $11 per unit selling price we also determine that Beachside needs to sell 19,500 T-shirts to earn the $27,000 target profit.

Discussion Questions

6-7. Prove that Claudia's sales must equal $214,500 to earn a $27,000 profit if she reduces the selling price per T-shirt from $12 to $11.

6-8. Why must we calculate a new contribution margin ratio when the per unit selling price changes?

6-9. Under what other circumstances must we calculate a new contribution margin ratio?

We can also use CVP Formula 2 to calculate the number of units Beachside must sell to earn a target profit of $27,000. When the selling price changes but variable cost does not, the number of units required to attain a target profit is determined using CVP Formula 2 and a recalculated contribution margin based on the new selling price. In the case of Beachside T-Shirt Shop, the new contribution margin is $2 (new selling price of $11 − variable cost of $9). We now apply this contribution margin to the formula.

CVP Formula 2—To Determine Required Sales in Units:

$$\frac{\text{Total fixed cost} + \text{target profit}}{\text{Contribution margin per unit}} = \text{Required sales in units}$$

$$\frac{\$12{,}000 + \$27{,}000}{\$2.00} = 19{,}500 \text{ T-shirts}$$

Our calculations confirm that with the lower selling price and revised contribution margin per unit, Beachside must sell 19,500 T-shirts to attain the target profit of $27,000. By multiplying the 19,500 units by the new $11 selling price, we can also confirm that Beachside's sales need to total $214,500 to earn the $27,000 target profit.

If Claudia reduces her selling price to $11, then Beachside must sell 19,500 T-shirts in 2010 to earn the target profit of $27,000. Claudia believes it would be impossible to sell that many shirts, so she begins to consider alternative ways to earn the target profit of $27,000 in such a competitive environment.

Discussion Question

6-10. If Claudia must lower her selling price to $11 per shirt to be competitive, and it would be impossible to sell 19,500 T-shirts, what are some of the alternatives she might consider to attain the $27,000 profit?

Change in Variable Cost and Fixed Cost

If Claudia does not want to change her selling price, there are alternatives—namely changing variable cost or fixed cost. Because Claudia believes the selling price per T-shirt must be $11, either the variable cost per unit or the total fixed cost must be reduced. We start with an analysis of possible changes in variable cost.

First, let's analyze how Beachside determined its original variable cost. We determine per unit variable cost by dividing the total variable cost by the number of units sold. Recall from our earlier discussion and Exhibit 6-3 that Beachside sold 3,000 T-shirts during 2007, and its total variable cost was $27,000. Therefore, the variable cost per unit was $9 ($27,000 variable cost ÷ 3,000 units sold).

To analyze how a change in variable cost will affect the variable cost per unit of $9, we must look at the three components of per unit variable cost: the cost of each T-shirt, the variable selling expenses, and the variable administrative expenses. We need to know what portion of the $9 variable unit cost relates to each component. We can determine these portions by dividing the 3,000 units sold into each of the three cost components. We use 3,000 because that number of units caused these costs to be incurred. We find the cost of each variable cost component in the contribution income statement presented in Exhibit 6-3. The cost and per unit calculation for each component are presented in Exhibit 6-12.

Exhibit 6-12 Analysis of Beachside's Variable Cost Components

	Total Cost		Units Sold		Unit Cost
Cost of Goods Sold (T-shirts)	$21,600	÷	3,000	=	$7.20
Variable Selling Expenses	3,800	÷	3,000	=	1.27
Variable Administrative Expenses	1,600	÷	3,000	=	0.53
Total Variable Cost	$27,000				$9.00 Per Unit

Claudia does not believe any change can be made in either the variable selling expenses or the variable administrative expenses. Any possible reduction in variable cost, then, must be in the cost of the T-shirts. Our calculations in Exhibit 6-12 show that the per unit cost of each T-shirt is $7.20.

Assume Claudia's shirt supplier has agreed to lower its price from $7.20 to $6 per T-shirt. This reduction of $1.20 ($7.20 − $6.00 = $1.20) will reduce Beachside's variable cost from $9 per shirt to $7.80 per shirt ($9.00 − $1.20 = $7.80). The new contribution margin is $3.20 ($11 selling price − $7.80 variable cost = $3.20), and the new contribution margin ratio is 29.091 percent ($3.20 contribution margin ÷ $11 selling price = 0.29091 or 29.091 percent rounded).

Now consider a change in Beachside's fixed cost. Recall that Beachside's total fixed cost is $12,000. Assume that Claudia has agreed to provide fellow businesswoman Susan Williams with space in her shop to sell bathing suits to Claudia's customers. Susan has agreed to pay Claudia $250 per month as rent for the space she will use. The $250 per month works out to be $3,000 per year ($250 per month × 12 months = $3,000). Thus, the $3,000 offset to rent effectively decreases Beachside's total fixed cost from $12,000 to $9,000.

Let's see what effect these changes would have on Claudia's company. To do this, again we will use CVP Formulas 1 and 2. We simply need to plug the new cost structures (variable and fixed) into the formulas as follows:

CVP Formula 1—To Determine Required Sales in Dollars

$$\frac{\text{Total fixed cost} + \text{target profit}}{\text{Contribution margin ratio}} = \text{Required sales in dollars}$$

$$\frac{\$9{,}000 + \$27{,}000}{29.091\%} = \$123{,}750 \text{ in sales (rounded)}$$

By using CVP Formula 1 (and Beachside's new variable and fixed cost structure), we found that if Beachside's sales total $123,750 in 2010, the company will earn a profit of $27,000. To calculate the unit sales required to attain Beachside's target profit of $27,000, we use the company's new contribution ratio and CVP Formula 2:

CVP Formula 2—To Determine Required Sales in Units

$$\frac{\text{Total fixed cost} + \text{target profit}}{\text{Contribution margin per unit}} = \text{Required sales in units}$$

$$\frac{\$9{,}000 + \$27{,}000}{\$3.20} = 11{,}250 \text{ T-shirts}$$

With the changes in cost structure Claudia has negotiated, she will be able to earn a $27,000 profit in 2010 even if her sales drop from 11,286 T-shirts (the 2009 sales level) to 11,250 T-shirts.

Discussion Questions

6-11. Prove that Claudia must have sales of $123,750 (11,250 T-shirts) to earn a $27,000 profit if she reduces the cost per T-shirt from $7.20 to $6 and reduces total fixed cost from $12,000 to $9,000.

6-12. If Claudia is more successful than anticipated in 2010 and sells 13,000 T-shirts by reducing her selling price to $11, and she also implements the variable and fixed cost changes described earlier, what will Beachside's profits be for 2010?

6-13. What complications do you foresee in using CVP analysis if, in addition to her existing line of shirts, Claudia begins selling a deluxe line of shirts that cost $11.50 each and sell for $17?

Multiple Products and CVP

In reality, most companies sell more than one product. Companies that sell multiple products can estimate *total* variable cost and *total* sales, but their various per unit variable costs and selling prices are of little use when they employ CVP for the company as a whole. These companies can still use CVP analysis, but they must use CVP Formula 1 or 3 which use the contribution ratio. CVP Formula 2 is useless in a multiproduct situation if the various products sold have different unit contribution margins as they do in most situations.

To demonstrate how managers use CVP analysis in a multiproduct situation or when per unit information is otherwise unavailable, let's consider the example of Margaret's Frame Factory. Margaret's Frame Factory makes and sells picture frames of various size and quality. Exhibit 6-13 presents Margaret's condensed contribution income statement for 2008.

Exhibit 6-13 Margaret's Condensed 2008 Contribution Income Statement

Margaret's Frame Factory Contribution Income Statement For the Year Ended December 31, 2008	Total	Percent of Sales
Sales	$ 500,000	100
Variable Cost	(315,000)	(63)
Contribution Margin	$ 185,000	37
Fixed Cost	(143,000)	
Operating Income	$ 42,000	

There is a per unit variable cost and selling price for each of the frame models Margaret's manufactures, but they are not included in Exhibit 6-13. All we have are the totals. The $185,000 contribution margin comes from the sale of several different products, each with its own contribution margin. The 37 percent contribution margin ratio, then, is an average contribution margin ratio based on the sales mix of these different products. Even with this limited information, however, we can use CVP analysis to both calculate a break-even point and predict target profits.

Break-Even Point in a Multiproduct Situation

To calculate the break-even point in a multiproduct situation, we use CVP Formula 1.

CVP Formula 1—To Determine Required Sales in Dollars

$$\frac{\text{Total fixed cost} + \text{target profit}}{\text{Contribution margin ratio}} = \text{Required sales in dollars}$$

$$\frac{\$143{,}000 + \$0}{37\%} = \$386{,}486 \text{ sales dollars (rounded)}$$

We know that Margaret's is well above the break-even point because the company earned a profit of $42,000 in 2008. The break-even calculation is still valuable to company management because it reveals how far sales could decline before the company would experience a loss. In this example, sales could decline by $113,514 ($500,000 2008 sales − $386,486 break-even point = $113,514 decline) before Margaret's would experience a loss.

Determining Required Sales in a Multiproduct Situation

Assume that Margaret's is interested in increasing profits to $80,000 in 2009. Based on the information contained in the 2008 contribution income statement presented in Exhibit 6-13, what would be the required sales to earn this target profit of $80,000? To find out, once again we use CVP Formula 1:

CVP Formula 1—To Determine Required Sales in Dollars

$$\frac{\text{Total fixed cost} + \text{target profit}}{\text{Contribution margin ratio}} = \text{Required sales in dollars}$$

Using the information from Margaret's Frame Factory's contribution income statement, we know that total fixed cost is $143,000 and the contribution margin ratio is

37 percent. The calculation of the required sales dollars to earn a target profit of $80,000 is as follows:

$$\frac{\$143{,}000 + \$80{,}000}{37\%} = \$602{,}703 \text{ sales dollars (rounded)}$$

Our calculations indicate that Margaret's Frame Factory will need $602,703 in sales to attain a target profit of $80,000.

Now assume that Margaret's desires a profit equal to 15 percent of sales. Based on the information contained in the 2008 contribution income statement presented in Exhibit 6-13, we can use CVP Formula 3 to determine the required sales to earn this target profit of 15 percent of sales as follows.

CVP Formula 3—To Determine Required Sales in Dollars to Earn a Percent of Sales Target Profit:

$$\frac{\text{Total fixed cost}}{\text{Contribution margin ratio} - \text{Target profit percentage}} = \text{Required sales in dollars}$$

Using the information from Margaret's Frame Factory's contribution income statement, we know that total fixed cost is $143,000 and the contribution margin ratio is 37 percent. The calculation of the required sales dollars to earn a profit of 15 percent of sales is as follows:

$$\frac{\$143{,}000}{37\% - 15\%} = \$650{,}000 \text{ sales dollars (rounded)}$$

Our calculations indicate that Margaret's Frame Factory will need $650,000 in sales to attain a target profit of 15% of sales, which is a profit of $97,500 ($650,000 × 15%).

Discussion Question

6-14. Using a contribution income statement, prove that Margaret's sales must total $602,703 to earn an $80,000 profit and they must total $650,000 to earn a profit equal to 15 percent of sales.

We have demonstrated how CVP analysis can provide useful information about how changes in selling price, variable cost, and fixed cost affect a company's break-even point. Managers can also use CVP analysis to see what sales (in either units or dollars) the company needs to attain target profits.

CVP analysis is highly adaptable. It works equally well when managers are trying to determine profit potential either of a small segment of a large business or of an entire company. Before a company expands an existing business market or makes the decision to enter new markets, management should invest some time in gathering revenue and cost data, separating the cost by cost behavior, developing a contribution income statement, and applying these simple CVP procedures.

CVP Assumptions

CVP analysis is a great "what if?" management tool because managers can use it to estimate a company's profit performance under a variety of different scenarios. It is, however, an estimation technique only, and the following assumptions are made when this type of analysis is used.

1. All costs can be classified as either fixed or variable. Implicit in this assumption is that a mixed cost can be separated into its fixed and variable components.
2. Fixed costs remain fixed throughout the range of activity.
3. Variable cost per unit remains the same throughout the range of activity.
4. Selling price per unit remains the same throughout the range of activity.
5. The average contribution margin ratio in a multiproduct company remains the same throughout the range of activity.

These assumptions rarely, if ever, match reality. Market pressures, inflation, and a myriad of other factors cause revenue and cost structures to change in ways that place limitations on CVP analysis. Notwithstanding these limitations, however, CVP helps managers make more realistic estimates of future profit potential. It is a technique available to managers of large and small companies worldwide as they attempt to better manage their businesses.

Absorption and Variable Costing—A Closer Look

When companies prepare traditional income statements they use absorption costing. Under absorption costing product cost includes all the costs to acquire products and get them ready to sell regardless of whether the costs are variable or fixed. When companies prepare contribution income statements they use variable costing. Under variable costing, only the variable costs to acquire products and get them ready to sell are treated as product costs. In other words, only variable product costs are treated as product costs. All fixed costs associated acquiring products or getting the products ready to sell are treated as period costs.

When a manufacturer uses absorption costing to determine the cost of manufacturing its goods, product cost includes the cost of direct material, direct labor, variable manufacturing overhead, and fixed manufacturing overhead. These costs are added to inventory and are not expensed as cost of goods sold until the products are sold. However, when a manufacturer uses variable costing, product cost includes only direct material, direct labor, and variable manufacturing overhead costs. Under variable costing, all of the fixed manufacturing overhead cost is treated as a period cost. When a manufacturer uses variable costing, only the variable costs are added to inventory (direct material, direct labor, and variable manufacturing overhead). Under variable costing, a manufacturer expenses fixed manufacturing overhead as it is incurred just like it expenses other period costs such as selling and administrative costs.

When companies prepare income statements under absorption costing, they use a traditional income statement format. On the other hand, when companies prepare income statements under variable costing, the companies generally use the contribution income statement format. We will first demonstrate how these income statements are prepared assuming beginning and ending inventories are zero. Let's assume that during its first year of business, Tim Chai Manufacturing produced and sold 600 units during 2007. The table that follows shows inventory information for the company.

Inventory Information:	
Beginning finished goods inventory (1/1/07)	0
Units produced	600
Units available for sale	600
Less units sold	(600)
Ending finished goods inventory (12/31/07)	0

We will further assume that the company sells its product for $100 per unit and that the cost information in Exhibit 6-14 is available:

Exhibit 6-14 Cost Information for Tim Chai Manufacturing for 2007

Variable costs per unit:	
Variable product cost:	
Direct material	$ 7
Direct labor	12
Variable manufacturing overhead	3
Total variable manufacturing cost per unit	$22
Variable selling and administrative expense	$19
Fixed cost per year:	
Fixed manufacturing overhead cost	$6,600
Fixed selling and administrative expense	$5,400

To calculate the product cost per unit for absorption costing we use per unit amounts from Exhibit 6-14 for direct material, direct labor, and variable manufacturing overhead. Under absorption costing, product cost includes fixed manufacturing overhead so we determine the fixed manufacturing overhead cost per unit by dividing the total fixed manufacturing overhead cost of $6,600 by the 600 units produced. In the table that follows we present the product cost per unit for absorption costing.

Absorption Cost per Unit:	
Direct material	$ 7
Direct labor	12
Variable manufacturing overhead	3
Fixed manuf. overhead cost ($6,600/600 units produced)	11
Total absorption cost per unit	$33

To calculate the product cost per unit for variable costing we use the per unit amounts from Exhibit 6-14 for direct material, direct labor, and variable manufacturing overhead. Since variable costing does not include fixed manufacturing overhead in product cost, there is no need to determine a fixed manufacturing overhead cost per unit. In the table that follows we present the product cost per unit for variable costing.

Variable Cost per Unit:	
Direct material	$ 7
Direct labor	12
Variable manufacturing overhead	3
Total variable cost per unit	$22

We now have enough information to prepare the absorption and variable costing income statement for Tim Chai Manufacturing for 2007 as shown in Exhibit 6-15.

Exhibit 6-15 Tim Chai Manufacturing 2007 Income Statements

Tim Chai Manufacturing, Inc.
Absorption Costing Income Statement
For the Year Ended December 31, 2007

Sales revenue (600 units sold × $100)		$60,000
Cost of goods sold:		
Beginning finished goods inventory (1/1/07)	$ 0	
Cost of goods manufactured		
(600 units produced × $33)	19,800	
Cost of goods available for sale	19,800	
Less ending finished goods inventory (12/31/07)	0	
Cost of goods sold		19,800
Gross profit		40,800
Selling and admin. exp. (600 units sold × $19 + $5,400)		16,800
Operating income		$23,400

Variable Costing Income Statement
For the Year Ended December 31, 2007

Sales revenue (600 units sold × $100)		$60,000
Variable cost of goods sold:		
Beginning finished goods inventory (1/1/07)	$ 0	
Variable cost of goods manufactured		
(600 units produced × $22)	13,200	
Cost of goods available for sale	13,200	
Less ending finished goods inventory (12/31/07)	0	
Variable cost of goods sold	13,200	
Variable selling and admin. exp. (600 units sold × $19)	11,400	
Total variable cost		24,600
Contribution margin		35,400
Fixed manufacturing overhead costs	6,600	
Fixed selling and administrative expense	5,400	
Total fixed costs		12,000
Operating income		$23,400

Notice that the income is the same amount for both methods. Sometimes this is not the case, however. The reason for the potential difference in income between the two methods has to do with how each method handles fixed manufacturing overhead.

Under absorption costing, fixed manufacturing overhead costs are added to inventory and only expensed as the products are sold. Basically, if all the products a company manufactures are sold within the accounting period then all of the fixed manufacturing overhead cost added to inventory is expensed as cost of goods sold in that period. In this case, none of the fixed manufacturing overhead cost is left in ending inventory. However if the company produces more units than it sells in a given period, all of the fixed manufacturing overhead is added to inventory but not all of it is expensed as cost of goods sold in that period. The fixed manufacturing overhead attributable to the unsold units remains in ending inventory instead of becoming part of the cost of goods sold in that period.

Under variable costing, fixed manufacturing overhead is expensed as a period cost. So, whether or not all the units produced are sold, the total fixed manufacturing overhead is expensed in the period in which it is incurred.

This difference in the treatment of fixed manufacturing overhead gives rise to two important differences between financial statements prepared using absorption costing and those prepared using variable costing. The dollar amount assigned to inventories and, in most cases, the amount of operating income for a given period will differ between the two methods based on the amount of fixed manufacturing overhead cost that remains in ending inventory at the end of that period under absorption costing.

Let's take another look at Tim Chai Manufacturing, but this time we will assume that the number of units produced differs from the number of units sold during each of the three years we will consider. In the income statements in Exhibit 6-15, the company produced 600 units and sold all of them so the ending inventory was zero. In our next presentation, we will assume that in 2008 the company's sales remain constant at 600 units, but the company produces 660 units which results in an ending inventory of 60 units. Then, in 2009, we will assume once again that sales remain constant at 600 units, but this time the company produces only 550 units. What changes from one year to the next is the number of units produced and the number of units remaining in ending inventory. We will assume that the number of units sold, selling price, all of the variable costs per unit and total fixed costs remain the same throughout the example. We do this to avoid distractions and to focus on the differences in inventory costs and operating income that are caused by increases or decreases in the number of units in inventory and the treatment of fixed manufacturing overhead cost. Exhibit 6-16 presents inventory and cost data for 2007, 2008, and 2009.

Exhibit 6-16 Chai Manufacturing Inventory and Cost Data for 2007, 2008, and 2009

Data for Three Years:

Inventory Information:	2007	2008	2009
Beginning finished goods inventory	0	0	60
Units produced	600	660	550
Units available for sale	600	660	610
Less units sold (The same each year.)	(600)	(600)	(600)
Ending finished goods inventory	0	60	10

Cost Information:			
Variable costs per unit (Exactly the same each year.):			
Variable product cost:	2007	2008	2009
Direct material	$ 7	$ 7	$ 7
Direct labor	12	12	12
Variable manufacturing overhead	3	3	3
Total variable manufacturing cost per unit	$22	$22	$22
Variable selling and administrative expense	$19	$19	$19
Fixed cost per year (Exactly the same each year):			
Fixed manufacturing overhead cost	$6,600	$6,600	$6,600
Fixed selling and administrative expense	$5,400	$5,400	$5,400

Based on the data in Exhibit 6-16, we can determine the absorption and variable costs per unit for 2007, 2008, and 2009 as shown in Exhibit 6-17.

Exhibit 6-17 Absorption and Variable Costs per Unit for 2007, 2008, and 2009

Absorption Cost per Unit:	2007	2008	2009
Direct material (Exactly the same each year)	$ 7	$ 7	$ 7
Direct labor (Exactly the same each year)	12	12	12
Variable manufacturing overhead (Exactly the same each year)	3	3	3
Fixed manufacturing overhead cost			
(2007: $6,600/600 units produced)	11		
(2008: $6,600/660 units produced)		10	
(2009: $6,600/550 units produced)			12
Total absorption cost per unit	$33	$32	$34
Variable Cost per Unit (Exactly the same each year):	2007	2008	2009
Direct material	$ 7	$ 7	$ 7
Direct labor	12	12	12
Variable manufacturing overhead	3	3	3
Total variable cost per unit	$22	$22	$22

Exhibit 6-18 presents the 2008 absorption costing and variable costing income statements for Tim Chai Manufacturing based on the cost data in Exhibit 6-16 and the cost per unit information in Exhibit 6-17. Note that companies generally base variable selling and administrative costs on the number of units sold, as opposed to the number of units produced.

Notice that the operating income for Tim Chai Manufacturing in Exhibit 6-18 for absorption costing is $600 higher than it is for variable costing ($24,000 − $23,400). This is because under absorption costing part of the fixed manufacturing overhead cost is not expensed and is instead included in the absorption costing ending inventory. In this simple situation the increase in the amount of fixed manufacturing overhead in ending absorption inventory can be calculated by multiplying the 60 units in ending inventory by the $10 fixed manufacturing overhead per unit from Exhibit 6-17. In this case the ending inventory under absorption costing increased by $600 more than the increase in inventory under variable costing, calculated as follows:

	Absorption Costing		**Variable Costing**		**Difference in Change in Inventory**
Beginning inventory	$ 0		$ 0		
Ending inventory	1,920		1,320		
Change in inventory	$1,920	−	$1,320	=	$600

Tracing the differences between income and inventory amounts becomes a bit more complex when both beginning and ending inventory amounts differ, as we will see in the next presentation.

Exhibit 6-18 Tim Chai Manufacturing 2008 Income Statements

Tim Chai Manufacturing, Inc.
Absorption Costing Income Statement
For the Year Ended December 31, 2008

Sales revenue (600 units sold × $100)		$60,000
Cost of goods sold:		
Beginning finished goods inventory	$ 0	
Cost of goods manufactured (660 units produced × $32)	21,120	
Cost of goods available for sale	21,120	
Less ending fin. goods inventory (60 units × $32)	(1,920)	
Cost of goods sold		19,200
Gross profit		40,800
Selling and admin. exp. (600 units sold × $19 + $5,400)		16,800
Operating income		$24,000

$1,920 change in inventory

Difference in the change in inventory = $1,920 − $1,320 = $600

Difference in income $24,000 −23,400 $ 600

Variable Costing Income Statement
For the Year Ended December 31, 2008

Sales revenue (600 units sold × $100)		$60,000
Variable cost of goods sold:		
Beginning finished goods inventory	$ 0	
Variable cost of goods manufactured (660 units produced × $22)	14,520	
Cost of goods available for sale	14,420	
Less ending finished goods inventory (10 units × $22)	(1,320)	
Variable cost of goods sold	13,200	
Variable selling and admin. exp. (600 units sold × $19)	11,400	
Total variable cost		24,600
Contribution margin		35,400
Fixed manufacturing overhead costs	6,600	
Fixed selling and administrative expense	5,400	
Total fixed costs		12,000
Operating income		$23,400

$1,320 change in inventory

Exhibit 6-19 presents the 2009 absorption costing and variable costing income statements for Tim Chai Manufacturing based on the inventory and cost data in Exhibit 6-16, the cost per unit information in Exhibit 6-17, and with ending inventory information from the income statements in Exhibit 6-18. The ending inventory for 2008 in Exhibit 6-18 becomes the beginning inventory we use for 2009 in Exhibit 6-19.

When inventory changes from one year to the next, the difference between absorption and variable costing operating income is explained by the difference between the change in inventory under absorption costing versus the change in inventory under variable costing. Notice that it is explained by the change in inventory during the period, not by the amount of ending inventory. In our example, the difference between the absorption and variable costing operating income for 2009 is $480 ($22,920 − $23,400). This difference can be explained by comparing the $1,580 ($1,920 − $340) change in inventory under absorption costing to the

Exhibit 6-19 Tim Chai Manufacturing 2009 Income Statements

Tim Chai Manufacturing, Inc.
Absorption Costing Income Statement
For the Year Ended December 31, 2009

Sales revenue (600 units sold × $100)		$60,000
Cost of goods sold:		
Beginning finished goods inventory (60 units × $32)	$ 1,920	
Cost of goods manufactured		
(550 units produced × $34)	18,700	
Cost of goods available for sale	20,620	
Less ending fin. goods inventory (10 units × $34)	(340)	
Cost of goods sold		20,280
Gross profit		39,720
Selling and admin. exp. (600 units sold × $19 + $5,400)		16,800
Operating income		$22,920

$1,580 change in inventory

Difference in the change in inventory = $1,580 − $1,100 = $480

Difference in income $23,400 −22,920 $ 480

Variable Costing Income Statement
For the Year Ended December 31, 2009

Sales revenue (600 units sold × $100)		$60,000
Variable cost of goods sold:		
Beginning finished goods inventory (60 units × $22)	$ 1,320	
Variable cost of goods manufactured		
(550 units produced × $22)	12,100	
Cost of goods available for sale	13,420	
Less ending finished goods inventory (10 units × $22)	(220)	
Variable cost of goods sold	13,200	
Variable selling and admin. exp. (600 units sold × $19)	11,400	
Total variable cost		24,600
Contribution margin		35,400
Fixed manufacturing overhead costs	6,600	
Fixed selling and administrative expense	5,400	
Total fixed costs		12,000
Operating income		$23,400

$1,100 change in inventory

$1,100 ($1,320 − $220) change in inventory under variable costing. The difference between the change in inventory for the two amounts equals the $480 difference in operating income. To summarize, for 2009 the ending inventory under absorption costing decreased by $480 more than the decrease in inventory under variable costing, calculated as follows:

	Absorption Costing		Variable Costing		Difference in Change in Inventory
Beginning inventory	$1,920		$1,320		
Ending inventory	340		220		
Change in inventory	$1,580	−	$1,100	=	$480

The difference in operating income can also be explained in a more detailed fashion by tracing the fixed cost through the absorption costing inventories and comparing the amount to the total fixed overhead, which is expensed under variable costing.

Background Data:						
Fixed manufacturing overhead in beginning absorption costing inventory	60	×	$10	=	$ 600	
Fixed manufacturing overhead in absorption costing current production	550	×	$12	=	6,600	
Calculation:						
Fixed manufacturing overhead in absorption cost of goods sold assuming FIFO inventory cost flow:						
Beginning inventory sold first	60 units	×	$10	=		600
Remaining sales from current production	540 units	×	$12	=		6,480
Fixed manufacturing overhead in cost of goods sold under absorption costing						7,080
Fixed manufacturing overhead expensed under variable costing						(6,600)
Difference between absorption and variable costing operating income						$ 480

Operating income for variable costing does not differ simply because a company produces more or fewer units than it sells. Under absorption costing, however, increasing inventories tends to increase operating income while decreasing inventories tends to decrease operating income. Even though managers may manipulate operating income somewhat under absorption costing by increasing or decreasing inventory levels, Generally Accepted Accounting Principles (GAAP) require businesses to use absorption costing for financial accounting. Although variable costing does not permit managers to manipulate income by increasing or decreasing inventory levels, variable costing is not permitted by GAAP for financial accounting. However, as we have seen in this chapter through the use of the contribution income statement and cost-volume-profit analysis, variable costing provides management with some very valuable information.

Summary

The traditional income statement, which separates the costs shown into product cost and period cost, is limited in its usefulness to managers as they attempt to plan and control their operations. It does not take into account that some costs change as volume changes, and some do not. The contribution income statement is more useful to managers as a planning tool because it separates the costs presented into fixed costs and variable costs rather than into product costs and period costs.

An integral part of the contribution income statement is the contribution margin, which is the amount remaining after all variable costs have been deducted from sales revenue. When the contribution margin is presented as a percentage of sales, it is called the contribution margin ratio. Both the contribution margin and the contribution margin ratio are used in cost-volume-profit analysis.

Cost-volume-profit (CVP) analysis is the analysis of the relationships between cost and volume, and the effect of those relationships on profit. The first application of CVP analysis is the calculation of break-even, which is the sales level resulting in neither a profit nor a loss. Break-even can be calculated either in sales dollars or in the number of units of product that must be sold.

Cost-volume-profit analysis can also be used to calculate the sales level required to achieve a target profit. As was the case with break-even, the sales level required to achieve a target profit can be calculated in both sales dollars and the number of units of product that must be sold.

Cost-volume-profit analysis can also be used to perform sensitivity analysis, which is a technique used to determine the effect on CVP when changes are made in the selling price, cost structure (variable and/ or fixed), and volume used in the calculations.

Although CVP analysis is easier to perform in a single-product situation, it can also be used to calculate break-even and sales required to achieve target profits in a multiple product situation.

Under absorption costing product cost includes all the costs to acquire products and get them ready to sell regardless of whether the costs are variable or fixed. Under variable costing, only the variable costs to acquire products and get them ready to sell are treated as product costs. All fixed costs associated with acquiring products or getting the products ready to sell are treated as period costs. When companies prepare traditional income statements they use absorption costing. When companies prepare contribution income statements they use variable costing.

Key Terms

Review the Facts

A. What is the difference between a contribution income statement and a traditional income statement?

B. What is the difference between absorption costing and variable costing?

C. What is the contribution margin?

D. What does the contribution margin "contribute toward"?

E. How does total contribution margin differ from contribution margin per unit?

F. What is the contribution margin ratio and how does it differ from the contribution margin?

G. What is cost-volume-profit (CVP) analysis?

H. What does the term break-even point mean?

I. In what ways does the calculation of the break-even point in units differ from the calculation of the break-even point in sales dollars?

J. How would you calculate the required sales in units to attain a target profit?

K. How would you calculate the required sales in dollars to attain a target profit?

L. What does the term sensitivity analysis mean in the context of CVP analysis?

M. What does the term average contribution margin ratio mean for a company that sells multiple products?

N. Which of the CVP formulas are used to calculate break-even and sales required to attain target profits for a multiproduct company?

O. Why is one of the CVP formulas useless in a multiproduct situation when contribution margins for individual products are unknown?

P. What generally causes the difference between the income calculated under absorption costing versus income calculated under variable costing?

Apply What You Have Learned

LO 4: Prepare a Contribution Income Statement

6-15. Fresh Baked Cookie Company sells cookies in a large shopping mall. The following multiple-step income statement was prepared for the year ending December 31, 2008.

Fresh Baked Cookie Company
Income Statement
For the Year Ended December 31, 2008

Sales		$36,000
Cost of Goods Sold		4,000
Gross Profit		$32,000
Operating Expense:		
Selling Expense	$18,000	
Administrative Expense	10,000	28,000
Operating Income		$ 4,000

Cost of goods sold is a variable cost. Selling expense is 20% variable and 80% fixed, and administrative expense is 5% variable and 95% fixed.

Required:

Prepare a contribution income statement for the Fresh Baked Cookie Company.

LO 4: Prepare a Contribution Income Statement

6-16. The following multiple-step income statement was prepared for Steinmann's Bait Shop for the year ending December 31, 2008.

Steinmann's Bait Shop **Income Statement** **For the Year Ended December 31, 2008**		
Sales		$98,000
Cost of Goods Sold		22,000
Gross Profit		$76,000
Operating Expense:		
Selling Expense	$27,000	
Administrative Expense	36,000	63,000
Operating Income		$13,000

Cost of goods sold is a variable cost. Selling expense is 30% variable and 70% fixed, and administrative expense is 10% variable and 90% fixed.

Required:

Prepare a contribution income statement for Steinmann's Bait Shop.

LO 4: Prepare a Contribution Income Statement

6-17. Quality Fishing Gear Company sells high-quality fiberglass fishing rods to retailers. The following multiple-step income statement was prepared for the year ending December 31, 2008.

Quality Fishing Gear Company **Income Statement** **For the Year Ended December 31, 2008**		
Sales		$540,000
Cost of Goods Sold		360,000
Gross Profit		$180,000
Operating Expense:		
Selling Expense	$88,000	
Administrative Expense	72,000	160,000
Operating Income		$ 20,000

Cost of goods sold is a variable cost. Selling expense is 65% variable and 35% fixed, and administrative expense is 25% variable and 75% fixed.

Required:

Prepare a contribution income statement for Quality Fishing Gear Company.

LO 4: Prepare a Contribution Income Statement

6-18. Ray Placid is considering opening the Placid Greeting Card Shop in a local mall. The store rent will be $550 per month, the cost of telephone service will be about $95 per month, and based on the size of the store, Ray believes that cost of electricity will average about $200 per month. Ray will be able to buy the greeting cards for $0.50 each and plans to sell them for $2 each. Salaries are expected to be $1,200 per month regardless of the number of cards sold. Ray estimates that other miscellaneous fixed costs will total $150 per month and miscellaneous variable cost will be $0.10 per card. Ray anticipates that he will be able to sell about 3,000 greeting cards per month. If Ray opens the store, his first month of business will be November 2010.

Required:

Prepare a projected contribution approach income statement for November 2010.

LO 4: Prepare a Contribution Income Statement

6-19. Joe's Pretzel Stand is located in the Orange Bowl stadium and sells pretzels during sporting events. The following information is available:

- Selling price per pretzel $2.00
- Cost of each pretzel $0.25
- Cost of renting the pretzel stand is $12,000 per year.
- Instead of an hourly wage, Joe pays college students $0.20 per pretzel sold to run the pretzel stand.

Required:

Prepare a contribution income statement for 2010 assuming that 8,000 pretzels are sold.

LO 4: Prepare a Contribution Income Statement

6-20. The following information is available for Blaire's Snow Cone Stand:

- Selling price per snow cone $1.25
- Cost of each snow cone $0.30
- Rent paid for the stand at a local flea market is $2,400 per year.
- Instead of an hourly wage, Blaire's pays high school students $0.40 per snow cone sold.

Required:

Prepare a contribution income statement for 2010 assuming that 6,000 snow cones are sold.

LO 4: Prepare a Condensed Contribution Income Statement

6-21. The following is the contribution income statement for The Bivans Company:

The Bivans Company Contribution Income Statement For the Year Ended December 31, 2009		
Sales		$800,000
Variable Cost:		
Cost of Goods Sold	$420,000	
Variable Selling Expense	75,000	
Variable Administrative Expense	33,000	
Total Variable Cost		528,000
Contribution Margin		$272,000
Fixed Cost:		
Fixed Selling Expense	$128,000	
Fixed Administrative Expense	53,000	
Total Fixed Cost		181,000
Operating Income		$ 91,000

Required:

Based on the contribution income statement for The Bivans Company, prepare a condensed contribution income statement.

LO 1: Prepare a Multiple-step Income Statement

6-22. Refer to the information presented in problem 6-21.

Required:

Prepare a multi-step income statement for the Bivans Company.

LO 4: Prepare a Condensed Contribution Income Statement

6-23. Following is the contribution income statement for The Lauren Company:

The Lauren Company Contribution Income Statement For the Year Ended December 31, 2009		
Sales		$4,800,000
Variable Cost:		
Cost of Goods Sold	$2,320,000	
Variable Selling Expense	265,000	
Variable Administrative Expense	484,000	
Total Variable Cost		3,069,000
Contribution Margin		$1,731,000
Fixed Cost:		
Fixed Selling Expense	$ 648,000	
Fixed Administrative Expense	973,000	
Total Fixed Cost		1,621,000
Operating Income		$ 110,000

Required:

Based on The Lauren Company's contribution income statement, prepare a condensed contribution income statement.

LO 1: Prepare a Multiple-step Income Statement

6-24. Refer to the information presented in problem 6-23.

Required:

Prepare a multi-step income statement for The Lauren Company.

LO 4: Prepare a Condensed Contribution Income Statement

6-25. The following is the contribution income statement for Karl's Athletic Shop:

Karl's Athletic Shop
Contribution Income Statement
For the Year Ended December 31, 2009

Sales		$422,000
Variable Cost:		
Cost of Goods Sold	$205,000	
Variable Selling Expense	55,000	
Variable Administrative Expense	22,000	
Total Variable Cost		282,000
Contribution Margin		$140,000
Fixed Cost:		
Fixed Selling Expense	$ 75,000	
Fixed Administrative Expense	34,000	
Total Fixed Cost		109,000
Operating Income		$ 31,000

Required:

Based on this contribution income statement, prepare a condensed contribution income statement for Karl's Athletic Shop.

LO 1: Prepare a Multiple-step Income Statement

6-26. Refer to the information presented in problem 6-25.

Required:

Prepare a multi-step income statement for Karl's Athletic Shop.

LO 4: Prepare a Contribution Income Statement

6-27. Paradise Manufacturing makes weight-lifting equipment. During 2008, the following costs were incurred:

	Amount	Percent Fixed	Percent Variable
Direct material	$680,000	—	100
Direct labor	420,000	—	100
Variable manufacturing overhead	130,000	—	100
Fixed manufacturing overhead	900,000	100	
Selling cost	300,000	20	80
Administrative cost	220,000	10	90

Sales for 2008 totaled $2,780,000 and there were no beginning or ending inventories.

Required:

Prepare a contribution income statement for the year ended December 31, 2008.

LO 4: Prepare a Contribution Income Statement

6-28. The following information is available for Nicole's Toy Manufacturing Company for 2008:

	Amount	Percent Fixed	Percent Variable
Direct material	$440,000	—	100
Direct labor	90,000	—	100
Variable manufacturing overhead	70,000	—	100
Fixed manufacturing overhead	800,000	100	—
Selling cost	950,000	45	55
Administrative cost	570,000	85	15

Sales for 2008 totaled $3,164,000 and there were no beginning or ending inventories.

Required:

Prepare a contribution income statement for the year ended December 31, 2008.

LO 4: Prepare a Contribution Income Statement

6-29. The following information is available for Rick's Watch Company for 2008:

	Amount	Percent Fixed	Percent Variable
Direct material	$534,000	—	100
Direct labor	129,000	—	100
Variable manufacturing overhead	397,000	—	100
Fixed manufacturing overhead	998,000	100	—
Selling cost	196,000	33	67
Administrative cost	243,000	78	22

Sales for 2008 totaled $2,745,000 and there were no beginning or ending inventories.

Required:

Prepare a contribution income statement for the year ended December 31, 2008.

LO 4: Prepare a Contribution Income Statement

6-30. Alumacraft Manufacturing makes aluminum serving carts for use in commercial jetliners. During 2009, the following costs were incurred:

	Amount	Percent Fixed	Percent Variable
Direct material	$2,600,000	100	—
Direct labor	1,820,000	100	—
Variable manufacturing overhead	540,000	—	100
Fixed manufacturing overhead	1,900,000	100	—
Selling cost	380,000	15	85
Administrative cost	230,000	5	95

Sales for 2009 totaled $7,900,000 and there were no beginning or ending inventories.

Required:

Prepare a contribution income statement for the year ended December 31, 2009.

LO 6: Determine Break-Even and Sales Required to Earn Target Profit Using Per Unit Amounts

6-31. The following information is available for Medical Testing Corporation.

Amount charged for each test performed	$	90
Annual fixed cost		200,000
Variable cost per test		25

Required:

a. Calculate how many tests Medical Testing Corporation must perform each year to break even.

b. Calculate how many tests Medical Testing Corporation must perform each year to earn a profit of $25,000.

LO 6: Determine Break-Even and Sales Required to Earn Target Profit Using Per Unit Amounts

6-32. The following information is available for Dottie's Donut Shop.

Amount charged per dozen doughnuts	$	0.90
Annual fixed cost		385,000.00
Variable cost per dozen doughnuts		0.22

Required:

a. Calculate how many dozen doughnuts Dottie must sell each year to break even.

b. Calculate how many dozen doughnuts Dottie must sell each year to earn a profit of $35,000.

LO 6: Determine Break-Even and Sales Required to Earn Target Profit Using Per Unit Amounts

6-33. Jim is considering starting a small company to paint driveways. The following information is available:

Amount charged per square yard painted	$	5
Annual fixed cost		3,000
Variable cost per square yard painted		2

Required:

a. Calculate how many square yards of driveway Jim must paint each year to break even.

b. Calculate how many square yards of driveway Jim must paint each year to earn a profit of $5,000.

c. Determine the dollar amount of the sales revenue Jim must have to earn a profit of 20% of sales.

LO 6: Determine Break-Even and Sales Required to Earn Target Profit Using Per Unit Amounts

6-34. Carbonnel Calendar Company is considering adding a new calendar design to their line. The following information is available:

Selling price per calendar	$ 3.97
Additional annual fixed cost	4,558.00
Variable cost per calendar	3.11

Required:

a. Calculate how many calendars must be sold each year to break even.

b. Calculate how many calendars must be sold each year to earn a profit of $2,580.

LO 3 & 6: Use Ratios to Determine Break-Even and Sales Required to Earn Target Profit

6-35. Melissa Valdez is planning to expand her clothing business by opening another store. In planning for the new store, Melissa believes that selling prices and costs of the various products sold will be similar to that of the existing store. In fact, she thinks that variable and fixed costs for the new store will be similar to that of the existing store, except that rent for the new store will be $300 per month more than the rent paid for the existing store. The following information is available for the existing store for the year ended December 31, 2008:

Sales	$200,000
Variable cost	130,000
Fixed cost	48,000

Required:

a. Determine the sales required for the new store to break even.

b. Determine the sales required for the new store to earn a profit of $20,000 per year. (Hint: Keep in mind that the $300 increase in rent is a monthly amount and the fixed cost of $48,000 is an annual amount.)

LO 3 & 6: Use Ratios to Determine Break-Even and Sales Required to Earn Target Profit

6-36. Emergency Medical, Inc. is considering opening a new emergency care facility. The fees charged and costs of the new facility will be similar to that of the existing facility. The only exception is that the annual fixed cost for the new facility is expected to be $75,000 more than that of the existing facility. The following information is available for Emergency Medical's existing facility for 2008:

Revenue	$1,250,000
Variable cost	600,000
Fixed cost	420,000

Required:

a. Determine the revenues required for the new emergency care facility to break even.

b. Determine the revenues required for the new emergency care facility to earn a profit of $120,000 per year.

c. Determine the revenues required for the new emergency care facility to earn a profit equal to 15% of revenues.

LO 3 & 6: Use Ratios to Determine Break-Even and Sales Required to Earn Target Profit

6-37. Wendt Industries is considering opening a second school supply store. The annual fixed cost of the new store is expected to be $225,000 per year. The following information is available for Wendt's first school supply store for 2008:

Revenue	$3,650,000
Variable cost	1,387,000

Required:

a. Based on this information, what is the required revenue for the second store to break even?

b. Based on this information, what is the required revenue for the second store to earn a profit of $125,000?

c. Based on this information, what is the required revenue for the second store to earn a profit of 8% of revenue?

LO 2, 4, & 6: Use Per Unit Amounts to Determine Break-Even and Sales Required to Earn Target Profit and Prepare a Contribution Income Statement

6-38. Richard Davenport owns a clothing store and is considering renting a soda vending machine for his store. He can rent the soda machine for $125 per month. Richard would supply the soda for the machine which he can buy for $3 per twelve pack. Richard plans to charge $0.75 per can.

Required:

a. List the fixed costs for renting and stocking the soda machine.

b. List the variable costs for renting and stocking the soda machine.

c. Calculate the contribution margin per can of soda.

d. 1. Calculate how many cans of soda Richard must sell each month to break even.

   2. Prepare a contribution income statement that proves the answer you just calculated.

e. 1. Calculate how many cans of soda Richard must sell each month to earn a profit of $50.

   2. Prepare a contribution income statement that proves your answer to the previous requirement.

LO 2, 4, & 6: Use Per Unit Amounts to Determine Break-Even and Sales Required to Earn Target Profit and Prepare a Contribution Income Statement

6-39. Erich Traebeecke owns the Kenpo Karate School in Miami. He is considering renting a candy vending machine for his school lobby. He can rent the candy machine for $90 per month. Erich would supply the candy bars for the machine. He can buy a box of eight candy bars for $1 per box. Erich plans to sell each candy bar for $0.35.

Required:

a. List the fixed costs of renting and stocking the candy machine.

b. List the variable costs of renting and stocking the candy machine.

c. Calculate the contribution margin per candy bar.

d. 1. Calculate how many candy bars must be sold each month to break even.

2. Prepare a contribution income statement that proves the answer you just calculated.

e. 1. Calculate how many candy bars must be sold each month to earn a profit of $180.

2. Prepare a contribution income statement that proves your answer to the previous requirement.

LO 2, 4, & 6: Use Per Unit Amounts to Determine Break-Even and Sales Required to Earn Target Profit and Prepare a Contribution Income Statement

6-40. Monica Llobet owns Monica's School of Dance. She is considering installing a cappuccino machine in the school's dance studio. Monica can rent the cappuccino machine for $48.88 per month. Coffee and supplies would cost about $.12 per cup of cappuccino. Monica plans to sell each cup of cappuccino for $2.

Required:

a. List the fixed costs of renting and stocking the cappuccino machine.

b. List the variable costs of renting and stocking the cappuccino machine.

c. Calculate the contribution margin per cup of cappuccino.

d. 1. Calculate how many cups of cappuccino must be sold each month to break even.

2. Prepare a contribution income statement that proves the answer you just calculated.

e. 1. Calculate how many cups of cappuccino must be sold each month to earn a profit of $100. (Round your answer to the nearest unit.)

2. Prepare a contribution income statement that proves your answer to the previous requirement.

LO 2 & 6: Use Per Unit Amounts to Determine Break-Even and Sales Required to Earn Target Profit

6-41. Alberto Pons is interested in selling pin-on buttons at school pep rallies. The button machine will cost $200, and the material to produce each button costs $0.15. In exchange for the right to sell the buttons, Alberto has agreed to donate $300 per year and $0.20 per button to the school's booster club. Alberto plans to sell the buttons for $1 each and to operate the service for four years. By then it will be time to graduate, and the button machine will be worn out.

Required:

a. Assuming the button machine will be able to produce buttons for four years, calculate the cost per year for the button machine.

b. Calculate the total fixed cost per year for Alberto's button business.

c. Calculate the variable cost per button.

d. Calculate the annual break-even point

1. in units.

2. in dollars.

e. Calculate how many buttons must be sold to earn an annual profit of $800.

f. Calculate the sales in dollars required to earn an annual profit of $800.

LO 2 & 6: Use Per Unit Amounts to Determine Break-Even and Sales Required to Earn Target Profit

6-42. Betty Lopez is interested in setting up a stand to sell Mylar helium balloons at a local roller rink. The stand would cost $250, and the material for each balloon would cost $0.75. In exchange for the right to sell the balloons, Betty has agreed to pay $500 per year and $0.50 per balloon to the roller rink's owner. Betty plans to sell the balloons for $3 each. Betty thinks the stand will last four years.

Required:

a. Assuming the balloon stand has an estimated useful life of four years with no salvage value, calculate the cost per year for the balloon stand.

b. Calculate the total fixed cost per year for Betty's balloon business.

c. Calculate the variable cost per balloon.

d. Calculate the annual break-even point

  1. in units.

  2. in dollars.

e. Calculate how many balloons must be sold to earn an annual profit of $2,000.

f. Calculate the sales in dollars required to earn an annual profit of $2,000.

LO 2 & 6: Use Per Unit Amounts to Determine Break-Even and Sales Required to Earn Target Profit

6-43. Bill Smith is interested in selling ice cream bars at school events. The vendor stand will cost $800, and the ice cream bars cost $0.65. In exchange for the right to sell the ice cream bars, Bill has agreed to donate $600 per year and $0.25 per ice cream bar to the school's booster club. Bill plans to sell the ice cream bars for $1.50 each. Bill intends to sell the ice cream bars and run the stand for four years.

Required:

a. Assuming the vendor stand can be used for four years, calculate the cost per year for the vendor stand.

b. Calculate the total fixed cost per year for Bill's ice cream business.

c. Calculate the variable cost per ice cream bar.

d. Calculate the annual break-even point.

  1. in units.

  2. in dollars.

e. Calculate how many ice cream bars must be sold to earn an annual profit of $3,000.

f. Calculate the sales in dollars required to earn an annual profit of $3,000.

g. Calculate Bill's profit if sales were $8,000 for this year.

LO 3 & 6: Determine the Contribution Margin Ratio and Determine Break-Even and Sales Required to Earn Target Profit

6-44. Amanda is considering opening a gift shop. She has collected the following information:

Monthly rent	$2,800
Monthly sales salaries	1,200

In addition to the sales salaries, Amanda intends to pay sales commissions of 5% of sales to her sales staff. The cost of the merchandise sold is expected to be 40% of sales.

Required:

a. Determine the following:

1. Amanda's break-even point in monthly sales dollars
2. The monthly sales dollars required to earn a profit of $2,000 per month
3. Amanda's break-even point if she is able to reduce rent by $200

b. Assume that Amanda has negotiated a 10% discount on all merchandise purchases. The new cost of merchandise will not change the selling price of product. Determine the following:

1. The new contribution margin ratio
2. The new break-even point in monthly sales dollars

LO 3 & 6: Determine the Contribution Margin Ratio and Determine Break-Even and Sales Required to Earn Target Profit

6-45. Noelle is considering opening a bookstore. She has collected the following information:

Monthly rent	$3,286
Monthly sales salaries	4,200

In addition to the sales salaries, Noelle intends to pay sales commissions of 10% of sales to her sales staff. The cost of the merchandise sold is expected to be 30% of sales.

Required:

a. Determine the following:

1. Noelle's break-even point in monthly sales dollars
2. The monthly sales dollars required to earn a profit of $1,500 per month
3. Noelle's break-even point if she is able to reduce rent by $300

b. Assume that Noelle has negotiated a 5% discount on all merchandise purchases. The new cost of merchandise will not change the selling price of product. Determine the following:

1. The new contribution margin ratio
2. The new break-even point in monthly sales dollars

LO 2 & 6: Use Per Unit Amounts to Determine Break-Even and Sales Required to Earn Target Profit

6-46. Clarice is considering buying a DVD rental business. If she finances the entire purchase price, the payments will be $2,900 per month. Store rent would be $2,000 per month and cost of sales clerks, replacement DVDs, and other expenses would b $1,200 per month. Clarice plans to rent the DVDs to her customers for $2 each.

Required:

a. Calculate the variable cost (if any) per DVD rental.

b. Calculate the total fixed cost per month.

c. Determine how many DVDs Clarice must rent each month to break even.

d. Determine how many DVDs Clarice must rent each month to earn a profit of $1,000 per month.

LO 3 & 6: Determine the Contribution Margin Ratio and Determine Break-Even and Sales Required to Earn Target Profit

6-47. Margaret Pitman is considering opening a gift shop. She has collected the following information:

Monthly rent	$1,800
Monthly sales salaries	1,200

The cost of the merchandise sold is expected to be 55% of sales.

Required:

a. What is the annual rent cost?

b. What is the annual sales salaries cost?

c. What is the contribution margin ratio?

d. What is the break-even point in dollars?

e. Determine the amount of sales needed to earn a profit of $12,000 for the year.

LO 3 & 6: Determine the Contribution Margin Ratio and Determine Break-Even and Sales Required to Earn Target Profit

6-48. Carol Jean is considering opening a frame shop. She has collected the following information:

Monthly rent	$ 600
Monthly sales salaries	1,100

The cost of the merchandise sold is expected to be 45% of sales.

Required:

a. What is the annual rent cost?

b. What is the annual sales salaries cost?

c. What is the contribution margin ratio?

d. What is the break-even point in dollars?

e. Determine the amount of sales needed to earn a profit of $18,000 for the year.

f. Determine the amount of sales needed to earn a profit equal to 15% of sales.

LO 3 & 6: Determine the Contribution Margin Ratio and Determine Break-Even and Sales Required to Earn Target Profit

6-49. Birdie Musicus is considering opening Musicus Beauty Supply. She has collected the following information:

Monthly rent	$3,400
Monthly sales salaries	2,800

The cost of the merchandise sold is expected to be 68% of sales.

Required:

a. What is the annual rent cost?

b. What is the annual sales salaries cost?

c. What is the contribution margin ratio?

d. What is the break-even point in dollars?

e. Determine the amount of sales needed to earn a profit of $36,000 for the year.

f. Determine the amount of sales needed to earn a profit equal to 10% or sales.

LO 3 & 6: Determine the Contribution Margin Ratio and Determine Break-Even and Sales Required to Earn Target Profit

6-50. Vivian Farias is considering opening Farias Music Store. She has collected the following information:

Monthly rent	$1,400
Monthly sales salaries	1,700

The cost of the merchandise sold is expected to be 52% of sales.

Required:

a. What is the annual rent cost?

b. What is the annual sales salaries cost?

c. What is the contribution margin ratio?

d. What is the break-even point in dollars?

e. Determine the amount of sales needed to earn a profit of $36,000 for the year.

LO 2, 3, 4, & 5: Analyze a Situation Using CVP

6-51. Quality Instrument Company manufactures various industrial thermometers. Last year the company sold 600 model QI-22 thermometers for $129 each. Managers are concerned that the profits from the QI-22 were only $7,740 last year. Fixed costs for this product are $50,000 per year. In an effort to increase profits, the company raised the price of the QI-22 to $148. Based on annual sales of 600 units, managers are confident that profits from the QI-22 will be increased to $19,140 next year.

The sales manager is concerned about the price increase. He believes the company should move more slowly in making the pricing decision and has suggested that a group be formed to explore the ramifications of such a pricing move.

Required:

Assume that you have been assigned to the group who will evaluate the proposed price change. The group is to create a report discussing the various ramifications of the price increase including its effect on projected sales and profits. Your report should make recommendations that are supported by calculations similar to those found in this chapter.

LO 2, 3, 4, & 5: Analyze a Situation Using CVP

6-52. Reuben Escobar's Door Company manufactured and sold 1,000 model SD4896 doors for $88 each. Managers are concerned that the profits from the SD4896 doors were only $8,000 last year. In an effort to increase profits, the company raised the price of the SD4896 to $106. Based on annual sales of 1,000 units, managers are con fident that profits from the SD4896 will increase to $26,000 next year. Fixed costs of $40,000 are allocated to the SD4896 based on the number of units produced.

The sales manager is concerned about the price increase. He believes the company should move more slowly in making the pricing decision and has suggested that a group be formed to explore the ramifications of such a pricing move.

Required:

Assume that you have been assigned to the group who will evaluate the proposed price change. The group is to create a report discussing the various ramifications of the price increase including its effect on projected sales and profits. Your report should make recommendations that are supported by calculations similar to those found in this chapter.

LO 2, 3, 4, & 5: Analyze a Situation Using CVP

6-53. Carol Werner is considering the purchase of a hot dog vending cart to sell hot dogs in a busy parking lot. The city of Panama City Beach requires that the cart be licensed at a cost of $500 per year.

Required:

a. 1. How would Carol determine the cost to rent a small space in the parking lot to operate the hot dog cart?

   2. How much do you think the monthly rent would be?

   3. How much do you think the hourly wage would be for an employee to operate the stand?

   4. How many hours per day do you think the stand should be open?

   5. Based on your answers to 3 and 4, what would you estimate monthly wage cost to be for the hot dog stand?

   6. How much do you think Carol should charge for each hot dog?

b. Answer the following questions using your answers to question 1.

   1. What is the variable cost per hot dog?

   2. What is the monthly fixed cost for operating the hot dog stand?

   3. What is the contribution margin per hot dog?

   4. What is the contribution margin ratio?

   5. What is the variable cost ratio?

   6. a. How many hot dogs must Carol sell each month to break even?

      b. Prepare a contribution income statement which proves your answer.

   7. a. How many hot dogs must Carol sell each month to earn a profit of $300?

      b. Prepare a contribution income statement that proves your answer.

LO 2 & 8: Determine Per Unit Amounts under Absorption and Variable Costing

6-54. The following information is available for the Tarrago Company:

Beginning finished goods inventory	0
Units produced	2,400
Units available for sale	2,400
Less units sold	(2,400)
Ending finished goods inventory	0

Selling price per unit	$ 100.00
Variable costs per unit:	
Variable product cost:	
Direct material	$ 9.00
Direct labor	$ 17.00
Variable manufacturing overhead	$ 6.00
Total variable manufacturing cost per unit	$ 22.00
Variable selling and administrative expense	$ 19.00
Fixed cost per year:	
Fixed manufacturing overhead cost	$13,200.00
Fixed selling and administrative expense	$10,800.00

Required:

a. Calculate the product cost per unit under absorption costing.

b. Calculate the product cost per unit under variable costing

LO 1, 2 & 8: Prepare Income Statements Under Absorption and Variable Costing When Beginning and Ending Inventories are Zero

6-55. The following information is available for the year ended December 31, 2008 for the Linda Tarrago Company:

Inventory information:	
Beginning inventory	0
Units produced	1,200
Units available for sale	1,200
Less units sold	(1,200)
Ending inventory	0
Selling price per unit	$ 175
Cost Information:	
Variable costs per unit:	
Variable product cost:	
Direct material	$ 10
Direct labor	$ 22
Variable manufacturing overhead	$ 13
Total variable manufacturing cost per unit	$ 45
Variable selling and administrative expenses	$ 6
Fixed cost per year:	
Fixed manufacturing overhead cost	$18,000
Fixed selling and administrative expenses	$58,000

Required:

a. Prepare an absorption costing multiple step income statement for the company

b. Prepare a variable costing contribution income statement for the company

c. Compare the income and ending inventory amounts under absorption and variable costing. If they are the same under each method, explain why this happened. If they are different under each method, explain why they are different.

LO 1, 2 & 8: Prepare Income Statements Under Absorption and Variable Costing When Inventory is Increasing from Zero to 300 Units

6-56. The following information is available for the year ended December 31, 2009 for the Linda Tarrago Company:

Inventory information:	
Beginning inventory	0
Units produced	1,500
Units available for sale	1,500
Less units sold	(1,200)
Ending inventory	300
Selling price per unit	$ 175
Cost Information:	
Variable costs per unit:	
Variable product cost:	
Direct material	$ 10
Direct labor	$ 22
Variable manufacturing overhead	$ 13
Total variable manufacturing cost per unit	$ 45
Variable selling and administrative expenses	$ 36
Fixed cost per year:	
Fixed manufacturing overhead cost	$18,000
Fixed selling and administrative expenses	$58,000

Required:

a. Prepare an absorption costing multiple step income statement for the company

b. Prepare a variable costing contribution income statement for the company

c. Compare the income and ending inventory amounts under absorption and variable costing. If they are the same under each method, explain why this happened. If they are different under each method, explain why they are different.

LO 1, 2 & 8: Prepare Income Statements Under Absorption and Variable Costing When Inventory is Decreasing from 300 Units to Zero

6-57. Note: This problem is a continuation of Problem 6-56. Problem 6-56 must be completed to determine the costs of the beginning inventory. The following information is available for the year ended December 31, 2010 for the Linda Tarrago Company:

Inventory information:	
Beginning inventory	300
Units produced	900
Units available for sale	1,200
Less units sold	(1,200)
Ending inventory	0
Selling price per unit	$ 175
Cost Information:	
Variable costs per unit:	
Variable product cost:	
Direct material	$ 10
Direct labor	$ 22
Variable manufacturing overhead	$ 13
Total variable manufacturing cost per unit	$ 45
Variable selling and administrative expenses	$ 36
Fixed cost per year:	
Fixed manufacturing overhead cost	$18,000
Fixed selling and administrative expenses	$58,000

Note: Problem 6-56 must be completed to determine the costs of the beginning inventory.

Required:

a. Prepare an absorption costing multiple step income statement for the company

b. Prepare a variable costing contribution income statement for the company

c. Compare the income and ending inventory amounts under absorption and variable costing. If they are the same under each method, explain why this happened. If they are different under each method, explain why they are different.

7

Making Decisions Using Relevant Information

When managers make decisions, it is critical that they base them on *relevant* information, disregarding all *irrelevant* information. To be relevant, the information must be pertinent to the decision at hand.

You may wonder why an entire chapter of this text is devoted to determining which costs and benefits are relevant. Isn't it understood that decision makers should disregard superfluous information and concentrate on the facts that relate to the decision at hand? Yes, but with so many considerations to muddy the water, determining what information is relevant is not always as easy as it might seem. For instance, consider an actual example about a couple that went to **Disney World** with their three-year-old daughter, Jessica. The family stayed at a **Disney** hotel to be close to the **Disney** attractions and to take advantage of the hotel's staff of baby-sitters. The baby-sitting service cost \$15 per hour and required a four-hour minimum. To get a sitter you must make arrangements well in advance and if you need to cancel, you must do it at least four hours in advance to avoid the \$60 minimum fee. Jessica's parents planned to take her to the **Magic Kingdom** early in the day and then leave her with a sitter in the late afternoon while they visited **EPCOT** on their own.

Jessica and her parents went to **Disney's Magic Kingdom** as they had planned and were having a wonderful time. As the day progressed, Jessica enjoyed the amusement park so much that her parents were having second thoughts about leaving her with the sitter. They had to make a decision: Should they take Jessica to **EPCOT** or leave her with the sitter as planned? What Jessica's parents really wanted to do was to take her to **EPCOT**. But, as they discussed the situation, the overwhelming focus of their decision became the troublesome \$60 minimum charge for the sitter. Because it was too late to cancel the sitter and avoid the \$60 cost, it seemed to follow that Jessica should stay with the sitter. But Jessica's parents were falling into a very common trap. They were allowing a cost that was actually irrelevant to sway their decision. Oddly enough, the element that had emerged as the central consideration, the \$60, was in fact, irrelevant to their decision. This is because the \$60 would have to be paid either way. That is, if Jessica's parents were to take her to the sitter, they would have to pay the \$60, or if they were to take her to **EPCOT**, they would still have to pay the \$60. Once Jessica's parents realized that the \$60 cost was irrelevant to their decision, they dismissed the sitter and took Jessica to **EPCOT** with them.

In business, the issue of what is relevant often confuses even the most seasoned business executive. To make the best possible decisions, decision makers must learn to consider only relevant information.

Learning Objectives

After completing your work on this chapter, you should be able to do the following:

1. Identify the characteristics of relevant costs and relevant benefits.
2. Explain why sunk costs and costs that do not differ between alternatives are irrelevant costs.
3. Describe the qualitative factors that decision makers should consider when making a business decision.
4. Use accounting information to determine the relevant cost of various decisions.
5. Explain the effects of fixed costs and opportunity costs on outsourcing decisions.
6. Prepare segment income statements and determine the relevant advantage or disadvantage of discontinuing a business segment.

Relevant Costs and Benefits

relevant information Information that is pertinent to a particular decision in that it has a bearing on which decision alternative is preferable.

relevant cost A cost or cash outflow that is pertinent to a particular business decision. A relevant cost is a future cost that differs between alternatives

relevant benefit A benefit (revenue or cash inflow) that is pertinent to a particular business decision. A relevant benefit is a future benefit that differs between alternatives.

sunk cost A past cost that cannot be changed by current or future actions.

Relevant information is information that is pertinent to a particular decision in that it has a bearing on which decision alternative is preferable. A **relevant cost** is a cost or cash outflow that is pertinent to a particular business decision. A **relevant benefit** is a benefit (revenue or cash inflow) that is pertinent to a particular business decision. Relevant costs and benefits possess two important characteristics: (1) The cost or benefit must be something that will happen in the future, and (2) the cost or benefit must differ between decision alternatives. A relevant cost is a future cost that differs between alternatives and a relevant benefit is a future benefit that differs between alternatives.

A relevant cost must be a future cost because current decisions can have no effect on past expenditures. Expenditures that have already occurred are called **sunk costs** and they cannot be changed by current or future actions. Because sunk costs are unaffected by current decisions, they are irrelevant and we should not consider them when evaluating current decision alternatives. For example, if your firm was deciding whether to replace an old printing press with a new, labor-saving model, the cost of the old press is irrelevant. Why? The firm already bought the old press. The purchase of the new printing press would not lessen or change the amount paid for the old press. Whether the company purchases the new press or not, the cost of the old press is a sunk cost: Nothing you do now can change it. Sunk costs include both amounts paid in the past and past commitments to pay. That is, once there is a binding commitment to pay cash or otherwise transfer resources, the cost associated with that commitment is a sunk cost.

To be relevant, a future cost or benefit must differ between decision alternatives. If a future cost or benefit will be the same regardless of the alternative we choose, it is irrelevant. Again, consider the decision of whether to buy a new printing press or to keep the old one. If the new printing press will use the same quantity and type of ink as the old one, the cost of ink is irrelevant no matter how large the dollar figure. If the revenue earned will be the same whether or not you replace the printing press, that benefit is irrelevant.

Discussion Questions

7-1. Refer to the decision faced by Jessica's parents in **Disney World**. Which criteria of relevance did the $60 baby-sitting cost fail to meet? Explain your reasoning.

7-2. Have you ever made a decision and later realized that you mistakenly let irrelevant factors affect your choice? Explain.

Quantitative factors are those that can be represented by numbers. Almost all accounting information is quantitative, including relevant cost and benefit information. However, managers often consider additional factors that cannot be quantified. **Qualitative factors** are factors that cannot be measured numerically—they must be described in words. Examples include customer satisfaction, product quality, employee morale, and customer perceptions.

quantitative factors Factors that can be measured by numbers.

qualitative factors Factors that cannot be measured by numbers-they must be described in words.

In addition to their financial impact, business decisions affect a multitude of non-financial areas. For example, closing an outdated factory may reduce production cost, but it will also adversely impact employee morale. The employees that remain after the plant closing may believe that the company's loyalty is to profits, not their well-being. Lower employee morale is likely to lead to less productivity and lower product quality. Qualitative factors should also be considered in smaller, routine decisions. For example, a furniture store manager considering a proposal to switch from company owned and operated delivery trucks to a delivery service should consider her lack of control if she uses the delivery service. Even though it may be less expensive to use a delivery service, the furniture store's manager may not want to lose the ability to select the most responsible truck drivers and to schedule deliveries exactly as she desires. When making a decision, managers should evaluate all relevant quantitative and qualitative factors.

Discussion Questions

Assume you are planning a trip from Miami to Texas to visit some friends. You have a job, but your boss will let you take off as many days as you wish for the trip. Your car is unreliable, so you compare two alternatives—take a bus or take an airplane.

7-3. What are the relevant quantitative factors you should consider in making your decision?

7-4. What are the relevant qualitative factors you should consider in making your decision?

Decision makers must question the relevance of accounting information. As discussed in Chapter 1, managers and engineers do not always specify accounting information requirements. When they don't, accountants provide them with information based on accepted accounting techniques and this information may not be relevant. Although management accounting information is generally relevant to internal decision makers, managers should be able to determine for themselves what information is relevant to their particular situation so they can make sound, well-informed decisions. As Exhibit 7-1 shows, whether an item is relevant or not hinges on the answers to the two important questions: (1) Is the item a future cost or benefit? And (2) Does the cost or benefit differ between decision alternatives?

Throughout the remainder of this chapter, we will explore several common business situations to demonstrate how to determine relevant cost and benefit information and its importance to good decision making. For each example, we will gather all costs

Exhibit 7-1 Determining Relevant Cost and Benefit

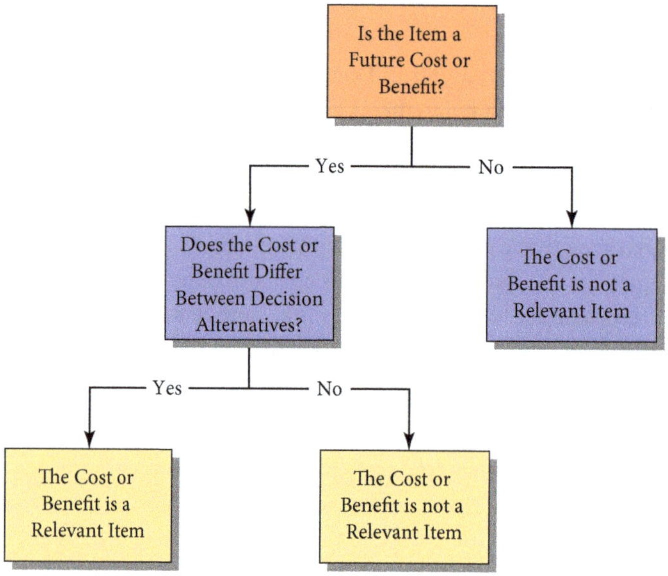

and benefits associated with the decision. Next, we will determine the relevant costs and benefits of each decision alternative. Finally, we will compare the relevant costs and benefits of the alternatives and determine the preferred alternative. The first example we will explore is an equipment replacement decision.

Equipment Replacement

As an example of how to determine relevant information, we examine a proposed equipment replacement project. Our example highlights the treatment of depreciation, sunk costs, and future costs and benefits that do not differ between alternatives.

Bill Smith & Partners, a local law firm, purchased and installed a sophisticated computer system two weeks ago at a cost of $35,500. Bill's brother, John, stops by the law office to say hello. While there, he notices the new system. He remarks that it is too bad the system is not the latest and quickest because, if it were, the data input time could be cut in half. John suggests that Bill consider updating. Bill responds, "I can't buy a new system. I just bought this one two weeks ago." John advises Bill to take a closer look before deciding.

Gather All Costs and Benefits Associated with the Decision

Bill turns to you for advice. He explains that the recently installed computer system cost $35,500 to purchase, has an estimated useful life of five years, with a residual value of $1,500. He notes that the firm plans to use straight-line depreciation, so it will recognize $6,800 depreciation per year. The cost of operating the recently installed system, which we will call the "old" system, includes three operators at $18,000 per year, and a maintenance contract at $1,000 per year. The maintenance agreement, however, can be canceled at any time. After calling around, Bill informs you that he can sell the old system now, but he will get only $10,000 for it (everyone wants the new model). The replacement system, which we call the "new" system, would cost $76,000 and has an estimated useful life of five years with a $2,000 residual value. Using the straight-line method, annual depreciation would be $14,800. Because data entry is faster, the new system would require only two operators at $18,000 per year. The maintenance contract on the new system would cost $1,000 per year and would be cancelable at any time.

A summary of the cost and benefit of each system is shown in Exhibit 7-2. These items are generally classified as start-up, operating, and shutdown.

Exhibit 7-2 Computer System Replacement Cost Summary

	Old System	New System
Start-up:		
Cost of system	$ 35,500	$ 76,000
Operating:		
Annual depreciation	$ 6,800	$ 14,800
Total depreciation	34,000	74,000
Annual labor cost	54,000	36,000
Total labor cost	270,000	180,000
Annual maintenance cost	1,000	1,000
Total maintenance cost	5,000	5,000
Shutdown:		
Residual value of system	$ 1,500	$ 2,000
Current sale price of old system	10,000	

To help Bill make a wise decision about whether to purchase the new computer system, you must first look at each item and determine whether it is relevant. To make an informed decision, a manager must consider the total cost and benefit of each alternative, including all the costs and benefits over the life of the alternative. For our computer replacement decision, the annual costs associated with each system are multiplied by the number of years the system will be used to determine the total cost of the system over its lifetime.

Determine the Relevant Cost and Benefit of Each Alternative

Next we determine the relevant cost and benefit of each decision alternative. As you consider each cost, try to determine whether it is relevant to the equipment replacement decision. Ask yourself the following two questions: (1) Is the cost a future cost? and (2) Does the cost differ between alternatives? We will examine the cost and benefit associated with the old system first.

Relevant Cost and Benefit of the Old Computer System

The $35,500 cost of the old system is not relevant because it is a sunk cost. Bill's decision to purchase or not to purchase the new system cannot change the past expenditure for the old one.

Although it may appear that depreciation is a future cost, it is nothing more than an allocation of an asset's original cost. The cost of an asset purchased in the past is a sunk cost, and depreciation simply allocates this sunk cost. Therefore, the depreciation for the old system is not relevant.

The total cost of $270,000 to pay for three operators is relevant, because it is a future cost and it differs between alternatives. The old system requires three operators, each costing $18,000 per year. Over the five-year expected life of the old system, that totals $270,000 (3 operators × $18,000 × 5 years).

The $5,000 total cost of the maintenance contract for the old system is irrelevant, because it does not differ between decision alternatives. The cost of the maintenance contract for the old system is the same as that for the new one. Therefore, although this is a future cost, it is irrelevant because it does not differ between alternatives.

The $1,500 residual value of the old system is relevant because it is a future benefit and it differs between alternatives. If Bill stays with the old system, he will be able to sell it at the end of its useful life for $1,500. If, he buys the new one however, he will sell the old one now for $10,000, and therefore he will be unable to sell it for its residual value in five years.

The $10,000 that Bill could get if he sells the old system now is a future benefit that differs between alternatives, and therefore it is relevant. If Bill buys the new system, he can sell the old one for $10,000, but if he does not buy the new system, he will need the old one so he would not sell it.

Relevant Costs and Benefits of the New Computer System

Next, we will analyze the start-up, operating, and shutdown of the new system. In our example, the only start-up cost for the new system is the $76,000 to purchase and install it. This cost is relevant because it is a future cost and it differs between alternatives.

The $74,000 in total depreciation on the new system is an allocation of the replacement system's cost. Because we have already considered the cost of the new system, we avoid double-counting by excluding its depreciation expense from our analysis of relevant costs.

The $180,000 (2 operators × $18,000 × 5 years) total labor cost for the new system's operators is relevant because it is a future cost that differs between alternatives. The labor cost for the old system is $270,000, whereas the labor cost for the new system is $180,000.

The total cost of the maintenance contract on the new system is $5,000. As it happens, the maintenance cost of the old system is also $5,000. In this situation, although maintenance cost is a future cost, it is irrelevant because it does not differ between the alternatives.

The $2,000 residual value for the new system is relevant because it is a future benefit that differs between alternatives. If Bill replaces his current system with a new one, then he can sell the new system for $2,000 at the end of its useful life (in the future). If he does not buy the new one, he obviously can't sell it.

Compare the Relevant Information and Select an Alternative

Now that we have determined which costs and benefits are relevant for each alternative, we compare them to see which alternative is best for Bill's firm. For each of our relevant cost examples, we will use a simple format that includes a column for the relevant items for each decision alternative. Once we list all the relevant items in the appropriate column, we will calculate the difference between the relevant costs and benefits and select the best decision alternative. It is important to differentiate between inflows and outflows. In Exhibit 7-3 we use parentheses to identify outflows.

As this analysis shows, Bill would save $24,500 over the next five years by buying the new computer system. So he should buy the new system to save money, right? From a purely monetary point of view, he should. However, the new system is not cheap. Often business decision makers determine the best alternative, only to learn the business does

Exhibit 7-3 Relevant Cost Comparison for Bill Smith & Partners

	Alternative One: Keep Old System	Alternative Two: Replace Old System
Start-up:		
Cost of new system		$ (76,000)
Operating:		
Labor cost:		
Old system (3 × 5 × $18,000)	$(270,000)	
New system (2 × 5 × $18,000)		(180,000)
Shutdown:		
Residual value of old system	1,500	
Sale price if old system sold now		10,000
Residual value of new system		2,000
Total relevant costs	$(268,500)	$(244,000)
Difference in relevant costs and benefits	$24,500 In favor of buying the new system	

not have enough available cash to take advantage of a course of action that would save money in the long run. Considering only relevant costs and benefits in decision making will lead to better business decisions, but it will not necessarily enable a company to take advantage of what can be learned in the process.

The Concept of an Incremental Cost or Benefit

We stated earlier that to be relevant, a cost or benefit must be (a) a future cost or benefit, and (b) the cost or benefit must differ between the alternatives. In the equipment replacement decision we just demonstrated, we listed the entire $270,000 to pay for three operators (3 × $18,000 × 5 years) as a relevant cost of the old system. We also listed $180,000 of operator cost (2 × $18,000 × 5 years) as a relevant cost of the new system. This treatment is not strictly correct, given our definition of relevant cost or benefit. Since the new system will require $180,000 to pay for two operators, only the incremental $90,000 of the operator cost under the old system is relevant ($270,000 under the old system minus $180,000 under the new system). The entire $180,000 operator cost under the new system is irrelevant, because that much operator cost will be incurred by the company whether it purchases the new system or keeps the old one.

In our example we also listed the residual value of the old system ($1,500) and the entire residual value of the new system ($2,000) as relevant benefits. Using the same reasoning as we did in the previous paragraph, we should list only the incremental $500 of residual value of the new system as a relevant benefit ($2,000 under the new system minus $1,500 under the old system). The entire $1,500 residual value of the old system is irrelevant because the company will receive that amount whether it keeps the old system or purchases the new one.

With all that said, we will get exactly the same result whether we treat the operator cost and residual value as we did in our original example, or if we include only incremental costs and benefits, as demonstrated in Exhibit 7-4.

Exhibit 7-4 Relevant Cost Comparison for Bill Smith & Partners Using only Incremental Costs and Benefits

		Incremental Benefit (Cost)
Start-up:		
Cost of new system		$(76,000)
Operating:		
Labor cost:		
Old system (3 × 5 × $18,000)	(270,000)	
New system (2 × 5 × $18,000)	(180,000)	
Cost reduction from new system		90,000
Shutdown:		
Residual value of old system	1,500	
Residual value of new system	2,000	
Excess residual value of new system		500
Sale price if old system sold now		10,000
Incremental relevant benefit in excess of costs in favor of buying the new system		$ 24,500

Discussion Questions

7-5. Assuming all purchases and sales of computer systems are cash transactions, how much cash would Bill need to buy the new system?

7-6. Now that we know the relevant quantitative information associated with the computer replacement, what qualitative factors should Bill consider before he makes his final decision?

Interest—The Time Value of Money

time value of money The interest earning potential of cash.

Equipment purchase decisions generally have long-term effects. Because of the long life of the equipment, the associated cash inflows and outflows will occur for many years. Therefore, decision makers should consider the interest-earning potential of the cash flows associated with equipment acquisitions. The interest earning potential of cash is sometimes called the **time value of money**. In this chapter we are focusing on relevant costs and benefits and have ignored the time value of money. However, Chapter 8 covers special techniques developed to incorporate the effect of interest and the timing of cash flows.

Special Orders

special order An order that is outside a company's normal scope of business activity.

Manufacturing businesses must often consider whether to accept a **special order**—an order that is outside its normal scope of business activity. As we will see, proper treatment of fixed cost is critical in making sound special order decisions.

Assume that your company, Alumafloat, makes small aluminum boats. Alumafloat has been in operation for almost 10 years and sells boats to retail boat dealers in southern Florida. One day, a **Sears** representative approaches you with an interesting proposition. **Sears** is interested in purchasing 1,000 of your boats for $125 each. The largest order your company has received to date was for 100 boats, so obviously, this huge order requires special consideration.

Gather All Costs and Benefits Associated with the Decision

The $125 offer from **Sears** is considerably less than Alumafloat's normal selling price of $160 per boat. In fact, the boats cost $130 each to produce, so the company would lose $5 per boat if it accepts **Sears'** $125 offer.

As you discuss the order with the representative from **Sears**, you tell her that you would be willing to sell the boats to **Sears** at a discounted price of $140 each because of the large quantity of boats they need. **Sears** refuses your offer. The store will only pay $125 per boat, and the representative expects you to accept or reject the order within five days.

You gather all the information necessary to make a wise decision. First, you meet with your company's cost accountant, who confirms that your cost per unit is $130. You also request a report detailing production cost so you can see how the cost per unit figure was calculated. Using expected total sales (excluding the special order from **Sears**) and production costs for this year, the cost accountant prepares the report shown in Exhibit 7-5.

Exhibit 7-5 Per Unit Cost and Sales Report for Alumafloat

Expected sales (5,500 units at $160 each)		$880,000
Less: Cost of goods sold (see detail below)		(715,000)
Expected gross margin		$165,000
Detailed calculation for cost of goods sold:		
	Per Unit	**Total**
Number of units	1	5,500
Direct material costs	$ 50	$275,000
Direct labor costs	55	302,500
Variable manufacturing overhead costs	10	55,000
Fixed manufacturing overhead costs	15	82,500
Total cost of goods sold	$130	$715,000

We must determine the potential effect on Alumafloat's revenues and expenses of accepting the order. Which costs shown in Exhibit 7-5 would be affected by the decision to accept the special order from **Sears**? To determine which costs are relevant, we will again ask the following two questions: (1) Is the cost a future cost? and (2) Does the cost differ between alternatives?

Determine the Relevant Cost and Benefit of Each Alternative

You must determine which costs and benefits are relevant. In this situation, the alternatives are to accept the order or reject it. Generally speaking, because no cost is associated with rejecting the order, our analysis focuses on the alternative to accept.

If you accept the order, sales will increase by $125,000 (1,000 boats × $125 per boat). The increase in sales due to the special order is a relevant benefit, because it is something that will happen in the future and it differs between alternatives.

All variable costs are relevant because they are future costs that differ between alternatives. If the special order is accepted, variable costs will be incurred to produce the 1,000 boats. In this example, variable cost includes direct material, direct labor, and variable manufacturing overhead.

Depending on the decision situation, fixed cost may or may not be relevant. Often fixed manufacturing overhead costs are not relevant costs because total fixed cost for the company will be unaffected by the increase in production volume. This fact holds true unless specific fixed cost increases occur due to the special order, or the order is so substantial that production would exceed the relevant range if the company accepts the order. As the report in Exhibit 7-5 indicates, the company expects total fixed manufacturing overhead cost to be $82,500. Assume in our example that the decision to accept or reject the special order from **Sears** would not affect total fixed manufacturing overhead cost. Therefore, in this case, fixed manufacturing overhead cost does not differ between alternatives and is irrelevant to the special order decision.

Compare the Relevant Costs and Benefits and Select an Alternative

Armed with information about relevant cost and benefit, you can make an informed decision about the **Sears** order. Exhibit 7-6 presents a schedule of relevant cost and benefit for this special order. The schedule excludes fixed manufacturing overhead cost because it is irrelevant.

Exhibit 7-6 Relevant Cost and Benefit for Special Order of 1,000 Boats

	Per Unit		Total	
Sales from special order		$ 125		$ 125,000
Direct material	$(50)		$(50,000)	
Direct labor	(55)		(55,000)	
Variable manufacturing overhead	(10)		(10,000)	
Total relevant production		(115)		(115,000)
Total increase in profit		$ 10		$ 10,000

Alumafloat's profit will increase by $10,000 if you accept the special order.

The reasoning in the Alumafloat example may seem logical, but companies often reject special orders that would increase profits, because managers do not understand the concept of relevant cost as it pertains to fixed cost. To avoid making poor decisions, managers must carefully consider how a special order will affect fixed cost.

Accounting information must sometimes be tailored by the information user to provide information that is relevant to the decision at hand. Regarding a huge international sale, an accountant for a **Fortune** 500 chemical company once remarked, "I can't believe that the product sales manager is selling below cost. He is disregarding fixed cost as he sets prices to move old stock." In fact, the manager may have made a good decision about the price of the product, depending on whether the fixed costs are relevant to the pricing decision. As a manager, you should know that routinely prepared accounting information cannot be relevant to every decision.

Discussion Questions

7-7. What would happen if you treated every order as a special order and routinely disregarded fixed cost considerations from your pricing decisions?

7-8. Assume that the production manager at Alumafloat reminds you that four years ago sales skyrocketed for a while. Demand was so great that production increased to the limit of the company's capacity. Alumafloat produced 6,950 boats in a 12-month period. What implications does this information have on your decision to accept the special order from **Sears**?

7-9. What qualitative factors should you consider regarding accepting an order to sell **Sears** the boats for less than the price you charge your regular customers? For example, what would your regular customers think if they found that **Sears** was selling the same style boat they buy from you?

Outsourcing—The Make or Buy Decision

Often companies purchase subcomponents used to manufacture their products instead of making them in their in-house manufacturing facilities. Buying services, products, or components of products from outside vendors instead of producing them is called **outsourcing**. Decision makers considering whether to make or buy subcomponents must pay close attention to fixed costs. Also, because the make or buy decision does not directly affect revenues or cash inflow (relevant benefits), we focus solely on identifying relevant costs.

outsourcing Buying services, products, or components of products instead of producing them.

Assume you are a product manager at Microbake, a plant that manufactures various products, including microwave ovens. A vendor has approached you about supplying the timer assemblies for your ovens for $12 each. Currently, Microbake makes the timers in its own subassembly department. The subassembly department makes many of the small component parts for the various products manufactured at the plant. When you review the cost sheets for the timers, you discover that the company uses 80,000 timers each year and they cost $14 each to produce in-house.

Gather All Costs Associated with the Decision

You call a meeting with Microbake's cost accounting department to discuss the situation and confirm that the $14 in-house manufacturing cost is correct. Even when pressed, the cost accountants are confident their cost figures are carefully prepared and accurate. In fact, they are surprised the company can buy the timers from the outside vendor for only $12 each. At your request, the cost accounting department prepares the cost breakdown for the timers shown in Exhibit 7-7.

Exhibit 7-7 Cost of Producing Oven Timers In-House

Number of timers produced each year		80,000
	Per Unit	**Total**
Direct material	$ 5	$ 400,000
Direct labor	4	320,000
Variable manufacturing overhead	1	80,000
Fixed manufacturing overhead	4	320,000
Total	$14	$1,120,000

Determine the Relevant Cost of Each Alternative

Once again we assess whether each cost is relevant by asking the following questions: (1) Is the cost a future cost? and (2) Does the cost differ between alternatives? The answers follow in Exhibit 7-8.

By definition, fixed manufacturing overhead remains constant in total regardless of the level of activity (in this case "activity" is the number of units produced). The fixed cost presented by the cost accountants is an allocation of the total fixed manufacturing overhead cost of the whole factory, or possibly of the subassembly department. If the company stops making the timers, the subassembly department will not go away and neither will its

Exhibit 7-8 Selecting Relevant Costs of Producing Oven Timers

	Future?	Differs?	Relevant?
Direct material:	yes	yes	yes
Direct labor:	yes	yes	yes
Variable manufacturing overhead:	yes	yes	yes
Fixed manufacturing overhead:	yes	no	no

fixed manufacturing overhead cost, because the company needs the subassembly department to produce other components. Unless fixed manufacturing overhead cost changes based on management's decision to buy the timers, it is irrelevant.

Compare the Relevant Costs and Select an Alternative

We compare the relevant costs of the make or buy decision in Exhibit 7-9.

Exhibit 7-9 Relevant Cost of Make or Buy Decision for Oven Timers

	Make	Buy
Cost to purchase		$960,000
Direct material	$400,000	
Direct labor	320,000	
Variable manufacturing overhead	80,000	
Total relevant cost	$800,000	$960,000
Difference in relevant costs	$160,000 In favor of making the oven timers in-house	

As Exhibit 7-9 indicates, once we have screened out the irrelevant fixed manufacturing overhead cost it becomes apparent that Microbake can save $160,000 per year by making the timers rather than buying them. Based on this relevant cost comparison, you decide not to purchase the timer assemblies from the outside vendor.

In a final effort to get the sale, the vendor contacts several people at Microbake informing them that you are squandering your company's money. The vendor points out to other Microbake managers that its price is $2 per unit less than your in-house production cost as determined by Microbake's highly trained cost accountants. Other managers are pressing to accept the outside vendor's proposal.

To settle the issue, you call a meeting of the managers and present your relevant cost findings. Several managers comment that your information disregards fixed manufacturing overhead. You explain that the fixed manufacturing overhead is irrelevant. The other managers argue that fixed manufacturing overhead is a very real part of business cost and that it should be included in your presentation. This presents no significant problem. Including fixed manufacturing overhead, although irrelevant, may highlight how fixed costs are affected (or in this case, unaffected) by changes in production. You must demonstrate, however, that if the units are manufactured in-house, there will be fixed manufacturing overhead cost; and that if the units are purchased from the outside vendor, there will still be fixed manufacturing overhead cost. The relevant cost comparison can include the irrelevant fixed manufacturing overhead cost as shown in Exhibit 7-10.

	Make	Buy
Cost to purchase		$ 960,000
Direct material	$ 400,000	
Direct labor	320,000	
Variable manufacturing overhead	80,000	
Fixed manufacturing overhead	320,000	320,000
Total relevant cost	$1,120,000	$1,280,000
Difference in relevant costs	$160,000 In favor of making the oven timers in-house	

Exhibit 7-10 Relevant Cost of Make or Buy Decision for Oven Timers with Fixed Costs Shown

As Exhibit 7-10 shows, because fixed manufacturing overhead is the same for the two alternatives, the outcome of the comparison is the same as that in Exhibit 7-9. Microbake can save $160,000 by making the timers instead of buying them.

Discussion Question

7-10. What would happen to the cost of producing other Microbake products if your decision is overturned and the company outsources the timer assemblies?

Special Relevant Cost Considerations for Fixed Costs

In some situations, the alternative selected affects fixed costs. For example, suppose Microbake could eliminate an entire eight-hour production shift if it no longer made the timers. Eliminating that shift thus eliminates one line supervisor whose annual salary is $45,000 per year and reduces other fixed manufacturing overhead cost by $150,000. Therefore, fixed manufacturing overhead would decrease by $195,000 ($45,000 + $150,000). Exhibit 7-11 shows the relevant cost of the make or buy decision when the alternative to buy the timers enables the company to eliminate a production shift.

	Make	Buy
Cost to purchase		$960,000
Direct material	$400,000	
Direct labor	320,000	
Variable manufacturing overhead	80,000	
Fixed manufacturing overhead	195,000	
Total relevant cost	$995,000	$960,000
Difference in relevant costs	$35,000 In favor of buying the oven timers from the outside vendor	

Exhibit 7-11 Relevant Cost of the Make or Buy Decision for Oven Timers with Relevant Fixed Manufacturing Overhead Cost

Exhibit 7-11 shows that the savings in fixed manufacturing overhead alters the cost comparison such that Microbake should opt to buy the timers. If the $195,000 reduction in fixed costs were realized, Microbake would save $35,000 by purchasing the timer assemblies from the vendor instead of making them.

Discussion Question

7-11. What qualitative factors should managers at Microbake consider with respect to their outsourcing decision?

Considering Opportunity Costs

opportunity cost The benefit foregone (given up) because one alternative is chosen over another.

Recall that an **opportunity cost** is the value of what a decision maker gives up because one alternative is chosen over another. For example, the opportunity cost of attending college rather than working full time is what you could have earned by working instead of going to college.

If Microbake buys the timer assemblies from an outside vendor, it may have an alternate use for the production capacity or assets used to make the timers—it may have an opportunity to enhance its earnings through an alternate use of the facilities. Assume that Microbake can use the production capacity freed up by purchasing the timers to make electronic alarm clocks. Assume further that the electronic alarm clocks would provide an annual contribution margin of $200,000 with no significant changes to fixed cost. If Microbake continues to make the timer assemblies, it would lose the opportunity to earn the $200,000. The lost $200,000 contribution margin on the electronic alarm clocks is an opportunity cost.

Because opportunity cost is the cost of not doing something, it is not reflected in the accounting records of a business and is not reported in the company's external financial statements or internal management reports. This does not mean an opportunity cost is not real—remember, reality and the measurement of reality are not the same thing. Opportunity cost is an economic reality. Although it is not generally part of financial accounting measures, opportunity cost is a relevant consideration in business decisions.

Returning to the Microbake timer example, the relevant costs of making or buying the 80,000 timers, including the $200,000 lost opportunity, is presented in Exhibit 7-12.

Exhibit 7-12 Relevant Cost of Make or Buy Decision for Oven Timers with Opportunity Cost

	Make	Buy
Cost to purchase		$960,000
Direct material	$ 400,000	
Direct labor	320,000	
Variable manufacturing overhead	80,000	
Opportunity cost	200,000	
Total relevant cost	$1,000,000	$960,000
Difference in relevant costs	$40,000 In favor of buying the oven timers from the outside vendor	

Exhibit 7-12 suggests that if the $200,000 contribution margin from the production of alarm clocks could be realized, Microbake should buy the timer assemblies from the outside vendor. The production capacity no longer needed to produce the timers could then be used to produce the alarm clocks, resulting in a $40,000 difference in the relevant cost in favor of buying the timers.

Microbake's outsourcing problem is an example of a very real business dilemma. Managers cannot rely solely on the cost information from accountants. They themselves must have enough accounting knowledge to determine the relevant cost of each decision alternative.

Discontinuing a Business Segment

When a particular division, department, product line, or product of a company is suffering losses, it seems to makes good sense to eliminate that unprofitable business segment. For example, assume one of ValueMart's three product lines, sporting goods, has been experiencing losses for some time. To improve the profits of the company as a whole, ValueMart managers are planning to eliminate the sporting goods line of products. Exhibit 7-13 presents a 2009 income statement for the company by business segment.

Exhibit 7-13 Segment Income Statement for ValueMart

ValueMart
Segment Income Statement
For the Year Ended December 31, 2009

	Total	Clothing	Housewares	Sporting Goods
Sales	$550,000	$250,000	$175,000	$125,000
Variable expense	211,250	75,000	61,250	75,000
Contribution margin	338,750	175,000	113,750	50,000
Fixed expenses				
Salaries	105,000	50,000	30,000	25,000
Store rent	50,000	25,000	15,000	10,000
Utilities	5,000	2,500	1,500	1,000
Advertising	24,000	9,000	7,000	8,000
Insurance	11,000	5,000	3,500	2,500
Depreciation of store equipment	13,000	6,000	4,000	3,000
Administrative expenses	44,000	20,000	14,000	10,000
Total fixed expenses	252,000	117,500	75,000	59,500
Operating income	$ 86,750	$ 57,500	$ 38,750	$ (9,500)

ValueMart's managers realize that their decision to discontinue the sporting goods product line will be quite unpopular and will be met with significant disappointment and resistance.

To help provide support for their decision to discontinue the segment, managers at ValueMart requested that their accountants provide them with a *pro forma* segment income statement for 2009 showing what the results would have been without the sporting goods product line. Their feeling was that once everyone saw that operating income would actually have been $9,500 higher without sporting goods, they would understand why the managers feel forced to discontinue that product line and would support the decision.

As it turned out, however, the managers were surprised when the pro forma income statement ValueMart's accountants prepared for 2009 showed a decrease in profits instead of an increase. The managers were also stunned to discover that the operating income of the two other product lines decreased instead of increasing or at least remaining constant (See Exhibit 7-14).

Exhibit 7-14 Pro Forma 2009 Segment Income Statement Without Sporting Goods

ValueMart
Pro Forma Segment Income Statement
For the Year Ended December 31, 2009

	Total	Clothing	Housewares
Sales	$425,000	$250,000	$175,000
Variable expense	136,250	75,000	61,250
Contribution margin	288,750	175,000	113,750
Fixed expenses			
Salaries	80,000	50,000	30,000
Store rent	50,000	30,000	20,000
Utilities	5,000	3,000	2,000
Advertising	16,000	9,000	7,000
Insurance	11,000	6,471	4,529
Depreciation of store equipment	10,000	6,000	4,000
Administrative expenses	44,000	25,882	18,118
Total fixed expenses	216,000	130,353	85,647
Operating income	$ 72,750	$ 44,647	$ 28,103

The managers demanded an explanation from their accountants. The accountants responded by saying that not all of the sporting goods product line's expenses would have been eliminated if the segment had been discontinued. They explained that some of the company's fixed costs were common to the entire company, and while they benefited the sporting goods product line, they benefited the other product lines, as well. They went on to explain that it was company practice to allocate a portion of these fixed costs to each of the product lines. Further, they explained that eliminating sporting goods would not reduce these common fixed costs at all. So, if the sporting goods product line had not been there in 2009, the accountants would simply have increased the allocation of the common fixed costs to the two remaining product lines. Thus, the operating income for the clothing and housewares product lines would have decreased as a result of eliminating sporting goods.

ValueMart's managers realized they needed to take another look at the decision before going forward with their plan. They realized that considering every item related to the sporting goods product line probably was a mistake and that they needed to focus solely on the relevant benefits and relevant costs of their decision.

Determine the Relevant Cost of Each Alternative

The managers requested a report from their accountants that shows the relevant as well as the irrelevant data surrounding the decision to discontinue the sporting goods line. Of course, to determine whether an item is relevant, they should focus on whether or not the item is a future item and whether it differs between alternatives. Considering only future items, if an item would be avoided by eliminating the sporting goods product line, the item differs between alternatives and is relevant. On the other hand, if a particular item is unavoidable regardless of whether the sporting goods product line is discontinued or not, the item does not differ between alternatives and is, therefore, irrelevant. Exhibit 7-15 presents a report prepared by the company's accountants showing the relevant benefits and costs of discontinuing the sporting goods product line. For

Exhibit 7-15 Relevant Benefits and Costs of Discontinuing the Sporting Goods Product Line

Sporting Goods Product Line Relevant Benefits and Costs of Discontinuing the Line	Total for Sporting Goods	Avoidable (Relevant) Amounts	Unavoidable (Irrelevant) Amounts
Sales	$125,000	$125,000	
Variable expense	75,000	75,000	
Contribution margin	50,000	50,000	
Fixed expenses			
Salaries	25,000	25,000	
Store rent	10,000		10,000
Utilities	1,000		1,000
Advertising	8,000	8,000	
Insurance	2,500		2,500
Depreciation of store equipment	3,000	3,000	
Administrative expenses	10,000		10,000
Total fixed expenses	59,500	36,000	23,500
Operating income	$ (9,500)	$ 14,000	$(23,500)

analytical purposes, the accountants assumed that the operating results for 2010 would be the same as in 2009.

The report in Exhibit 7-15 may seem a bit confusing to you, so we'll take a few minutes to explain it. Based on the accountants' assumption that the operating results for 2010 would be the same as in 2009, the first column shows what the operating results will be in 2010 for sporting goods if the product line is not eliminated. If you look back at the segment income statement for 2009 in Exhibit 7-13, you will see that this is so. The second column in Exhibit 7-15 presents the amounts associated with sporting goods that will disappear from the company if the product line is eliminated. Obviously the sales of $125,000 will be gone. The variable expense of $75,000 will no longer be incurred because they are all associated specifically with sporting goods. All of the fixed expenses in the second column are directly associated with sporting goods, so they will disappear if the product line is eliminated. The third column presents fixed expenses that ValueMart will incur regardless of whether or not the sporting goods line is eliminated.

Now let's talk about the operating income line of the second and third columns in Exhibit 7-15. The operating income in the second column means that if we consider only the relevant items associated with sporting goods (the ones that would disappear if that product line is eliminated), the sporting goods line will contribute $14,000 to the ValueMart's operating income. Further, the total at the bottom of the second column represents the amount by which the company's operating income will decrease if the sporting goods product line is eliminated. The third column represents the amount that will remain part of the company's operating income regardless of whether or not the sporting goods product line is discontinued. This is so because $23,000 of common fixed cost that has been allocated to sporting goods will now simply be allocated to the other product lines, thereby reducing the overall company's operating income by that amount.

Special Cost Considerations for Common Fixed Costs

To avoid making a costly mistake, special care should be taken regarding common fixed costs. Common fixed costs can be handled in any one of three ways. 1) Companies can allocate common fixed costs and include them with other costs. This can present a significant problem because it is difficult to determine which costs are direct costs and which are simply allocated to the segment. 2) Companies can allocate common fixed costs but then be sure to separate them from direct costs to assess segment performance and the income generated by the segment. When companies use this approach, fixed costs are classified as either direct fixed costs or common (indirect) fixed costs. Direct fixed costs are subtracted from the contribution margin to determine the segment margin for each segment. The amount of income that pertains to a particular segment is called the **segment margin**. 3) Companies can refrain from allocating common fixed costs at all. All three approaches are used in practice. Exhibit 7-16 demonstrates how the segment income statements for ValueMart would appear under the second method—allocating common fixed costs, but keeping them separate. Exhibit 7-16 also shows the detailed calculations to allocate the common fixed costs in proportion to relative sales.

segment margin The amount of income that pertains to a particular part (segment) of a company.

Exhibit 7-16 Segment Income Statement Separating Direct and Common Fixed Costs

ValueMart
Segment Income Statement
For the Year Ended December 31, 2009

	Total	**Clothing**	**Housewares**	**Sporting Goods**
Sales	$550,000	$250,000	$175,000	$125,000
Variable expense	211,250	75,000	61,250	75,000
Contribution margin	338,750	175,000	113,750	50,000
Direct fixed expenses:				
Salaries	105,000	50,000	30,000	25,000
Advertising	24,000	9,000	7,000	8,000
Depreciation of store equipment	13,000	6,000	4,000	3,000
Total direct fixed expense	142,000	65,000	41,000	36,000
Segment margin	**196,750**	**110,000**	**72,750**	**14,000**
Indirect fixed expenses:				
Store rent	50,000	25,000*	15,000*	10,000*
Utilities	5,000	2,500*	1,500*	1,000*
Insurance	11,000	5,000**	3,500**	2,500**
Administrative expenses	44,000	20,000**	14,000**	10,000**
Total indirect fixed expense	110,000	52,500	34,000	23,500
Operating income	$ 86,750	$ 57,500	$ 38,750	$ (9,500)

* These amounts were allocated based on square footage occupied by each of the three product lines in the company's single building. Of the total 5,000 square footage available, Clothing occupies 2,500 square feet, Housewares occupies 1,500 square feet and Sporting Goods occupies 1,000 square feet.

Rent allocation:

Clothing	$50,000 × (2,500/5,000) = $25,000
Housewares	$50,000 × (1,500/5,000) = $15,000
Sporting Goods	$50,000 × (1,000/5,000) = $10,000

(Continued)

Exhibit 7-16 (*Continued*)

Utilities allocation:

Clothing	$5,000 × (2,500/5,000) = $2,500
Housewares	$5,000 × (1,500/5,000) = $1,500
Sporting Goods	$5,000 × (1,000/5,000) = $1,000

** These amounts were allocated based on the relative sales of each of the three product lines.

Insurance allocation:

Clothing	$11,000 × ($250,000/$550,000) = $5,000
Housewares	$11,000 × ($175,000/$550,000) = $3,500
Sporting Goods	$11,000 × ($125,000/$550,000) = $2,500

Administrative expense allocation:

Clothing	$44,000 × ($250,000/$550,000) = $20,000
Housewares	$44,000 × ($175,000/$550,000) = $14,000
Sporting Goods	$44,000 × ($125,000/$550,000) = $10,000

To determine whether a part of a company should be eliminated, companies should pay special attention to common fixed costs and are wise to focus on the segment margin as opposed to the operating income of the segment.

Although we have explored relevant information using only four examples, it is important to understand that relevant cost concepts apply to almost every business decision. Knowing how to determine which information is relevant is even helpful with personal decisions such as whether to attend summer school at a local university or enroll in a student exchange program and study abroad. Business situations and life in general provide an array of quantitative and qualitative considerations for every decision alternative. As a decision maker, you must be able to seek out the relevant considerations and disregard the irrelevant ones.

Summary

To make the best decision possible, a manager must consider only relevant information. What is relevant in one situation may not be relevant in another. A relevant cost or benefit is an item that makes a difference in a given decision situation. Relevant costs are also always future costs, because past costs cannot be changed by any current or future actions. Further, a future cost or benefit must differ between the alternatives to be considered relevant. Opportunity costs are often relevant and should be considered by managers making decisions. An opportunity cost is the value of benefits given up because one alternative is chosen over another. The treatment of common fixed costs requires special consideration when deciding whether a business segment should be discontinued.

In addition to the quantitative information managers must consider in making decisions, qualitative information such as customer satisfaction, product quality, and employee morale must also be considered. Oftentimes the qualitative considerations should outweigh purely quantitative considerations.

Key Terms

Review the Facts

A. What is a relevant benefit?

B. What is a relevant cost?

C. What two important characteristics do all relevant costs possess?

D. What is a sunk cost?

E. Describe the difference between qualitative and quantitative factors.

F. When trying to determine whether a cost is relevant, what are the two questions the decision maker should ask?

G. Why is the depreciation for existing assets considered irrelevant for equipment replacement decisions?

H. What is the time value of money?

I. Why is the time value of money important for decisions involving the purchase of long-lived assets?

J. What would cause a fixed cost to be relevant for a special order decision?

K. What is outsourcing?

L. Define opportunity cost.

M. How should common fixed costs be treated when evaluating business segments?

N. The concepts of relevant information apply to what types of decisions?

Apply What You Have Learned

LO 1: Determine Which Costs Are Relevant

7-12. The production manager at Ace Manufacturing is contemplating whether he should upgrade some old production equipment. He is considering the following factors:

1. _____ The cost of the old equipment
2. _____ The cost of the new equipment
3. _____ Depreciation on the old equipment
4. _____ Depreciation on the new equipment
5. _____ Trade-in value of the old equipment
6. _____ Residual value of the old equipment
7. _____ Residual value of the new equipment

Required:

For each item listed, indicate whether it is relevant (R) or irrelevant (I).

LO 3: Quantitative and Qualitative Considerations

7-13. Tom Robinson is thinking about buying a portable computer. He has a computer at home, but the portable computer would allow him to work during his frequent business trips. Tom is trying to convince his boss that the computer would save the company some money. Tom hopes that his company will pay at least part of the computer's purchase price and the monthly fee for internet service.

Tom has asked a group of friends to help him think of all the advantages of buying the computer. Assume you are part of the group.

Group Requirements:

a. Prepare an informal schedule of the costs associated with the computer purchase.

b. List as many quantitative benefits as you can that the company will gain if Tom buys the portable computer.

c. List as many quantitative benefits as you can that Tom will gain if he buys the portable computer.

d. List as many qualitative benefits as you can that the company will gain if Tom buys the portable computer.

e. List as many qualitative benefits as you can that Tom will gain if he buys the portable computer.

f. How much of the computer's cost do you think Tom should pay? How much should Tom's employer pay?

LO 3 & 4: Determine Relevant Cost Schedule and Qualitative Factors

7-14. Tina Alberts is thinking about trading her car for a new one. Her present car is only three years old, completely paid for, but out of warranty. The car's original cost was $22,000. Lately, the car has been somewhat undependable and the repair bills have been quite high. In the last three months, Tina paid over $1,200 for repairs. Tina intends to use her trade-in as the down payment and then finance the balance. She is looking at a new Nissan which she can get for about $23,000, less her trade.

Tina has asked a group of close friends to help her think of all the relevant advantages and disadvantages of getting the new car. Assume you are part of this group.

Group Requirements:

a. Prepare an informal schedule listing the relevant quantitative factors that Tina should consider. Do not limit your answer to the items found in the problem. Include all the factors you can think of. When possible, try to include estimated dollar amounts in your schedule.

b. Prepare an informal schedule listing the relevant qualitative factors that Tina should consider.

c. From a quantitative point of view, do you think Tina should buy the new car?

d. Considering both quantitative and qualitative factors, do you think Tina should buy the new car?

LO 1: Determine Which Costs Are Relevant

7-15. Jean Parks is a salesperson for Quality Food Products, Inc. She is considering a 250-mile trip to visit a potential customer, ByLots. Following are factors she is pondering.

1. _____ The cost of traveling the 250 miles to ByLots

2. _____ The time she will spend on the road

3. _____ The time she will spend visiting with ByLots's executives

4. _____ The amount of time already devoted to ByLots

5. _____ The revenue potential from ByLots
6. _____ The cost of her last visit to ByLots
7. _____ The probability that her visit will result in new sales
8. _____ The cost of lunch for herself if she visits ByLots
9. _____ The cost of the lunch she would buy for ByLots's executives

Required:

For each item listed, indicate whether it is relevant (R) or irrelevant (I).

LO 3: Determine Quantitative and Qualitative Factors

7-16. This question is based on the same situation as 7-15. Jean Parks is a salesperson for Quality Food Products, Inc. She is considering a 250-mile trip to visit a potential customer, ByLots. Following are factors she is pondering.

1. _____ The cost of traveling the 250 miles to ByLots
2. _____ The time she will spend on the road
3. _____ The time she will spend visiting with ByLots's executives
4. _____ The amount of time already devoted to ByLots
5. _____ The revenue potential from ByLots
6. _____ The cost of her last visit to ByLots
7. _____ The probability that her visit will result in new sales
8. _____ The cost of lunch for herself if she visits ByLots
9. _____ The cost of the lunch she would buy for ByLots's executives

Required:

For each item listed, indicate whether it is quantitative (A) or qualitative (B).

LO 3: Determine Quantitative and Qualitative Factors

7-17. Managers at Ace Manufacturing are considering upgrading some production equipment. They are considering the following factors:

1. _____ Maintenance cost
2. _____ Changes in product quality
3. _____ Residual value of the old equipment
4. _____ Cost of new equipment
5. _____ Difficulty of training employees to use new equipment
6. _____ Residual value of the new equipment
7. _____ The ill feelings due to the possible reduction in the labor force

Required:

For each item listed, indicate whether it is quantitative (A) or qualitative (B).

LO 1, 2, 3, & 5: List All Costs, Indicate Relevant Costs, Indicate Qualitative Factors

7-18. Assume that you are deciding whether to live in a campus dormitory room or an off-campus apartment.

Required:

a. List all the costs that come to mind as you think about this decision.

b. Review your list and indicate which costs are relevant and which are irrelevant to the decision.

c. What are some qualitative factors that you should consider when making this decision?

LO 1, 2, 3, & 5: List Costs, Indicate Relevant Costs, Indicate Qualitative Factors

7-19. Assume that you are deciding what to do next summer. You are considering two alternatives: Go to summer school, or tour Europe.

Required:

a. List all the costs that come to mind as you think about this decision.

b. Review your list and indicate which costs are relevant and which are irrelevant to your decision.

c. What are some qualitative factors that you should consider when making this decision?

LO 1, 2, 3, & 5: List Costs, Indicate Relevant Costs, Indicate Qualitative Factors

7-20. George Binkley's car is seven years old. The car is no longer under warranty and requires frequent repairs. George is trying to decide whether to buy a new car. He has asked you what you think about his idea.

Required:

a. List all the costs that come to mind as you think about his decision.

b. Review your list and indicate which costs are relevant and which are irrelevant to the decision.

c. What are some qualitative factors that he should consider when making this decision?

LO 4: Determine Relevant Cost for Equipment Replacement

7-21. The managers at Miami Manufacturing Company are considering replacing the industrial mixer used in the company's factory.

Information about the old mixer:	
Cost	$28,000
Estimated useful life	10 years
Estimated residual value	$ 0
Current age	5 years
Estimated current fair value	$ 8,000
Annual operating cost	$15,000
Information about the new mixer:	
Cost	$34,000
Estimated useful life	5 years
Estimated residual value	$ 0
Annual operating cost	$12,000

Required:

Prepare a relevant cost schedule showing the benefit of keeping the old mixer or buying the new one.

LO 4: Determine Relevant Cost for Equipment Replacement

7-22. The managers at General Manufacturing Company are considering replacing the industrial lathe used in the company's factory.

Information about the old lathe:	
Cost	$57,000
Estimated useful life	8 years
Estimated residual value	$ 0
Current age	2 years
Estimated current fair value	$32,000
Annual operating cost	$32,000
Information about the new lathe:	
Cost	$61,000
Estimated useful life	6 years
Estimated residual value	$ 0
Annual operating cost	$24,000

Required:

Prepare a relevant cost schedule showing the benefit of keeping the old lathe or buying the new one.

LO 4: Determine Relevant Cost for Equipment Replacement

7-23. John Paul Hudik, president of J. P. Hudik Boat Hauling, is considering replacing the company's industrial lift used to haul boats. The new lift would allow the company to lift larger boats out of the water.

Information about the old lift:	
Cost	$94,000
Estimated useful life	12 years
Estimated residual value	$10,000
Current age	4 years
Estimated current fair value	$48,000
Annual contribution margin	$50,000
Information about the new lift:	
Cost	$128,000
Estimated useful life	8 years
Estimated residual value	$25,000
Annual contribution margin	$65,000

Required:

Prepare a relevant cost schedule showing the benefit of keeping the old lift or buying the new one.

LO 4: Determine Relevant Cost for Equipment Replacement

7-24. The managers at Wilma Manufacturing are considering replacing a printing press with a new, high-speed model.

Information about the old printing press:	
Cost	$255,000
Estimated useful life	10 years
Estimated residual value	$ 25,000
Annual depreciation	$ 23,000
Current age	3 years
Accumulated depreciation to date	$184,000
Estimated current fair value	$150,000
Annual contribution margin	$110,000
Information about the new printing press:	
Cost	$535,000
Estimated useful life	7 years
Estimated residual value	$ 45,000
Annual depreciation	$ 70,000
Annual contribution margin	$150,000

Required:

Prepare a relevant cost schedule showing the benefit of keeping the old printing press or buying the new one.

LO 4: Determine Relevant Cost for New Business Segment

7-25. Photo Express operates a small camera store in Ft. Lauderdale, Florida. The store has two departments, camera sales and photo finishing. Rent, utilities, and other operating expenses are allocated to the departments based on the square footage occupied by the department. Currently, the camera sales department occupies 3,000 square feet and the photo finishing department occupies 2,000 square feet.

Photo Express president, Billy Clifford, is thinking about buying a computer system to produce poster prints. The poster printing system would occupy 200 square feet of the store's floor space.

Budgeted monthly information for the store:	
Store rent	$ 5,000
Salaries and wages	10,500
Utilities	750
Other operating expenses	3,000
Sales	125,000
Cost of goods sold	95,000
Information about the poster printing system:	
Cost of the poster system	$25,700
Estimated useful life	5 years
Estimated residual value	$ 500
Floor space required	200 square feet
Monthly cost of electricity used by poster system	$ 50
Budgeted monthly amounts:	
Poster sales revenue	$ 1,200
Poster supplies	200
Wages for poster operation	250
Store rent	200
Utilities	32
Other operating expenses	120

Clifford believes the company should not buy the poster system because it will show a loss every month. Because he is not sure, he has contacted a small consulting group to seek advice. Assume you are part of the consulting group.

Required:

a. Would the poster system show a loss every month as Clifford suggests? Prepare a schedule to substantiate your answer.

b. Would the company's overall monthly profits increase or decrease as a result of buying the poster system? Prepare a schedule to substantiate your answer.

c. Prepare a relevant cost schedule showing the advantage or disadvantage of buying the poster system.

LO 4: Determine Relevant Cost for New Business Segment

7-26. The Largo Gift Hut operates a small souvenir shop in Key Largo, Florida. The shop has two departments, retail sales and mail order. Rent, utilities, and other operating expenses are allocated to the departments based on the square footage occupied by the department. Currently, the retail sales department occupies 5,000 square feet and the mail order department occupies 1,000 square feet.

Largo's president, Bobbye Kenyon, is thinking about buying a silk screen machine to make souvenir T-shirts. The silk screen machine would occupy 500 square feet of the souvenir shop's floor space.

Budgeted monthly information for the store:	
Store rent	$ 5,100
Salaries and wages	8,500
Utilities	1,000
Other operating expenses	3,000
Sales	80,000
Cost of goods sold	57,000
Information about the silk screen machine:	
Cost of the silk screen machine	$ 9,640
Estimated useful life	5 years
Estimated residual value	$ 400
Floor space required	500 square feet
Monthly cost of electricity used by silk screen machine	$ 20
Budgeted monthly amounts:	
T-shirt sales revenue	$ 1,700
Cost of T-shirts	450
Cost of T-shirt supplies	100
Wages for the T-shirt operation	250
Store rent	425
Utilities	85
Other operating expenses	250

Kenyon believes she should not buy the silk screen machine because it will show a loss every month. Because she is not sure, she has contacted a small consulting group to seek advice. Assume you are part of the consulting group.

Required:

a. Would the silk screen machine show a loss every month as Kenyon suggests? Prepare a schedule to substantiate your answer.

b. Would the company's overall monthly profits increase or decrease as a result of buying the silk screen machine? Prepare a schedule to substantiate your answer.

c. Prepare a relevant cost schedule showing the advantage or disadvantage of buying the silk screen machine.

LO 4: Determine Relevant Cost for Equipment Replacement

7-27. Frank's Marine Service purchased a forklift five years ago for $16,000. When it was purchased the forklift had an estimated useful life of 10 years and a residual value of $4,000. The forklift can be sold now for $6,000. The operating cost for the forklift is $4,500 per year.

Frank is thinking about buying a newer forklift for $17,000. The newer model would have an estimated useful life of five years and a residual value of $7,000. The operating cost for the newer forklift would be $3,000 per year.

Required:

a. What are the relevant costs associated with the decision to replace the forklift?

b. Prepare a relevant cost schedule showing the advantage or disadvantage of buying the forklift.

LO 4: Determine Relevant Cost for Equipment Replacement

7-28. Al Hart of Hart Engineering is considering whether to purchase a new copy machine. He purchased the old machine two years ago for $8,500. When purchased, the old machine had an estimated useful life of eight years and a residual value of $500. The operating cost of the old machine is $3,000 per year. The old machine can be sold today for $2,000. A new machine can be bought today for $10,000 and would have an estimated useful life of six years with a residual value of $1,000. The operating cost of the new copy machine is expected to be $1,500 per year.

Required:

a. Prepare a schedule showing all the costs associated with the current copy machine.

b. Prepare a schedule showing all the costs associated with the new copy machine.

c. Prepare a schedule showing the relevant cost of the copy machine replacement decision and the favored alternative.

d. Discuss the qualitative factors that Hart should consider.

e. Would you buy the newer copy machine?

LO 4: Determine Relevant Cost for Equipment Replacement

7-29. Mike Thomlinson is considering whether to replace one of his delivery trucks. He purchased the current delivery truck four years ago for $24,000, and it came with a three-year, 75,000-mile warranty. When purchased, the current truck had an estimated useful life of five years and a residual value of $2,000. Thomlinson uses the straight-line method for depreciation. The new truck would be identical to the current truck, except it would be new and would have the three-year new truck warranty. The operating cost for the current truck is $4,000 for fuel, $23,200 for the driver's salary, and maintenance cost is about $5,000 per year. If Thomlinson keeps the old truck, it will last another five years, but would require the $5,000 in maintenance each year. The current truck can be sold now for $4,000, or it can be sold in five years for $1,000. The new truck would cost $25,500, has an estimated useful life of five years, and can be sold at the end of the five years for $4,000. At the end of the warranty period, the new truck will require maintenance of $5,000 per year.

Required:

a. Prepare a schedule showing all the costs associated with the current truck.

b. Prepare a schedule showing all the costs associated with the new truck.

c. Prepare a schedule showing the relevant cost of the truck replacement decision and the favored alternative.

d. Discuss the qualitative factors that Thomlinson should consider.

e. If the old truck had an estimated useful life of five years when it was purchased, and it has already been used for four years, discuss the ramifications of using the truck for another five years.

f. Would you buy the new truck? Why or why not?

LO 4: Determine Relevant Cost for Equipment Replacement

7-30. Jack Owens is considering whether to replace a piece of production equipment with a new model. The new machine would cost $170,000, have an eight-year life, and have no residual value. The variable cost of operating the machine would be $180,000 per year. The present machine was purchased one year ago, and could be used for the next eight years. When it was purchased, the present machine had an estimated useful life of nine years and a residual value of zero. The present machine can be sold now for $28,000, but will have no residual value in eight years. The variable cost of operating the present machine is $200,000 per year.

Required:

a. Prepare a schedule showing the costs associated with the present machine.

b. Prepare a schedule showing the costs associated with the new machine.

c. Prepare a schedule showing the relevant cost of the equipment replacement decision and the favored alternative.

d. Discuss the qualitative factors that Owens should consider.

LO 3 & 4: Determine the Relevant Cost of Buying a House and List Qualitative Factors

7-31. Lowell Elsea is in the process of buying a house. He is interested in two houses. One house is two miles from his work; the other is on the outskirts of town, 34 miles from work. Surprisingly, the two houses are nearly identical, except the closer house is much more expensive. The house that is two miles from Lowell's work is $127,000, whereas the other house is only $109,000. Maintenance, taxes, insurance, and other costs would be the same for both houses.

Lowell goes to work about 250 days each year. Lowell has just traded his old car for a new one. Each time his car reaches 80,000 miles, Lowell trades it for a new model. Generally, he expects to pay about $20,000 when he trades for a new car. His cars usually get about 20 miles per gallon of regular, $3.25-per-gallon gasoline. Maintenance on his car runs about 5 cents per mile on average. Other than driving to and from work, Lowell drives about 15,000 miles each year.

Regardless of which house Lowell buys, he expects to be transferred to another area of the country in five years.

Lowell is about to buy the less expensive house when he asks your advice.

Required:

a. Which house should Lowell buy?

b. How much will Lowell save if he follows your advice? (Disregard the time value of money.)

c. What qualitative factors should Lowell consider?

LO 4: Relevant Cost of a Make or Buy Decision

7-32. Microline is considering buying computer cabinets from an outside vendor. Currently, Microline makes the cabinets in its own manufacturing facility. Microline can buy the cabinets for $15 each. The company uses 15,000 cabinets each year. Information about Microline's cost to manufacture the 15,000 cabinets follows:

	Per Unit	Total
Direct material	$ 4	$ 60,000
Direct labor	6	90,000
Variable overhead	7	105,000
Fixed overhead	5	75,000
Total	$22	$330,000

Fixed cost for Microline would not change if the company stopped making the cabinets.

Required:

Prepare a relevant cost schedule that indicates whether Microline should buy the cabinets or continue to make them.

LO 4: Relevant Cost of a Make or Buy Decision

7-33. Gem Products is considering buying the casters it uses in the manufacture of office chairs from an outside vendor. Currently, Gem Products makes the casters in its own manufacturing facility. Gem Products can buy the casters for $1.15 each. The company uses 450,000 casters each year. Information about Gem Products' cost to manufacture the 450,000 casters follows:

	Per Unit	Total
Direct material	$ .50	$225,000
Direct labor	.10	45,000
Variable overhead	.40	180,000
Fixed overhead	.25	112,500
Total	$1.25	$562,500

Fixed cost for Gem Products would not change if the company stopped making the casters.

Required:

Prepare a relevant cost schedule that indicates whether Gem Products should buy the casters or continue to make them.

LO 4: Relevant Cost of a Make or Buy Decision

7-34. RJ Manufacturing is considering buying the mounting brackets it uses to make its fire extinguishers from an outside supplier. Currently, RJ Manufacturing makes the brackets in its own manufacturing facility. RJ Manufacturing can buy the brackets for $0.75 each. The company uses 700,000 brackets each year. Information about RJ Manufacturing's cost to manufacture the 700,000 brackets follows:

	Per Unit	Total
Direct material	$.30	$210,000
Direct labor	.10	70,000
Variable overhead	.40	280,000
Fixed overhead	.15	98,000
Total	$.94	$658,000

Fixed cost for RJ Manufacturing would not change if the company stopped making the brackets.

Required:

Prepare a relevant cost schedule that indicates whether RJ Manufacturing should buy the brackets or continue to make them.

LO 4: Relevant Cost of an Outsourcing Decision

7-35. Jumbo Chinese Restaurant operates a small laundry facility to launder the uniforms, tablecloths, and other linens used by its restaurant chain. Jumbo's laundry operation occupies space in an industrial area close to the company's home office and its largest restaurant. Jumbo is considering using a laundry service to perform the laundering needed by the company.

Jumbo's $180,000 administrative expense is allocated based on the number of employees. Jumbo employs 90 people. Information about the laundry facilities follows:

Direct cost information:	
Wages for two employees	$38,000
Cost of equipment	$ 7,500
Original estimated useful life of equipment	5 years
Estimated remaining useful life of equipment	1 year
Building rent per year	$ 3,000
Utilities	$ 2,000
Miscellaneous cost	$ 1,500
Indirect cost information:	
Administrative expense	$ 4,000

An outside laundry service has offered to provide Jumbo's laundering services for $50,000 per year. The fee is guaranteed for one year. If the offer is accepted, Jumbo will scrap the laundry equipment and close down its laundry operation completely.

Required:

The president of Jumbo has asked you to prepare a report that details the qualitative and quantitative factors that should be considered in making the decision about whether to close the laundry operation. Your report should discuss the relevant qualitative and quantitative factors for each alternative and include a relevant cost schedule. Your report should conclude with a well-supported recommended course of action.

LO 4: Relevant Cost of an Outsourcing Decision

7-36. Fast Track Delivery Service operates a small auto repair facility to service its fleet of 35 delivery vehicles. Fast Track's repair facility occupies space in an industrial area close to the company's home office. Fast Track is considering using a local repair shop to service its vehicles. Fast Track's $120,000 administrative expense is allocated based on the number of employees. Fast Track employs 50 people. Information about the repair facility follows:

Direct cost information:	
Wages for three employees	$64,000
Cost of equipment used	$33,500
Original estimated useful life of equipment	12 years
Estimated remaining useful life of equipment	9 years
Building rent per year	$ 6,000
Utilities	$ 2,000
Cost of automobile parts	$30,000
Miscellaneous cost	$ 1,500
Indirect cost information:	
Administrative expense	$ 7,200

A dependable automotive service center has offered to provide maintenance contracts of each vehicle for $3,000 per vehicle. If Fast Track accepts the offer it would close the maintenance facility. The company estimates that it can sell the maintenance equipment for $10,000.

Required:

The president of Fast Track has asked you to prepare a report that details the qualitative and quantitative factors that should be considered in making the decision about whether to close the maintenance facility. Your report should discuss the relevant qualitative and quantitative factors for each alternative and include a relevant cost schedule. Your report should conclude with a well-supported recommendation.

LO 3 & 4: Relevant Cost and Qualitative Factors of a Special Order Decision

7-37. Abraham Manufacturing produces 22,000 rubber engine mounts each year for use in its electric cart manufacturing plant. Abraham's engine mounts have an excellent reputation for strength and durability. At a production level of 22,000, the cost per unit is as follows:

Direct material	$ .53
Direct labor	1.45
Variable overhead	.92
Fixed overhead	1.27
Total	$4.17

A competitor, Jenkins Cart Company, is interested in purchasing 14,000 rubber engine mounts from Abraham. Jenkins has offered to pay $4.17 each for the engine mounts. Abraham Manufacturing has the capacity and can easily manufacture the engine mounts for Jenkins.

Several managers at Abraham are concerned that there would be no financial benefit whatsoever for Abraham if the engine mounts are sold at cost.

Required:

a. Prepare a schedule that details the advantage or disadvantage of selling the 14,000 engine mounts to Jenkins.

b. Discuss the qualitative aspects of selling the parts to Jenkins.

LO 3 & 4: Relevant Cost and Qualitative Factors of a Special Order Decision

7-38. Kelly Gas Grill Company produces 200,000 RV22 propane gas regulator and valve assemblies each year for use in its gas grill factory. Kelly's gas grills are known for quality and have a reputation of lasting a lifetime. At 200,000 units per year, the cost per unit is as follows:

Direct material	$ 3.02
Direct labor	2.44
Variable overhead	1.20
Fixed overhead	5.60
Total	$12.26

A competitor, Econo Grill, is interested in purchasing 80,000 RV22 assemblies from Kelly. Econo Grill has offered to pay $12.30 per unit. Kelly has the capacity and can easily manufacture the parts for Econo Grill.

Several managers at Kelly are concerned that there would be almost no financial benefit if the RV22 assemblies are sold for $12.30 each.

Required:

a. Prepare a schedule that details the advantage or disadvantage of selling the 80,000 RV22 assemblies to Econo Grill.

b. Discuss the qualitative aspects of selling the parts to Econo Grill.

LO 3 & 4: Relevant Cost and Qualitative Factors of a Special Order Decision

7-39. Eiroa Marine Cable Company produces 400,000 feet of SS316 cable each year. At 400,000 feet per year, the cost per foot is as follows:

Direct material	$ .32
Direct labor	.14
Variable overhead	.08
Fixed overhead	.73
Total	$1.27

A competitor, Garcia Marine, is interested in purchasing 175,000 feet of SS316 cable from Eiroa. Garcia has offered to pay $0.92 per foot for the cable. Eiroa has the capacity and can easily manufacture the cable for Garcia Marine.

Frank Eiroa, president of Eiroa Marine Cable, is concerned that there is no financial benefit for the company if it sells the cable for only $0.92 per foot.

Required:

a. Prepare a schedule that details the advantage or disadvantage of selling the 175,000 feet of cable to Garcia Marine.

b. Discuss the qualitative aspects of selling the cable to Garcia.

LO 3 & 4: Relevant Cost and Qualitative Factors of a Special Order Decision

7-40. Gator Corporation manufactures camping equipment. One of the Gator's most popular products is its Tl012 tent which the company sells for $28 each. Gator sells about 9,000 Tl0l2 tents each year through its mail-order business. Another camping equipment company, TreeClimb Corporation has approached Gator about purchasing 2,000 Tl012 tents. The tents would be the same as the T1012 except they would bear the TreeClimb brand. TreeClimb is willing to pay $20 per tent. Although Gator has plenty of plant capacity to produce the additional 2,000 tents, the company's manufacturing cost is $23 per unit, or $3 more per tent than TreeClimb is willing to pay. The following per unit information pertains to Gator's cost to produce 9,000 Tl0l2 tents:

Direct material	$ 9
Direct labor	4
Variable manufacturing overhead	2
Fixed manufacturing overhead	5
Total	$20

Required:

a. By what amount would Gator's operating income increase or decrease if the company accepts the special order?

b. Discuss the qualitative aspects of this special order decision.

LO 3 & 4: Relevant Cost and Qualitative Factors of a Special Order Decision

7-41. Refer to problem 7-40. Assume that Gator Corporation would have to purchase an additional sewing machine to accept the special order from TreeClimb. The cost of the new sewing machine is $2,500.

Required:

a. By what amount would Gator's operating income increase or decrease if the company accepts the special order under these circumstances?

b. Discuss the qualitative aspects of this special order decision.

LO 4: Relevant Cost of a Special Order Decision

7-42. Hi-Cast Corporation manufactures fishing rods. Part of Hi-Cast's sales success comes from a patented material, tuflex, used to make the fishing rods. Tuflex allows the fishing rods to be very flexible, yet nearly unbreakable. Hi-Cast sells about 150,000 fishing rods annually to wholesalers for $18 each. A major department store chain, Sale-Mart, is interested in purchasing 30,000 fishing rods that would bear the Sale-Mart's brand name. Sale-Mart is willing to pay only $9 per fishing rod, considerably less than Hi-Cast's normal selling price. Although Hi-Cast has plenty of plant capacity available to make the additional 30,000 fishing rods, the company's manufacturing cost is $11 per fishing rod, or $2 more per rod than Sale-Mart is willing to pay. Sale-Mart has indicated that the 30,000 fishing rods do not have to be as flexible and tough as the regular Hi-Cast rods. The following per unit information pertains to Hi-Cast's cost to produce 150,000 fishing rods:

Direct material:	
Tuflex	$ 4
Other material	1
Direct labor	3
Variable manufacturing overhead	1
Fixed manufacturing overhead	2
Total	$11

If fiberglass is used in place of tuflex, the direct material cost can be reduced by $2 per rod.

Required:

By what amount would Hi-Cast's operating income increase or decrease if the company accepts the special order?

LO 3 & 4: Relevant Cost and Qualitative Factors of an Outsourcing Decision

7-43. John Tullis Equipment Company makes high-pressure pumps. Tullis makes 10,000 VI valve assembles per year for use in production. The manufacturing facilities used to make the VI valves are also used to produce a variety of other subassemblies and products. Accordingly, no special production equipment is needed to make the VI valves. The production cost for VI valve assembles is as follows:

Direct material	$ 55,000
Direct labor	140,000
Variable manufacturing overhead	70,000
Fixed manufacturing overhead	210,000
Total	$475,000

Sure Flow Valve Company has offered to supply the VI valve assemblies to Tullis for $32 each.

Required:

a. Prepare a schedule that shows whether Tullis should buy the valves from Sure Flow or continue to make them.

b. Discuss the qualitative factors that Tullis should consider in this make or buy decision.

LO 3 & 4: Relevant Cost and Qualitative Factors of an Outsourcing Decision

7-44. Refer to problem 7-43. Assume Tullis could use the manufacturing facilities which are no longer needed to make the VI valves to produce a new line of small pumps. The small pumps would provide a contribution margin of $60,000.

Required:

a. Prepare a schedule that shows whether Tullis should buy the valves from Sure Flow or continue to make them.

b. Discuss the qualitative factors that Tullis should consider in this make or buy decision.

LO 3 & 4: Relevant Cost and Qualitative Factors of an Outsourcing Decision

7-45. General Manufacturing Company makes residential aluminum windows. A company has offered to supply General with the window crank assembly it needs for $3.50 each. General uses 50,000 crank assemblies each year. The machinery used to make the window cranks is used to produce a variety of other subassemblies and products. The production cost for the window crank assemblies is as follows:

Direct material	$ 70,000
Direct labor	40,000
Variable manufacturing overhead	55,000
Fixed manufacturing overhead	35,000
Total	$200,000

Required:

a. Prepare a schedule that shows the relevant cost and the preferred alternative of this make or buy decision.

b. Discuss the qualitative factors that General should consider when deciding whether to buy the window cranks from the outside supplier.

LO 3 & 4: Relevant Cost and Qualitative Factors of an Outsourcing Decision

7-46. Hutchens Electric produces electric fans. Hutchens manufactures 19,000 small electric fan motors each year. Dalta Motor Company has offered to supply Hutchens with the small electric motors for $12.50 each. The facilities that Hutchens uses to make the small motors are used to make larger motors and other components. Hutchens's production cost for the small electric fan motors is as follows:

Direct material	$132,000
Direct labor	26,500
Variable manufacturing overhead	43,500
Fixed manufacturing overhead	77,500
Total	$279,500

Required:

a. Prepare a schedule that shows whether Hutchens Electric should buy the electric fans or continue to make them.

b. Discuss the qualitative factors that Hutchens should consider when making this make or buy decision.

LO 3 & 4: Relevant Cost and Qualitative Factors of an Outsourcing Decision

7-47. Refer to problem 7-46. Assume that Hutchens Electric can use the facilities freed up by purchasing the electric motors from Dalta Motor Company to produce a new model fan that would have a contribution margin of $95,000.

Required:

a. Prepare a relevant cost schedule that shows whether Hutchens Electric should buy the electric fans or continue to make them.

b. Discuss the qualitative factors that Hutchens should consider when making this make or buy decision.

LO 3 & 4: Relevant Cost and Qualitative Factors of an Outsourcing Decision

7-48. Nunez, Inc. requires 12,000 units of part X45 per year. At the current level of production, the cost per unit is as follows:

Direct material	$ 3
Direct labor	1
Variable overhead	2
Fixed overhead	4
Total	$10

JLW, Inc. has offered to sell Nunez 12,000 units of X45 for $8 each. If Nunez is no longer required to produce the X45s, a supervisor can be eliminated. The supervisor's salary of $24,000 is part of fixed overhead cost. Other fixed overhead costs would remain the same.

Required:

a. Prepare a schedule that details the advantage or disadvantage of buying the 12,000 units of X45 from JLW, Inc.

b. Discuss the qualitative aspects of purchasing the parts from JLW, Inc.

LO 3 & 4: Relevant Cost and Qualitative Factors of an Outsourcing Decision

7-49. Cox, Inc. requires 3,000 spindles per year. At the current level of production, the cost per unit is as follows:

Direct material	$ 38
Direct labor	12
Variable overhead	14
Fixed overhead	44
Total	$108

AMW, Inc. has offered to sell Cox the 3,000 spindles for $100 each. If Cox is no longer required to produce the spindles, a supervisor can be eliminated. The supervisor's salary of $36,000 is part of fixed overhead cost. Other fixed overhead costs would remain the same.

Required:

a. Prepare a schedule that details the advantage or disadvantage of buying the 300 spindles from AMW, Inc.

b. Discuss the qualitative aspects of purchasing the parts from AMW, Inc.

LO 3 & 4: Relevant Cost and Qualitative Factors of an Outsourcing Decision

7-50. Adcox, Inc. requires 4,000 switch assemblies per year. At the current level of production, the cost per unit is as follows:

Direct material	$ 3
Direct labor	3
Variable overhead	2
Fixed overhead	2
Total	$10

Camron, Inc. has offered to sell Adcox, Inc. the 4,000 switch assemblies for $9 each. If Adcox is no longer required to produce the switch assemblies, part of the building can be leased to another company for $10,000 per year. Other fixed overhead costs would remain the same.

Required:

a. Prepare a schedule that details the advantage or disadvantage of buying the 4,000 switch assemblies from Camron, Inc.

b. Discuss the qualitative aspects of purchasing the parts from Camron, Inc.

LO 1, 2, & 4: Prepare a Report for Equipment Replacement Decision

7-51. The Sakura Company operates a chain of Japanese restaurants. Restaurant managers are paid bonuses based on the financial profits of their restaurants.

Last year, the manager of the South Miami Sakura Restaurant installed a new oven that cost $5,000. At the time, the oven had an estimated useful life of five years with no residual value. Annual repair and maintenance on the oven is $900, and the cost of electricity used by the oven is $3,400 per year. The old oven can be sold now for $1,500.

A salesperson is trying to convince the store manager to replace the oven purchased last year with a new, energy-efficient model. The salesperson says the new oven will increase company profits. The new oven can be purchased for $6,000, and has an estimated useful life of four years with a residual value of $1,000. The annual repair and maintenance would be the same as the old oven, or $900 per year, but the annual cost of electricity used by the oven would drop to $1,800.

The manager is not convinced by the salesperson. "If I buy this new oven, my financial income will drop and I'll never get my bonus. The loss in the first year will make me look like a fool!"

Required:

a. Prepare a report showing the relevant cost of keeping the old oven versus buying the new one.

b. Based on your report, what do you think of the restaurant manager's comments?

LO 1 & 6: Prepare Reports Regarding the Discontinuance of a Business Segment

7-52. Sherry Shoe Stores operates a chain of three retail shoe stores in the Miami area. The following information is available for the year ended December 31, 2009:

Sherry Shoe Stores
Segment Income Statement
For the Year Ended December 31, 2009

	Total	Store A	Store B	Store C
Sales	$1,800,000	$600,000	$800,000	$400,000
Variable expense	940,000	365,000	385,000	190,000
Contribution margin	860,000	235,000	415,000	210,000
Fixed expenses				
Store salaries and wages	272,000	155,000	92,000	25,000
Store rent	92,000	32,000	34,000	26,000
Store utilities	14,400	5,200	4,700	4,500
Advertising	95,000	31,667	42,222	21,111
General insurance	50,000	16,667	22,222	11,111
Depreciation of store equipment	13,000	6,000	4,000	3,000
Administrative exp.	135,000	45,000	60,000	30,000
Total fixed expenses	671,400	291,534	259,144	120,722
Operating income	$ 188,600	$(56,534)	$155,856	$ 89,278

Advertising is done in Miami area newspapers and cable television. The insurance policy for the chain is purchased by the home office. The costs of general business expenses of operating the retail chain are included in administrative expenses. These costs are allocated to the three stores in proportion to sales. Other amounts are directly related to the individual stores.

Sherry's owner is exploring the possibilities of reorganizing the chain to increase income. As part of the plan, Store A will be closed in order to eliminate its significant losses.

Required:

a. Based on the amounts for 2009, prepare a segment income statement for the company assuming the retail chain did not include Store A. Your answer should include a column for the total company and columns for each of the remaining segments.

b. Based on the amounts for 2009, prepare a schedule that reflects the relevant benefits and costs of discontinuing Store A.

c. Based on the amounts for 2009, prepare a segment income statement through operating income that includes the segment margin for each store. Your answer should include a column for the total company and columns for each segment.

d. Prepare a brief report to Sherry's owner to explain the situation and to make your recommendations. Be sure your report includes the details necessary to support your recommendations.

LO 1 & 6: Prepare a Segment Income Statement with and without the Allocation of Common Fixed Costs to Segments

7-53. The Albert Pons Company has two divisions. The following information is available for the year ended December 31, 2008.

The sales for the company are $200,000 for the Central Division, and $400,000 for the South Division. Variable costs for the Central Division are $150,000, whereas variable costs for the South Division are $300,000. Direct fixed costs of the Central Division are $19,000 and direct fixed costs of the South Division are $54,000. The company allocates common fixed costs to segments based on relative sales. Common fixed costs for the company are $27,000.

Required:

a. Prepare a segment income statement for the company which distributes common fixed costs to segments based on relative sales. Your answer should include a column for the total company and columns for each segment.

b. Do you think it is wise to evaluate the performance of a business segment based on income that includes an allocation for common fixed costs? Why or why not?

c. Prepare a segment income statement for the company which does not distribute common fixed cost to segments. Your answer should include a column for the total company and columns for each segment.

LO 1 & 6: Prepare a Segment Income Statement with and without the Allocation of Common Fixed Costs to Segments

7-54. The Peppermill Company has three divisions. The following information is available for the year ended December 31, 2008.

The sales for the company are $200,000 for the Central Division, and $400,000 for the South Division, and $600,000 for the West Division. Variable costs for the Central Division are $150,000, variable costs for the South Division are $300,000, and variable costs for the West Division are $450,000. Direct fixed costs of the Central Division are $20,000, direct fixed costs of the South Division are $54,000, and direct fixed costs of the West Division are $100,000. The company allocates common fixed costs to segments based on relative sales. Common fixed costs for the company are $102,000.

Required:

a. Prepare a segment income statement for the company which distributes common fixed costs to segments based on relative sales. Your answer should include a column for the total company and columns for each segment.

b. Based on your answer for part a, which segment seems to have generated the least profit?

c. Prepare a segment income statement for the company which does not distribute common fixed cost to segments. Your answer should include a column for the total company and columns for each segment.

d. Based on your answer for part c, which segment seems to have generated the most profit?

LO 1 & 6: Prepare a Segment Income Statement with and without the Allocation of Common Fixed Costs to Segments

7-55. The Pitman Sales Company has three divisions. The following information is available for the year ended December 31, 2008.

The sales for the company are $100,000 for Division A, and $200,000 for Division B, and $300,000 for Division C. Variable costs for Division A are $50,000, variable costs for Division B are $100,000, and variable costs for Division Care $150,000. Direct fixed costs of Division A are $20,000, direct fixed costs of Division B are $30,000, and direct fixed costs of Division C are $60,000. The company allocates common fixed costs to segments based on relative sales. Common fixed costs for the company are $186,000.

Required:

a. Prepare a segment income statement for the company which distributes common fixed costs to segments based on relative sales. Your answer should include a column for the total company and columns for each segment.

b. Based on your answer for part a, which segment seems to have generated the least profit?

c. Prepare a segment income statement for the company which does not distribute common fixed cost to segments. Your answer should include a column for the total company and columns for each segment.

d. Based on your answer for part c, which segment seems to have generated the most profit?

LO 1 & 6: Prepare a Segment Income Statement with and without the Allocation of Common Fixed Costs to Segments

7-56. The Porter Sales Company has three divisions. The following information is available for the year ended December 31, 2008.

The sales for the company are $100,000 for Division 101, and $100,000 for Division 202, and $200,000 for Division 303. Variable costs for Division 101 are $50,000, variable costs for Division 202 are $60,000, and variable costs for Division 303 are $110,000. Direct fixed costs of Division 101 are $20,000, direct fixed costs of Division 202 are $30,000, and direct fixed costs of Division 303 are $50,000. The company allocates common fixed costs to segments based on relative sales. Common fixed costs for the company are $40,000.

Required:

a. Prepare a segment income statement for the company which distributes common fixed costs to segments based on relative sales. Your answer should include a column for the total company and columns for each segment.

b. Based on your answer for part a, does it appear that one of the segments should be closed?

c. Prepare a segment income statement for the company which does not distribute common fixed cost to segments. Your answer should include a column for the total company and columns for each segment.

d. Based on your answer for part c, does it still seem that one of the segments should be closed?

LO 1 & 6: Analyze Segment Cost and Prepare a Memo

7-57. The following segment income statement has been prepared for the Albertson Sales Company.

Albertson Sales Company
Segment Income Statement
For the Year Ended December 31, 2008

	Company Total	Medical Division	Industrial Division	Consumer Division
Sales	$750,000	$337,500	$157,500	$255,000
Variable cost	499,425	211,500	110,625	177,300
Contribution margin	250,575	126,000	46,875	77,700
Direct fixed cost	112,500	48,000	30,000	34,500
Segment margin	138,075	78,000	16,875	43,200
Common fixed cost	90,000	40,500*	18,900**	30,600***
Net income	$ 48,075	$ 37,500	$ (2,025)	$ 12,600

*$337,500/$750,000 = 45% × $90,000 = $40,500
**$157,500/$750,000 = 21% × $90,000 = $18,900
***$255,000/$750,000 = 34% × $90,000 = $30,600

The company President, Bob Albertson, is calling a management meeting to explore the idea of closing or selling the Industrial Division. Many managers are complaining that the division is "dragging the company down."

Assume that, in preparation for the meeting, Mr. Albertson has contacted you and asked that you explore the situation.

Required:

Based on the information presented for the Albertson Sales Company, prepare a memo to Mr. Albertson which includes a brief summary of the problem and a proposed solution.

8

The Capital Budget: Evaluating Capital Expenditures

Let's say you're considering two very different purchases: a compact disc and a new car. Certainly, each of these purchases will require different amounts of time and effort. For instance, you probably won't review your long-term goals and annual budget before you buy the CD, nor will you likely create a list of costs and benefits to determine which CD to buy. However, when thinking about buying a new car, you'll probably first spend considerable time deciding whether you really need one, and whether you can afford it. Then, if you decide to go forward, you'll likely spend a significant amount of time determining what kind of car to buy.

The purchase of an expensive item such as a car warrants careful planning. For one thing, once you have bought something expensive it's usually costly to change your mind. In our example, you would have to sell or trade the new car, probably at a substantial loss. What is true in your personal financial decisions is also true in business. Unlike personal expenditures made for comfort or convenience, companies make business expenditures (large and small) to further the goals of the business. In fact, companies make most business expenditures to increase profits. For this reason, business expenditures are really investments, from which the company hopes to earn both a return *of* the investment and a return *on* the investment.

Business expenditures for acquiring expensive assets that will be used for more than one year are called **capital investments**. Because of the cost and extended useful life of these assets, companies devote tremendous time and energy to evaluating potential capital investments. For example, according to information in its annual reports, **Motorola, Inc.** invested approximately $2.6 billion in capital expenditures in the five years ending December 31, 2008. Even for a company as large as **Motorola**, $2.6 billion is an enormous amount of money. If **Motorola** made these investments in projects that did not perform as the company hoped they would, it could lead to disaster. Certainly, this magnitude of investment required serious analysis on the part of this company before it committed to the various projects those dollars represent.

capital investments Business expenditures in acquiring expensive assets that will be used for more than one year.

capital projects Another name for capital investments.

capital budgeting The planning and decision process for making investments in capital projects.

Generally, capital investments—also known as **capital projects**—are investments in property, plant, and equipment. Examples include investments in computer equipment, production equipment, another factory, a new wing of a hospital, or a new campus dormitory. **Capital budgeting** is the planning and decision process for making investments in capital projects. Although we focus on business firms in our discussion, all types of organizations can use capital budgeting techniques—not-for-profit, for profit, and social organizations.

In this chapter, we explain how firms make capital budgeting decisions. Capital budgeting, however, is only part of a much more involved planning process, which we also discuss in this chapter.

Two of the evaluation techniques used to assess potential capital projects rely heavily on a knowledge of the time value of money. For this reason, we have included two appendices to the chapter that deal with the time value of money. The first details calculations for the time value of money using financial tables and the second details similar calculations using a financial calculator.

Learning Objectives

After completing your work on this chapter, you should be able to do the following:

1. Describe the overall business planning process and where the capital budget fits in that process.
2. Explain in your own words the process of capital budgeting.
3. Discuss the four shared characteristics of all capital projects.
4. Describe the cost of capital and the concept of scarce resources.
5. Determine the information relevant to the capital budgeting decision.
6. Evaluate potential capital investments using four capital budgeting decision models: net present value, internal rate of return, payback period, and accounting rate of return.
7. Determine present and future values using present value tables and future value tables (Appendix A).
8. Determine present and future values using a financial calculator (Appendix B)

The Business Planning Process

Managers use accounting information for two main types of business decisions, planning and control. In this section, we give an overview of how organizations plan for the future. We discuss the why, the what, the how, and the who of business planning. Though management accounting information is used in all steps in the planning process, it is especially important to the what, the how, and the who decisions.

The Mission—Overall Company Goals: The Why

People form an organization to accomplish a purpose or several purposes—the organization's goals. These goals define *why* the organization exists; goals are the why of the business.

Organizational goals constitute the overall objectives the company, so those goals should not be subject to short-term economic pressures. Examples of some organizational goals might be to earn money, to save lives, or to improve communication among employees. Most companies' goals are stated in general terms that are not easily quantified, which means that although progress toward fulfillment can be measured, it is not really possible to determine when the goals have been attained. For instance, a firm with the goal of earning money usually does not specify exactly how much money it must earn to meet its goal.

organizational goals The overall objectives of the company. They outline why the organization exists and are a combination of financial and nonfinancial goals.

The goals of a business organization are usually a combination of nonfinancial and financial aspirations. Whether nonfinancial or financial, however, almost all goals have either a direct or indirect effect on the company's financial well-being. Does this sound strange? The next section explains why almost all goals can affect the financial health of a business.

Nonfinancial Goals

Typically, nonfinancial goals do not mention money. Rather, they refer to activities that may or may not result in profits. A hospital's nonfinancial goals, for instance, might be to provide the best health care possible to its patients; to recruit and employ highly qualified workers; to provide a safe, pleasant environment for its employees and patients; and to create an atmosphere of caring for both the physical and the emotional concerns of its patients.

Discussion Questions

8-1. Consider the hospital's nonfinancial goals. What financial effect will occur if the hospital *does* work toward those goals?

8-2. What financial effect will result if the hospital *does not* work toward those goals?

8-3. Review the hospital's nonfinancial goals. How would you determine when those goals have been reached?

Note that the nonfinancial goals for the hospital are stated in very general language. More than specific results, these goals represent standards of conduct and performance toward which the hospital should always be striving. They are stated in such a way that it is very difficult, if not impossible, to determine when the goals have been attained.

Financial Goals

For most business organizations, the primary financial goal is to earn a profit. What this really means, of course, is that the goal is to earn a return on investment for the business owner or owners. This goal may be worded as "achieving superior financial performance," "earning a reasonable return for the stockholders," "maximizing shareholder value," or similar language. As was the case with the nonfinancial goals, it is difficult to determine when these financial goals have been attained.

Goal Awareness

Once goals have been set, the company should communicate them to every person in the organization. This communication maximizes the likelihood that a business will achieve its goals. Many companies use a **mission statement**—a summary of the main goals of the organization—to communicate the firm's goals to all employees.

mission statement A summary of the main goals of the organization.

The goals in the **Johnson & Johnson** mission statement, for example, address the concerns of all parties who have a stake in how the company conducts its business. For instance, **Johnson & Johnson's** stakeholders include health care providers, consumers, suppliers, employees, the community, and stockholders. **Johnson & Johnson's** mission statement communicates the firm's goals and presents the image of a responsible, ethical business.

Stating lofty goals in a mission statement is not a guarantee of reaching those goals. Businesses must act in a manner consistent with their goals to ensure progress. Consider the following two examples. In 1982 **Johnson & Johnson** demonstrated the company's commitment to its goals after two fatalities occurred in the Chicago area when someone injected cyanide into six bottles of Tylenol. Once aware of these events, **Johnson & Johnson** immediately responded by recalling all Tylenol throughout the United States. The company also instituted a nationwide advertising campaign advising consumers *not* to use Tylenol and provided full disclosure about the situation. In short, the company responded in a manner consistent with its goals.

Compare **Johnson & Johnson's** actions to **Ford Motor Company**'s 1996 response to faulty ignition systems in some of its cars. These faulty ignition systems caught fire without warning and created a dangerous and potentially fatal situation. **Ford's** response was to wait for the federal government to tell the company which cars it had to recall. Legal? Certainly. A smart way to conduct business? Well, while it cost **Ford** less than a total recall of the affected vehicles, the company's reputation suffered, and many people agree that **Ford** did not conduct its business in a way consistent with its stated goal of total quality.

Core Values: What the Company Stands For

core values What defines our perception of what is most important in life and also defines a sense of right and wrong, of just or unjust.

Each of us has personal core values that define who we are, how we act, and what we stand for. **Core values** define our perception of what is most important in life and also define a sense of right and wrong, of just or unjust. Companies must have a similar set of core values in order to succeed. Company values include a sense of caring and a commitment to the health and well being of people and the environment.

Vision: The Hope for the Future

vision Management's dream for the company's future—the hope for where the company is going and how will it get there.

Company leadership must develop a vision of the company's future. **Vision** is where is the company going and how will it get there. What products and services will the company sell and how will it sell them? Where will the company conduct its business and how will the company learn, innovate, and grow as the future unfolds? These are all questions that are answered by vision.

Generally, company vision is not all about income and financial results. Of course, without financial prosperity, companies are unable to fulfill other aspects of their corporate vision so future financial success, growth and prosperity are also an important aspect of vision.

Strategy: The Business Plan of Attack

Once a company has established its mission, its core values, and its vision for the future, it must establish a workable strategy to achieve them. It is not enough for a business to have a mission and vision that includes building wealth through corporate earnings, it must also have a plan of attack or a **strategy** to create those earnings. For some companies, a strategy includes low prices and high volume. For others the strategy is high quality, superior service, and high prices. Some companies have profit strategy based on fast inventory turnover, while others have an earnings strategy based on higher margins and slower turnover.

strategy The plan of attack for furthering the company's vision and creating earnings.

Putting together a successful business strategy involves analyzing the situation that exists and the situation that is anticipated which includes among other things, evaluating the company, competitors, and social, economic, and market conditions. A three step approach to establishing a strategy is to determine where you are today, where you would like to be in the future, and finally, how you are going to get there. How you are going to get there is the business strategy. In forming a successful strategy, it is important to avoid focusing on the narrow view of business. For example, it is not wise to prepare a business strategy that focuses primarily on the financial aspirations of the company.

In the past, business in the United States has focused almost exclusively on financial amounts to measure success. Success has been gauged by how much revenue can be generated, how much costs can be reduced, or how much profit can be earned. Recently, however, many companies have begun to also consider nonfinancial performance measures in evaluating business performance. Managers are finding that a more strategic, balanced approach is necessary to drive corporate performance. Harvard professor Robert Kaplan and consultant David Norton have developed a management technique called the balanced scorecard. The **balanced scorecard** is an integrated set of performance measures organized around four distinct perspectives—financial, customer, internal, and innovation and learning as shown in Exhibit 8-1.

balanced scorecard An integrated set of performance measures organized around four distinct perspectives—financial, customer, internal, and innovation and learning

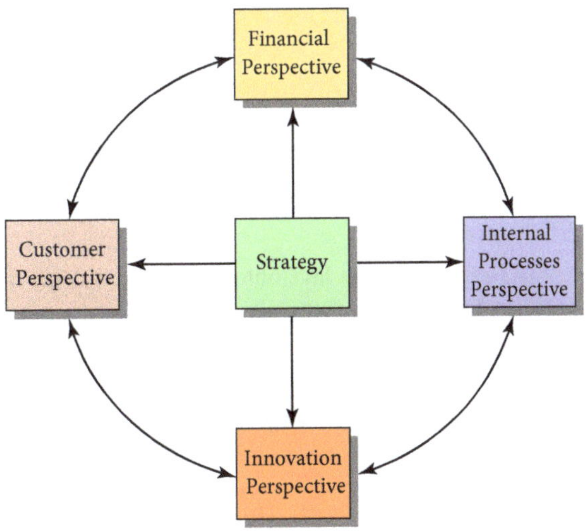

Exhibit 8-1 The Four Perspectives of the Balanced Scorecard

The balanced scorecard can help managers successfully create and implement a balanced business strategy. Successful strategy execution doesn't just happen. In fact, in recent years many businesses have failed, not because they lacked a good strategy, but rather because they failed to adequately implement their strategy. The balanced scorecard can help with strategy execution through the use of objectives, measures, and targets. When a company adopts the balanced scorecard, managers must create objectives, measures, and performance targets for each scorecard perspective. The balanced scorecard is discussed in greater depth in Chapter 11.

strategic plan A long-range plan that sets forth the actions a company will take to attain its organizational goals.

Once a business has established its mission, vision, and strategy, the firm must then create a **strategic plan**—a long-range plan that sets forth the actions the firm will take to attain its goals. In the following section, we explore briefly how firms develop strategic plans.

The Strategic Plan: The What

The steps outlined in the strategic plan, sometimes referred to as a long-range budget, are the *what* of doing business. The actions specified in the strategic plan describe what actions a business must take to implement its goals. To be effective, then, strategic plans should support—not conflict—with the company's goals.

Companies make long-range plans so they are well positioned to reach their goals as the future unfolds. For example, it can take **Dow Chemical Company** five years or longer to build a production facility, so **Dow** managers must anticipate product demand accurately in advance, in order to build a plant of the appropriate size in time to produce enough to meet consumer demand.

A company's strategic plan tends to have objectives that are quantifiable, and a time frame for attainment of the objectives. A company might specify, for instance, that it plans to replace its four least efficient production facilities over the next five years, reduce customer complaints by 20 percent over the next three years, or increase market share for its newest product by 25 percent within 10 years. As you can readily see, a firm can determine exactly when it has met all these objectives.

After an organization develops a strategic plan that specifies the actions it will take to reach its goals, the company then decides how to allocate its monetary resources to implement its strategies, and who will be responsible for the day-to-day activities of the business. This step in the planning process is the preparation of budgets.

The Capital Budget: The How

capital budget The budget that outlines how a company intends to invest its scarce resources in long-lived productive assets.

The capital budget is the *how* of the planning process. The **capital budget** is the budget that outlines how a firm intends to invest its scarce resources in long-lived productive assets.

The capital budget lays out plans for acquiring and replacing long-lived expensive assets such as land, buildings, machinery, and equipment. During the capital budgeting process, companies decide whether and what items they should purchase, how much they should spend, and how much profit the items can generate. Capital budgeting decisions, then, should further the strategic plan and goals of the business.

The Operating Budget: The Who

operating budget The budget that plans a company's routine day-to-day business activities for one to five years.

Companies not only must budget for long-term activities, they also must plan and budget for day-to-day business activities. The budget that pertains to routine company operations for one to five years in the future is called the **operating budget**. The operating budget establishes who is responsible for the day-to-day operation of the organization, so we refer to it as the *who* of the planning process. The operating budget will be our focus in Chapter 9.

An important thing to understand about the planning process is the interrelationship among goals, strategic plan, capital budget, and operating budget. Exhibit 8-2 demonstrates that interrelationship.

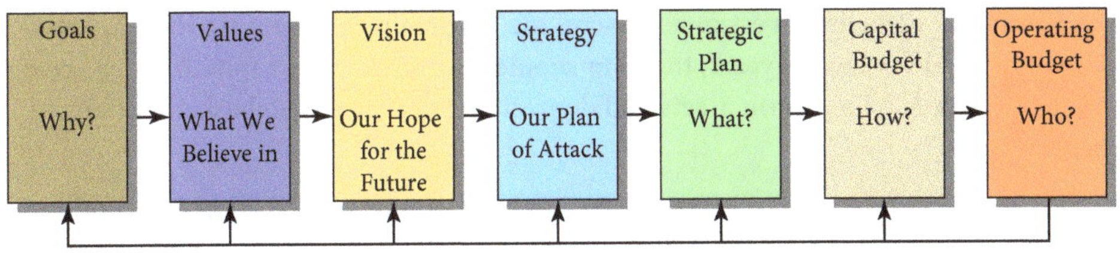

Exhibit 8-2 Interrelationship among the Planning Elements

The overall function of management accounting in this process is to provide a substantial portion of the information that company management needs not only to achieve the *what*, the *how*, and the *who*, but also to ensure that these functions are achieved within the context of the *why*.

The Capital Budget: What Is It?

The capital budget plans for the acquisition and replacement of long-lived expensive items such as land, buildings, machinery, and equipment. These long-lived items are called **capital assets**. The capital budget focuses on the long-term operations of the company to determine how an organization intends to invest its scarce resources in long-lived productive assets. Thus, we refer to this part of the planning process as the *how* of being in business and doing business.

capital assets Long-lived expensive items such as land, buildings, machinery, and equipment.

During the capital budgeting process, companies determine whether they should purchase items, how much they should spend, and how much profit the items promise to generate. No decisions made in the capital budgeting process, however, should conflict with the company's strategic plan or organizational goals.

Capitalizing Assets

Capital budgeting deals with decisions regarding investments that will benefit the company for many years, so most companies do not use capital budgeting techniques for small purchases or for those that provide benefits for only the current year.

When a company makes an expenditure, the cost of the item purchased will be reflected either as an expense on the company's income statement for the year of purchase, or as an increase in the company's assets on its balance sheet. Theoretically, the distinction lies in whether the item purchased will provide economic value to the company beyond the year of purchase. If a purchased item is expected to provide economic benefits beyond the year in which it is purchased, it should be capitalized, which means that its cost is recorded as an increase in long-term assets and will be depreciated (converted from asset to expense) over the item's estimated useful life. Conversely, if a purchased item is not expected to provide economic benefit to the company beyond the year of purchase, its cost should be reflected as an expense on the income statement for that year.

To illustrate, the cost of a delivery truck should be reflected as an increase in assets because the truck will likely be used for several years. In contrast, the cost of last month's lawn service does not provide any future value and therefore should be reflected as an expense immediately.

Judgment plays an important role in determining whether a purchased item should be capitalized or expensed. For example, how should a company record the cost of a $3 wastebasket with an estimated useful life of three years? Because the wastebasket will be used for several years, the item should theoretically be capitalized—its cost should be added to long-term assets and depreciated over the wastebasket's estimated useful life.

From a practical standpoint, it is senseless to expend the additional accounting effort to capitalize and then depreciate the wastebasket. Why? Because, whether the wastebasket is capitalized and depreciated over its estimated useful life or expensed immediately, the effect on a company's financial statements would be so minimal that no economic decision maker will be influenced by the alternative selected. Thus, the cost of the wastebasket is immaterial, so due to the modifying convention of materiality discussed in financial accounting, the wastebasket is expensed when purchased.

Capitalization Amount

Generally, companies set a cost threshold that helps determine the appropriate accounting treatment for capitalizing long-lived items. For example, a company might say that any long-lived item costing less than $3,000 will be expensed when purchased, while those costing $3,000 or more will be capitalized. There are no hard and fast rules for setting the capitalization threshold, but most businesses choose an amount between $500 and $5,000 as their capitalization amount.

Characteristics of Capital Projects

Capital budgeting deals with planning for purchases of items that will be capitalized, meaning they will be classified as assets when purchased and then depreciated over their estimated useful lives. While the capitalization amount and the evaluation process for capital projects vary from company to company, all capital projects share certain characteristics. The four main shared characteristics include:

1. *Long life*. Capital projects are expected to benefit the company for at least two years, which is the whole idea behind capitalizing the cost of a purchased item. As discussed in the previous section, if a purchased item will benefit the company only in the year of purchase, the cost of the item is expensed immediately. If the item purchased is likely to benefit a company in years beyond the year of purchase, the cost of that item is capitalized. Usually, the kinds of purchases we are discussing in this chapter benefit the company longer than two years—perhaps five, 10, or an even greater number of years.
2. *High cost*. Technically, the purchase of any long-lived item for which the cost exceeds a company's capitalization amount is considered a capital project. As stated earlier, this may be as low as $500 for some firms. As a practical matter, however, the capital budgeting techniques we consider in this chapter are used to evaluate high-cost projects. A good example is the cost of a new factory built by **Motorola** or **Intel**. Such a factory may cost $500 million or more. Another example is the decision by **Wal-Mart** or **Kmart** to open a new store in a particular location. Many millions of dollars are involved in opening a store for these companies.
3. *Quickly sunk costs*. Costs that cannot be recovered are called sunk costs. A capital project usually requires a firm to incur substantial cost in the early stages

of the project. As new information about market size, technology, and so on becomes available, the company's management may decide the project should be abandoned. Unfortunately, the company may not be able to recoup much of the cost already incurred. For example, consider the case of a manufacturer that begins construction on a new factory with an estimated cost of $500 million. After spending $200 million on construction, the company decides the new factory is not needed because the product it planned to manufacture in the facility has become obsolete. The company cannot sell the partially completed factory and has no other use for it. The $200 million is a sunk cost because it cannot be recovered.

4. *High degree of risk.* Capital projects have a high degree of business risk because they involve the future, which always entails uncertainty. Because of the long lives, high costs, and sunk costs of capital projects, companies must try to estimate the returns from those projects in future years. These characteristics increase the likelihood of erroneous estimates. The uncertainty of the future coupled with the high initial investment make capital projects quite risky.

Discussion Question

Consider these questions: "Will I be paid?" "How much will I be paid?" and "When will I be paid?"

8-4. Why do you think these questions were extremely difficult for **Microsoft** to answer as the company considered the development of *Windows 7* as a potential capital project?

The Cost of Capital and the Concept of Scarce Resources

When you put money into a savings account, you expect to earn interest. This interest is the return on your investment. Like most people, you would like the return to be as high as possible. If you were going to deposit $5,000 in a savings account, you would probably shop for a secure bank, with a return as high as or higher than that of competing banks.

Businesses shop for capital projects the same way you would shop for a bank in which to deposit your $5,000. If it appears that a capital project will be profitable, how does a company determine whether it will be profitable enough to warrant investing its money? A proposed project should promise a return that is equal to or exceeds the firm's cost of capital.

In evaluating potential capital projects, a company must determine a benchmark rate of return to help select which capital project or projects it will undertake. The benchmark return rate for selecting projects is usually the company's **cost of capital** , which is the cost of obtaining financing from all available financing sources. Cost of capital is also referred to as the **cost of capital rate**, the **required rate of return**, or the **hurdle rate**. For the sake of consistency, we use cost of capital throughout all our discussions in this chapter.

As you may recall from financial accounting, companies can obtain financing from two sources, borrowing from creditors (debt financing) and investments by

cost of capital The cost of obtaining financing from all available financing sources. Generally the rate of return required for capital investments.

cost of capital rate Another name for cost of capital.

required rate of return Another name for cost of capital.

hurdle rate Another name for cost of capital.

owners (equity financing). When a company invests in a capital project, the money must come from one or both of these sources. Both creditors and owners require a return on the funding they provide to the company, and the company must seek investments that provide a return at least equal to the cost of obtaining funding from debt and equity sources. If a company borrows funds at an interest rate of 9 percent, then the expected return on a capital project must be at least 9 percent. Similarly, if a company's owners provide the financing and expect a return of 20 percent on their investment, then the expected return from a capital project should be at least 20 percent to be acceptable.

Weighted Average Cost of Capital

weighted average cost of capital The combined cost of debt financing and equity financing.

blended cost of capital Same thing as the weighted average cost of capital.

cost of debt capital The interest a company pays to its creditors.

cost of equity capital What equity investors give up when they invest in one company rather than another.

The funding for a company's capital projects usually comes from a combination of debt and equity financing. The combined cost of debt and equity financing is called the **weighted average cost of capital**. The rate for the weighted average cost of capital represents the combined rate of the cost of both debt and equity financing. The weighted average cost of capital is sometimes referred to as the **blended cost of capital**.

The **cost of debt capital** is the interest a company pays on all forms of borrowing. The interest rate, say 8 percent, is agreed upon when a company borrows from either the bank or the bond market. The amount of interest a company pays is easy to determine because it is reported on the company's income statement as interest expense.

The cost of a company's equity financing is more challenging to determine than the cost of its debt financing, because the **cost of equity capital** is what equity investors relinquish when they invest in one company rather than another. To illustrate, assume Elizabeth Todd has $5,000 to invest and she is considering the purchase of either Boardman Company stock or Hoffman Company stock. What does Elizabeth give up if she invests her $5,000 in Boardman? She relinquishes what she would have earned had she invested in Hoffman. That is, she lost the opportunity to earn whatever she would have earned had she purchased Hoffman's stock rather than Boardman's.

The amount an equity investor earns is a combination of dividends received and the appreciation in the market value of the stock the investor owns. In Elizabeth's case, the amount earned if she buys the Boardman Company stock is a combination of the dividends she receives from Boardman, plus any increase in the market value of the Boardman stock she owns.

Discussion Question

Assume Elizabeth buys the Boardman stock and consistently earns an 8% return on her investment (dividends plus appreciation of the Boardman stock).

8-5. If Elizabeth could earn a 17% return on an investment in Hoffman Company stock (or some other company), what would you advise her to do? Explain your reasoning.

It's all well and good for us to discuss this topic from the investor's point of view (in this case Elizabeth Todd), but what has this to do with the cost of equity capital for Boardman Company? Well, if Boardman wants to keep Elizabeth as a stockholder, it must return to her an amount at least as great as she could earn by investing her money somewhere else. If Elizabeth can earn 17 percent from an investment in Hoffman, Boardman must give her that kind of return or she may sell her Boardman stock and invest in Hoffman (or some other company). Boardman, then, would use 17 percent as the cost of the equity capital it received from Elizabeth, because that is what she could earn elsewhere. In other words, that is what she gave up by investing in Boardman.

In a real-world situation, Boardman Company would not know about the alternatives being considered by Elizabeth Todd and her $5,000. Therefore, the company cannot determine the specific percentage return Elizabeth must earn to keep her happy. What Boardman must do is try to determine what percentage return equity investors can generally expect on their investments and use that percentage as the cost of equity capital.

Unlike debt financing costs (interest expense), the cost of equity financing is not reported in financial statements in its entirety. Firms do report profit distributions to stockholders in the form of dividends, but the larger part of the cost of equity capital is the appreciation in the market value of stockholders' ownership interest. This market value is not reported on financial statements.

Most equity investors want to own stock in high return companies because they naturally want their investment to earn the highest possible return. Many high return companies in the stock market yield as high as 17 percent to 20 percent annually to their stockholders in the form of dividends and appreciation in stock value.

Discussion Questions

Assume you own stock in a publicly traded company and you consistently earn an 8% return on your investment (dividends plus appreciation of the company's stock).

8-6. If you are certain you could earn a 20% return on an investment in some other company's stock, what would you do? Explain your reasoning.

8-7. Because a publicly traded company receives money only when its stock is originally issued, why do you think it would care about the stock's market value in the stock market?

It is important to note here that the issue is not whether investors can, in fact, earn a 17 to 20 percent return by selling their stock in one company and investing in another. They only need to *think* they can earn the higher return.

If enough of a company's stockholders begin selling their stock, the market price of the stock will drop—the economic law of supply and demand at work. As the stock price drops, more stockholders may decide to sell their stock before the price drops even lower. This, of course, makes the stock price drop further.

Discussion Question

8-8. What would you think about a company whose stock was selling for $50 a share in January and $12 a share in December?

Stock analysts, customers, suppliers, and many other parties have a tendency to gauge a company's health by the market value of its stock. For this reason, companies have a vested interest in making sure the market value of their stock does not begin a downward spiral.

Because the investors in the stock market think they can earn a 17 to 20 percent return by investing in the top performing companies, a company must return 17 to 20 percent annual return to its stockholders to be considered one of the high performing companies. Publicly traded companies usually consider their cost of equity financing to be as high as 20 percent. This percentage is commonly used to compute the company's weighted average cost of capital.

To illustrate the calculation of the weighted average cost of capital, we consider the case of Adler Enterprises, which has $2,000,000 in assets. A total of $1,200,000 or 60 percent ($1,200,000/$2,000,000) of these assets are financed by debt (borrowing) with an interest rate of 7.5 percent. The remaining $800,000 or 40 percent ($800,000/$2,000,000) are financed by equity (the sale of Adler Enterprises stock) and the company uses a 20 percent cost of equity financing. We find the weighted average cost of capital for Adler Enterprises using the calculation in Exhibit 8-3.

Exhibit 8-3 Weighted Average Cost of Capital Calculation

Method of Financing	Proportion of Financing Provided		Cost of Financing		Weighted Cost of Financing
Debt	60%	×	7.5%	=	4.5%
Equity	40%	×	20.0%	=	8.0%
			Weighted average Cost of Capital		12.5%

We see that Adler's weighted cost of debt financing is the proportion of debt financing (60 percent) multiplied by the cost of that financing (7.5 percent). The company's weighted cost of equity financing is the proportion of equity financing (40 percent) times the cost of the equity financing (20 percent). Its weighted average cost of capital is the sum of the weighted cost of each type of financing—12.5 percent.

Firms use their weighted average cost of capital as a benchmark rate of return to evaluate capital projects. For example, suppose Adler Enterprises is considering a capital project that requires an investment of $200,000. If Adler decides to undertake this project, it must obtain $200,000 to fund it. Recall that Adler's weighted average cost of capital is 12.5 percent. Unless the expected rate of return on the project is 12.5 percent or higher, Adler's management will probably reject the project. Otherwise, it would cost more to fund the project than the project could earn.

Discussion Questions

8-9. When you consider that companies are generally in business to earn a profit, why might it be acceptable to select a capital project that promises a return that is just equal to the weighted average cost of capital?

8-10. Under what circumstances do you think a company might accept one capital project over another even though the project selected promises a lower return?

8-11. Do you think there would ever be a situation when a company should proceed with a capital project even though the project promises a return lower than the cost of capital? Explain your reasoning.

8-12. What do you think might cause a company to reject a proposed capital project even though it promises a return significantly higher than the cost of capital?

Scarce Resources

In our personal lives, what we buy is usually not limited by how much we want, but rather by how much money we have available to spend. Well, what is true for individuals is also true for businesses. The number and size of capital projects a company undertakes is not limited by a lack of viable alternative projects. What limits companies is that they simply do not have access to enough money to take advantage of all the opportunities available to them. This limitation on the amount available to spend is commonly called **scarce resources**. Even huge multinational companies must select only investments they consider most favorable from a virtually unlimited pool of possible investment opportunities, because firms do not have access to enough money to invest in every good project that comes along. Managers must carefully evaluate the alternative capital projects available to their companies so they can select the projects that promise the highest return (as long as the projects are consistent with the company's goals and strategies).

scarce resources A term describing the limited amount of money a company has to invest in capital projects.

Evaluating Potential Capital Projects

Because capital projects are usually long lived, costly, and high risk, managers must carefully evaluate capital expenditure decisions, especially in light of their financial limitations. The evaluation process generally includes the following four steps:

1. Identifying possible capital projects
2. Determining the relevant cash flows for alternative projects
3. Selecting a method of evaluating the alternatives
4. Evaluating the alternatives and selecting the capital project or projects to be funded

Let us investigate each of these steps from the manager's point of view.

Identifying Possible Capital Projects

Businesses usually make capital expenditures to maximize profits by increasing revenue, reducing costs, or a combination of the two. A project that satisfies the company's desire to maximize profits will be identified as a potential capital expenditure.

Firms often generate revenue increases by investing in projects that increase capacity or draw more customers. For a hotel chain, an increase in available rooms might increase revenue. For a restaurant, revenue might be enhanced by investing in cooking equipment that prepares food more rapidly. For a hospital, the ability to provide additional services or increasing the number of beds might be the key to added revenue.

To reduce operating costs a manufacturer might upgrade production equipment so less direct labor or less electricity is required. An airline catering company could invest in more energy-efficient ovens to reduce food preparation cost. Reducing cost has exactly the same effect as increasing revenue. As Benjamin Franklin said, "A penny saved is a penny earned." If you think about it, this really makes sense. If a company saves $1 by reducing costs by $1, the cost reduction has the same impact on profits as increasing selling price to increase revenue by $1.

Although the majority of potential capital projects are intended to either increase revenue or reduce costs, in certain instances a company must make a capital expenditure that will result in neither. These projects are usually concerned with safety or environmental issues and may come as a result of governmental regulation requirements; or, a company may simply determine such an expenditure is necessary given its goal of worker safety or good corporate citizenship.

In any event, capital projects a company deems necessary but do not promise either to increase revenue or reduce costs are usually not evaluated using the same criteria as those projects that do promise increased profits. In this chapter, we restrict ourselves to the evaluation of potential capital projects that promise to either increase revenue or reduce costs.

As the need for increasing revenue or reducing costs presents itself, a company should explore all alternative courses of action. Brainstorming sessions and input from multiple sources both within and outside a firm can help generate ideas for alternative options.

Determining Relevant Cash Flows for Alternative Projects

Throughout our discussion of capital budgeting, we have discussed capital projects that promise to increase a company's profits by either increasing revenue or reducing costs (expenses). Recall, however, that under accrual accounting, revenue is not the same as cash inflow and expense is not the same as cash outflow in the short run.

net cash flows Cash inflow less cash outflow.

Because capital projects usually are long lived, most business managers believe it is appropriate to analyze an alternative using cash inflow and cash outflow over the life of the project. They do this by determining the **net cash flow** of a project—the project's expected cash inflows minus its cash outflows for a specific time period. For example, if a manager estimates that investing in a new production machine will yield \$40,000 in cash inflows during the useful life of the machine but will require spending \$30,000 for the same period, the net cash flow would be \$10,000 (\$40,000 − \$30,000).

relevant net cash flows Future net cash flows that differ between or among the alternatives being considered.

Only relevant net cash flows should be considered in a capital budgeting decision. **Relevant net cash flows** are future cash flows that differ between or among alternatives. Thus, a relevant cash flow must be one that will occur in the future, not one that has already occurred, and it must be affected by the investment decision. Past cash flows, or cash flows that will not change as a result of the investment decision, are irrelevant and should not be considered in the decision process. This concept should seem familiar because it follows the same reasoning as our discussion of relevant costs, the subject of Chapter 7.

Once a company obtains and assesses the relevant net cash flows for each alternative project, the next step is to choose a method to measure the value of each project.

Selecting a Method of Evaluating the Alternatives

Over time, accountants and managers have developed many capital budgeting decision methods to evaluate potential capital projects. In this chapter, we present four methods:

1. Net present value
2. Internal rate of return
3. Payback period
4. Accounting rate of return

Each of these methods offers a different way to measure a project's value, and sometimes the different methods render conflicting rankings. In such a case, managers should be aware of the strengths and weaknesses of each capital budgeting method. In the next major section we discuss each of the four methods and the advantages and disadvantages of each.

Selecting Capital Projects

To select a capital project, firms decide first whether to accept or reject a project using one or more capital budgeting techniques to measure the project's value. If the project does not generate an acceptable rate of return, it will probably be rejected. Furthermore, a company should reject any proposed capital project that is inconsistent with the company's goals and strategic plan, even if the promised return on that project is higher than some other potential project.

Once a project has been accepted as viable, that project can then be ranked with other acceptable projects based on expected performance.

Capital Budgeting Decision Methods

In this section, we present four capital budgeting methods: net present value, internal rate of return, payback period, and accounting rate of return. The first two methods, which are discounted cash flow methods, are used more frequently in business because they include the concept of the time value of money.

A dollar received or paid at some point in the future does not have the same value as a dollar received or paid today. The reason for the difference in value is that if cash is available now, it can be invested now and earn a return as time passes. This increase in the value of cash over time due to investment income is referred to as the **time value of money**. The concept of the time value of money is used to determine either the future value of money invested today or the present value of money to be received at some point in the future.

time value of money The increase in the value of cash over time due to investment income.

In the following discussion of net present value and internal rate of return, we assume you have a working knowledge of the time value of money, discussed in detail in Appendix A to this chapter. Refer to it now if you need to refresh your understanding. In addition, Appendix B to this chapter demonstrates how to do present value and future value calculations using a financial calculator. Throughout the remainder of this chapter, we will demonstrate present value calculations using both present value tables and a financial calculator. The amounts will differ somewhat due to rounding. Because not all students have access to a financial calculator, we will demonstrate both, but in our discussions we will use only the amounts derived from using the tables.

Capital projects deal with cash flows that begin in the present and extend into the future, sometimes for many years. Therefore, the evaluation of these kinds of projects uses the concept of present value. Determining the present value of cash to be received in future periods is called **discounting cash flows**.

discounting cash flows Determining the present value of cash to be received in the future.

Discounted Cash Flow Methods

Business managers use two discounted cash flow methods to evaluate potential capital projects: net present value and internal rate of return.

Net Present Value

net present value (NPV) The present value of all cash inflows associated with a proposed capital project minus the present value of all cash outflows associated with the proposed capital project.

The **net present value (NPV)** of a proposed capital project is the present value of cash inflows minus the present value of cash outflows associated with a capital project. Note that NPV is different from the present value. The former is the difference between the present value of a capital project's cash inflow and the present value of its cash outflow. The latter is the amount a future payment or series of payments is in today's dollars evaluated at the appropriate discount rate. NPV is used to determine whether a proposed capital project's anticipated return is higher or lower than the weighted average cost of capital.

A company calculates the NPV of a capital project by discounting the net cash flows for all years of the project using the company's weighted average cost of capital as the discount rate. A positive NPV indicates that the expected return on a proposed project is higher than the company's cost of capital. A negative NPV indicates that the expected return on a proposed project is lower than the company's cost of capital. An NPV of zero shows that the expected return on a project is exactly equal to the company's cost of capital.

To illustrate the NPV calculations, assume Whitewater Adventure Company is considering a computer hardware upgrade that would require an investment of \$100,000. Assume further that the enhanced speed of the computer is expected to save \$31,000 annually in operator salaries. Remember, this reduction of cash outflow is a cash inflow in NPV analysis. The computer has an estimated useful life of five years with no residual value.

The cash flows associated with the computer upgrade are shown in Exhibit 8-4.

Exhibit 8-4 Expected Cash Flows for Whitewater Adventure Company Computer Upgrade

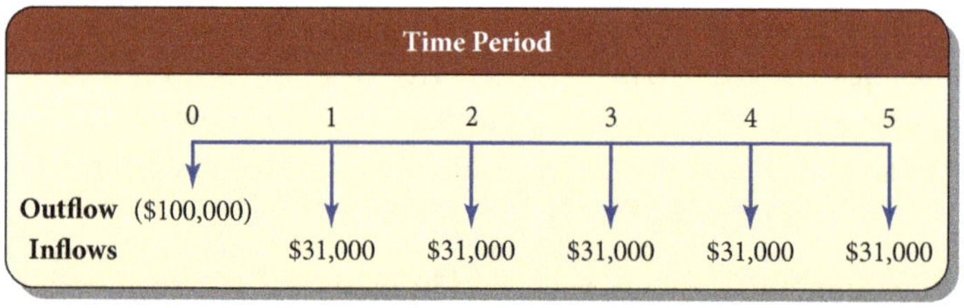

Notice in Exhibit 8-4 that the initial cash outlay of \$100,000 occurs at "time 0." When working with present values, time 0 is considered today, or the present. Unless otherwise specified, we assume all other cash flows for this project will occur at the end of each period. We also ignore depreciation in our analysis because depreciation is a noncash expense under accrual accounting and the NPV method focuses on cash flow rather than accrual operating income.

Whitewater has a 14 percent weighted average cost of capital so we use 14 percent as the discount rate to evaluate whether the company should accept the computer upgrade project; that is, we use a 14 percent discount rate to calculate the present value of the project's cash outflows and cash inflows. In this case, the project's \$100,000 cash outflow occurs today (time 0), so that amount is already stated in present value terms.

Next, we must find the present value of the project's cash inflows, which occur at the end of each of the next five years. Because the stream of \$31,000 positive cash flows constitutes an annuity, we use the *Present Value of an Annuity of \$l Table,* found in Exhibit A8-10 of Appendix A at the end of this chapter. In this case, we use the table to find the present value factor of a five-year annuity, with a discount rate of 14 percent. We have reproduced a portion of the table as Exhibit 8-5. As you can see from the highlighted portion in this exhibit, the factor for five years with a discount rate of 14 percent is 3.433.

Exhibit 8-5 Partial Present Value of an Annuity of $1 Table

Present Value of an Annuity of $1 Table

Period	8%	9%	10%	11%	12%	13%	14%	15%
1	0.926	0.917	0.909	0.901	0.893	0.885	0.877	0.870
2	1.783	1.759	1.736	1.713	1.690	1.668	1.647	1.626
3	2.577	2.531	2.487	2.444	2.402	2.361	2.322	2.283
4	3.312	3.240	3.170	3.102	3.037	2.974	2.914	2.855
5	3.993	3.890	3.791	3.696	3.605	3.517	3.433	3.352
6	4.623	4.486	4.355	4.231	4.111	3.998	3.889	3.784
7	5.206	5.033	4.868	4.712	4.564	4.423	4.288	4.160
8	5.747	5.535	5.335	5.146	4.968	4.799	4.639	4.487
9	6.247	5.995	5.759	5.537	5.328	5.132	4.946	4.772
10	6.710	6.418	6.145	5.889	5.650	5.426	5.216	5.019

We multiply $31,000, the amount of the annuity, by the 3.433 present value factor and find that the present value of the annuity is $106,423 ($31,000 × 3.433 = $106,423). See Exhibit 8-6 for instructions on how to use a financial calculator to determine this.

Exhibit 8-6 How to Use a Financial Calculator

USING A FINANCIAL CALCULATOR

To calculate the present value of the $31,000 payments using a financial calculator we would enter the information in our financial calculator and solve for a solution as follows:

Input:	5	14	?	31,000	0
	n	i	PV	PMT	FV
Answer:			−106,426		

Notice that the amount is $3 more than the amount we obtained when we used the present value table. This is because financial calculators typically round to 12 decimal places while our tables round to only three. What this means is that the answer we get from the calculator is more precise than the one from the tables. Although we will demonstrate each present value calculation using both tables and a financial calculator, because not all students have access to a financial calculator, throughout the remainder of the chapter we will use the amounts from the tables in our discussions.

Finally, we find the NPV of the project by subtracting the present value of cash outflows from the present value of cash inflows. In our example, the net present value calculations are presented in Exhibit 8-7.

Exhibit 8-7 Net Present Value Calculations

Time Period

	0	1	2	3	4	5
	($100,000)					
$31,000 × 3.433 =	106,423	$31,000	$31,000	$31,000	$31,000	$31,000
Net Present Value	$ 6,423					

NPV = PV of Project's Expected Returns − Initial Cash Outlay
NPV = $106,423 − $100,000
NPV = $6,423

As Exhibit 8-7 shows, the positive NPV of $6,423 indicates that the project's expected return exceeds Whitewater's 14 percent weighted average cost of capital.

A word of caution here. A net present value of $6,423 does not mean that the project's return is only $6,423. Rather, it means that the project's return *exceeds* the company's 14 percent cost of capital by $6,423.

Discussion Questions

8-13. How would you explain the difference between present value and net present value?

8-14. Should a business accept or reject a project with an NPV of zero? Explain your reasoning.

Net Present Value Calculations with Uneven Cash Flows

The Whitewater Adventure Company example was relatively easy to calculate because the project's expected cash flows were the same each year (an annuity). When the expected cash flows are uneven, we find the present value of each year's net cash flow and then add those amounts. To demonstrate, assume that Whitewater's computer upgrade has expected annual returns of $31,000, but in year 3 the computer system will require $12,000 in maintenance fees (a cash outflow), and at the end of year 5, the system can be sold for $6,000 (a cash inflow). A time line showing these additional cash flows is shown in Exhibit 8-8.

Exhibit 8-8 Uneven Expected Cash Flows for Whitewater Adventure Company Computer Upgrade

Time Period

	0	1	2	3	4	5
Initial Investment	($100,000)					
Maintenance				($12,000)		
Operating Costs		$31,000	$31,000	$31,000	$31,000	$31,000
Residual Value						$ 6,000
Net Cash Flow	($100,000)	$31,000	$31,000	$19,000	$31,000	$37,000

Each of the amounts for the five years shown in Exhibit 8-8 can be discounted to present value using the *Present Value of $1 Table*, found in Exhibit A8-5 of Appendix A at the end of the chapter, a portion of which is reproduced as Exhibit 8-9.

Exhibit 8-9 Partial Present Value of $1 Table

Present Value of $1 Table

Period	8%	9%	10%	11%	12%	13%	14%	15%
1	0.926	0.917	0.909	0.901	0.893	0.885	0.877	0.870
2	0.857	0.842	0.826	0.812	0.797	0.783	0.769	0.756
3	0.794	0.772	0.751	0.731	0.712	0.693	0.675	0.658
4	0.735	0.708	0.683	0.659	0.636	0.613	0.592	0.572
5	0.681	0.650	0.621	0.593	0.567	0.543	0.519	0.497
6	0.630	0.596	0.564	0.535	0.507	0.480	0.456	0.432
7	0.583	0.547	0.513	0.482	0.452	0.425	0.400	0.376
8	0.540	0.502	0.467	0.434	0.404	0.376	0.351	0.327
9	0.500	0.460	0.424	0.391	0.361	0.333	0.308	0.284
10	0.463	0.422	0.386	0.352	0.322	0.295	0.270	0.247

The calculation of the present values, using the highlighted factors in the 14 percent discount rate column, is shown in Exhibit 8-10.

Exhibit 8-10 Net Present Value Calculations with Uneven Cash Flows

	Time Period					
	0	1	2	3	4	5
Initial Investment	($100,000)					
Maintenance				($12,000)		
Operating Costs		$31,000	$31,000	$31,000	$31,000	$31,000
Residual Value						$ 6,000
Net Cash Flow	($100,000)	$31,000	$31,000	$19,000	$31,000	$37,000

$31,000 × 0.877 =	27,187
$31,000 × 0.769 =	23,839
$19,000 × 0.675 =	12,825
$31,000 × 0.592 =	18,352
$37,000 × 0.519 =	19,203
Net Present Value	$ 1,406

As Exhibit 8-9 demonstrates, the positive $1,406 NPV indicates that the computer upgrade exceeds Whitewater's 14 percent weighted average cost of capital. This positive

NPV indicates that the project is acceptable for the company. See Exhibit 8-11 for instructions on calculating the present value of the net cash flows for each year using a financial calculator.

Exhibit 8-11 Calculating the Present Value of the Net Cash Flows for Each Year

USING A FINANCIAL CALCULATOR

To calculate the present value of the net cash flows for each year using a financial calculator we would enter the information in our financial calculator and solve for a solution as follows:

YEAR 1

Input:	1	14	?	0	31,000
	n	**i**	**PV**	**PMT**	**FV**
Answer:			−27,193		

YEAR 2

Input:	2	14	?	0	31,000
	n	**i**	**PV**	**PMT**	**FV**
Answer:			−23,853		

YEAR 3

Input:	3	14	?	0	19,000
	n	**i**	**PV**	**PMT**	**FV**
Answer:			−13,824		

YEAR 4

Input:	4	14	?	0	31,000
	n	**i**	**PV**	**PMT**	**FV**
Answer:			−18,354		

YEAR 5

Input:	5	14	?	0	37,000
	n	**i**	**PV**	**PMT**	**FV**
Answer:			−19,217		

Notice that the amounts are different than those we obtained when we used the present value of $1 table. Again, this is due to rounding.

Although the NPV method indicates whether a proposed capital project is acceptable, it does have limitations as a ranking method to compare alternative projects. A direct comparison of the NPVs of various projects may lead to poor decisions regarding project selection, because NPV is measured in dollars rather than percentages. For example, assume that management intends to select one of two projects, Project A or Project B. Calculations indicate that the NPV of Project A is $5,000, whereas the NPV of Project B is $6,000.

While choosing the project with the higher NPV seems wise, this is not always a good choice because NPV analysis does not consider the relative investments required by the projects. In our example, for instance, say the present value of Project A's net cash inflows is $105,000 and its required investment is $100,000. Then suppose that the present value of Project B's net cash inflows is $206,000 and its required investment is $200,000. We see that Project A requires an investment of $100,000, whereas Project B requires double that investment amount. The relatively small increase in the NPV from $5,000 to $6,000 does not justify selecting a project that requires double the amount of investment. How then can the NPV method be used when ranking various projects? We solve the problem of selecting among projects by using a profitability index.

Profitability Index

The **profitability index** provides a means of ranking alternative but acceptable capital projects by using an index calculated by dividing the present value of the project's net cash inflows by its required investment. To illustrate, we return to our example of Projects A and B. We know that both projects have positive NPVs and are acceptable projects.

profitability index A method used to rank acceptable proposed capital projects.

By dividing its present value of net cash inflows by the required investment, we determine that the profitability index for Project A is 1.05 ($105,000 ÷ $100,000 = 1.05). The profitability index for Project B is 1.03 ($206,000 ÷ $200,000 = 1.03). The higher the profitability index, the higher the rate of return for the project. Accordingly, we would rank Project A higher than Project B because Project A's index value is 1.05 compared to Project B's lower index value of 1.03.

Although the NPV method indicates whether a project's return is lower or higher than the required rate of return, it does not provide the project's expected percentage return. Many managers find it helpful to know the expected rate of return of projects when making capital budgeting decisions. The internal rate of return method, discussed in the following section, is a technique that provides this information.

Internal Rate of Return

The **internal rate of return (IRR)** of a proposed capital project is the calculated expected percentage return promised by a project. Just like the NPV method, the IRR method considers all cash flows for a proposed project and adjusts for the time value of money. However, the IRR results are expressed as a percentage, not a dollar amount. This method, also known as the **real rate of return**, or the **time-adjusted rate of return**, determines the discount rate that makes the present value of a project's cash inflows and the present value of a project's outflows exactly the same.

internal rate of return (IRR) The calculated expected percentage return promised by a proposed capital project.

real rate of return Another name for internal rate of return.

time-adjusted rate of return Another name for internal rate of return.

To calculate a project's IRR, we use the same present value tables we use to calculate net present value, but we apply them differently. In this application, we use the tables to determine a discount rate (a percentage), rather than using a pre-selected discount rate to determine present value amounts (expressed in dollars).

As an example, assume that Project C requires an initial investment of $300,000 and will provide net cash inflows of $56,232 per year for eight years. Because this project is an annuity, to determine the IRR we will use the *Present Value of an Annuity of $1 Table,* found in Exhibit A8-10 of Appendix A at the end of this chapter. a portion of which is reproduced as Exhibit 8-12.

This time when we use the table, instead of using an interest rate to determine the present value factor, we will use a present value factor to determine the interest rate. To do this, the first step is to determine the present value factor we will look up on the table. To calculate the present value factor we divide the required initial investment by the annual net cash inflow as follows:

$$\frac{\text{Required initial investment}}{\text{Annual net cash inflow}} = \text{Present value factor}$$

$$\frac{\$300{,}000}{\$56{,}232} = 5.335 \text{ Present value factor}$$

Now that we know the present value factor, we can find Project C's IRR by moving down the time period column on the table in Exhibit 8-12 to eight periods, as that is the life of the project. Next we follow across the row corresponding to eight periods until we find a factor that is close to the one we calculated (5.335). As we follow across the row for eight periods, we find a factor that is not just close but matches exactly. The factor of 5.335 is in the 10 percent column, which indicates the IRR for Project C is 10 percent. Thus, the actual rate of return promised by Project C is 10 percent.

Exhibit 8-12 Partial Present Value of an Annuity of $1 Table

Present Value of an Annuity of $1 Table

Period	7%	8%	9%	10%	11%	12%	13%	14%
1	0.935	0.926	0.917	0.909	0.901	0.893	0.885	0.877
2	1.808	1.783	1.759	1.736	1.713	1.690	1.668	1.647
3	2.624	2.577	2.531	2.487	2.444	2.402	2.361	2.322
4	3.387	3.312	3.240	3.170	3.102	3.037	2.974	2.914
5	4.100	3.993	3.890	3.791	3.696	3.605	3.517	3.433
6	4.767	4.623	4.486	4.355	4.231	4.111	3.998	3.889
7	5.389	5.206	5.033	4.868	4.712	4.564	4.423	4.288
8	5.971	5.747	5.535	5.335	5.146	4.968	4.799	4.639
9	6.515	6.247	5.995	5.759	5.537	5.328	5.132	4.946
10	7.024	6.710	6.418	6.145	5.889	5.650	5.426	5.216

Once we determine the IRR we compare it to the cost of capital to gauge the project's acceptability. An IRR that exceeds the firm's cost of capital indicates an acceptable project. For example, if the company's cost of capital is nine percent, Project C's 10 percent IRR shows that the firm would find the project acceptable.

In the example for Project C, we contrived the dollar amounts so that the factor we calculated exactly equaled one of the factors in the present value table. In a real-life situation, the calculated factor will usually fall between two factors on the present value table. For example, assume Project D would require an investment of $330,000 and would generate estimated annual net cash inflows of $64,900 for eight years. The present value factor for this project is 5.085, determined as follows:

$$\frac{\text{Required initial investment}}{\text{Annual net cash inflow}} = \text{Present value factor}$$

$$\frac{\$330{,}000}{\$64{,}900} = 5.085 \text{ Present value factor}$$

Returning to the table in Exhibit 8-12 and following across the year 8 row, we find that our calculated 5.085 factor is between the factors 5.146 (the 11 percent column) and 4.968 (the 12 percent column), but is closer to 5.146. Therefore, the project's IRR would fall between 11 and 12 percent, but would be closer to 11 percent. We then estimate that the IRR for Project D is slightly more than 11 percent.

For instructions on how to calculate the IRR using a financial calculator, see Exhibit 8-13.

Exhibit 8-13 Calculating the Internal Rate of Return

USING A FINANCIAL CALCULATOR

To calculate the internal rate of return using a financial calculator, we simply enter all the data we have for the project, and solve for the information we need. In other words, we enter the number of years (n = 8), the project's required initial investment as a negative amount (PV = −330,000), the project's annual net cash inflows as a positive amount (PMT = 64,900), the project's residual value, if any as a positive amount (FV = 0) and then solve for the project's rate of return, i. We would enter the information in our financial calculator and solve as follows:

Input:	8	?	−330,000	64,900	0
	n	**i**	**PV**	**PMT**	**FV**
Answer:		11.34%			

When calculating the IRR, a financial calculator not only makes the calculations easier to do, but the result is much more precise as well. Additionally, when using a financial calculator you can easily calculate the IRR for any project that has a residual value by simply entering the amount as the FV. What's more, although it is beyond the scope of this text, many financial calculators can also easily accommodate situations where cash flows differ from year to year. (Note: To avoid an "ERROR 5" message, enter the PV as a negative number and the PMT and FV as positive numbers.)

Comparing Projects Using the IRR Method Managers can use the IRR to rank projects. For example, the IRR of Project C (10 percent), can be compared to the approximate IRR of Project D (just over 11 percent). Assuming both projects were acceptable, Project D would be ranked higher than Project C because it promises a higher IRR.

Comparing NPV and IRR Both NPV and IRR are well-respected techniques used to determine the acceptability of a proposed capital project for two reasons. First, they are based on cash flows, not accounting income. Second, both methods consider the time value of money.

NPV is used to determine whether the promised return from a proposed capital project meets the minimum acceptable return requirements (cost of capital). A drawback of this method is that the calculated NPV is stated in dollars rather than percentages. Thus, comparison between projects of different size is difficult. The profitability index overcomes this difficulty.

IRR is used to calculate a proposed capital project's actual expected rate of return. Because this method is calculated using percentages rather than dollars, it can be used as a direct comparison of various proposed projects.

Nondiscounted Cash Flow Methods

Decision makers generally consider the NPV and IRR methods the most reliable techniques available because they utilize the time value of money in their evaluation of potential capital projects. Other methods that ignore the time value of money exist, however, and many companies use them to some degree. We now discuss two of them—the payback period and the accounting rate of return.

Payback Period

payback period A capital budgeting technique that measures the length of time a capital project must generate positive cash flows that equal the original investment in the project.

As its name implies, the **payback period** is a capital budgeting technique that measures the length of time a capital project must generate positive net cash flows to equal, or "pay back," the original investment in the project. For instance, assume that a project's estimated initial outlay is $40,000. Assume further that the project is expected to generate a net cash inflow of $12,500 per year. When net cash inflows are equal from one year to the next, we determine the payback period by dividing the required initial investment by the annual net cash inflows. In our example, we find that the payback period is 3.2 years. The calculations follow:

$$\frac{\text{Required initial investment}}{\text{Annual net cash inflow}} = \text{Payback period in years}$$

$$\frac{\$40{,}000}{\$12{,}500} = 3.2 \text{ years}$$

If a project has uneven cash flows, we can determine the payback period by adding the net cash inflows year by year until the total equals the required initial investment. For example, suppose a project requires an initial investment of $50,000 and is expected to generate the following net cash inflows:

2009	$12,000
2010	$15,000
2011	$18,000
2012	$15,000
2013	$12,000

We find the payback period by totaling the net cash inflows until we reach $50,000 as shown in Exhibit 8-14.

Exhibit 8-14 Payback Period with Uneven Cash Flows

Year	Net Cash Received in Prior Years		Net Cash Received in Current Year		Accumulated Net Cash Received
1	0	+	$12,000	=	$12,000
2	$12,000	+	$15,000	=	$27,000
3	$27,000	+	$18,000	=	$45,000
4	$45,000	+	$15,000	=	$60,000
5	$60,000	+	$12,000	=	$72,000

As Exhibit 8-14 shows, the initial investment will be "paid back" after the third year, but before the end of the fourth year. At the end of the third year, it is anticipated that $45,000, or all but $5,000 of the initial $50,000 investment will be recouped. The remaining $5,000 will be received during the fourth year as part of the $15,000 net cash inflows anticipated for that year. It will take about one third ($5,000 ÷ $15,000) of the fourth year to collect the final $5,000 to make up the $50,000 needed to payback the initial investment. Therefore the payback period is 3⅓ years.

The payback period highlights the liquidity of an investment and companies use it as a screening device to reject projects with unreasonably low net cash flow expectations. This method is simple to use, is easily understood, and offers some limited insight into a project's liquidity.

The payback period is not often used to make final capital investment decisions because it does not consider three crucial elements: (1) the expected returns of a project after the payback period, (2) how the returns will compare to the firm's cost of capital or (3) the time value of money.

Because the payback period ignores the firm's cost of capital, total cash flow, and time value of money concerns, managers do not normally accept or reject a project based solely on the payback period method. If used at all the payback period is usually a screening device only to eliminate potential projects from further evaluation. Companies often establish a maximum payback period for potential projects. If a proposed capital project promises a payback of longer than the established maximum period, that project would be eliminated from further consideration. For example, assume a company has established a maximum payback period of three years. Using this standard, the project presented in Exhibit 8-14 would be rejected because its payback period is longer than three years.

Accounting Rate of Return

In our discussion so far, we have emphasized that the focus in capital budgeting decisions should be on cash flows. Over time, however, the net cash flow associated with a capital project should approximate operating income as determined using accrual accounting revenue and expense recognition. The **accounting rate of return** method uses accrual accounting operating income, rather than net cash flow, as the basis for evaluating alternative capital budgeting projects.

accounting rate of return The rate of return for a capital project based on the anticipated increase in accounting operating income due to the project. relative to the amount of capital investment required.

The accounting rate of return is the rate of return for a capital project based on the anticipated increase in accounting operating income due to the project, relative to the amount of capital investment required.

This method focuses on a proposed project's required investment and how that project changes a company's operating income. As an example, let's reexamine the computer hardware upgrade project for the Whitewater Adventure Company discussed earlier in the chapter. As you recall, the computer hardware upgrade would require an initial investment of $100,000. Additionally, the upgrade would reduce operating expenses by $31,000 per year for five years. The computer has an estimated useful life of five years with no residual value. Accounting operating income would be affected in two ways by the computer upgrade. First, the reduced operating expenses would increase operating income by $31,000 each year. Second, depreciation for the computer upgrade would decrease operating income. With this information, we can calculate the straight line depreciation expense and accounting rate of return as follows:

Straight-Line Depreciation

$$\frac{\text{Asset's cost} - \text{estimated residual value}}{\text{Estimated useful life}} = \text{Straight-line depreciation}$$

$$\frac{\$100{,}000 - \$0}{5 \text{ years}} = \$20{,}000 \text{ Annual depreciation expense}$$

Accounting Rate of Return

$$\frac{\text{Increase in operating income}}{\text{Required investment}} = \text{Accounting rate of return}$$

$$\frac{\$31{,}000 - \$20{,}000}{\$100{,}000} = 11\% \text{ Accounting rate of return}$$

The accounting rate of return is simple to calculate and provides some measure of a project's profitability; however, it has two major drawbacks. First, the accounting rate of return method focuses on accounting income rather than cash flow. In capital budgeting, most analysts believe that a focus on cash flow is preferable to a focus on accounting income. Second, like the payback period method, the accounting rate of return does not consider the time value of money.

Many managers consider the accounting rate of return to be superior to the payback period because it offers at least a limited measure of a proposed capital project's rate of return. As with the payback period, however, managers should not accept or reject a project based solely on the accounting rate of return. Both of these methods should be used only as screening devices or in conjunction with discounted cash flow methods of evaluating capital project alternatives.

Factors Leading to Poor Capital Project Selection

The process of determining which capital projects to select is a serious matter for any company. If managers do not treat capital budgeting with the seriousness it deserves, they run the risk of making poor decisions as to the capital projects selected. At the very least, selecting the wrong capital projects is enormously costly. At worst, investing in the wrong projects can lead to financial ruin for any company, regardless of its size or past performance. In addition to the difficulties inherent in the capital budgeting process caused by the uncertainty associated with the future, there are two factors that can lead to poor capital project selection. They are natural optimism on the part of managers and the tendency of some managers to turn the capital project evaluation process into a game.

Natural Optimism

Human beings are essentially optimistic. As managers they have a natural tendency to estimate both the cash inflows and outflows associated with a proposed project they are sponsoring with an overly optimistic outlook. This means they will likely overstate the estimated cash inflows and understate the estimated cash outflows. At the very minimum, this natural optimism limits the effectiveness of any of the evaluation techniques we have discussed in this chapter, because all of them use inflow and outflow estimates as the basis of evaluation.

There is nothing wrong with thinking positively. Optimism is, in fact, a desirable trait. Managers must understand, however, that such optimism can cloud their judgment as they assess potential capital projects. Good managers attempt to be as realistic as possible as they prepare proposals for the evaluation of potential capital projects.

Capital Budgeting Games

The managers who propose potential capital projects understand that there is usually not enough money available to fund all projects, even if they all promise a return greater than the cost of capital. A manager who proposes a capital project is, in fact, competing with other managers' projects for a limited number of capital investment dollars. For this reason, the capital project evaluation process is sometimes treated like some sort of game with little consideration of the potentially disastrous consequences. Some managers manipulate the estimates of cash inflow and cash outflow to get "pet" projects approved, often at the expense of other, more deserving projects. Do not confuse this idea with the natural optimism we discussed a moment ago. The manipulation we are talking about here is an additional factor that can lead to selecting the wrong capital projects.

Summary

There are four elements in the overall planning process for any organization. These elements include the establishing of goals, formulating a strategic plan, preparing the capital budget, and preparing the operating budget.

The capital budgeting process has been described as the *how* of being in business and doing business, which means that the capital budget outlines how a company will invest its scarce resources in long-lived productive assets.

All capital projects have at least four shared characteristics. Such projects are usually long lived, carry with them high costs, have costs associated with the project that usually become sunk almost immediately, and usually involve a high degree of risk.

In the long run, the capital projects a company undertakes must cover at least the cost of the company's capital. The cost of capital is the cost of obtaining financing from both debt and equity sources. The combination of the cost of debt financing and equity financing is referred to as the weighted average cost of capital. If the capital project being considered does not at least cover the cost of capital, it makes no sense, from a purely financial standpoint, to undertake it.

Over time, accountants and managers have developed several methods to evaluate potential capital projects. Among these are the net present value (NPV), the internal rate of return (IRR), the payback period, and the accounting rate of return. Each of these four methods has certain advantages and disadvantages relative to the other methods. Managers generally consider the NPV and IRR methods to be superior to the payback and accounting rate of return methods because they incorporate the time value of money in their approach to evaluating potential capital projects.

Appendix A: The Time Value of Money

The Time Value of Money—The Concept of Interest

A dollar received or paid at some point in the future does not have the same value as a dollar received or paid today. If you were asked why this is so, you might think the change in value is due to inflation. Even if inflation did not exist, however, a dollar received or paid in the future would not have the same value as a dollar received or paid today. The reason for the difference in value is that if cash is available now, it can be invested now and earn a return as time passes. This increase in the value of cash over time, due to its earning potential, is referred to as the time value of money. We use the concept of the time value of money to determine either the future value of money invested today or the present value of money to be received or paid at some point in the future.

Learning Objectives

After completing your work in this appendix, you should be able to do the following:

1. Explain the concept of simple interest and compound interest.
2. Determine the future value of a single amount invested today using a future value table.
3. Determine the present value of a single amount to be received at some point in the future using a present value table.
4. Describe the concept of an annuity.
5. Determine the future value of an annuity using a future value table.
6. Determine the present value of an annuity using a present value table.

Future Value

future value The value of a payment, or series of payments, at some future point in time calculated at some interest rate.

Future value is the value of a payment, or series of payments, at some future point in time calculated at some interest rate. For example, if you were to invest $2,000 at an annual interest rate of 10 percent, your investment would grow to $2,200 in one year. How? The amount of the increase is calculated by multiplying the principal—the original investment—by the interest rate. In our case the principal is $2,000, the interest rate is 10 percent, so the total return on your investment is $200. The $200 is added to the $2,000 investment for a total of $2,200. So far, so good. But suppose you left the investment untouched for three years. What would be its total value at the end of the three years? The answer depends on whether we calculate the interest as simple interest or compound interest.

simple interest Interest calculated on the original principal amount invested only.

Simple interest is interest calculated only on the original principal. A calculation of interest earned at 10 percent per year for three years on a $2,000 principal using simple interest is presented in Exhibit A8-1.

Exhibit A8-1 Simple Interest Calculation

	Year 1	Year 2	Year 3
Principal	$2,000	$2,000	$2,000
Times the interest rate	× 10%	× 10%	× 10%
Equals interest earned	$ 200	$ 200	$ 200

Note in Exhibit A8-1 that we calculate interest for each of the three years only on the original investment of $2,000. At the end of three years you would receive your $2,000 (return of your investment) and $600 interest (return on your investment).

Compound interest is interest calculated on the investment principal *plus* all previously earned interest. Continuing with our example, a principal of $2,000 that earns a compounded rate of 10 percent interest per year for three years is shown in Exhibit A8-2.

compound interest Interest calculated on the original principal amount invested plus all previously earned interest.

Exhibit A8-2 Compound Interest Calculations

	Year 1	Year 2	Year 3
Principal	$2,000	$2,000	$2,000
Previously earned interest	+ 0	+ 200*	+ 420**
Total	2,000	2,200	2,420
Times the interest rate	× 10%	× 10%	× 10%
Equals interest earned	$ 200	$ 220	$ 242

* Interest earned in year 1 ($200) becomes part of the amount earning interest in year 2.
** Interest earned in year 1 ($200) and the interest earned in year 2 ($220) becomes part of the amount earning interest in year 3.

Note in Exhibit A8-2 that we calculate interest for each of the three years not only on the original investment of $2,000, but also on the interest earned in previous years. At the end of three years you would receive your $2,000 back (return of your investment) and $662 interest (return on your investment). The difference of $62 between the interest earned using compound interest ($662) and the interest earned using simple interest ($600) is interest earned on your previously earned interest.

The power of compounding is tremendous. To demonstrate, let us extend our example of the $2,000 investment. Suppose Dick Gustufson invests $2,000 at 10 percent annual interest when he is 18 years old and leaves it untouched until he is 38 years old. Using the simple interest calculation, Dick's investment will earn interest of $4,000 ($2,000 × 10% × 20 years). If, however, the interest over that same 20 years is compounded, the total interest earned would be $11,454. The $7,454 difference in interest earned is due entirely to interest earning interest on previously earned interest.

Future Value of a Single Sum

We could calculate the amount of compound interest on Dick's investment by extending the three-year example presented in Exhibit A8-2 for another 17 years. This, however, would be cumbersome, time consuming, and tiresome. Fortunately, future value tables greatly simplify the calculation of compound interest.

Future value tables are previously calculated values of $1 at various rates of interest and time periods. The tables are used to determine either the future value of a single payment or the future value of an annuity—that is, a stream of equal payments made at equal intervals.

We use the *Future Value of $1 Table* (Exhibit A8-3) to determine the future value of a single amount deposited today. With this information, we can quickly determine the future value of Dick Gustufson's $2,000 investment at a 10 percent interest rate compounded annually.

As we see in Exhibit A8-3, by moving across the interest rate column headings to the 10 percent column, and then down the time period row to the 20 time periods row, we

Exhibit A8-3 Future Value of $1 Table

Future Value of $1 Table

Period	3%	4%	5%	6%	7%	8%	9%	10%	11%	12%	13%	14%	15%	16%	17%	18%
1	1.030	1.040	1.050	1.060	1.070	1.080	1.090	1.100	1.110	1.120	1.130	1.140	1.150	1.160	1.170	1.180
2	1.061	1.082	1.103	1.124	1.145	1.166	1.188	1.210	1.232	1.254	1.277	1.300	1.323	1.346	1.369	1.392
3	1.093	1.125	1.158	1.191	1.225	1.260	1.295	1.331	1.368	1.405	1.443	1.482	1.521	1.561	1.602	1.643
4	1.126	1.170	1.216	1.262	1.311	1.360	1.412	1.464	1.518	1.574	1.630	1.689	1.749	1.811	1.874	1.939
5	1.159	1.217	1.276	1.338	1.403	1.469	1.539	1.611	1.685	1.762	1.842	1.925	2.011	2.100	2.192	2.288
6	1.194	1.265	1.340	1.419	1.501	1.587	1.677	1.772	1.870	1.974	2.082	2.195	2.313	2.436	2.565	2.700
7	1.230	1.316	1.407	1.504	1.606	1.714	1.828	1.949	2.076	2.211	2.353	2.502	2.660	2.826	3.001	3.185
8	1.267	1.369	1.477	1.594	1.718	1.851	1.993	2.144	2.305	2.476	2.658	2.853	3.059	3.278	3.511	3.759
9	1.305	1.423	1.551	1.689	1.838	1.999	2.172	2.358	2.558	2.773	3.004	3.252	3.518	3.803	4.108	4.435
10	1.344	1.480	1.629	1.791	1.967	2.159	2.367	2.594	2.839	3.106	3.395	3.707	4.046	4.411	4.807	5.234
11	1.384	1.539	1.710	1.898	2.105	2.332	2.580	2.853	3.152	3.479	3.836	4.226	4.652	5.117	5.624	6.176
12	1.426	1.601	1.796	2.012	2.252	2.518	2.813	3.138	3.498	3.896	4.335	4.818	5.350	5.936	6.580	7.288
13	1.469	1.665	1.886	2.133	2.410	2.720	3.066	3.452	3.883	4.363	4.898	5.492	6.153	6.886	7.699	8.599
14	1.513	1.732	1.980	2.261	2.579	2.937	3.342	3.797	4.310	4.887	5.535	6.261	7.076	7.988	9.007	10.147
15	1.558	1.801	2.079	2.397	2.759	3.172	3.642	4.177	4.785	5.474	6.254	7.138	8.137	9.266	10.539	11.974
16	1.605	1.873	2.183	2.540	2.952	3.426	3.970	4.595	5.311	6.130	7.067	8.137	9.358	10.748	12.330	14.129
17	1.653	1.948	2.292	2.693	3.159	3.700	4.328	5.054	5.895	6.866	7.986	9.276	10.761	12.468	14.426	16.672
18	1.702	2.026	2.407	2.854	3.380	3.996	4.717	5.560	6.544	7.690	9.024	10.575	12.375	14.463	16.879	19.673
19	1.754	2.107	2.527	3.026	3.617	4.316	5.142	6.116	7.263	8.613	10.197	12.056	14.232	16.777	19.748	23.214
20	1.806	2.191	2.653	3.207	3.870	4.661	5.604	6.727	8.062	9.646	11.523	13.743	16.367	19.461	23.106	27.393
21	1.860	2.279	2.786	3.400	4.141	5.034	6.109	7.400	8.949	10.804	13.021	15.668	18.822	22.574	27.034	32.324
22	1.916	2.370	2.925	3.604	4.430	5.437	6.659	8.140	9.934	12.100	14.714	17.861	21.645	26.186	31.629	38.142
23	1.974	2.465	3.072	3.820	4.741	5.871	7.258	8.954	11.026	13.552	16.627	20.362	24.891	30.376	37.006	45.008
24	2.033	2.563	3.225	4.049	5.072	6.341	7.911	9.850	12.239	15.179	18.788	23.212	28.625	35.236	43.297	53.109
25	2.094	2.666	3.386	4.292	5.427	6.848	8.623	10.835	13.585	17.000	21.231	26.462	32.919	40.874	50.658	62.669

Exhibit A8-4 Future Value of an Annuity of $1 Table

Future Value of an Annuity of $1 Table

Period	3%	4%	5%	6%	7%	8%	9%	10%	11%	12%	13%	14%	15%	16%	17%	18%
1	1.000	1.000	1.000	1.000	1.000	1.000	1.000	1.000	1.000	1.000	1.000	1.000	1.000	1.000	1.000	1.000
2	2.030	2.040	2.050	2.060	2.070	2.080	2.090	2.100	2.110	2.120	2.130	2.140	2.150	2.160	2.170	2.180
3	3.091	3.122	3.153	3.184	3.215	3.246	3.278	3.310	3.342	3.374	3.407	3.440	3.473	3.506	3.539	3.572
4	4.184	4.246	4.310	4.375	4.440	4.506	4.573	4.641	4.710	4.779	4.850	4.921	4.993	5.066	5.141	5.215
5	5.309	5.416	5.526	5.637	5.751	5.867	5.985	6.105	6.228	6.353	6.480	6.610	6.742	6.877	7.014	7.154
6	6.468	6.633	6.802	6.975	7.153	7.336	7.523	7.716	7.913	8.115	8.323	8.536	8.754	8.977	9.207	9.442
7	7.662	7.898	8.142	8.394	8.654	8.923	9.200	9.487	9.783	10.089	10.405	10.730	11.067	11.414	11.772	12.142
8	8.892	9.214	9.549	9.897	10.260	10.637	11.028	11.436	11.859	12.300	12.757	13.233	13.727	14.240	14.773	15.327
9	10.159	10.583	11.027	11.491	11.978	12.488	13.021	13.579	14.164	14.776	15.416	16.085	16.786	17.519	18.285	19.086
10	11.464	12.006	12.578	13.181	13.816	14.487	15.193	15.937	16.722	17.549	18.420	19.337	20.304	21.321	22.393	23.521
11	12.808	13.486	14.207	14.972	15.784	16.645	17.560	18.531	19.561	20.655	21.814	23.045	24.349	25.733	27.200	28.755
12	14.192	15.026	15.917	16.870	17.888	18.977	20.141	21.384	22.713	24.133	25.650	27.271	29.002	30.850	32.824	34.931
13	15.618	16.627	17.713	18.882	20.141	21.495	22.953	24.523	26.212	28.029	29.985	32.089	34.352	36.786	39.404	42.219
14	17.086	18.292	19.599	21.015	22.550	24.215	26.019	27.975	30.095	32.393	34.883	37.581	40.505	43.672	47.103	50.818
15	18.599	20.024	21.579	23.276	25.129	27.152	29.361	31.772	34.405	37.280	40.417	43.842	47.580	51.660	56.110	60.965
16	20.157	21.825	23.657	25.673	27.888	30.324	33.003	35.950	39.190	42.753	46.672	50.980	55.717	60.925	66.649	72.939
17	21.762	23.698	25.840	28.213	30.840	33.750	36.974	40.545	44.501	48.884	53.739	59.118	65.075	71.673	78.979	87.068
18	23.414	25.645	28.132	30.906	33.999	37.450	41.301	45.599	50.396	55.750	61.725	68.394	75.836	84.141	93.406	103.740
19	25.117	27.671	30.539	33.760	37.379	41.446	46.018	51.159	56.939	63.440	70.749	78.969	88.212	98.603	110.285	123.414
20	26.870	29.778	33.066	36.786	40.995	45.762	51.160	57.275	64.203	72.052	80.947	91.025	102.444	115.380	130.033	146.628
21	28.676	31.969	35.719	39.993	44.865	50.423	56.765	64.002	72.265	81.699	92.470	104.768	118.810	134.841	153.139	174.021
22	30.537	34.248	38.505	43.392	49.006	55.457	62.873	71.403	81.214	92.503	105.491	120.436	137.632	157.415	180.172	206.345
23	32.453	36.618	41.430	46.996	53.436	60.893	69.532	79.543	91.148	104.603	120.205	138.297	159.276	183.601	211.801	244.487
24	34.426	39.083	44.502	50.816	58.177	66.765	76.790	88.497	102.174	118.155	136.831	158.659	184.168	213.978	248.808	289.494
25	36.459	41.646	47.727	54.865	63.249	73.106	84.701	98.347	114.413	133.334	155.620	181.871	212.793	249.214	292.105	342.603

find a number on the table at the point where the row and column intersect, at a value of 6.727. This number is called a future value factor. Because we are using the *Future Value of $1 Table*, the 6.727 factor tells us that the value of a single dollar 20 years into the future is $6.727, or about $6.73. That is to say that if $1 is invested today at 10 percent, it will be worth $6.73 in 20 years.

But Dick invested $2,000, not $1. To determine the future value of $2,000, we multiply $2,000 by the factor of 6.727 to determine that $2,000 invested today at 10 percent will be worth $13,454 after 20 years ($2,000 × 6.727 = $13,454). If you subtract his initial investment of $2,000, the amount of interest he will earn is $11,454.

Future Value of an Annuity

We use the *Future Value of an Annuity of $1* Table, presented as Exhibit A8-4, to determine the future value of a stream of cash flows when the stream of cash flows constitutes an **annuity**. An annuity is a stream of cash flows where the dollar amount of each payment and the time interval between each payment are uniform.

annuity A stream of equal periodic cash flows.

To see how the table in Exhibit A8-4 is used, assume Susan King intends to deposit $2,000 in an account at the end of each year for four years at a compound interest rate of 12 percent per year. Using the *Future Value of an Annuity of $1* Table we determine that the factor for 4 years at 12 percent is 4.779. Accordingly, if Susan deposits $2,000 at the end of each year for four years at 12 percent, the account balance will be approximately $9,558 ($2,000 × 4.779).

Present Value (Discounting)

The basic premise of the present value of money is that it is more valuable to receive cash today (so it can be invested to receive interest) than to receive the cash later. The question is, just how valuable is it to receive cash sooner rather than later?

If we know the expected rate of return, we can actually calculate the value of receiving cash sooner rather than later. For example, if you are offered the option of receiving $1,000 today or $1,000 one year from now, how much more valuable is it to receive the $1,000 today? If the $1,000 received today can be invested in a savings account earning six percent interest, then it will grow by $60 during the year. At the end of one year, it will be worth $1,060 and you would be $60 richer than if you had opted to receive the $1,000 one year from now. The $60 growth in value over time exemplifies the time value of money. Clearly, if money is available and invested, it grows as time passes.

If cash can be invested at six percent, $1,000 received today is equivalent to receiving $1,060 one year from now. The amount a future cash flow or stream of cash flows is worth today evaluated at the appropriate interest rate is the cash flow's **present value**. Determining the present value of an amount of cash to be received in the future is called *discounting*.

present value The amount future cash flows are worth today based on an appropriate interest rate.

Present value tables greatly simplify the calculation of discounting to find the present value of a single amount or an annuity. Present value tables are previously calculated values of $1 at various interest rates and time periods. The tables are used to determine either the present value of a single amount or the present value of an annuity.

Present Value of a Single Sum

We use the *Present Value of $1 Table*, presented as Exhibit A8-5, to determine the present value of a single amount to be received at some point in the future.

To see how we use the *Present Value of $1 Table*, suppose you visited your rich Aunt Hattie and helped her wash her dog. Your aunt was so touched by your kindness, she offers you a gift of $1,000. You are excited and hold out your hand for the money, but she informs you that she is not going to give you the money now. Rather she intends to give you the money one year from now. Her only request is that you tell her how much to deposit in a six percent savings account today so that the account will equal $1,000 one year from now.

In this case, you know that the future value of the amount is $1,000 one year from now. The amount your Aunt Hattie wants to know is the present value, the amount that must be deposited today at six percent so that the account will be worth $1,000 in one year. To find out how much Aunt Hattie must deposit, we use the *Present Value of $1 Table* in Exhibit A8-5. We quickly scan the table to find the point of intersection between the six percent interest rate column and the number of time periods row which is 1. The point of intersection, the present value factor, is 0.943. This factor indicates that the present value of one dollar discounted at six percent is $0.943, or about 94 cents. Thus, if $0.943 is invested today at six percent, it will be worth $1 one year from now.

But Aunt Hattie is going to give you $1,000, not $1. To determine the present value of $1,000, we simply multiply $1,000 by the factor of 0.943 to determine that $943 invested today at six percent will be worth $1,000 in one year, as shown by the time line presentation in Exhibit A8-6.

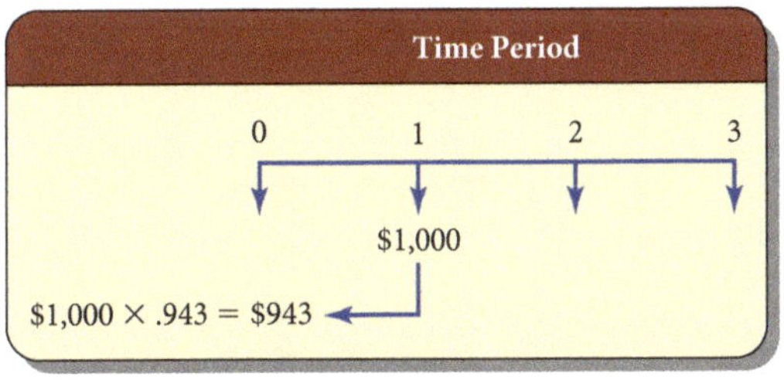

Exhibit A8-6 Time Line Presentation of Present Value of $1

Exhibit A8-6 shows that to have $1,000 a year from now, given an expected rate of interest of six percent per year, Aunt Hattie must deposit $943. So, the present value of $1,000 to be received one year from now at six percent is $943. The $943 will grow in value as it accumulates interest. This growth is the time value of money. You immediately inform your aunt Hattie that she must deposit $943 today at six percent to have the $1,000 gift ready for you one year from now.

Aunt Hattie is so happy with your quick response that she offers you an additional $1,000 gift. The second $1,000 gift, however, will be given two years from now, which means you will receive the first $1,000 gift at the end of year 1, and the second $1,000 gift at the end of year 2. You are thrilled, but again, your Aunt Hattie requests that you tell her exactly how much she must deposit today at six percent to have the additional $1,000 in two years. We use the *Present Value of $1 Table* in Exhibit A8-5 to find that the present value factor for a time period of two and an interest rate of six percent is 0.890. Accordingly, the present value of $1,000 to be received two years from now is $890 ($1,000 × 0.890). You quickly inform your aunt that she must deposit a total of $1,833 ($943 + $890) today to pay both the $1,000 at the end of year 1, and the $1,000 at the end of year 2. The time line and calculations are shown in Exhibit A8-7.

Exhibit A8-5 Present Value of $1 Table

Present Value of $1 Table

Period	3%	4%	5%	6%	7%	8%	9%	10%	11%	12%	13%	14%	15%	16%	17%	18%
1	0.971	0.962	0.952	0.943	0.935	0.926	0.917	0.909	0.901	0.893	0.885	0.877	0.870	0.862	0.855	0.847
2	0.943	0.925	0.907	0.890	0.873	0.857	0.842	0.826	0.812	0.797	0.783	0.769	0.756	0.743	0.731	0.718
3	0.915	0.889	0.864	0.840	0.816	0.794	0.772	0.751	0.731	0.712	0.693	0.675	0.658	0.641	0.624	0.609
4	0.888	0.855	0.823	0.792	0.763	0.735	0.708	0.683	0.659	0.636	0.613	0.592	0.572	0.552	0.534	0.516
5	0.863	0.822	0.784	0.747	0.713	0.681	0.650	0.621	0.593	0.567	0.543	0.519	0.497	0.476	0.456	0.437
6	0.837	0.790	0.746	0.705	0.666	0.630	0.596	0.564	0.535	0.507	0.480	0.456	0.432	0.410	0.390	0.370
7	0.813	0.760	0.711	0.665	0.623	0.583	0.547	0.513	0.482	0.452	0.425	0.400	0.376	0.354	0.333	0.314
8	0.789	0.731	0.677	0.627	0.582	0.540	0.502	0.467	0.434	0.404	0.376	0.351	0.327	0.305	0.285	0.266
9	0.766	0.703	0.645	0.592	0.544	0.500	0.460	0.424	0.391	0.361	0.333	0.308	0.284	0.263	0.243	0.225
10	0.744	0.676	0.614	0.558	0.508	0.463	0.422	0.386	0.352	0.322	0.295	0.270	0.247	0.227	0.208	0.191
11	0.722	0.650	0.585	0.527	0.475	0.429	0.388	0.350	0.317	0.287	0.261	0.237	0.215	0.195	0.178	0.162
12	0.701	0.625	0.557	0.497	0.444	0.397	0.356	0.319	0.286	0.257	0.231	0.208	0.187	0.168	0.152	0.137
13	0.681	0.601	0.530	0.469	0.415	0.368	0.326	0.290	0.258	0.229	0.204	0.182	0.163	0.145	0.130	0.116
14	0.661	0.577	0.505	0.442	0.388	0.340	0.299	0.263	0.232	0.205	0.181	0.160	0.141	0.125	0.111	0.099
15	0.642	0.555	0.481	0.417	0.362	0.315	0.275	0.239	0.209	0.183	0.160	0.140	0.123	0.108	0.095	0.084
16	0.623	0.534	0.458	0.394	0.339	0.292	0.252	0.218	0.188	0.163	0.141	0.123	0.107	0.093	0.081	0.071
17	0.605	0.513	0.436	0.371	0.317	0.270	0.231	0.198	0.170	0.146	0.125	0.108	0.093	0.080	0.069	0.060
18	0.587	0.494	0.416	0.350	0.296	0.250	0.212	0.180	0.153	0.130	0.111	0.095	0.081	0.069	0.059	0.051
19	0.570	0.475	0.396	0.331	0.277	0.232	0.194	0.164	0.138	0.116	0.098	0.083	0.070	0.060	0.051	0.043
20	0.554	0.456	0.377	0.312	0.258	0.215	0.178	0.149	0.124	0.104	0.087	0.073	0.061	0.051	0.043	0.037
21	0.538	0.439	0.359	0.294	0.242	0.199	0.164	0.135	0.112	0.093	0.077	0.064	0.053	0.044	0.037	0.031
22	0.522	0.422	0.342	0.278	0.226	0.184	0.150	0.123	0.101	0.083	0.068	0.056	0.046	0.038	0.032	0.026
23	0.507	0.406	0.326	0.262	0.211	0.170	0.138	0.112	0.091	0.074	0.060	0.049	0.040	0.033	0.027	0.022
24	0.492	0.390	0.310	0.247	0.197	0.158	0.126	0.102	0.082	0.066	0.053	0.043	0.035	0.028	0.023	0.019
25	0.478	0.375	0.295	0.233	0.184	0.146	0.116	0.092	0.074	0.059	0.047	0.038	0.030	0.024	0.020	0.016

Exhibit A8-10 Present Value of an Annuity of $1 Table

Present Value of an Annuity of $1 Table

Period	3%	4%	5%	6%	7%	8%	9%	10%	11%	12%	13%	14%	15%	16%	17%	18%
1	0.971	0.962	0.952	0.943	0.935	0.926	0.917	0.909	0.901	0.893	0.885	0.877	0.870	0.862	0.855	0.847
2	1.913	1.886	1.859	1.833	1.808	1.783	1.759	1.736	1.713	1.690	1.668	1.647	1.626	1.605	1.585	1.566
3	2.829	2.775	2.723	2.673	2.624	2.577	2.531	2.487	2.444	2.402	2.361	2.322	2.283	2.246	2.210	2.174
4	3.717	3.630	3.546	3.465	3.387	3.312	3.240	3.170	3.102	3.037	2.974	2.914	2.855	2.798	2.743	2.690
5	4.580	4.452	4.329	4.212	4.100	3.993	3.890	3.791	3.696	3.605	3.517	3.433	3.352	3.274	3.199	3.127
6	5.417	5.242	5.076	4.917	4.767	4.623	4.486	4.355	4.231	4.111	3.998	3.889	3.784	3.685	3.589	3.498
7	6.230	6.002	5.786	5.582	5.389	5.206	5.033	4.868	4.712	4.564	4.423	4.288	4.160	4.039	3.922	3.812
8	7.020	6.733	6.463	6.210	5.971	5.747	5.535	5.335	5.146	4.968	4.799	4.639	4.487	4.344	4.207	4.078
9	7.786	7.435	7.108	6.802	6.515	6.247	5.995	5.759	5.537	5.328	5.132	4.946	4.772	4.607	4.451	4.303
10	8.530	8.111	7.722	7.360	7.024	6.710	6.418	6.145	5.889	5.650	5.426	5.216	5.019	4.833	4.659	4.494
11	9.253	8.760	8.306	7.887	7.499	7.139	6.805	6.495	6.207	5.938	5.687	5.453	5.234	5.029	4.836	4.656
12	9.954	9.385	8.863	8.384	7.943	7.536	7.161	6.814	6.492	6.194	5.918	5.660	5.421	5.197	4.988	4.793
13	10.635	9.986	9.394	8.853	8.358	7.904	7.487	7.103	6.750	6.424	6.122	5.842	5.583	5.342	5.118	4.910
14	11.296	10.563	9.899	9.295	8.745	8.244	7.786	7.367	6.982	6.628	6.302	6.002	5.724	5.468	5.229	5.008
15	11.938	11.118	10.380	9.712	9.108	8.559	8.061	7.606	7.191	6.811	6.462	6.142	5.847	5.575	5.324	5.092
16	12.561	11.652	10.838	10.106	9.447	8.851	8.313	7.824	7.379	6.974	6.604	6.265	5.954	5.668	5.405	5.162
17	13.166	12.166	11.274	10.477	9.763	9.122	8.544	8.022	7.549	7.120	6.729	6.373	6.047	5.749	5.475	5.222
18	13.754	12.659	11.690	10.828	10.059	9.372	8.756	8.201	7.702	7.250	6.840	6.467	6.128	5.818	5.534	5.273
19	14.324	13.134	12.085	11.158	10.336	9.604	8.950	8.365	7.839	7.366	6.938	6.550	6.198	5.877	5.584	5.316
20	14.877	13.590	12.462	11.470	10.594	9.818	9.129	8.514	7.963	7.469	7.025	6.623	6.259	5.929	5.628	5.353
21	15.415	14.029	12.821	11.764	10.836	10.017	9.292	8.649	8.075	7.562	7.102	6.687	6.312	5.973	5.665	5.384
22	15.937	14.451	13.163	12.042	11.061	10.201	9.442	8.772	8.176	7.645	7.170	6.743	6.359	6.011	5.696	5.410
23	16.444	14.857	13.489	12.303	11.272	10.371	9.580	8.883	8.266	7.718	7.230	6.792	6.399	6.044	5.723	5.432
24	16.936	15.247	13.799	12.550	11.469	10.529	9.707	8.985	8.348	7.784	7.283	6.835	6.434	6.073	5.746	5.451
25	17.413	15.622	14.094	12.783	11.654	10.675	9.823	9.077	8.422	7.843	7.330	6.873	6.464	6.097	5.766	5.467

Exhibit A8-7 Time Line Presentation

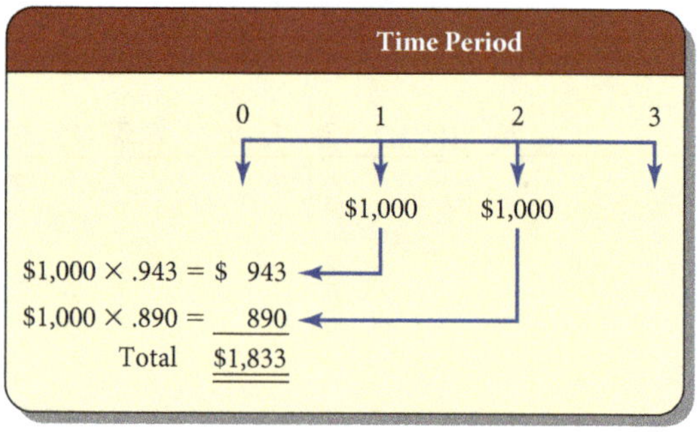

Now suppose your Aunt Hattie plans to give you a gift of $1,000 per year for the next three years. We could rely on the *Present Value of $1 Table* and add the totals for each year as shown in Exhibit A8-8.

Exhibit A8-8 Time Line Presentation

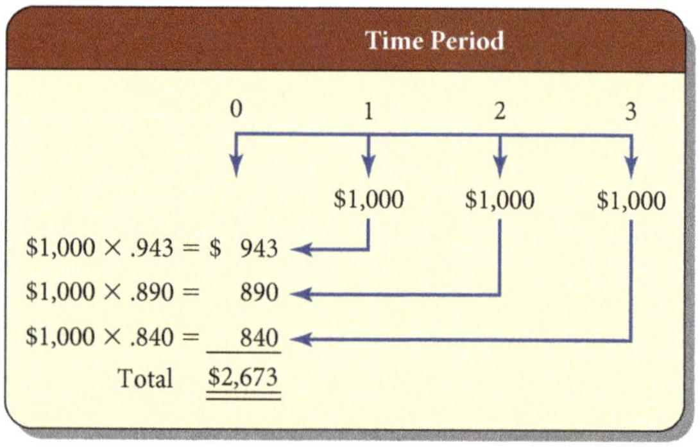

We can simplify the calculations, however, by multiplying the $1,000 by the sum of the three present value factors, which is 2.673. Accordingly, instead of multiplying $1,000 by 0.943, then $1,000 by 0.890, then $1,000 by 0.840, and summing the total, we simply multiply the $1,000 by the sum of the factors as shown in Exhibit A8-9.

Exhibit A8-9 Time Line Presentation

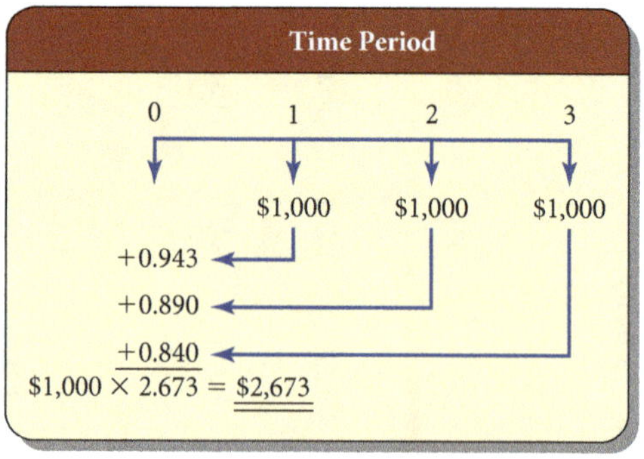

Present Value of an Annuity

Because the stream of cash flows in our example is an annuity—three equal payments made at regular intervals of one year—we can use the *Present Value of an Annuity of $1 Table*, presented as Exhibit A8-10.

By examining the table in Exhibit A8-10, we find that the present value factor of an annuity for three periods at six percent is 2.673. Notice that the 2.673 equals the sum of the individual present value of $1 factors for each of the three years in Exhibit A8-9. Next, we multiply the $1,000 by the 2.673 factor to find that the present value of Aunt Hattie's $1,000, three-year annuity paid yearly is $2,673.

As you use the future value and present value tables provided in this book, note that the number of interest rates and time periods is limited. Although these smaller tables are useful for learning the basics, in business practice future value and present value tables include a much larger number of interest rates and time periods. If needed, comprehensive tables are available at bookstores and office supply stores.

A working knowledge of present and future value concepts will be extremely important to you not only in your college course work but also in your professional career. Whether the task is evaluating potential capital projects, as in this chapter, or any of its many other applications, you will find these concepts invaluable throughout your life.

Most computers can also be used to solve present value and future value problems. Many software packages now include modules that can handle simple and advanced calculations dealing with the time value of money.

As an alternative to using a computer or future and present value tables, we can compute future value and present value using nothing more than a handheld financial calculator. It must be a financial or business calculator. Engineering and scientific calculators generally do not have present value and future value functions. In the business world, most managers rely on calculators and computers to calculate future and present values. Appendix B of this chapter describes how to use a financial calculator for present value and future value computations.

Appendix B: Using a Financial Calculator

Once you have mastered Appendix A and know about the time value of money and how financial tables work, you are ready to learn about the modern-day equivalent of the tables—the financial calculator. A **financial calculator** can provide all the information that financial tables provide and more.

financial calculator A calculator that can provide an array of information regarding the time value of money including future and present values.

Learning Objectives

After completing your work in this appendix, you should be able to do the following:

1. Use a financial calculator for future value calculations.
2. Use a financial calculator for present value calculations
3. Use a financial calculator for auto loan calculations.
4. Use a financial calculator for home mortgage calculations.

Recall that in Appendix A we calculated several amounts as we demonstrated the future value and present value tables. In this appendix, we will use the same information to re-calculate those same amounts, but this time we will use a financial calculator. In addition, we will demonstrate how to use the calculator for common situations such as auto financing and home mortgages. Once you understand how to use a financial calculator, calculating loan payments, present values, and future values will be quick and easy.

Calculator Differences

The way financial calculators work is quite simple. Generally, we know four of the variables and must use the calculator to solve for the one that's missing. Almost all financial calculators use the following five keys:

n	i	PV	PMT	FV

Where:

n—Is the number of periods.
i—Is the interest rate per period
PV—Is the present value.
PMT—Is the amount of the payments per period. It is the amount of the annuity.
FV—Is the future value. It is the cash flow that occurs at the end of the last period.

Although they all use the same financial keys (n, i, PV, PMT, and FV), not all financial calculators work exactly the same way. Consult your calculator's instruction manual to figure out just how your calculator works. Afterwards, it will be easy to do future value and present value calculations. Then, as you read this appendix, you can experiment with your calculator by entering each of our examples into it to make sure you get the same solution we do. Here are some of the calculator differences you may encounter:

Buttons vs. Display Many calculators have separate buttons on the face of the calculator for the financial function. On others, however, the financial function keys are shown on the display after the operator has accessed the calculator's present value menu.

Determining the Solution On many calculators you simply press the key corresponding to the amount you are trying to determine and the calculator provides the solution. But some calculators require that you press a *compute* key or *start* key and then the key corresponding to the amount you need to know.

Compounding Periods Another difference among calculators has to do with the interest rate and compounding. In business, interest is most often compounded monthly. Accordingly, some calculators are programmed so that the calculator automatically converts the interest rate you enter to monthly compounding. With these calculators, when you enter the interest rate the calculator automatically converts it to a monthly rate by dividing the rate by 12. This is fine if you are truly doing a problem with monthly compounding of interest, but for academic problems, compounding is often assumed to occur yearly so you must either re-program your calculator for yearly compounding or you can fool the calculator by multiplying the interest rate by 12 so that when the calculator divides it by 12 you end up with the correct rate.

Pluses and Minuses Some calculators are programmed so the cash inflows and cash outflows offset each other. But for many calculators, the operator must indicate whether the cash flow is an inflow or an outflow or an error message may appear. If you notice that error messages appear, try entering all cash inflows as positive amounts and all cash outflows as negative amounts. This may solve the problem. For our examples, we will use positive and negative amounts to show inflows and outflows respectively.

Timing of Cash Flows All financial calculators are able to do future value and present value calculation assuming the cash flow takes place at the end of the period or at the beginning of the period. For this appendix, we will assume that cash flows take place at the end of each period. In the case of annuities, if the cash flow takes place at the end of each period it is sometimes called an *ordinary annuity,* and if the cash flow takes place at the beginning of each period it is often called an *annuity due.* For the calculations in this appendix, you should be sure your calculator is set to assume that cash flows take place at the end of the period. This is the default setting for most financial calculators.

In the following sections, we will re-calculate each of the examples we presented in Appendix A. We will indicate the amounts we enter into our financial calculator followed by the solution.

Future Value of a Single Sum

As we did in Appendix A, let's assume that Dick Gustufson invests $2,000 today at 10 percent interest compounded annually, and would like to know how much his investment will be worth in 20 years. Keep in mind that the when Dick invests, he has a $2,000 outflow because he is taking the cash and putting it into the investment. Therefore we will enter a negative amount in our calculator for this $2,000 outflow. We would enter the information in our financial calculator and solve as follows:

Input:	20	10	−2,000	0	?
	n	i	PV	PMT	FV
Answer:					13,455

In this case, we entered 20 for n, 10 for i, −2,000 for the PV, and zero for PMT. We then press the FV key to determine that the future value of Dick's investment is $13,455. This amount is $1 more than the amount we obtained when we used the future value tables in Appendix A because the calculator rounds to 12 decimal places and our tables round to only three. What this means is that the answer we get from the calculator is more precise than the one from the tables.

What if Dick wanted to determine how much less he would earn if he could only find a 9 percent investment? The information is already in our calculator, but we need to change the interest rate from 10 percent to 9 percent. All we need to do is enter 9 for i and then press the FV key again to calculate the new future value. When an element of the calculation changes, you only need to re-enter that element. If the other amounts stay the same, we need not re-enter them.

Already in Calculator	20	10	−2,000	0	13,455
New Input:		9			?
	n	i	PV	PMT	FV
Answer:					11,209

So if Dick can only find a 9 percent investment compounded annually, his $2,000 investment will be worth $11,209 at the end of 20 years.

Future Value of an Annuity

As we did in Appendix A, let's say Susan King intends to deposit $2,000 in an account at the end of each year for four years at a compound interest rate of 12 percent per year. We would enter the information in our financial calculator and solve as follows:

Input:	4	12	0	−2,000	?
	n	**i**	**PV**	**PMT**	**FV**
Answer:					9,559

In this case, we entered 4 for n, 12 for i, zero for the PV, and −2,000 for PMT. We then press the FV key to determine that the future value of Susan's investment is $9,559. As it happens, this is the same amount we obtained when we used the future value tables in Appendix A. Bear in mind, however, because financial calculators round to 12 decimal places and financial tables usually do not, differences between the results of the two methods are likely to occur.

Present Value of a Single Sum

To demonstrate how to determine present value of a single sum, let's revisit the Aunt Hattie example in Appendix A. Remember that your aunt was touched by your kindness, so she offered to give you a gift of $1,000. Her only request is that you tell her how much to deposit in a six percent savings account today so that the account will equal $1,000 one year from now. We would enter the information in our financial calculator and solve as follows:

Input:	1	6	?	0	1,000
	n	**i**	**PV**	**PMT**	**FV**
Answer:			−943		

In this case, we entered 1 for n, 6 for i, 0 for PMT, and 1,000 for FV. We then press the PV key to determine that the present value, or the amount Aunt Hattie should deposit, is $943.

Now assume your Aunt Hattie is so happy with your quick response that she offers you an additional $1,000 gift. The second $1,000 gift, however, will be given two years from now, which means you will receive the first $1,000 gift at the end of year 1, and the second $1,000 gift at the end of year 2. As we enter the amounts in our calculator for the second $1,000 payment we should keep in mind that most of the amounts stay the same. Only the number of years changes. Accordingly, we would enter the information in our financial calculator and solve as follows:

Already in Calculator:	1	6	−943	0	1,000
New Input:	2		?		
	n	**i**	**PV**	**PMT**	**FV**
Answer:			−890		

So your aunt must deposit a total of $1,833 ($943 + $890) today to pay both the $1,000 at the end of year 1, and the $1,000 at the end of year 2.

Now suppose your Aunt Hattie planned to give you a gift of $1,000 per year for the next three years. We would enter the information in our financial calculator and solve as follows:

	n	i	PV	PMT	FV
Already in Calculator:	2	6	−890	0	1,000
New Input:	3		?		
Answer:			−840		

So your aunt must deposit a total of $2,673 ($943 + $890 + $840) today to pay $1,000 at the end of each of the next three years.

Present Value of an Annuity

Because the stream of cash flows in our example is an annuity—three equal payments made at regular intervals of one year—we can find the present value of the stream of $1,000 payments using the PMT key instead of calculating the present value of each individual cash flow. We would enter the information in our financial calculator and solve as follows:

	n	i	PV	PMT	FV
Input:	3	6	?	$1,000	0
Answer:			−2,673		

So again we determine that your aunt must deposit a total of $2,673 today to pay $1,000 at the end of each of the next three years.

Common Uses of a Financial Calculator

Having a financial calculator and knowing the basics of how to use it provides you with a valuable business decision tool. The information a financial calculator offers can help you make adjustments in financing and investment situations so they best fit your needs and abilities. We have already discussed how to determine the future value and present value of investments. In the following sections we will use a financial calculator to provide valuable information for auto loans and home mortgages.

Auto Loans

Let's say you're buying a new car. You have $6,000 as a down payment and the total price of the car you have selected is $24,000. Accordingly, you intend to finance $18,000 ($24,000 − $6,000). The bank offers to make the loan at 7 percent. You have looked over your finances and feel you could pay $300 a month and would like the term of the auto loan to be four years, or 48 monthly payments. Unlike the academic problems we have been working so far, interest is compounded monthly for an auto loan, not annually. The bank's interest rate is an annual rate, not a monthly one. For some financial calculators, we must divide the 7 percent annual rate by 12 to determine the monthly rate of interest that we will enter for the i key. We would enter the information in our financial calculator and solve as follows:

	n	i	PV	PMT	FV
Input:	48	7/12= .583333	18,000	?	0
Answer:				−431	

So we enter 48 for n, .583333 for i, 18,000 for PV and 0 for FV. Then we press the PMT key and the calculator determines that the payment will be $431. But wait. Although the loan term is 48 months, the monthly payment is more than your $300 limit. Let's assume that you decide that a longer-term loan would be easier to manage than a higher monthly payment. If you want to know how much the payments would be for a 60 month loan instead of a 48 month loan, just enter 60 for n and then press the PMT key again to calculate the new monthly payment amount. When only the length of the loan changes, the interest rate (i) and the amount of the loan (PV) stay the same, so we need not re-enter them. Accordingly, we would enter the information in our financial calculator and solve as follows:

	n	i	PV	PMT	FV
Already in Calculator	48	7/12= .583333	18,000	−431	0
New Input:	60			?	
Answer:				−356	

The monthly loan payment for a 60 month loan is $356. If the maximum you can pay per month is $300, how much can you borrow for 60 months? Well, to find out we enter an acceptable payment amount, the $300, and press PV to determine the amount we can borrow. All the other amounts in the calculator are fine and do not need to be changed. We would enter the information in our financial calculator and solve as follows:

	n	i	PV	PMT	FV
Already in Calculator	60	7/12= .583333	18000	−356	0
New Input:			?	−300	
Answer:			15,151		

So for a 60 month loan at 7 percent interest with a monthly payment of $300, you can borrow $15,151. What this means is that, with your $6,000 down payment, you'd better look for a car that costs about $21,151 or less.

Home Mortgages

The calculations for a home mortgage are exactly the same as they are for an auto loan. The only difference is that the loan amounts and terms are usually much longer for home mortgages.

Assume that you are thinking about buying a home and have $10,000 available as a down payment. Assume further that you have found a house that you can buy for $150,000 and have been pre-approved for a 6.5 percent, 30 year mortgage loan. Accordingly, you intend to finance $140,000 ($150,000 − $10,000). As was the case in the auto loan example, interest is compounded monthly for home mortgages. The bank's 6.5 percent interest rate is an annual rate, not a monthly one. For some financial calculators, we must divide the 6.5 percent annual rate by 12 to determine the monthly rate of interest that we will enter for the i key. We would enter the information in our financial calculator and solve as follows:

	30 × 12	6.5/12=			
Input:	360	.541667	140,000	?	0
	n	**i**	**PV**	**PMT**	**FV**
Answer:				−885	

So we enter 360 for n, .541667 for i, 140,000 for PV and 0 for FV. Then we press the PMT key and the calculator determines that the payment will be $885. Keep in mind that the $885 only pays the interest and principal on the loan. You will also have to pay homeowner's insurance and property taxes on the property, which could add significantly to the monthly payment. For our purposes, we will focus on the $885 principal and interest.

Assume that you feel the payment amount is affordable, but the term of the loan seems way too long. What if the term of the loan were cut in half? Instead of a 30 year loan, the term would be only 15 years. Will the payments nearly double if you have to pay the loan off in half the time? No, the monthly payment will increase substantially, but the new payment will be far less than double. We would enter the change in our financial calculator and solve as follows:

Already in	30 × 12	6.5/12=			
Calculator:	360	.541667	140,000	−885	0
New Input:	15 × 12				
	180			?	
	n	**i**	**PV**	**PMT**	**FV**
Answer:				−1,220	

Assume that the $1,220 payment is acceptable and you inform the bank that you would like a 15 year loan. The interest rate for a 15 year loan will probably be less than that for a 30 year loan. Assume the bank reduces the rate to 6.25% due to the shorter loan term. We would enter the change in our financial calculator and solve as follows:

Already in	15 × 12	6.5/12 =			
Calculator:	180	.541667	140,000	−1,220	0
New Input:		6.25/12			
		.520833			
	n	**i**	**PV**	**PMT**	**FV**
Answer:				−1,200	

By reducing the interest rate from 6.5 percent to 6.25 percent, your monthly payment would go down by $20 per month.

Whether you are evaluating potential capital projects or a home mortgage, a financial calculator can quickly and easily provide you with a wealth of valuable information. A financial calculator is truly worth every penny it costs and learning how to use one is time very well spent.

Key Terms

- **accounting rate of return** 305
- **annuity** 312
- **balanced scorecard** 285
- **blended cost of capital** 290
- **capital assets** 287
- **capital budget** 286
- **capital budgeting** 282
- **capital investments** 281
- **capital projects** 282
- **compound interest** 309
- **core values** 284
- **cost of capital** 289
- **cost of capital rate** 289
- **cost of debt capital** 290
- **cost of equity capital** 290
- **discounting cash flows** 295
- **financial calculator** 317
- **future value** 308
- **hurdle rate** 289
- **internal rate of return (IRR)** 301
- **mission statement** 283
- **net cash flow** 294
- **net present value (NPV)** 296
- **operating budget** 286
- **organizational goals** 283
- **payback period** 304
- **present value** 312
- **profitability index** 301
- **real rate of return** 301
- **relevant net cash flows** 294
- **required rate of return** 289
- **scarce resources** 293
- **simple interest** 308
- **strategic plan** 286
- **strategy** 285
- **time value of money** 295
- **time-adjusted rate of return** 301
- **vision** 284
- **weighted average cost of capital** 290

Review the Facts

A. What constitutes a firm's goals?

B. What is a mission statement and how does it relate to a company's goals?

C. Describe core values, vision and strategy.

D. List the perspectives of the balanced scorecard.

E. What is a strategic plan and how does it relate to a company's goals?

F. What is the purpose of a capital budget and how does it relate to the strategic plan and a company's goals?

G. What is the purpose of an operating budget and how does it relate to the capital budget, the strategic plan, and a company's goals?

H. What are capital investments?

I. What is the difference between a capital investment and a capital project?

J. What is the focus of the capital budget?

K. What does it mean when the cost of a purchased item is capitalized?

L. What does it mean when the cost of a purchased item is expensed?

M. What are the four shared characteristics of virtually all capital projects?

N. What are some other terms used to describe the cost of capital?

O. Describe what is meant by the net present value of an investment.

P. With respect to net present value calculations, what is the advantage of calculating the profitability index?

Q. What is determined by the internal rate of return?

R. What is determined by the payback method?

S. What is the accounting rate of return?

T. What are two factors that can lead to poor capital project selection?

U. What is the basic difference between simple interest and compound interest? (Appendix A)

V. What is an annuity? (Appendix A)

Apply What You Have Learned

LO 1: Match Elements of Planning to Characteristics

8-15. Following are the elements of the planning process as discussed in this chapter, with some characteristics pertaining to those elements.

a. Goals b. Strategic plan c. Capital budget d. Operating budget

1. _____ Pertains to day-to-day activities
2. _____ Pertains to the long term investment of scarce resources
3. _____ Consists of both financial and nonfinancial considerations
4. _____ Stated in terms that are not easily quantified
5. _____ Stated in terms that are easily quantified
6. _____ Constitutes the who of business planning
7. _____ Constitutes the why of business planning
8. _____ Constitutes the how of business planning
9. _____ Constitutes the what of business planning
10. _____ Relates to long-lived, expensive assets

Required:

Match each element of the planning process with the appropriate characteristics. Each letter may be used more than once.

LO 4: Discuss and Calculate the Cost of Capital

8-16. The Marcus Company is in the process of determining a return rate to use for its cost of capital. Upon review of the financial statements it was determined that the total interest bearing debt is $1,400,000 and total stockholders equity is $1,000,000. In addition, it was determined that the cost of debt financing is 8%, and the cost of equity financing is 18%.

Required:

a. What proportion of the Marcus Company's total financing comes from debt?

b. What proportion of the Marcus Company's total financing comes from equity?

c. Calculate the Marcus Company's weighted average cost of capital.

LO 4: Discuss and Calculate the Cost of Capital

8-17. The Byrne Company is in the process of determining a return rate to use for its cost of capital. Upon review of the financial statements it was determined that the total interest bearing debt is $4,800,000 and total stockholders' equity is $14,400,000. In addition, it was determined that the cost of debt financing is 7%, and the cost of equity financing is 22%.

Required:

a. What proportion of The Byrne Company's total financing comes from debt?

b. What proportion of The Byrne Company's total financing comes from equity?

c. Calculate The Byrne Company's weighted average cost of capital.

LO 4: Discuss and Calculate the Cost of Capital

8-18. The Cunningham Company is in the process of determining a return rate to use for its cost of capital.

Upon review of the financial statements it was determined that the total interest bearing debt is $800,000 and total stockholders' equity is $1,700,000. In addition, it was determined that the cost of debt financing is 9%, and the cost of equity financing is 20%.

Required:

a. What proportion of The Cunningham Company's total financing comes from debt?

b. What proportion of The Cunningham Company's total financing comes from equity?

c. Calculate The Cunningham Company's weighted average cost of capital.

LO 2: Determine the Sequence of Evaluating Capital Expenditures

8-19. Following in random order are the five steps for evaluating a capital expenditure.

a. _____ Identify alternative capital projects.

b. _____ Identify the need for a capital expenditure.

c. _____ Select a method for evaluating the alternatives.

d. _____ Evaluate the alternatives and select the project or projects to be funded.

e. _____ Determine relevant cash inflow and cash outflow information.

Required:

In the space provided, indicate a logical sequence of the steps for evaluating a capital expenditure.

LO 6 & 7: Determine Net Present Value, No Residual Value

8-20. Florence Kundrat owns Discount Fashions. She is contemplating the purchase of a soda machine which would be used to sell soft drinks to customers for $0.75 each. The following estimates are available:

Initial outlay	$3,500
Annual cash inflow	$1,000
Cost of capital	10%
Estimated useful life of the soda machine	5 years
Estimated residual value of the soda machine	$ 0

Required:

Determine the net present value of the soda machine purchase.

LO 6 & 7: Determine Net Present Value, No Residual Value

8-21. Brianna Garcia is contemplating the purchase of an ice cream vending machine which would be used to sell ice cream to customers for $2 each. The following estimates are available.

Initial outlay	$4,000
Annual cash inflow	$1,200
Cost of capital	12%
Estimated useful life of the ice cream machine	5 years
Estimated residual value of the ice cream machine	$ 0

Required:

Determine the net present value of the ice cream machine purchase.

LO 6 & 7: Determine Net Present Value, No Residual Value

8-22. Javier Cruz is contemplating the purchase of a machine which will automate the production of baseball bats in his factory. The following estimates are available.

Initial outlay	$97,000
Annual reduction in manufacturing labor cost	$22,500
Cost of capital	14%
Estimated useful life of the baseball bat machine	8 years
Estimated residual value of the bat machine	$ 0

Required:

Determine the net present value of the baseball bat machine purchase.

LO 6 & 7: Determine Net Present Value, No Residual Value

8-23. Dahlia Garcia is contemplating the purchase of a machine which will automate the production of hosiery in her factory. The following estimates are available.

Initial outlay	$112,000
Annual reduction in manufacturing labor cost	$ 22,500
Cost of capital	12%
Estimated useful life of the hosiery machine	8 years
Estimated residual value of the hosiery machine	$ 0

Required:

Determine the net present value of the hosiery machine purchase.

LO 6 & 7: Determine Net Present Value and Profitability Index, Various Rates, No Residual Value

8-24. Michael Diaz Sporting Goods is considering the purchase of a machine that is used to cut material to make baseball gloves. The cost of the machine is $265,000. The machine has an estimated useful life of eight years, with no residual value. Currently, the company leases a similar machine for $50,000 per year. If the new machine is purchased, the company's cost of labor would be reduced by $12,000 per year.

Required:

a. Determine the net present value of the machine under each of the following assumptions.
   1. The cost of capital is 12%
   2. The cost of capital is 14%
   3. The cost of capital is 16%
b. Determine the profitability index under each of the following assumptions.
   1. The cost of capital is 12%
   2. The cost of capital is 14%
   3. The cost of capital is 16%

LO 6 & 7: Determine Net Present Value and Profitability Index, Various Rates, No Residual Value

8-25. Carlos Urriola Manufacturing is considering the purchase of a computer controlled manufacturing machine that is used in its factory. The cost of the machine is $3,600,000. The machine has an estimated useful life of 10 years, with no residual value. If the new machine is purchased, the company's cost of labor would be reduced by $650,000 per year.

Required:

a. Determine the net present value of the machine under each of the following assumptions.
   1. The cost of capital is 10%
   2. The cost of capital is 12%
   3. The cost of capital is 14%
b. Determine the profitability index under each of the following assumptions.
   1. The cost of capital is 10%
   2. The cost of capital is 12%
   3. The cost of capital is 14%

LO 6 & 7: Determine Net Present Value, No Residual Value

8-26. Frank Eiroa is considering the purchase of an engine lift for use in his marine repair business. He has determined that a used lift is available for $5,500. The engine lift has an estimated useful life of eight years and a residual value of zero. Currently, Frank rents engine lifts as needed. If the lift is purchased, annual rental payment of $1,400 would be saved. The cost of capital is 16%.

Required:

Calculate the net present value of the engine lift purchase.

LO 6 & 7: Determine Net Present Value, No Residual Value

8-27. Alfredo Lomando is considering the purchase of an industrial glass cutting machine for use in his business. He has determined that a used glass cutter is available for

$25,800. The cutter has an estimated useful life of 10 years and a residual value of zero. Currently, Alfredo rents an industrial cutter for $4,400 annually. The cost of capital is 14%.

Required:

Calculate the net present value of the industrial glass cutter.

LO 6 & 7: Determine Net Present Value, with Residual Value

8-28. The owner of Wynn Sports Cards is contemplating the purchase of a machine which will automate the production of baseball cards in her factory. The following estimates are available.

Initial outlay	$35,000
Annual reduction in manufacturing labor cost	$ 8,500
Cost of capital	14%
Estimated useful life of the card machine	5 years
Estimated residual value of the card machine	$ 2,000

Required:

Determine the net present value of the baseball card machine purchase.

LO 6 & 7: Determine Net Present Value, with Residual Value

8-29. Kevin Petty owns Discount Parts, Inc. He is contemplating the purchase of a brake lathe that could be used to refurbish brake parts for customers. The following estimates are available.

Initial outlay	$6,500
Annual cash inflow	$1,500
Cost of capital	16%
Estimated useful life of the brake lathe	6 years
Estimated residual value of the brake lathe	$1,000

Required:

Determine the net present value of the brake lathe purchase.

LO 6 & 7: Determine Net Present Value, with Residual Value

8-30. Paola Grillon owns Grillon Skin Care Products. She is contemplating the purchase of an industrial mixer that would be used to mix cosmetics in her factory. The following estimates are available.

Initial outlay	$78,500
Annual cash inflow	$19,500
Cost of capital	16%
Estimated useful life of the mixer	7 years
Estimated residual value of the mixer	$ 4,000

Required:

Determine the net present value of the industrial mixer purchase.

LO 6 & 7: Determine Net Present Value, with Residual Value

8-31. Elianne Vinas owns Vinas Shoe Company. She is contemplating the purchase of a cutting machine that would be used to make shoes in her factory. The following estimates are available.

Initial outlay	$58,000
Annual cash inflow from reduced labor cost	$11,500
Cost of capital	12%
Estimated useful life of the cutter	8 years
Estimated residual value of the cutter	$ 2,000

Required:

Determine the net present value of the cutting machine purchase.

LO 6 & 7: Determine Net Present Value and Profitability Index, Various Rates, with Residual Value

8-32. George Gonzalez Construction Company is considering the purchase of a new road grader. The cost of the road grader is $68,000. The road grader has an estimated useful life of seven years and an estimated residual value of $5,000. Currently, the company rents road graders as needed. If the road grader is purchased, annual rental payments of $17,000 would be saved.

Required:

a. Determine the net present value of the grader purchase under each of the following assumptions.

1. The cost of capital is 12%
2. The cost of capital is 14%
3. The cost of capital is 16%

b. Determine the profitability index under each of the following assumptions.

1. The cost of capital is 12%
2. The cost of capital is 14%
3. The cost of capital is 16%

LO 6 & 7: Determine Net Present Value and Profitability Index, Various Rates, with Residual Value

8-33. Wesley Parks Pencil Company is considering the purchase of a new machine to make pencils. The cost of the machine is $248,000. The pencil machine has an estimated useful life of 10 years and an estimated residual value of $25,000. Currently, the company leases a similar machine for $45,000 per year.

Required:

a. Determine the net present value of the pencil machine purchase under each of the following assumptions.

1. The cost of capital is 10%
2. The cost of capital is 12%
3. The cost of capital is 14%

b. Determine the profitability index under each of the following assumptions.

   1. The cost of capital is 10%

   2. The cost of capital is 12%

   3. The cost of capital is 14%

LO 6 & 7: Determine Net Present Value and Profitability Index, Various Rates, with Residual Value

8-34. Sylvia Heain's Catering Service is considering the purchase of new energy-efficient cooking equipment. The cost of the new equipment is $78,000. The equipment has an estimated useful life of eight years and an estimated residual value of $5,000. Currently, the company leases similar cooking equipment for $10,000 per year. If the new cooking equipment is purchased, the company's cost of electricity would be reduced by $8,000 per year.

Required:

a. Determine the net present value of the cooking equipment under each of the following assumptions.

   1. The cost of capital is 12%

   2. The cost of capital is 14%

   3. The cost of capital is 16%

b. Determine the profitability index under each of the following assumptions.

   1. The cost of capital is 12%

   2. The cost of capital is 14%

   3. The cost of capital is 16%

LO 6 & 7: Determine Internal Rate of Return, Various Rates, No Residual Value

8-35. Penny Williams is contemplating the purchase of a new computer system for her company, Williams Manufacturing. She has made the following estimates.

Initial outlay	$18,023.88
Annual cash savings	$ 5,000.00
Estimated useful life of the computer	5 years
Estimated residual value of the computer	$ 0

Required:

a. Determine the internal rate of return for the computer purchase.

b. Indicate whether the computer purchase should be accepted under each of the following assumptions.

   1. The cost of capital is 9%

   2. The cost of capital is 11%

   3. The cost of capital is 13%

   4. The cost of capital is 15%

LO 6 & 7: Determine Internal Rate of Return, Various Rates, No Residual Value

8-36. Valdez Moving and Storage is contemplating the purchase of a new delivery truck. The following estimates are available.

Initial outlay	$ 51,590
Annual cash flow from the new truck	$14,000
Estimated life of the truck	6 years
Estimated residual value of the truck	$ 0

Required:

a. Determine the internal rate of return for the truck purchase.

b. Indicate whether the truck purchase should be accepted under each of the following assumptions.

1. The cost of capital is 14%
2. The cost of capital is 16%
3. The cost of capital is 18%

LO 6 & 7: Determine Internal Rate of Return for Three Projects, Select Project, No Residual Value

8-37. Hank Maupin & Company is in the process of replacing its existing computer system. The following three proposals are being considered.

	System A	System B	System C
Initial outlay	$18,023.88	$22,744.72	$24,031.57
Annual cash savings	$ 5,000.00	$ 6,000.00	$ 7,000.00
Estimated useful life	5 years	5 years	5 years

The estimated residual value of all computer systems under consideration is zero.

Required:

a. Determine the internal rate of return for each of the proposed computer systems.

b. Which computer system would you recommend? Explain your reasoning.

LO 6 & 7: Determine Internal Rate of Return for Three Projects, Select Project, No Residual Value

8-38. David Wilson Equipment Company is in the process of selecting some new manufacturing equipment. The following three proposals are being considered.

	Equipment A	Equipment B	Equipment C
Initial outlay	$14,902.92	$18,555.46	$26,674.63
Annual cash savings	$ 3,000.00	$ 4,000.00	$ 5,000.00
Estimated useful life	8 years	8 years	8 years

The estimated residual value of all equipment under consideration is zero.

Required:

a. Determine the internal rate of return for each of the proposed pieces of equipment.

b. Which piece of equipment would you recommend? Explain your reasoning.

LO 6 & 7: Determine Net Present Value, Profitability Index, and Internal Rate of Return, Various Rates, No Residual Value

8-39. Dunn Manufacturing Company is considering the purchase of a factory that makes valves. These valves would be used by Dunn to manufacture water pumps. The purchase would require an initial outlay of $1,564,800. The factory would have an estimated useful life of 10 years and no residual value. Currently, the company buys 500,000 valves per year at a cost of $1.50 each. If the factory were purchased, the valves could be manufactured for $0.90 each.

Required:

a. Determine the net present value of the proposed project and whether it should be accepted under each of the following assumptions.

   1. The cost of capital is 12%
   2. The cost of capital is 14%
   3. The cost of capital is 16%

b. Determine the profitability index under each of the following assumptions.

   1. The cost of capital is 12%
   2. The cost of capital is 14%
   3. The cost of capital is 16%

c. Determine the internal rate of return of the proposed project and indicate whether it should be accepted under each of the following assumptions.

   1. The cost of capital is 12%
   2. The cost of capital is 14%
   3. The cost of capital is 16%

LO 6: Determine Payback Period, Even Cash Flows

8-40. Tom Robinson owns Discount Hardware. He is contemplating the purchase of a copy machine which would be used to make copies to sell to customers for five cents each. The following estimates are available.

Initial outlay	$4,500
Annual cash inflow	$1,800

Required:

Determine the payback period for the copy machine purchase.

LO 6: Determine Payback Period, Even Cash Flows

8-41. Rebecca Pons owns Pons Magic Makers Manufacturing. She is contemplating the purchase of a machine that would be used to manufacture various products that would be sold to magic shops. The following estimates are available.

Initial outlay	$23,539.20
Annual cash inflow	$ 7,356.00

Required:

Determine the payback period for the machine purchase.

LO 6: Determine Payback Period, Even Cash Flows

8-42. Claudia Vargas is contemplating the purchase of a machine that would be used in her business. The following estimates are available.

Initial outlay	$5,826.50
Annual cash inflow	$1,355.00

Required:

Determine the payback period for the machine purchase.

LO 6: Determine Payback Period, Even Cash Flows

8-43. Cesar Nieto is contemplating the purchase of a machine that would be used in his business. The following estimates are available.

Initial outlay	$323,400.00
Annual cash inflow	$ 33,000.00

Required:

Determine the payback period for the machine purchase.

LO 6: Determine Payback Period, Uneven Cash Flows

8-44. Junior Gonzales Racing Fuel is considering the purchase of a fuel truck that he would use to sell gasoline at motor sport racing events in Puerto Rico. He has determined that a used truck is available for $11,000. He believes that the cash inflows would grow each year as he is able to sign fuel supply contracts at more and more events. He has made the following cash inflow estimates.

First year	$3,000
Second year	$4,500
Third and subsequent years	$5,000

Required:

Determine the payback period for the purchase of the fuel truck.

LO 6: Determine Payback Period, Uneven Cash Flows

8-45. Veronica Torres is considering opening a ceramic studio. She has determined that it would require an investment of $14,000 to open the store. She believes that the cash inflows would grow each year as more and more people learn of the store. She has made the following cash inflow estimates.

First year	$2,000
Second year	$4,000
Third and subsequent years	$5,000

Required:

Determine the payback period for the ceramic studio.

LO 6: Determine Payback Period, Uneven Cash Flows

8-46. Karen Calloway is considering adding a new style of gym shorts to her product line. She has determined that it would require an investment of $22,000 to add the new style shorts. She believes that the cash inflows would grow each year as the new style becomes more popular. She has made the following cash inflow estimates.

First year	$ 4,000
Second year	$ 6,000
Third and subsequent years	$10,000

Required:

Determine the payback period for the new style of gym shorts.

LO 6: Determine Accounting Rate of Return

8-47. BRV Construction Company is contemplating the purchase of scaffolding at the cost of $32,000. Currently, the company rents similar scaffolding for use at each of its construction sites. The scaffolding has an estimated useful life of five years and an estimated residual value of $2,000. By purchasing the scaffolding, BRV could save rental fees of $11,760 per year.

Required:

Determine the accounting rate of return for BRV's investment in the scaffolding.

LO 6: Determine Accounting Rate of Return

8-48. Smith and Smith & Associates is contemplating the purchase of equipment that would cost $196,600. Currently, the company rents similar equipment for $45,076 per year. The proposed new equipment has an estimated useful life of eight years and an estimated residual value of $9,000.

Required:

Determine the accounting rate of return for the Smith and Smith & Associates investment in the new equipment.

LO 6: Determine Accounting Rate of Return

8-49. Condore & Company is contemplating the purchase of a machine that would cost $142,790. The machine would provide an annual contribution margin of $47,262.55 each year. The proposed new machine has an estimated useful life of five years and an estimated residual value of $10,000.

Required:

Determine the accounting rate of return for Condore & Company's investment in the new machine.

LO 5, 6, & 7: Determine Relevant Information, Net Present Value, Screen Project, with Residual Value

8-50. Frank's Marine Service purchased a forklift five years ago for $16,000. When it was purchased, the forklift had an estimated useful life of 10 years and a residual value of $4,000. The forklift can be sold now for $6,000. The operating cost for the forklift is $4,500 per year.

Frank is thinking about buying a newer forklift for $17,000. The newer forklift would have an estimated useful life of five years and a residual value of $7,000. The operating cost for the newer forklift would be $3,000 per year.

The company's cost of capital is 10%.

Required:

a. Prepare a relevant cost schedule showing the benefits of buying the new forklift. (For this requirement, ignore the time value of money.)

b. How much must the company invest today to replace the old forklift?

c. If the company replaces the old forklift, what is the increase in the company's annual contribution margin?

d. If the company sells the old forklift now to make room for the new one, it will not receive the $4,000 residual value at the end of its useful life. Instead, the company will receive the $7,000 residual value from the new forklift. With this in mind, if the company buys the forklift, what is the change in the residual value the company is to receive at the end of the five-year life of the equipment?

e. Calculate the net present value of replacing the old forklift.

f. Do you think the company should replace the old forklift?

LO 5, 6, & 7: Determine Relevant Information, Net Present Value, Screen Project, with Residual Value

8-51. Al Hart of Hart Engineering is considering the purchase of a new copy machine. He purchased the old machine two years ago for $8,500. When it was purchased the old machine had an estimated useful life of eight years and a residual value of $500. The operating cost of the old machine is $3,000 per year. The old machine can be sold today for $2,000. A new machine can be bought today for $10,000 and would have an estimated useful life of six years with a residual value of $1,000. The operating cost of the new copy machine is expected to be $1,500 per year. The company's cost of capital is 8%.

Required:

a. Prepare a relevant cost schedule showing the benefit of buying the new copy machine. (For this requirement, ignore the time value of money.)

b. How much must the company invest today to replace the old copy machine?

c. If the company replaces the old copy machine, what is the increase in the company's annual contribution margin?

d. If the company sells the old copy machine now to make room for the new one, it will not receive the $500 residual value at the end of its useful life. Instead, the company will receive the $1,000 residual value from the new copy machine. With this in mind, if the company buys the copy machine, what is the change in the residual value the company is to receive at the end of the six-year life of the equipment?

e. Calculate the net present value of replacing the old copy machine.

f. Do you think the company should replace the old copy machine?

LO 5, 6, & 7: Determine Relevant Information, Net Present Value, Screen Project, No Residual Value

8-52. The managers at AAA Manufacturing Company are considering replacing an industrial mixer used in the company's factory. The company's cost of capital is 10%.

Information about the old mixer:	
Cost	$28,000
Estimated useful life	10 years
Estimated residual value	$ 0
Current age	5 years
Estimated current fair value	$ 8,000
Annual operating cost	$18,000
Information about the new mixer:	
Cost	$34,000
Estimated useful life	5 years
Estimated residual value	$ 0
Annual operating cost	$12,000

Required:

a. Prepare a relevant cost schedule showing the benefit of buying the new mixer.

b. How much must the company invest today to replace the industrial mixer?

c. If the new mixer is purchased, how much would be saved in operating costs each year?

d. How much would the company receive at the end of the five-year useful life of the new mixer?

e. Calculate the net present value of replacing the old mixer.

f. Do you think the company should replace the old mixer?

LO 5, 6, & 7: Determine Relevant Information, Net Present Value, Screen Project, No Residual Value

8-53. The managers at General Manufacturing Company are considering replacing the industrial lathe used in the company's factory. The company's cost of capital is 12%.

Information about the old lathe:	
Cost	$57,000
Estimated useful life	8 years
Estimated residual value	$ 0
Current age	2 years
Estimated current fair value	$32,000
Annual operating cost	$32,000
Information about the new lathe:	
Cost	$61,000
Estimated useful life	6 years
Estimated residual value	$ 0
Annual operating cost	$24,000

Required:

a. Prepare a relevant cost schedule showing the benefit of buying the new lathe. (For this requirement, ignore the time value of money.)

b. How much must the company invest today to replace the old lathe?

c. If the company replaces the old lathe, how much will be saved in operating costs each year?

d. Calculate the net present value of replacing the old lathe.

e. Do you think the company should replace the old lathe?

LO 5, 6, & 7: Determine Relevant Information, Net Present Value, Screen Project, with Residual Value

8-54. John Paul Hudik, president of Hudik Boat Hauling, is considering replacing the company's industrial lift used to haul boats. The new lift would allow the company to lift larger boats out of the water. The company's cost of capital is 14%.

Information about the old lift:	
Cost	$ 94,000
Estimated useful life	12 years
Estimated residual value	$ 10,000
Current age	4 years
Estimated current fair value	$ 48,000
Annual contribution margin	$ 50,000
Information about the new lift:	
Cost	$128,000
Estimated useful life	8 years
Estimated residual value	$ 25,000
Annual contribution margin	$ 65,000

Required:

a. Prepare a relevant cost schedule showing the benefit of buying the new lift. (For this requirement, ignore the time value of money.)

b. How much must the company invest today to replace the old lift?

c. If the company replaces the old lift, what is the increase in the company's annual contribution margin?

d. If the company sells the old lift now to make room for the new one, it will not receive the $10,000 residual value at the end of its useful life. Instead, the company will receive the $25,000 residual value from the new lift. With this in mind, if the company buys the new lift, what is the change in the residual value the company is to receive at the end of the eight-year life of the equipment?

e. Calculate the net present value of replacing the old lift.

f. Do you think the company should replace the old lift?

LO 5, 6, & 7: Determine Relevant Information, Net Present Value, Screen Project, with Residual Value

8-55. The managers at Wilma Manufacturing are considering replacing a printing press with a new, high-speed model. The company's cost of capital is 12%.

Information about the old printing press:	
Cost	$255,000
Estimated useful life	10 years
Estimated residual value	$ 25,000
Annual depreciation	$ 23,000
Current age	3 years
Accumulated depreciation to date	$184,000
Estimated current fair value	$150,000
Annual contribution margin	$110,000
Information about the new printing press:	
Cost	$535,000
Estimated useful life	7 years
Estimated residual value	$ 45,000
Annual depreciation	$ 70,000
Annual contribution margin	$150,000

Required:

a. Prepare a relevant cost schedule showing the benefit of buying the new printing press. (For this requirement, ignore the time value of money.)

b. How much must the company invest today to replace the old printing press?

c. If the company replaces the old printing press, what is the increase in the company's annual contribution margin?

d. If the company sells the old printing press now to make room for the new one, it will not receive the $25,000 residual value at the end of its useful life. Instead, the company will receive the $45,000 residual value from the new printing press. With this in mind, if the company buys the printing press, what is the change in the residual value the company is to receive at the end of the seven-year life of the equipment?

e. Calculate the net present value of replacing the old printing press.

f. Do you think the company should replace the old printing press?

Appendix

LO 7: Calculate Simple, Compound Interest, Full Years

8-56. Greg Gluck Marine borrowed $5,000 from National Bank on January 1, 2008.

Required:

a. Assuming 9% simple interest is charged, calculate interest for 2008, 2009, and 2010.

b. Assuming 9% annually compounded interest is charged, calculate interest for 2008, 2009, and 2010.

LO 7: Calculate Simple, Compound Interest, Full Years

8-57. Gary borrowed $8,000 from Orlando National Bank on January 1, 2008.

Required:

a. Assuming 8% simple interest is charged, calculate interest for 2008, 2009, and 2010.

b. Assuming 8% annually compounded interest is charged, calculate interest for 2008, 2009, and 2010.

LO 7: Calculate Simple, Compound Interest, Full Years

8-58. Cam borrowed $2,000 from Miami National Bank on January 1 2008.

Required:

a. Assuming 6% simple interest is charged, calculate interest for 2008, 2009, and 2010.

b. Assuming 6% annually compounded interest is charged, calculate interest for 2008, 2009, and 2010.

LO 7: Calculate Future Value, Single Cash Flow, Various Rates and Maturities

8-59. Susan Jones made the following investments on January 1, 2008:

1. $2,000 at 10% for 5 years
2. $12,000 at 4% for 8 years
3. $9,000 at 14% for 15 years

Assume the interest on each investment is compounded annually.

Required:

Calculate the future value of each of the investments listed above at their maturity.

LO 7: Calculate Future Value, Single Cash Flow, Various Rates and Maturities

8-60. Ivan Zhang made the following investments on January 1 2008:

1. $3,000 at 8% for 6 years
2. $4,000 at 6% for 8 years
3. $5,000 at 10% for 5 years

Assume the interest on each investment is compounded annually.

Required:

Calculate the future value of each of the investments listed above at their maturity.

LO 7: Calculate Future Value, Single Cash Flow, Various Rates and Maturities

8-61. Orlando Gonzalez made the following investments on January 1 2008:

1. $1,000 at 14% for 3 years
2. $2,000 at 10% for 5 years
3. $4,000 at 8% for 8 years

Assume the interest on each investment is compounded annually.

Required:

Calculate the future value of each of the investments listed above at their maturity.

LO 7: Calculate Future Value, Yearly Cash Flows, Various Rates and Maturities

8-62. Consider the following investments:

1. $2,000 at the end of each of the next five years at 10% interest compounded annually.
2. $12,000 at the end of each of the next eight years at 4% interest compounded annually.
3. $9,000 at the end of each of the next 15 years at 14% interest compounded annually.

Required:

Calculate the future value of each of the investments listed above at their maturity.

LO 7: Calculate Future Value, Yearly Cash Flows, Various Rates and Maturities

8-63. Consider the following investments.

1. $12,000 at the end of each of the next three years at 12% interest compounded annually.
2. $16,000 at the end of each of the next five years at 10% interest compounded annually.
3. $20,000 at the end of each of the next 10 years at 8% interest compounded annually.

Required:

Calculate the future value of each of the investments listed above at their maturity.

LO 7: Calculate Future Value, Yearly Cash Flows, Various Rates and Maturities

8-64. Consider the following investments.

1. $1,000 at the end of each of the next five years at 6% interest compounded annually.
2. $1,000 at the end of each of the next five years at 8% interest compounded annually.
3. $1,000 at the end of each of the next five years at 10% interest compounded annually.

Required:

Calculate the future value of each of the investments listed above at their maturity.

LO 7: Calculate Present Value, Single Cash Flow, Single Rate

8-65. Jim Johnson is planning to buy a new car when he graduates from college in three years. He would like to invest a single amount now, in order to have the $24,000 he estimates the car will cost.

Required:

Calculate the amount Jim must invest today, to have enough to buy the new car assuming his investment will earn 4% compounded annually for the three-year investment.

LO 7: Calculate Present Value, Single Cash Flow, Single Rate

8-66. Lowell Pitman needs to have $50,000 at the end of five years. Lowell would like to invest a single amount now, to have the $50,000 in five years.

Required:

Calculate the amount Lowell must invest today, to have the amount of money he needs assuming his investment will earn 8% compounded annually for the five year investment.

LO 7: Calculate Present Value, Single Cash Flow, Single Rate

8-67. Lauren Elsea is planning to buy a house when she graduates from college. She would like to have $20,000 for the down payment. Lauren would like to invest a single amount now, to have the $20,000 at the end of three years.

Required:

Calculate the amount Lauren must invest today, to have the amount of money she needs assuming her investment will earn 6% compounded annually for the three year investment.

LO 7: Calculate Present Value, Yearly Cash Flows, Single Rate

8-68. Linda Chidister is planning to send her son, Edward, to college. While he is in college, Linda intends to give him $3,000 at the end of each year.

Required:

How much must Linda invest today so she will have enough to give Edward $3,000 at the end of each of the next four years assuming the investment will earn 6% interest compounded annually?

LO 7: Calculate Present Value, Yearly Cash Flows, Single Rate

8-69. Alex Malpin is planning to spend the next three years doing research in China. An Asian studies research institute has agreed to pay Alex $20,000 at the end of each of the three years he is in China.

Required:

How much must be invested today to have enough to pay Alex $20,000 at the end of each of the next three years assuming the investment will earn 10% interest compounded annually.

LO 7: Calculate Present Value, Yearly Cash Flows, Single Rate

8-70. Photo Factory is planning to purchase some photo processing equipment from Ace Equipment Company. The equipment will provide cash flow of $15,000 at the end of each of the next eight years.

Required:

How much should Photo Factory pay for the equipment assuming it will provide $15,000 at the end of each of the next eight years and Ace has promised that it will earn a return of exactly 14%?

9

The Operating Budget

Imagine that one morning midway through your accounting class, you and three of your classmates decide to go to Paris. The four of you stand up, excuse yourselves, and set out for the airport, where you discover that the next flight to France departs in four hours and that there are only three seats available. You buy three tickets, send one friend back to class, and head to the gate.

When you arrive in Paris, one of your friends asks, "Well, we're here. What now?" You respond, "I don't know, this was a spur-of-the-moment thing. We have the freedom to do whatever we want!" But suddenly your classmates are not feeling so spontaneous. In fact, they're riddled with concerns. "Where will we stay? Did you bring any money? Who has a French/English dictionary? Now that we're here, how long will we stay? What will we do? We didn't bring any clothes. How are we getting home?"

What's wrong with this adventure? Well, let's just say it could have used a bit more planning. Thoughtful planning increases the possibility of succeeding in almost anything we undertake.

Careful planning is in fact, a key element of business success. Without planning, business activities founder and a company almost certainly loses direction. In Chapter 8 we described planning as the *why*, the *what*, the *how*, and the *who* of being in business and doing business. Recall that the *why* is the process of setting company goals. The *what* is the strategic plan to implement those goals in the long-term. These two planning elements were discussed in some detail in Chapter 8. The *how* is the process of capital budgeting to allocate scarce resources and was the major focus of Chapter 8.

The *who* is the final step—the operating budget. The **operating budget** is a budget for a specific time, usually one to five years, that establishes who is responsible for the day-to-day operation of the business during that time. This budget is also sometimes called the **master operating budget** or simply the **master budget**. For the sake of consistency, we will use the term *operating budget* throughout our discussions of this topic.

operating budget A budget for a specific period. Usually one to five years, that establishes who is responsible for the day-to-day operation of a business during that time.

master operating budget Another name for operating budget.

master budget Another name for operating budget.

The operating budget will be an important part of your business life, regardless of your occupation or the type of company for which you choose to work. Whether the organization is profit or not-for-profit, and whether it is a service, merchandising, or manufacturing firm, budgeting has become increasingly important in charting the success of today's organizations. Gone are the days when companies could succeed on simple luck and optimism. Gone, too, are the days when a select group of top managers prepared operating budgets with little input from others in the organization. Many companies today involve all managers and employees in the budgeting process. Fortune 500 companies such as **General Dynamics**, **Honeywell**, **General Motors**, and others have recognized that better budgeting is achieved when they involve those who actually work in the area or function for which the budget is being prepared. As you read the pages that follow, we hope you remember that budgets will be an important ingredient in your personal business success, and that you will very likely be involved in the budgeting process much earlier in your career than you may expect.

The chapter is divided into two main parts. Part One is an overview of the operating budget, its purpose, and where it fits into the overall management process. Part Two is a detailed presentation of how the operating budget is actually prepared and how it should and should not be used by managers.

Learning Objectives

After completing your work on this chapter, you should be able to do the following:

1. Describe some of the benefits of the operating budget.
2. Describe the three budgeted financial statements contained in the operating budget and the other budgets that support the budgeted financial statements.
3. Compare and contrast various approaches to preparing and using the operating budget.
4. Describe the role of the sales forecast in the budgeting process.
5. Prepare various budgets included in the operating budget.
6. Describe the flexible budget and the flexible budget performance report.
7. Describe the appropriate use of the operating budget in the overall management process.

PART ONE: AN OVERVIEW OF THE OPERATING BUDGET

The Operating Budget: What Is It?

What exactly is an operating budget? We know it is the plan for a company's operating activities for some period of time, but what is in that plan? The operating budget includes a set of estimated financial statements.

Recall that the three main financial statements are the balance sheet, the income statement, and the statement of cash flows. Businesses prepare these statements at the end of a given time period to show the effects of past transactions and events. An operating budget contains those same three financial statements, except they are estimates—or forecasts—of future transactions and events. The forecasted financial statements in the operating budget are sometimes called pro forma financial statements. *Pro forma* is a Latin phrase meaning "provided in advance."

Because the operating budget is a set of estimated financial statements, much of what we will cover in this chapter will at least be familiar to you. The only difference between the financial statements businesses use to show the effects of past events and transactions and the ones you will explore in this chapter is that the budgeted financial statements are used to predict future events.

Benefits of Budgeting

A well-prepared operating budget can create many benefits for the company. In this section, we will explore four of them. First, budgeting serves as a guide. Second, it helps organizations allocate resources. Third, it encourages communication and coordination. Fourth, it sets performance standards, or *benchmarks*.

Serves as a Guide

The operating budget should serve as a guide for a company to follow during the budgeted period. Recall the hypothetical trip to Paris we described in the chapter opener. Now let's assume that our travelers did have a plan after all. Suppose that while touring France, our travelers heard about a fantastic side trip (a terrific art show in Nice) not included in their original itinerary. Based on this new information, our travelers would probably adjust their original plan to allow for this side trip. And so it should be with a budget, because companies should adjust their budgets when desirable or necessary.

To illustrate, suppose the budget for Pam's Flower Shop forecasted sales revenue of $310,000 for the first three months of 2010. Business was better than expected and the flower shop had sales of $310,000 by the end of February. Should Pam close the flower shop until April 1 because she attained her budgeted sales figure for the quarter? Of course not. Or suppose Pam has the opportunity to purchase 20 dozen roses just before Valentine's Day at a bargain basement price. She can probably sell all of them for a whopping profit, but she didn't budget for this special purchase. What should she do? It may seem obvious that she should take advantage of this terrific opportunity, but a surprising number of businesses view the budget as "set in stone," so to speak, and meeting the budget becomes the primary business objective. An unwillingness to adjust a budget based on new information can be detrimental to a company because opportunities are missed and poor decisions made.

Assists in Resource Allocation

As discussed in Chapter 8, all organizations have scarce resources. No company can afford to do everything it desires, or even everything it needs to do within a given time period. A budget can help management decide where to allocate its limited resources.

The budgeting process may uncover potential bottlenecks and allow managers to address these issues in advance as the budget is being prepared, rather than as problems occur during the year. An example of a bottleneck in a manufacturing environment is presented for Montrose Manufacturing Company in Exhibit 9-1.

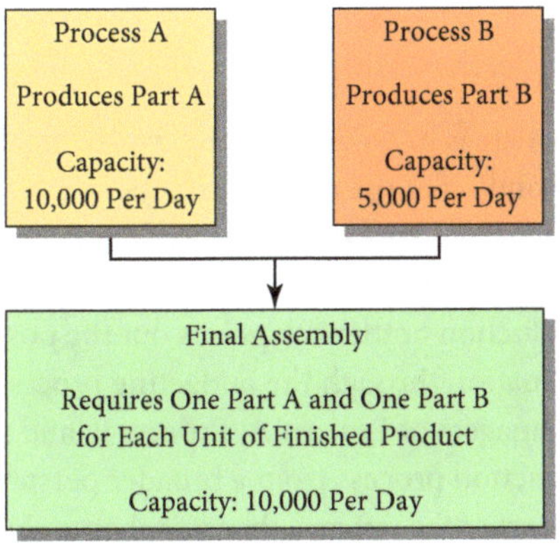

Exhibit 9-1 Example of Production Bottleneck at Montrose Manufacturing

As you can see from Exhibit 9-1, each unit of finished product Montrose manufactures requires one Part A and one Part B. The maximum number of finished units of product the company can produce per day is 5,000 even though the capacity of both Process A and Final Assembly is 10,000 units per day. The limiting factor is Process B, which can produce only 5,000 parts per day. Montrose could increase the capacity of Process A from 10,000 parts per day to 100,000 parts per day and the company *still* could produce only 5,000 finished units per day. The same would be true with Final Assembly. Montrose could increase Final Assembly capacity, but it still could only assemble 5,000 units per day. Process B is the bottleneck in this company's production process.

Assume Montrose Manufacturing Company moved some production machinery from Process A to Process B. This change reduces the capacity of Process A by 2,500 parts per day, but increases the capacity of Process B by 2,500 parts per day as reflected in Exhibit 9-2.

Exhibit 9-2 Elimination of Production Bottleneck at Montrose Manufacturing

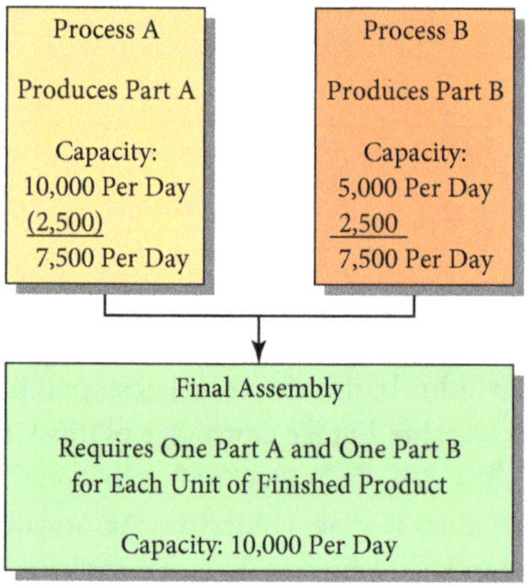

As you can see by looking at Exhibit 9-2, Montrose has increased its capacity to produce finished units by 50 percent (from 5,000 units to 7,500 units) without adding any additional machinery to its operation, which is a significant factor if you recall our discussion of capital expenditures in Chapter 8.

The issue of resource allocation is also important for a merchandising business. For example, February may be so busy for a Pam's Flower Shop that she will need extra workers. If Pam knows this in advance, she will have time to hire the needed workers at the least cost so she can offer quality service and sell more flowers. In contrast, if Pam did not plan for the February rush, she would find herself understaffed and unable to provide quality, timely service. She might lose customers before she could hire more workers, and sales could drop. Budgeting, then, helps Pam make good decisions about how to allocate her resources.

Fosters Communication and Coordination

As managers from different functional areas in an organization work together to prepare the budget, they gain a better understanding of the entire business. When managers from all areas learn of difficulties facing others and spot duplication of effort, the firm can then solve problems and coordinate efforts more effectively. Our previous example of Montrose Manufacturing Company and its production bottleneck points out the possibilities of increased communication and coordination through the budgeting process. In working to solve this production problem, the managers of Process A, Process B, and Final Assembly had the opportunity to view the production process from a broader perspective. Rather than concentrating only on their own part of the process, they were better able to understand the problems facing managers in other areas of the company's operations. They were forced to communicate with one another and to better coordinate their efforts.

Even for a small company like Pam's Flower Shop, success can depend on coordinating many activities. For example, Pam expects sales to increase in February because of Valentine's Day. She anticipates she will need more flowers to sell, and more labor to sell them. The number of extra workers, however, may depend on the amount of additional flowers ordered. When she prepares the budget, Pam speaks to the inventory manager and the personnel manager about the February rush to better coordinate their activities. Then the managers know in advance exactly what needs to be done.

Establishes Performance Standards

The operating budget also sets performance standards for an organization. As managers prepare budgets for their companies, they should establish performance goals they both want and can attain. If a company's actual sales, for example, are less than its budgeted sales for a particular period, the sales manager will review the deficit and ask why. Once she has learned why, she may be able to correct the problem causing the lagging sales, or she may find it necessary to adjust the budget for next time. Without a budget she might not notice the sales shortfall and therefore would not even know the problem exists.

Budgeted performance standards become benchmarks against which firms can compare their actual results. Differences between the actual results and the budget can be explored and improvements made. The improvements may focus on performance, the budgeting process, or both.

Discussion Question

9-1. In what other ways do you think a company might benefit from preparing an operating budget?

Contents of the Operating Budget

Many of us have had to prepare a personal cash budget, in which we compare the amount of cash coming in to the amount of cash going out. Because of this personal experience with budgeting, many people think that business budgeting focuses only on budgeting for cash inflows and outflows. This view, however, is far too narrow. Remember, the operating budget is a set of estimated financial statements that includes the balance sheet, income statement, and statement of cash flows, regardless of whether the business preparing the budget is a manufacturer, a merchandiser, or a service company.

Sales Budget

The sales budget is the first budget prepared and is based on a sales forecast. A **sales forecast** is a prediction of sales in units or dollars for the budget period. We'll discuss the sales forecast in more detail later in this chapter. As the name implies, the **sales budget** details the expected sales revenue from a company's primary operating activities during a certain time period. Because manufacturers and merchandisers sell tangible, physical product, the sales budget is based on the number of units the firm expects to sell. The sales budget of a service business is based on the amount of services the firm expects to render.

sales budget Details the expected sales revenue from a company's primary operating activities during a certain time period.

Because sales revenue is an income statement item, companies use the information provided by the sales budget to construct the budgeted income statement.

Production or Purchases Budget

production budget Details the cost and number of units that must be produced by a manufacturer to meet the sales forecast and the desired ending inventory.

purchases budget Details the cost and number of units that must be purchased by a merchandiser to meet the sales forecast and the desired ending inventory.

For manufacturers, the budget that plans for the cost and number of units of product that must be manufactured to meet the sales forecast and the desired quantity of ending finished goods inventory is known as the **production budget**. For merchandisers, this budget is called the **purchases budget**, but the two are functionally equivalent. Their names reflect the source of the items sold: Manufacturers produce the products they sell, and merchandisers purchase the products they sell.

The production budget and the purchases budget are simply pro forma versions of the cost of goods manufactured schedule and the cost of purchases schedule, as discussed in Chapter 2. A production budget is usually more complicated than a purchases budget because, as discussed in Chapter 2, costing manufactured product is more complicated than costing purchased product. A production budget includes schedules for materials, labor, and manufacturing overhead. An operating budget for a service business does not include a production budget or purchases budget because a service company does not sell tangible, physical product.

Only some of the product scheduled to be produced by a manufacturer or purchased by a merchandiser is intended to be sold during the period covered by the budget. The product not projected to be sold is called *ending finished goods inventory* for a manufacturer and *ending merchandise inventory* for a merchandiser. In either case, this projected ending inventory is classified as an asset. Therefore, companies use some of the information provided by the production budget or purchases budget to construct the budgeted balance sheet.

The product that is projected to be sold during the period covered by the budget is classified as an expense item and will be shown on the budgeted income statement. As you recall, this expense item is called cost of goods sold. The cost of goods sold information needed to construct the budgeted income statement comes from the cost of goods sold budget.

Cost of Goods Sold or Cost of Services Budget

cost of goods sold budget Calculates the total cost of all of the product a manufacturing or merchandising company estimates it will sell during the period covered by the budget.

cost of services budget Calculates the total cost of all the services a service type business estimates it will provide during the period covered by the budget.

A **cost of goods sold budget** calculates the total cost of all the product a company estimates it will sell during the period covered by the operating budget. This budget differs from the production (purchases) budget because of inventory requirements. Under accrual accounting, we do not recognize the cost of product as an expense (cost of goods sold) on the income statement until it is sold. Until then, we record it as an asset (inventory) and show it as such on the balance sheet. For a service type business, this budget is called the **cost of services budget**.

Whether we are talking about the cost of goods sold budget or the cost of services budget, they are similar to the schedules in Chapter 2 regarding the costing of products and services. The only difference is that the budgets discussed in this chapter pertain to the future.

Because cost of goods sold or cost of services is an income statement item, companies use the information provided by the cost of goods sold budget or cost of services budget to construct the budgeted income statement.

Selling and Administrative Expense Budget

selling and administrative expense budget Calculates all costs other than the cost of product or services required to support a company's forecasted sales.

After a company makes its sales forecast and estimates its product (or service) cost, it can estimate all other costs needed to support that level of sales. A **selling and administrative expense budget** calculates all costs other than the cost of product or services required to support a company's forecasted sales. The kinds of items included in this budget are identical to those included in the income statements we have discussed throughout this text. They are what we described as period costs in Chapter 2 and include such items as advertising, administrative salaries, rent, and utilities.

Budgeted Income Statement

A **budgeted income statement** shows the expected revenues, expenses, and net income for the period covered by the operating budget. Companies prepare this budget using information from the sales budget, the cost of goods sold (or cost of services) budget, and the selling and administrative expense budget.

budgeted income statement Shows the expected net income for the period covered by the operating budget.

Cash Budget

A **cash budget** shows whether the expected amount of cash generated by operating activities will be sufficient to pay anticipated expenses during the period covered by the operating budget. It also reveals whether a company should expect a need for short-term external financing during the budget period. Be careful not to confuse the cash budget with the budgeted statement of cash flows, as discussed later in the chapter. The budgeted statement of cash flows is more comprehensive than a cash budget.

cash budget Shows whether the expected amount of cash generated by operating activities will be sufficient to pay anticipated expenses during the period covered by the operating budget.

Budgeted Balance Sheet

A **budgeted balance sheet** presents estimated assets, liabilities, and owners' equity at the end of the budgeted period. It is created exactly the way a balance sheet based on actual historical results is prepared. At the start of the period being budgeted, a company has a balance sheet that presents its assets, liabilities, and owners' equity. The estimated results of operations (budgeted income statement) will change most (if not all) of the company's asset, liability, and equity items. The result is an estimated balance sheet at the end of the budget period.

budgeted balance sheet A presentation of estimated assets, liabilities, and owners' equity at the end of the budgeted period.

Manufacturing and merchandising companies prepare the budgeted balance sheet using information from the actual balance sheet at the beginning of the period covered by the budget, the production (purchases) budget, and the budgeted income statement. Service type companies have no production or purchases budget, so they prepare the budgeted balance sheet using information from the actual balance sheet at the beginning of the budget period and the budgeted income statement.

Budgeted Statement of Cash Flows

A **budgeted statement of cash flows** is a statement of a company's expected sources and uses of cash during the period covered by the operating budget. Manufacturers, merchandisers, and service companies create the budgeted statement of cash flows the same way they create the budgeted balance sheet. At the start of the period being budgeted, they report their cash balance. Based on the estimated results of operations (budgeted income statement) and other business activities that either generate or use cash, they estimate the cash balance at the end of the budget period. The purpose of the budgeted statement of cash flows is to explain what will cause that change in cash.

budgeted statement of cash flows A statement of a company's expected sources and uses of cash during the period covered by the operating budget.

Discussion Question

9-2. In what ways do you think the cash budget described earlier differs from the budgeted statement of cash flows?

Interrelationship Among the Budgets

The budgets we have discussed are closely interrelated. A change in any one of them will cause a ripple effect throughout all the others. Exhibit 9-3 shows the extent of this interrelationship.

Exhibit 9-3 Interrelationship Among the Budgets

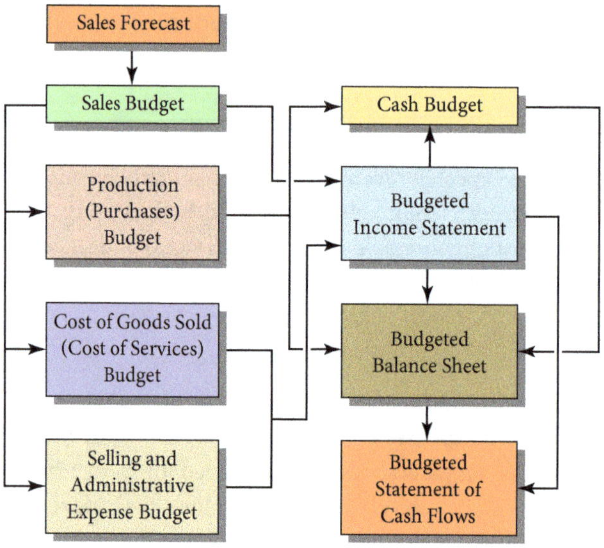

To demonstrate the interrelationship among the budgets, we return to Pam's Flower Shop. Because Pam's company is a merchandiser, the operating budget she prepares will include a sales budget, a purchases budget, a cost of goods sold budget, a selling and administrative expense budget, a cash budget, a budgeted income statement, a budgeted balance sheet, and a budgeted statement of cash flows.

Pam prepared the various budgets described for the first three months of 2010 based on the following sales forecast.

Pam's Flower Shop
Sales Forecast
For the Three Months Ended March 31, 2010

	January	February	March	Total
Sales	$90,000	$120,000	$100,000	$310,000

Discussion Question

9-3. From what you have learned so far about the operating budget, which of the budgets for Pam's Flower Shop will the amounts in this sales forecast affect? Explain how each is affected.

Now assume that a new flower shop opened just down the street from Pam's after she had prepared her operating budget. Pam believes that to be realistic in her planning, she needs to revise her sales forecast as follows:

Pam's Flower Shop
Revised Sales Forecast
For the Three Months Ended March 31, 2010

	January	February	March	Total
Sales	$75,000	$100,000	$90,000	$265,000

Discussion Question

9-4. Which of the budgets for Pam's Flower Shop will the changes in her sales forecast affect? Explain how each is affected.

Because sales revenue is changed in Pam's revised sales forecast, the sales budget will be different. Even without any information about purchases, you should intuitively recognize that lower sales probably means fewer flowers sold; therefore, Pam will need to purchase fewer flowers, meaning that the purchases budget must be revised. The same holds true for the cost of goods sold budget. The selling and administrative expense budget may need to be revised based on the new forecast, because lower sales probably means fewer sales clerks, at least. The cash budget will need to be revised because lower sales means less cash collected and lower purchases means less cash spent. The budgeted income statement must surely be revised, because we use the sales budget, the cost of goods sold budget, and the selling and administrative expense budget to construct the budgeted income statement. If those budgets must be revised, the budgeted income statement must also be revised. If the budgeted income statement is affected, the budgeted balance sheet must be revised because the results from the income statement are reflected in the balance sheet. If cash is affected in any way (and we already determined it would be), the budgeted statement of cash flows must be revised.

As you can see, a change in any of the budgets has a ripple effect throughout all the other budgets. For example, if sales volume changes, then not only will the sales budget change but also most of the amounts in the other budgets will change as well. Companies often prepare an initial operating budget based on a particular forecasted level of sales. A budget that is based on one level of activity is called a **static budget**.

static budget A budget that is based on one level of activity.

Because the various budgets contained in the operating budget are so closely tied together, preparing the operating budget in most organizations is extremely time consuming and complicated. Depending on the size of the company, it may take several months to prepare the operating budget. For example, a manufacturer or merchandiser prepares a sales budget for each product the company sells. If the company sells 80 products, then 80 sales budgets must be prepared. If the company also has 80 sales territories, a whopping 6,400 sales budgets must be prepared (80 products × 80 sales territories). Companies must begin the budgeting process early enough to allow sufficient time for completion. If the budgeted period begins on January 1, 2010, for example, the budgeting process may begin in August or September 2009, or even earlier.

For some large, multinational companies, the process never ends. They work on the 2010 budget from January through December 2009. Then they turn right around in January 2010 and begin work on the 2011 budget, and so on. It takes so long to complete the process that by they time they finish one year, it is time to start again for the next year.

Different Approaches to Budgeting

We now know what an operating budget is, but exactly how do businesses prepare one? The answer depends on the needs of the business and the approach it takes to the budgeting process. Next we investigate several budgeting approaches: perpetual, incremental, zero-based, top-down, bottom-up, imposed, and participative approaches.

Perpetual Budgeting

Some companies continually update their operating budgets. As one month ends, another month's budget is added to the end of the budget. Therefore, at any given time, the budget

perpetual budgeting The budgeting approach of updating the budget every month.

continual budgeting Another name for perpetual budgeting.

rolling budget Another name for a perpetual budget.

projects 12 months into the future. This budgeting approach is called **perpetual budgeting**, sometimes called **continual budgeting** or a **rolling budget**. Companies that use perpetual budgeting always budget 12 months in advance.

One advantage of perpetual budgeting is that it spreads the workload for budget preparation evenly over the year, which allows employees to incorporate the work required to prepare the budget into their routine work schedule. Another advantage of a perpetual budget is that the budget always extends 12 months into the future. In contrast, when perpetual budgeting is *not* used, the new operating budget is typically prepared when only a couple of months are left on the old budget. One disadvantage of perpetual budgeting may be that the budget preparation process becomes so routine that employees lose the motivation and creativity required to prepare an innovative operating budget. An important aspect of solid budgeting is looking for better ways to do things. Think back to the example we used earlier for Montrose Manufacturing Company, which was able to restructure its production process because its managers were serious about looking for a better way. If preparing the budget becomes routine—just another bunch of forms to fill out—managers may stop this critical evaluation and become satisfied with the status quo. Another disadvantage is that many managers believe they do not have sufficient time to do all that is asked of them in their regular day-to-day responsibilities. Adding the responsibility of preparing a perpetual budget to a heavy workload can lead to sloppy budgeting.

Incremental Budgeting

incremental budgeting The process of using the prior year's budget or the company's actual results to build the new operating budget.

The process of using the prior year's budget or the company's actual results to build the new operating budget is called **incremental budgeting**. If, for example, a company's 2009 budget included $200,000 for maintenance and repairs on the machinery and equipment in its production facility, $200,000 becomes the starting point for this item in preparing the 2010 budget. The only question managers need to answer is whether the company needs to include *more* than $200,000 for repairs and maintenance in 2010. This budgeting approach is used by many companies.

The trouble with the incremental budgeting approach is that if the prior year's budget includes unnecessary costs, or items that do not optimize performance, this waste may be simply rolled over into the next year's budget. The advantage to this approach is its simplicity. Some practitioners and many experts believe the disadvantages greatly outweigh the advantages.

Discussion Question

9-5. In what ways, if any, do you think the use of incremental budgeting contributes to wasteful spending?

Zero-Based Budgeting

zero-based budgeting A process of budgeting in which manager's start from scratch, or zero, when preparing a new budget.

An alternative to the incremental budgeting approach is zero-based budgeting. In **zero-based budgeting**, managers start from scratch, or zero, when preparing a new budget. Each item on the budget must be justified every year as though it were a new budget item. Zero-based budgeting is much more difficult and time consuming than incremental budgeting, but many organizations believe the results are worth that time and effort because managers are forced to reexamine the items included in the budget and justify their continuation.

Top-Down versus Bottom-Up Budgeting

Budgeted information can flow either from the upper levels of management in a company down to managers and employees at lower levels, or vice versa. For fairly obvious reasons, the former approach is known as the top-down approach and the latter as the bottom-up approach. Each has distinct advantages and disadvantages.

Top-Down Budgeting

When top managers in the company prepare the budget, the process is called **top-down budgeting**. The top executives prepare the budget, and lower-level managers and employees work to meet that budget.

top-down budgeting A budget prepared by top managers in a company.

The top-down approach has several advantages. First, a company's upper management is usually most knowledgeable about the company's overall operation. It makes sense (on the surface, at least) that upper managers be responsible for the information contained in the operating budget because they are the most experienced and knowledgeable individuals in the company. Second, top management is keenly aware of company goals and strategic plans, so they will prepare the budget with these goals and plans in mind. Third, the top-down budgeting approach involves fewer people, so it causes fewer disruptions, is more efficient, and is less time consuming than the bottom-up approach. Finally, when companies use top-down budgeting, it is less likely that padding the budget or budget slack will occur. Padding the budget or introducing budget slack is when employees purposely try to influence the budgeting process so resulting budgeted performance targets are very easy for them to achieve. Generally top managers are less likely to be swayed by employees vying for lower sales targets or budgets that include higher costs.

The top-down approach to budgeting has several disadvantages. First, top managers may be keenly aware of the big picture, but they do not have the working knowledge of daily activities needed to prepare the detailed budgets for all company activities. Second, lower-level managers and employees are usually less accepting of budgets when they have no part in setting the standards. Third, without involving lower level employees in the planning process, the employees are less likely to think about the company's goals and the various activities they will be involved in that will affect the company's future.

Most large, publicly traded companies in the United States use some form of top-down budgeting. Why? If you recall our discussion of the cost of equity capital in Chapter 8, you know that a firm's top management fully understands the need to maximize returns for stockholders. Most of that return is in the form of stock appreciation (increase in the market price of the stock), rather than dividends. The greatest influence on the selling price of a company's stock price is company profits. So, to ensure maximum stock appreciation, a company must be as profitable as possible. The top management of these publicly traded companies generally have a better sense than lower-level managers and employees of how much profit the company must have in a given year to maintain (or attain) a high return for stockholders. In top-down budgeting, the target profit figures become the starting point of the budgeting process.

Traditionally, most firms that used top-down budgeting also used an imposed budgeting process. An **imposed budget** is a budget in which upper management sets figures for all operating activities that the rest of the company rarely, if ever, can negotiate. Top management expects all other managers to "do whatever it takes to make it happen." This type of budgeting process can do more harm than good, because it can lead to business practices that conflict with the company's stated goals. Today, however, not all top-down budgets are imposed budgets, as we will see shortly.

imposed budget A budget in which upper management sets figures for all operating activities that the rest of the company rarely, if ever, can negotiate.

Bottom-Up Budgeting

In **bottom-up budgeting**, lower-level managers and employees prepare the initial budget. For example, members of the sales force prepare the sales budget for their own sales territories.

bottom-up budgeting A budget initially prepared by lower-level managers and employees.

The sales manager then reviews these sales budgets, makes any necessary changes, and combines them to form the overall company sales budget. Likewise, employees in the production facility prepare budgets for production, including schedules for direct material, direct labor, and manufacturing overhead.

Bottom-up budgeting has three main advantages. First, the budget may be more realistic. Those who work in a functional area are usually better informed about what should be included in the budget than upper-level managers. If lower-level managers and employees take the budgeting process seriously, they are likely to create an operating budget based on accurate, realistic information. Second, lower-level managers and employees are more likely to work toward budgeted performance standards because they helped to set those standards. Third, as employees prepare the budget, they learn to think about the company's goals, how various activities can affect the future, and how they personally will participate. In short, they begin to think about the work they will need to do in the coming year.

Bottom-up budgeting has several disadvantages. First, lower-level managers may be less aware and concerned with the company's overall goals and strategic plans so they are less likely to incorporate them into the budget. Second, employees at every level must take time from their day-to-day responsibilities to work on the budget as it is prepared, reviewed, revised, and approved – all of which adds up to substantial time and effort. Finally, some employees may pad their budgets or to introduce budget slack. In other words they may try to prepare a budget that is so generous they can effortlessly outperform it. For example, sales representatives may budget sales of $300,000, when they can achieve sales of $350,000 with little effort. Thus, their actual sales performance looks great compared with budgeted sales. Manipulating the budget to make certain that the actual performance exceeds budgeted performance is one example of a budget game. A *budget game* is the game of using the budget to do things it was never intended to do, such as ensuring a strong performance appraisal.

participative budget A budget in which managers and employees at many levels of the company are involved in setting the performance standards and preparing the budget.

Bottom-up budgeting is always a participative budgeting process. A **participative budget** is one in which managers and employees at many levels of the company are involved in setting the performance standards and preparing the budget. Recent developments have expanded the use of participative budgeting to top-down budgeting, so it is beneficial to discuss imposed and participative budget philosophies a little further.

Imposed versus Participative Budgets

A bottom-up budget will always be a participative budget. Managers and employees at all levels of the company participate in preparing a bottom-up budget. A top-down budget, however, can be either imposed or participative.

In recent years, companies have discovered that by allowing more participation, they empower their employees. To empower employees means to give employees the authority to make decisions concerning their job responsibilities, including decisions about items in the operating budget.

A company committed to both top-down budgeting and empowered employees must combine the top-down and bottom-up approaches to budgeting. Rather than having all budget information flow from the top of the company downward to lower levels, upper management provides profit targets to managers at lower levels. These lower-level managers then prepare the operating budget for their functional areas, given the profit targets upper management provides.

Discussion Questions

9-6. What possible positive results do you think can come from more empowerment:

a. for the company? Explain your reasoning.

b. for managers and employees? Explain your reasoning.

9-7. What possible negative results do you think can come from more empowerment:

a. for the company? Explain your reasoning.

b. for managers and employees? Explain your reasoning.

As an example of combining thc top-down and bottom-up approaches to budgeting, we look at Preston Nydegger Company. Upper management at Nydegger has established a target profit of $1 million for the upcoming year. The company has three divisions (A, B, & C), and each must earn some part of the targeted $1 million profit. Division C is the smallest of the three, and corporate headquarters has assigned this division a target profit of $150,000 for the next year.

Now that Division C has received its target profit (this is the top-down part), the division manager, Joenne Moss, and her managers and employees set about to prepare the operating budget for the year (this is the participative part). When they have completed their budgeting process, the result in summary form is as follows:

Sales	$500,000
Expenses	(450,000)
Net Income	$150,000

Wait a minute! Something's wrong. The numbers just don't add up. Well, what we see is a conflict between the top-down target profit ($150,000) and what Joenne and her people at Division C think they can accomplish in the upcoming year ($500,000 in sales and $450,000 in expenses). What happens next will determine whether this budget is imposed or participative.

If the upper management of Nydegger Company refuses to negotiate and compromise with Division C, the budget becomes imposed. Remember, there is little room for negotiation between upper management and the rest of the company as to the amounts included in an imposed operating budget. If, however, upper management is willing to yield somewhat on its profit targets, the budget becomes participative.

It is unrealistic to think Nydegger will simply adjust its target from $150,000 to $50,000, which would certainly make the arithmetic in the budgeted income statement work. More than likely, Nydegger's upper management will meet with Joenne and her staff to negotiate a compromise target profit. Let's say they did just that, and the negotiations led to a revised target profit of $90,000 for the division. The revised summary budgeted income statement, then, would be as follows:

Sales	$500,000
Expenses	(450,000)
Net Income	$ 90,000

The math still doesn't work! Management at the division level must now either forecast more sales or find some way to reduce expected expenses (or some combination of the two) to project an additional $40,000 in profit for the year.

The key to making a top-down budget a participative budget is the ability and willingness on the part of upper management to negotiate and compromise.

Discussion Questions

9-8. If you were the chief executive officer of your company, would you prefer a top-down or bottom-up budgeting process? Why?

9-9. If you were in middle management, would you prefer a top-down or bottom-up budgeting process? Why?

9-10. If you were the company CEO, do you think it would be wise for you to spend time tending to the details of the various budgets, given all your other responsibilities?

The overall approach a company takes to preparing its operating budget may actually be a combination of several of the approaches we have discussed here. For example, one company may have a top-down, participative, zero-based budgeting approach. Another company may be committed to an incremental, participative, bottom-up, perpetual budgeting philosophy. The object is not to select a particular approach from a laundry list. Rather, managers must approach preparing the operating budget in a way that makes sense in the circumstances.

The Sales Forecast

> *After analyzing all available data, the certified meteorologists at the U.S. Weather Service predicted sunny and warm weather for the next five days, with only a 10 percent chance of rain. It rained every day for the next five days.*

What is true for predicting future weather conditions is also true for predicting a company's future sales performance. Although technological advances over the past 30 years have improved financial forecasting methods, predicting future sales still remains largely an educated guess. The prediction of sales for the period covered by the operating budget is called the **sales forecast**.

sales forecast The prediction of sales for the period covered by the operating budget.

Cornerstone and Keystone of Budgeting

A solid, realistic sales forecast is perhaps the most critical feature of a solid, realistic operating budget. Why? Once the sales forecast has been developed, the business can prepare the sales budget, the production or purchases budget, the cost of goods or cost of services budget, the selling and administrative expense budget, the cash budget, and the three budgeted financial statements (income statement, balance sheet, and statement of cash flows).

The sales forecast is often called the cornerstone of budgeting. In the construction of a building, the first brick or stone laid is called the cornerstone. The remainder of the entire building is built off this cornerstone. If this brick is strong and placed properly the rest of the wall will be straight. In the construction of the operating budget, the sales forecast is the first step; all the budgets are built from the sales forecast. The sales forecast, then, is the cornerstone of the budgeting process, as depicted in Exhibit 9-4.

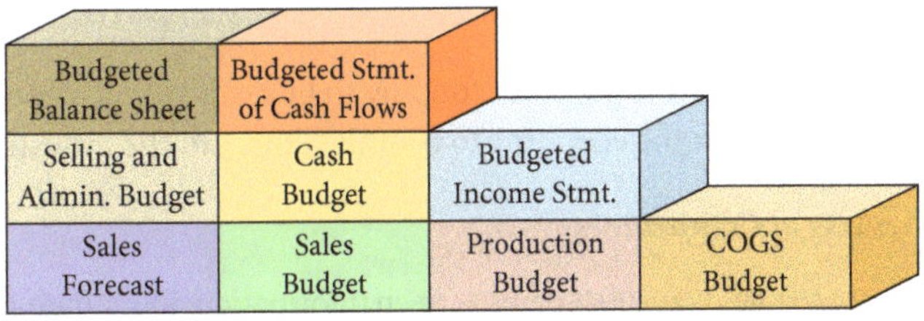

Exhibit 9-4 The Sales Forecast as the Cornerstone of Budgeting

The sales forecast has also been called the keystone of budgeting. This description clearly reflects the importance of the sales forecast. In the building of a stone archway, the keystone is the stone placed at the exact center at the top of the arch. If this stone is strong and placed properly, the arch will last. In fact, some arches built without mortar more than 1,000 years ago are still standing. They are held together solely from the strength of the keystone. If the keystone is weak, however, or is improperly set, the arch will collapse; and so it is with budgeting. The quality of the entire operating budget depends on the quality and accuracy of the sales forecast as depicted in Exhibit 9-5.

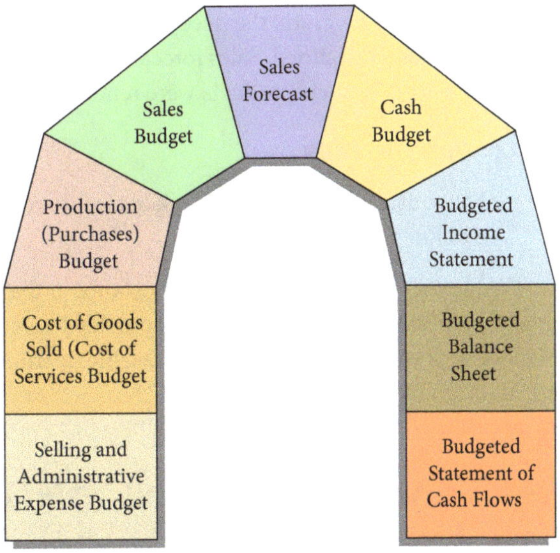

Exhibit 9-5 The Sales Forecast as the Keystone of Budgeting

As an archway made of stones depends on the keystone for its strength, the reliability of the operating budget depends on the strength of the sales forecast. If the sales forecast does not reasonably reflect the actual sales during the operating budget period, the budget will not reasonably estimate the actual results for the period. Thus, there will be differences between the actual income statement, balance sheet, and statement of cash flows and the budgeted income statement, balance sheet, and statement of cash flows.

Factors Affecting the Accuracy of the Sales Forecast

Many factors influence the accuracy of the sales forecast. We have chosen four to discuss here: the general economy, industry conditions, competition, and technology.

General Economy

If the economy goes into a recession, consumer saving and spending patterns change. Sales forecasts are usually affected as a result. The problem is, most economists estimate that the economy can be entering or moving out of a recession for at least six to nine months before we realize it. Thus, when a firm creates its sales forecast for the next year's budget, it may be unaware of what the actual state of the economy will be throughout the period covered by the operating budget.

Industry Conditions

It is possible for the general economy to be healthy and a particular industry to be in a recession or for the economy to be unhealthy and the industry quite healthy.

Actions of Competitors

All companies take great pains to keep information about their plans from their competitors. Therefore, all companies make their sales forecasts without information that has a tremendous impact on the accuracy of the forecast. For example, imagine **Intel** is about to launch a revolutionary product that could absolutely devastate its competitors. **Motorola** does not know this, so it creates a sales forecast that is inaccurate because it is unaware of **Intel's** planned actions.

Technological Developments

Technological developments can greatly influence the quality of the sales forecast. It is possible that the market for a particular product may not be as strong—or may not even exist—when the time the period being budgeted for arrives. When **Microsoft** introduced its *Windows Vista* program, the need for products compatible with Microsoft's old operating system sharply declined. Sales forecasts for software companies that did not expect the drop in demand for their products were rendered unreliable.

Discussion Question

9-11. What other factors can you think of that would influence the accuracy of a company's sales forecast?

We cannot overemphasize the importance of the sales forecast in the budgeting process, despite the difficulty of being completely accurate. It is worth the time and effort. Managers, however, must prepare and use the operating budget with a solid understanding of its limitations.

PART TWO: PREPARING AND USING THE OPERATING BUDGET

Preparing a Master Operating Budget

Marcy's Surf Shop is a retail store that sells only one product (surfboards) and deals in only one product model. The company's fiscal year ends June 30. At Marcy's request, we will prepare the operating budget for the first quarter of the fiscal year ending June 30, 2011. Thus, we will be budgeting for the quarter ending September 30, 2010.

We start with Marcy's budgeted income statement and the budgets that provide information we use to construct that budgeted financial statement. We will then prepare the budgeted balance sheet along with all other budgets required to prepare the budgeted balance sheet. Finally, we will prepare the budgeted statement of cash flows.

Because we focus on a merchandising company rather than a manufacturer, we will work with a purchases budget rather than a production budget.

Budgeted Income Statement

To prepare the budgeted income statement, we need information about sales, cost of goods sold, and selling and administrative expenses for the period covered by the budget. Therefore, we must prepare a budget for each of those items before we can construct the budgeted income statement.

Sales Budget

The first information we need to build the budgeted income statement is found in the sales budget. Our first task, then, is to request that Marcy's marketing and sales personnel provide a sales forecast. They tell us that they will be happy to do so, but are not sure how. Should we suggest they take last year's sales numbers and increase them by, say, five percent? This would be incremental budgeting, and without a critical look at market factors that affect sales it is a poor approach to budgeting. If simply increasing last year's amounts by a constant percentage were adequate, a computer could easily be programmed to do the job.

Before Marcy's Surf Shop can forecast its sales realistically, sales management and the sales personnel must first consider the factors that influence market conditions. After much discussion, Marcy's staff decided to research the following items:

- Current customer spending patterns
- The ability to attract new customers through market promotions
- The introduction of any new products
- The discontinuation of any products
- The competition
- Price changes
- The general economy
- Technological changes

Marcy's sales team researches each of the items chosen for evaluation by the company and examines the results to make sales forecasting something more than just a guessing game. Once the sales team considers all its research, it develops a forecast of unit sales for each month in the quarter. The sales team forecasts sales for Marcy's Surf Shop of 30 units in July, 50 units in August, and 40 units in September, as shown in Exhibit 9-6.

Exhibit 9-6 Sales Forecast for Marcy's Surf Shop

Marcy's Surf Shop
Sales Forecast
For the Quarter Ended September 30, 2010

	July	**August**	**September**	**Total**
Forecasted Sales in Units	30	50	40	120

Based on this forecast, we can prepare Marcy's sales budget for the quarter, as shown in Exhibit 9-7.

Exhibit 9-7 Sales Budget for Marcy's Surf Shop

Marcy's Surf Shop
Sales Budget
For the Quarter Ended September 30, 2010

	July	**August**	**September**	**Total**
Forecasted Sales in Units	30	50	40	120
× Forecasted Sales Price	$ 200	$ 200	$ 200	$ 200
= Budgeted Sales Dollars	$6,000	$10,000	$8,000	$24,000

We simply used the sales forecast of unit sales and the projected selling price of $200 per surfboard to develop the sales budget.

A real sales budget for an actual company is no more complicated than this one. Of course, in our example, Marcy's sells only one product. Remember from our earlier discussion that if Marcy's sold 80 different products, the company would need to prepare 80 of these sales budgets. If Marcy's sold 80 different products in 80 different locations, the company would need to prepare 6,400 of these sales budgets (80 products × 80 locations).

Discussion Question

9-12. What factors should Marcy's management consider when setting the $200 budgeted selling price for its surfboards?

Cost of Goods Sold Budget

Once we know how many units Marcy's Surf Shop plans to sell, and the cost per unit, we can prepare a cost of goods sold budget. As its name implies, we use this budget to determine how much cost of goods sold should be based on forecasted sales. Preparing the cost of goods sold budget consists of multiplying forecasted unit sales by the cost per unit. The cost of goods sold budget for Marcy's Surf Shop is presented in Exhibit 9-8.

Exhibit 9-8 Cost of Goods Sold Budget for Marcy's Surf Shop

Marcy's Surf Shop
Cost of Goods Sold Budget
For the Quarter Ended September 30, 2010

		July	August	September	Total
	Forecasted Unit Sales	30	50	40	120
×	Forecasted Unit Cost	$ 120	$ 120	$ 120	$ 120
=	Budgeted Cost of Goods Sold	$3,600	$6,000	$4,800	$14,400

Exhibit 9-8 shows that Marcy's forecasted cost of goods sold for the quarter is $14,400 ($3,600 + $6,000 + $4,800 = $14,400). The cost of goods sold budget provides the forecasted product cost information we use to prepare the budgeted income statement. This product cost information helps Marcy's management determine whether the company will be profitable based on its budget, or whether changes should be planned now to ensure profits in the budget period.

Discussion Questions

Compare the sales budget in Exhibit 9-7 with the cost of goods sold budget in Exhibit 9-8.

9-13. What are the similarities?

9-14. What are the differences?

Realistically, Marcy's will need to purchase more units of product than just the ones it expects to sell in July, August, and September. Thus, in addition to the budgets required to prepare the budgeted income statement, we will need to prepare a purchases budget. For our demonstration purposes, however, we will wait until after we have prepared the budgeted income statement to present the purchases budget. The only additional budget we need to prepare before we can prepare the budgeted income statement is the selling and administrative expense budget.

Selling and Administrative Expense Budget

The various expenses associated with the selling and administrative functions are estimated and used to prepare this budget. Selling and administrative expenses include salaries, advertising, rent, utilities, etc. Some of these costs are fixed while others are variable. For example, salaries and wages for the company run $1,000 per month plus 10% of sales. The table that follows depicts the breakdown of fixed and variable selling and administrative expenses.

	Fixed Cost Per Month	Variable Cost
Salaries and Wages	$1,000	10% of Sales
Rent	200	None
Depreciation for July and August	100	None
Depreciation for September	104	None
Others	500	5% of Sales

Next we prepare the selling and administrative expense budget based on the sales budget and the additional information presented above. The selling and administrative expense budget for Marcy's Surf Shop is presented in Exhibit 9-9.

Exhibit 9-9 Selling and Administrative Expense Budget for Marcy's Surf Shop

Marcy's Surf Shop
Selling and Administrative Expense Budget
For the Quarter Ended September 30, 2010

	July	August	September	Total for the Quarter
Variable Selling and Administrative Expenses:				
Var. Salaries and Wages (10% of sales)	$ 600*	$1,000*	$ 800*	$2,400
Other Var. S.&A. Exp.(5% of sales)	300**	500**	400**	1,200
Total Variable Selling and Admin. Exp.	900	1,500	1,200	3,600
Fixed Selling and Administrative Expenses:				
Fixed Salaries and Wages	1,000	1,000	1,000	3,000
Rent	200	200	200	600
Depreciation	100	100	104	304
Other Fixed Selling and Admin Exp.	500	500	500	1,500
Total Fixed Selling and Admin. Exp.	1,800	1,800	1,804	5,404
Total Selling and Administrative Expenses	$2,700	$3,300	$3,304	$9,004

*$6,000 × 10% = $600
$10,000 × 10% = $1,000
$8,000 × 10% = $800

** $6,000 × 5% = $300
$10,000 × 5% = $500
$8,000 × 5% = $400

The types of items and the amounts included in the selling and administrative expense budget vary from company to company. As we said earlier, the items included in this budget are determined by what is required to support the level of sales in the sales budget.

Discussion Questions

9-15. If you were preparing a selling and administrative expense budget, what are some of the things you would consider as you mapped out strategies to increase sales?

9-16. Besides those included in Exhibit 9-9, what are some other administrative costs you think would normally be included in a selling and administrative expense budget?

9-17. What do you think might explain the increase in anticipated depreciation expense in September from $100 to $104?

Building the Budgeted Income Statement

To prepare the budgeted income statement, we use information from the sales, cost of goods sold, and selling and administrative expense budgets. The budgeted income statement depicts the amount of profit or loss a business can expect from its budgeted operating activities. First, we take the total forecasted sales revenue from the sales budget. Next, we list variable costs such as cost of goods sold from the cost of goods sold budget and the variable selling and administrative expenses from the selling and administrative expense budget. We then subtract total variable cost from sales revenue to determine the forecasted contribution margin. We then list the fixed costs, in this case, all from the selling and administrative expense budget. By subtracting the total fixed cost from the contribution margin we determine the company's operating income for the period covered by the budget. The budgeted income statement for Marcy's Surf Shop is presented in Exhibit 9-10.

Exhibit 9-10 Budgeted Income Statement for Marcy's Surf Shop

Marcy's Surf Shop
Budgeted Income Statement
For the Quarter Ended September 30, 2010

Sales in Units	July 30	August 50	September 40	Total for the Quarter 120
Sales ($200 per unit)	$6,000	$10,000	$8,000	$24,000
Variable Costs:				
Cost of Goods Sold ($120 per unit)	(3,600)	(6,000)	(4,800)	(14,400)
Var. Salaries and Wages (10% of sales)	(600)	(1,000)	(800)	(2,400)
Other Var. S.&A. Exp.(5% of sales)	(300)	(500)	(400)	(1,200)
Total Variable Cost	(4,500)	(7,500)	(6,000)	(18,000)
Contribution Margin	1,500	2,500	2,000	6,000
Fixed Costs:				
Fixed Salaries and Wages	(1,000)	(1,000)	(1,000)	(3,000)
Rent	(200)	(200)	(200)	(600)
Depreciation	(100)	(100)	(104)	(304)
Other Fixed Selling and Admin Exp.	(500)	(500)	(500)	(1,500)
Total Fixed Cost	(1,800)	(1,800)	(1,804)	(5,404)
Operating Income	$ (300)	$ 700	$ 196	$ 596

We see from Exhibit 9-10 that Marcy's Surf Shop is projecting a $300 operating loss for July. In August Marcy's is projecting a operating income of $700 and in September it is $196. The total operating income for the quarter, then, is $596.

After Marcy's management team has looked at the budgeted income statement we have prepared, they may want to make some changes in their plans. For instance, management may find the $300 loss in July unacceptable. If so, they would review all the information used to build the budgeted income statement and either adjust their expectations or adjust the assumptions we used to prepare the budget.

Whatever the outcome of this evaluation, Marcy's Surf Shop has a better chance of planning for a successful future if management takes the budgeting process seriously. If budgets are used properly, managers will have an opportunity to see trouble spots in advance and make the required adjustments before it is too late.

Budgeted Balance Sheet

Now that we have prepared the budgeted income statement, we have much of the information we need to prepare the budgeted balance sheet. First, however, we must prepare two more budgets: the purchases budget, as mentioned when we were preparing the budgeted income statement, and the cash budget.

Purchases Budget

The cost of goods sold budget we prepared accounts only for the units projected to be sold during the period covered by the budget. If Marcy's planned to begin and end the period covered by the budget with no inventory on hand and planned to purchase only the amount of inventory during the budgeted period sufficient to support the level of projected sales, there would be no need for a separate purchases budget. Rather, the company could just use the information from the cost of goods sold budget. This plan is unrealistic, however, because a company like Marcy's must begin and end each period with a certain amount of merchandise on hand. These inventory requirements create the need for the purchases budget. Marcy's purchases budget for the three months ended September 30, 2010, is presented as Exhibit 9-11.

Marcy's Surf Shop
Purchases Budget
For the Quarter Ended September 30, 2010

		July	August	September	Total	
	Forecasted Unit Sales	30	50	40	120	(a)
+	Desired Ending Inventory*	20*	16*	24*	24	(b)
=	Total Units Needed	50	66	64	144	(c)
−	Beginning Inventory	(8)	(20)	(16)	(8)	(d)
=	Units to Be Purchased	42	46	48	136	(e)
×	Cost Per Unit	$ 120	$ 120	$ 120	$ 120	(f)
=	Cost of Purchases	$5,040	$5,520	$5,760	$16,320	(g)

* 40% of the next month's sales requirements

Exhibit 9-11 Purchases Budget for Marcy's Surf Shop

As you can see by looking at Exhibit 9-11, the purchases budget, even for a small company like Marcy's Surf Shop, can seem rather complicated. A line-by-line analysis, however, reveals that much of the information it contains is already known, and the new information is basically straightforward.

a. *Forecasted Unit Sales.* These numbers should look familiar to you because you have seen them three times already. They come directly from the sales forecast presented in Exhibit 9-6 and we used them to construct the sales budget in Exhibit 9-7 and the cost of goods sold budget in Exhibit 9-8.

b. *Desired Ending Inventory.* These numbers represent the number of units of product the company believes it needs on hand at the end of a given period to support sales in the early days of the next period. As the asterisk note in Exhibit 9-11 explains, Marcy's has decided it should have inventory of product on hand at the end of any given month equal to 40 percent of the next month's sales requirements. At the end of July, for example, Marcy's desires an ending inventory of 20 units, which is 40 percent of August's sales of 50 units (50 × 40% = 20 units).

   The amount of desired ending inventory is determined by at least two factors. First, the company must consider how long it usually takes to get product from the company's suppliers. This information is obtained from the purchasing records and discussions with the purchasing department. Second, the company must estimate the number of units of product it will sell in the early days of each month. This information comes from historical sales records and discussions with sales personnel.

   The desired ending inventory amounts for July, August, and September will be important to us when we construct the budgeted balance sheet, but we will defer our discussion of how they are used until we actually prepare that budget.

Discussion Question

9-18. Can you tell by looking at the purchases budget in Exhibit 9-11 how many surfboards Marcy's has forecasted it will sell in October? Explain your reasoning.

c. *Total Units Needed.* This figure is the sum of (a) and (b).

d. *Beginning Inventory.* Because the purpose of the purchases budget is to determine how many units of inventory Marcy's must purchase during each of the months included in the budget period, we must subtract any inventory forecasted to be on hand at the beginning of each month from the total units needed to determine how many units the company must purchase during the month.

   The beginning inventory for any period is the ending inventory for the previous period. You will note in the purchases budget in Exhibit 9-11 that the beginning inventory for August (20 units) is the same as the desired ending inventory for July, and the beginning inventory for September (16 units) is the same as the desired ending inventory for August. You should also note that the beginning inventory in the total column (eight units) is the same as the beginning inventory for July, because the total column is for the entire quarter and the quarter begins in July.

Discussion Question

9-19. The purchases budget in Exhibit 9-11 indicates that Marcy's desires ending inventory equal to 40% of the next month's sales requirements. Because sales in July are expected to be 30 surfboards, the beginning inventory in July (which is the ending inventory for June) should be 12 units (30 × 40%). Why do you think the beginning inventory in July is only eight surfboards?

e. *Units to Be Purchased.* This figure is simply (c) minus (d) and tells us the number of surfboards that Marcy's must purchase in each of the three months of the budget period and the total for the quarter.

f. *Cost Per Unit.* The cost per unit is what Marcy's must pay for each surfboard it purchases. Note that this cost is the same as the cost per unit used when we prepared the cost of goods sold budget presented in Exhibit 9-8.

g. *Cost of Purchases.* This figure is simply (e) multiplied by (f) and tells us what the purchase of surfboards will cost Marcy's in each of the three months of the budget period and the total for the quarter.

Cash Budget

When a company uses accrual accounting, it recognizes revenue when it is earned rather than when the cash associated with that revenue is collected, and expenses when the benefit is received rather than when the cash associated with the expenses is paid. This means, of course, that while the budgeted income statement (including the sales budget, cost of goods sold budget, and the selling and administrative expense budget) provides information about Marcy's projected earnings activities for the budget period, it does not provide direct information about what is projected to happen during that period in terms of cash. Also, unless Marcy's pays cash for its purchase of surfboards, the purchases budget suffers from the same limitation.

Before we can prepare the budgeted balance sheet, we must determine the effect on cash of the budgets we have prepared so far. We do that by preparing a cash budget, which is composed of a cash receipts schedule and a cash payments schedule.

Cash Receipts Schedule

The **cash receipts schedule** presents the amount of cash a company expects to collect during the budget period from the sales of its product. Before we can prepare Marcy's cash receipts schedule, we must make certain estimates about the composition of the company's sales (cash or credit) and the pattern of collecting the accounts receivable created by the credit sales. We estimate that 25 percent of Marcy's sales are for cash and the remaining 75 percent are on account (credit sales). Of the sales on account, we estimate that 30 percent are collected in the month of the sale, 60 percent in the month following the sale, and 10 percent in the second month following the sale. Because of the lag between the time a credit sale is made and the time cash is collected, some of the cash for credit sales made in May and June will not have been collected by the end of June, which means that those amounts will be collected during the three months included in our budget period. Therefore, we need to know that May credit sales were $4,500, and June credit sales were $6,000.

cash receipts schedule Presents the amount of cash a company expects to collect during the budget period.

Using the credit sales figures from May and June, and our assumptions about when cash is collected, we can prepare Marcy's cash receipts schedule for the three months ended September 30, 2010 as shown in Exhibit 9-12.

Although the cash receipts schedule presented in Exhibit 9-12 seems quite complex, it is more straightforward than it first appears. It is broken into two major parts. The first presents the amount of cash collected from credit sales during the period covered by the schedule (a through c) and the second part presents the amount of cash collected from cash sales during the budget period (d).

Exhibit 9-12 Cash Receipts Schedule for Marcy's Surf Shop

Marcy's Surf Shop
Cash Receipts Schedule
For the Quarter Ended September 30, 2010

	July	**August**	**September**	**Total**	
Credit Sales Collected:					
From Accounts Receivable at June 30, 2010:					
May Credit Sales ($4,500)					
Collected in July (10%)	$ 450			$ 450	(a)
June Credit Sales ($6,000)					
Collected in July (60%)	3,600			3,600	
Collected in August (10%)		$ 600		600	
From New Credit Sales:					
July Credit Sales ($4,500)					
Collected in July (30%)	1,350			1,350	(b)
Collected in August (60%)		2,700		2,700	
Collected in September (10%)			$ 450	450	
August Credit Sales ($7,500)					
Collected in August (30%)		2,250		2,250	
Collected in September (60%)			4,500	4,500	
September Credit Sales ($6,000)					
Collected in September (30%)			1,800	1,800	
Budgeted Receipts from Credit Sales	$5,400	$5,550	$6,750	$17,700	(c)
Cash Sales:					
July Cash Sales	1,500			1,500	(d)
August Cash Sales		2,500		2,500	
September Cash Sales			2,000	2,000	
Budgeted Cash Receipts	$6,900	$8,050	$8,750	$23,700	(e)

Let's take a few minutes to examine this schedule and see where the numbers came from and what they mean.

a. *From Accounts Receivable at June 30, 2010.* The accounts receivable balance at the end of June is composed of receivables arising from sales in May and June. May's credit sales were $4,500. Based on our collection assumption, 30 percent of that amount was collected in May and 60 percent in June. If 90 percent had been collected by the end of June, the remaining $450 ($4,500 × 10%) had not and was included in the balance of accounts receivable at the end of June. Since July is the second month following the credit sales in May, the $450 balance is shown as a collection in July ($4,500 × 10%).

   Credit sales in June totaled $6,000. Only $1,800 of that amount was collected in June ($6,000 × 30%). If 30 percent had been collected by the end of June, $4,200 ($6,000 × 70%) had not and was included in the balance of accounts receivable at the end of June. Since July is the month following the credit sales in June, $3,600 is shown as a collection in July ($6,000 × 60%); and because August is the second month following the credit sales in June, the remaining $600 balance is shown as a collection in August ($6,000 × 10%).

b. *From New Sales.* Recall from the sales budget in Exhibit 9-7 that budgeted sales for the three months covered by our budget example were $6,000 in July, $10,000 in August, and $8,000 in September. One of the assumptions we made as we began our discussion of the cash receipts schedule was that 75 percent of Marcy's sales were credit sales. Therefore, the sales on account used in this section of the schedule are \$4,500 for July (\$6,000 × 75%), \$7,500 for August (\$10,000 × 75%), and \$6,000 for September (\$8,000 × 75%).

The collection pattern for each of the three months is the same: 30 percent of credit sales are collected in the month of sale, 60 percent in the month following the sale, and 10 percent in the second month following the sale. So for July's credit sales, for example, the schedule shows \$1,350 will be collected in July (\$4,500 × 30%), \$2,700 will be collected in August (\$4,500 × 60%), and \$450 (\$4,500 × 10%) in September. The amounts projected to be collected for August and September credit sales are calculated exactly the same way.

c. *Budgeted Receipts from Credit Sales.* This figure is simply the sum of (a) and (b). It presents the total amount of cash Marcy's expects to collect during the period covered by the schedule from credit sales.

d. *Cash Sales.* This section is the least complicated of the schedule. For the three months included in the schedule it presents the portion of sales that will be cash sales. If 75 percent of the sales made in a given month are credit sales, then 25 percent will be cash sales. Therefore, in July the cash sales will be \$1,500 (\$6,000 × 25%) and that amount is shown as a cash receipt in July. The amount for August is \$2,500 (\$10,000 × 25%), and for September \$2,000 (\$8,000 × 25%).

e. *Budgeted Cash Receipts.* This figure is simply the sum of (c) and (d). As the description indicates, it presents the total amount of cash Marcy's plans to collect from the accounts receivable balance at the end of June, the credit sales it will have during the period covered by the schedule, and the cash sales made during the period.

Cash Payments Schedule

The **cash payments schedule** presents the amount of cash a company expects to pay out during the budget period. Before we can prepare Marcy's cash payments schedule, we must make certain assumptions about the company's pattern of cash payments. We assume that payment for the purchase of surfboards is made in the month following the purchase. Because of the lag time between the time a purchase is made and the time cash is paid, the purchases made in June will not have been paid by the end of June, which means that this amount will be paid in July, one of the months included in our budget period. Therefore, we need to know that purchases of merchandise in June totaled \$5,200. All cash selling and administrative expenses are paid in the month incurred.

cash payments schedule Presents the amount of cash a company expects to payout during the budget period.

Using these assumptions about when cash is paid and the purchases figure from June, we can prepare Marcy's cash payments schedule for the three months ended September 30, 2010, as shown in Exhibit 9-13.

Exhibit 9-13 Cash Payments Schedule for Marcy's Surf Shop

Marcy's Surf Shop
Cash Payments Schedule
For the Quarter Ended September 30, 2010

	July	August	September	Total	
Purchases	\$5,200	\$5,040	\$5,520	\$15,760	(a)
Selling and Admin. Expense:					
Salaries and Wages	1,600	2,000	1,800	5,400	(b)
Rent	200	200	200	600	(b)
Other Selling and Admin. Expense	800	1,000	900	2,700	(b)
Purchase of Display Case		240			(c)
Budgeted Cash Payments	\$7,800	\$8,480	\$8,420	\$24,700	(d)

As you can see from Exhibit 9-13, the cash payments schedule is not nearly as complex as either the purchases budget or the cash receipts schedule. There are a couple of tricky parts, however, so let us examine the items included.

a. *Purchases.* These are payments for the purchase of surfboards. Recall our assumption that payment for the purchase of merchandise is made in the month following purchase. The projected payment of $5,200 in July, then, is for purchases made in June, the payment of $5,040 in August will be for July purchases, and the $5,520 payment in September will be for August purchases.

Discussion Question

9-20. In our assumptions about cash payments, we said that June purchases of merchandise totaled $5,200 so it is easy to see where the July payment originated. Where do you suppose the payment amounts ($5,040 and $5,520) originated for August and September?

b. *Selling and Administrative Expense.* These are payments for the support costs Marcy's anticipates for each month of the budget period. The amounts come directly from the selling and administrative expense budget in Exhibit 9-9.

Discussion Question

9-21. Look back at the selling and administrative expense budget in Exhibit 9-9. All the expense items included in that budget are included in the cash payments schedule except depreciation. Why do you think depreciation expense was included in the selling and administrative expense budget but excluded from the cash payments schedule?

c. *Purchase of Display Case.* Evidently, Marcy's is planning to purchase a new display case for the showroom during the month of August. This purchase will be added to Marcy's property, plant, and equipment and will be important to us when we prepare the budgeted balance sheet and the budgeted statement of cash flows. Incidentally, the planned purchase of this display case is what caused depreciation expense in Exhibit 9-9 to increase by $4 in September.

d. *Budgeted Cash Payments.* This figure is simply the sum of (a), (b), and (c). As the description indicates, it presents the total amount of cash Marcy's plans to pay out during the period covered by the schedule.

Building the Cash Budget

Now that we have prepared the cash receipts schedule and the cash payments schedule, we can prepare Marcy's cash budget for the quarter ended September 30, 2010. As was the case with the schedules, we must make some assumptions for the cash budget. First, we estimate that Marcy's Surf Shop will have a cash balance of $2,170 on June 30, 2010. Second, Marcy's desires to maintain a cash balance of at least $1,900 at all times. If cash falls below $1,900, the company will borrow from a local bank. Finally, we ignore the interest Marcy's would be required to pay on any borrowings from the bank.

Using the assumption about Marcy's desired minimum cash balance, and the information from the cash receipts schedule and the cash payments schedule, we can prepare the company's cash budget for the quarter ending September 30, 2010, as shown in Exhibit 9-14.

The cash budget itself may not seem as complicated as the purchases budget, the cash receipts schedule, or the cash payments schedule. There are, however, some potential pitfalls in your understanding of the way this budget is constructed, so we will take a few minutes and discuss the items included.

Exhibit 9-14 Cash Budget for Marcy's Surf Shop

Marcy's Surf Shop
Cash Budget
For the Quarter Ended September 30, 2010

		July	August	September	Total	
	Beginning Cash Balance	$2,170	$ 1,900	$ 1,900	$ 2,170	(a)
+	Cash Receipts	6,900	8,050	8,750	23,700	(b)
=	Cash Available	$9,070	$ 9,950	$10,650	$25,870	(c)
−	Cash Payments	(7,800)	(8,480)	(8,420)	(24,700)	(d)
=	Balance before Borrowing	$1,270	$ 1,470	$ 2,230	$ 1,170	(e)
+/−	Borrowing/(Repayment)	$ 630	$ 430	$ (330)	$ 730	(f)
=	Ending Cash Balance	$1,900	$ 1,900	$ 1,900	$ 1,900	(g)

a. *Beginning Cash Balance.* Like all balance sheet items, the beginning cash balance for any period is the ending cash balance for the previous period. As mentioned earlier, the ending cash balance for June will be $2,170. Therefore, July's beginning cash balance will be June's ending cash balance. The same pattern holds true for the other months presented. August's beginning balance is July's ending balance and September's beginning balance is August's ending balance. Note, however, that the beginning balance in the total column ($2,170) is the same as the beginning balance for July. Likewise, the ending balance in the total column ($1,900) is the same as the ending balance for September, because the total column represents the entire quarter. The beginning balance for the quarter is July's beginning balance and the ending balance for the quarter is September's ending balance.

b. *Cash Receipts.* The cash receipts amounts are taken directly from the budgeted cash receipts line of the cash receipts schedule shown in Exhibit 9-12.

c. *Cash Available.* This figure is simply the sum of (a) and (b). This amount represents the total cash Marcy's expects to be available before deducting any payments.

d. *Cash Payments.* The cash payments amounts are taken directly from the budgeted cash payments line of the cash payments schedule shown in Exhibit 9-13.

e. *Balance before Borrowing.* This amount is calculated by simply subtracting (d) from (c). It represents the anticipated ending cash balance before any adjustments for borrowing or loan payments.

f. *Borrowing/(Repayment).* Marcy's wants to maintain a cash balance of at least $1,900. If the balance before borrowing drops too low, Marcy's will borrow enough money from the bank to bring the balance up to the desired ending cash balance of $1,900. As you can see, July's balance before borrowing is expected to be only $1,270. Therefore, Marcy's can anticipate the need to borrow $630 to bring the balance up to $1,900. So, if the balance before borrowing is less than the desired ending cash balance, as it will be in July and again in August, the amount that must be borrowed to bring the cash balance to the desired amount can be easily calculated. If, on the other hand, the expected balance before borrowing is greater than $1,900, as is the case in September, any amount in excess of the desired ending cash balance will be used to repay the loan ($330 in this instance).

g. *Ending Cash Balance.* This figure is simply (e) plus the borrowing or less the repayment shown in (f). As we said earlier, this ending cash amount also becomes the next month's beginning cash balance.

Now we can use the information from the cash budget and other budgets to prepare the budgeted balance sheet.

Building the Budgeted Balance Sheet

We assume that you already know the basics of how to construct a balance sheet, so for our presentation of the budgeted balance sheet, we focus on how to determine the various asset, liability, and equity items and dollar amounts for these items.

Although some of the amounts needed to prepare the budgeted balance sheet are taken directly from the budgets already prepared, many amounts are not specifically included in any of those budgets. For example, we have not prepared a budget or schedule that shows the ending balances for accounts receivable, inventory, property, plant, and equipment, accumulated depreciation, accounts payable, bank loans payable, common stock, additional paid-in capital, or retained earnings. For each of these items, we will present a brief discussion and a schedule to show how to calculate the amounts that should appear on the budgeted balance sheet. You will find as you examine each of these items that the budgeted ending balance is calculated by taking the beginning balance and adding or subtracting the changes that are expected to occur during the budget period. So, for each of these items, the beginning balance is our starting point. As discussed, the *beginning* balance of any balance sheet item is the prior month's *ending* balance. Therefore, all we need is the balance sheet for June 30 to determine the beginning balance for July. The balance sheet as of June 30, 2010, for Marcy's Surf Shop is shown in Exhibit 9-15.

Exhibit 9-15 Balance Sheet as of June 30, 2010, for Marcy's Surf Shop

Marcy's Surf Shop Balance Sheet As of June 30, 2010	
Assets	
Current Assets	
Cash	$ 2,170
Accounts Receivable	4,650
Inventory	960
Total Current Assets	$ 7,780
Property, Plant, and Equipment	
Equipment	6,000
Less Accumulated Depreciation	(1,200)
Equipment, Net	$ 4,800
Total Assets	$12,580
Liabilities	
Current Liabilities	
Accounts Payable	$ 5,200
Total Liabilities	$ 5,200
Owner's Equity	
Paid-in Capital	
Common Stock	$ 1,000
Additional Paid-in Capital	5,475
Total Paid-in Capital	$ 6,475
Retained Earnings	$ 905
Total Equity	$ 7,380
Total Liabilities and Equity	$12,580

Using the June 30, 2010 balance sheet in Exhibit 9-15 and information from the other budgets we have prepared so far, we can prepare a budgeted balance sheet for each of the three months included in our budget period, as shown in Exhibit 9-16.

Exhibit 9-16 Budgeted Balance Sheets for Marcy's Surf Shop

Marcy's Surf Shop
Budgeted Balance Sheet
As of July 31, August 31, and September 30, 2010

	July	August	September	
Assets:				
Current Assets				
Cash	$ 1,900	$ 1,900	$ 1,900	(a)
Accounts Receivable, Net	3,750	5,700	4,950	(b)
Inventory	2,400	1,920	2,880	(c)
Total Current Assets	$ 8,050	$ 9,520	$ 9,730	
Property, Plant, and Equipment				
Equipment	$ 6,000	$ 6,240	$ 6,240	(d)
Less Accumulated Depreciation	(1,300)	(1,400)	(1,504)	(e)
Equipment, Net	$ 4,700	$ 4,840	$ 4,736	
Total Assets	$12,750	$14,360	$14,466	
Liabilities:				
Current Liabilities				
Accounts Payable	$ 5,040	$ 5,520	$ 5,760	(f)
Bank Loan Payable	630	1,060	730	(g)
Total Liabilities	$ 5,670	$ 6,580	$ 6,490	
Owner's Equity				
Paid-in Capital				
Common Stock	$ 1,000	$ 1,000	$ 1,000	
Additional Paid-in Capital	5,475	5,475	5,475	(h)
Total Paid-in Capital	$ 6,475	$ 6,475	$ 6,475	
Retained Earnings	$ 605	$ 1,305	$ 1,501	(i)
Total Equity	$ 7,080	$ 7,780	$ 7,976	
Total Liabilities and Equity	$12,750	$14,360	$14,466	

The balance sheets presented in Exhibit 9-16 are much like the other balance sheets you have seen throughout your studies. The essential difference is not the format, but rather, the time frame. These are projected balance sheets whereas the others have presented past results. There is no total column for this budget, because the balance sheet is a financial snapshot of a business taken at the end of a period. Therefore, in a very real sense, the snapshot taken at the end of September is the total column.

As we have done with the other budgets prepared in this chapter, we will now take a few minutes and explain how the items on the budgeted balance sheet were determined.

a. *Cash.* This amount is taken directly from the ending cash balance line of the cash budget shown in Exhibit 9-14. For example, the amount shown as the ending cash balance of $1,900 in the July column of the cash budget is shown as cash in the July column of the budgeted balance sheet.

b. *Accounts Receivable.* To determine the ending accounts receivable balance for each month shown in Exhibit 9-16, we simply take the beginning accounts receivable balance, add budgeted credit sales for that month, and subtract budgeted collections for that month.

		July	August	September
	Beginning Balance	$4,650	$3,750	$ 5,700
+	Credit sales	4,500	7,500	6,000
−	Collections	(5,400)	(5,550)	(6,750)
=	Ending Balance	$3,750	$5,700	$ 4,950

The beginning accounts receivable balance of $4,650 for July is taken from the June 30, 2010, balance sheet shown in Exhibit 9-15. The cash receipts budget provides the rest of the information we need. The cash receipts budget shows the projected credit sales, and the total expected to be collected from credit sales. For July, the cash receipts budget shows credit sales of $4,500 and a total of $5,400 collected from credit sales. After adding the credit sales of $4,500 to the beginning balance of $4,650, we subtract the collections of $5,400 to arrive at the ending accounts receivable balance of $3,750. This amount is shown on the budgeted balance sheet for July. The ending accounts receivable amounts for other months are calculated the same way.

c. *Inventory*. To determine the ending inventory balance for each month shown in Exhibit 9-16, we simply take the beginning inventory balance, add purchases made during the month, and subtract that month's cost of goods sold.

		July	August	September
	Beginning Balance	$ 960	$2,400	$ 1,920
+	Purchases	5,040	5,520	5,760
−	Cost of goods sold	(3,600)	(6,000)	(4,800)
=	Ending Balance	$2,400	$1,920	$ 2,880

The beginning inventory balance for July of $960 is taken from the June 30, 2010, balance sheet shown in Exhibit 9-15. By looking at the purchases budget in Exhibit 9-11 and the cost of goods sold budget in Exhibit 9-8, we find that expected purchases for July are $5,040 and cost of goods sold are expected be $3,600. After adding the purchases of $5,040 to the beginning balance of $960, we subtract the cost of goods sold of $3,600 to arrive at the ending inventory balance of $2,400. This amount is shown on the budgeted balance sheet for July. The ending inventory amounts for other months are calculated the same way.

d. *Equipment*. To determine the ending balance in the equipment, we adjust the beginning balance by adding the cost of equipment purchased and subtracting the cost of any equipment sold. In our example, the only change in equipment is the $240 for the showcase the company is planning to buy in August. We add $240 to the $6,000 beginning balance to arrive at the budgeted ending balance of $6,240.

e. *Accumulated Depreciation*. To determine the ending balance for accumulated depreciation, we adjust the beginning balance by adding the depreciation for the period and subtracting the accumulated depreciation associated with any assets that have been sold or scrapped. In our example, the company does not expect to sell or otherwise dispose of any equipment, so the only changes to accumulated depreciation are increases relating to the budgeted monthly depreciation. You might notice that the amount added to accumulated depreciation in September is slightly higher than that for July and August. This is so because of the added depreciation for the showcase the company expects to buy in August.

f. *Accounts Payable.* To determine the ending accounts payable balance for each month shown in Exhibit 9-16, we simply take the beginning accounts payable balance, add budgeted purchases for that month, and subtract budgeted payments for that month.

		July	August	September
	Beginning Balance	$5,200	$5,040	$5,520
+	Purchases	5,040	5,520	5,760
−	Payments	(5,200)	(5,040)	(5,520)
=	Ending Balance	$5,040	$5,520	$5,760

The beginning accounts payable balance for July of $5,200 is taken from the June 30, 2010, balance sheet shown in Exhibit 9-15. By looking at the purchases budget in Exhibit 9-11 and the cash payments budget in Exhibit 9-13, we find that expected purchases for July are $5,040 and cash payments are expected be $5,200. After adding the purchases of $5,040 to the beginning balance of $5,200, we subtract the cash payments of $5,200 to arrive at the ending accounts payable balance of $5,040. This amount is shown on the budgeted balance sheet for July. The ending accounts payable amounts for other months are calculated the same way.

g. *Bank Loan Payable.* To determine the ending bank loans payable balance for each month shown in Exhibit 9-16, we simply take the beginning bank loans payable balance, add the budgeted borrowing for that month, and subtract budgeted payments for that month.

		July	August	September
	Beginning Balance	$ 0	$ 630	$1,060
+	Borrowing	630	430	0
−	Repayments	0	0	(330)
=	Ending Balance	$630	$1,060	$ 730

The beginning bank loans payable balance for July would normally come from the June 30, 2010, balance sheet shown in Exhibit 9-15; however, in this example the beginning balance for bank loans payable on June 30, 2010, is zero, so bank loans payable does not appear. By looking at the cash budget in Exhibit 9-14, we find that borrowing of $630 is expected in July, borrowing of $430 is expected in August, and a repayment of $330 is expected in September.

h. *Common Stock and Additional Paid-in Capital.* In this example, no common stock or additional paid in capital transactions are expected during the budget period. Therefore, the beginning July balance for these items found on the June 30, 2010, balance sheet in Exhibit 9-15 remains unchanged during the budget period.

i. *Retained Earnings.* To determine the ending retained earnings balance, we add the income for the period or, if the company has a loss, subtract the loss and deduct dividends, if they exist, from the beginning retained earnings balance.

		July	August	September
	Beginning Balance	$905	$ 605	$1,305
+	Income/Loss	(300)	700	196
−	Dividends	0	0	0
=	Ending Balance	$605	$1,305	$1,501

In our example, the $905 beginning balance of retained earnings is found on the June 30, 2010, balance sheet shown in Exhibit 9-15. To find the ending retained earnings that should appear on the budgeted balance sheet for July, we deduct the budgeted loss for that month of $300 from the beginning retained earnings balance of $905. That figure becomes the beginning balance in August. To determine the August ending balance of retained earnings we simply add August's budgeted income. September's ending balance would be calculated the same way. There are no dividends in our example so the dividend amount is zero for each month presented.

Budgeted Statement of Cash Flows

Now that we have prepared all the other budgets, we can now prepare the budgeted statement of cash flows. This budgeted financial statement must be the final budget prepared because, as you recall from your earlier study of this financial statement, it is a form of financial statement analysis. A statement of cash flows prepared on historical results analyzes the income statement and the balance sheet to explain what caused cash to change from the beginning of a period to the end of the period. The budgeted statement of cash flows does exactly the same thing, except that it analyzes the budgeted income statement and the budgeted balance sheet to explain what will cause the projected change in cash from the start to the end of the budget period.

A budgeted statement of cash flows for Marcy's Surf Shop is presented as Exhibit 9-17.

Exhibit 9-17 Budgeted Statement of Cash Flows for Marcy's Surf Shop

Marcy's Surf Shop
Budgeted Statement of Cash Flows
For the Quarter Ended September 30, 2010

	July	August	September	Total	
Cash Flows from Operating Activities:					
Income	$ (300)	$ 700	$ 196	$ 596	(a)
Add: Depreciation	100	100	104	304	(b)
Changes in CA & CL:					
Accounts Receivable	900	(1,950)	750	(300)	
Inventory	(1,440)	480	(960)	(1,920)	(c)
Accounts Payable	(160)	480	—	560	
Net Cash Flow from Op Act	$ (900)	$ (190)	330	$ (760)	
Cash Flow From Investing Activities:					
Cash Paid for Showcase	—	(240)	—	(240)	(d)
Net Cash Flow from Inv Act		$ (240)		$ (240)	
Cash Flow From Financing Activities:					
Borrowing	$ 630	$ 430		$1,060	(e)
Loan Payments	—	—	$ (330)	(330)	
Net Cash Flow from Fin Act	$ 630	$ 430	$ (330)	$ 730	
Increase/(Decrease) in Cash	$ (270)	$ 0	$ 0	$ (270)	
Budgeted Beginning Cash Balance	2,170	1,900	1,900	2,170	
Budgeted Ending Cash Balance	$1,900	$1,900	$1,900	$1,900	

To fully understand the preparation of the statement in Exhibit 9-17, it is best if you have a basic understanding of how the statement of cash flows is generally prepared. If this is not the case, we suggest that you review this area in any introductory financial accounting text.

a. The income amounts are taken directly from the budgeted income statements.

b. Adjust for non-cash items—Since depreciation is a non-cash expense, we add it back to income.

c. Adjust for changes in operating balance sheet accounts—To do this, we adjust income by adding the amount of any decreases in operating assets (such as accounts receivable and inventory) and increases in operating liabilities (such as accounts payable). Next, we adjust income by subtracting the amount of any increases in operating assets and decreases in operating liabilities.

d. Any purchases of investments, such as property, plant and equipment or certain financial investments are shown as a decrease to cash. In our example, we show the purchase of the display case found on the cash payments schedule in Exhibit 9-13. If there were any sales of investments, they would have been shown as an increase to cash.

e. Any increases in cash from general borrowing or sales of the company's stock are added while any decreases in cash due to repaying general borrowing, dividend payments, or repurchasing company stock (the purchase of treasury stock) are subtracted. In our example, we show the borrowing and loan payments found on the cash budget in Exhibit 9-14.

In the normal course of business, a company can obtain cash from only three sources: borrowing, owner contributions, and profitable operations. Unfortunately, it seems Marcy's does not anticipate generating enough cash through operations to run the business and must, therefore, borrow the money. If Marcy finds this unacceptable, she may want to continue the budgeting process and make adjustments to her business plan.

You will be delighted to know we are not going to do that for Marcy. We hope, however, that you have learned what a powerful tool the operating budget can be by going through the steps required to prepare one.

We have seen that the operating budget can serve as a guide for the company to follow, assist a company in allocating its scarce resources, and foster communication and coordination among managers from different functional areas within the company. It can also establish performance standards, or benchmarks, against which the company can compare its actual results. This fourth application presents some serious challenges to managers, however. Misunderstanding how to set and use performance standards can lead to behavior that is actually detrimental to the organization.

Once upon a time, in the United States at least, someone figured out that the operating budget could be used as a means of controlling a company's activities. It's really a pretty simple concept. Once you establish the operating budget for the year, you keep one eye on the budget and one eye on the actual results. The idea is that if you prepare a solid budget and then perform to meet that budget, you will naturally keep control of your operation. Before long, this way of using the operating budget had become quite common among U.S. companies. As this practice became more popular, firms began evaluating the performance of their managers based on how they performed against the budget as well. This practice is known as the **performance to budget** evaluation. Salary increases, year-end bonuses, and promotions to senior management began to depend at least partially on a manager's ability to "meet or beat" the budget. By now, the operating budget had become the principal means used to control costs. It was felt that if managers performed well against the budget, they were doing a good job of controlling the operations they managed, which makes sense, right? Wrong! Unfortunately, that is not what happens when the budget is used as the primary control device in a company. What happens is that using the budget for this purpose actually encourages managers to make bad decisions and discourages them from making good decisions.

performance to budget A process of evaluating managers and employees based on how they perform against the budget.

The Static Budget Performance Report

budget performance report The evaluation instrument used to evaluate a manager's performance to budget.

As performance to budget became a popular way of measuring management performance, an instrument known as the **budget performance report** evolved to capture the information management thought was needed to perform the evaluation. The report compares budgeted amounts to actual results to calculate favorable and unfavorable variances.

According to the operating budget for Marcy's Surf Shop, the company forecasted sales of 120 units and operating income of $596 for the quarter ending September 30, 2010. Let's assume that the company was actually able to sell 140 units and its actual operating income was $3,556. The performance report in Exhibit 9-18 compares the static budget income statement to Marcy's Surf Shop's actual results.

Exhibit 9-18 Static Budget Income Statement Performance Report for Marcy's Surf Shop

Marcy's Surf Shop
Static Budget Income Statement Performance Report
For the Quarter Ended September 30, 2010

(a) Description	(b) Static Budget	(c) Actual Results	(d) Static Budget Variances	
Units	120	140	20	Favorable
Sales	$24,000	$29,500	$ 5,500	Favorable
Variable Costs:				
Cost of Goods Sold	(14,400)	(16,350)	(1,950)	Unfavorable
Variable Salaries and Wages	(2,400)	(2,750)	($350)	Unfavorable
Other Variable Selling and Admin. Exp.	(1,200)	(1,325)	($125)	Unfavorable
Total Variable Cost	(18,000)	(20,425)	(2,425)	Unfavorable
Contribution Margin	6,000	9,075	3,075	Favorable
Fixed Costs:				
Fixed Salaries and Wages	(3,000)	(3,075)	(75)	Unfavorable
Rent	(600)	(660)	(60)	Unfavorable
Depreciation	(304)	(304)	0	
Other Fixed Selling and Admin Exp.	(1,500)	(1,480)	20	Favorable
Total Fixed Cost	(5,404)	(5,519)	(115)	Unfavorable
Operating Income	$ 596	$ 3,556	$ 2,960	Favorable

variance The difference between the amount budgeted and the actual amount.

As you can see, the report is not terribly complicated. The description column (a), lists the items for which the manager being evaluated is responsible. The budget column (b), lists the budgeted amount for each of those items. The actual column (c), lists the actual operating results for the period covered by the budget. The difference between the budgeted amount and the actual amount is called a **variance**. The variances in our example appear in column (d) along with an indication as to whether the variances are favorable or unfavorable. Sales or income amounts that are greater than budgeted amounts result in favorable variances whereas sales that are less than budgeted amounts result in unfavorable variances. As you might imagine, expenses and costs that are greater than budgeted amounts result in unfavorable variances while expenses and costs that are less than budgeted amounts result in favorable variances.

Discussion Question

9-22. What do the words favorable and unfavorable mean to you?

Notice that while sales and income exceed budgeted amounts resulting in favorable variances, many of the costs and expenses also exceed the budget resulting in a significant number of unfavorable variances. It might seem that it would be wise to focus attention on these unfavorable variances so management can take corrective action. However, after closer consideration, it is likely that the costs were actually greater than budget amounts due to the increased sales volume and not due to a lack of control over spending. In order to really tell whether cost variances are truly unfavorable, we must determine what the costs should be based on the actual level of sales activity. Flexible budgets can help us with this problem.

The Flexible Budget

Earlier in the chapter we presented an exhibit that showed the interrelationship among all the budgets. We have reproduced that presentation as Exhibit 9-19. As we said in that earlier discussion, a change in any one of the budgets has a ripple effect throughout all the other budgets. A little logic tells us that if there are variances in any one of the budgets there will also be a ripple effect throughout all the other budgets.

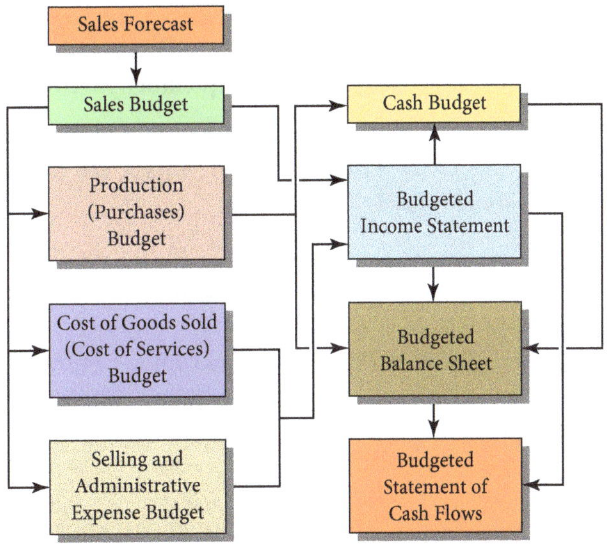

Exhibit 9-19 Interrelationship Among the Budgets

Perhaps a more important cause of variances than the interrelationship among the budgets is the role of the sales forecast in the budgeting process. Note in Exhibit 9-19 that all the budgets included in the operating budget are dependent upon the sales forecast, which explains why we described the sales forecast as both the cornerstone and the keystone of the operating budget in our earlier discussions.

The sales forecast is so critical in the budgeting process that we will end this section by sharing three truths with you about the sales forecast and the operating budget:

Truth 1: If the sales forecast is inaccurate, the operating budget will be inaccurate. Do not confuse *inaccurate* with *bad*. A bad sales forecast comes from lack of effort and attention. An inaccurate sales forecast simply means that the actual results are different from the operating budget because the future did not turn out the way company management predicted.

Truth 2: The sales forecast will be inaccurate. Recall the items we discussed earlier in the chapter that affect a company's ability to forecast sales. The state of the general economy, actions of competitors, technological developments, and many other factors make an accurate sales forecast literally impossible.

Truth 3: The operating budget will be inaccurate. Once again, do not confuse inaccurate with bad. Inaccurate simply means that the actual results are going to be different from what was budgeted, meaning, of course, that variances will always exist.

Some approaches to the budget performance report help overcome the variances caused by actual sales being different from budgeted sales. The most popular of these is the flexible budget performance report, which we will cover next.

Preparing the Flexible Budget

flexible budget A budget that takes into consideration how changes in the level of activity affect revenues and costs. A flexible budget can be prepared for any level of activity.

As we mentioned earlier, a budget that is based on one level of activity is called a static budget. The variances depicted in the performance report in Exhibit 9-18 are based on the company's static budget. In addition to the static budget, it is also useful to prepare budgets based on other levels of sales activity as well. **Flexible budgets** take into consideration how changes in the level of activity affect revenues and costs. A flexible budget can be prepared for any level of activity. Exhibit 9-20 depicts flexible budget income statements for Marcy's Surf Shop for various levels of sales activity.

Exhibit 9-20 Flexible Budget Income Statements for Marcy's Surf Shop

Marcy's Surf Shop
Flexible Budget Income Statements
For the Quarter Ended September 30, 2010

	Sales of 110 Units	Sales of 120 Units	Sales of 130 Units	Sales of 140 Units	Sales of 150 Units	
Units	110	120	130	140	150	(a)
Sales ($200 per unit)	$22,000	$24,000	$26,000	$28,000	$30,000	(b)
Variable Costs:						
Cost of Goods Sold ($120 per unit)	(13,200)	(14,400)	(15,600)	(16,800)	(18,000)	(c)
Var. Salaries and Wages (10% of sales)	(2,200)	(2,400)	(2,600)	(2,800)	(3,000)	(d)
Other Var. S.& A. Exp. (5% of sales)	(1,100)	(1,200)	(1,300)	(1,400)	(1,500)	(e)
Total Variable Cost	(16,500)	(18,000)	(19,500)	(21,000)	(22,500)	(f)
Contribution Margin	5,500	6,000	6,500	7,000	7,500	(g)
Fixed Costs:						
Fixed Salaries and Wages	(3,000)	(3,000)	(3,000)	(3,000)	(3,000)	(h)
Rent	(600)	(600)	(600)	(600)	(600)	(h)
Depreciation	(304)	(304)	(304)	(304)	(304)	(h)
Other Fixed Selling and Admin Exp.	(1,500)	(1,500)	(1,500)	(1,500)	(1,500)	(h)
Total Fixed Cost	(5,404)	(5,404)	(5,404)	(5,404)	(5,404)	(i)
Operating Income	$ 96	$ 596	$ 1,096	$ 1,596	$ 2,096	(j)

As we have done with the static budgets presented earlier in this chapter, we will now take a few minutes and explain how we determined the amounts on the flexible budget income statement.

a. *Units.* This is simply the number of unit sales we use to prepare the budget. It can be any number of units, however, in our example, we selected amounts that were reasonable based on sales in the static budget of 120 units for the quarter. Because our example assumes actual sales for the quarter of 140 units, we were sure to include a column for this level of sales activity.

b. *Sales*. To determine the sales in dollars we multiply the $200 selling price per unit by the budgeted number of units sold.

c. *Cost of goods sold*. To determine the cost of goods sold we multiply the $120 cost per unit by the budgeted number of units sold.

d. *Variable salaries and wages*. To determine the variable salaries and wages we multiply the budgeted sales dollars in item (b) by the salaries and wages variable percentage, which is 10 percent.

e. *Other variable selling and administrative expense*. To determine the budgeted variable selling and administrative expense we multiply the sales dollars in item (b) by the other selling and administrative variable percentage, which is five percent.

f. *Total variable cost*. Total variable cost is determined by simply adding up all of the variable costs.

g. *Contribution Margin*. The contribution margin is sales less total variable cost.

h. *Fixed Costs*. Unless we exceed the relevant range, fixed costs should not change as activity increases so we use the same fixed cost amounts we used to prepare the static budget. For this example we will assume that each of our flexible budget columns is within the relevant range.

i. *Total fixed cost*. Total fixed cost is determined by adding up all of the fixed costs.

j. *Operating income*. We determine operating income by subtracting total fixed cost from the contribution margin.

As you can see by looking at the operating income for each column in the flexible budget, income increases significantly as the number of units sold increases.

The Flexible Budget Performance Report

In our example for Marcy's Surf Shop, the company actually sold 140 units instead of the 120 units forecasted in the static budget. According to the flexible budget, operating income at this level of sales should have been $1,596. However the company's actual operating income was $3,556 as mentioned earlier. In order to provide a better assessment of the company's performance, we will examine two performance reports. The first, the **sales volume variance performance report**, presented in Exhibit 9-21, depicts the static budget compared to the flexible budget and the variances the company should expect due to the difference in sales volume.

sales volume variance performance report A report that depicts the static budget compared to the flexible budget and the variances the company should expect due to the difference in sales volume.

The performance report in Exhibit 9-21 compares the static budget to a flexible budget prepared based on the actual level of activity. That is, since actual sales were 140 units, the flexible budget we use in the performance report is based on sales of 140 units (one of the levels we budgeted for in Exhibit 9-20). Variances that represent the differences between the static budget and a flexible budget prepared for the actual level of sales volume are called **sales volume variances**. Notice that the sales volume variance for operating income is $1,000 favorable. This indicates that the company's operating income is theoretically $1,000 higher due to the increased sales volume. The unfavorable sales volume variances for variable costs are of no concern whatever. In fact, we would expect variable costs to be higher due to the increased sales volume. These unfavorable variances actually equal the amount of the expected increases in variable costs due to the increase in sales volume. Budgeted fixed costs remain constant within the relevant range regardless of the level of sales activity, so the sales volume variances for fixed cost are zero.

sales volume variances Variances that represent the differences between the static budget and a flexible budget prepared for the actual level of sales volume.

Exhibit 9-21 Sales Volume Variance Performance Report for Marcy's Surf Shop

Marcy's Surf Shop
Sales Volume Variance Performance Report
For the Quarter Ended September 30, 2010

	Static Budgeted	Flexible Budget	Sales Volume Variances	
Units	120	140	20	F
Sales	$24,000	$28,000	$4,000	F
Variable Costs:				
Cost of Goods Sold	(14,400)	(16,800)	(2,400)	U
Variable Salaries and Wages	(2,400)	(2,800)	(400)	U
Other Var. S. &A. Exp.	(1,200)	(1,400)	(200)	U
Total Variable Cost	(18,000)	(21,000)	(3,000)	U
Contribution Margin	6,000	7,000	1,000	F
Fixed Costs:				
Fixed Salaries and Wages	(3,000)	(3,000)	—	
Rent	(600)	(600)	—	
Depreciation	(304)	(304)	—	
Other Fixed Selling and Admin Exp.	(1,500)	(1,500)	—	
Total Fixed Cost	(5,404)	(5,404)	—	
Operating Income	$ 596	$ 1,596	$1,000	F

F = Favorable
U = Unfavorable

flexible budget performance report A report that depicts the variances that result from a comparison of the flexible budget to the company's actual results

flexible budget variances Variances that represent the differences between actual results and the flexible budget prepared based on the actual level of activity.

Next we will examine the **flexible budget performance report**, presented in Exhibit 9-22, which depicts the flexible budget variances that result from a comparison of the flexible budget to the company's actual results.

The flexible budget performance report in Exhibit 9-22 compares the flexible budget to actual results. Variances that represent the differences between actual results and the flexible budget prepared based on the actual level of activity are called **flexible budget variances**.

Based on the flexible budget, operating income should have been $1,596, but the actual operating income for the company was $3,556. How could this be? Well, for one thing, the favorable flexible budget variance for sales is an indication that the company was able to sell its surf boards for a higher price than the $200 per unit they budgeted. This means that the sales staff not only sold more units, as indicated by the sales volume variances, but also sold their products for a higher per unit price than they had anticipated.

The flexible budget variances for the variable and fixed costs indicate how well managers were able to keep costs under control. For example, based on the flexible budget, cost of goods sold should have been $16,800. However, the actual amount for cost of goods sold was only $16,350, which resulted in a $450 favorable flexible budget variance. Other variable costs can be analyzed in the same fashion. It appears that the company's managers had trouble controlling the fixed costs. For example, the actual rent of $660 is $60 more than the budgeted amount. Comparing the actual rent cost of $660 to the budgeted amount of $600 results in a $60 unfavorable flexible budget variance for rent.

Exhibit 9-22 Flexible Budget Performance Report for Marcy's Surf Shop

Marcy's Surf Shop
Flexible Budget Performance Report
For the Quarter Ended September 30, 2010

	Flexible Budget	Actual	Flexible Budget Variances	
Units	140	140	—	
Sales	$28,000	$29,500	$1,500	F
Variable Costs:				
Cost of Goods Sold	(16,800)	(16,350)	450	F
Variable Salaries and Wages	(2,800)	(2,750)	50	F
Other Var. S. &A. Exp.	(1,400)	(1,325)	75	F
Total Variable Cost	(21,000)	(20,425)	575	F
Contribution Margin	7,000	9,075	2,075	F
Fixed Costs:				
Fixed Salaries and Wages	(3,000)	(3,075)	(75)	U
Rent	(600)	(660)	(60)	U
Depreciation	(304)	(304)	—	
Other Fixed Selling and Admin Exp.	(1,500)	(1,480)	20	F
Total Fixed Cost	(5,404)	(5,519)	(115)	U
Operating Income	$ 1,596	$ 3,556	$1,960	F

F = Favorable
U = Unfavorable

To get a clearer picture of the breakdown of the differences between the amounts originally included in a company's static budget and its actual results, we can prepare a report that includes columns for the static budget, the flexible budget, and actual results with appropriate variances placed between the first and third columns and between the third and fifth columns. Exhibit 9-23 presents this report for Marcy's Surf Shop.

Although the report in Exhibit 9-23 may seem difficult to follow at first, upon closer examination we find that it is simply the information from Exhibits 9-21 and 9-22 combined into one presentation. The disadvantage of the report is that it is complicated, but its advantage is that it traces various amounts from the company's original business plans (the static budget), through to the actual results. Importantly, the report also presents appropriate variances to help managers understand the nature of the differences between their static budget and actual results.

Although we have only presented the flexible budget for the income statement, in practice, companies prepare flexible budgets for virtually all of their budgets.

For manufacturers, flexible budgets can become quite involved. Manufacturers often determine budgeted amounts for the direct material, direct labor, variable manufacturing overhead, and fixed manufacturing overhead for each individual unit of production. This practice is called standard costing, a topic covered in the next chapter.

Exhibit 9-23 Income Statement Performance Report for Marcy's Surf Shop

Marcy's Surf Shop
Income Statement Performance Report
For the Quarter Ended September 30, 2010

	Static Budgeted 1	Sales Volume Variances 2 = 3 − 1	Flexible Budget 3	Flexible Budget Variances 4 = 5 − 3	Actual 5
Units	120	20 F	140	—	140
Sales	$24,000	$4,000 F	$28,000	$1,500 F	$29,500
Variable Costs:					
Cost of Goods Sold	(14,400)	(2,400) U	(16,800)	450 F	(16,350)
Variable Salaries and Wages	(2,400)	(400) U	(2,800)	50 F	(2,750)
Other Var. S. & A. Exp.	(1,200)	(200) U	(1,400)	75 F	(1,325)
Total Variable Cost	(18,000)	(3,000) U	(21,000)	575 F	(20,425)
Contribution Margin	6,000	1,000 F	7,000	2,075 F	9,075
Fixed Costs:					
Fixed Salaries and Wages	(3,000)	—	(3,000)	(75) U	(3,075)
Rent	(600)	—	(600)	(60) U	(660)
Depreciation	(304)	—	(304)	—	(304)
Other Fixed Selling and Admin Exp.	(1,500)	—	(1,500)	20 F	(1,480)
Total Fixed Cost	(5,404)	—	(5,404)	(115) U	(5,519)
Operating Income	$ 596	$ 1,000 F	$1,596	$ 1,960 F	$ 3,556

$1,000 F — Sales volume variance

$1,960 F — Flexible budget variance

$2,960 F — Static budget variance

F = Favorable
U = Unfavorable

Using (and Misusing) the Operating Budget

> *If I get bigger pants, does that mean I've lost weight?*
>
> —Paul Valenzuela

What may have caused Marcy's favorable flexible budget variances? It could be that company managers did their very best to keep costs as low as possible. But there is a possibility that when the budget was originally prepared, employees used sales and cost targets that could be easily achieved. This way, they could achieve their budgeted operating income and favorable variances without having to work very hard. It is difficult to say what really happened without further examination of the facts. But one thing is clear, a *favorable* variance is not always *good*. It simply means *under budget*.

What about the performance evaluation for the staff at Marcy's Surf Shop? Once again, it depends greatly on how company management views the performance relative to the budget. In all too many companies, favorable variances are rewarded in two ways. First, the staff would receive congratulations from everyone involved in the evaluation on what a great job they did to boost sales and keep costs under control for the quarter. Second, the budgets for the following periods would be adjusted to reflect the possible higher sales volume, higher sales prices, and lower costs. That's right! When managers keep costs under control, resulting in favorable cost variances, their budgets are often cut so they must keep costs down to the new low level from then on. The reasoning is that if costs are low in the current period, we can keep them just as low in the future. Some managers figure this out and to avoid having their cost budgets cut they purposely increase spending to avoid favorable cost variances. This is sometimes called "use it or lose it" and is a practice that flourishes in many companies in the United States today.

In many companies, if no variance exists for a particular cost item, management assumes that there is no problem with the amount spent on that item. This is a wrong assumption. This is the point Paul Valenzuela—a former executive of **Ford Motor Company**—was making in the quotation that opened this section. Buying bigger clothes makes it appear you have lost weight, when in fact you may not have lost any. The way this translates into the topic we are discussing is that if managers are able to secure a large budget for a particular item, they will appear to be efficient simply by spending less than, or exactly, the amount budgeted. Spending the amount budgeted means spending the amount budgeted—nothing more, nothing less. It certainly doesn't mean that the amount spent was what should have been spent.

Often, managers use variances to direct their attention to trouble spots in the organization. This is called **management by exception**. When using management by exception the focus is primarily on items with large variances. Further, when these variances are investigated, the analysis usually focuses on the actual performance column of the performance report. If a large, unfavorable variance exists, managers are often required to explain why they spent more than the budget allowed. On the other hand, if a favorable variance exists, the item becomes a target for reducing costs next year, so the budget is cut.

management by exception When managers use variances to direct their attention to trouble spots in the organization.

What is bizarre about this method of using the budget performance report is that everyone knows budgets are established for the future. Everyone also knows that the future is to a great extent unknown to us. Yet, once the budget is established it becomes set in stone, so to speak, and it is most often assumed that any variance between the budgeted cost and the actual cost can be traced to the actual results and not to the budget.

Are we suggesting that managers should be free to spend whatever amount they see fit on the cost items for which they are responsible? Absolutely not! This idea makes no sense, and it runs counter to everything we have said throughout this chapter, and indeed, throughout this book. Managers should be working every day to control costs and run their operations more efficiently. What we are saying is that this has very little to do with the operating budget. Cost control is an ongoing management process, of which the operating budget is only a part. Using the budget as the primary cost control device in a business is done in place of real control. Perhaps worse than that, using performance to budget as the evaluation instrument for managers encourages them to focus on the elimination of variances as their primary goal. As stated, because the budget is often considered to be set in stone, the only way to eliminate variances is to manipulate the actual performance to match the budget. This is what leads to silly budget games, such as padding the budget and the "use it or lose it" phenomenon we mentioned earlier.

If we lived in a perfect world where we could predict the future accurately, there would be no problem with the performance to budget evaluation technique. Unfortunately, we do not live in such a perfect world, and the future is largely unknown to us. When we prepare the operating budget we are attempting to predict the future. Differences are bound to exist between what we predict and what actually happens.

So, how do managers overcome the problems we have been discussing in this section? Well, they do it by using the budget as it was intended to be used—as a guide for the business. Managers must be prepared to respond to changing circumstances and updated information.

On June 6, 1944, the United States military and its allies invaded Europe in perhaps the largest and most complicated military action in the history of the world. Operation Overlord, as it was called, involved many thousands of troops, and the outcome of World War II was at stake. The allies, under the supreme command of General Dwight D. Eisenhower, spent well over a year preparing for D-Day. Every detail of the invasion was meticulously planned and the various military units involved spent months practicing their roles. The plan called for split-second timing and total coordination among all units involved.

When the invasion was launched, however, almost nothing went according to plan. Landing craft carrying the soldiers missed their target beaches, some by as much as four miles. High winds caused paratroop units to land as far as ten miles behind enemy lines. Everything went wrong. And yet, the allies ultimately won a total and complete victory in the invasion of Normandy. When he was asked how this could be when nothing went according to plan, General Eisenhower (who later became President of the United States) responded with a statement that speaks volumes to the subject of planning and control. He said "Plans are nothing; planning is everything". What he meant was that the planning and practice the military undertook to prepare for the invasion prepared them to respond and adjust to changing conditions.

As it was in the invasion of Europe, so must it be in business. Managers should not hesitate to adjust their budgets when desirable or necessary. Further, when the period covered by the operating budget is over, an analysis should be performed to compare the actual results to the budget. The focus of this analysis, however, should be on how to improve the budgeting process rather than on the inevitable variances that have occurred.

Summary

The operating budget is an integral part of the overall planning process for any company. Besides serving as a guide for the business throughout the period covered by the budget, the operating budget can assist management in allocating resources, fostering communication and coordination among various segments of the company, and establishing performance standards.

The operating budget is a set of estimated financial statements. These are the budgeted income statement, the budgeted balance sheet, and the budgeted statement of cash flows. Besides the budgeted financial statements, the operating budget includes several other budgets prepared to support the budgeted financial statements. These are the sales budget, the production (or purchases) budget, the cost of goods sold (or cost of services) budget, the selling and administrative expense budget, and the cash budget (including the cash receipts schedule and the cash payments schedule).

There are several different approaches to preparing the operating budget. Perpetual, incremental, zero-based, top-down, bottom-up, imposed, and participative approaches to budgeting are just some that have developed over time. Each approach has certain advantages and certain disadvantages relative to the other approaches.

All the budgets included in the operating budget are dependent on the sales forecast. Indeed, the accuracy of the entire budget is dependent on the accuracy of the forecast. Many factors, including the state of the general economy, the condition of the company's industry, the actions of competitors, and technological developments all influence a company's ability to forecast its sales reasonably.

Flexible budgeting is a technique that adjusts a static budget (one prepared for a specific level of activity) to the actual level of activity, thus showing what the results should have been at the actual level of activity. This provides management a clearer comparison between a period's actual results and the budget for that same period.

The operating budget was never meant to be used as the principal cost control device in business. Using the budget for this purpose actually encourages managers to make decisions that are detrimental to the business. If used properly, however, as a guide and coordination instrument, the operating budget can be of tremendous benefit for any company.

Key Terms

Review the Facts

A. What is the operating budget?

B. What is the master budget?

C. Which financial statements are part of the operating budget?

D. What is the difference between the financial statements included in the operating budget and other financial statements you have learned about in this course?

E. List the main benefits of budgeting.

F. What is the basic difference between the production budget and the purchases budget?

G. What are two advantages of perpetual budgeting?

H. What is a disadvantage of perpetual budgeting?

I. What is incremental budgeting?

J. What problem is associated with incremental budgeting?

K. What is zero-based budgeting?

L. Describe the differences between top-down and bottom-up budgeting.

M. Describe the differences between an imposed budget and a participative budget.

N. Why is the sales forecast often called the cornerstone of budgeting?

O. Why is the sales forecast often called the keystone of budgeting?

P. List three factors that should be considered when preparing the sales forecast.

Q. Why does the number of units budgeted to be purchased differ from the number of units budgeted to be sold?

R. When preparing the purchases budget, what two factors should be considered when determining the budgeted ending inventory?

S. What is presented on the cash receipts schedule?

T. For a particular budget period, why don't the budgeted cash collections from customers equal budgeted sales?

U. What is the basic difference between a budgeted balance sheet and an historical balance sheet?

V. In the normal course of business, what are the three sources from which a company can obtain cash?

W. How does the flexible budget differ from the static budget?

X. How do sales volume variances differ from flexible budget variances?

Y. What is a performance to budget evaluation?

Apply What You Have Learned

LO 3 & 4: Determine Order of Operating Budget Preparation

9-23. During the budgeting process, not all budgets are prepared at the same time. Following are several operating budgets.

1. _____ Cash budget
2. _____ Budgeted financial statements
3. _____ Purchases budget
4. _____ Sales budget
5. _____ Administrative expense budget
6. _____ Selling expense budget

Required:

Indicate a logical sequence for the preparation of the master budget.

LO 3: Indicate Advantages and Disadvantages of Top-Down, Bottom-Up Approaches

9-24. The master budget can be prepared using either the top-down or bottom up approach. Following in random order are several advantages and disadvantages of each approach.

1. _____ Budgeting process forces managers at various levels to think about future activities.
2. _____ Top manager is more knowledgeable.
3. _____ Employees at various levels must take time from their schedules to work on the budget.
4. _____ Employees will be more eager to work toward goals they helped set.
5. _____ Employees feel more like part of the company team.
6. _____ Top manager is more aware of company goals.
7. _____ Employees may try to pad the budget.

8. ______ Employees are less accepting of budgeted goals if they had no part in setting them.

9. ______ Top manager lacks detailed knowledge required to prepare budgets.

Required:

For each of these items, indicate whether it is associated with top-down (T) or bottom-up (B), and whether it is an advantage (A) or disadvantage (D).

LO 3: Indicate Budgeting Approaches

9-25. Following are approaches to budgeting, with a partial definition of those items in scrambled order.

a. Perpetual budgeting

b. Incremental budgeting

c. Zero-based budgeting

d. Top-down budgeting

e. Bottom-up budgeting

1. ______ Lower-level managers and employees initially prepare the budget.

2. ______ Each item on the budget must be justified each year.

3. ______ The budget is updated every month.

4. ______ Lower-level managers generally do not participate in budget preparation.

5. ______ Uses the prior year's budget to build the new budget.

Required:

For each partial definition, identify the budgeting approach to which it refers.

LO 5: Prepare a Sales Budget

9-26. For 2011, Tom Norris Computer Game Company expects to sell 6,000 games in the first quarter, 7,000 games in the second quarter, 9,000 games in the third quarter, and 12,000 games in the fourth quarter. Each game sells for $11.

Required:

Prepare the 2011 sales budget for Tom Norris Computer Game Company.

LO 5: Prepare a Sales Budget

9-27. For 2011, Paul Elsea's Barber Supply Company expects to sell 100 hair dryers in the first quarter, 90 hair dryers in the second quarter, 130 hair dryers in the third quarter, and 150 hair dryers in the fourth quarter. Each hair dryer sells for $67.

Required:

Prepare the 2011 sales budget for hair dryers for Paul Elsea's Barber Supply Company.

LO 5: Prepare a Sales Budget

9-28. For 2011, Taub Yo Yo Company expects to sell 20,000 units in January, 25,000 units in February, and 30,000 units in March. Each unit sells for $1.20.

Required:

Prepare the sales budget for Taub Yo Yo Company for the first quarter of 2011.

LO 5: Prepare a Sales Budget

9-29. The Golden Bird Cage Company intends to sell 11,500 bird cages during 2011. The budgeted selling price per cage is $88. The following sales forecast is available:

	Units
First quarter	2,500
Second quarter	2,100
Third quarter	3,800
Fourth quarter	3,100

Required:

Prepare the 2011 sales budget for Golden Bird Cage Company.

LO 5: Prepare a Sales Budget

9-30. Easy-Glide Strollers intends to sell 73,000 baby strollers in the first quarter of 2011. The budgeted selling price per stroller is $59. The following sales forecast is available:

	Units
January	22,500
February	22,500
March	28,000

Required:

Prepare the sales budget for Easy-Glide Strollers for the first quarter of 2011.

LO 5: Prepare a Purchases Budget

9-31. Florence Marie's Hat Shop plans to sell the following quantity of hats during the first four months of 2011.

	Units
January	200
February	250
March	300
April	320

Florence pays $6 for each hat which she sells for $15.

At the beginning of January, Florence plans to have 40 hats on hand, and hopes to maintain an ending inventory equal to 20% of next month's sales.

Required:

Prepare a purchases budget for the first quarter of 2011 for Florence Marie's Hat Shop. Remember, the first quarter is January, February, and March. April sales are only provided to help compute the ending inventory for March.

LO 5: Prepare a Sales Budget and Cost of Goods Sold Budget

9-32. Refer to the information in problem 9-31.

Required:

a. Prepare a sales budget for the first quarter of 2011 for Florence Marie's Hat Shop.

b. Prepare a cost of goods sold budget for the first quarter of 2011 for Florence Marie's Hat Shop.

LO 5: Prepare a Purchases Budget.

9-33. Cathy Norris Art Supplies plans to sell the following quantity of model AB222 airbrush during the first four months of 2011.

	Units
January	400
February	260
March	220
April	200

The company pays $44 for each airbrush and sells them for $65. At the beginning of January, Cathy Norris Art Supplies plans to have 60 airbrushes on hand, and hopes to maintain an ending inventory equal to 15% of next month's sales.

Required:

Prepare a purchases budget for the first quarter of 2011 for Cathy Norris Art Supplies. Remember, the first quarter is January, February, and March. April sales are only provided to help compute the ending inventory for March.

LO 5: Prepare a Sales Budget and Cost of Goods Sold Budget

9-34. Refer to the information in problem 9-33.

Required:

a. Prepare a sales budget for the first quarter of 2011 for Cathy Norris Art Supplies.

b. Prepare a cost of goods sold budget for the first quarter of 2011 for Cathy Norris Art Supplies.

LO 5: Prepare a Sales Budget, Cost of Goods Sold Budget, and Purchases Budget

9-35. Diaz Lumber plans to sell the following quantity of BC Grade 1/2-inch plywood during the first four months of 2011.

January	220 sheets
February	250 sheets
March	200 sheets
April	300 sheets

Diaz pays $7 for each sheet of plywood and sells them for $12. At the beginning of January, Diaz plans to have 66 sheets of plywood on hand, and hopes to maintain an ending inventory equal to 30% of next month's sales.

Required:

a. Prepare a sales budget for the first quarter of 2011 for Diaz Lumber.

b. Prepare a cost of goods sold budget for the first quarter of 2011 for Diaz Lumber.

c. Prepare a purchases budget for the first quarter of 2011 for Diaz Lumber.

LO 5: Prepare a Budgeted Income Statement Using Information Provided in Other Budgets

9-36. Smith Manufacturing has prepared the following budgeted information for January 2011.

Smith Manufacturing
Sales Budget
For January 2011

	Budgeted Sales in Units	3,300
×	Budgeted Sales Price	$ 200
=	Budgeted Sales Dollars	$660,000

Smith Manufacturing
Cost of Goods Sold Budget
For January 2011

	Budgeted Sales in Units	3,300
×	Budgeted Cost Per Unit	$ 110
=	Budgeted Cost of Goods Sold	$363,000

Smith Manufacturing
Selling and Administrative Expense Budget
For January 2011

Salaries and Wages	$101,500
Rent	64,000
Depreciation	53,200
Other	2,300
Budgeted S & A Expense	$221,000

Required:

Prepare a budgeted income statement for January 2011 for Smith Manufacturing.

LO 5: Prepare a Budgeted Income Statement Using Information Provided in Other Budgets

9-37. Gomez Sales Company has prepared the following budgeted information for March 2011.

Gomez Sales Company
Sales Budget
For March 2011

	Budgeted Sales in Units	110,000
×	Budgeted Sales Price	$ 4.95
=	Budgeted Sales Dollars	$544,500

Gomez Sales Company
Cost of Goods Sold Budget
For March 2011

	Budgeted Sales in Units	110,000
×	Budgeted Cost Per Unit	$ 3.35
=	Budgeted Cost of Goods Sold	$368,500

(Continued)

Gomez Sales Company Selling and Administrative Expense Budget For March 2011	
Sales Salaries	$ 51,500
Sales Commission	11,000
Other Salaries and Wages	35,000
Store Rent	24,000
Other Expenses	$ 10,500
Budgeted S & A Expense	$132,000

Required:

Prepare a budgeted income statement for March 2011 for Gomez Sales Company.

LO 5: Prepare a Budgeted Income Statement Using Information Provided in Other Budgets

9-38. Copas Company has prepared the following budgeted information for December 2011.

Copas Company Sales Budget For December 2011		
	Budgeted Sales in Units	10,000
×	Budgeted Sales Price	$ 12.00
=	Budgeted Sales Dollars	$120,000

Copas Company Cost of Goods Sold Budget For December 2011		
	Budgeted Sales in Units	10,000
×	Budgeted Cost Per Unit	$ 8.00
=	Budgeted Cost of Goods Sold	$80,000

Copas Company Selling and Administrative Expense Budget For December 2011	
Sales Salaries	$18,500
Sales Commission	3,000
Store Rent	9,000
Other Expenses	1,500
Budgeted S & A Expense	$32,000

Required:

Prepare a budgeted income statement for December 2011 for Copas Company.

LO 5: Prepare a Budgeted Income Statement

9-39. For the first quarter of 2011, Philip's Sales Corporation has budgeted sales of $390,000 and budgeted cost of goods sold of $280,000. In addition, the budget for the first quarter of 2011 includes wages and salaries of $42,000, rent of $9,000, utilities of $2,000, maintenance of $1,000, and other expenses of $3,000.

Required:

Prepare a budgeted income statement for the first quarter of 2011 for Philip's Sales Corporation.

LO 5: Prepare a Budgeted Income Statement

9-40. For January 2011, Edwardo Manufacturing has budgeted sales of $1,200,000 and budgeted cost of goods sold of $980,000. In addition, the budget for January 2011 includes sales salaries of $98,000, administrative salaries of $54,000, rent of $24,000, utilities of $8,000, and other expenses of $9,000.

Required:

Prepare a budgeted income statement for January 2011 for Edwardo Manufacturing.

LO 5: Prepare a Budgeted Income Statement

9-41. For the year 2011, Martin Sales Corporation has budgeted sales of $3,500,000 and budgeted cost of goods sold of $2,800,000. In addition, the budget for 2011 includes sales salaries of $220,000, administrative salaries of $130,000, depreciation of $180,000, utilities of $38,000, and other expenses of $22,000.

Required:

Prepare a budgeted income statement for 2011 for Martin Sales Corporation.

LO 5: Prepare a Budgeted Income Statement for One Quarter

9-42. The following budgets were prepared for Gary's Jean Store.

Gary's Jean Store
Sales Budget
For the Quarter Ended June 30, 2010

	Apr	May	Jun	Total
Budgeted Sales in Units	300	350	400	1,050
× Budgeted Sales Price	$ 27	$ 27	$ 27	$ 27
= Budgeted Sales Dollars	$8,100	$9,450	$10,800	$28,350

Gary's Jean Store
Cost of Goods Sold Budget
For the Quarter Ended June 30, 2010

	Apr	May	Jun	Total
Budgeted Sales in Units	300	350	400	1,050
× Budgeted Cost Per Unit	$ 14	$ 14	$ 14	$ 14
= Budgeted Cost of Goods Sold	$4,200	$4,900	$5,600	$14,700

Gary's Jean Store
Selling and Administrative Expense Budget
For the Quarter Ended June 30, 2010

	Apr	May	Jun	Total
Salaries and Wages	$1,800	$2,200	$1,900	$ 5,900
Rent	500	500	500	1,500
Depreciation	100	100	100	300
Other	600	900	800	2,300
Budgeted Sales Dollars	$3,000	$3,700	$3,300	$10,000

Required:

Prepare a budgeted income statement for the second quarter of 2010 for Gary's Jean Store.

LO 5: Prepare a Budgeted Income Statement for One Quarter

9-43. Franco's Cart Company manufactures small carts that are designed to be pulled behind a small tractor or riding lawn mower. The following budgets were prepared for Franco's Cart Company.

Franco's Cart Company
Sales Budget
For the Quarter Ended March 31, 2010

		Jan	Feb	Mar	Total
	Budgeted Sales in Units	1,300	1,450	1,700	4,450
×	Budgeted Sales Price	$ 186	$ 186	$ 186	$ 186
=	Budgeted Sales Dollars	$241,800	$269,700	$316,200	$827,700

Franco's Cart Company
Cost of Goods Sold Budget
For the Quarter Ended March 31, 2010

		Jan	Feb	Mar	Total
	Budgeted Sales in Units	1,300	1,450	1,700	4,450
×	Budgeted Cost Per Unit	$ 154	$ 154	$ 154	$ 154
=	Budgeted Cost of Goods Sold	$200,200	$223,300	$261,800	$685,300

Franco's Cart Company
Selling and Administrative Expense Budget
For the Quarter Ended March 31, 2010

	Jan	Feb	Mar	Total
Salaries and Wages	$21,950	$22,200	$23,600	$67,750
Rent	4,000	4,500	4,500	13,000
Depreciation	3,200	3,200	3,200	9,600
Other	2,300	2,500	2,800	7,600
Budgeted S & A Expense	$31,450	$32,400	$34,100	$97,950

Required:

Prepare a budgeted income statement for the first quarter of 2010 for Franco's Cart Company.

LO 5: Prepare a Budgeted Income Statement for One Quarter

9-44. The following budgets were prepared for Byrne Manufacturing.

Byrne Manufacturing
Sales Budget
For the Quarter Ended September 30, 2011

		Jul	Aug	Sep	Total
	Budgeted Unit Sales	900	1,100	1,300	3,300
×	Budgeted Sales Price	$ 225	$ 225	$ 225	$ 225
=	Budgeted Sales Dollars	$202,500	$247,500	$292,500	$742,500

Byrne Manufacturing
Cost of Goods Sold Budget
For the Quarter Ended September 30, 2011

	Jul	Aug	Sep	Total
Budgeted Unit Sales	900	1,100	1,300	3,300
× Budgeted Cost Per Unit	$ 204	$ 204	$ 204	$ 204
= Budgeted Cost of Goods Sold	$183,600	$224,400	$265,200	$673,200

Byrne Manufacturing
Selling and Administrative Expense Budget
For the Quarter Ended September 30, 2011

	Jul	Aug	Sep	Total
Salaries and Wages	$ 4,800	$ 5,200	$ 5,800	$15,800
Rent	2,400	2,400	2,400	7,200
Depreciation	1,150	1,150	1,150	3,450
Other	1,800	2,000	2,200	6,000
Budgeted S &A Expense	$10,150	$10,750	$11,550	$32,450

Required:

Prepare a budgeted income statement for the third quarter of 2011 for Byrne Manufacturing.

LO 5: Prepare a Cash Receipts Schedule for One Quarter

9-45. The Deacon Company is preparing a cash receipts schedule for the first quarter of 2010. Sales for November and December of 2009 are expected to be $180,000 and $200,000, respectively. Budgeted sales for the first quarter of 2010 are presented here.

The Deacon Company
Sales Budget
For the Quarter Ended March 31, 2010

	Jan	Feb	Mar	Total
Budgeted Sales	$220,000	$240,000	$260,000	$720,000

Twenty percent of sales are for cash, the remaining 80% are on account. Ten percent of the sales on account are collected in the month of the sale, 60% in the month following the sale, and the remaining 30% in the second month following the sale. There are no uncollectible accounts receivable.

Required:

Prepare a cash receipts schedule for the first quarter of 2010.

LO 5: Prepare a Cash Receipts Schedule for One Quarter

9-46. The V & A Velez Company is preparing a cash receipts schedule for the first quarter of 2010. Sales for November and December of 2009 are expected to be $300,000 and $310,000, respectively. Budgeted sales for the first quarter of 2010 are presented here.

The V & A Velez Company Sales Budget For the Quarter Ended March 31, 2010	Jan	Feb	Mar	Total
Budgeted Sales	$220,000	$290,000	$340,000	$850,000

Ten percent of sales are for cash, the remaining 90% are on account. Twenty percent of the sales on account are collected in the month of the sale, 70% in the month following the sale, and the remaining 10% in the second month following the sale. There are no uncollectible accounts receivable.

Required:

Prepare a cash receipts schedule for the first quarter of 2010.

LO 5: Prepare a Cash Receipts Schedule for One Quarter

9-47. The Arauz Company is preparing a cash receipts schedule for the first quarter of 2011. Sales for November and December of 2010 are expected to be $30,000 and $50,000, respectively. Budgeted sales for the first quarter of 2011 are presented here.

The Arauz Company Sales Budget For the Quarter Ended March 31, 2011	Jan	Feb	Mar	Total
Budgeted Sales	$20,000	$25,000	$40,000	$85,000

Fifteen percent of sales are for cash, the remaining 85% are on account. Twenty percent of the sales on account are collected in the month of the sale, 50% in the month following the sale, and the remaining 30% in the second month following the sale. There are no uncollectible accounts receivable.

Required:

Prepare a cash receipts schedule for the first quarter of 2011.

LO 5: Prepare a Cash Receipts Schedule for One Quarter

9-48. The Phillips Company is preparing a cash receipts schedule for the first quarter of 2011. Sales for November and December of 2010 are expected to be $33,000 and $55,000, respectively. Budgeted sales for the first quarter of 2011 are presented here.

The Phillips Company Sales Budget For the Quarter Ended March 31, 2011	Jan	Feb	Mar	Total
Budgeted Sales	$20,000	$30,000	$45,000	$95,000

Fifteen percent of sales are for cash, the remaining 85% are on account. Twenty percent of the sales on account are collected in the month of the sale, 50% in the month following the sale, 30% in the second month following the sale. There are no uncollectible accounts receivable.

Required:

Prepare a cash receipts schedule for the first quarter of 2011.

LO 5: Prepare a Cash Receipts Schedule for One Quarter

9-49. The Aimin Company is preparing a cash receipts schedule for the first quarter of 2011. Sales for November and December of 2010 are expected to be $40,000 and $80,000, respectively. Budgeted sales for the first quarter of 2011 are presented here.

The Aimin Company
Sales Budget
For the Quarter Ended March 31, 2011

	Jan	Feb	Mar	Total
Budgeted Sales	$30,000	$40,000	$50,000	$120,000

Ten percent of sales are for cash, the remaining 90% are on account. Fifteen percent of the sales on account are collected in the month of the sale, 60% in the month following the sale, 25% in the second month following the sale. There are no uncollectible accounts receivable.

Required:

Prepare a cash receipts schedule for the first quarter of 2011.

LO 5: Prepare a Cash Receipts Schedule for One Quarter

9-50. The Gabriel Diaz Company is preparing a cash receipts schedule for the first quarter of 2011. Sales on account for November and December of 2010 are expected to be $500,000 and $750,000, respectively. Budgeted sales for the first quarter of 2011 are presented here.

The Gabriel Diaz Company
Sales Budget
For the Quarter Ended March 31, 2011

	Jan	Feb	Mar	Total
Budgeted Cash Sales	$ 40,000	$ 45,000	$ 55,000	$ 140,000
Budgeted Sales on Account	400,000	450,000	550,000	1,400,000
Total Sales	$440,000	$495,000	$605,000	$1,540,000

Expected collection pattern for sales on account:

15% in the month of sale
60% in the month following the sale
25% in the second month following the sale
0% uncollectible

Required:

Prepare a cash receipts schedule for the first quarter of 2011.

LO 5: Prepare a Cash Receipts Schedule for One Quarter

9-51. The Lila Steinman Company is preparing a cash receipts schedule for the first quarter of 2011. Sales on account for November and December of 2010 are expected to be $200,000 and $400,000, respectively. Budgeted sales for the first quarter of 2011 are presented here.

The Lila Steinman Company
Sales Budget
For the Quarter Ended March 31, 2011

	Jan	Feb	Mar	Total
Budgeted Cash Sales	$ 20,000	$ 25,000	$ 27,000	$ 72,000
Budgeted Sales on Account	180,000	210,000	250,000	640,000
Total Sales	$200,000	$235,000	$277,000	$712,000

Expected collection pattern for sales on account:

10% in the month of sale
70% in the month following the sale
20% in the second month following the sale
0% uncollectible

Required:

Prepare a cash receipts schedule for the first quarter of 2011.

LO 5: Prepare a Cash Receipts Schedule for One Quarter

9-52. The Lowensohn Company is preparing a cash receipts schedule for the first quarter of 2011. Sales on account for November and December of 2010 are expected to be $320,000 and $550,000, respectively. Budgeted sales for the first quarter of 2011 are presented here.

The Lowensohn Company
Sales Budget
For the Quarter Ended March 31, 2011

	Jan	Feb	Mar	Total
Budgeted Cash Sales	$120,000	$150,000	$125,000	$395,000
Budgeted Sales on Account	180,000	225,000	190,000	595,000
Total Sales	$300,000	$375,000	$315,000	$990,000

Expected collection pattern for sales on account:

30% in the month of sale
50% in the month following the sale
20% in the second month following the sale
0% uncollectible

Required:

Prepare a cash receipts schedule for the first quarter of 2011.

LO 5: Prepare a Cash Receipts Schedule for One Quarter

9-53. The S.R. Jackson Company is preparing a cash receipts schedule for the second quarter of 2011. Sales on account for February and March of 2011 are expected to be $50,000 and $60,000, respectively. Budgeted sales for the second quarter of 2011 are presented here.

The S.R. Jackson Company
Sales Budget
For the Quarter Ended June 30, 2011

	Apr	May	Jun	Total
Budgeted Cash Sales	$15,000	$20,000	$25,000	$ 60,000
Budgeted Sales on Account	30,000	40,000	50,000	120,000
Total Sales	$45,000	$60,000	$75,000	$180,000

Expected collection pattern for sales on account:

25% in the month of sale
50% in the month following the sale
25% in the second month following the sale
0% uncollectible

Required:

Prepare a cash receipts schedule for the second quarter of 2011.

LO 5: Prepare a Cash Receipts Schedule for One Quarter

9-54. The Hodson Company is preparing a cash receipts schedule for the third quarter of 2011. Sales on account for May and June of 2011 are expected to be $100,000 and $120,000, respectively. Budgeted sales for the third quarter of 2011 are presented here.

The Hudson Company
Sales Budget
For the Quarter Ended September 30, 2011

	Jul	Aug	Sep	Total
Budgeted Cash Sales	$ 8,000	$ 9,000	$ 11,000	$ 28,000
Budgeted Sales on Account	80,000	90,000	110,000	280,000
Total Sales	$88,000	$99,000	$121,000	$308,000

Expected collection pattern for sales on account:

10% in the month of sale
60% in the month following the sale
30% in the second month following the sale
0% uncollectible

Required:

Prepare a cash receipts schedule for the third quarter of 2011.

LO 5: Prepare a Cash Receipts Schedule for One Quarter

9-55. The A.R. Oddo Company is preparing a cash receipts schedule for the fourth quarter of 2011. Sales on account for August and September of 2011 are expected to be

$200,000 and $220,000, respectively. Budgeted sales for the fourth quarter of 2011 are presented here.

The A.R. Oddo Company Sales Budget For the Quarter Ended December 31, 2011	Oct	Nov	Dec	Total
Budgeted Cash Sales	$ 42,000	$ 46,000	$ 60,000	$148,000
Budgeted Sales on Account	210,000	230,000	300,000	740,000
Total Sales	$252,000	$276,000	$360,000	$888,000

Expected collection pattern for sales on account:

20% in the month of sale
70% in the month following the sale
10% in the second month following the sale
0% uncollectible

Required:

Prepare a cash receipts schedule for the fourth quarter of 2011.

LO 5: Prepare a Cash Receipts Schedule for One Quarter

9-56. The law firm of Hendricks & Hendricks is preparing a cash receipts schedule for the first quarter of 2011. Service revenue for November and December of 2010 are expected to be $90,000 and $50,000, respectively. All billings are on account. There are no "cash sales." Budgeted service revenue for the first quarter of 2011 is presented here.

Hendricks & Hendricks Service Revenue Budget For the Quarter Ended March 31, 2011	Jan	Feb	Mar	Total
Budgeted Service Revenue	$40,000	$50,000	$65,000	$155,000

Expected collection pattern:

30% in the month of sale
60% in the month following the sale
10% in the second month following the sale
0% uncollectible

Required:

Prepare a cash receipts schedule for the first quarter of 2011.

LO 5: Prepare a Cash Receipts Schedule for One Quarter

9-57. The medical practice of Healit & Quick is preparing a cash receipts schedule for the first quarter of 2011. Service revenue for November and December of 2010 are expected to be $120,000 and $110,000, respectively. All billings are on account. There are no "cash sales." Budgeted service revenue for the first quarter of 2011 is presented here.

Healit & Quick
Service Revenue Budget
For the Quarter Ended March 31, 2011

	Jan	Feb	Mar	Total
Budgeted Service Revenue	$120,000	$130,000	$140,000	$155,000

Expected collection pattern:

20% in the month of sale
60% in the month following the sale
20% in the second month following the sale
0% uncollectible

Required:

Prepare a cash receipts schedule for the first quarter of 2011.

LO 5: Prepare a Cash Payments Schedule for One Quarter

9-58. Marcy Steinmann and Company has prepared the following budgets for the first quarter of 2011.

Marcy Steinmann and Company
Selling and Administrative Expense Budget
For the Quarter Ended March 31, 2011

	Jan	Feb	Mar	Total
Salaries and Wages	$1,700	$2,200	$1,900	$ 5,800
Rent	300	300	300	900
Depreciation	200	200	200	600
Other	900	1,200	1,000	3,100
Total	$3,100	$3,900	$3,400	$10,400

Marcy Steinmann And Company
Purchases Budget
For the Quarter Ended March 31, 2011

		Jan	Feb	Mar	Total
	Forecasted Unit Sales	50	60	70	180
+	Desired Ending Inventory	12	14	16	16
=	Total Units Needed	62	74	86	196
−	Beginning Inventory	(10)	(12)	(14)	(10)
=	Units to Be Purchased	52	62	72	186
×	Cost Per Unit	$ 220	$ 220	$ 220	$ 220
=	Cost of Purchases	$11,440	$13,640	$15,840	$40,920

Selling and administrative expenses are paid in the month incurred and purchases are paid in the month following the purchase. Purchases for December 2010 are $10,500. No equipment purchases or additional expenditures are made during the quarter.

Required:

Prepare a cash payment schedule for the first quarter of 2011.

LO 5: Prepare a Cash Payments Schedule for One Quarter

9-59. Jackson Sales Company has prepared the following budgets for the second quarter of 2011.

Jackson Sales Company Selling and Administrative Expense Budget For the Quarter Ended June 30, 2011	Apr	May	Jun	Total
Salaries	$1,000	$1,200	$1,300	$3,500
Rent	200	200	200	600
Utilities	120	180	220	520
Depreciation	80	80	80	240
Other	500	600	650	1,750
Total	$1,900	$2,260	$2,450	$6,610

Jackson Sales Company Selling and Administrative Expense Budget For the Quarter Ended June 30, 2011	Apr	May	Jun	Total
Forecasted Unit Sales	70	80	90	240
+ Desired Ending Inventory	16	18	19	19
= Total Units Needed	86	98	109	259
− Beginning Inventory	(15)	(16)	(18)	(15)
= Units to Be Purchased	71	82	91	244
× Cost Per Unit	$ 100	$ 100	$ 100	$ 100
= Cost of Purchases	$7,100	$8,200	$9,100	$24,400

Selling and administrative expenses are paid in the month incurred and purchases are paid in the month following the purchase. Purchases for March 2011 are $6,800. No equipment purchases or additional expenditures are made during the quarter.

Required:

Prepare a cash payment schedule for the second quarter of 2011.

LO 5: Prepare a Cash Payments Schedule for One Month

9-60. The following budgeted information is available for the Top Coat Clothing Company for January 2011.

Salaries	$120,000
Rent	9,000
Electricity	1,200
Depreciation	3,200
Others Expenses	1,500
Purchases	380,000

Selling and administrative expenses are paid in the month incurred and purchases are paid in the month following the purchase. Purchases for December 2010 are $350,000. No equipment purchases or additional expenditures are made during the month.

Required:

Prepare a cash payment schedule for January 2011.

LO 5: Prepare a Cash Payments Schedule for One Month

9-61. The following budgeted information is available for Jack's Feed Store in June 2011.

Salaries	$12,000
Rent	600
Electricity	140
Depreciation	800
Others Expenses	700
Purchases	80,000

Selling and administrative expenses are paid in the month incurred and purchases are paid in the month following the purchase. Purchases for May 2011 are $75,000. No equipment purchases or additional expenditures are made during the month.

Required:

Prepare a cash payment schedule for June 2011.

LO 5: Prepare a Cash Budget for One Quarter

9-62. The following information is available for the Art Kriner Company for the first quarter of 2011.

	Jan	Feb	Mar
Budgeted Receipts from Credit Sales	$5,000	$5,500	$5,800
Budgeted Cash Sales	1,200	1,250	1,300
Budgeted Cash Payments	6,300	7,185	6,520

Beginning cash balance for January 2011 is expected to be $1,500. The company intends to maintain a cash balance of at least $1,000. The company has made arrangements to borrow from a local bank if necessary.

Required:

Prepare a cash budget for the first quarter of 2011.

LO 5: Prepare a Cash Budget for One Quarter

9-63. The following information is available for the Dixon Company for the second quarter of 2011.

	Apr	May	Jun
Budgeted Receipts from Credit Sales	$500,000	$520,000	$550,000
Budgeted Cash Sales	100,000	105,000	112,000
Budgeted Cash Payments	670,000	615,000	627,000

Beginning cash balance for April 2011 is expected to be $90,000. The company intends to maintain a cash balance of at least $50,000. The company has made arrangements to borrow from a local bank if necessary.

Required:

Prepare a cash budget for the second quarter of 2011.

LO 5: Prepare a Cash Budget for One Quarter

9-64. The following information is available for the Ortega Company for the first quarter of 2011.

	Jan	Feb	Mar
Budgeted Receipts from Credit Sales	$100,000	$110,000	$115,000
Budgeted Cash Sales	80,000	95,000	98,000
Budgeted Cash Payments	178,000	215,000	206,000

Beginning cash balance for January 2011 is expected to be $20,000. The company intends to maintain a cash balance of at least $15,000. The company has made arrangements to borrow from a local bank if necessary.

Required:

Prepare a cash budget for the first quarter of 2011.

LO 5: Prepare a Cash Budget for One Month

9-65. The following information is available for November 2011.

Budgeted Receipts from Credit Sales	$25,100
Budgeted Cash Sales	5,900
Budgeted Cash Payments	32,600

Beginning cash balance for November is expected to be $5,800. The company intends to maintain a cash balance of at least $5,000. The company has made arrangements to borrow from a local bank if necessary.

Required:

Prepare a cash budget for November 2011.

LO 5: Prepare a Cash Budget for One Month

9-66. The following information is available for October 2011.

Budgeted Receipts from Credit Sales	$300,000
Budgeted Cash Sales	80,000
Budgeted Cash Payments	410,000

Beginning cash balance for October is expected to be $60,000. The company intends to maintain a cash balance of at least $50,000. The company has made arrangements to borrow from a local bank if necessary.

Required:

Prepare a cash budget for October 2011.

LO 5: Prepare a Cash Budget for One Month

9-67. The following information is available for July 2011.

Budgeted Receipts from Credit Sales	$500,000
Budgeted Cash Sales	40,000
Budgeted Cash Payments	577,000

Beginning cash balance for July is expected to be $95,000. The company intends to maintain a cash balance of at least $75,000. The company has made arrangements to borrow from a local bank if necessary.

Required:

Prepare a cash budget for July 2011.

LO 5: Prepare a Budgeted Balance Sheet and Budgeted Statement of Cash Flows for Three Months

9-68. The following information is available for the Perlmuter Printing Supply Company.

Perlmuter Printing Supply Company
Sales Budget
For the Quarter Ended September 30, 2010

	July	August	September
Budgeted Sales Dollars	$90,000	$80,000	$70,000

Perlmuter Printing Supply Company
Cost of Goods Sold Budget
For the Quarter Ended September 30, 2010

	July	August	September
Budgeted Cost of Goods Sold	$54,000	$48,000	$42,000

Perlmuter Printing Supply Company
Selling and Administrative Expense Budget
For the Quarter Ended September 30, 2010

	July	August	September
Salaries and Wages	$12,600	$12,000	$11,800
Rent	1,000	1,000	1,000
Depreciation	1,800	1,800	1,800
Other	3,800	3,000	2,900
Total	$19,200	$17,800	$17,500

Perlmuter Printing Supply Company
Budgeted Income Statement
For the Quarter Ended September 30, 2010

	July	August	September
Sales	$90,000	$80,000	$70,000
Cost of Goods Sold	54,000	48,000	42,000
Gross Profit	36,000	32,000	28,000
Selling and Admin. Expense	19,200	17,800	17,500
Net Income	$16,800	$14,200	$10,500

Perlmuter Printing Supply Company
Purchases Budget
For the Quarter Ended September 30, 2010

	July	August	September
Cost of Purchases	$52,000	$46,000	$41,000

Perlmuter Printing Supply Company
Cash Receipts Schedule
For the Quarter Ended September 30, 2010

	July	August	September
Budgeted Receipts from Credit Sales	$78,000	$76,000	$68,000
Budgeted Cash Sales	9,000	8,000	7,000
Total Cash Receipts	$87,000	$84,000	$75,000

Perlmuter Printing Supply Company
Cash Payments Schedule
For the Quarter Ended September 30, 2010

	July	August	September
Purchases	$56,000	$52,000	$46,000
Selling and Admin. Expense:			
Salaries and Wages	$12,600	$12,000	$11,800
Rent	1,000	1,000	1,000
Other	3,800	3,000	2,900
Budgeted Cash Payments	$73,400	$68,000	$61,700

Perlmuter Printing Supply Company
Cash Budget
For the Quarter Ended September 30, 2010

		July	August	September
	Beginning Cash Balance	$ 18,500	$ 32,100	$ 48,100
+	Cash Receipts	87,000	84,000	75,000
=	Cash Available	$105,500	$116,100	$123,100
	Cash Payments	(73,400)	(68,000)	(61,700)
=	Balance before Borrowing	$ 32,100	$ 48,100	$ 61,400
+/−	Borrowing/(Repayment)	0	0	0
=	Ending Cash Balance	$ 32,100	$ 48,100	$ 61,400

Perlmuter Printing Supply Company
Balance Sheet
June 30, 2010

Assets	
Current Assets	
Cash	$ 18,500
Accounts Receivable	20,000
Inventory	16,000
Total Current Assets	$ 54,500
Property, Plant, and Equipment	
Equipment	108,000
Less Accumulated Depreciation	(43,200)
Equipment, Net	$ 64,800
Total Assets	$119,300
Liabilities	
Current Liabilities	
Accounts Payable	$ 56,000
Total Liabilities	$ 56,000
Stockholders' Equity	
Paid-in Capital	
Common Stock	$ 1,000
Additional Paid-in Capital	10,000
Total Paid-in Capital	$ 11,000
Retained Earnings	$ 52,300
Total Stockholders' Equity	$ 63,300
Total Liabilities and Equity	$119,300

Required:

a. Prepare budgeted balance sheets for July, August, and September of 2010.

b. Prepare budgeted statements of cash flows for July, August, and September of 2010.

LO 5: Determine Missing Budget Information

9-69. Following is a partial performance report.

Description	Budget	Actual	Variance
Wages	$5,000	$5,200	$?
Store Rent	6,000	?	200 F
Utilities Expense	?	1,200	50 U

Required:

Provide the missing information.

LO 5: Determine Budget Variances

9-70. Following is a partial performance report.

Description	Budget	Actual	Variance
Sales	$25,000	$22,000	$?
Cost of Goods Sold	20,000	17,600	?
Gross Profit	5,000	4,400	?

Required:

Calculate the variances for this information and indicate whether they are favorable (F) or unfavorable (U).

LO 5: Determine Budget Variances

9-71. Following is a partial performance report.

Description	Budget	Actual	Variance
Rent Revenue	$15,000	$14,000	$?
Interest Expense	15,000	14,000	?

Required:

Calculate the variances for this information and indicate whether they are favorable (F) or unfavorable (U).

LO 6: Discuss Variances

9-72. Robin Wince owns a small chain of frame shops. All the frames and other merchandise the company sells is purchased by the company's central purchasing department. A partial performance report showing the direct costs for one of Robin's stores appears as follows:

	Budget	Actual	Variance
Sales	$200,000	$200,000	$ 0
Cost of Goods Sold	120,000	110,000	10,000 F
Selling and Admin. Expense	40,000	50,000	10,000 U
Income	$ 40,000	$ 40,000	$ 0

Required:

Robin is concerned even though the variance in income is zero. Because the total variance is zero, the store manager believes that there is no problem. Do you agree with the manager? Why?

LO 6: Prepare a Memo Regarding Variances

9-73. Matt Lehti owns the Zap Record Shop. He is in the process of examining the following performance report.

	Budget	Actual	Variance
Sales	$100,000	$120,000	$20,000 F
Cost of Goods Sold	60,000	72,000	12,000 U
Selling and Admin. Expense	10,000	9,000	1,000 F
Income	$ 30,000	$ 39,000	$ 9,000 F

Matt is very pleased that the company had favorable variances for sales and income. However, he finds the sizable unfavorable variance for cost of goods sold very disturbing. He is preparing himself for a serious discussion with the purchasing agent who is responsible for purchasing the merchandise sold.

Required:

Assume that Matt Lehti has asked you for assistance in preparing for the meeting with the purchasing agent. Prepare a memo to Matt that provides him with any information you think would be helpful.

LO 5 & 6: Flexible Budget and Performance Report Preparation

9-74. Marla Swartz Company's 2010 operating budget is based on sales of 90,000 units at $112 per unit. Budgeted variable costs are $88 per unit, while fixed costs total $2,100,000.

For 2010 actual sales were 89,000 units at $111 each. Actual variable costs were $86 per unit and fixed costs totaled $2,080,000.

Required:

Based on the budgeted sales and costs figures, prepare a flexible-budget contribution income statement for the company for sales of 89,000 units.

LO 5 & 6: Flexible Budget and Performance Report Preparation

9-75. KH Company's 2010 operating budget is based on sales of 89,000 units at $111 per unit. Budgeted variable costs are $86 per unit, while fixed costs total $2,080,000.

For 2010 actual sales were 90,000 units at $112 each. Actual variable costs were $88 per unit and fixed costs totaled $2,100,000.

Required:

Based on the budgeted sales and costs figures, prepare a flexible-budget contribution income statement for the company for sales of 90,000 units.

LO 5 & 6: Flexible Budget and Performance Report Preparation

9-76. Stefani DeMoss Table Company manufactures tables for schools. The 2010 operating budget is based on sales of 20,000 units at $100 per table. Operating income is anticipated to be $120,000. Budgeted variable costs are $64 per unit, while fixed costs total $600,000.

Actual income for 2010 was a surprising $354,000 on actual sales of 21,000 units at $104 each. Actual variable costs were $60 per unit and fixed costs totaled $570,000.

Required:

Prepare a variance analysis report with both flexible-budget and sales-volume variances using the following format:

	Static Budget	Sales Volume Variances	Flexible Budget	Flexible Budget Variances	Actual Results
Units	20,000	________	21,000	________	21,000
Sales	$________	$________	$________	$________	$________
Variable Costs	________	________	________	________	________
Contribution Margin	________	________	________	________	________
Fixed Cost	________	________	________	________	________
Operating Income	$________.	$________.F	$________.	$________.	$________.

LO 5 & 6: Flexible Budget and Performance Report Preparation

9-77. Clay Johnson Company's 2010 operating budget is based on sales of 50,000 units at $135 per unit. Operating income is anticipated to be $250,000. Budgeted variable costs are $88 per unit, while fixed costs total $2,100,000.

Actual income for 2010 was a surprising $367,000 on actual sales of 53,000 units at $138 each. Actual variable costs were $89 per unit and fixed costs totaled $2,230,000.

Required:

Prepare a variance analysis report with both flexible-budget and sales-volume variances using a format similar to the one presented for the preceding problem.

LO 5 & 6: Flexible Budget and Performance Report Preparation

9-78. The following static budgets are available for the McVay Company for January 2011.

McVay Company Sales Budget For January 2010	
Budgeted Sales in Units	3,300
Budgeted Sales Price	$ 200
Budgeted Sales Dollars	$660,000

McVay Company Cost of Goods Sold Budget For January 2010	
Budgeted Sales in Units	3,300
Budgeted Cost Per Unit	$ 110
Budgeted Cost of Goods Sold	$363,000

McVay Company Selling and Administrative Expense Budget For January 2011		
Salaries and Wages:		
Variable Salaries and Wages	$16,500	
Fixed Salaries and Wages	85,000	
Total Salaries and Wages		$101,500
Rent (Fixed)		64,000
Depreciation (Fixed)		53,200
Other Expenses		
Variable Other Expenses	825	
Fixed Other Expenses	1,475	
Total Other Expenses		2,300
Budgeted S & A Expense		$221,000

The actual results of the company's operations appear in the following income statement:

McVay Company Income Statement For January 2010	
Unit Sales	3,600
Sales	$718,300
Variable Cost:	
Cost of Goods Sold	399,600
Variable Salaries and Wages	17,500
Variable Other Expenses	1,000
Total Variable Cost	418,100
Contribution Margin	300,200
Fixed Cost:	
Fixed Salaries and Wages	86,800
Rent (Fixed)	65,000
Depreciation (Fixed)	58,200
Fixed Other Expenses	1,375
Total Fixed Cost	211,375
Operating Income	$ 88,825

The company's president, John McVay is quite pleased with the 2010 results because they are so much higher than the $76,000 in operating income he was expecting expected. He is planning a party to celebrate the achievement and everyone in the company is invited. John plans to make some comments during the party to congratulate each manager that contributed to the cause. He has asked you to review the numbers to provide input regarding which managers he should thank during the party.

Required:

a. Prepare flexible budgets similar to those in Exhibit 9-20 for the company assuming sales levels of 3,000, 3,300, 3,600, and 3,900 units.

b. Prepare a static budget performance report similar to the one in Exhibit 9-18.

c. Prepare a sales volume variance report similar to the one in Exhibit 9-21.

d. Prepare a flexible budget performance report similar to the one in Exhibit 9-22.

e. Prepare a performance report with columns for the static budget, sales volume variances, the flexible budget, flexible budget variances, and actual results. Your report should be similar to the one in Exhibit 9-23.

f. Based on the reports you have prepared, comment on how well the company performed during the year relative to the budget. Be sure to comment on various areas including sales, variable cost control, and fixed cost control.

LO 5 & 6: Flexible Budget and Performance Report Preparation

9-79. The following static budgets are available for the COACE Company for 2010.

COACE Company
Sales Budget
For the Year Ended December 31, 2010

Budgeted Sales in Units	10,000
Budgeted Sales Price	$ 850
Budgeted Sales Dollars	$8,500,000

COACE Company
Cost of Goods Sold Budget
For the Year Ended December 31, 2010

Budgeted Sales in Units	10,000
Budgeted Cost Per Unit	$ 500
Budgeted Cost of Goods Sold	$5,000,000

COACE Company
Selling and Administrative Expense Budget
For the Year Ended December 31, 2010

Salaries and Wages:		
Variable Salaries and Wages	$ 200,000	
Fixed Salaries and Wages	950,000	
Total Salaries and Wages		$1,150,000
Rent (Fixed)		120,000
Depreciation (Fixed)		60,000
Other Expenses		
Variable Other Expenses	400,000	
Fixed Other Expenses	1,300,000	
Total Other Expenses		1,700,000
Budgeted S & A Expense		$3,030,000

The actual results of the company's operations appear in the following income statement:

COACE Company Income Statement For the Year Ended December 31, 2010	
Unit Sales	11,000
Sales	$9,362,000
Variable Cost:	
Cost of Goods Sold	5,455,000
Variable Salaries and Wages	215,000
Variable Other Expenses	439,000
Total Variable Cost	6,109,000
Contribution Margin	3,253,000
Fixed Cost:	
Fixed Salaries and Wages	957,000
Rent (Fixed)	132,000
Depreciation (Fixed)	61,000
Fixed Other Expenses	1,358,000
Total Fixed Cost	2,508,000
Operating Income	$ 745,000

The company's president, Mr. Lin is somewhat pleased with the 2010 results, but questions why both variable and fixed costs increased as they did. He feels confident that if the managers had done a better job keeping costs in check, income would have been significantly greater. When he approached the managers, the managers in charge of fixed costs were quick to point out that their costs had only increased by a small amount, whereas the variable costs skyrocketed. It seems these managers have a good point, so Mr. Lin intends to pressure the managers responsible for variable costs to take corrective action to bring the costs into line. Before directing his attention to variable cost control, Mr. Lin has asked you to review the numbers to provide input regarding the manager's inability to control costs.

Required:

a. Prepare flexible budget income statements for the year assuming sales levels of 9,000, 10,000, 11,000, and 12,000 units. (Similar to those in Exhibit 9-20)

b. Prepare a static budget performance report similar to the one in Exhibit 9-18.

c. Prepare a sales volume variance report similar to the one in Exhibit 9-21.

d. Prepare a flexible budget performance report similar to the one in Exhibit 9-22.

e. Prepare a performance report with columns for the static budget, sales volume variances, the flexible budget, flexible budget variances, and actual results. Your report should be similar to the one in Exhibit 9-23.

f. Based on the reports you have prepared, comment on how well the company performed during the year relative to the budget. Be sure to comment on various areas including sales, variable cost control, and fixed cost control.

LO 5: Prepare a Budgeted Income Statement for One Quarter

9-80. The following budgets were prepared for Meg's Jean Store.

Meg's Jean Store
Sales Budget
For the Quarter Ended June 30, 2010

		Apr	May	Jun	Total
	Budgeted Sales in Units	300	350	400	1,050
×	Budgeted Sales Price	$ 27	$ 27	$ 27	$ 27
=	Budgeted Sales Dollars	$8,100	$9,450	$10,800	$28,350

Meg's Jean Store
Cost of Goods Sold Budget
For the Quarter Ended June 30, 2010

		Apr	May	Jun	Total
	Budgeted Sales in Units	300	350	400	1,050
×	Budgeted Cost Per Unit	$ 14	$ 14	$ 14	$ 27
=	Budgeted Cost of Goods Sold	$4,200	$4,900	$5,600	$14,700

Meg's Jean Store
Selling and Administrative Expense Budget
For the Quarter Ended June 30, 2010

	Apr	May	Jun	Total
Salaries and Wages	$1,800	$1,950	$2,100	$5,850
Rent	500	500	500	1,500
Depreciation	100	100	100	300
Other	600	660	720	1,980
Budgeted Selling & Admin. Expense	$3,000	$3,210	$3,420	$9,630

Required:

Based on the information for Meg's Jean Store, prepare flexible budget income statements for the year ended December 31, 2010 similar to those in Exhibit 9-20. Assume sales levels of 3,000, 3,500, 4,000, and 4,500 units.

Hint: Keep in mind that the fixed costs and other amounts presented above are monthly amounts and your flexible budget will be for the entire year. Also, you will need to separate Meg's mixed costs into their variable and fixed cost components using one of the methods presented in Chapter 5, such as the high-low method.

10

Standard Costing

How do managers know which problems are the most pressing ones? How do they know how much time to spend solving such problems? Suppose, for example, that you are the production manager for Inline Skate Company. Your responsibilities include making sure that the plant produces high-quality skates at a relatively low cost. If the actual production cost for a pair of skates is $12.87, how would you know whether this amount is acceptable? In addition, how would you know which specific costs are too high, too low, or just right? You could focus on a selected cost area such as direct material, but you might be spending valuable time trying to control costs that are already under control.

Fortunately, standard costing can help overcome some of the guesswork inherent to operating a business. **Standard costing** is the process of setting cost performance goals that benchmark desirable performance and then using these cost goals to evaluate performance. Under standard costing, employees work to establish performance goals that can be used as benchmarks for good performance. As these goals are being set, employees are planning how factory resources will be acquired and used. Then, once operations begin, employees strive to control costs so the goals can be met.

standard costing The process of setting cost performance goals that benchmark acceptable performance and then using these cost goals to evaluate performance.

The goals also provide management with a basis for performance evaluation when actual results are compared to goals to help find areas of weakness.

If the Inline Skate Company used standard costing, you could evaluate the $12.87 cost per pair of skates by comparing it to the amount budgeted. In fact, standard costing would allow you to review each component of production cost. You would be able to detect cost overruns for direct material, direct labor, variable manufacturing overhead, or fixed manufacturing overhead. In short, standard costing provides managers with a means to quickly focus their attention on problem areas.

Learning Objectives

After completing your work on this chapter, you should be able to do the following:

1. Describe standard costing and indicate why standard costing is important.
2. Explain the concept of management by exception.
3. Contrast ideal and practical standards.

4. Identify and discuss the weaknesses of standard costing.
5. Compare standard costing, actual costing, and normal costing.
6. Determine standards for a manufacturing company.
7. Calculate standard cost variances for direct material, direct labor, variable manufacturing overhead, and fixed manufacturing overhead.
8. Describe the meaning of standard cost variances for direct material, direct labor, variable manufacturing overhead, and fixed manufacturing overhead.
9. Prepare journal entries to record standard costs and variances.

Why Is Standard Costing Used?

In today's competitive environment, business success depends in large part on solid planning, as discussed in Chapter 9. Standard costing is often a key planning tool. When a company uses standard costing, it establishes performance standards for the coming year. A **standard** is a preestablished benchmark for desirable performance. A **standard cost system** is one in which a company, after careful analysis, sets cost standards and then uses them to evaluate actual performance.

standard A pre-established benchmark for desirable performance.

standard cost system A system in which cost standards are set after careful analysis and then the standards are used to evaluate actual performance. A system that uses estimated amounts (standards) for direct material, direct labor, and manufacturing overhead to determine the cost of products.

Standard costing is used to bolster business success. In general, the use of standard costing encourages planning, establishes performance targets, and provides a basis for evaluating actual performance.

Planning is a critical part of any standard cost system. Managers and other employees work to gather information and investigate ways of achieving acceptable performance at the lowest cost. With this information, standards are established. For example, standards are created for the amount and cost of direct material, and for the number of direct labor hours and their cost. The process of planning provides benefits to the company because, once employees have established standards during the planning process, they know what needs to be done and how to do it most efficiently.

Once standards have been set, they can be used as performance targets. Managers and employees are encouraged to act so that actual results meet the expectations established by the standards. For example, if the production cost standard (the cost goal) for a pair of skates made by the Inline Skate Company is $13, employees are encouraged to make the skates for $13 or less. In an ideal situation, every employee would work to make the highest quality skates for less than the $13 standard cost.

To determine whether and where problems exist, managers compare actual results to the standards. A **variance** is the difference between actual performance and the standard. Variances can be used to help determine where managers should focus their attention.

variance The difference between actual performance and the standard.

Actual performance that falls below standard results in an **unfavorable variance**. Essentially, an unfavorable variance reflects a situation in which the cost of actual performance is higher than planned performance. For example, if the standard direct labor time to manufacture a desk is 12 minutes and it actually takes 15 minutes, the three minute difference constitutes an unfavorable variance of three minutes. Because it is more costly to the company when three minutes of additional labor is used than was planned, an unfavorable variance is an indication that a problem may exist and management attention is needed.

unfavorable variance The difference between actual performance and standard performance when the actual performance falls below the standard.

When actual performance exceeds the expectations established by the standard, a **favorable variance** results. In our desk example, if it actually takes 11 minutes to make

favorable variance The difference between actual performance and standard performance when the actual performance exceeds the standard.

the desk instead of the standard 12 minutes, the difference constitutes a favorable variance of one minute because cost to the company is reduced if labor time is one minute less than planned.

It might seem that a favorable variance indicates that management attention is not needed, but such is not always the case. Managers should review all variances, favorable and unfavorable, and use judgment and additional information to prioritize problem-solving efforts. For example, if a purchasing agent is able to buy direct material for less than the standard price, a favorable variance will occur. If the lower price is the result of purchasing substandard material, the "favorable" variance may not actually be to the company's benefit at all. Another reason to look into the cause of favorable variances is to learn how performance was improved. If the favorable variance is the result of improved performance, management may be able to learn how to make similar performance improvements in other areas of the company.

Items that have no variance should also be investigated. As discussed in Chapter 9, the absence of a variance should not be construed as meaning that everything is as it should be with that particular item. Managers must also remember that the cause of a variance may be the standard and not the performance. Standard setting is not an exact science. Standards must be reviewed often and changed as circumstances warrant.

It is most helpful if managers are able to review related standard cost variances together. For this purpose, a performance report is often prepared that summarizes variances for a particular operation of the company and shows where attention is needed. The process of focusing management attention on areas where actual performance deviates from the preestablished standards is called **management by exception**.

management by exception The process of focusing management attention on areas where actual performance deviates from the preestablished standards.

Under management by exception, managers first tend to problems associated with large variances. Then, once the large problems have been addressed, managers can turn to areas associated with smaller variances. Finally, as time permits, items where no variances exist are examined.

Standards—A Closer Look

Most companies set cost standards once each year. Even if variances occur, it is generally unwise to casually adjust standards during the year, because managers might be too quick to adjust them to eliminate unfavorable variances instead of working to improve performance. Also, if standards are adjusted too often, performance becomes difficult to track. Performance that results in an unfavorable variance one month might result in a favorable variance the next month once the standard has been changed. Standards should be altered only if conditions change so significantly that the established standards lose their effectiveness as performance targets.

Quantity and Price Standards

Performance standards can be set for almost any business activity. For example, standards can be set for the number of product returns, or for the amount of employee turnover. In practice, however, standards are used most often to help control costs.

Two things can cause cost to increase: the quantity used and the price paid. It is better to establish both a quantity standard and a separate price standard for each material used in production. For example, to say the direct material for product X should cost $3 per unit is not as helpful in controlling cost as saying that it should take 1.5 pounds of material at $2 per pound to make product X. Establishing a quantity and price standard provides performance targets for the amount of material used in production and a separate target for finding the material at the best purchase price.

Although it is also helpful to establish quantity and price standards for direct labor, we generally do not refer to labor in terms of *quantity* and *price*. Instead, we use the equivalent terms *hours* and *rate*. The quantity standard for labor is the number of hours, and the price standard is the rate.

Ideal versus Practical Standards

During the planning process, managers and other employees work to set standards that will both help provide performance targets and provide a basis for performance evaluation. If we were setting a price standard for the purchase of gasoline, for example, we could set a cost goal of $0.50 per gallon, $5 per gallon, or any price in between. The object would be to select a standard that would challenge employees to find gasoline at the best price. If the standard is set at $0.50 per gallon, it is unlikely that employees will even try to achieve this impossible standard. On the other hand, if the standard is set at $5 per gallon, employees will be able to achieve the standard so easily that it will offer no incentive to find low-cost gasoline. Generally it is best to select a standard that offers a challenging, yet achievable, performance goal.

Ideal Standards

ideal standard A standard that is attainable only under perfect conditions.

A standard that is attainable only under perfect conditions is called an **ideal standard**. Under ideal standards, there is no room for substandard performance of any kind. In a manufacturing setting, for instance, ideal standards assume that the plant operates in a perfect world with no machine downtime, no waste of direct material for any reason, and no employee rest breaks. In the real world, ideal standards are nearly impossible to achieve. Such standards may frustrate employees because, no matter how hard they try, they will never be able to meet them. In time, employees may throw up their hands and stop trying to meet the standards altogether.

Practical Standards

practical standard A standard that allows for normal, recurring inefficiencies.

A standard that allows for normal, recurring inefficiencies is called a **practical standard**. For example, in manufacturing, a practical standard for the quantity of direct material would allow for waste due to expected defects in the material. For labor, a practical standard would provide for employees working at a normal pace with adequate rest periods. When compared to ideal standards, practical standards are more realistic and less likely to result in unreasonable unfavorable variances. In addition, when practical standards are used, an unfavorable variance indicates that a true problem exists. Accordingly, most companies use practical standards.

Setting Standards

Often, standards are based on past performance. For example, if material Y was purchased for $4.45 per pound last year, it is likely it can be purchased for about $4.45 the next year; but using last year's actual amounts as next year's standards is overly simplistic. When setting standards, it is best to use historical information, and then incorporate any anticipated changes in efficiency or price.

It is usually best to use a team approach to evaluate each standard. Whether formal or informal, a team approach for gathering input from various knowledgeable employees will result in better, more appropriate standards. For example, when setting direct material standards for a manufacturer, a team approach would likely be better than a single employee setting the standards based solely on his or her own limited knowledge. The team might include accountants, production-line workers, production supervisors, purchasing agents, and others who are knowledgeable about the quality, use, sources, and prices of direct material. Then, the historical information provided by the accountants, information about usage and quality requirements provided by production personnel, and information about sourcing and pricing from the purchasing agent can be analyzed. Once the team has examined all this information, appropriate direct material standards can be set.

If reasonable standards are established, actual performance is accurately measured and compared to the standards, and a system to provide performance reports is put in place, standard costing can be a valuable management tool. A flowchart of how standard costing works is shown in Exhibit 10-1. Managers can then encourage employees to strive to meet the performance goals established by the standards, and can use performance reports and management by exception to help direct their attention to troubled areas. Unfortunately, standard costing is not the answer to all management's problems, and when managers rely too heavily on standard costing, serious problems can occur.

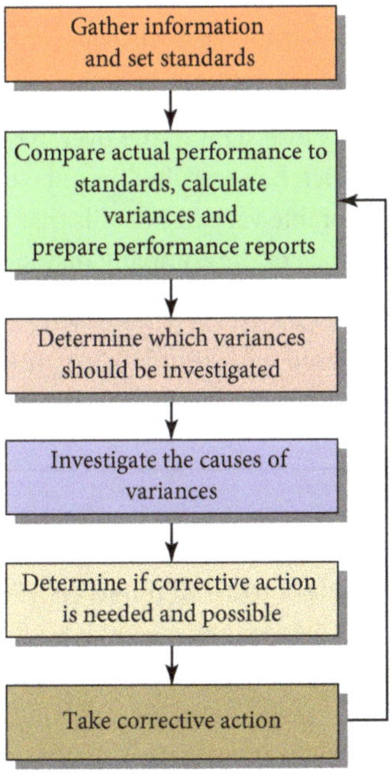

Exhibit 10-1 The Standard-Costing Process

Problems with Standard Costing

To use standard costing as an effective management tool, managers must be aware of its potential problems. The first problems may occur when standards are being set. Employees with relevant expertise are often consulted to help establish an appropriate standard. Most of these employees are keenly aware that the standard will be used later to evaluate their performance. With lax standards, employees will not have to work as hard to meet the goals set by the standard, and unfavorable variances will be less likely. With stringent standards, employees will have to work much harder to meet targeted goals. Accordingly, employees often try to ensure that the standards adopted by the company are lax, resulting in suboptimal performance goals.

Another problem with standard costing stems from relying on historical information to set standards. If past performance was less than optimal, the new standards will call for performance that is less than optimal. The inefficiency of the past may be built into the new standards. Sometimes employees and lower-level managers deliberately manipulate actual performance so it appears that less stringent standards should be maintained. This way, employees are less likely to face the consequences of unfavorable performance variances in the future.

Still another problem associated with standard costing is that managers tend to manage everything "by the numbers." When a standard cost system is well established, managers often focus almost entirely on significant, unfavorable variances and overlook serious problems that do not give rise to unfavorable variances. For example, a manager may try desperately to reduce an unfavorable direct material variance while completely overlooking a significant product quality problem. Why? The product quality problem does not result in a variance; therefore, a manager whose attention is directed solely by management by exception would have no "exception" to direct him or her to the quality problem. Managers may get so engrossed in chasing down problems associated with unfavorable variances that they waste company time and resources as they try to rectify insignificant problems.

In addition, managers who use management by exception may spend so much time on unfavorable variances that they fail to recognize employees who are responsible for favorable variances. By failing to recognize employees who do a good job, managers lose the benefit of positive reinforcement as a management tool.

Yet another problem is that managers lose sight of the overall business operation as they focus on the multitude of details which have resulted in unfavorable variances. In time, managers focus so much on unfavorable variance details that they cannot see the forest for the trees. The overall performance of the company may suffer because managers are managing details while ignoring the big picture.

A summary of the problems associated with standard costing is presented in Exhibit 10-2. Take some time to become familiar with these problems.

Exhibit 10-2 Summary of Standard Costing Problems

PROBLEMS WITH STANDARD COSTING

1. Employees who help set standards try to avoid unfavorable variances by setting lax standards.
2. Reliance on historical information may perpetuate past inefficiencies in current standards.
3. Managers that manage "by the numbers" may overlook significant problems that do not result in an unfavorable variances or waste time on insignificant unfavorable variances.
4. Managers may focus so much on unfavorable variances that they fail to recognize employees who are doing a good job.
5. Managers may focus so much on variances that they fail to see the big picture.

Who Uses Standard Costing?

Almost any business entity can use standard costing regardless of whether it is a for-profit or a not-for-profit organization. Although it is most often used by manufacturers, service and merchandising often use standard costing. Whenever it is appropriate to establish standards of performance for purposes of planning and control, standard costing can be used. For example, a tire store might establish a standard for the amount of time it should take to change a set of tires. An oil change center might establish a standard for the amount of time it should take to change the oil and service an automobile. A catering company could develop standards for the quantity and price of each food item, the labor hours and labor rate to prepare each item, and a standard for the amount of overhead cost associated with the preparation of each item it sells.

In a manufacturing environment, companies use a standard cost system to budget the cost of producing each individual unit of product. In effect, standard costing is like preparing a budget for a single unit of production. Managers estimate the cost of direct material, direct labor, variable manufacturing overhead, and fixed manufacturing overhead required to produce each item.

In Chapter 3 we discussed two types of cost systems. In an **actual cost system** we compute actual direct material, direct labor, and manufacturing overhead costs. In a **normal cost system** we compute actual direct material and actual direct labor costs, and use a predetermined application rate for manufacturing overhead. A **standard cost system** goes one step further. In a standard cost system, estimated amounts are used for direct material, direct labor, and manufacturing overhead. Exhibit 10-3 compares the three cost systems.

actual cost system A system that uses actual direct material cost, actual direct labor cost, and actual manufacturing overhead cost to determine the cost of products.

normal cost system A system that uses actual direct material cost and actual direct labor cost but uses a predetermined application rate based on estimates for manufacturing overhead to determine the cost of products.

standard cost system A system that uses estimated amounts (standards) for direct material, direct labor, and manufacturing overhead to determine the cost of products.

Exhibit 10-3 Comparison of Actual, Normal, and Standard Cost Systems

Cost Classification	Actual Cost System	Normal Cost System	Standard Cost System
Direct Material	Actual	Actual	Estimated
Direct Labor	Actual	Actual	Estimated
Manufacturing Overhead	Actual	Estimated	Estimated

In the sections that follow, we discuss the details of how standard costing is used in manufacturing.

Basic Standard Costing for a Manufacturer

When manufacturing companies use standard costing, standards are set for direct material, direct labor, variable manufacturing overhead, and fixed manufacturing overhead. We will walk through the most commonly used standards and variances using the Tree Top Mailbox Company as an example. Tree Top is a small company that makes a single product.

Tree Top Mailbox Company was founded by three college sophomores, Ali, Maria, and Bill. They started the company to earn spending money while they attended college. The trio had done some market research and determined that they could sell decorative wooden mailboxes for $10 each. They each planned to work about 60 hours a month for $10 per hour. Any remaining profits would be left in the company to be divided equally at the end of their venture.

The three entrepreneurs rented a garage to house the small company for $200 per month plus utilities. They purchased equipment—a table saw and drill press, for $900. The estimated useful life of the equipment is three years.

In October, Tree Top's first month of operation, the company was able to sell every mailbox produced. By the end of October, they had made and sold 300 boxes.

As shown on the income statement in Exhibit 10-4, the company's profits for October totaled $305.

Exhibit 10-4 Tree Top's October 2009 Income Statement

Tree Top Mailbox Company
Income Statement
For the Month Ended October 31, 2009

Sales (300 mailboxes at $10 each)		$3,000
Variable Cost:		
Direct Material	$ 600	
Direct Labor (180 hours at $10 per hour)	1,800	
Utilities	40	
Miscellaneous Variable Cost	30	
Total Variable Cost		2,470
Contribution Margin		530
Fixed Cost:		
Rent	200	
Depreciation	25	
Total Fixed Cost		225
Net Income		$ 305

Discussion Questions

10-1. How did Ali, Maria, and Bill calculate the depreciation expense of $25 per month?

10-2. Can you tell from Exhibit 10-4 whether the three Tree Top employees met their business goals in the month of October? Why or why not?

Ali, Maria, and Bill were thrilled that their equity in the company had grown by $305 in the first month. They felt that information for October's business activity could be used to develop a standard cost system to help manage their company.

Setting Direct Material Standards

As stated, setting direct material standards involves two important considerations: the quantity of material and the price paid. We now discuss each of these in some detail.

Direct Material Quantity Standard

direct material quantity standard The amount of direct material it should take to manufacture a single unit of product.

bill of materials A listing of the quantity and description of each item of direct material used to manufacture an individual product.

The amount of direct material it should take to make a single unit of production is called the **direct material quantity standard**. A bill of materials is often used to help establish this standard. A **bill of materials** is a listing of the quantity and description of each item of direct material used to manufacture an individual product. The bill of material for the 7ULTRA-A CB radio made by **Cobra Electronics Corporation** includes just under than 300 items, as shown in Exhibit 10-5.

Each item of direct material, from the speaker to the smallest resistor, is listed. With input from engineering, production, and other personnel, a bill of materials can be prepared and direct material quantity standards can be set. For the Tree Top Mailbox Company, the bill of materials would be quite simple. Basically it involves only one direct material—wood.

Exhibit 10-5 Bill of Materials for 7ULTRA-A CB Radio.

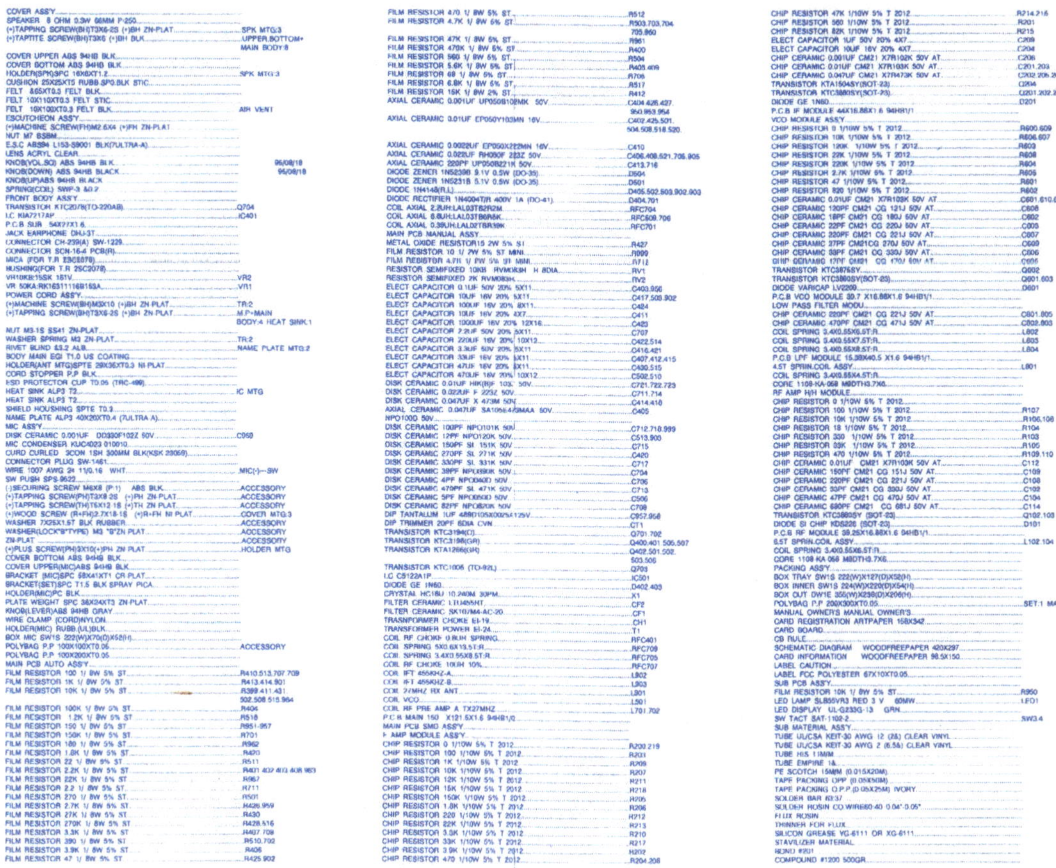
BILL OF MATERIAL FOR 7ULTRA-A

To determine the direct material quantity standard for the Tree Top Mailbox Company using practical standards, Ali measured the wood included in a single mailbox. He determined that each mailbox was made of 16 feet of 1/4 × 2 inch pine. Then he examined the scrap wood from the prior month's production and estimated that the amount of wood to make a single mailbox should be increased by 35 percent to allow for scrap due to knots and other expected defects in the wood. Accordingly, Tree Top adopted a practical direct material quantity standard of 21.6 feet (16 feet × 1.35% = 21.6 feet) per mailbox.

Direct Material Price Standard

In addition to the amount of direct material used, the price per measure of direct material will affect the total cost of direct material. The **direct material price standard** is the anticipated cost for each item of direct material used in the manufacture of a product. For the plastic used to make golf balls, the direct material price standard would be the cost per pound of plastic. For wire used in a CD player, the direct material price standard would be the cost per foot of wire. Notice that the direct material price standard reflects a price per measure of direct material (e.g., per foot of wire), *not* per unit of production (e.g., per CD player).

direct material price standard The anticipated cost for each item of direct material used in the manufacture of a product.

Because purchasing agents are generally knowledgeable about the price paid for direct material, they are likely to be key players in determining direct material price standards.

Purchasing agents would also gather historical direct material price information, making necessary adjustments for any anticipated price changes.

As indicated, Tree Top uses wood that measures 1/4 × 2 inches. The direct material price standard is expressed as an amount per foot of this wood. The Tree Top Mailbox Company has no purchasing agent, so Ali shopped around and found that good quality pine wood could be purchased for $0.70 per 8 foot length. Also, Ali determined that no price increases were expected during the year. Accordingly, Tree Top established a standard price per foot of wood of $0.0875 ($0.70 ÷ 8 feet = $0.0875) per foot.

Although only a single direct material is used to make Tree Top's mailboxes, most products require the use of many different raw materials. Separate standards must be established for each direct material used in production. If production required the use of material A, material B, and material C, separate quantity and price standards must be prepared for each.

Once a manufacturer knows the direct material quantity standard and the direct material price standard, it can determine the standard cost for direct material per unit of product. For Tree Top, the standard cost for direct material of $1.89 is calculated by multiplying the standard quantity of 21.60 feet by the standard price of $0.0875, shown as follows:

Standard Quantity	×	Standard Price	=	Standard Direct Material Cost Per Unit
21.60 Feet	×	$0.875	=	$1.89

Setting Direct Labor Standards

As with direct material, setting direct labor standards involves two important considerations: the number of direct labor hours and the wage rate per hour.

Direct Labor Efficiency Standard

direct labor efficiency standard The estimated number of direct labor hours required to produce a single unit of product.

The estimated number of direct labor hours required to produce a single unit of product is called the **direct labor efficiency standard**. When the direct labor force works efficiently, labor hours are kept to a minimum. Conversely, too many hours of direct labor relative to production would indicate direct labor inefficiency. The standard for the number of direct labor hours could be called the direct labor quantity standard, or the direct labor hours standard, but neither of these terms sounds quite right, which explains why this standard has come to be known as the direct labor efficiency standard.

Production supervisors and other production employees are often key players in establishing direct labor efficiency standards. Historical information about direct labor and production volumes are used to help establish an appropriate standard for the number of direct labor hours per unit of production. Also, information from industrial engineers, such as the results of time-and-motion studies, may be helpful in determining the amount of direct labor time it should take to efficiently produce a unit of product.

Tree Top's founders wanted to select a standard that would help encourage them to make as many mailboxes as possible, but allow them to work at a quick, yet reasonable pace. After reviewing their activities for October, the three agreed that the standard hours allowed for a single unit of production should be 0.6 hours (36 minutes). This time, then, became Tree Top's direct labor efficiency standard.

Direct Labor Rate Standard

The **direct labor rate standard** is the planned hourly wage paid to production workers. The personnel manager is often a key player in determining the direct labor rate standard. Sometimes direct labor rates are established through collective bargaining or other employment agreements. Other times a less formal procedure is used to set hourly pay rates. In either case, historical information coupled with information regarding anticipated pay rate changes establishes the direct labor rate standard. Often, companies compute an expected average hourly direct labor rate, which is used as the plant-wide direct labor rate standard. For Tree Top, Ali, Maria, and Bill agreed that, based on their original plan, the direct labor rate standard of $10 per hour should be used.

direct labor rate standard The planned hourly wage paid to production workers.

Once a company knows the direct labor efficiency standard and the direct labor rate standard, it can determine the standard labor cost per unit of product. In the case of Tree Top, based on the direct labor efficiency standard of 0.6 hours and the direct labor rate standard of $10 per direct labor hour, the standard direct labor cost to make a single mailbox is $6, shown as follows:

Direct Labor Efficiency Standard	×	Direct Labor Rate Standard (per Hour)	=	Standard Direct Labor Cost Per Unit
0.6 Hours	×	$10 Per Hour	=	$6

Setting Variable Manufacturing Overhead Standards

Recall that manufacturing overhead includes all production costs that are not part of direct materials or direct labor. Manufacturing overhead includes costs of operating the factory such as rent, insurance, depreciation, supplies, taxes, raw materials handling, and so forth. Recall also that costs can be classified as either fixed or variable. Fixed costs are those that remain constant in total, even as activity changes. Variable costs, in contrast, increase in total as activity changes. Therefore, variable manufacturing overhead would include those manufacturing overhead costs that increase in total as production increases.

In Chapter 3, we saw that manufacturing overhead is often allocated to production based on direct labor hours, direct labor cost, machine hours, or some other allocation base. In this section, we illustrate how a standard cost system works when manufacturing overhead is allocated using direct labor hours as the allocation base. Although the specific calculations would be somewhat different, other allocation bases can be used in standard costing, as well.

To set standards for variable manufacturing overhead, managers must first estimate variable manufacturing overhead costs. Once they estimate total variable manufacturing overhead, they can then determine a cost per direct labor hour, or per unit of some other allocation base.

For Tree Top Mailbox Company, variable manufacturing overhead cost includes utilities and miscellaneous variable cost, as shown on October's income statement presented in Exhibit 10-4. The miscellaneous variable cost includes the cost of indirect material such as glue, small nails, and wood stain. Based on October's results, Ali, Maria, and Bill estimated that variable manufacturing overhead cost would be about $63 to make 300 mailboxes. The $63 includes $33 for utilities and $30 for other miscellaneous variable costs. Tree Top planned to allocate this variable overhead cost to production based on direct labor hours.

The Standard Variable Manufacturing Overhead Rate

standard variable manufacturing overhead rate The rate used to apply variable manufacturing overhead to units of manufactured product.

The rate used to apply variable manufacturing overhead to units of product is known as the **standard variable manufacturing overhead rate**. As stated, Ali, Maria, and Bill expected to work about 60 hours each, or a total of 180 direct labor hours per month. Based on the planned variable manufacturing overhead cost of $63 and 180 estimated direct labor hours, we compute a standard variable manufacturing overhead rate of $0.35 by dividing the $63 budgeted variable manufacturing overhead by the 180 estimated direct labor hours, shown as follows:

Budgeted Variable Manufacturing Overhead	÷	Budgeted Direct Labor Hours	=	Standard Variable Manufacturing Overhead Rate
$63	÷	180 Hours	=	$0.35 Per Hour

When the variable manufacturing overhead allocation is based on direct labor hours, once a manufacturer knows the direct labor efficiency standard and the standard variable manufacturing overhead rate per direct labor hour, it can determine the standard variable manufacturing overhead cost per unit. The standard variable manufacturing overhead cost to build a single unit of product is calculated by multiplying the direct labor efficiency standard (the estimated direct labor hours per unit) by the standard variable manufacturing overhead rate. For Tree Top, the standard cost per unit for variable manufacturing overhead is $0.21, shown as follows:

Direct Labor Efficiency Standard	×	Standard Variable Manufacturing Overhead Rate	=	Standard Variable Mfg Overhead Cost Per Unit
0.6 Hours	×	$0.35 Per Hour	=	$0.21

Setting Fixed Manufacturing Overhead Standards

Unlike variable manufacturing overhead cost, which changes in total as production increases or decreases, fixed manufacturing overhead cost remains constant in total regardless of how many units are produced.

To set the fixed manufacturing overhead standards, manufacturers must first estimate the total cost of fixed manufacturing overhead. For Tree Top Mailbox Company, this amount consists of rent of $200 per month and monthly depreciation of $25 for the equipment used to make the mailboxes. Fixed manufacturing overhead then totals $225 per month ($200 + $25 = $225).

Standard Fixed Manufacturing Overhead Rate

As with variable manufacturing overhead, fixed manufacturing overhead can be allocated to production based on units of production, direct labor hours, direct labor dollars, machine hours, or some other allocation base. The rate used to apply fixed manufacturing overhead to units of product is known as the **standard fixed manufacturing overhead rate.**

standard fixed manufacturing overhead rate The rate used to apply fixed manufacturing overhead to units of manufactured product.

Our illustration assumes that Tree Top Mailbox Company allocates fixed manufacturing overhead to production based on direct labor hours. In such a case, we determine the standard fixed manufacturing overhead rate by dividing the total estimated fixed manufacturing overhead cost by the total estimated direct labor hours. In the case of Tree Top, we calculate the standard fixed manufacturing overhead rate of $1.25 per direct labor hour by dividing the budgeted fixed manufacturing overhead cost of $225 by the budgeted direct labor hours of 180 shown as follows:

Budgeted Fixed Mfg Overhead	÷	Budgeted Direct Labor Hours	=	Standard Fixed Mfg Overhead Rate
$225	÷	180 Hours	=	$1.25

We calculate the standard fixed manufacturing overhead cost to build a single unit of product by multiplying the direct labor efficiency standard per unit by the standard fixed manufacturing overhead rate. For Tree Top, the standard cost per unit for fixed manufacturing overhead is $0.75, shown as follows:

Direct Labor Efficiency Standard	×	Standard Fixed Mfg Overhead Rate	=	Standard Fixed Mfg Overhead Cost Per Unit
0.6 Hours	×	$1.25 Per Hour	=	$0.75

Total Standard Cost Per Unit

Once standards have been set for direct material, direct labor, variable manufacturing overhead, and fixed manufacturing overhead, the total standard cost per unit can be calculated. This amount reflects how much it *should* cost to produce a unit of product. The standard cost per unit represents a useful estimate that can be helpful for planning and setting selling prices. For Tree Top, the total standard cost per mailbox is $8.85 as shown in Exhibit 10-6.

Exhibit 10-6 Total Standard Cost Per Mailbox Built

Standard Direct Material Cost Per Mailbox	$1.89
Standard Direct Labor Cost Per Mailbox	6.00
Standard Variable Manufacturing Overhead Cost Per Mailbox	.21
Standard Fixed Manufacturing Overhead Cost Per Mailbox	.75
Total Standard Cost Per Mailbox	$8.85

As you might imagine, the *actual* cost of producing an item is almost never exactly the same as the *standard* cost. When actual cost exceeds standard cost, management should take steps to determine the cause of the variance, and, if necessary, take corrective action.

Actual total production cost that exceeds the standard may indicate that a general problem exists, but it provides almost no information that can help managers focus on the true cause of the problem. Managers need access to information they can use to isolate and address specific cost problems.

The next sections show how managers use standard costing to isolate specific problems for each production cost category.

Variance Analysis

Standard costs can help control costs by serving as benchmarks to compare with actual production costs. To use standard costing as a control device, managers compare *standard costs* to *actual costs* to see whether variances exist. Instead of calculating a single variance for total production cost, they make variances specific enough to isolate a particular production process problem. In this section we examine how we can calculate detailed standard cost variances for direct material, direct labor, variable manufacturing overhead, and fixed manufacturing overhead. We will walk through the calculations for each standard cost variance using Tree Top Mailbox Company as an example.

Unfortunately for Tree Top, November was not nearly as successful as October. The company produced and sold only 225 mailboxes in spite of demand for many more. The income statement for the month of November appears in Exhibit 10-7.

Exhibit 10-7 Tree Top's November 2009 Income Statement

Tree Top Mailbox Company
Income Statement
For the Month Ended November 30, 2009

Sales (225 mailboxes at $10 each)		$2,250
Variable Cost:		
Direct Material (6,000 feet of wood)	$ 477	
Direct Labor (162 hours at $10.50 per hr)	1,701	
Utilities (all variable)	50	
Miscellaneous Variable Costs	90	
Total Variable Cost		2,318
Contribution Margin		(68)
Fixed Cost:		
Rent	200	
Depreciation	35	
Total Fixed Cost		235
Net Income		$ (303)

November's loss disturbed Ali, Maria, and Bill because they had spent nearly as much time at the shop as in October, but produced far fewer mailboxes. What changes should Tree Top make to get the company back on track? We can answer this question once we have calculated the variances and examined their causes.

To calculate standard cost variances, we use the standard costs discussed in the preceding sections, and compare them with Tree Top's actual performance. Actual performance data are obtained from various sources, including company reports and files. In our Tree Top Mailbox Company example, we have included the key details in November's income statement, presented in Exhibit 10-7.

Direct Materials Variances

Direct material variances can be used to answer three important questions.

1. Did the company pay more or less than it should have when the direct material was purchased from the supplier based on the standards set?
2. Did the company use more or less direct material that it should have, based on the standards set?
3. What was the cost impact of these price and quantity differences?

Direct Material Price Variance

The **direct material price variance** is a measure of the difference between the amount the company *planned* to pay for direct material and the amount it *actually* paid. This variance provides an indication of whether the price paid to suppliers for direct material compares favorably to the standard price. To find the direct material price variance we use a two-step process. First, we determine the amount that should have been paid for the direct material. Second, we calculate the dollar amount of the direct material variance.

direct material price variance A measure of the difference between the amount the company planned to pay for direct material purchased and the amount it actually paid for the direct material.

Step 1: *Determine the amount that should have been paid for the direct material purchased according to the standard price.*

According to the detailed information on November's income statement, Tree Top Mailbox Company purchased 6,000 feet of wood. How much should the company have paid for the 6,000 feet of wood if it had been able to purchase it at the standard price? We determine this amount by multiplying the actual quantity of direct material purchased by the standard price. Often the quantity of material purchased differs from the quantity of material used in production. Which amount should we use? For this calculation remember to use the quantity of material purchased, not the quantity used in production, shown as follows:

Actual Quantity Purchased		Direct Material Price Standard		Quantity Purchased Priced at Standard
6,000 Feet	×	$0.0875	=	$525

Our calculations show that, based on the standard price of $0.0875 per foot, the 6,000 feet of wood purchased should have cost $525.

Step 2: *Calculate the dollar amount of the direct material price variance.*

We calculate the dollar amount of the direct material price variance by subtracting the actual cost of direct material purchased from the standard cost of the direct material purchased (determined in step 1). According to the detailed information on November's income statement, Tree Top purchased the 6,000 feet of wood for $477. By comparing the standard cost of $525 to the actual cost of $477, we determine that the price variance is $48 favorable, shown as follows:

Quantity Purchased Priced at Standard	–	Actual Direct Material Cost	=	Direct Material Price Variance
$525	–	$477	=	$48 Favorable

To review the calculations for the direct material price variance in dollars, we compare the amount the wood purchased *should* have cost, $525, to what the wood *actually* cost, $477, to determine the direct material price variance.

When a product requires the use of multiple direct materials, a manufacturer must compute a separate material price variance for each direct material used. The logic and computations, however, are similar to those presented here.

Once management calculates the direct material price variance, it can assess the situation and, if necessary, take corrective action. In most manufacturing companies, direct material is purchased by purchasing agents working in the company's purchasing department. Therefore, direct material price variances are brought to the attention of the purchasing agent responsible for buying the particular direct material so that the price can be evaluated and corrective action taken when necessary.

In the case of Tree Top, the actual price paid for the wood was lower than the standard price, resulting in a favorable direct material price variance. It may seem that a favorable variance would not warrant investigation, but this is not always the case. A significant favorable variance is worth examining for several reasons. First, repeated favorable variances may be an indication that the standard is too lax. Second, management should investigate the variance to see whether the techniques used to achieve the favorable variance can be used by other areas of the company to help reduce cost. Third, a favorable variance may have occurred because of a trade-off between price and quality. For example, a favorable variance might be achieved by purchasing direct material of a substandard quality.

Bill purchased the wood for Tree Top from the lumber company at a discounted price. The lumber company was able to offer the discount because another customer had refused the wood and the lumber company was overstocked. As it turned out, the wood had an unusually high number of knots and other blemishes. The substandard wood, then, may have caused the use of more direct material and direct labor than would have otherwise been required for production.

Discussion Questions

10-3. How might the purchase of wood at a discount affect the amount of direct material used to make the mail boxes?

10-4. If there had been no variance, would this mean Tree Top paid what it should have for the wood used to build its mailboxes in November? Explain your reasoning.

Direct Material Quantity Variance

The **direct material quantity variance**, sometimes called the **direct material usage variance** or the **direct material efficiency variance**, is a measure of the over- or

direct material quantity variance A measure of the over- or under consumption of direct material for the number of units actually manufactured.

direct material usage variance Another name for the direct material quantity variance.

direct material efficiency variance Another name for the direct material quantity variance.

under-consumption of direct material for the number of units actually manufactured. It informs management whether too much or too little direct material is used in the manufacturing process based on the standards. The direct material quantity variance is the difference between the standard quantity and the actual quantity of direct materials used. We follow three steps to calculate the direct material quantity variance. First, we calculate the standard quantity of direct material allowed for actual production. Second, we calculate the variance in units of direct material. Finally, we calculate the variance in dollars.

Step 1: *Calculate the standard quantity of direct material allowed for actual production.*

The standard quantity of direct material allowed is the amount needed for actual production, according to the standard. It is the amount allowed for actual production. To calculate this amount, we determine how much direct material should have been used according to the standard to make the units actually produced.

Recall that Tree Top produced 225 mailboxes in November. To determine the quantity of the wood that *should* have been used to make 225 mailboxes, we multiply the direct material quantity standard (21.60 feet per unit) by the number of mailboxes produced (225). For Tree Top, the standard quantity of direct material allowed for the actual production of 225 mailboxes is 4,860 feet, shown as follows:

Direct Material Quantity Standard	×	Number of Units Produced	=	Standard Quantity of Direct Material Allowed
21.60 Feet	×	225 Units	=	4,860 Feet

We see from the calculations that 4,860 feet of wood is the standard direct material quantity allowed for the units produced—the direct material quantity that should have been used based on the number of units *actually* produced.

Step 2: *Calculate the direct material quantity variance in units of direct material.*

We calculate the direct material quantity variance in units of direct material by subtracting the actual quantity of direct material used from the standard quantity of direct material allowed. For Tree Top Mailbox Company, the direct material quantity variance in feet is determined by comparing the quantity of wood it *should* have taken to make the 225 mailboxes (determined in step 1) to the quantity of wood it *actually* took to make the mailboxes (the actual quantity).

Discussion Question

10-5. If the actual amount of wood used was more than the standard quantity of wood, do you think the direct material quantity variance would be favorable or unfavorable? Explain your reasoning.

To use standard costing, a manufacturer must maintain a record of the quantity of direct material used in production. In the case of Tree Top, this information is found in the income statement as presented in Exhibit 10-7. A review of that income statement shows that the actual quantity of direct material Tree Top used to make the 225 mailboxes in November was 6,000 feet of wood. Often the quantity of material used in production differs from the quantity of material purchased. For this calculation it is important to remember to use the quantity of material used, not the quantity purchased.

We calculate Tree Top's direct material quantity variance by finding the difference between the standard quantity of direct material allowed and the quantity of direct material used in production. In this case the variance is 1,140 unfavorable, shown as follows:

Standard Quantity of Direct Material Allowed		Actual Quantity Used		Quantity Variance in Units of Direct Material (feet)
4,860 Feet	−	6,000 Feet	=	1,140 Unfavorable

We can see from the presentation that Ali, Maria, and Bill used 1,140 more feet of wood than the standard allowed to make the 225 mailboxes. Does this overuse of direct material really matter? Even if the direct material quantity variance in feet is 1,140 unfavorable, it *may* represent an insignificant dollar amount. To evaluate whether this variance is worthy of attention, we need to assign a dollar amount.

Step 3: *Calculate the direct material quantity variance in dollars.*

To avoid contaminating the quantity variance with problems relating to the actual price paid for material, the dollar amount assigned to the direct material quantity variance is based on the standard direct material price, not the actual price. Tree Top's direct material quantity variance in dollars is $99.75. We calculate this amount by multiplying the direct material quantity variance (1,140 feet) by the direct material price standard of $0.0875, shown as follows:

Quantity Variance in Units of Direct Material (Feet)		Direct Material Price Standard		Direct Material Quantity Variance in Dollars
1,140 Unfavorable	×	$0.0875	=	$99.75 Unfavorable

The direct materials quantity variance in dollars provides valuable information about the cost of using too much direct material to make the mailboxes. Now that a dollar amount has been assigned to the variance, we can evaluate its importance and devote the amount of management attention that is appropriate.

Discussion Questions

10-6. Based on Tree Top Mailbox Company's direct material quantity variance, do you think that Ali, Maria, and Bill need to examine reasons for using so much wood? Explain your reasoning.

10-7. If the dollar amount of a variance is insignificant, does the variance information help Tree Top's management team determine where it should focus attention? Explain.

10-8. If there had been no variance, would this mean Tree Top used the appropriate amount of wood to build its mailboxes in November? Explain your reasoning.

We assume that only one direct material is used to make the mailboxes for Tree Top. In practice most products require several different direct materials, ranging from one to thousands, and a manufacturer must compute a separate material quantity variance for each direct material used. The logic and computations, however, are similar to those presented here.

Once management calculates the direct material quantity variance, it can assess the situation and, if necessary, take corrective action. Generally, a quantity variance should be discussed with the individuals who are responsible for the amount of direct material used. The focus of the discussion should be on finding and eliminating the cause of the variance. In many companies, the person responsible for direct material consumption is the production supervisor, who would attempt to determine the cause of the variance and take steps to eliminate it.

Direct Labor Variances

Direct labor variances help managers answer three key questions.

1. Was the company's hourly direct labor rate more or less than it should have been based on the standards set?
2. Did it take more or fewer direct labor hours than it should have taken for the company to manufacture its products based on the standards set?
3. What was the cost impact of these differences in the hourly direct labor rate and the number of direct labor hours?

It may be helpful to consider some parallels between direct material and direct labor. Instead of using the terms *price* and *quantity* as we did for direct material, we use *rate* and *hours* for direct labor. In reality, only the descriptive words change—the meanings stay the same. The price per measure of direct material is similar to the rate per hour of direct labor. Likewise, the quantity of direct material is similar to the hours of direct labor. Because of these similarities, the steps and calculations of standard cost variances for direct labor are comparable to direct material variances.

Direct Labor Rate Variance

The **direct labor rate variance** is a measure of the difference between the actual wage rate paid to employees and the direct labor rate standard. This variance shows the effect of unanticipated wage rate changes. The direct labor rate standard for the company is $10 per hour. As you will note by looking at the November income statement in Exhibit 10-7, each of the three owners received a $0.50 raise during November. So, for Tree Top, the direct labor rate variance will indicate added cost caused by the pay raises. We use a two-step process to calculate the direct labor rate variance. First, we find the amount the company should have paid for direct labor for the hours worked. Second, we determine the dollar amount of the direct labor rate variance.

direct labor rate variance A measure of the difference between the actual wage rate paid to employees and the direct labor rate standard.

Step 1: *Determine the amount that should have been paid for the actual direct labor hours worked according to the direct labor rate standard.*

In this step we determine how much the company should have paid for the direct labor hours actually worked, based on the direct labor rate standard. For Tree Top, the actual direct labor hours totaled 162 for November. By multiplying the 162 actual direct labor hours by the direct labor rate standard of $10, we determine that the company should have paid $1,620, shown as follows:

Actual Direct Labor Hours	×	Direct Labor Rate Standard	=	Actual Direct Labor Hours at the Standard Rate
162 Hours	×	$10	=	$1,620

Once we determine what the company should have paid according to the standard, we can compare it to the amount actually paid to determine the direct labor rate variance.

Step 2: *Calculate the dollar amount of the direct labor rate variance.*

We compute the dollar amount of the direct labor rate variance by subtracting the actual cost of direct labor from the standard cost of the direct labor actually worked. The direct labor rate variance compares the amount the actual direct labor hours should have cost to the actual cost. In the case of Tree Top, we find that the actual direct labor cost for November was $1,701, as shown on the November income statement in Exhibit 10-7. Tree Top's direct labor hours at standard should have cost $1,620. When we compare actual labor cost ($1,701) to standard cost ($1,620), we find an unfavorable direct labor rate variance of $81, shown as follows:

Actual Direct Labor Hours at the Standard Rate	−	Actual Direct Labor Cost	=	Direct Labor Rate Variance
$1,620	−	$1,701	=	$81 Unfavorable

The calculated variance is unfavorable because the actual direct labor cost is higher than the cost based on the standard rate. This $81 unfavorable variance provides useful information to Ali, Maria, and Bill about the effect of their $0.50 per hour raise.

Discussion Questions

10-9. What effect did the $0.50 per hour pay raise have on November's profits?

10-10. In light of the financial problems that occurred in November, do you think Tree Top's owners should roll back the wage rate to $10 per hour? Explain your reasoning.

As with other variances, once management calculates the direct labor rate variance, it can assess the variance and, if necessary, take corrective action. Direct labor rate variances are caused by labor rate changes that are unanticipated. Generally, when labor rates are contractually set or a result of collective bargaining with labor unions, labor rate changes are not unexpected. Accordingly, these labor rates are factored into the direct labor rate standard. A direct labor rate variance can be caused by an unexpected rate change of some kind, or perhaps an unanticipated change in the makeup of the labor force. For example, if the company retains more experienced workers and has fewer new workers, an unfavorable direct labor rate variance is likely because new employees generally begin their employment at a lower hourly wage than experienced employees.

In the case of Tree Top Mailbox Company, the November income statement shows that Ali, Maria, and Bill gave themselves an unplanned $0.50 per hour raise. Although no corrective action will likely be taken, the trio now knows how the raise affected profits.

Direct Labor Efficiency Variance

direct labor efficiency variance A measure of the difference between the planned number of direct labor hours and the actual number of direct labor hours for the units actually manufactured.

The **direct labor efficiency variance** is a measure of the over- or under-consumption of direct labor for the number of units actually manufactured. In other words, the direct labor efficiency variance informs management whether too much or too little direct labor is used in the manufacturing process based on the standards. This variance is comparable to the direct material quantity variance. Both are used to evaluate the quantity of something used. In the case of the direct material quantity variance, the focus is on the quantity of direct material used. In the case of the direct labor efficiency variance, the focus is on the quantity of direct labor hours used.

We use three steps to calculate this variance. First, we find the standard number of direct labor hours allowed for production. Second, we determine the variance in hours. Finally, we calculate the variance in dollars.

Step 1: *Calculate the standard number of direct labor hours allowed for actual production.*

In this first step we determine the amount of direct labor time it *should* have taken to make all the units that were *actually* made during the period. According to the direct labor efficiency standard for Tree Top, it should have taken 0.6 hours (36 minutes) to make each mailbox. Because 225 mailboxes were made in November, the total amount of direct labor hours should have been 135 hours ($225 \times 0.6 = 135$).

Step 2: *Calculate the direct labor efficiency variance in hours.*

We compute the direct labor efficiency variance in hours by subtracting the standard direct labor hours allowed from the actual number of direct labor hours worked. According to information taken from Tree Top's November income statement presented in Exhibit 10-7, the actual number of direct labor hours used in November was 162. By comparing the standard hours allowed for the 225 mailboxes, 135 hours, to the actual direct labor hours, 162 hours, we see that the direct labor efficiency variance in hours is 27 hours unfavorable, shown as follows:

Standard Direct Labor Hours Allowed		Actual Direct Labor Hours		Direct Labor Efficiency Variance in Hours
135 Hours	−	162 Hours	=	27 Hours Unfavorable

The variance between the standard direct labor hours allowed and actual number of direct labor hours worked indicates that Tree Top's employees did not work very efficiently. If they had, they would have completed the 225 mailboxes in 135 hours, or maybe even less.

To grasp the true magnitude of the 27 hour unfavorable variance, we must assign a dollar amount.

Step 3: *Calculate the direct labor efficiency variance in dollars.*

To avoid contaminating the direct labor efficiency variance with problems relating to the actual labor rate, we calculate the direct labor efficiency variance in dollars by multiplying the variance in hours by the direct labor rate standard, not the actual labor rate. In the case of Tree Top, we multiply the 27-hour unfavorable direct labor efficiency variance by the direct labor rate standard of $10, shown as follows:

Direct Labor Efficiency Variance in Hours		Direct Labor Rate Standard		Direct Labor Efficiency Variance in Dollars
27 Hours	×	$10	=	$270 Unfavorable

Once management calculates the direct labor efficiency variance, it can assess the variance and, if necessary, take corrective action. The plant manager would probably ask the production supervisor or production-line employees to help determine why the unfavorable variance occurred. Once the cause of the problem is found, corrective action can be taken.

Tree Top determined that substandard wood caused the unfavorable direct labor efficiency variance. To make mailboxes of sufficient quality, Ali, Maria, and Bill needed extra time to cut the knots and other blemishes from the wood. The solution to the variance problem is to purchase only good quality wood in the future.

The direct labor variances reveal that Ali, Maria, and Bill had two important problems in November regarding direct labor cost. First, the hourly wage paid to Ali, Maria, and Bill was higher than the planned $10 direct labor rate standard. This higher wage rate increased direct labor cost by $81. Second, it took 27 extra hours to make the 225 mailboxes. The extra 27 hours increased labor cost by $270. The total effect of these two direct labor problems is $351 unfavorable.

Manufacturing Overhead Variances

Manufacturing overhead variances help managers answer two vital questions.

1. Did the company spend more or less on manufacturing overhead items than it should have, based on the standards that were set?
2. Did the company utilize its production facility efficiently?

In this section we look at four different manufacturing overhead variances, two that deal with variable manufacturing overhead and two with fixed manufacturing overhead.

Variable Manufacturing Overhead Spending Variance

variable manufacturing overhead spending variance The difference between how much was actually spent on variable manufacturing overhead and the amount that should have been spent based on the actual direct labor hours worked.

The **variable manufacturing overhead spending variance** is the difference between what was *actually* spent on variable manufacturing overhead and what *should* have been spent, based on the actual direct labor hours worked. The question this variance answers is, based on the actual number of direct labor hours worked, is variable manufacturing overhead cost in line? In the case of Tree Top, given that production took 162 direct labor hours, was variable manufacturing overhead more or less than it should have been for that many direct labor hours? We use two steps to find the answer. First, we must determine the standard variable manufacturing overhead for the actual number of direct labor hours worked. Second, we calculate the variable manufacturing overhead spending variance in dollars. Let's look at the first step in this process.

Step 1: *Determine the standard variable manufacturing overhead for the actual number of direct labor hours worked.*

To determine the standard variable manufacturing overhead for the actual direct labor hours worked, we multiply the standard variable manufacturing overhead rate by the actual number of direct labor hours. This calculation shows us the amount that should have been spent for variable manufacturing overhead based on the actual direct labor hours worked. Based on Tree Top's standard variable manufacturing overhead rate of $0.35 per hour, the standard variable manufacturing overhead cost for the 162 actual direct labor hours is $56.70, shown as follows:

Actual Direct labor Hours		Standard Variable Mfg Overhead Rate		Standard Variable Mfg Overhead for Actual Direct Labor Hours
162 Hours	×	$0.35	=	$56.70

Now that we know how much Tree Top's variable manufacturing overhead should have been, we can compare it to the actual variable manufacturing overhead amount to determine the amount of the variance.

Step 2: *Calculate the variable manufacturing overhead spending variance.*

We calculate the variable manufacturing overhead spending variance by comparing standard variable manufacturing overhead for the actual number of direct labor hours worked to the amount actually spent for variable manufacturing overhead. This calculation compares *actual* variable manufacturing overhead cost to what it *should* have been for the actual direct labor hours worked. In the case of Tree Top, the actual amount spent for variable manufacturing overhead in November was $140. By comparing this amount to the standard of $56.70, we determine that the variable manufacturing overhead spending variance is $83.30 unfavorable, shown as follows:

Standard Variable Mfg Overhead Cost for Actual Direct Labor Hours		Actual Variable Mfg Overhead Cost		Variable Mfg Overhead Spending Variance
$56.70	−	$140.00	=	$83.30 Unfavorable

Discussion Questions

10-11. What are some possible reasons why Tree Top Mailbox Company's variable manufacturing overhead spending was much higher than it should have been based on the standards?

10-12. If there had been no variance, would this mean Tree Top paid what it should have for variable manufacturing overhead in November? Explain your reasoning.

As managers assess the variable manufacturing overhead spending variance, they should keep in mind that it is a result of many different variable manufacturing overhead expenditures. In practice, most companies break down the variable manufacturing overhead spending variance into separate variances for each variable manufacturing overhead item. For example, a manufacturer would have separate variance calculations for electricity, water, telephone, cleaning supplies, maintenance supplies, and so forth. The logic and calculations for each variance, however, would be similar to what we have presented here.

Variable Manufacturing Overhead Efficiency Variance

The **variable manufacturing overhead efficiency variance** is a measure of the variable manufacturing overhead cost attributable to the difference between the planned and

variable manufacturing overhead efficiency variance A measure of the variable manufacturing overhead cost attributable to the difference between the planned and actual direct labor hours worked.

actual activity of the allocation base. Recall that companies select an allocation base that they think reflects the actual consumption of factory resources. Common allocation bases include direct labor hours, direct labor cost, and machine hours. Since Tree Top has selected direct labor hours as its allocation base, our treatment of this topic will use direct labor hours as the allocation base. If some other allocation base is used, the concepts presented and the computations would differ only slightly.

When direct labor hours is used as the allocation base, the variable manufacturing overhead efficiency variance relates more to the efficiency of direct labor than anything else. While production workers work in the factory, they consume electricity as they use lights and air conditioning and operate machinery. They also use supplies and other factory resources that all are part of manufacturing overhead. So, as workers work longer, they use more factory resources. How much more? The variable manufacturing overhead efficiency variance helps answer this question.

An unfavorable variable manufacturing overhead efficiency variance is a measure of the variable manufacturing overhead cost associated with the extra hours worked by direct labor. A direct relationship exists between the direct labor efficiency variance and the variable manufacturing overhead efficiency variance. Therefore, if the direct labor efficiency variance is unfavorable, the variable manufacturing overhead efficiency variance will also be unfavorable. Likewise, if the direct labor efficiency variance is favorable, the variable manufacturing overhead efficiency variance will also be favorable.

We use three steps to calculate this variance. First, we find the standard number of direct labor hours allowed for production. Second, we determine the variance in hours. Finally, we calculate the variance in dollars.

Step 1: *Calculate the standard number of direct labor hours allowed for actual production.*

Step 2: *Calculate the direct labor efficiency variance in hours.*

We have listed the first two steps for calculating the variable manufacturing overhead efficiency variance without any explanation because they are the same as those for determining the direct labor efficiency variance. These steps are to find the standard number of direct labor hours allowed for actual production and then to calculate the direct labor efficiency variance in hours.

Assuming then, that we have calculated the direct labor efficiency variance, we review the information learned from those calculations before moving to the third step of the calculations, which is determining the variable manufacturing overhead efficiency variance in dollars.

Recall that our calculation showed that Tree Top used an extra 27 direct labor hours to make the 225 mailboxes in November. The extra 27 direct labor hours not only increased direct labor cost, but it also increased other costs. While Ali, Maria, and Bill worked the extra 27 hours, they consumed electricity, supplies, and other factory resources. In sum, the inefficiency of the workforce increased variable manufacturing overhead cost. Had they not worked the extra 27 hours, Tree Top's owners would have saved not only the labor cost, but also the factory resources they consumed as they worked the extra time.

Step 3: *Calculate the variable manufacturing overhead efficiency variance in dollars.*

To calculate the variable manufacturing overhead efficiency variance in dollars, we multiply the direct labor efficiency variance in hours by the standard variable manufacturing overhead rate.

For Tree Top, the direct labor efficiency variance in hours we calculated earlier is 27 hours. We multiply this amount by the standard variable manufacturing overhead rate we calculated earlier of $0.35. This results in an unfavorable variable manufacturing overhead efficiency variance of $9.45 shown as follows:

Direct Labor Efficiency Variance in Hours	×	Standard Variable Mfg Overhead Rate	=	Variable Mfg Overhead Efficiency Variance
27 Hours	×	$0.35	=	$9.45 Unfavorable

Once management calculates the variable manufacturing overhead efficiency variance, it can assess the variance and take corrective action if necessary. Because the variable manufacturing overhead efficiency variance is based on direct labor efficiency, improving the direct labor efficiency variance will solve the variable manufacturing overhead efficiency variance problem.

Tree Top's variable manufacturing overhead efficiency variance is so small that it may warrant no management attention. Even so, as Ali, Maria, and Bill work to bring the direct labor efficiency variance under control, the variable manufacturing overhead variance will also improve.

Discussion Questions

10-13. If variable manufacturing overhead is allocated to production based on direct labor hours, why will an unfavorable variable manufacturing overhead efficiency variance always accompany an unfavorable direct labor efficiency variance?

10-14. If the direct labor efficiency variance is zero, will the variable manufacturing overhead efficiency variance also be zero? Explain your reasoning.

For Tree Top Mailbox Company, the trouble with variable manufacturing overhead cost is a combination of an unfavorable spending variance of $83.30 and an unfavorable efficiency variance of $9.45. Although the unfavorable efficiency variance will require little or no attention, the spending variance is sizeable and should be investigated. Each component of variable manufacturing overhead should be reviewed to see whether spending can be reduced.

Fixed Manufacturing Overhead Budget Variance

The **fixed manufacturing overhead budget variance**, also called the **fixed manufacturing overhead spending variance**, is a measure of how actual total fixed manufacturing overhead compares to budgeted fixed manufacturing overhead. For example, if a company expects fixed manufacturing overhead cost to be $200,000 per month, the fixed manufacturing overhead budget variance indicates whether the actual fixed manufacturing overhead is more or less than the $200,000.

fixed manufacturing overhead budget variance The difference between the actual amount of total fixed manufacturing overhead cost and the budgeted fixed manufacturing overhead cost.

fixed manufacturing overhead spending variance Another name for the fixed manufacturing overhead budget variance.

We take only one step to compute the fixed manufacturing overhead budget variance. The dollar amount is calculated simply by subtracting actual fixed manufacturing overhead cost from the budgeted fixed manufacturing overhead. For Tree Top, the fixed manufacturing overhead budget variance for November is $10 unfavorable, because actual fixed manufacturing overhead cost exceeded the amount budgeted, shown as follows:

Budgeted Fixed Mfg Overhead Cost	–	Actual Fixed Mfg Overhead Cost	=	Fixed Mfg Overhead Budget Variance
$225	–	$235	=	$10 Unfavorable

Our example company has only two fixed manufacturing overhead items, rent and depreciation. Rent was $200 as planned, but apparently the company purchased a new piece of equipment, which resulted in a $10 increase in fixed manufacturing overhead. Tree Top purchased additional production equipment resulting in higher depreciation cost, and therefore an unfavorable fixed manufacturing overhead budget variance occurred.

Fixed manufacturing overhead costs are generally associated with long-term commitments for specific factory resources. Examples of fixed manufacturing overhead include the cost of depreciation on factory equipment, factory rent, insurance, and property taxes. Unlike other factory costs, fixed manufacturing overhead is less likely to be affected by the routine decisions that managers and employees make daily. For example, Tree Top did not overspend on fixed manufacturing overhead, rather the budget was flawed because they forgot to include depreciation of a new piece of equipment when they prepared the budget.

The variance between the amount budgeted and the actual fixed manufacturing overhead incurred is just as likely to be caused by a flawed budget as it is by spending decisions made during the budget period. For example, if a company budgets $50,000 for property taxes but the taxes are actually $51,000, the $1,000 variance that results is caused by a flawed budget, not by uncontrolled spending. Accordingly, fixed manufacturing overhead budget variances should be closely scrutinized to determine whether the required corrective action is to improve the budgeting process or to modify spending during the period.

Like variable manufacturing overhead, fixed manufacturing overhead comprises many different items. In practice, separate budget variances are calculated for each fixed manufacturing overhead item.

Fixed Manufacturing Overhead Volume Variance

fixed manufacturing overhead volume variance A measure of the utilization of plant capacity. This variance is caused by manufacturing more or less product during a particular production period than planned.

The last standard cost variance we discuss is the **fixed manufacturing overhead volume variance**, which measures utilization of plant capacity. This variance is caused by the manufacture of more or less product during a particular production period than planned. When a manufacturer invests in expensive production machinery, it does so in anticipation of producing a given amount of product. If the company expects to produce only a small amount of product, it invests in inexpensive, low-volume equipment. If, however, the company expects to produce a large volume of product, it usually acquires more costly, high-volume equipment. If expensive, high-volume equipment is purchased but actual production is low, then it is likely that the company spent too much on production capacity. The fixed manufacturing overhead volume variance focuses on this relationship between production capacity and the actual volume produced.

When Ali, Maria, and Bill formed their manufacturing company, they could have set up shop to produce a very small number of mailboxes using hand tools; or they could have chosen to invest heavily in a building and automated equipment, thereby greatly increasing their plant capacity. They chose to rent a small garage and invest a small amount in power tools that gave them a capacity to produce about 300 mailboxes per month. If they produce more than 300 mailboxes, that's great, but if they produce fewer, they are underutilizing their capacity to produce. In November, they produced only 225 mailboxes. Tree Top Mailbox Company, then, underutilized its capacity to produce by 75 mailboxes. Is this a big problem? To evaluate the magnitude of the problem we need to assign a dollar amount to the underutilization.

In the case of Tree Top Mailbox Company, the monthly fixed cost of $225 (later increased to $235) provides a capacity to produce 300 mailboxes. We follow three steps to calculate the fixed manufacturing overhead volume variance. First, we find the difference between expected and actual production. Second, we determine the standard number of direct labor hours associated with the production. Finally, we calculate the dollar amount of the fixed manufacturing overhead volume variance. We examine these steps in detail next.

Step 1: *Calculate the difference between expected (budgeted) production and actual production.*

The budgeted production for Tree Top is 300 mailboxes per month. Tree Top's actual production was less than its budgeted production by 75 mailboxes, shown as follows:

Budgeted Production	−	Actual Number of Units Produced	=	Under- Or Overproduction in Units
300 Units	−	225 Units	=	75 Units Under

Because Tree Top allocates fixed manufacturing overhead based on direct labor hours, the direct labor efficiency standard, with the standard fixed manufacturing overhead rate per direct labor hour is used to calculate the dollar amount of the fixed manufacturing overhead volume variance.

Step 2: *Determine the standard number of direct labor hours associated with the under- or over-production.*

We determine the standard number of direct labor hours associated with the under- or over-production by multiplying the under- or over-production by the direct labor efficiency standard. In the case of Tree Top, the direct labor efficiency standard is 0.6 hours per unit. Accordingly, the standard direct labor hours associated with the underproduction of 75 mailboxes is 45 hours (75 units × 0.6 hours per unit), shown as follows:

Amount of Under- or Overproduction	×	Direct Labor Efficiency Standard	=	Standard Direct Labor Hours for Under- or Overproduction
75 Units	×	0.6 Hours Per Unit	=	45 Hours

Now that we know the number of standard hours associated with the over- or underproduction, we can assign a dollar amount based on the standard fixed manufacturing overhead rate per hour.

Step 3: *Calculate the dollar amount of the fixed manufacturing overhead volume variance.*

We calculate the dollar amount of the fixed manufacturing overhead volume variance by multiplying the standard number of direct labor hours associated with the under- or overproduction by the standard fixed manufacturing overhead rate per direct labor hour. In the case of Tree Top, the fixed manufacturing overhead volume variance is $56.25, shown as follows:

Standard Direct Labor Hours for Under- or Overproduction	×	Standard Fixed Mfg Overhead Rate	=	Fixed Mfg Overhead Volume Variance
45 Hours	×	$1.25	=	$56.25 Unfavorable

Once management calculates the fixed manufacturing overhead volume variance, it can attempt to determine what caused it. In the case of Tree Top, the variance resulted primarily from inefficiencies caused by substandard direct material. Surprisingly, however, fixed manufacturing overhead volume variances are often caused by marketing and sales activities, rather than by the production department. In general, production occurs in response to sales demand. If the product is selling poorly, production volume will be low because little product is needed to fulfill demand. Conversely, if sales demand is high, production volume is likely to be large to meet demand.

Using Standard Cost Variances to Manage by Exception

Once all the standard cost variances have been calculated, the accounting department prepares a performance report that lists each variance. Then managers can use management by exception to address the problems associated with the unfavorable variances, beginning with the largest. A performance report is presented in Exhibit 10-8 for Tree Top Mailbox Company.

Exhibit 10-8 Tree Top's November Performance Report

Tree Top Mailbox Company
Performance Report
For November 2009

Variance	Amount	Favorable/ Unfavorable
Direct material price variance	$ 48.00	Favorable
Direct material quantity variance	99.75	Unfavorable
Direct labor rate variance	81.00	Unfavorable
Direct labor efficiency variance	270.00	Unfavorable
Variable mfg overhead spending variance	83.30	Unfavorable
Variable mfg overhead efficiency variance	9.45	Unfavorable
Fixed mfg overhead budget variance	10.00	Unfavorable
Fixed mfg overhead volume variance	56.25	Unfavorable
Total	$561.75	Unfavorable

As the Tree Top Mailbox Company example shows, sometimes relationships among standard cost variances can occur that help explain the cause of some variances. Also, managers must develop the skill to review the variances and then seek out their causes and possible remedies. Even though managers can use standard costing to spot pressing issues, they must be aware of its shortcomings. Standard costing is one management tool, but not the only tool.

Alternate Calculations for Standard Cost Variances

So far we have presented but one of the many ways to calculate standard cost variances. Another way of calculating the variance which is quite popular is called the graphical approach. The following tables present this alternate method for calculating standard cost variances.

Direct Material Variances

AQP Actual **Q**uantity of direct material **P**urchased
AQU Actual **Q**uantity of direct material **U**sed in production
AP Actual **P**rice per measure of direct material (This amount is often unknown and is unnecessary as long as the total cost of the direct material purchased is known.)
SP **S**tandard **P**rice per measure of direct material (The direct material price standard.)
SQA **S**tandard **Q**uantity allowed for **A**ctual production (Units actually produced × the direct material quantity standard.)

AQP × AP	AQP × SP
6,000 × $0.0795	6,000 × $0.0875
$477.00	$525.00

Direct Material Price Variance
$48.00 F

AQU × SP	SQA × SP
6,000 × $0.0875	225 × 21.6 Feet × $0.0875
$525.00	4860 Feet × $.0875
	$425.25

DM Quantity Variance
$99.75 U

Direct Labor Variances

AH Actual direct labor **H**ours
AR Actual labor **R**ate per direct labor hour (This amount is often unknown and is unnecessary as long as the total actual direct labor cost is known.)
SR Standard labor **R**ate per direct labor hour (The direct labor rate standard.)
SHA Standard direct labor **H**ours allowed for **A**ctual production (Units actually produced × the direct labor efficiency standard.)

Actual Direct Labor Cost AH × AR	AH × SR	SHA × SR
162 × $10.50	162 × $10.00	225 × 0.6 Hours × $10.00
$1,701.00	$1,620.00	135 Hours × $10.00
		$1,350.00

Dir. Labor Rate Variance
$81.00 U

Dir. Labor Eff. Variance
$270.00 U

Variable Manufacturing Overhead Variances

AH Actual direct labor **H**ours
AR Actual variable manufacturing overhead **R**ate per direct labor hour (This amount is often unknown and unnecessary because the total actual variable manufacturing overhead cost is generally provided.)
SR Standard variable manufacturing overhead **R**ate per direct labor hour
SHA Standard direct labor **H**ours allowed for **A**ctual production (Units actually produced × the direct labor efficiency standard.)

Actual VMOCost AH × AR	AH × SR	SHA × SR
162 × $?	162 × $0.35	225 × 0.6 Hours × $0.35
$140.00	$56.70	135 Hours × $0.35
		$47.25

VMO Spending Variance
$83.30 U

VMO Efficiency Variance
$9.45 U

Fixed Manufacturing Overhead Variances

AH Actual direct labor **H**ours
AR **A**ctual fixed manufacturing overhead **R**ate per direct labor hour (This amount is often unknown and unnecessary because the total actual fixed manufacturing overhead cost is generally provided.)
SR **S**tandard fixed manufacturing overhead **R**ate per direct labor hour
SHA **S**tandard direct labor **H**ours allowed for **A**ctual production (Units actually produced × the direct labor efficiency standard.)

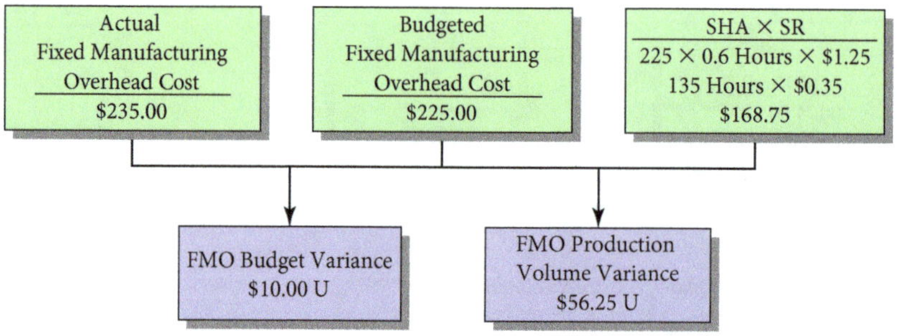

Recording Product Cost Using Standard Costing

This section is intended to provide an overview of the accounting entries to record product costs using standard costing. To fully understand the material in this part of the chapter, it is best if you have a basic understanding of debit and credit accounting procedures including general journal entries and the use of t-accounts. If this is not the case, we suggest that you review the accounting procedures section of any introductory financial accounting text.

The recording process for standard costing involves ten basic types of transactions:

Transaction 1—Record the purchase of direct material and the direct material price variance.

Transaction 2—Record the use of direct material and the direct material quantity variance.

Transaction 3—Record the use of direct labor and the direct labor rate and efficiency variances.

Transaction 4—Record actual variable manufacturing overhead cost incurred.

Transaction 5—Record the application of variable manufacturing overhead to production.

Transaction 6—Close the variable manufacturing overhead accounts and record the variable manufacturing overhead variances.

Transaction 7—Record actual fixed manufacturing overhead cost incurred.

Transaction 8—Record the application of fixed manufacturing overhead to production.

Transaction 9—Close the fixed manufacturing overhead accounts and record the fixed manufacturing overhead variances.

Transaction 10—Close the standard cost variances to cost of goods sold.

To record these transactions we will use the following general ledger accounts:

1. *Cash*
2. *Raw materials inventory*

3. *Work-in-process inventory*
4. *Direct materials price variance*
5. *Direct materials quantity variance*
6. *Direct labor efficiency variance*
7. *Direct labor rate variance*
8. *Variable manufacturing overhead efficiency variance*
9. *Variable manufacturing overhead spending variance*
10. *Fixed manufacturing overhead budget variance*
11. *Fixed manufacturing overhead volume variance*
12. *Variable manufacturing overhead incurred*
13. *Variable manufacturing overhead applied*
14. *Fixed manufacturing overhead incurred*
15. *Fixed manufacturing overhead applied*
16. *Accumulated depreciation*
17. *Accounts payable*
18. *Cost of goods sold*

As we demonstrate the journal entries, we will analyze each transaction using the following four steps.

1. Determine if and when a transaction occurred, what accounts were affected, which account balances should increase, which should decrease, and by how much.
2. Determine which accounts we should debit and which we should credit.
3. Make the journal entry.
4. Review the entry to ensure it is in proper form and that the debits equal the credits.

The entries that follow are based on information from the Tree Top Mailbox Company example presented in this chapter.

Before we begin, it is important to know that when companies use standard costing, they maintain their direct materials, work-in-process, and finished goods inventories at standard cost. The standard cost variances account for the differences between the standard costs maintained in inventories and actual costs. Also keep in mind that when we record a standard cost variance, we need to credit the variance account if the variance is favorable and we need to debit the variance account if it is unfavorable.

Transaction 1—*Record the purchase of direct material and the direct material price variance.*

1. Let's assume the Tree Top purchased the 6,000 feet of wood for $477.00 on November 1, 2009. This transaction affects the raw materials inventory account, the accounts payable account and direct material price variance account. Because Tree Top is using a standard cost system, we should increase the balance in the raw materials inventory account by the 6,000 feet of wood priced at standard. At Tree Top's $0.0875 per foot standard direct material price, the standard cost of the 6,000 feet of wood is $525.00 (6,000 × $0875). Also, we should increase accounts payable by the $477.00 actual cost of the material. After all, that is how much Tree Top must pay for the wood. Finally,

we should place the $48.00 favorable variance, the difference between the material's standard cost and its actual cost, in the direct material price variance account.

2. Because raw materials inventory is an asset account we increase it with a debit. Accounts payable is a liability account so we increase it with a credit. As we mentioned previously, if a variance is favorable, we should credit the variance account and if it is unfavorable, we should debit the variance account. Therefore, because it is a favorable variance, we credit the direct materials price variance account.

3. The general journal entry:

2009				
Nov	1	Raw Materials Inventory	525.00	
		Accounts Payable		477.00
		Direct Material Price Variance		48.00
		To record the purchase of raw material and		
		the direct material price variance.		

4. A final check of the entry reveals that we dated it correctly, made the debit part of the entry first, indented the credit account title, and the dollar amount of the debits equals that of the credits. The entry is fine.

Transaction 2—*Record the use of direct material and the direct material quantity variance.*

1. We will assume this transaction took place on November 2, 2009. The transaction affects the work-in-process inventory, raw materials inventory, and the direct material quantity variance accounts. We should decrease the balance of the raw materials inventory account based on the actual quantity of material used, priced at standard cost. Therefore we will decrease raw materials inventory by 6,000 feet actually used in production multiplied by the direct material price standard of $.0875, or $525.00. When standard costing is used, we increase work-in-process inventory by the standard quantity of material allowed multiplied by the direct material price standard. In Tree Top's case, we would increase work-in-process inventory by $425.25, shown as follows:

Number of Mailboxes Produced	×	Direct Material Quantity Standard	×	Direct Material Price Standard	=	Amount to Add to Work-in-Process
225	×	21.6 Feet	×	$.0875	=	$425.25

Finally, we should place the $99.75 unfavorable variance in the direct material quantity variance account.

1. Because work-in-process materials inventory is an asset account, we increase it with a debit. Raw materials inventory is also an asset account so we decrease it with a credit. Because it is an unfavorable variance, we debit the direct materials quantity variance account.

2. The general journal entry:

2009				
Nov.	2	Work-In-Process Inventory	425.25	
		Direct Material Quantity Variance	99.75	
		Raw Materials Inventory		525.00
		To record the use of direct material and the direct material quantity variance.		

3. A final check of the entry reveals that it is fine.

Transaction 3—*Record the use of direct labor and the direct labor rate and efficiency variances.*

2. We will assume this transaction took place on November 30, 2009. As we learned in Chapter 2, direct labor cost increases the work-in-process inventory account. When standard costing is used, we increase work-in-process inventory by the standard hours allowed multiplied by the direct labor rate standard. In Tree Top's case, we would increase work-in-process inventory by $1,350.00, shown as follows:

Number of Mailboxes Produced	×	Direct Labor Efficiency Standard	×	Direct Labor Rate Standard	=	Amount to Add to Work-in-Process
225	×	.6	×	$10	=	$1,350.00

We should decrease cash based on the amount actually paid to the labor force, or $1,701.00. The combination of the unfavorable direct labor efficiency variance of $270.00 and the unfavorable direct labor rate variance of $81.00 make up the difference between the amount recorded in work-in-process inventory and the amount paid out as wages.

3. Because work-in-process inventory is an asset account, we increase it with a debit. Cash is also an asset account so we decrease it with a credit. Because the variances are both unfavorable, we debit both the direct labor efficiency variance and the direct labor rate variance accounts.

4. The general journal entry:

2009				
Nov.	30	Work-In-Process Inventory	1,350.00	
		Direct Labor Efficiency Variance	270.00	
		Direct Labor Rate Variance	81.00	
		Cash		1,701.00
		To record direct labor cost and variances		

5. A final check of the entry reveals that it is fine.

Transaction 4—*Record actual variable manufacturing overhead cost incurred.*

1. Let's assume Tree Top's actual variable manufacturing overhead costs totaling $140.00 were paid in cash on November 30, 2009. This entry is relatively straightforward and one you should be familiar with if you studied the manufacturing overhead entries we demonstrated near the end of Chapter 3. We should increase the variable manufacturing overhead incurred account for the actual cost of the variable manufacturing overhead and decrease cash for the amount paid.
2. We increase the variable manufacturing overhead incurred account with a debit and we decrease the cash account with a credit.
3. The general journal entry:

2009				
Nov.	30	Variable Manufacturing Overhead Incurred	140.00	
		Cash		140.00
		To record actual variable manufacturing		
		overhead cost for November.		

4. A final check of the entry reveals that it is fine.

Transaction 5—*Record the application of variable manufacturing overhead to production.*

1. The variable manufacturing overhead cost allocated to production becomes part of work-in-process inventory so this transaction affects the work-in-process inventory account. Because Tree Top uses a standard cost system, the transaction also affects an account called variable manufacturing overhead applied. If you studied the manufacturing overhead entries we covered in Chapter 3, you will already be familiar with this entry. When we allocate manufacturing overhead to production in a standard cost system, we use a different account than the one we used when we recorded the actual manufacturing overhead costs. By using two separate accounts, managers can keep track of both the actual manufacturing overhead costs incurred and the amount applied to production. The amount of variable manufacturing overhead allocated to production is based on the variable manufacturing overhead standard rate. In other words, we allocate variable manufacturing overhead to production at standard. In Tree Top's case, we would increase work-in-process inventory and variable manufacturing overhead applied $47.25, shown as follows:

Number of Mailboxes Produced	×	Direct Labor Efficiency Standard	×	Variable Overhead Rate Standard	=	Amount to Add to Work-in-Process
225	×	.6	×	$0.35	=	$47.25

2. We increase the work-in-process inventory account with a debit and the variable manufacturing overhead applied account with a credit.

3. The general journal entry:

2009				
Nov.	30	Work-In-Process Inventory	47.25	
		Variable Manufacturing Overhead Applied		47.25
		To record the allocation of variable		
		manufacturing overhead to production.		

4. A final check of the entry reveals that it is fine.

Transaction 6—*Close the variable manufacturing overhead accounts and record the variable manufacturing overhead variances.*

1. The difference between the $140.00 balance in the variable manufacturing overhead incurred account and the $47.25 balance in the variable manufacturing overhead applied account equals the combination of the $9.45 unfavorable variable manufacturing overhead efficiency variance and the $83.30 unfavorable variable manufacturing overhead spending variance. These variance accounts are established when the variable manufacturing overhead incurred and the variable manufacturing overhead applied accounts are closed. Companies generally do this closing procedure only at year end. For demonstration purposes, we will assume that Tree Top has elected to close the manufacturing overhead accounts to establish the variable manufacturing overhead efficiency and spending variances at the end of November.
2. Because the variable manufacturing overhead incurred account has a debit balance, we close it with a credit, and because the variable manufacturing overhead applied account has a credit balance, we close it with a debit. As we previously mentioned, if the variance is favorable, we should credit the variance account. Conversely, if the variance is unfavorable, we should debit the variance account. For Tree Top, both the efficiency variance and the spending variance are unfavorable so the variance accounts will be debited.
3. The general journal entry:

2009				
Nov.	30	Variable Manufacturing Overhead Applied	47.25	
		Variable Manufacturing Overhead Efficiency Variance	9.45	
		Variable Manufacturing Overhead Spending Variance	83.30	
		Variable Manufacturing Overhead Incurred		140.00
		To close variable manufacturing overhead accounts and record		
		the variable manufacturing variances		

4. A final check of the entry reveals that it is fine.

Transaction 7—*Record actual fixed manufacturing overhead cost incurred.*

1. Tree Top's actual fixed manufacturing overhead costs consist of $200.00 for rent and $35.00 for depreciation. We will assume the rent was paid on November 1 and

the depreciation is recorded on November 30. We should increase the fixed manufacturing overhead incurred account for the actual cost of the fixed manufacturing overhead. We should decrease cash for the $200.00 rent and increase accumulated depreciation for the $35.00 in depreciation.

2. We increase the fixed manufacturing overhead incurred account with a debit, and we decrease the cash account and increase the accumulated depreciation account with credits.
3. The general journal entries:

2009				
Nov.	1	Fixed Manufacturing Overhead Incurred	200.00	
		Cash		200.00
		To record rent for November		
	30	Fixed Manufacturing Overhead Incurred	35.00	
		Accumulated Depreciation		35.00
		To record depreciation for November		

4. A final check of the entries reveals that they are fine.

Transaction 8—*Record the application of fixed manufacturing overhead to production.*

1. As with variable manufacturing overhead, fixed manufacturing overhead cost allocated to production becomes part of work-in-process inventory. Because Tree Top uses a standard cost system, the transaction also affects an account called fixed manufacturing overhead applied. As was the case with variable manufacturing overhead, we allocate fixed manufacturing overhead to production at standard. In Tree Top's case, we would increase work-in-process inventory and fixed manufacturing overhead applied by $168.75, shown as follows:

Number of Mailboxes Produced		Direct Labor Efficiency Standard		Fixed Mfg Overhead Rate Standard		Amount to Add to Work-in-Process
225	×	.6	×	$1.25	=	$168.75

2. We increase the work-in-process inventory with a debit and the fixed manufacturing overhead applied account with a credit.
3. The general journal entry:

2009				
Nov.	30	Work-In-Process Inventory	168.75	
		Fixed Manufacturing Overhead Applied		168.75
		To record the allocation of fixed manufacturing		
		overhead to production.		

4. A final check of the entry reveals that it is fine.

Transaction 9—*Close the fixed manufacturing overhead accounts and record the fixed manufacturing overhead variances.*

1. The difference between the $235.00 balance in the fixed manufacturing overhead incurred account and the $168.75 balance in the fixed manufacturing overhead applied account is equal to the combination of company's fixed manufacturing overhead budget variance and its fixed manufacturing overhead volume variance. In Tree Top's case, the company's fixed manufacturing overhead budget variance is $10.00, and its fixed manufacturing overhead volume variance totaled $56.25. As was the case with the variable manufacturing overhead variances, the fixed manufacturing overhead variance accounts are established when the fixed manufacturing overhead incurred and the fixed manufacturing overhead applied accounts are closed. For demonstration purposes, we will assume once more that Tree Top has elected to close the fixed manufacturing overhead accounts to establish the fixed manufacturing overhead volume and budget variances at the end of November.
2. Because the fixed manufacturing overhead incurred account has a debit balance, we close it with a credit, and because the fixed manufacturing overhead applied account has a credit balance, we close it with a debit. As we previously mentioned, if the variance is favorable, we should credit the variance account. Conversely, if the variance is unfavorable, we should debit the variance account. For Tree Top, both the fixed manufacturing overhead budget and the fixed manufacturing overhead volume variance are unfavorable so we will debit those variance accounts to increase them.
3. The general journal entry:

2009				
Nov.	30	Fixed Manufacturing Overhead Applied	168.75	
		Fixed Manufacturing Overhead Budget Variance	10.00	
		Fixed Manufacturing Overhead Volume Variance	56.25	
		Fixed Manufacturing Overhead Incurred		235.00
		To close fixed manufacturing overhead accounts and record		
		the fixed manufacturing overhead variances		

4. A final check of the entry reveals that it is fine.

Transaction 10—*Close the standard cost variances to cost of goods sold.*

1. The variance accounts are monitored during the year but generally no accounting entries are made to dispense with the amounts until the end of the year. For demonstration purposes, we will assume that Tree Top has elected to close the variance accounts at the end of November.

   In most cases an accounting entry is made to close the standard cost variances to cost of goods sold. Because the amount of the variances is generally relatively small and most product cost ends up in cost of goods sold by year end, closing the variance accounts to cost of goods sold is adequate for most companies.

At this point, Tree Top's variance accounts have the following balances:

	Debit Balance	Credit Balance
Direct Material Price Variance		48.00
Direct Material Quantity Variance	99.75	
Direct Labor Efficiency Variance	270.00	
Direct Labor Rate Variance	81.00	
Variable Manufacturing Overhead Efficiency Variance	9.45	
Variable Manufacturing Overhead Spending Variance	83.30	
Fixed Manufacturing Overhead Budget Variance	10.00	
Fixed Manufacturing Overhead Volume Variance	56.25	

2. To close Tree Top's variance accounts, if the variance account has a debit balance, we close the account with a credit and if the account has a credit balance, we will close it with a debit. Once this is done, we will enter an amount in the cost of goods sold account that will balance the entry.

3. The general journal entry:

2009				
Nov.	30	Cost of Goods Sold	561.75	
		Direct Material Price Variance	48.00	
		Direct Material Quantity Variance		99.75
		Direct Labor Efficiency Variance		270.00
		Direct Labor Rate Variance		81.00
		Variable Manufacturing Overhead Efficiency Variance		9.45
		Variable Manufacturing Overhead Spending Variance		83.30
		Fixed Manufacturing Overhead Budget Variance		10.00
		Fixed Manufacturing Overhead Volume Variance		56.25
		To close standard cost variance accounts to		
		cost of goods sold.		

4. A final check of the entry reveals that it is fine.

Summary

In the process of operating businesses, managers must focus their valuable time on areas that need to be improved. One area that requires constant attention is controlling the costs of operations. A process designed to help managers focus on cost items that need attention is standard costing, which sets cost performance goals and then uses these cost goals to evaluate performance.

Differences between the costs incurred by actual performance and what the costs should have been, based on the standards, are called variances. A favorable variance results when the actual cost is lower than cost based on standard. An unfavorable variance results when the actual cost is higher than cost based on standard.

In establishing performance standards, managers can use either ideal standards, which can be attained only under perfect conditions, or practical standards, which allow for normal working conditions.

Although a standard costing system can be extremely helpful to managers, it has several potential problems. These include employees setting lax standards to avoid unfavorable variances, relying on historical information that may perpetuate past inefficiencies, and managing "by the numbers" thus overlooking significant problems that do not result in variances.

A standard cost system in a manufacturing environment uses estimates for the cost of direct materials, direct labor, and manufacturing overhead. This system is in contrast to both an actual cost system, which uses the actual cost for direct materials, direct labor, and manufacturing overhead, and a normal cost system, which uses actual costs for direct materials and direct labor, and estimates for manufacturing overhead.

The standards used in manufacturing companies generally include a direct material quantity standard, a direct material price standard, a direct labor efficiency standard, a direct labor rate standard, a standard variable manufacturing overhead rate, and a standard fixed manufacturing overhead rate.

To use standard costing as a control device, managers compare standard costs to actual costs to see whether variances exist. Then they investigate variances, as appropriate, which is known as variance analysis. The variances most commonly used are the direct material quantity variance, the direct material price variance, the direct labor efficiency variance, the direct labor rate variance, the variable manufacturing overhead efficiency variance, the variable manufacturing overhead spending variance, the fixed manufacturing overhead budget variance, and the fixed manufacturing overhead volume variance.

When a company uses standard costing, it maintains raw materials, work-in-process, and finished goods inventories at standard cost. The standard cost variances account for the difference between the standard cost maintained in inventory and actual costs. When we record a variance, we should credit the variance account if the variance is favorable and we should debit the variance account if it is unfavorable. Companies generally close the standard cost variance accounts to cost of goods sold at year end.

Key Terms

actual cost system....421

bill of materials....422

direct labor efficiency standard....424

direct labor efficiency variance....434

direct labor rate standard....425

direct labor rate variance....433

direct material efficiency variance....430

direct material price standard....423

direct material price variance....429

direct material quantity standard....422

direct material quantity variance....430

direct material usage variance....430

favorable variance....416

fixed manufacturing overhead budget variance....439

fixed manufacturing overhead spending variance....439

fixed manufacturing overhead volume variance....440

ideal standard....418

management by exception....417

normal cost system....421

practical standard....418

standard....416

standard cost system....416

standard costing....415

standard fixed manufacturing overhead rate....427

standard variable manufacturing overhead rate....426

unfavorable variance....416

variable manufacturing overhead efficiency variance....437

variable manufacturing overhead spending variance....436

variance....416

Review the Facts

A. What is standard costing?

B. What is a standard?

C. What is a variance?

D. Describe management by exception.

E. How often do most companies set cost standards?

F. What are the two things that can cause cost to increase?

G. What is the difference between an ideal standard and a practical standard?

H. Briefly describe five problems with standard costing.

I. What is a bill of material?

J. What are the two direct material standards?

K. What are the two direct labor standards?

L. How can standard costs be used to control cost?

M. What is measured by the direct material quantity variance?

N. What is measured by the direct material price variance?

O. What is measured by the direct labor efficiency variance?

P. What is measured by the direct labor rate variance?

Q. What is measured by the variable manufacturing overhead efficiency variance?

R. What is measured by the variable manufacturing overhead spending variance?

S. What is measured by the fixed manufacturing overhead budget variance?

T. What is measured by the fixed manufacturing overhead volume variance?

Apply What You Have Learned

LO 7 & 9: Determine Direct Material Variances and Prepare Journal Entries

10-15. The Zhang Manufacturing Company purchased 4,000 pounds of direct material at $5.20 per pound. It used 2,700 pounds to make 5,000 finished units. The standard cost for direct material is $5.00 per pound and the quantity standard is 0.5 (one-half) pound per finished unit.

Required:

a. According to the appropriate standard, how much should the company have paid for the 4,000 pounds of direct material purchased?

b. Determine the direct material price variance based on the amount of direct material purchased.

c. According to the appropriate standard, how many pounds of direct material should have been used to make the 5,000 finished units?

d. Determine the direct material quantity variance in pounds of direct material.

e. Determine the direct material quantity variance in dollars.

f. Prepare the following journal entries:

   1. Record the purchase of direct material.

   2. Record the use of direct material.

LO 7 & 9: Determine Direct Material Variances and Prepare Journal Entries

10-16. The Carbonnell Manufacturing Company purchased 15,000 pounds of direct material at $1.30 per pound. It used 14,700 pounds to make 5,000 finished units. The standard cost for direct material is $1.35 per pound and the quantity standard is three pounds per finished unit.

Required:

a. According to the appropriate standard, how much should the company have paid for the 15,000 pounds of direct material purchased?

b. Determine the direct material price variance based on the amount of direct material purchased.

c. According to the appropriate standard, how many pounds of direct material should have been used to make the 5,000 finished units?

d. Determine the direct material quantity variance in pounds of direct material.

e. Determine the direct material quantity variance in dollars.

f. Prepare the following journal entries:

   1. Record the purchase of direct material.

   2. Record the use of direct material.

LO 7 & 9: Determine Direct Material Variances and Prepare Journal Entries

10-17. The Smithstone Company purchased 2,500 square feet of direct material at $6.30 per square foot. It used 2,055 square feet of material to make 500 finished units. The standard cost for direct material is \$6.15 per square foot and the quantity standard is four pounds per finished unit.

Required:

a. According to the appropriate standard, how much should the company have paid for the 2,500 square feet of direct material purchased?

b. Determine the direct material price variance based on the amount of direct material purchased.

c. According to the appropriate standard, how many square feet of direct material should have been used to make the 500 finished units?

d. Determine the direct material quantity variance in square feet of direct material.

e. Determine the direct material quantity variance in dollars.

f. Prepare the following journal entries:

   1. Record the purchase of direct material.

   2. Record the use of direct material.

LO 7: Determine Direct Material Variances

10-18. Econo Manufacturing purchased 20,000 square feet of direct material at \$0.54 per square foot. It used 12,625 square feet to make 1,250 finished units. The standard cost for direct material is \$0.55 per square foot and the quantity standard is 10 square feet per finished unit.

Required:

a. According to the appropriate standard, how much should the company have paid for the 20,000 square feet of direct material purchased?

b. Determine the direct material price variance based on the amount of direct material purchased.

c. According to the appropriate standard, how many square feet of direct material should have been used to make the 1,250 finished units?

d. Determine the direct material quantity variance in square feet of direct material.

e. Determine the direct material quantity variance in dollars.

LO 7: Determine Direct Material Variances

10-19. The following information is presented for the Scout Manufacturing Company.

- Direct material price standard is \$1.55 per gallon.
- Direct material quantity standard is 2.5 gallons per finished unit.
- Budgeted production is 1,000 finished units.
- 4,000 gallons of direct material were purchased for \$6,000.
- 2,800 gallons of direct material were used in production.
- 1,100 finished units of product were produced.

Required:

a. Determine the direct material price variance.

b. Determine the direct material quantity variance in dollars.

LO 7: Determine Direct Material Variances

10-20. The following information is presented for the Flowvalve Manufacturing Company.

- Direct material price standard is $15 per pound.
- Direct material quantity standard is 1/4 pound per finished unit.
- Budgeted production is 20,000 finished units.
- 6,000 pounds of direct material were purchased for $91,320.
- 4,650 pounds of direct material were used in production.
- 18,000 finished units of product were produced.

Required:

a. Determine the direct material price variance.

b. Determine the direct material quantity variance in dollars.

LO 7: Determine Direct Material Variances

10-21. The following information is presented for the Munter Manufacturing Company.

- Direct material price standard is $3.25 per pound.
- Direct material quantity standard is six pounds per finished unit.
- Budgeted production is 25,000 finished units.
- 175,000 pounds of direct material were purchased for $559,650.
- 155,200 pounds of direct material were used in production.
- 25,600 finished units of product were produced.

Required:

a. Determine the direct material price variance.

b. Determine the direct material quantity variance in dollars.

LO 7: Determine Direct Material Variances

10-22. Information from the Quincy Company is as follows:

Actual cost of 33,000 pounds of direct material purchased	$97,350
Direct material used in production	30,575 pounds
Actual production	2,980 units
Direct material price standard	$3.00 per pound
Direct material quantity standard per finished unit of production	10 pounds
Budgeted production	3,000 units

Required:

a. Determine the direct material price variance.

b. Determine the direct material quantity variance in dollars.

LO 7: Determine Direct Material Variances

10-23. Information from the Wayne Manufacturing is as follows:

Actual cost of 10,000 pounds of direct material purchased	$2,400
Direct material used in production	9,177pounds
Actual production	980 units
Direct material price standard	$0.25 per pound
Direct material quantity standard per finished unit of production	9 pounds
Budgeted production	1,000 units

Required:

a. Determine the direct material price variance.

b. Determine the direct material quantity variance in dollars.

LO 7: Determine Direct Material Variances

10-24. Information from the Myco Manufacturing Company is as follows:

Actual cost of 120,000 feet of direct material purchased	$427,200
Direct material used in production	111,100 feet
Actual production	3,200 units
Direct material price standard	$3.50 per foot
Direct material quantity standard per finished unit of production	35 feet
Budgeted production	3,500 units

Required:

a. Determine the direct material price variance.

b. Determine the direct material quantity variance in dollars.

LO 7 & 9: Determine Direct Labor Variances and Prepare Journal Entries

10-25. The direct labor rate standard for Amy Manufacturing is $12 per direct labor hour. The direct labor efficiency standard is two hours per finished unit. Last month, the company completed 8,000 units of product using 16,350 direct labor hours at an actual cost of $194,565.

Required:

a. According to the appropriate standard, how much should the company have paid for the 16,350 actual direct labor hours?

b. Determine the direct labor rate variance.

c. According to the appropriate standard, how many hours of direct labor should it have taken to produce the 8,000 units?

d. Determine the direct labor efficiency variance in hours.

e. Determine the direct labor efficiency variance in dollars.

f. Prepare a journal entry to record the direct labor and the direct labor rate and efficiency variances.

LO 7 & 9: Determine Direct Labor Variances and Prepare Journal Entries

10-26. The direct labor rate standard for Calspan Manufacturing is $18.50 per direct labor hour. The direct labor efficiency standard is six minutes or 1/10 of an hour per finished unit. Last month, the company completed 105,650 units of product using 10,400 direct labor hours at an actual cost of $191,360.

Required:

a. According to the appropriate standard, how much should the company have paid for the 10,400 actual direct labor hours?

b. Determine the direct labor rate variance.

c. According to the appropriate standard, how many hours of direct labor should it have taken to produce the 105,650 units?

d. Determine the direct labor efficiency variance in hours.

e. Determine the direct labor efficiency variance in dollars.

f. Prepare a journal entry to record the direct labor and the direct labor rate and efficiency variances.

LO 7: Determine Direct Labor Variances

10-27. The direct labor rate standard for Key Largo Manufacturing is $10 per direct labor hour. The direct labor efficiency standard is three hours per finished unit. Last month, the company completed 2,800 units of product using 8,620 direct labor hours at an actual cost of $88,355.

Required:

a. According to the appropriate standard, how much should the company have paid for the 8,620 actual direct labor hours?

b. Determine the direct labor rate variance.

c. According to the appropriate standard, how many hours of direct labor should it have taken to produce the 2,800 units?

d. Determine the direct labor efficiency variance in hours.

e. Determine the direct labor efficiency variance in dollars.

LO 7 & 9: Determine Direct Labor Variances and Prepare Journal Entries

10-28. The direct labor rate standard for Sakura Manufacturing is $15.25 per direct labor hour. The direct labor efficiency standard is 30 minutes or 1/2 of an hour per finished unit. Last month, the company completed 27,800 units of product using 14,050 direct labor hours at an actual cost of $215,246.

Required:

a. Determine the direct labor rate variance.

b. Determine the direct labor efficiency variance in dollars.

c. Prepare a journal entry to record the direct labor and the direct labor rate and efficiency variances.

LO 7 & 9: Determine Direct Labor Variances and Prepare Journal Entries

10-29. The direct labor rate standard for Melissa Valdez Manufacturing is $10 per direct labor hour. The direct labor efficiency standard is 0.25 (one quarter) hour per finished unit. Last month, the company completed 38,000 units of product using 9,280 direct labor hours at an actual cost of $97,904.

Required:

a. Determine the direct labor rate variance.

b. Determine the direct labor efficiency variance in dollars.

c. Prepare a journal entry to record the direct labor and the direct labor rate and efficiency variances.

LO 7: Determine Direct Labor Variances

10-30. The following information is presented for the Marathon Manufacturing Company.

- Direct labor rate standard is $11.55.
- Direct labor efficiency standard is 2.5 hours per finished unit.
- Budgeted production is 1,200 finished units.
- Production required 2,910 direct labor hours at a cost of $33,174.
- 1,150 finished units of product were produced.

Required:

a. Determine the direct labor rate variance.

b. Determine the direct labor efficiency variance in dollars.

LO 7: Determine Direct Labor Variances

10-31. The following information is presented for the Picas Manufacturing Company.

- Direct labor rate standard is $12.
- Direct labor efficiency standard is two hours per finished unit.
- Budgeted production is 2,200 finished units.
- Production required 4,560 direct labor hours at a cost of $54,036.
- 2,250 finished units of product were produced.

Required:

a. Determine the direct labor rate variance.

b. Determine the direct labor efficiency variance in dollars.

LO 7: Determine Direct Labor Variances

10-32. The following information is presented for the Lew Green Manufacturing Company.

- Direct labor rate standard is $24.
- Direct labor efficiency standard is three hours per finished unit.
- Budgeted production is 775 finished units.
- Production required 2,375 direct labor hours at a cost of $57,475.
- 810 finished units of product were produced.

Required:

a. Determine the direct labor rate variance.

b. Determine the direct labor efficiency variance in dollars.

LO 7: Determine Direct Labor Variances

10-33. Information from the Spin Manufacturing Company is presented as follows:

Actual number of direct labor hours	275
Actual direct labor cost	$4,620
Actual number of units produced	800 units
Direct labor rate standard	$16.10
Direct labor efficiency standard	3 hours per unit
Budgeted production	850 units

Required:

a. Determine the direct labor rate variance.

b. Determine the direct labor efficiency variance in dollars.

LO 7: Determine Direct Labor Variances

10-34. Information from the Popular Manufacturing Company is as follows:

Actual number of direct labor hours	1,275
Actual direct labor cost	$16,065
Actual number of units produced	1,255 units
Direct labor rate standard	$12
Direct labor efficiency standard	1 hour per unit
Budgeted production	1,200 units

Required:

a. Determine the direct labor rate variance.

b. Determine the direct labor efficiency variance in dollars.

LO 7: Determine Direct Labor Variances

10-35. Information from the Electronic Manufacturing Company is as follows:

Actual number of direct labor hours	12,830
Actual direct labor cost	$292,524
Actual number of units produced	2,040 units
Direct labor rate standard	$23.10
Direct labor efficiency standard	6 hour per unit
Budgeted production	2,000 units

Required:

a. Determine the direct labor rate variance.

b. Determine the direct labor efficiency variance in dollars.

LO 7: Determine Direct Material and Direct Labor Variances

10-36. Information from the Atlantic Company is presented as follows:

Actual cost of 30,000 pounds of direct material purchased	$97,500
Direct material used in production	28,100 pounds
Actual number of direct labor hours	12,850
Actual direct labor cost	$165,765
Actual production	2,500 units
Direct material price standard	$3.30 per pound
Direct material quantity standard per finished unit of production	11 pounds
Direct labor rate standard	$13
Direct labor efficiency standard	5 hour per unit
Budgeted production	2,400 units

Required:

a. Determine the direct material price variance.

b. Determine the direct material quantity variance in dollars.

c. Determine the direct labor rate variance.

d. Determine the direct labor efficiency variance in dollars.

LO 7: Determine Direct Material and Direct Labor Variances

10-37. Information from the Progressive Company is presented as follows:

Actual cost of 9,000 pounds of direct material purchased	$2,200
Direct material used in production	7,800 pounds
Actual number of direct labor hours	980
Actual direct labor cost	$14,945
Actual production	240 units
Direct material price standard	$0.25 per pound
Direct material quantity standard per finished unit of production	30 pounds
Direct labor rate standard	$15
Direct labor efficiency standard	4 hour per unit
Budgeted production	250 units

Required:

a. Determine the direct material price variance.

b. Determine the direct material quantity variance in dollars.

c. Determine the direct labor rate variance.

d. Determine the direct labor efficiency variance in dollars.

LO 7: Determine Direct Material and Direct Labor Variances

10-38. Information from the Packard Company is presented as follows:

Actual cost of 1,000 pounds of direct material purchased	$10,300
Direct material used in production	830 pounds
Actual number of direct labor hours	1,220
Actual direct labor cost	$13,176
Actual production	400 units
Direct material price standard	$10 per pound
Direct material quantity standard per finished unit of production	2 pounds
Direct labor rate standard	$11
Direct labor efficiency standard	3 hour per unit
Budgeted production	450 units

Required:

a. Determine the direct material price variance.

b. Determine the direct material quantity variance in dollars.

c. Determine the direct labor rate variance.

d. Determine the direct labor efficiency variance in dollars.

LO 7: Determine Variable Manufacturing Overhead Variances

10-39. Billy Clifford Manufacturing applies variable manufacturing overhead to production on the basis of $15 per direct labor hour. The direct labor efficiency standard is five hours per finished unit. Last month the company produced 12,000 units and used 62,000 direct labor hours. Actual variable manufacturing overhead cost incurred totaled $920,000.

Required:

a. Determine the variable manufacturing overhead spending variance.

b. According to the appropriate standard, how many direct labor hours should it have taken to produce the 12,000 units?

c. Determine the direct labor efficiency variance in hours.

d. Determine the variable manufacturing overhead efficiency variance in dollars.

LO 7: Determine Variable Manufacturing Overhead Variances

10-40. Clifford Knapp Manufacturing applies variable manufacturing overhead to production on the basis of $5 per direct labor hour. The direct labor efficiency standard is two hours per finished unit. Last month the company produced 11,000 units and used 22,400 direct labor hours. Actual variable manufacturing overhead cost incurred totaled $111,700.

Required:

a. Determine the variable manufacturing overhead spending variance.

b. According to the appropriate standard, how many direct labor hours should it have taken to produce the 11,000 units?

c. Determine the direct labor efficiency variance in hours.

d. Determine the variable manufacturing overhead efficiency variance in dollars.

LO 7 & 9: Determine Variable Manufacturing Overhead Variances and Prepare Journal Entries

10-41. Carlos Gonzalez Marine Manufacturing applies variable manufacturing overhead to production on the basis of $6 per direct labor hour. The direct labor efficiency standard is three hours per finished unit. Last month the company produced 15,000 units and used 45,650 direct labor hours. Actual variable manufacturing overhead cost incurred totaled $277,800.

Required:

a. Determine the variable manufacturing overhead spending variance.

b. According to the appropriate standard, how many direct labor hours should it have taken to produce the 15,000 units?

c. Determine the direct labor efficiency variance in hours.

d. Determine the variable manufacturing overhead efficiency variance in dollars.

e. Prepare the following journal entries:

   1. Record the actual variable manufacturing overhead. (Use "various accounts" for the credit side of the entry.)

   2. Record the variable manufacturing overhead applied to production.

   3. Close the variable manufacturing overhead accounts and establish the variable overhead variance accounts.

   4. Close the variance accounts to cost of goods sold.

LO 7 & 9: Determine Variable Manufacturing Overhead Variances and Prepare Journal Entries

10-42. Alpine Manufacturing applies variable manufacturing overhead to production on the basis of $13 per direct labor hour. The direct labor efficiency standard is four hours per finished unit. Last month the company produced 3,000 units and used 11,700 direct labor hours. Actual variable manufacturing overhead cost incurred totaled $157,200.

Required:

a. Determine the variable manufacturing overhead spending variance.

b. Determine the variable manufacturing overhead efficiency variance in dollars.

c. Prepare the following journal entries:

   1. Record the actual variable manufacturing overhead. (Use "various accounts" for the credit side of the entry.)

   2. Record the variable manufacturing overhead applied to production.

   3. Close the variable manufacturing overhead accounts and establish the variable overhead variance accounts.

   4. Close the variance accounts to cost of goods sold.

LO 7: Determine Variable Manufacturing Overhead Variances

10-43. The Adler Manufacturing Company applies variable manufacturing overhead to production on the basis of $22 per direct labor hour. The direct labor efficiency standard is 0.5 hours per finished unit. Last month the company produced 14,500 units and used 7,300 direct labor hours. Actual variable manufacturing overhead cost incurred totaled $162,000.

Required:

a. Determine the variable manufacturing overhead spending variance.

b. Determine the variable manufacturing overhead efficiency variance in dollars.

LO 7: Determine Variable Manufacturing Overhead Variances

10-44. The following information is presented for the Carol Green Manufacturing Company.

- Standard variable manufacturing overhead rate is $3.50 per direct labor hour.
- Direct labor efficiency standard is three hours per finished unit.
- Budgeted production is 810 finished units.
- Production required 2,370 direct labor hours.
- Variable manufacturing overhead cost was $8,500.
- 775 finished units of product were produced.

Required:

a. Determine the variable manufacturing overhead spending variance.

b. Determine the variable manufacturing overhead efficiency variance in dollars.

LO 7: Determine Variable Manufacturing Overhead Variances

10-45. The following information is presented for the Anne Reed Manufacturing Company.

- Standard variable manufacturing overhead rate is $7.00 per direct labor hour.
- Direct labor efficiency standard is six hours per finished unit.
- Budgeted production is 500 finished units.
- Production required 3,400 direct labor hours.
- Variable manufacturing overhead cost was $23,600.
- 550 finished units of product were produced.

Required:

a. Determine the variable manufacturing overhead spending variance.

b. Determine the variable manufacturing overhead efficiency variance in dollars.

LO 7: Determine Variable Manufacturing Overhead Variances

10-46. The following information is presented for the Willie Kemp Manufacturing Company.

- Standard variable manufacturing overhead rate is $2 per direct labor hour.
- Direct labor efficiency standard is four hours per finished unit.
- Budgeted production is 1,500 finished units.
- Production required 6,100 direct labor hours.
- Variable manufacturing overhead cost was $12,325.
- 1,550 finished units of product were produced.

Required:

a. Determine the variable manufacturing overhead spending variance.

b. Determine the variable manufacturing overhead efficiency variance in dollars.

LO 7: Determine Variable Manufacturing Overhead Variances

10-47. Information from the Systems Manufacturing Company is as follows:

Actual number of direct labor hours	12,000
Actual variable manufacturing overhead cost	$145,965
Actual number of units produced	2,440 units
Standard variable manufacturing overhead rate	$12.10 per direct labor hour
Direct labor efficiency standard	5 hours
Budgeted production	2,500 units

Required:

a. Determine the variable manufacturing overhead spending variance.

b. Determine the variable manufacturing overhead efficiency variance in dollars.

LO 7: Determine Variable Manufacturing Overhead Variances

10-48. Information from the Altos Manufacturing Company is as follows:

Actual number of direct labor hours	12,330
Actual variable manufacturing overhead cost	$74,490
Actual number of units produced	12,540 units
Standard variable manufacturing overhead rate	$6 per direct labor hour
Direct labor efficiency standard	1 hour
Budgeted production	12,000 units

Required:

a. Determine the variable manufacturing overhead spending variance.

b. Determine the variable manufacturing overhead efficiency variance in dollars.

LO 7: Determine Variable Manufacturing Overhead Variances

10-49. Information from the Aspen Manufacturing Company is as follows:

Actual number of direct labor hours	175,000
Actual variable manufacturing overhead cost	$2,400,000
Actual number of units produced	21,740 units
Standard variable manufacturing overhead rate	$14 per direct labor hour
Direct labor efficiency standard	8 hours
Budgeted production	20,000 units

Required:

a. Determine the variable manufacturing overhead spending variance.

b. Determine the variable manufacturing overhead efficiency variance in dollars.

LO 7 & 9: Determine Fixed Manufacturing Overhead Variances and Prepare Journal Entries

10-50. The Hill Manufacturing Company applies fixed manufacturing overhead at the rate of $5.50 per direct labor hour. Fixed manufacturing overhead is budgeted to be $330,000 per month. The direct labor efficiency standard is five hours per finished unit. Although budgeted production for the month was 12,000, the company only produced 11,800 units. Production required actual direct labor hours of 60,000 and actual fixed manufacturing overhead cost incurred was $325,000.

Required:

a. Determine the fixed manufacturing overhead budget variance.

b. What is the difference between the planned number of units and the number of units actually produced?

c. Determine the fixed manufacturing overhead volume variance.

d. Prepare the following journal entries:

   1. Record the actual fixed manufacturing overhead. (Use "various accounts" for the credit side of the entry.)

   2. Record the fixed manufacturing overhead applied to production.

   3. Close the fixed manufacturing overhead accounts and establish the fixed manufacturing overhead variance accounts.

   4. Close the variance accounts to cost of goods sold.

LO 7 & 9: Determine Fixed Manufacturing Overhead Variances and Prepare Journal Entries

10-51. The Johnson Manufacturing Company applies fixed manufacturing overhead at the rate of $4.60 per direct labor hour. Fixed manufacturing overhead is budgeted to be $910,800 per month. The direct labor efficiency standard is three hours per finished unit. Although budgeted production for the month was 66,000, the company produced 67,800 units. Production required actual direct labor hours of 203,000 and actual fixed manufacturing overhead cost incurred was $920,000.

Required:

a. Determine the fixed manufacturing overhead budget variance.

b. What is the difference between the planned number of units and the number of units actually produced?

c. Determine the fixed manufacturing overhead volume variance.

d. Prepare the following journal entries:

   1. Record the actual fixed manufacturing overhead. (Use "various accounts" for the credit side of the entry.)

   2. Record the fixed manufacturing overhead applied to production.

   3. Close the fixed manufacturing overhead accounts and establish the fixed manufacturing overhead variance accounts.

   4. Close the variance accounts to cost of goods sold.

LO 7: Determine Fixed Manufacturing Overhead Variances

10-52. The Quality Manufacturing Company applies fixed manufacturing overhead at the rate of $7 per direct labor hour. Fixed manufacturing overhead is budgeted to be $336,000 per month. The direct labor efficiency standard is three hours per finished unit. Although budgeted production for the month was 16,000, the company only produced 15,500 units. Production required actual direct labor hours of 60,000 and actual fixed manufacturing overhead cost incurred was $344,000.

Required:

a. Determine the fixed manufacturing overhead budget variance.

b. Did the company produce as many units as it had planned? What is the difference between the planned number of units and the number of units actually produced?

c. Determine the fixed manufacturing overhead volume variance.

LO 7: Determine Fixed Manufacturing Overhead Variances

10-53. The following information is presented for the Oddo Manufacturing Company.

- Standard fixed manufacturing overhead rate is $2 per direct labor hour.
- Direct labor efficiency standard is four hours per finished unit.
- Budgeted production is 2,500 finished units.
- Budgeted fixed manufacturing overhead is $20,000.
- Actual fixed manufacturing overhead cost was $17,750.
- 2,150 finished units of product were produced.

Required:

a. Determine the fixed manufacturing overhead budget variance.

b. Determine the fixed manufacturing overhead volume variance in dollars.

LO 7: Determine Fixed Manufacturing Overhead Variances

10-54. The following information is presented for the Alexander Manufacturing Company.

- Standard fixed manufacturing overhead rate is $6.50 per direct labor hour.
- Direct labor efficiency standard is two hours per finished unit.
- Budgeted production is 5,000 finished units.
- Budgeted fixed manufacturing overhead is $65,000.
- Actual fixed manufacturing overhead cost was $66,100.
- 5,150 finished units of product were produced.

Required:

a. Determine the fixed manufacturing overhead budget variance.

b. Determine the fixed manufacturing overhead volume variance in dollars.

LO 7: Determine Fixed Manufacturing Overhead Variances

10-55. The following information is presented for the Adcox Manufacturing Company.

- Standard fixed manufacturing overhead rate is $9.50 per direct labor hour.
- Direct labor efficiency standard is nine hours per finished unit.
- Budgeted production is 9,000 finished units.
- Budgeted fixed manufacturing overhead is $769,500.
- Actual fixed manufacturing overhead cost was $755,360.
- 8,500 finished units of product were produced.

Required:

a. Determine the fixed manufacturing overhead budget variance.

b. Determine the fixed manufacturing overhead volume variance in dollars.

LO 7: Determine Fixed Manufacturing Overhead Variances

10-56. Information from the Michael Manufacturing Company is as follows:

Actual number of direct labor hours	12,200
Actual fixed manufacturing overhead cost	$145,900
Actual number of units produced	2,400 units
Standard fixed manufacturing overhead rate	$12 per direct labor hour
Direct labor efficiency standard	5 hours
Budgeted production	2,500 units
Budgeted fixed manufacturing overhead	$150,000

Required:

a. Determine the fixed manufacturing overhead budget variance.

b. Determine the fixed manufacturing overhead volume variance in dollars.

LO 7: Determine Fixed Manufacturing Overhead Variances

10-57. Information from the Jennings Manufacturing Company is as follows:

Actual number of direct labor hours	5,130
Actual fixed manufacturing overhead cost	$24,900
Actual number of units produced	5,400 units
Standard fixed manufacturing overhead rate	$5 per direct labor hour
Direct labor efficiency standard	1 hour
Budgeted production	5,000 units
Budgeted fixed manufacturing overhead	$25,000

Required:

a. Determine the fixed manufacturing overhead budget variance.

b. Determine the fixed manufacturing overhead volume variance in dollars.

LO 7: Challenging—Determine Fixed Manufacturing Overhead Variances

10-58. Information from the Cathy Manufacturing Company is as follows:

Actual number of direct labor hours	5,200
Actual fixed manufacturing overhead cost	$88,960
Actual number of units produced	2,700 units
Standard fixed manufacturing overhead rate	$15 per direct labor hour
Direct labor efficiency standard	2 hours
Budgeted production	3,000 units
Budgeted fixed manufacturing overhead	$90,000

Required:

a. Determine the fixed manufacturing overhead budget variance.

b. Determine the fixed manufacturing overhead volume variance in dollars.

LO 7: Determine Fixed Manufacturing Overhead Variances

10-59. Todd Manufacturing Company's budgeted production is 200,000 units per month. Budgeted monthly fixed manufacturing overhead is $2,400,000 and is applied to production at a rate of $4 per direct labor hour. The direct labor efficiency standard is three direct labor hours per unit of production. Last month it took 520,000 actual direct labor hours to produce 175,000 units. Actual fixed manufacturing overhead for the month was $2,435,000.

Required:

a. Determine the fixed manufacturing overhead budget variance.

b. Determine the fixed manufacturing overhead volume variance.

LO 7: Challenging—Determine Budgeted Production and Fixed Manufacturing Overhead Variances

10-60. The E. O. Mast Manufacturing Company applies fixed manufacturing overhead at the rate of $20 per direct labor hour. Fixed manufacturing overhead is budgeted to be $4,000,000 per month. The direct labor efficiency standard is two hours per finished unit. Last month the company produced 89,000 units using 180,000 direct labor hours and incurring fixed manufacturing overhead cost of $4,100,000.

Required:

a. Determine the fixed manufacturing overhead budget variance.

b. Did the company produce as many units as it had planned? What is the difference between the planned number of units and the number of units actually produced?

c. Determine the fixed manufacturing overhead volume variance.

LO 7: Challenging—Determine Budgeted Production and Fixed Manufacturing Overhead Variances

10-61. The Annie Manufacturing Company applies fixed manufacturing overhead at the rate of $10 per direct labor hour. Fixed manufacturing overhead is budgeted to be $418,000 per month. The direct labor efficiency standard is four hours per finished unit. Last month the company produced 9,800 units using 36,500 direct labor hours and incurring fixed manufacturing overhead cost of $410,000.

Required:

a. Determine the fixed manufacturing overhead budget variance.

b. Did the company produce as many units as it had planned? What is the difference between the planned number of units and the number of units actually produced?

c. Determine the fixed manufacturing overhead volume variance.

LO 7: Challenging—Determine Budgeted Production and Fixed Manufacturing Overhead Variances

10-62. The St. Hill Manufacturing Company applies fixed manufacturing overhead at the rate of $15 per direct labor hour. Fixed manufacturing overhead is budgeted to be $247,500 per month. The direct labor efficiency standard is six hours per finished unit. Last month the company produced 2,500 units using 15,500 direct labor hours and incurring fixed manufacturing overhead cost of $230,000.

Required:

a. Determine the fixed manufacturing overhead budget variance.

b. Did the company produce as many units as it had planned? What is the difference between the planned number of units and the number of units actually produced?

c. Determine the fixed manufacturing overhead volume variance.

LO 7: Challenging—Determine Budgeted Fixed Manufacturing Overhead and Fixed Manufacturing Overhead Variances

10-63. Information from the South Manufacturing Company is as follows:

Actual number of direct labor hours	32,500
Actual fixed manufacturing overhead cost	$428,000
Actual number of units produced	8,000 units
Standard fixed manufacturing overhead rate	$12 per direct labor hour
Direct labor efficiency standard	4 hours
Budgeted production	9,000 units
Budgeted fixed manufacturing overhead	$?

Required:

a. Determine the fixed manufacturing overhead budget variance.

b. Determine the fixed manufacturing overhead volume variance in dollars.

LO 7: Challenging—Determine Fixed Manufacturing Overhead Variances

10-64. Information from the North Manufacturing Company is as follows:

Actual number of direct labor hours	13,000
Actual fixed manufacturing overhead cost	$50,000
Actual number of units produced	2,120 units
Standard fixed manufacturing overhead rate	$4 per direct labor hour
Direct labor efficiency standard	6 hours
Budgeted production	2,000 units
Budgeted fixed manufacturing overhead	$?

Required:

a. Determine the fixed manufacturing overhead budget variance.

b. Determine the fixed manufacturing overhead volume variance in dollars.

LO 7: Challenging—Determine Fixed Manufacturing Overhead Variances

10-65. Information from the West Manufacturing Company is as follows:

Actual number of direct labor hours	27,000
Actual fixed manufacturing overhead cost	$260,000
Actual number of units produced	3,250 units
Standard fixed manufacturing overhead rate	$9 per direct labor hour
Direct labor efficiency standard	8 hours
Budgeted production	3,500 units
Budgeted fixed manufacturing overhead	$?

Required:

a. Determine the fixed manufacturing overhead budget variance.

b. Determine the fixed manufacturing overhead volume variance in dollars.

LO 7: Determine Direct Material, Direct Labor, Variable Manufacturing Overhead and Fixed Manufacturing Overhead Variances

10-66. Information from the Quintana Company is as follows:

Actual costs and amounts:	
Actual production	3,800 units
Actual cost of 23,000 pounds of direct material purchased	$89,700
Actual amount of direct material used	22,950
Actual direct labor cost	$23,205
Actual direct labor hours	1,950 hours
Actual variable manufacturing overhead cost	$12,000
Actual fixed manufacturing overhead cost	$18,000
Standards and other budgeted amounts:	
Budgeted production	4,000 units
Direct material price standard	$3.85
Direct material quantity standard	6 pounds per unit
Direct labor rate standard	$11 per hour
Direct labor efficiency standard per unit	0.5 hours
Standard variable mfg. overhead rate	$5.50 per direct labor hour
Standard fixed mfg. overhead rate	$10 per direct labor hour
Budgeted fixed manufacturing overhead	$20,000

Required:

Determine the following variances:

a. Direct material price variance

b. Direct material quantity variance in dollars

c. Direct labor rate variance

d. Direct labor efficiency variance in dollars

e. Variable manufacturing overhead spending variance

f. Variable manufacturing overhead efficiency variance in dollars

g. Fixed manufacturing overhead budget variance

h. Fixed manufacturing overhead volume variance in dollars

LO 7: Determine Direct Material, Direct Labor, Variable Manufacturing Overhead and Fixed Manufacturing Overhead Variances

10-67. Information from the Holzmann Company is as follows:

Actual costs and amounts:	
Actual production	6,300 units
Actual cost of 20,000 pounds of direct material purchased	$40,000
Actual amount of direct material used	19,100
Actual direct labor cost	$386,100
Actual direct labor hours	26,000 hours
Actual variable manufacturing overhead cost	$165,000
Actual fixed manufacturing overhead cost	$310,000
Standards and other budgeted amounts:	
Budgeted production	6,000 units
Direct material price standard	$2.10
Direct material quantity standard	3 pounds per unit
Direct labor rate standard	$15 per hour
Direct labor efficiency standard per unit	4 hours
Standard variable mfg. overhead rate	$6.50 per direct labor hour
Standard fixed mfg. overhead rate	$12.75 per direct labor hour
Budgeted fixed manufacturing overhead	$306,000

Required:

Determine the following variances:

a. Direct material price variance

b. Direct material quantity variance in dollars

c. Direct labor rate variance

d. Direct labor efficiency variance in dollars

e. Variable manufacturing overhead spending variance

f. Variable manufacturing overhead efficiency variance in dollars

g. Fixed manufacturing overhead budget variance

h. Fixed manufacturing overhead volume variance in dollars

LO 7: Determine Direct Material, Direct Labor, Variable Manufacturing Overhead and Fixed Manufacturing Overhead Variances

10-68. Information from the Collins Company is as follows:

Actual costs and amounts:	
Actual production	2,300 units
Actual cost of 16,000 pounds of direct material purchased	$19,360
Actual amount of direct material used	12,000
Actual direct labor cost	$46,410
Actual direct labor hours	4,750 hours
Actual variable manufacturing overhead cost	$29,100
Actual fixed manufacturing overhead cost	$50,125
Standards and other budgeted amounts:	
Budgeted production	3,000 units
Direct material price standard	$1.10
Direct material quantity standard	5 pounds per unit
Direct labor rate standard	$12 per hour
Direct labor efficiency standard per unit	2 hours
Standard variable mfg. overhead rate	$6 per direct labor hour
Standard fixed mfg. overhead rate	$8 per direct labor hour
Budgeted fixed manufacturing overhead	$48,000

Required:

Determine the following variances:

a. Direct material price variance

b. Direct material quantity variance in dollars

c. Direct labor rate variance

d. Direct labor efficiency variance in dollars

e. Variable manufacturing overhead spending variance

f. Variable manufacturing overhead efficiency variance in dollars

g. Fixed manufacturing overhead budget variance

h. Fixed manufacturing overhead volume variance in dollars

11

Evaluating Performance and Emerging Management and Accounting Techniques

Imagine for a moment that you open "The Right Step," a small shoe store in a local shopping center. After you're in business about six months, the store's success prompts you to open a second store in a shopping area across town. The second store also does very well, so you open a third, and in time, your shoe store chain grows to five stores.

For each store you open, you hire a store manager, because it is impossible to give each store your personal, hands-on management attention. Each store manager is responsible for the success of his or her location. You now oversee the managers at all of your stores, and one of your most important roles has become assessing the performance of these store managers.

As any business grows, the diversity of knowledge required to effectively manage, combined with time constraints, reduce the ability of a single manager to run the entire enterprise. When a manager can no longer manage the whole company single handedly, she must delegate management responsibility to subordinate managers. Evaluating the performance of these managers is the focus of this chapter.

Learning Objectives

After completing your work on this chapter, you should be able to do the following:

1. Describe centralized and decentralized management styles.
2. Describe the different types of business segments and the problems associated with determining segment costs.
3. Prepare a segment income statement.
4. Describe and calculate the return on investment.

5. Describe and calculate residual income and economic value added (EVA)™.
6. Describe various emerging management and management accounting techniques.
    - The Balanced Scorecard
    - E-commerce
    - Enterprise Information System
    - Six Sigma
    - Theory of Constraints
    - Lean Manufacturing

Business Segments

business segment A part of a company managed by a particular individual or a part of a company about which separate information is needed.

To help make businesses more manageable, their owners often divide them into parts. A **business segment** represents a part of a company managed by a particular individual, or a part of a company about which separate information is needed, perhaps to evaluate management performance or to help managers make better management decisions.

Companies can be segmented by geographic area or location, business function, product, product line, or department. A segment can be described as a department, a division, an area, a region, a product line, or some other designation. Examples of business segments include the Latin American Area of the **Dow Chemical Company**, an individual **Target** department store, a **Motorola** manufacturing plant, and the Department of Accounting at the **University of Miami**.

segment reports Reports that provide information pertaining to a particular business segment.

Obtaining detailed information about business segments is a vital part of the management decision process. Managers need information that relates to their business segment. Reports that provide information pertaining to a particular business segment are called **segment reports**. Segment reports should not be clouded by data that relate to other segments or by general information pertaining to the company as a whole. For example, if you were hired to be the manager of the **Hard Rock Cafe** in Orlando, Florida, and responsible for enhancing the restaurant's profits, you would benefit by having information about your particular restaurant. Although it might be somewhat helpful to know the overall profitability of the entire restaurant chain, specific information about the Orlando **Hard Rock Cafe** would be much more useful. You might want to know detailed sales information by product, by server, and by time of day. You would also want a comprehensive listing of your restaurant's expenses. Reports that include revenues and expenses for your restaurant only would help you to find opportunities to increase profits.

Discussion Question

11-1. If you were the manager of the **Contemporary Hotel at Disney World**, what information would you want to help maximize the performance of the hotel?

Segment Information

Depending on the needs of management and the availability of information, segment reports may be simple and include little detail, or they may be quite elaborate and include an abundance of detailed segment information. For example, it is possible for segment reports to consist simply of a listing of the segment's sales by product; or, segment reports may include sales, expenses, and other information. The extent of the information included in segment reports depends on management's need to know, balanced with the cost of providing the information.

The Segment Income Statement

An income statement prepared for a business segment is called a **segment income statement.** When preparing a segment income statement, companies use either the traditional income statement (sometimes called the functional income statement) or the contribution income statement format. Recall from our discussions in Chapter 6 that the traditional income statement separates costs into product and period costs. The contribution income statement classifies costs by behavior, either variable or fixed. We know that a variable cost is one that changes in total based on some activity, whereas a fixed cost is one that remains unchanged regardless of the level of activity. To be sure you remember these two income statement formats, we reproduce them in Exhibit 11-1.

segment income statement An income statement prepared for a business segment.

Exhibit 11-1 Traditional and Contribution Income Statement Formats

	Traditional (Functional) Format		Contribution Income Format
	Sales		Sales
–	Cost of Goods Sold (Product Cost)	–	All Variable Costs (Product and Period)
=	Gross Profit	=	Contribution Margin
–	Selling & Admin. Exp. (Period Cost)	–	All Fixed Costs (Product and Period)
=	Net Income	=	Net Income

To prepare a segment income statement, we gather revenue and expense information that pertains to the particular segment and then arrange it in the appropriate income statement format. As we mentioned in Chapter 7, the amount of income that pertains to a particular segment is called the **segment margin**. Because the contribution income statement format is particularly well-suited for our work in this chapter, we use that format in all our remaining presentations. A segment income statement for the Miami office of the Quintana Company appears in Exhibit 11-2.

segment margin The amount of income that pertains to a particular segment.

Exhibit 11-2 Segment Income Statement for the Miami Office

Quintana Company Miami Office
Segment Income Statement
For the Year Ended December 31, 2008

Sales	$1,200,000
Variable cost	800,000
Contribution margin	400,000
Fixed cost for Miami office	300,000
Segment margin	$ 100,000

It is important that the segment income statement for the Miami office of the Quintana Company include all the appropriate information for the Miami office, and no more. Often, this is easier said than done. Generally, revenue can easily be traced to individual business segments, therefore obtaining detailed revenue information by segment is not too difficult. Unfortunately, however, the same cannot always be said for cost information.

It is often difficult (if not impossible) to obtain cost information that includes all the costs for a particular segment and excludes costs associated with other segments. There are several reasons for this. First, it may be difficult to identify all the costs that relate to the segment. For example, say that the Norris Division of the NHL Company has three copiers. Certainly the cost of these copiers should be included in any evaluation of the Norris Division. These three copiers, however, are just three of the 27 copiers owned by the NHL Company (the other 24 copiers are in other segments). The problem is that all 27 copiers were purchased by the central company purchasing department and Norris has no record of the cost of its three copiers.

Discussion Question

11-2. What are three other costs that relate directly to the Norris Division, but for which the division probably does not have information?

The second reason it may be difficult to identify costs to particular segments is that costs are often mixed together in the accounting process. An example of this might be advertising purchased by the NHL Company, which benefits not only the Norris Division, but also the five other divisions of the company. The exact amount that should be charged to the Norris Division is virtually impossible to determine accurately.

Discussion Question

11-3. What are three other costs that benefit the Norris Division but benefit at least one other division as well?

To help manage a business segment, we should include all the costs associated with the segment on cost reports prepared for it. It is equally important that costs that do not pertain to the segment be excluded from the segment's cost reports. In the case of variable costs, this is fairly straightforward. Variable costs can be traced directly to the business segments to which they pertain and then be included on the appropriate segment reports.

direct fixed cost Fixed costs incurred to support a single business segment.

traceable fixed cost Another name for direct fixed cost.

common fixed cost Fixed costs incurred to support more than one business segment, or the company as a whole.

indirect fixed cost Another name for common fixed cost.

Fixed costs are more difficult to trace to individual business segments and therefore present more of a challenge. One problem with tracing fixed costs to business segments is that some fixed costs pertain to a single business segment whereas others benefit several segments or perhaps the company as a whole. Fixed costs that arise to support a single segment are called **direct fixed costs** or **traceable fixed costs**. These fixed costs can be traced to an individual business segment. Direct fixed costs should be included on the cost reports for the segment to which they pertain. Fixed costs that arise to support more than one segment or the company as a whole are called **common fixed costs** or **indirect fixed costs**.

This discussion of direct and indirect costs should not seem entirely new. It is a subject we covered in some depth in Chapter 2 when we discussed the concept of a cost object. As you recall, a cost object is any activity or item for which a separate cost measurement is desired. A cost that can be traced directly to a cost object is a direct cost, whereas a cost that is incurred to support multiple cost objects is an indirect cost. In our present discussion, the cost object is the business segment.

Because common fixed costs benefit several segments or the company in general, segment managers often have little control over them. A simple question can be asked to determine whether a cost is a common cost or a direct cost:

Would the cost continue if the segment were to disappear?

If the cost will continue even if the segment disappeared, the cost is a common fixed cost. If, on the other hand, the cost would disappear if the segment disappears, the cost is a direct fixed cost. There are very few, if any, common variable costs; thus, in virtually all instances, the common costs we must consider are fixed.

For many years there has been debate as to whether cost reports prepared for an individual segment should include some allocated amount of common fixed costs. Proponents of allocation maintain that common fixed costs benefit the entire company and therefore each segment should be charged for its "fair share" of the common cost. Further, they argue that it is impossible to determine true segment profitability if common costs are excluded. Opponents of allocation argue just the opposite. They maintain that because segment managers have little or no authority to control common fixed costs, these costs should not be included in segment reports. These folks believe it is unfair to charge a manager's department for costs that are out of his or her control. In addition, common fixed costs are generally distributed to various business segments based on an arbitrary allocation scheme and, as we covered in Chapter 7, can make a segment appear to be unprofitable when, in fact, that segment is contributing to the overall profitability of the company. Another problem is that managers may attempt to "control" the common fixed costs allocated to their segment by manipulating the allocation base.

Discussion Question

11-4. Let's say you are a segment manager at **Motorola**. How would you react to a charge made to your department for a portion of the cost of the fleet of corporate aircraft, even though you have never even seen one of the planes?

Both proponents and opponents of common fixed cost allocation to business segments feel strongly about their positions. There seems to be little question, however, that the practice of including common fixed costs in segment reports is losing popularity. This fact is not surprising when we consider that the main purpose of management accounting is to influence managers to act to benefit the company. It seems clear that including common fixed costs in segment reports can lead managers toward behavior that is counterproductive. Restricting a segment cost report to costs over which a manager has control makes it a more useful tool for supporting sound business decisions.

Allocating Service Department Cost

The main operation of a merchandiser is selling products. For a manufacturer, the main operation is manufacturing and selling products, and for a service business, the main operation is providing services to customers. In addition to any company's main business operation, however, secondary support operations also occur. Most companies, whether merchandisers, manufacturers, or service-type businesses, also have an accounting department, a personnel department, and other departments that provide support to the various functions of the company. Further, telephone service and a facility (building) within which to operate must be provided. The business segments that handle these and other secondary operations are called **service departments**. These departments provide necessary services to the main business operations and other service departments.

service department A business segment responsible for secondary (support) functions. Service departments provide service to the main business operations and to other service departments.

Discussion Question

11-5. Besides the ones listed in the previous paragraph, what are five other service departments you think most companies have?

The cost of operating a service department can be substantial. This cost is allocated to the departments that use the services provided. In other words, if a particular department receives benefit from a service department, that department should be charged for the cost of the service.

Determining the amount of service department cost to charge various user departments is not an exact science. For some kinds of service cost, a direct correlation can be found between the amount of service provided to a department and the cost charged to that department. In these instances, the manager of the user department rarely disputes the charge. For other types of service cost, however, no direct cause and effect can be found. In that event, the cost charged to departments for services is based on an allocation method that may or may not be accurate or even fair. This allocation is much like that of common fixed cost to segments we discussed earlier. The allocation of service department cost when no correlation can be found between the service and the cost can actually cloud management's vision about the performance of a department.

As was the case with allocating fixed common cost to segments, certain managers believe that service department costs should be allocated whereas others believe the practice should be stopped. As usual, both sides hold strongly to their views. Although some companies have stopped allocating service department cost, the majority of companies still maintain this practice. The responsibility of department managers is to be vigilant in making certain that the costs charged to their departments reasonably reflect the amount of service received. Examples of service departments and possible allocation bases are shown in Exhibit 11-3.

Exhibit 11-3 Representative Service Departments and Possible Allocation Bases

Service Department	Allocation Basis
Personnel Department	• Number of employees
Telephone	• Number of phones • Number of lines • Long-distance charges

Copy Machine or Copy Center	• Quantity of services used:
	  • Number of single-sided copies
	  • Number of double-sided copies
	  • Number of bindings
	• Number of employees

Employee Cafeteria	• Number of meals served
Finance Department	• Amount of capital invested
Building Occupancy	• Square footage of building occupied
Computer Operations	• Computer mainframe time • Number of personal computers • Number of reports generated
Computer Programming	• Hours of programming
Office Services	• Square footage of office occupied • Number of offices
Engineering Department	• Number of engineering changes • Hours of engineering services
Maintenance	• Square footage of building occupied • Hours of maintenance
Aircraft Operations	• Number of passenger miles • Number of hours flown • Weight of load and distance flown

Activity-Based Service Department Cost Allocation

Activity-based costing is a topic we covered in Chapter 4 when we discussed alternative ways to allocate manufacturing overhead to units of product produced. Activity-based costing can also be a valuable tool for allocating service department cost to other departments. When possible, the allocation base used to allocate cost should be an activity that causes the cost. As stated in Chapter 4, an activity that causes cost to occur is called a cost driver. The two major benefits to using cost drivers to allocate service department cost are (1) this cost allocation method tends to be more fair and accurate, and (2) in attempting to control the cost allocated to their departments, managers will work to reduce the allocation base—the cost driver. Because the cost driver is also the cost cause, reducing the cost driver will actually reduce the amount paid by the company for goods and services. For example, when the cost driver used to allocate basic phone service is the number of phone lines, reducing the number of phone lines not only reduces the allocation of phone cost, but it also reduces the amount the company spends for phone service. This reduction results in true cost savings for the company.

Discussion Question

11-6. Refer to the list of five service departments you made in response to Discussion Question 11-5. What is a possible allocation base for each of the departments you listed?

It is important to know about service department cost allocation for several reasons. First, as a department manager, you will need to know how to control service department costs allocated to your department. Second, you should be able to discriminate between costs that are arbitrarily allocated to your department and those that are equitable. Third, as a high-level manager, you should be able to recognize when an allocation method should be modified or replaced, because it does not result in information that provides incentives for managers to act in fulfillment of company goals.

Sometimes the allocation method can cause managers to do counterproductive things, especially when activity-based cost allocation is not used. For example, consider what occurred in a major corporation when it changed the allocation base it used to distribute the cost of office space. Top managers felt that departments should not be charged for halls, elevator waiting areas, or other common areas but only for the office space dedicated entirely to the departments' use. So, from a charge for all the square footage the departments occupied, the firm changed to a charge for only the square footage of the *enclosed* office space occupied by the departments. Some managers then recognized that their department's allocation for office space could be cut if they were to reduce the square footage used for enclosed offices. Accordingly, they removed the separating cubicle walls of several offices occupied by department secretaries and created for them work space in the new "common" area. The result was an increase in the amount of common space, and a marked decrease in the amount of square footage used for enclosed offices. Because the departments were only charged for enclosed office space, their office space cost allocation was reduced.

The change in allocation base worked to the detriment of the company as a whole, of course, because it incurred the cost of remodeling the office space even though the remodeling was completely unnecessary. Interestingly, only managers who had a working knowledge of how service department costs were allocated knew how to take advantage of the situation.

Discussion Question

11-7. Do you think the cost previously described should even be allocated? If not, explain your reasoning. If you answered yes, what would you suggest to the company to overcome the dysfunctional management behavior described?

Reducing the service cost allocated to a particular department is not a difficult task to accomplish. First, the department manager must determine what allocation base is being used. Second, the manager must reduce the amount of the allocation base consumed by the department. If the allocation base used is a cost driver, the actual cost involved will decrease. If the allocation base is arbitrary and unrelated to the actual cost, the amount allocated to the department will decrease, but the actual cost to the company will continue and simply be shifted to other managers' departments.

As an example of how to control service department cost allocation, assume that the cost of photocopies is allocated based on the number of copies made. A reduction in the number of copies made will reduce the copy cost allocated to the user department. Attempting to reduce the number of copies would include reviewing department procedures to ensure that only necessary copies are made. It might also include reviewing alternate imaging technology to find ways to reduce the need for photocopies. This same logic can be used to control the cost allocation for telephone use, which is often allocated to departments based on the number of phone lines used. To reduce the cost allocation, unnecessary telephones are eliminated.

In each of these two examples, because the allocation base is a cost driver, a reduction in the base would not only cause a reduction in the cost allocated to the department but would also cause a true reduction in cost to the company.

Approaches to Segment Management

The strategy used to manage business segments varies from company to company. Some companies prefer that top management make all but the most routine decisions, whereas other companies prefer that lower-level managers make most or all of the decisions within their area. When almost all decisions are made by the top managers and little is left to the discretion of lower-level managers, the company is said to have a centralized management style. Conversely, if management decisions are made at the lowest possible management level, the company is said to have a decentralized management style. These management styles have both advantages and disadvantages.

Centralized Management

centralized management A management style in which top managers make most management decisions.

When a company uses a **centralized management** style, top management makes most management decisions. Middle- and lower-level managers are responsible only for routine decisions and supervisory functions. This management style ensures that the wishes of top management are incorporated into each management decision. Top managers often have the most experience, which could lead to wise business decisions. However, a centralized management style has certain disadvantages: (1) Top managers must spend their valuable time making many routine, low-level business decisions. (2) Top managers may not be intimately familiar with the various routine aspects of the business. (3) Lower-level employees have little opportunity to gain experience in decision making.

decentralized management A management style in which lower-level managers are responsible for decisions that relate to their segment of the company.

Decentralized Management

When a company uses a **decentralized management** style, lower-level managers are responsible for management decisions that relate to their segment of the business. When a highly decentralized management style is used, decisions are made at the lowest possible level in the organization.

A decentralized management style has several advantages. It helps spread the decision making responsibilities among the various management levels of the company and allows lower-level managers greater control over their business segments. Another benefit is that a decentralized management style provides an opportunity for lower-level managers to sharpen their decision making skills, thus providing the company with experienced managers to progress through the ranks to top management positions. Decentralization also means that decisions are made by the managers who are most familiar with the problems and opportunities occurring in the routine operations of the company. Top managers may be somewhat removed from the intimacies of the daily routine business operations and therefore would be hard pressed to make well informed decisions. Another advantage is that it relieves top managers of the responsibility of routine decisions and allows them to focus on strategic decisions and the overall goals of the organization.

A disadvantage of decentralized management is that decisions may not entirely reflect the views of top managers who likely have a better understanding of the company's strategic initiatives. Also, decisions are made by managers who may be less experienced than the top managers.

Discussion Questions

11-8. If you were the chief executive officer of your company, would you prefer a centralized or decentralized management style? Explain your reasoning.

11-9. If you were a lower-level manager in your company, would you prefer a centralized or decentralized management style? Explain your reasoning.

11-10. What similarities do you see between our discussion here of centralized and decentralized management and our discussion in Chapter 9 of top-down and bottom-up budgeting?

Evaluating Business Segments

To evaluate the performance of business segments, we must first determine just what constitutes good performance. To establish whether a manager is doing a good job, for example, we must first have some idea of just what a "good job" means. To evaluate segment performance, a standard must be developed that establishes just what constitutes good performance.

The performance of a business segment can be evaluated based on a number of criteria. The most logical evaluation criteria match the scope of responsibility and authority afforded the segment's manager. That is, if a particular segment's manager has the responsibility and authority only to control costs, the segment performance should be evaluated based on criteria that focus on cost control. Conversely, if the segment manager has the responsibility to generate revenue and also to control costs, the segment's performance should be evaluated based on criteria that focus on profits. Segments may be categorized based on the criteria used for their evaluation. The most popular segment categories are revenue centers, cost centers, profit centers, and investment centers.

revenue center A business segment in which the manager has responsibility and authority to act to increase revenues but has little or no control over costs and the amount invested in the segment.

Revenue Centers

A **revenue center** is a business segment whose manager has responsibility and authority to act to increase revenues but has little control over costs and the amount invested in the segment. The performance of a revenue center is evaluated based on the amount of revenue generated by the segment, and the manager is evaluated based on his or her ability to generate sales revenue.

An example of a business segment properly designated as a revenue center is a sales office whose segment manager has little or no control over costs. The results of the manager's actions would affect sales revenue but have minimal effect on cost.

Cost Centers

cost center A business segment where the manager has responsibility and authority to act to decrease or at least control costs but has little or no control over the revenues generated or the amount invested in the segment.

A **cost center** is a business segment whose manager has responsibility and authority to decrease or at least control costs while keeping output high. Generally, cost center managers are not responsible for generating revenue, nor do they have control over the amount invested in the segment. The performance of a cost center is evaluated based on the amount of cost incurred by the segment and the manager is evaluated based on his or her ability to control these costs.

Business segments that provide service to the company or customers but do not contribute directly to revenues are good candidates to be designated as cost centers. Examples of cost centers include the accounting department of a hospital, a repair department that handles warranty repair work, an assembly department, and an inspection facility in a manufacturing plant.

Profit Centers

profit center A business segment in which the manager has the responsibility and authority to act to increase revenue and decrease or at least control costs, but has little or no control over the amount invested in the segment.

A **profit center** is a business segment whose manager has the responsibility and authority to act to increase revenue and decrease or at least control costs but does not have control over the amount invested in the segment. The performance of a profit center is evaluated based on the amount of profits it generates. The manager of a profit center is evaluated based on his or her ability to increase revenue and control expenses, because profits are increased by increasing revenue and/or decreasing expenses.

Examples of profit centers include individual stores in a department store chain, a college bookstore, and a pathology testing center.

Measuring Performance of Revenue, Cost, and Profit Centers

The most commonly used method of evaluating the performance of revenue centers, cost centers, and profit centers is performance to budget. The sales goals established during the budgeting process can be used as a basis for evaluating the performance of revenue centers. If, for example, actual sales are higher than budgeted sales, this would be a favorable indication. If, on the other hand, actual sales are lower than budgeted sales, this would be an unfavorable indication. For a cost center, the goals established during the budgeting process for output and cost can be used as a basis for evaluating cost center performance. Actual production that exceeds budgeted production, for example, would be a favorable indication. Costs per unit of output that are lower than budgeted would also be a favorable indication. Obviously, favorable performance would be indicated by high output and low cost relative to output volume. For a profit center, the profit goals established during the budgeting process can be compared to actual profits to evaluate profit center performance. Favorable performance would be indicated by actual profits that meet or exceed budgeted profits.

It is often argued that having managers strive to meet budgeted performance targets is so simplistic that it leads to suboptimal performance. Managers may simply strive to meet the expectations established by the budget instead of trying to maximize sales. Another potential problem is that managers who are evaluated based on performance to budget can make themselves look good by negotiating relatively low budgeted sales and relatively high budgeted costs. Then when the actual sales are higher than budgeted, and the actual costs are lower than budgeted, the manager appears to have performed well. This information may seem familiar to you. Other chapters in the text included brief discussions of the problems associated with performance to budget as a way to measure managers' performance—a subject addressed in Chapter 9 when we presented the operating budget and again in Chapter 10 in the presentation of standard costing. Everything about the potential for counterproductive behavior inherent in the performance to budget evaluation technique applies to measuring the performance of revenue centers, cost centers, and profit centers.

If we move away from performance to budget as a means of evaluating revenue center managers, however, what do we put in its place? This topic has been a topic of debate for some time in management accounting circles. The answer, we suspect, is not to drop performance to budget as a performance measure entirely. Rather, it should be supplemented with other types of measures, some of which are presented later in this chapter. For now, just remember that a company runs a real risk of encouraging silly management behavior if it relies too heavily on performance to budget as a means of evaluating its managers.

Investment Centers

Does earning a profit of $100,000 constitute good performance? Before we can tell just how good it is, we should also consider the amount of investment required. Surely, almost any business segment can be profitable if there is an unlimited amount to invest in assets and technology. In business, the hope is to keep the profit high and the amount invested low.

An **investment center** is a business segment that is evaluated based on the amount of profit generated relative to the amount invested in the segment. An investment center manager should strive to maximize profit while minimizing the amount of investment used to earn the profit. Reducing the investment in a given segment allows the freed-up funds to be used by other segments. If the funds are not needed by the company elsewhere, financing can be reduced.

investment center A business segment that is evaluated based on the amount of profit generated relative to the amount invested in the segment.

If a segment manager has responsibility and authority for revenues, costs, and capital investment in the segment, it should probably be designated an investment center. Examples of business segments that might be designated investment centers are individual stores in a department store chain, a college bookstore, and a pathology testing center. Note that these examples are the same as those given for segments designated as profit centers in our earlier discussion, because the classification of a business segment as a revenue center, profit center, cost center, or investment center depends not only on the operation of the segment but also, and as importantly, on the responsibility and authority afforded the segment's manager. If a manager's responsibility includes the generation of revenue, cost control, and control of the amount invested in the segment, then the business segment she or he manages should be designated an investment center.

As stated earlier, an investment center should be evaluated not only on the income generated by the segment, but also on the amount of investment required to earn the income. Obviously the higher the net income, the better, and the lower the investment required to generate that net income, the better. To evaluate the performance of an investment center we must be able to quantify the relationship between income earned and the investment required. For example, if you are about to invest in a savings account, it might be beneficial to know that a $5,245 deposit will earn interest of $183.57 in one year's time. Without knowing the percentage interest rate of return, however, the amounts have little meaning when evaluating the performance of the savings account. In business, the percentage return on an amount invested is called return on investment.

Return on Investment

In 1903, Pierre DuPont and two of his cousins, Alfred and Coleman, formed the E.I. DuPont de Nemours Powder Company by combining several gunpowder companies they had purchased from other DuPont family members. When the cousins purchased the companies, they paid for them by issuing bonds equal in value to the expected future earnings potential of the companies acquired to form the new business. Pierre and his cousins could realize a profit only when the income from the new company exceeded the projected income of the individual companies they had purchased. Therefore, if income did not increase, there would only be enough profits to pay the bonds, leaving no profit for the cousins. This transaction is an early example of a leveraged buyout.

Knowing only the amount of income was not enough to monitor the success of the new organization. Accordingly, Pierre DuPont devised the return on investment model to calculate the percentage return on the cousins' investment. The return on investment could be used to assess whether the returns of the individual segments of the DuPont Company exceeded the rate used to calculate the purchase price and interest payments on the bonds. Of course, the hope was that each of the segments of the DuPont Company would have a return on investment that exceeded the rate used to determine the purchase price. The company went on to become the **DuPont Chemical Company** of today.

Discussion Question

11-11. What similarities do you see between our discussion here of return on investment and our discussion in Chapter 8 of capital expenditures?

return on investment (ROI) The percentage return generated by an investment in a business or a business segment.

Since its inception, DuPont's return on investment model has been a popular method of evaluating investment centers. **Return on investment (ROI)** is the percentage return generated by an investment in a business or business segment. ROI is calculated by dividing the amount of income by the amount invested. For example, assume that the Eastern Division of the Lisa Company generated a segment margin of \$896,750 for 2009 and the amount invested in the division was \$10,550,000. This information is interesting, but it is probably more meaningful to know the percentage return that the investment generated. The ROI for the Eastern Division is 8.5 percent, shown as follows:

$$\frac{\text{Segment income}}{\text{Investment in the segment}} = \text{Return on investment}$$

$$\frac{\$896{,}750}{\$10{,}550{,}000} = 8.5\%$$

After we determine the ROI for the division, the next question is, is the ROI adequate? If a company uses ROI as the measurement criterion for evaluating segment performance, it must establish a required rate for the ROI. The required rate of return that companies normally use is the weighted average cost of capital rate, as discussed in Chapter 8 concerning capital expenditures. Once established, the required ROI rate is used as a benchmark to evaluate the performance of the various investment centers in the company. A segment with an ROI that equals or exceeds the company's required rate will be viewed favorably, whereas a segment with an ROI that is lower than the required rate will be viewed as deficient. If we assume that the required rate for the ROI for the Lisa Company is 8 percent, then the Eastern Division's performance is certainly adequate.

Discussion Question

11-12. What similarities do you see between our discussion here of the ROI calculation and our discussion in Chapter 8 of the internal rate of return?

In evaluating segment performance, we can rank segments by their return on investment. For example, if the Western Division of the Lisa Company has income of $857,500 with an investment of $9,800,000, how does the performance of the Western Division compare to that of the Eastern Division? The return on investment of both divisions is presented as Exhibit 11-4.

Exhibit 11-4 Return on Investment for Both Divisions of Lisa Company

Eastern Division	Western Division
$\frac{\text{Segment income}}{\text{Investment in the segment}} = \text{ROI}$	$\frac{\text{Segment income}}{\text{Investment in the segment}} = \text{ROI}$
$\frac{\$896{,}750}{\$10{,}550{,}000} = 8.5\%$	$\frac{\$857{,}500}{\$9{,}800{,}000} = 8.75\%$

Based on the ROI, the performance of the Western Division is superior to that of the Eastern Division because its ROI is greater. In this case, the Western Division's manager may be rewarded because of that division's better performance. As you might imagine, the use of ROI tends to encourage competition among segment managers, who strive to enhance performance evaluation by choosing investments that will work to increase their segment's ROI.

For the ROI to increase, the ROI of any new investment must exceed the segment's current ROI. If a new investment promises an ROI that is equal to the segment's current ROI, the segment's ROI will remain unchanged. However, if the new investment's ROI is less than the segment's current ROI, the segment's ROI will decrease. For example, assume that the manager of the Eastern Division is contemplating a new investment in the hope of improving his or her performance evaluation. An investment opportunity is available that promises additional income of $123,750 and requires an additional investment of $1,500,000. The ROI for this new investment opportunity is 8.25 percent calculated as follows:

$$\frac{\text{New investment income}}{\text{Investment in the new project}} = \text{ROI}$$

$$\frac{\$123{,}750}{\$1{,}500{,}000} = 8.25\%$$

Based on the company's required rate of return of 8 percent, it seems that the project should be accepted. Will the manager of the Eastern Division accept the project because it exceeds the company's required ROI and would benefit the company as a whole? Unfortunately, the answer is probably no. The manager of the Eastern Division may not select this project because it would work to reduce the segment's current ROI, as shown in Exhibit 11-5.

Exhibit 11-5 Effect of New Project on Eastern Division's Segment ROI

Eastern Division *Without* the New Investment Opportunity	Eastern Division *With* the New Investment Opportunity
$\frac{\text{Segment income}}{\text{Investment in the segment}} = \text{ROI}$	$\frac{\text{Segment income}}{\text{Investment in the segment}} = \text{ROI}$
$\frac{\$896{,}750}{\$10{,}550{,}000} = 8.5\%$	$\frac{\$896{,}750 + \$123{,}750}{\$10{,}550{,}000 + \$1{,}500{,}000} = 8.47\%$

Although the Eastern Division's ROI would still be higher than the required ROI rate of 8 percent, the new investment would reduce the division's ROI from 8.5 percent to approximately 8.47 percent.

When ROI is used as the segment performance measure, the evaluation is usually based not only on how the segment's ROI compares to the company's required rate, but also on how segment's ROI compares to the ROI of other segments. Therefore, managers will only select projects that will enhance their current ROI. Unfortunately this often works to the detriment of the company as a whole, because projects that meet the company's required ROI rate are rejected simply because they will not increase the segment's ROI. Fortunately, another evaluation technique encourages managers to accept projects that have an ROI exceeding the company's required ROI rate. This evaluation technique is called residual income.

Residual Income and Economic Value Added (EVA)™

residual income The amount by which a segment's actual income exceeds the income needed to meet a company's required rate of return.

economic value added (EVA) Almost the same as residual income except that it is adjusted for certain accounting distortions.

Residual income is a technique used to evaluate investment centers by focusing on the amount by which a segment's actual income exceeds the income needed to meet the company's required rate of return. **Economic value added (EVA)**, which is trademarked by the consulting firm of Stern Stewart & Co., is similar to residual income except that Stern Stewart adjusted the calculation for certain distortions that stem from generally accepted accounting principles (GAAP). For example, EVA calculations require research and development (R&D) costs to be capitalized as an asset and amortized over the periods benefited, whereas R&D costs are treated as period expenses under GAAP. EVA has become very popular and many managers attribute significant improvements in company performance to its use in evaluating their managers. For our purposes, we will make no distinction between residual income and EVA.

To demonstrate residual income, let's take another look at the Lisa Company. Recall that the investment in the Eastern Division of the Lisa Company is $10,550,000 and that the company's required rate of return is 8 percent. With that said, the Eastern Division must earn $844,000 ($10,550,000 × 8%) just to equal the 8 percent required rate of return. This required earnings amount represents the dollar amount of earnings the segment must earn to equal the required rate of return for the company. Any earnings in excess of the required earnings (in this case $844,000) constitute the segment's residual income. For the Eastern Division, the $896,750 actual income exceeds the $844,000 required income by $52,750. Therefore, the residual income for the Eastern Division is $52,750, shown as follows:

Actual Income	$ 896,750
Less Required Income ($10,550,000 × 8%)	$(844,000)
Equals Residual Income	$ 52,750

This is not to say that the Eastern Division only earned $52,750. Rather, the Eastern Division's income exceeded the company's required earnings by $52,750.

If the division's actual income were less than the income required to meet the company's required rate of return, the residual income amount would be a negative number. In our example, the positive residual income amount indicates that the segment's actual earnings exceed the company's required rate of return. In the unlikely event that residual income is zero, it would indicate that the actual income for the segment exactly equals the company's required rate of return.

Discussion Question

11-13. What similarities do you see between our discussion here of the residual income calculation and our discussion in Chapter 8 of net present value?

We now calculate the residual income for the Western Division so we can evaluate the relative performance of the two divisions. Using the amounts previously presented for the Western Division, we calculate residual income as $73,500:

Actual Income	$ 857,500
Less Required Income ($9,800,000 × 8%)	$(784,000)
Equals Residual Income	$ 73,500

Notice that the residual income of the Western Division exceeds that of the Eastern Division. Accordingly, the performance of the Western Division would be viewed more favorably than that of the Eastern Division. In an attempt to improve the Eastern Division's relative performance, managers would strive to increase revenue, decrease expenses, or seek new, high-return investment opportunities.

When ROI is used to evaluate potential investment opportunities, managers invest only in projects with an anticipated return that exceeds the segment's current ROI. Projects that exceed the company's required rate of return but do not exceed the segment's current ROI would likely be rejected. Look again at the investment opportunity proposed for the Eastern Division. Recall that the project would require an investment of $1,500,000 with anticipated additional income of $123,750. Therefore, the total investment of the Eastern Division would increase to $12,050,000 ($10,550,000 + $1,500,000), while total segment income would increase to $1,020,500 ($896,750 + $123,750).

If residual income were used to evaluate segment performance, management of the Eastern Division would tend to accept the proposed project if it worked to increase residual income. The residual income for the Eastern Division both with and without the proposed investment opportunity is presented in Exhibit 11-6.

Exhibit 11-6 Residual Income for Eastern Division with and without Proposed Investment

Eastern Division *Without* the New Investment Opportunity		**Eastern Division *With* the New Investment Opportunity**	
Actual Income	$896,750	Actual Income	$1,020,500
Required Income		Required Income	
($10,550,000 × 8%) =	($844,000)	($12,050,000 × 8%) =	$ (964,000)
Residual Income	$ 52,750	Residual Income	$ 56,500

As you can see, the investment opportunity for the Eastern Division would increase residual income. Therefore, management of the Eastern Division would tend to favor the investment. Notice that the residual income method, unlike ROI, prompts managers to accept projects with return rates that exceed the company's required rate of return even if the project's rate of return falls short of the segment's current ROI.

Emerging Management and Management Accounting Techniques

Chapter 1 of this text began with a discussion of the worldwide economic problems facing businesses today. In that chapter, we said that in the current global business environment it is not enough for business men and woman to simply be familiar with the management accounting techniques their companies currently use. Instead, they must be aware of the various techniques they can employ to improve their management and decision making capabilities as needs arise. In the following section we provide an introduction to several emerging management concepts and techniques that are helping managers to improve their business success. With the emergence of each of these, management accounting has a key role to play in providing managers with a critical portion of the information they need to implement and use the techniques.

The Balanced Scorecard

When you're driving a car, you can't focus just on your speedometer. Nor can you focus just on your gas gauge, or temperature gauge, or any single one of the gauges intended to provide you with information about your automobile and how you are driving. Not only do you have to steer the car, watch the road, and pay attention to the traffic, but periodically you must check the gauges. Well, like a driver that becomes fixated on only one gauge, business in the United States has focused almost exclusively on financial measures (particularly the income statement) to assess performance. Success has been gauged by how much revenue can be generated, how much costs can be reduced, or how much profit can be earned. Recently, however, many companies have begun to also consider nonfinancial performance measures in evaluating business performance. Managers are finding that a more strategic, balanced approach is necessary to drive corporate performance. Harvard professor Robert Kaplan and consultant David Norton have developed a management technique called the balanced scorecard. The balanced scorecard doesn't focus solely on the financial objectives of the firm. Instead the **balanced scorecard** is an integrated set of performance measures organized around four distinct perspectives—financial, customer, internal, and innovation and learning as depicted in Exhibit 11-7. The innovation and learning perspective is also called the learning and growth perspective. The balanced scorecard suggests these perspectives, but managers generally tailor them to suit their own business needs.

balanced scorecard An integrated set of performance measures organized around four distinct perspectives—financial, customer, internal, and innovation and learning.

The balanced scorecard can help managers successfully implement business strategy. Typically the problem with strategy is not its creation but rather its implementation. According to Fortune Editor at Large, Patricia Sellers in her December 2008 article, *Execution, execution, execution!*, strategy execution has always been the number one reason why CEOs fail.[i] Sellers states that this point has been preached by her colleague Geoff Colvin and management guru Ram Charan over the past decade. In a 1999 cover story on prominent CEO failures, Fortune estimates that in 70 percent of cases the problem was not a bad strategy, but rather failure to implement the strategy. Although having a good business

[i]Patricia Sellers, *Execution, execution, execution!*, Fortune Postcards, December 18, 2008

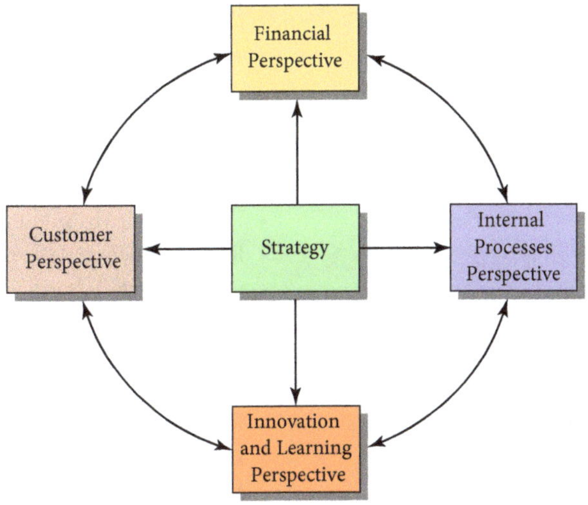

Exhibit 11-7 The Four Perspectives of the Balanced Scorecard

strategy is critically important, it is safe to say that with strategy implementation failure rates of 70 percent to 90 percent, execution of strategy is even more critically important.

Successful strategy execution doesn't just happen. Just because managers are very much aware of the business strategy, it does not mean they will act to achieve it. However, the balanced scorecard can help businesses execute their strategy through the use of objectives, measures, and targets. When a company adopts the balanced scorecard, managers must create objectives, measures, and performance targets for each scorecard perspective. **Objectives** are concise statements for each balanced scorecard perspective that articulate what the organization hopes to accomplish. It is critically important that each objective support the company's business strategy. If an objective does not support the business strategy, either the objective should be eliminated or the strategy changed to accommodate the objective. **Measures** are descriptions of how success in achieving scorecard objectives will be measured. **Targets** express the level of performance or rate of improvement desired for each measure.

balanced scorecard objectives Concise statements for each balanced scorecard perspective that articulate what the organization hopes to accomplish.

balanced scorecard measures Descriptions of how success in achieving scorecard objectives will be measured.

balanced scorecard targets The level of performance or rate of improvement desired for each measure.

Once managers establish the company's overall objectives, they can create appropriate detailed departmental objectives and measures. Still, it is important that the detailed objectives support the business strategy. Exhibit 11-8 shows examples of objectives and measures for the four balanced scorecard perspectives.

Sometimes it is impossible to achieve company objectives without establishing some new significant programs. These short-term programs and actions that will help achieve the established balanced scorecard objectives and performance targets are called **initiatives**. Examples of initiatives include the following:

balanced scorecard initiatives Short-term programs and actions that will help achieve the established balanced scorecard objectives and performance targets.

- Establishing a new maintenance program
- Upgrading selected equipment
- Establishing new performance benchmarks
- Establishing a new employee training program
- Establishing a new frequent purchase program

Unfortunately, employees seldom act to execute strategy simply because a good strategy exists and they are aware of it. But the balanced scorecard can help. The scorecard helps because once objectives and initiatives are established and communicated to the workforce, employees have a clearer picture of what they need to accomplish for the company.

Exhibit 11-8 Examples of Objectives and Measures for the Four Balanced Scorecard Perspectives

Perspective	Overall Objective	Examples of Measures
Financial	To succeed financially	• Operating income • Return on investment (ROI) • Residual income (RI) and Economic value added (EVA) • Sales growth • Cost reductions
Customer	To achieve our vision of how we should appear to our customers	• Number of new customers, • Customer retention • Depth of customer relationships • Market share • Time required to fill orders • On-time deliveries • Customer complaints • Time to resolve complaints • Completeness of product-line offering • Customer satisfaction with products and services • Customer satisfaction with company employees
Internal	To excel at having superior business processes to satisfy our shareholders and customers	• Process quality measures • Lead-time (time between when a customer places an order and when it is delivered) • Defect rates • Yield ratios of good items to items entering process • Waste, scrap and rework measures • Returns
Innovation and Learning (Learning and growth)	To sustain our ability to change and improve. (Employee capabilities and innovation are key ingredients to this objective.)	• Employee retention • Average revenue per employee • Employee training • Number of products under development • Amount of research and development cost • Number of new products • Number of new, lower cost supply channels • Number of items from new, low cost supply channels • Information system capabilities (Availability of useful information to employees.)

Additionally, measures and targets not only help gauge the degree to which employees are meeting scorecard objectives, they also greatly encourage employees to act so that the differences between the established performance targets and their actual performance do not result in unfavorable variances. And most importantly, since the targets are tied to measures and objectives that are tied to the company's business strategy, employees will conduct themselves in a way that is likely to achieve strategy execution.

Although the balanced scorecard is often viewed as a performance measurement technique, Kaplan and Norton report that it can be much more.

> *. . . innovating CEOs used the balanced scorecard not only to clarify and communicate strategy, but also to manage strategy. They are using the measurement focus of the scorecard to accomplish critical management processes:*
>
> 1. *Clarify and translate vision and strategy*
> 2. *Communicate and link strategic objectives and measures*
> 3. *Plan, set targets, and align strategic initiatives*
> 4. *Enhance strategic feedback and learning*
>
> —Robert S. Kaplan and David P. Norton

(From: The Balanced Scorecard: Translating Strategy Into Action, Robert S. Kaplan and David P. Norton, Harvard Business School Press, Pages—preface page ix and page 10).

To assure that the balanced scorecard is not only a measurement and reporting tool but a management technique that will effectively enhance a company's performance, it is important that each objective, measure, target, and initiative be closely aligned with the firm's overall goals and business strategy.

Setting objectives and a basis for measurement for each of the four scorecard perspectives allows managers and employees to focus on the success of each perspective, and to avoid making the mistake of attending to one perspective while neglecting another. Attention to each of the four perspectives is critical to the success of all types of businesses. As we said at the beginning of this section, when you're driving a car, you can't just focus on your speedometer. When managing a business in today's competitive business environment, you can't focus solely on financial performance measures.

For more information about the balanced scorecard you can visit the **Palladium Group** at its website at www.thepalladiumgroup.com. The **Palladium Group** is an organization founded by Kaplan and Norton which is devoted to helping firms execute strategy. The **Palladium Group** provides various courses and seminars concerning the balanced scorecard and strategy execution. Some of the seminars can be attended online free of charge. In association with **Harvard Business Publishing** , the **Palladium Group** also conducts a four-day Balanced Scorecard Certification Boot Camp which is endorsed by Kaplan and Norton.

E-Commerce

Electronic commerce, commonly called **e-commerce**, refers to the buying and selling of products or services and other business activities conducted over the internet. Today, most people associate e-commerce with purchasing goods and services via the internet using secure web sites and electronic payment. This application of e-commerce, however, did not begin until the mid to late 1990s.

electronic commerce Buying and selling of products or services and other business activities conducted over the internet.

e-commerce The same thing as electronic commerce.

The term electronic commerce was first applied in the late 1970s to commercial transactions conducted electronically, such as Electronic Funds Transfer (EFT) and Electronic Data Interchange (EDI). This made it possible for businesses to send commercial documents like purchase orders, invoices, and payments electronically. Throughout the 1980s additional electronic applications were developed, such as telephone banking, automated teller machines, airline reservation systems, and the growth and acceptance of credit cards.

The most significant influence on the growth and diversification of e-commerce was the emergence of the internet in the 1990s. Commercial use of the internet started to catch on in 1995 with an estimated 18 million users. The rise in usage meant an untapped market—an international market. Before long, an entirely new industry (dot.com) was born. In the year 1999 alone, there were over 450 initial public offerings (IPOs) of internet and technology related companies. Of those companies, more than 100 saw their stock price double in price on the first day of trading. By 2001, however, the dot.com bubble had burst. In that year, the number of IPOs dwindled to fewer than 80, and none of their stock prices doubled on the first day of trading.

By the end of 2002, the vast majority of all the dot.com companies started in the 1990s were gone. E-commerce, however, has flourished in the first decade of the 21st century. Some dot.com companies such as **Amazon.com**, **Taobao**, and **Ebay** have survived and are very successful. Additionally, many traditional retailers such as **Target** and **Wal-Mart** have electronic commerce presence on the internet.

business-to-consumer (B2C) Commerce conducted between businesses and consumers.

business-to-business (B2B) Commerce conducted between businesses.

business-to-government (B2G) Commerce conducted between businesses and government agencies.

Commerce conducted between businesses and consumers is called **business-to-consumer or B2C**. Individual consumers can go online to purchase anything from books or groceries, to expensive items like real estate. Commerce conducted between businesses is referred to as **business-to-business or B2B** and commerce conducted between businesses and government agencies is referred to as **business-to-government or B2G**. Manufacturers, wholesalers, retailers and financial institutions use the internet to buy and sell products, and exchange financial data to facilitate domestic and international business.

Process Management

business process A stream of connected activities that begins with research and development, through product design, then to manufacturing, then marketing and distribution, all with the focus on customer satisfaction. (Sometimes called the *value chain*.)

value chain A stream of connected activities that begins with research and development, through product design, then to manufacturing, then marketing and distribution, all with the focus on customer satisfaction. Each step in the process should add value to products and ultimately to the value of the entire organization (Sometimes called the *business process*.)

process management Managing the various interconnected business activities (business processes) in an enterprise.

In this age of integrated systems that cross organizational functions in a business enterprise, it's sometimes hard to remember that such integration was unheard of just a few short years ago. In times past, about the only communication that existed between different functional areas in a company were reports passed back and forth. Not only was coordination of effort lacking, but because managers of various functions had no real knowledge of what other departments did, they often didn't understand the information in those reports, so the reports were largely ignored.

Well, those days are gone forever. In Chapter 1 we stressed that the last couple of decades have been a period of rapid change in the business environment. The explosion of worldwide competition, the serious financial scandals in the United States and other countries, and technological development have forced the managers of businesses worldwide to rethink the way they operate their companies. Rather than looking at the different functional areas of the business as separate, discrete areas of emphasis with little or no coordination, managers have begun to view their companies as a stream of activities that begins with research and development, through product design, then to manufacturing, then marketing and distribution, all with the focus on customer satisfaction. This series of connected activities is known as the **business process**. It is also referred to as a **value chain**, because each step in the process should add value to the products produced and ultimately to the value of the entire organization (See Exhibit 11-9).

Managing various interconnected business activities (business process) is known as **process management**. As the notion of business as an integrated series of steps in a

Exhibit 11-9 The Value Chain

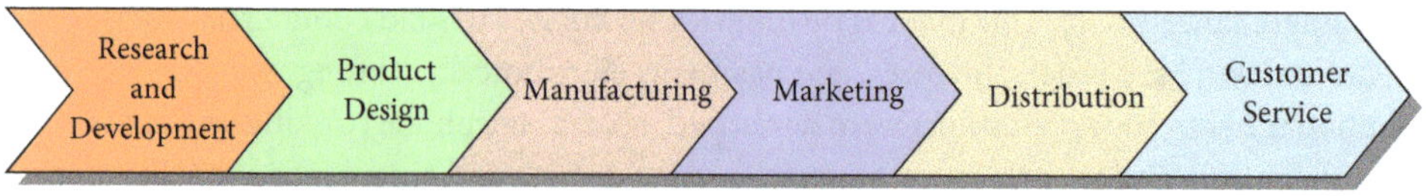

process has grown, a number of innovative approaches to managing that process have emerged. In this section we will discuss four of them. They are the Enterprise Information System, Six Sigma, the Theory of Constraints, and Lean Manufacturing. Although they all share the common goal of managing the business process, each has unique characteristics.

Enterprise Information Systems

In times past, most companies had separate computer software programs for use by the various functional units of the company. Accounting had one software program, manufacturing another, marketing yet another, and so on. Because these software programs were not integrated, the various functional areas of the company found it difficult to communicate information to one another. Aside from the excess cost associated with maintaining multiple software programs, there was unavoidable duplication of effort and inconsistent results based on the same data.

The solution to the problems inherent to maintaining multiple computer software programs is an enterprise information system. In the broadest general sense, an **enterprise information system** is an integrated computer system capable of supporting an entire organization with quality service while processing large volumes of data. An enterprise information system is actually an interrelated set of information systems that work together to facilitate planning, control, and coordination in businesses.

enterprise information system An integrated computer system capable of supporting an entire organization with quality service while processing large volumes of data.

A typical enterprise information system utilizes a central database. A **database** is an electronic filing system that contains various facts and figures in an organized fashion. All data are entered into the database only once. When any new data are added to the system, or if any data are changed, the new information is available immediately to everyone in the organization, regardless of the functional area. In traditional systems, it is not uncommon for changes in a customer's status, for example, to be reflected in the company's accounting system, but not in the marketing system, or the shipping department's records. The potential problems caused by this inconsistent update of records are obvious. With an enterprise system, because all records are kept in a centralized database, when a customer's status changes, all relevant functional areas have access to the update immediately.

database An electronic filing system that contains various facts and figures in an organized fashion.

Enterprise information systems are expensive to install and require a significant investment in training of personnel. Once installed and mastered, however, more and more companies are finding the time and money well spent.

Six Sigma

Six Sigma is a business management strategy that seeks to identify and remove the causes of defects and errors (anything that could lead to customer dissatisfaction) in manufacturing and other business processes. The Six Sigma process was developed by engineers at **Motorola** in the 1980s, and the company has reported over $17 billion in cost savings since it was implemented. Other companies, including **General Electric** and **Honeywell** were quick to adopt Six Sigma, and by the late 1990s, about two-thirds of the Fortune 500 companies had begun to use the process with the aim of reducing costs and improving quality.

Six Sigma A business management strategy that seeks to identify and remove the causes of defects and errors (anything that could lead to customer dissatisfaction) in manufacturing and other business processes.

In the Six Sigma process, sigma (the lower-case Greek letter σ) represents one standard deviation (a measure of variation) of a statistical population. The number six refers to the number of standard deviations from zero defects a particular manufacturing process is allowed. This is based on the notion that if the process has six standard deviations (or less) from zero defects, there will be practically no items that fail to meet specifications. In fact statistically, processes that operate with six sigma quality produce long-term defect levels below 3.4 defects per million opportunities (DPMO). Six Sigma's implicit goal is to improve all processes to that level of quality or better. Exhibit 11-10 presents DPMO and yield rates for various sigma levels. Most companies operate at about 3 sigma.

Exhibit 11-10 DPMO and Yield Rates for Various Sigma Levels

Sigma	Defects Per Million Opportunities	Yield
1	690,000.0	30.9%
2	308,000.0	69.2%
3	66,800.0	93.3%
4	6,210.0	99.4%
5	320.0	99.98%
6	3.4	99.9997%

When managers use Six Sigma they are trying to reduce the number of defects per opportunity, not per unit of product. For example, when **Motorola** manufactures a mobile telephone, there are thousands of opportunities for a defect to occur. **Motorola** managers break down telephone manufacturing into various processes and each of these processes is examined with an eye toward eliminating every opportunity for a defect to occur. The idea is to break down each business function to its most basic processes and then eliminate anything in the process that might cause a defect to occur.

The Six Sigma approach incorporates five processes: define, measure, analyze, improve and control.

- *Define*. This step concentrates on defining project goals and boundaries, and identifying issues that managers must address to achieve an improved sigma level. An improved sigma level signifies a reduced defect rate.
- *Measure*. In this step, information about the current situation is gathered to obtain baseline information on current process performance and identify problem areas.
- *Analyze*. This step focuses on identifying the causes of quality problems and confirming those causes through the use of appropriate data analysis tools.
- *Improve*. In this step solutions are implemented that address the causes of problems identified during the analysis phase.
- *Control*. In this step the improvements put in place are evaluated and monitored to prevent problems from reoccurring.

A firm adopting six sigma identifies problem areas, measures them, identifies their root causes, takes corrective action and then puts controls in place to prevent the problem from reoccurring.

There is an ongoing debate as to the benefits and costs of six sigma. On the surface it would appear that there could really be no downside risk associated with implementing a process whose only purpose is to increase the quality of processes within a company. So, except for the natural human tendency to resist change, why would anyone have reservations about a process such as six sigma? The reason is simply this: In the broadest sense, there are only two ways to increase a company's profits. The first is to increase revenues, and the second is to reduce costs. The promise of six sigma is that it will do both. By increasing the quality of products, existing customers will be more satisfied and the company should be able to attract new customers, thereby increasing revenue. The elimination of defects and errors should naturally reduce costs, because expensive rework and the enormous cost of scrapping inferior quality units of product will be greatly reduced or eliminated. Further, because of the critical analyses of processes within the company, unnecessary steps in the production process can be streamlined and eliminated. As revenues increase and costs decrease, profits will naturally increase.

A very real potential problem exists with the process of reducing costs. As surely as night follows day, if the employees of a company perceive that such cost cutting measures will lead to layoffs, they have a vested interest in making sure the process is unsuccessful. Fredrick Winslow Taylor in his landmark book, *Principles of Scientific Management*, published way back in 1911 stated that when a new method is found to be markedly superior to an existing one, it should be adopted. He also warned explicitly against cutting piece rates (or, by implication, cutting wages or discharging workers) when efficiency improvements reduce the need for raw labor:

> *". . . after a workman has had the price per piece of the work [wages] he is doing lowered two or three times as a result of his having worked harder and increased his output, he is likely entirely to lose sight of his employer's side of the case and become imbued with a grim determination to have no more cuts if soldiering [marking time, just doing what he is told] can prevent it."*

So managers must be very careful about translating six sigma improvements into improved financial results. If improvement is to occur, employees must be convinced that the result will be more job security for them as those improvements result in improved financial performance.

Theory of Constraints

A **constraint** is anything that does not allow you to do something you want to do or even need to do. Everyone is constrained by something. For you it might be not having enough money to buy that new car you would like to have, or maybe you are taking so many classes at school that you can't enjoy the social life some of your friends do. What is true for individuals is true for business organizations, as well. No company can do everything it desires to do at any given time. If this sounds familiar to you it is because we discussed it in Chapter 8 under the topic of scarce resources. We also touched on the subject in Chapter 9 when we discussed the benefits of the operating budget. Recall that in that discussion we examined a situation at the Montrose Manufacturing Company. We have reproduced Montrose production process as Exhibit 11-11

constraint Anything that does not allow you to do something you want or need to do.

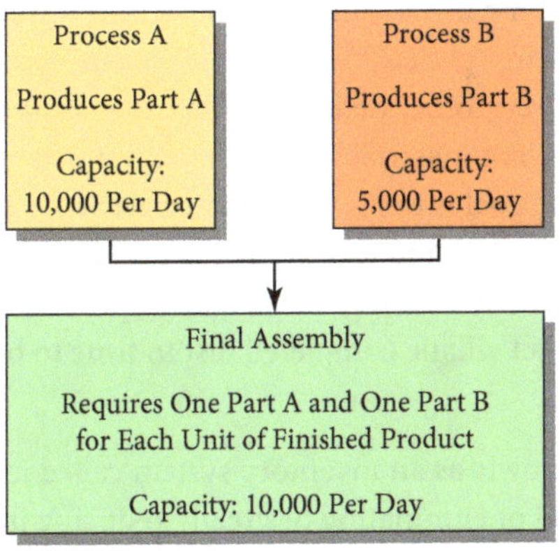

Exhibit 11-11 Diagram of Montrose Manufacturing Production Process

As you can see from Exhibit 11-11, each unit of finished product Montrose manufactures requires one Part A and one Part B. The maximum number of finished units of product the company can produce per day is 5,000. The limiting factor is Process B, which can produce only 5,000 parts per day. Montrose could increase the capacity of Process A from 10,000 parts per day to 100,000 parts per day and the company *still* could produce only 5,000 finished units per day because of the constraint caused by Process B. The same would be true with Final Assembly. Montrose could increase Final Assembly capacity, but it still could only assemble 5,000 units per day. In Chapter 9 we called Process B a bottleneck in the production process; here we refer to it as a constraint.

theory of constraints (TOC) An overall management philosophy introduced by Dr. Eliyahu M. Goldratt in his 1984 book titled *The Goal* which is based on the premise that the ability to achieve a goal is limited by at least one constraining process.

The **theory of constraints (TOC)** is an overall management philosophy introduced by Dr. Eliyahu M. Goldratt in his 1984 book titled *The Goal*. TOC is based on the premise that the ability to achieve a goal is limited by at least one constraining process. An analogy of a chain has been used to describe the nature of constraints. A chain is composed of a series of links. There is an old saying that a chain is only as strong as its weakest link. The truth of this saying should be clear. If a chain has ten links and only one of those links is not strong, the chain cannot fulfill its purpose. In the case of Montrose discussed above, let's say that its production process is a chain with only three links. Process B is the weak link in this chain. As we said earlier, it doesn't matter what steps Montrose takes in the other two links in the chain (Process A and Final Assembly), because the weak link (constraint) is Process B. Any improvement in the entire production process must begin with addressing Process B. Only by increasing throughput (flow) at the bottleneck process can overall throughput be increased.

TOC has been described as a four step process whose aim is to ensure ongoing improvement efforts centered around the organization's constraints:

1. Identify the constraint.
2. Decide how to address the constraint.
3. Work only on the selected constraint until a solution is achieved.
4. If, as a result of steps 1-3, the constraint has moved, return to Step 1.

As you can see TOC is actually a circular process. Once the selected constraint is removed, a new constraint will naturally emerge. Then the process begins again.

Lean manufacturing A production practice that focuses on reducing waste and inefficiencies in the production of product. The lean philosophy considers the expenditure of resources for any goal other than creating value for the end customer to be wasteful, and thus a target for elimination. The idea is to keep things trim and slim, or *lean*.

Lean production The same thing as lean manufacturing.

Lean The same thing as lean manufacturing.

just-in-time (JIT) A method of eliminating or greatly reducing inventory by delaying the purchase of material until it is actually needed for immediate use. Sometimes Lean is described too narrowly as just-in-time.

Lean Manufacturing

Lean manufacturing or **Lean Production**, which is often known simply as **Lean**, is a production practice that focuses on reducing waste and inefficiencies in the production of product. The lean philosophy considers the expenditure of resources for any goal other than creating value for the end customer to be wasteful, and thus a target for elimination. This means limiting the use of company resources until they are absolutely needed to fulfill customer demand. Products are "pulled" through the system. That is, products are made in response to the *pull* from customer demand, rather than to the *push* to have product to fill orders that may or may not materialize. Lean is sometimes referred to as a just-in-time philosophy, because the goal is to have raw materials arrive just in time to enter the production process. Then, as those materials make their way through the factory, partially completed units of product will arrive at the next step in production just in time to be worked on there. Units of product will be completed just in time to be shipped to the customer.

Often, Lean is described too narrowly as an inventory system called just-in-time. **Just-in-time (JIT)** is simply a method of eliminating or greatly reducing inventory by delaying the purchase of material until it is actually needed for immediate use. This view of Lean is incomplete and prompts many managers to reject the whole idea of lean manufacturing. In a more basic sense, Lean simply means more value with less work. It is a generic process management philosophy derived mostly from the **Toyota Production System (TPS)** and identified as Lean only in the last few years.

Toyota's development of ideas that later became Lean may have started as early as 1934 when it produced its first car. Kiichiro Toyoda, founder of Toyota, directed the engine casting work and was unhappy with the poor quality of the company's manufactured engines. He decided he must stop the wasted effort of repairing the poor quality engines; rather, he believed it would be more efficient and cost effective to repair the process used to produce the engines. He studied each stage of the production process and did, in fact, find ways to eliminate the waste and inefficiency of Toyota's production process. In 1936, when Toyota won its first truck contract, his processes hit new problems and he developed new ways of improving production efficiency.

Eventually, management at Toyota realized that the scheduling of work should not be driven by sales or production targets but by actual sales. By making this change, over-production could be avoided and thus the notion of *pull* (build to order) rather than target driven *push* came into being.

In a very real sense, however, the production philosophy that came to be known as Lean can be traced back to Henry Ford and the mass production process he developed at **Ford Motor Company** in the first decade of the 20th century. When asked in 1980 how Toyota had developed TPS, an executive of the company answered that they had learned it all from Henry Ford's book *Today and Tomorrow.*

Overview of Lean Manufacturing

Limiting the use of company resources until they are needed for production cannot be achieved by simply adopting a mind-set that purchases will be delayed until the last possible minute. Instead, the Lean philosophy focuses on delaying expenditures for inventory and reducing inventory levels to near zero by creating very efficient production processes that require only a minimal amount of inventory to successfully manufacture high-quality products.

One key component of Lean is that manufacturers must be able to depend on their suppliers for 100 percent on-time deliveries of 100 percent defect-free material. When Lean is implemented, manufacturers defer quality inspections to their suppliers and insist upon parts and components that are free of defects. **Zero defects** is a term that is often used to describe the concept of products that are completely free of imperfections. In a Lean environment, zero defects becomes the norm.

zero defects Describes the concept of products that are completely free of imperfections.

For Lean to be successful, manufacturers must develop close relationships with suppliers who can provide absolutely on-time deliveries and absolutely consistent high quality. As part of the program to develop these close relationships, firms greatly reduce the number of their suppliers. By working with a core of carefully selected suppliers, the manufacturer is able to make substantial purchase commitments that help compensate suppliers for the added effort required to meet the manufacturer's demands. Also, the financial benefits they gain from receiving on-time deliveries of consistently high-quality products make it possible for manufacturers to justify paying a premium price for the goods they purchase.

setup time The time it takes to prepare manufacturing equipment for the production of particular products.

In a Lean environment, setup times must be reduced to the lowest possible levels. As mentioned in Chapter 4, **setup time** is the time it takes to prepare manufacturing equipment for the production of a particular product. One major problem with long setup times is that while production equipment is being set up, it cannot be used to produce anything. The trouble does not end there, however. If setup time is substantial, fewer and longer production runs must be made to justify the substantial setup effort. It makes no sense to go through a long setup process to produce only a few units. The result of long production runs is higher inventory levels. This method is in direct conflict with the Lean philosophy. Conversely, if setup time is very short, running a short production run to produce fewer units of product is more feasible. With shorter production runs making fewer units, inventories can be reduced.

In Lean environments, setup time is now measured and average setup times are used to evaluate the performance of segment managers. In factories using Lean production, setup time is reduced from hours or days to minutes.

throughput time The time that passes from the time a unit of product enters the production process until it emerges as a finished product.

Another benefit of Lean is reduced throughput time. **Throughput time** is the time between the entrance of raw materials into the production process and the time it emerges as a finished product. It is an important measure of plant efficiency because the amount of money invested in work-in-process inventory can be lowered by reducing the time products are in the production process. In addition to reducing inventories, shorter throughput time frees production equipment so it can be used to make other products. Throughput time can thus be measured and used as a basis for evaluating performance.

lead time The time that passes from the time an order is received until the product is complete and ready for shipment.

Another hallmark of the Lean philosophy is reduced lead time. **Lead time** is the time between the receipt of an order and the completion of a product ready for shipment. Decreasing setup and throughput times can greatly reduce lead time. Many manufacturers that have adopted Lean have reduced lead time from months or years, to days or even hours. Lead time can be measured and used as a basis for evaluating plant performance.

unscheduled downtime The amount of time production equipment is out of service due to unscheduled repairs and maintenance.

In a further effort to increase efficiency, managers are working to reduce unscheduled downtime. **Unscheduled downtime** is the amount of time production equipment is out of service due to unscheduled repairs and maintenance. To keep this factor low, managers implement routine maintenance programs that not only keep unscheduled downtime to a minimum but also keep machinery running at peak performance. Companies are now tracking unscheduled downtime and using the information to evaluate plant performance.

By now, you may be wondering just how these Lean production improvements can be achieved. They do not come cheaply or easily. A great deal of time and money must be spent to achieve the added efficiency that comes with a Lean production environment. Some key factors are improved plant layout and product flow, mechanized procedures for machine setup, convenient storage and labeling of machine parts used in the setup process, and a formal plant maintenance program.

The production plant layout should be designed so that raw materials enter the production process with little or no need to be transported to work stations. For example, when a new **Saturn** automobile is made, the truck that transports the seats to the factory is literally connected to the production building, and the seats are fed to the production line, in the proper order, through conveyors in the truck to conveyers in the factory. At **Saturn**, the days of buying an assortment of seats and storing them in a warehouse are gone. Gone too are the days when personnel picked through massive inventories of seats to find a particular color and style and transported the selected seats to the production line. By cooperating with the seat manufacturer and a transportation company, **Saturn** can depend on the seats not only arriving on time but being received in the correct order by color and style with zero defects. A backup plan for shipment delays is the responsibility of the supplier and transportation company.

In addition to facilitating efficient handling of raw material, a Lean environment should also strive to streamline the movement of material from one production process to the next. For example, the **Dunlop** golf ball factory in South Carolina has eliminated the use of hopper carts to transport golf balls from the painting process to the packaging process. This was achieved by changing the plant layout so that golf balls travel by conveyor from one process to the next. This production improvement saves time and eliminates the need for handling the golf balls between processes. An added feature of this change was the elimination of inspection stations between the painting department and the packaging department, as the golf balls were no longer subject to blemishes caused by rough treatment in the hopper carts. The production change worked to greatly increase plant efficiency and improve product quality.

Each manufacturing environment is unique. Managers and plant workers must cooperate to continually reinvent the production environment. Old production techniques and strategies must be set aside in favor of new standards of production excellence, efficiency, and product quality. Company management and production personnel must work together to achieve the world-class production excellence required in today's competitive business environment. It takes a team effort characterized by an innovative spirit and a willingness to invest in grand-scale changes.

Lean manufacturing is really nothing more than the latest variation on the themes of efficiency and waste elimination. It is a present-day instance of the larger recurring theme in human life of increasing efficiency, decreasing waste, and using empirical methods to decide what matters, rather than uncritically accepting pre-existing ideas of what matters. Lean manufacturing should be viewed, with the benefit of hindsight, as a progression from, or a better attempt at the same goal of, earlier efficiency efforts—that is, picking up where earlier leaders like Henry Ford left off, and learning from their successes, *and* their mistakes.

The Lean mindset can also be used in coordinating business activities between and among companies, such as manufacturers, wholesalers, and retailers. The term **supply chain management** is commonly used to describe the relationship between companies as products move from the manufacturer to the ultimate end consumer. **Wal-Mart** must be able to depend on the distributors of the products it sells to its retail customers throughout the world. Those distributors must be able to depend on the manufacturers of the products they sell to **Wall-Mart**, **Target**, **Costco** and others. All of the businesses in the supply chain, from the manufacturers of consumer products, such as **Colgate-Palmolive**, **Unilever**, and **Procter & Gamble (P&G)** to the retail outlets that sell those products to the final consumer, understand that their success depends on their working together. They all have a vested interest in making sure the supply chain is not disrupted.

supply chain management A term commonly used to describe the coordination of business activities between companies as products move from the manufacturer to the ultimate end consumer.

Summary

As companies grow and the products and services they provide become more diversified, it becomes a virtual impossibility for one person to perform all management functions. More managers are required to operate and control the various facets of what we call management. A natural outgrowth of a company's evolution is the creation of business segments. A segment is any part of a company about which separate information is required to evaluate performance.

When a company is segmented, it will employ either a centralized management style or a decentralized management style. In a centralized company, upper management makes most of the important business decisions. In a decentralized company, lower-level managers are responsible for virtually all decisions that relate to their segment of the company.

Determining what costs should be charged to a particular business segment and the amount of those costs is sometimes very difficult. Some costs associated with operating a business segment are directly incurred by that segment. Others, however, are incurred to support more than one segment. These common costs must be allocated in some way to the segments receiving the benefit of the costs.

The four most commonly used designations of business segments are revenue centers, cost centers, profit centers, and investment centers. Revenue centers, cost centers, and profit centers are usually evaluated based on performance to budget. The performance of investment centers is most often evaluated using the return on investment (ROI), residual income (RI), or economic value added (EVA)™.

Although performance to budget and either return on investment or residual income are still commonly used to evaluate business segment performance, other nonfinancial measures have become popular in recent years. The balanced scorecard is an integrated set of performance measures organized around four distinct perspectives—financial, customer, internal, and innovation and learning. Many companies are now emphasizing such elements as product quality, customer satisfaction, employee morale, safety in the workplace, and efficiency as ways to better measure and improve company performance.

In recent years, a number of innovative management techniques have begun to emerge. Among these are e-commerce, enterprise information systems, six sigma, the theory of constraints, and lean manufacturing. With the emergence of each of these, management accounting has a key role to play in providing managers with a critical portion of the information they need to implement and use the techniques.

Key Terms

Review the Facts

A. Describe a business segment.
B. What is the difference between direct fixed cost and common fixed cost?
C. What is a service department?
D. Why is it important to know about service department cost allocation?
E. Describe the difference between centralized and decentralized management.
F. Describe a revenue center.
G. Describe a cost center.
H. What is the difference between a profit center and an investment center?
I. Why is residual income sometimes preferred to return on investment?
J. Describe the balanced scorecard.
K. What are the four perspectives of the balanced scorecard?
L. What are balanced scorecard objectives, measures, and targets?
M. What is E-commerce?
N. Describe the value chain.

O. What is meant by process management?

P. What is an enterprise information system?

Q. What is the primary motivation behind Six-Sigma?

R. Describe the theory of constraints.

S. Describe lean manufacturing.

T. What is meant by the just-in-time philosophy?

Apply What You Have Learned

LO 6: Matching—Emerging Management and Management Accounting Techniques

11-14. Required:

In the blank spaces provided, match the term to its definition.

A. balanced scorecard
B. balanced scorecard measures
C. balanced scorecard targets
D. balanced scorecard initiatives
E. balanced scorecard objectives
F. e-commerce
G. value chain
H. process management
I. enterprise information system
J. database
K. Six Sigma
L. constraint
M. theory of constraints (TOC)
N. Lean manufacturing
O. just-in-time (JIT)
P. zero defects
Q. setup time
R. throughput time
S. lead time
T. unscheduled downtime
U. supply chain management

_____ 1. An electronic filing system that contains various facts and figures.

_____ 2. Buying and selling of products or services and other business activities conducted over the internet.

_____ 3. A stream of connected activities that begins with research and development, through product design, then to manufacturing, then marketing and distribution, all with the focus on customer satisfaction.

_____ 4. An integrated set of performance measures organized around distinct perspectives.

_____ 5. A business management strategy that seeks to identify and remove the causes of defects and errors (anything that could lead to customer dissatisfaction) in manufacturing and other business processes.

_____ 6. An overall management philosophy introduced by Dr. Eliyahu M. Goldratt in his 1984 book titled *The Goal* which is based on the premise that the ability to achieve a goal is limited by at least one constraining process.

_____ 7. A production practice that focuses on reducing waste and inefficiencies in the production of product. This philosophy considers the expenditure of resources for any goal other than creating value for the end customer to be wasteful, and thus a target for elimination.

_____ 8. The amount of time production equipment is out of service due to unscheduled repairs and maintenance.

_____ 9. Concise statements for each balanced scorecard perspective that articulate what the organization hopes to accomplish.

_____ 10. A term commonly used to describe the coordination of business activities between companies as products move from the manufacturer to the ultimate end consumer.

_____ 11. Descriptions of how success in achieving scorecard objectives will be measured.

_____ 12. An integrated computer system capable of supporting an entire organization with quality service while processing large volumes of data.

_____ 13. Anything that does not allow you to do something you want or need to do.

_____ 14. Managing the various interconnected business activities in an enterprise.

_____ 15. A method of eliminating or greatly reducing inventory by delaying the purchase of material until it is actually needed for immediate use.

_____ 16. Describes the concept of products that are completely free of imperfections.

_____ 17. The level of performance or rate of improvement desired for each measure.

_____ 18. The time it takes to prepare manufacturing equipment for the production of particular products.

_____ 19. The time that passes from the time a unit of product enters the production process until it emerges as a finished product.

_____ 20. The time that passes from the time an order is received until the product is complete and ready for shipment.

_____ 21. Short-term programs and actions that will help achieve the established balanced scorecard objectives and performance targets.

LO 2 & 3: Prepare a Segment Income Statement with and without the Allocation of Common Fixed Costs to Segments

11-15. The Almer Sales Company has two divisions. The following information is available for the year ended December 31, 2008.

The sales for Almer are $300,000 for the Eastern Division and $200,000 for the Western Division. Variable costs for the Eastern Division are $250,000, whereas variable costs for the Western Division are $170,000. Direct fixed costs of the Eastern Division are $20,000 and direct fixed costs of the Western Division are $15,000. The Almer Company allocates common fixed costs to segments based on relative sales. Common fixed costs for the company are $25,000.

Note: Exhibit 7-16 in Chapter 7 provides calculations details that can help with preparing the solution to this exercise.

Required:

a. Prepare a segment income statement for the company which distributes common fixed costs to segments based on relative sales. Your answer should include a column for the total company and columns for each segment.

b. Do you think it is wise to evaluate the performance of a business segment based on income that includes an allocation for common fixed costs? Why or why not?

c. Prepare a segment income statement for the company which does not distribute common fixed cost to segments. Your answer should include a column for the total company and columns for each segment.

LO 2 & 3: Prepare a Segment Income Statement with and without the Allocation of Common Fixed Costs to Segments

11-16. The Ted Green Sales Company has two divisions. The following information is available for the year ended December 31, 2008.

The sales for the company are $30,000 for the North Division, and $90,000 for the South Division. Variable costs for the North Division are $18,000, while variable costs for the South Division are $54,000. Direct fixed costs of the North Division are $5,000 and direct fixed costs of the South Division are $15,000. The company allocates common fixed costs to segments based on relative sales. Common fixed costs for the company are $10,000.

Note: Exhibit 7-16 in Chapter 7 provides calculations details that can help with preparing the solution to this exercise.

Required:

a. Prepare a segment income statement for the company which distributes common fixed costs to segments based on relative sales. Your answer should include a column for the total company and columns for each segment.

b. Do you think it is wise to evaluate the performance of a business segment based on income that includes an allocation for common fixed costs? Why or why not?

c. Prepare a segment income statement for the company which does not distribute common fixed cost to segments. Your answer should include a column for the total company and columns for each segment.

LO 2: Identify the Area of Responsibility Associated with Different Types of Business Segments

11-17. Following are some popular segment classifications followed by three areas of management responsibility.

Segment Classification:			
Revenue center	_____	_____	_____
Cost center	_____	_____	_____
Profit center	_____	_____	_____
Investment center	_____	_____	_____

R —Revenue
C — Cost
I — Amount invested

Required:

In the blank spaces provided, match the area or responsibility, revenue (R), cost (C), and amount invested (I) to the appropriate segment classification. Although not all the blank spaces will be used, some segment classifications will have more than one area of responsibility.

LO 4: Determine Return on Investment

11-18. The Chemical Division of CalChem Incorporated generated a segment margin of $220,680 for the year 2008 and the amount invested in the division was $1,226,000.

Required:

Determine the return on investment for the Chemical Division.

LO 4: Determine Return on Investment

11-19. The Southern Division of the Benson Sales Company generated a segment margin of $790,020 for the year 2008 and the amount invested in the division was $4,158,000.

Required:

Determine the return on investment for the Southern Division.

LO 4: Determine Return on Investment

11-20. The Automotive Division of the Bascom Company generated a segment margin of $1,916,800 for the year 2008 and the amount invested in the division was $11,980,000.

Required:

Determine the return on investment for the Automotive Division.

LO 4: Determine Return on Investment

11-21. The Alcad Farm Products Company generated income of $558,620 for the year 2008 and the amount invested in the division was $3,286,000.

Required:

Determine the return on investment for Alcad.

LO 2 & 4: Determine and Interpret Return on Investment

11-22. The following information is available for the three divisions of the Pompano Company.

Amount invested in each division:	
Division A	$3,255,000
Division B	$2,145,000
Division C	$3,587,000
Segment margin of each division:	
Division A	$553,350
Division B	$407,550
Division C	$573,920

The required rate of return for the company is 16%.

Required:

a. Determine the return on investment for each division.

b. Rank the three divisions assuming they are considered profit centers.

c. Rank the three divisions assuming they are considered investment centers and performance is evaluated based on return on investment.

d. Why do the rankings for parts b and c differ?

LO 2 & 4: Determine and Interpret Return on Investment

11-23. The following information is available for the three divisions of the Stevens Company.

Amount invested in each division:	
Division 101	$1,255,000
Division 202	$2,445,000
Division 303	$3,697,000
Segment margin of each division:	
Division 101	$198,450
Division 202	$371,640
Division 303	$569,338

The required rate of return for the company is 15%.

Required:

a. Determine the return on investment for each division.

b. Rank the three divisions assuming they are considered profit centers.

c. Rank the three divisions assuming they are considered investment centers and performance is evaluated based on return on investment.

d. Why do the rankings for parts b and c differ?

LO 2 & 4: Determine and Interpret Return on Investment

11-24. The following information is available for the three divisions of the Reed Company.

Amount invested in each division:	
North Division	$7,225,000
South Division	$5,105,000
Central Division	$4,322,000
Segment margin of each division:	
North Division	$1,336,625
South Division	$ 898,480
Central Division	$ 816,585

The required rate of return for the company is 14%.

Required:

a. Determine the return on investment for each division.

b. Rank the three divisions assuming they are considered profit centers.

c. Rank the three divisions assuming they are considered investment centers.

d. Why do the rankings for parts b and c differ?

LO 5: Determine Residual Income

11-25. The Eastern Division of the Key Largo Company generated a segment margin of $1,836,800 for the year 2008 and the amount invested in the division was $12,780,000. The company's required rate of return is 14%.

Required:

Determine the residual income for the Eastern Division.

LO 5: Determine Residual Income

11-26. Division A of the Emry Company generated a segment margin of $522,567 for the year 2008 and the amount invested in the division was $2,778,450. The company's required rate of return is 18%.

Required:

Determine the residual income for Division A.

LO 5: Determine Residual Income

11-27. Central Division of the Craft Company generated a segment margin of $244,765 for the year 2008 and the amount invested in the division was $1,335,500. The company's required rate of return is 17%.

Required:

Determine the residual income for the Central Division.

LO 2, 4, & 5: Determine and Interpret Return on Investment and Residual Income

11-28. The following information is available for the three divisions of the Top Company.

Amount invested in each division:	
Division D	$7,555,000
Division E	$5,995,000
Division F	$3,082,000
Segment margin of each division:	
Division D	$1,133,250
Division E	$ 911,240
Division F	$ 493,120

The required rate of return for the company is 14%.

Required:

a. Determine the return on investment for each division.

b. Determine the residual income for each division.

c. Rank the three divisions assuming they are considered profit centers.

d. Rank the three divisions assuming they are considered investment centers and performance is evaluated based on return on investment.

e. Rank the three divisions assuming they are considered investment centers and performance is evaluated based on residual income.

f. Why do some of the rankings for parts c, d, and e differ?

LO 2, 4, & 5: Determine and Interpret Return on Investment and Residual Income

11-29. The following information is available for the three divisions of the Slick Company.

Amount invested in each division:	
Division 1	$1,155,000
Division 2	$3,988,000
Division 3	$3,080,000
Segment margin of each division:	
Division 1	$196,350
Division 2	$634,092
Division 3	$492,800

The required rate of return for the company is 15%.

Required:

a. Determine the return on investment for each division.

b. Determine the residual income for each division.

c. Rank the three divisions assuming they are considered profit centers.

d. Rank the three divisions assuming they are considered investment centers and performance is evaluated based on return on investment.

e. Rank the three divisions assuming they are considered investment centers and performance is evaluated based on residual income.

f. Why do some of the rankings for parts c, d, and e differ?

LO 2, 4, & 5: Determine and Interpret Return on Investment and Residual Income

11-30. The following information is available for the three divisions of the Kenyon Company.

Amount invested in each division:	
Division H	$5,188,000
Division I	$2,588,000
Division J	$6,386,000
Segment margin of each division:	
Division H	$ 933,840
Division I	$ 491,720
Division J	$1,136,708

The required rate of return for the company is 16%.

Required:

a. Determine the return on investment for each division.

b. Determine the residual income for each division.

c. Rank the three divisions assuming they are considered profit centers.

d. Rank the three divisions assuming they are considered investment centers and performance is evaluated based on return on investment.

e. Rank the three divisions assuming they are considered investment centers and performance is evaluated based on residual income.

f. Why do some of the rankings for parts c, d, and e differ?

LO 2 & 4: Determine and Interpret Return on Investment

11-31. The following information is available for the three divisions of the Planet Company.

Amount invested in each division:	
Automotive Division 1	$1,235,000
Industrial Division 2	$2,005,000
Consumer Division 3	$6,022,000
Segment margin of each division:	
Automotive Division 1	$202,540
Industrial Division 2	$332,830
Consumer Division 3	$963,520

The required rate of return for the company is 14%.

The company uses return on investment to evaluate segment performance.

The company is considering acquiring an automotive parts manufacturing company that is expected to provide income of $36,450. The acquisition would require an investment of $225,000. Although the prospective acquisition would fit nicely into the Automotive Division's operation, the Automotive Division's manager has voiced considerable reservations. He believes it would not be in the company's best interest to acquire the new segment.

The manager of the Industrial Division concurs with the Automotive Division manager. Oddly enough, the Consumer Division manager not only thinks the acquisition is a good idea, but has volunteered to accept it in her division.

Required:

a. Determine the return on investment for each division.

b. Do you feel that it is in the company's best interest to acquire the automotive parts manufacturer? Explain your answer.

c. Why are the Automotive and Industrial Division managers reluctant to recommend the acquisition?

d. Why would the Consumer Division manager volunteer to accept the proposed acquisition into her division?

LO 2 & 5: Determine and Interpret Residual Income

11-32. Refer to the information in problem 11-31.

Required:

Explain how each of the managers' feelings about the acceptability of the proposed acquisition would differ if the company used residual income to evaluate segment performance instead of return on investment.

Glossary

A

absorption costing A costing method where product cost includes all the costs to acquire products and get them ready to sell regardless of whether the costs are variable or fixed. Generally Accepted Accounting Principles require businesses to use absorption costing for financial accounting. (p. 195)

accounting rate of return The rate of return for a capital project based on the anticipated increase in accounting operating income due to the project relative to the amount of capital investment required. (p. 305)

activity based costing A technique to allocate indirect cost to cost objects based on activities that cause the cost to occur. It is more accurate than traditional cost allocation. (p. 132)

actual cost system A system that uses actual direct material cost, actual direct labor cost, and actual manufacturing overhead cost to determine the cost of products. (pp. 86, 129, 421)

administrative cost All costs incurred by a company that are not product costs or selling costs. Includes the cost of accounting, finance, employee relations, and executive functions. (p. 23)

allocation base An item or activity associated with cost objects that can be used to proportionately distribute manufacturing overhead costs to each cost object. (p. 84)

annuity A stream of equal periodic cash flows. (p. 312)

B

balanced scorecard An integrated set of performance measures organized around four distinct perspectives—financial, customer, internal, and innovation and learning. (pp. 285, 490)

balanced scorecard initiatives Short-term programs and actions that will help achieve the established balanced scorecard objectives and performance targets. (p. 491)

balanced scorecard measures Descriptions of how success in achieving scorecard objectives will be measured. (p. 491)

balanced scorecard objectives Concise statements for each balanced scorecard perspective that articulate what the organization hopes to accomplish. (p. 491)

balanced scorecard targets The level of performance or rate of improvement desired for each measure. (p. 491)

bill of materials A listing of the quantity and description of each item of direct material used to manufacture an individual product. (p. 422)

blended cost of capital Same thing as the weighted average cost of capital. (p. 290)

bottom-up budgeting A budget initially prepared by lower-level managers and employees. (p. 353)

break-even The point at which sales and costs are equal so the enterprise generates neither a profit nor a loss. (p. 200)

break-even point The level of sales required to achieve breakeven. This can be expressed either in sales dollars or in the number of units sold. (p. 200)

budget performance report The evaluation instrument used to evaluate a manager's performance to budget. (p. 376)

budgeted balance sheet A presentation of estimated assets, liabilities, and owners' equity at the end of the budgeted period. (p. 349)

budgeted income statement Shows the expected net income for the period covered by the operating budget. (p. 349)

budgeted statement of cash flows A statement of a company's expected sources and uses of cash during the period covered by the operating budget. (p. 349)

business process A stream of connected activities that begins with research and development, through product design, then to manufacturing, then marketing and distribution, all with the focus on customer satisfaction. (Sometimes called the value chain.) (p. 494) *business segment* A part of a company managed by a particular individual or a part of a company about which separate information is needed. (p. 476)

business-to-business (B2B) Commerce conducted between businesses. (p. 494)

business-to-consumer (B2C) Commerce conducted between businesses and consumers. (p. 494)

business-to-government (B2G) Commerce conducted between businesses and government agencies. (p. 494)

C

capital assets Long-lived expensive items such as land, buildings, machinery, and equipment. (p. 287)

capital budget The budget that outlines how a company intends to invest its scarce resources in long-lived productive assets. (p. 286)

capital budgeting The planning and decision process for making investments in capital projects. (p. 282)

capital investments Business expenditures in acquiring expensive assets that will be used for more than one year. (p. 281)

capital projects Another name for capital investments. (p. 282)

cash budget Shows whether the expected amount of cash generated by operating activities will be sufficient to pay anticipated expenses during the period covered by the operating budget. (p. 349)

cash payments schedule Presents the amount of cash a company expects to payout during the budget period. (p. 367)

cash receipts schedule Presents the amount of cash a company expects to collect during the budget period. (p. 365)

centralized management A management style in which top managers make most management decisions. (p. 482)

Certified Management Accountant (CMA®) Certification awarded to highly qualified accountants intended for those providing accounting services to a particular company or organization in industry. (p. 3)

Certified Public Accountant (CPA) A license awarded by a state government to highly qualified accountants and is intended for accountants that work for accounting firms that provide accounting services to the public. (p. 3)

common cost Another name for indirect cost. (p. 21)

common fixed cost Fixed costs incurred to support more than one business segment, or the company as a whole. (p. 478)

compound interest Interest calculated on the original principal amount invested plus all previously earned interest. (p. 309)

constraint Anything that does not allow you to do something you want or need to do. (p. 497)

continual budgeting Another name for perpetual budgeting. (p. 352)

contribution income statement An income statement that classifies cost by behavior (fixed cost and variable cost). (p. 195)

contribution margin The amount remaining after all variable costs have been deducted from sales. (p. 196)

contribution margin ratio The contribution margin expressed as a percentage of sales. (p. 198)

controller A company's chief accountant responsible for preparing accounting reports for both external and internal decision makers. (p. 9)

conversion cost The combined total of direct labor cost and manufacturing overhead cost. (p. 26)

core values What defines our perception of what is most important in life and also defines a sense of right and wrong, of just or unjust. (p. 284)

cost accounting A narrow application of management accounting dealing specifically with procedures designed to determine how much a particular item (usually a unit of manufactured product) costs. (p. 2)

cost allocation base An item or activity associated with cost objects that is used to proportionately distribute cost to each cost object. (p. 130)

cost behavior The reaction of costs to changes in levels of activity. (p. 156)

cost center A business segment where the manager has responsibility and authority to act to decrease or at least control costs but has little or no control over the revenues generated or the amount invested in the segment. (p. 484)

cost driver An activity used as an allocation base for a particular cost that causes the cost to occur. (p. 132)

cost object Any activity or item for which a separate cost measurement is desired. (p. 21)

cost of capital rate Another name for cost of capital. (p. 289)

cost of capital The cost of obtaining financing from all available financing sources. Generally the rate of return required for capital investments. (p. 289)

cost of debt capital The interest a company pays to its creditors. (p. 290)

cost of equity capital What equity investors give up when they invest in one company rather than another. (p. 290)

cost of goods sold budget Calculates the total cost of all the product a manufacturing or merchandising company estimates it will sell during the period covered by the budget. (p. 348)

cost of services budget Calculates the total cost of all the services a service type business estimates it will provide during the period covered by the budget. (p. 348)

cost pool An accumulation of the costs associated with a specific cost object. (pp. 84, 129) *cost* The resources forfeited to receive some goods or services. (p. 20)

cost-volume-profit (CVP) analysis The analysis of the relationships between cost and volume and the effect of these relationships on profit. (p. 199)

D

database An electronic filing system that contains various facts and figures in an organized fashion. (p. 495)

decentralized management A management style in which lower-level managers are responsible for decisions that relate to their segment of the company. (p. 482)

direct cost A cost that can be easily traced to an individual cost object. (p. 21)

direct fixed cost Fixed costs incurred to support a single business segment. (p. 478)

direct labor cost The cost of all production labor that can be traced directly to a unit of manufactured product. (p. 26)

direct labor efficiency standard The estimated number of direct labor hours required to produce a single unit of product. (p. 424)

direct labor efficiency variance A measure of the difference between the planned number of direct labor hours and the actual number of direct labor hours for the units actually manufactured. (p. 434)

direct labor hours The time spent by production workers as they transform raw materials into units of finished products. (p. 29)

direct labor rate standard The planned hourly wage paid to production workers. (p. 425)

direct labor rate variance A measure of the difference between the actual wage rate paid to employees and the direct labor rate standard. (p. 433)

direct material efficiency variance Another name for the direct material quantity variance. (p. 430)

direct material price standard The anticipated cost for each item of direct material used in the manufacture of a product. (p. 423)

direct material price variance A measure of the difference between the amount the company planned to pay for direct material purchased and the amount it actually paid for the direct material. (p. 429)

direct material quantity standard The amount of direct material it should take to manufacture a single unit of product. (p. 422)

direct material quantity variance A measure of the over- or under consumption of direct material for the number of units actually manufactured. (p. 430)

direct material The raw material that becomes a part of the final product and can be easily traced to the units produced. (p. 28)

direct material usage variance Another name for the direct material quantity variance. (p. 430)

direct materials cost The cost of all raw materials that can be traced directly to a unit of manufactured product. (p. 26)

discounting cash flows Determining the present value of cash to be received in the future. (p. 295)

E

e-commerce The same thing as electronic commerce. (p. 493)

economic value added (EVA) Almost the same as residual income except that it is adjusted for certain accounting distortions. (p. 488)

electronic commerce Buying and selling of products or services and other business activities conducted over the internet. (p. 493)

engineering approach A method of separating a mixed cost into its fixed and variable components using experts that are familiar with the technical aspects of the activity and associated cost. (p. 163)

enterprise information system An integrated computer system capable of supporting an entire organization with quality service while processing large volumes of data. (p. 495)

equivalent units The theoretical number of units that would have been completed if all production efforts resulted in only completed units. (p. 90)

F

factory burden Another name for manufacturing overhead cost. (p. 29)

factory overhead Another name for manufacturing overhead cost. (p. 29)

favorable variance The difference between actual performance and standard performance when the actual performance exceeds the standard. (p. 416)

financial accounting The branch of accounting designed to provide information to external decision makers such as stockholders and creditors. (p. 6)

financial calculator A calculator that can provide an array of information regarding the time value of money including future and present values. (p. 317)

finished goods inventory Products that have been completed and are ready to sell. (p. 27)

fixed cost A cost that remains constant in total regardless of the level of activity. (p. 156)

fixed manufacturing overhead budget variance The difference between the actual amount of total fixed manufacturing overhead cost and the budgeted fixed manufacturing overhead cost. (p. 439)

fixed manufacturing overhead spending variance Another name for the fixed manufacturing overhead budget variance. (p. 439) *fixed manufacturing overhead volume variance* A measure of the utilization of plant capacity. This variance is caused by manufacturing more or less product during a particular production period than planned. (p. 440)

flexible budget A budget that takes into consideration how changes in the level of activity affect revenues and costs. A flexible budget can be prepared for any level of activity. (p. 378)

flexible budget performance report A report that depicts the variances that result from a comparison of the flexible budget to the company's actual results. (p. 380)

flexible budget variances Variances that represent the differences between actual results and the flexible budget prepared based on the actual level of activity. (p. 380)

functional income statement Another name for the traditional income statement. (p. 195)

future value The value of a payment, or series of payments, at some future point in time calculated at some interest rate. (p. 308)

G

Generally Accepted Accounting Principles (GAAP) Financial accounting rules establishing how financial accounting information is to be prepared and presented. (p. 7)

H

high-low method A method of separating a mixed cost into its fixed and variable components using the mathematical differences between the highest and lowest levels of activity and cost. (p. 171)

hurdle rate Another name for cost of capital. (p. 289)

hybrid firms Companies that generate revenue from both providing services and selling products. (p. 39)

I

ideal standard A standard that is attainable only under perfect conditions. (p. 418)

imposed budget A budget in which upper management sets figures for all operating activities that the rest of the company rarely, if ever, can negotiate. (p. 353)

incremental budgeting The process of using the prior year's budget or the company's actual results to build the new operating budget. (p. 352)

indirect cost A cost that supports more than one cost object. (p. 21)

indirect fixed cost Another name for common fixed cost. (p. 478)

indirect labor The labor incurred in support of multiple cost objects (p. 30)

indirect materials Materials consumed in support of multiple cost objects. (p. 29)

Industrial Revolution A term used to describe the transition in the United States from an agricultural-based economy to a manufacturing-based economy. (p. 11)

internal rate of return (IRR) The calculated expected percentage return promised by a proposed capital project. (p. 301)

International Financial Reporting Standards (IFRS) International financial accounting rules establishing how financial accounting information is to be prepared and presented. (p. 7)

inventoriable cost Another name for product cost. (p. 22)

investment center A business segment that is evaluated based on the amount of profit generated relative to the amount invested in the segment. (p. 485)

J

job cost sheet A document that tracks the cost of products and organizes and summarizes the cost information for each job. (p. 78)

job order costing A costing method that accumulates cost by a single unit or production or batch of units. (p. 77)

just-in-time (JIT) A method of eliminating or greatly reducing inventory by delaying the purchase of material until it is actually needed for immediate use. Sometimes Lean is described too narrowly as just-in-time. (p. 498)

L

labor time ticket A document that tracks the amount of time each employee works on a particular job or a particular task in a factory or organization. (p. 83)

lead time The time that passes from the time an order is received until the product is complete and ready for shipment (p. 500)

Lean The same thing as lean manufacturing. (p. 498)

Lean manufacturing A production practice that focuses on reducing waste and inefficiencies in the production of product. The lean philosophy considers the expenditure of resources for any goal other than creating value for the end customer to be wasteful, and thus a target for elimination. The idea is to keep things trim and slim, or lean. (p. 498)

Lean production The same thing as lean manufacturing. (p. 498)

least-squares method Another name for regression analysis. (p. 173)

linear regression analysis Another name for regression analysis. (p. 173)

M

management accounting The branch of accounting designed to provide information to the firm's internal economic decision makers. (p. 2)

management by exception When managers use variances to direct their attention to trouble spots in the organization. (pp. 383, 417)

managerial accounting Another name for management accounting. (p. 2)

manufacturing overhead All activities involved in the manufacture of products besides direct materials or direct labor. (p. 29)

manufacturing overhead allocation The process of assigning or allotting an amount of manufacturing overhead cost to each unit of product produced based on some reasonable basis of distribution. (p. 128)

manufacturing overhead cost All costs associated with the operation of the manufacturing facility besides direct materials cost and direct labor cost. It is composed entirely of indirect manufacturing cost incurred to support multiple cost objects. (p. 26)

master budget Another name for operating budget. (p. 343)

master operating budget Another name for operating budget. (p. 343)

material stores Another name for raw materials inventory (p. 27)

materials requisition A formal request for material to be transferred from the raw materials storage area to production. (p. 81)

mission statement A summary of the main goals of the organization. (p. 283)

mixed cost A cost that has both a fixed cost and a variable cost component. (p. 161)

N

net cash flows Cash inflow less cash outflow. (p. 294)

net present value (NPV) The present value of all cash inflows associated with a proposed capital project minus the present value of all cash outflows associated with the proposed capital project. (p. 296)

normal cost system A system in which product cost reflects actual direct material cost, actual direct labor cost and estimated manufacturing overhead cost. (pp. 86, 129)

O

operating budget The budget that plans a company's routine day-to-day business activities for one to five years. (pp. 286, 343)

opportunity cost The benefit foregone (given up) because one alternative is chosen over another. (p. 252)

organizational goals The overall objectives of the company. They outline why the organization exists and are a combination of financial and nonfinancial goals. (p. 283)

outsourcing Buying services, products, or components of products instead of producing them. (p. 249)

over applied manufacturing overhead When more manufacturing overhead cost is applied to production than the actual manufacturing overhead costs incurred. (p. 87)

overhead In a manufacturing company, another name for manufacturing overhead cost; in a service type business, the indirect service cost. (p. 29)

P

participative budget A budget in which managers and employees at many levels of the company are involved in setting the performance standards and preparing the budget. (p. 354)

payback period A capital budgeting technique that measures the length of time a capital project must generate positive cash flows to equal the original investment in the project. (p. 304)

performance to budget A process of evaluating managers and employees based on how they perform against the budget. (p. 375)

period cost All costs incurred by a company that are not considered product cost. Includes selling and administrative cost. (p. 22)

perpetual budgeting The budgeting approach of updating the budget every month. (p. 352)

practical standard A standard that allows for normal, recurring inefficiencies. (p. 418)

predetermined manufacturing overhead application rate An overhead allocation rate calculated using estimated annual manufacturing overhead cost and an annual estimated amount for the allocation base. (pp. 86, 129)

present value The amount future cash flows are worth today based on an appropriate interest rate. (p. 312)

prime cost The combined total of direct material cost and direct labor cost. (p. 26)

process costing A method of allocating manufacturing cost to products to determine an average cost per unit. (p. 77)

process management Managing the various interconnected business activities (business processes) in an enterprise. (p. 494)

product cost The cost of the various products a company sells. (p. 22)

production budget Details the cost and number of units that must be produced by a manufacturer to meet the sales forecast and the desired ending inventory. (p. 348)

profit center A business segment in which the manager has the responsibility and authority to act to increase revenue and decrease or at least control costs, but has little or no control over the amount invested in the segment. (p. 484)

profitability index A method used to rank acceptable proposed capital projects. (p. 301) *purchase order* A document a company or organization uses to order materials from a vendor. (p. 80)

purchase requisition A request form that lists the quantity and description of the materials needed. (p. 79)

purchases budget Details the cost and number of units that must be purchased by a merchandiser to meet the sales forecast and the desired ending inventory. (p. 348)

purchasing department A department that specializes in purchasing all the goods required by a company or organization. (p. 80)

Q

qualitative factors Factors that cannot be measured by numbers-they must be described in words. (p. 241)

quantitative factors Factors that can be measured by numbers. (p. 241)

R

raw materials inventory Materials that have been purchased but have not yet entered the production process. (p. 27)

real rate of return Another name for internal rate of return. (p. 301)

receiving report A document that indicates the quantity and condition of each item received. (p. 80)

regression analysis A method of separating a mixed cost into its fixed and variable components using fairly complex mathematical formulas. (p. 173)

relevant benefit A benefit (revenue or cash inflow) that is pertinent to a particular business decision. A relevant benefit is a future benefit that differs between alternatives. (p. 240)

relevant cost A cost or cash outflow that is pertinent to a particular business decision. A relevant cost is a future cost that differs between alternatives (p. 240)

relevant information Information that is pertinent to a particular decision in that it has a bearing on which decision alternative is preferable. (p. 240)

relevant net cash flows Future net cash flows that differ between or among the alternatives being considered. (p. 294)

relevant range The range of activity within which cost behavior assumptions are valid. (p. 160)

required rate of return Another name for cost of capital. (p. 289)

residual income The amount by which a segment's actual income exceeds the income needed to meet a company's required rate of return. (p. 488)

return on investment (ROI) The percentage return generated by an investment in a business or a business segment. (p. 486)

revenue center A business segment in which the manager has responsibility and authority to act to increase revenues but has little or no control over costs and the amount invested in the segment. (p. 483)

rolling budget Another name for a perpetual budget (p. 352)

S

sales budget Details the expected sales revenue from a company's primary operating activities during a certain time period. (p. 347)

sales forecast The prediction of sales for the period covered by the operating budget. (p. 356)

sales volume variance performance report A report that depicts the static budget compared to the flexible budget and the variances the company should expect due to the difference in sales volume. (p. 379)

sales volume variance Variances that represent the differences between the static budget and a flexible budget prepared for the actual level of sales volume. (p. 379)

Sarbanes-Oxley Act A United States federal law enacted in 2002 that establishes new or strengthened standards for all U.S. publicly traded companies boards of directors, management, and the public accounting firms that deal with them. (p. 4)

scarce resources A term describing the limited amount of money a company has to invest in capital projects. (p. 293)

scatter graph approach A method of separating a mixed cost into its fixed and variable components by plotting historical activity and cost data to determine how the cost relates to various levels of activity. (p. 163)

scientific management A management philosophy based on the notion that management should maximize the prosperity of the employer and employees by improving worker efficiency through the use of standard amounts of time it should take workers to produce whatever the company manufactures. (p. 12)

segment income statement An income statement prepared for a business segment. (p. 477)

segment margin The amount of income that pertains to a particular part (segment) of a company. (p. 256)

segment margin The amount of income that pertains to a particular segment. (p. 477)

segment reports Reports that provide information pertaining to a particular business segment. (p. 476)

selling and administrative expense budget Calculates all costs other than the cost of product or services required to support a company's forecasted sales. (p. 348)

selling cost The cost of locating customers, attracting customers, convincing customers to buy, and the cost of necessary paperwork to document and record sales. (p. 22)

sensitivity analysis A technique used to determine the effect on cost-volume-profit when changes are made in the selling price, cost structure (variable and/or fixed) and/or volume used in the CVP calculations. Also called what-if analysis. (p. 206)

service department A business segment responsible for secondary (support) functions. Service departments provide service to the main business operations and to other service departments. (p. 479)

setup time The time it takes to prepare manufacturing equipment for the production of particular products. (p. 499)

simple interest Interest calculated on the original principal amount invested only (p. 308)

Six Sigma A business management strategy that seeks to identify and remove the causes of defects and errors (anything that could lead to customer dissatisfaction) in manufacturing and other business processes. (p. 495)

special order An order that is outside a company's normal scope of business activity. (p. 246)

standard A pre-established benchmark for desirable performance. (p. 416)

standard cost system A system that uses estimated amounts (standards) for direct material, direct labor, and manufacturing overhead to determine the cost of products. (p. 421)

standard cost system A system in which cost standards are set after careful analysis and then the standards are used to evaluate actual performance. A system that uses estimated amounts (standards) for direct material, direct labor, and manufacturing overhead to determine the cost of products. (p. 416)

standard costing The process of setting cost performance goals that benchmark acceptable performance and then using these cost goals to evaluate performance. (p. 415)

standard fixed manufacturing overhead rate The rate used to apply fixed manufacturing overhead to units of manufactured product. (p. 427)

standard variable manufacturing overhead rate The rate used to apply variable manufacturing overhead to units of manufactured product. (p. 426)

static budget A budget that is based on one level of activity. (p. 351)

strategic plan A long-range plan that sets forth the actions a company will take to attain its organizational goals. (p. 286)

strategy The plan of attack for furthering the company's vision and creating earnings. (p. 285)

sunk cost A past cost that cannot be changed by current or future actions. (p. 240)

supply chain management A term commonly used to describe the coordination of business activities between companies as products move from the manufacturer to the ultimate end consumer. (p. 501)

T

theory of constraints (TOC) An overall management philosophy introduced by Dr. Eliyahu M. Goldratt in his 1984 book titled The Goal which is based on the premise that the ability to achieve a goal is limited by at least one constraining process. (p. 498)

throughput time The time that passes from the time a unit of product enters the production process until it emerges as a finished product. (p. 500)

time value of money The increase in the value of cash over time due to investment income. The interest earning potential of cash. (pp. 246, 295)

time-adjusted rate of return Another name for internal rate of return. (p. 301)

top-down budgeting A budget prepared by top managers in a company. (p. 353)

traceable fixed cost Another name for direct fixed cost. (p. 478)

traditional income statement An income statement prepared in the multiple-step or single-step income statement format which conforms to Generally Accepted Accounting Principles (GAAP) and can be used for external financial reporting. (p. 195)

treasurer The corporate officer that is generally responsible for cash and credit management, obtaining external financing, and making investments for the company. (p. 9)

U

under applied manufacturing overhead. When less manufacturing overhead cost is applied to production than the actual manufacturing overhead costs incurred. (p. 87)

unfavorable variance The difference between actual performance and standard performance when the actual performance falls below the standard. (p. 416)

unscheduled downtime The amount of time production equipment is out of service due to unscheduled repairs and maintenance. (p. 500)

V

value chain A stream of connected activities that begins with research and development, through product design, then to manufacturing, then marketing and distribution, all with the focus on customer satisfaction. Each step in the process should add value to products and ultimately to the value of the entire organization (Sometimes called the business process.) (p. 494)

variable cost A Cost that changes in total proportionately with changes in the level of activity. (p. 157)

variable costing A method of costing where only the costs to acquire products or to get them ready to sell that vary with output are treated as product costs. In other words, only variable product costs are treated as product costs. (p. 195)

variable manufacturing overhead efficiency variance A measure of the variable manufacturing overhead cost attributable to the difference between the planned and actual direct labor hours worked. (p. 437)

variable manufacturing overhead spending variance The difference between how much was actually spent on variable manufacturing overhead and the amount that should have been spent based on the actual direct labor hours worked. (p. 436)

variance The difference between actual performance and the standard. The difference between the amount budgeted and the actual amount. (pp. 376, 416)

vision Management's dream for the company's future—the hope for where the company is going and how will it get there. (p. 284)

W

weighted average cost of capital The combined cost of debt financing and equity financing. (p. 290)

work-in-process inventory Products that have entered the production process but have not yet been completed. (p. 27)

Z

zero defects Describes the concept of products that are completely free of imperfections. (p. 499)

zero-based budgeting A process of budgeting in which manager's start from scratch, or zero, when preparing a new budget. (p. 352)